cum sesquipedale (Tafel 5113), *Coelogyne pandurata* (Tafel 5084), *Grammatophyllum speciosum* (Tafel 5157), *Dimorphorchis lowii* (Tafel 5475) und die erste künstliche Hybride *Calanthe × dominyi* (Tafel 5042).

Fitch überlebte seinen Arbeitgeber viele Jahre: William Hooker (dann Sir William) verstarb im Jahre 1865. Es war ein glücklicher Umstand, daß ihm sein Sohn, der gleichermaßen bedeutende Botaniker Joseph Dalton Hooker (1817–1911), sowohl als Direktor von Kew wie auch als Herausgeber des *Botanical Magazine* nachfolgte.

Wie sein Vater verband er seine Fähigkeiten als Botaniker mit der Kunst des Zeichnens. Unter seiner Führung florierte das *Magazine* zu einer Zeit, in der die interessantesten und spektakulärsten Orchideenarten entdeckt und in die Kultur eingeführt wurden. Er machte endgültig Schluß mit der Klassifizierung der Orchideen nach dem Linnéschen System und gab auch den Weg frei für die Mitarbeit anderer Autoren; besonders zu erwähnen sind James Bateman (1864–1866), der einige der Orchideenbeschreibungen durchführte, und J.G. Baker, dem die Bearbeitung der petaloiden Monokotyledonen oblag. Nach einer Auseinandersetzung mit Hooker wegen der Anstellung seiner Schwiegertochter Harriet Thiselton-Dyer als Zeichnerin zog sich Fitch zurück, und damit wurde die Familienverknüpfung der Hookers noch enger. Allerdings war es dann Matilda Smith (1854–1926), eine Kusine Hookers, die nach 1878 die Hauptlast zu tragen hatte. Wenn ihr Talent auch keinesfalls dem von Fitch gleichkam, so war sie doch ausreichend begabt, und dank der feinen Lithographie von J. Nugent Fitch (1840–1927), einem Neffen von Walter Hood Fitch, sind auch die Arbeiten von Matilda Smith als Gewinn für das *Botanical Magazine* anzusehen.

Im Jahre 1904 übergab Joseph Hooker (jetzt Sir Joseph) die Herausgeberschaft an seinen Schwiegersohn Sir William Thiselton-Dyer, die Erarbeitung der Texte jedoch wurde den in Kew angestellten Botanikern zugewiesen; das wird auch heute noch so gehandhabt. Die zahlreichen Orchideenbeschreibungen wurden von Robert Allen Rolfe (1855–1921) ausgeführt, den Hooker zum ersten (vollangestellten) Kurator des Orchideenherbariums ernannt hatte. Rolfes berühmteste Hinterlassenschaft für die Orchideenwelt war die Begründung der »Orchid Review«, (1893), die noch heute erscheint.

Das *Botanical Magazine* litt dann stark unter den wirtschaftlichen Folgen des ersten Weltkrieges. Die Lage verschlechterte sich nach 1918 derartig, daß sich Lovell Reeve & Co., die Eigentümer und Verleger seit 1845, entschlossen, die Herausgabe des Blattes von Dezember 1920 an einzustellen. Da aber brachte der weitbekannte Gartenbaufachmann und Reisende Henry John Elwes (1846–1922) während der Gartenbauausstellung in Chelsea im Mai 1922 die Probleme des *Botanical Magazine* der Royal Horticultural Society zur Kenntnis. Bereits im Oktober des gleichen Jahres wurden die Rechte des *Botanical Magazine* dieser Gesellschaft übertragen und die Veröffentlichungen wieder aufgenommen, wobei Kew weiterhin die Verantwortung für Redaktion, Texterstellung und Illustration behielt.

Der zweite Weltkrieg hatte dann erneut eine Krise zur Folge. Während der Kriegsjahre nahm die Häufigkeit der Herausgabe ständig ab, und bei Kriegsende überwogen die Herstellungskosten, hauptsächlich wegen der traditionellen und damit veralteten Fertigung, die Einkünfte. Von 1787 bis 1948 wurden nahezu alle Tafeln nach Farbvorlagen der Zeichner, von geschulten Hilfskräften mit Wasserfarben handkoloriert. Das war ein kostspieliger Vorgang, für den sich zudem kaum noch entsprechende Leute finden ließen. Um weiterzubestehen, mußte eine neue Farbrepro- bzw. -druckmethode gefunden werden. Für den außerhalb der Reihe 1937 gedruckten Band 147 (den sogenannten »Cory«-Band) hatte man bereits mit Farblithographie gearbeitet, und für den Band 165 war mit einem Vierfarbhalbtonprozeß auf Glanzpapier experimentiert worden. Mit dem Band 166 kam dann ein Vier-oder Mehrfarbdruckverfahren zur Anwendung, das Farbtafeln hervorbrachte, die sich mit den handkolorierten früherer Zeiten vergleichen ließen.

Dank aller dieser Umstände konnte die Produktion des *Botanical Magazine* mit höchster Qualität aufrechterhalten werden. Die Technik von Illustratorinnen wie Lilian Snelling (1879–1972), Stella Ross-Craig (geb. 1906), Ann Webster (geb. 1930) und Margaret Stones (geb. 1920) ist von größter Perfektion. Die Qualität der Texte ist damit vergleichbar. Auf Victor Summerhayes (1897–1974), eine Autorität auf dem Gebiet europäischer und afrikanischer Orchideen, folgte Rolfe als Kurator des Orchideenherbariums in Kew, und nach dessen Eintritt in den Ruhestand übernahmen nacheinander Peter Francis Hunt (geb. 1936), Peter Taylor (geb. 1926) und Phillip Cribb (geb. 1946) die Leitung des Herbariums. Sie sind alle mit zahlreichen Veröffentlichungen im *Botanical Magazine* vertreten.

Seit 1971 liegt die Verantwortung für das *Botanical Magazine* in den Händen des Bentham-Moxon Trusts in Kew. Bis zum Jahre 1983 wurde es im gleichen Format fortgeführt, das Sir William Hooker eingesetzt hatte. Hohe Herstellungskosten, verbunden mit einem verhältnismäßig geringen Absatz in den letzten Jahren, machten dann aber eine kühne Umstellung notwendig – vielleicht die gründlichste in der langen Geschichte dieses Unternehmens. Das *Botanical Magazine* war schon seit langem in »new series« (neuen Reihen) erschienen, um neue Subskribenten zu gewinnen. Im April 1984 wurde nun *Curtis's Botanical Magazine* dem »Kew Magazine« einverleibt und auf diese Weise zugleich das langdauernde Verhältnis zwischen dem *Botanical Magazine* und den Königlichen Botanischen Gärten in Kew zum Ausdruck gebracht.

In vieler Hinsicht ist »The Kew Magazine« seinem berühmten Vorgänger ähnlich. Jeder Band erscheint in vier Teilen, von denen jeder mit sechs Farbdarstellungen höchster Qualität von Pflanzen von wissenschaftlichem oder gartenbaulichem Interesse versehen ist. Jede Farbtafel wird von einem allgemeinen Einführungstext, einer Kulturanleitung und einer botanischen Beschreibung begleitet. Als Neuerung enthält das Magazin zusätzlich Artikel von allgemeinem Interesse, wie Naturschutz und Sammeln von Pflanzen. Es ist nicht ohne Bedeutung, daß die allererste Abbildung des ersten Bandes in der neuen Aufmachung die letzthin wiederentdeckte Frauenschuhart *Paphiopedilum sanderianum* darstellt.

Die Illustratoren und ihre Arbeiten

Der Erfolg des *Botanical Magazine* beruht großenteils auf dem Talent und der Kunst seiner Zeichner, dem Geschick der Stecher und Lithographen und nicht zuletzt auf der hohen Qualität des Druckes. Man kann nicht bezweifeln, daß der von William Curtis festgelegte Plan wohldurchdacht war und er auf die richtige Karte gesetzt hatte. Dafür spricht nicht nur der Erfolg seiner Arbeit, sondern auch die Zahl seiner Nachahmer. Gute botanische Illustratoren sind selten zu finden, müssen sie doch neben künstlerischem Talent auch ein hohes Maß an botanischen Kenntnissen besitzen. Curtis hatte das Glück, James Sowerby anzustellen, der sein Können schon in der »Flora Londinensis« bewiesen hatte. Sydenham Edwards wurde ein Jahr nach der Begründung des *Botanical Magazine* Curtis vorgestellt, der sofort von der Begabung dieses Mannes beeindruckt war. Schon bald war er als alleiniger Illustrator für das *Magazine* tätig; er behielt diese Position für die nächsten 27 Jahre, in denen er 1650 Tafeln erstellte. Viele seiner Originalzeichnungen befinden sich in Kew.

Edwards langes Wirken war so etwas wie ein Präzedenzfall. Obgleich mehr als 30 Zeichner im Verlauf der Zeit für das *Botanical Magazine* tätig waren, war es nur eine Handvoll von ihnen, die mit ihren Beiträgen dominierten. Der berühmteste ist Walter Hood Fitch, ein Schützling von Sir William Hooker, er war als Zeichner für das *Botanical Magazine* von 1834 bis 1877 tätig. Wilfred Blunt (1950) beschreibt ihn in seinem Buch »The Art of Botanical Illustration« als den produktivsten von allen botanischen Illustratoren. Sir Joseph Hooker hat ihn des öfteren wegen seiner unnachahmlichen Begabung, das Charakteristische in einer Pflanze zu sehen und darzustellen, gelobt. Blunt preist ihn zwar als den bedeutendsten botanischen Illustrator seiner Zeit in Europa, stellt aber fest, daß es seinen Zeichnungen trotz der präzisen Darstellungsweise ein wenig an Subtilität fehlt. Fitch selbst hat eine aufschlußreiche Darstellung seiner Technik für die botanische Illustration im »Gardeners' Chronicle« (1869) gegeben.

Es ist traurig zu hören, daß Fitch aus dem *Botanical Magazine*, dem er unter dem alten und dem jungen Hooker gedient hatte, wegen einer Auseinandersetzung ausschied. Sein Weggang hinterließ eine Lücke, die sich nur schwer füllen ließ. Zum Glück war Matilda Smith, eine Kusine Sir Joseph Hookers, gerade aus Indien zurückgekehrt, so daß Hooker sie im Präparieren und Zeichnen von Blüten unterrichten konnte. Sie wurde für ihre hingebungsvolle Arbeit bekannt. Ihre erste Tafel (6386) erschien 1878, und sie setzte ihre Tätigkeit als hauptsächliche und die meiste Zeit über einzige Illustratorin bis zum Jahre 1921 fort. Sie zeichnet allein für 384 Orchideentafeln verantwortlich. Blunt (1950) bemerkt, daß sie ein wenig plump gezeichnet habe, was allerdings ein zu hartes Urteil sein mag. Schließlich darf nicht übersehen werden, daß John Nugent Fitch als Lithograph aus ihren leicht skizzenhaften Arbeiten oft Hervorragendes zu machen wußte.

Eine derartige Kritik trifft keineswegs auf die Aquarellarbeit ihrer Nachfolgerin Lilian Snelling zu. Sowohl die künstlerische Qualität als auch die botanische Genauigkeit ihrer Darstellungen kann sich mit den entsprechenden Tugenden von Walter Hood Fitch messen. Blunt preist ihre Arbeiten wegen der anmutigen Eleganz der Darstellung. Wie Fitch meisterte auch sie die Kunst der Lithographie, und sie war außerdem imstande, ihre eigenen Zeichnungen – später auch die von Stella Ross-Craig – auf die Zinkplatte zu übertragen. Die Arbeiten von Lilian Snelling begleiteten das *Botanical Magazine* über 30 Jahre und gereichen ihm noch heute zur Zierde.

Im Laufe der letzten Jahre erschienen zahlreiche Aquarellzeichnungen hervorragender Illustratoren, die auch heute noch alle tätig sind. Eine Anzahl überdurchschnittlich guter Beiträge stammt von der Hand der offiziellen Illustratorin von Kew, Mary Grierson. Die australische Zeichnerin Margaret Stones wie auch die in Kew beschäftigte Joanna Langhorne (vormals Lowe) haben in den vergangenen Jahren wesentliche Beiträge geleistet. Ihre Arbeiten kann man auch in David Hunts »Orchids from Curtis's Botanical Magazine« (1971–1981) bewundern. In den letzten fünf Jahren erschienen Illustrationen von Pandora Sellars; ihre Orchideenzeichnungen gehören zu den besten und schönsten, die im *Botanical Magazine* erschienen sind.

Wenn man die Stellung des *Botanical Magazine* in der Geschichte der Gartenkultur in Europa und auf den Britischen Inseln im Verlauf des 18. und 19. Jahrhunderts ermessen will, sollte man den Beitrag von A. B. Hemsley, das Vorwort zum Index des *Botanical Magazine* von 1904, lesen. Die Geschichte des *Magazine* von der Begründung bis zum Band 164 wurde von F. J. Chittenden dem Index der Bände 1 bis 164 vorangestellt. Eine kritische Würdigung der am *Magazine* beteiligten Illustratoren findet man in Wilfred Blunts prägnantem Beitrag in seinem herrlichen Buch »The Art of Botanical Illustration« (Die Kunst der botanischen Illustration).

Die folgenden biographischen Einzelheiten beziehen sich auf Illustratoren, die im *Botanical Magazine* zwischen 1787 und 1984 mit ihren Darstellungen vertreten sind, und zwar in ihrer zeitlichen Reihenfolge.

Sydenham Edwards (1769?–1819) war der Sohn eines Lehrers aus Abergavenny in Wales. Abgesehen von Nr. 75 zeichnete er die ersten 1721 Tafeln. Wegen einer Meinungsverschiedenheit mit Dr. John Sims verließ er seine Stellung 1815 und begründete kurz danach das »Botanical Register« in Nachahmung und als Konkurrenz des *Botanical Magazine*. Diese Zeitschrift lebte nach seinem Tode unter der Redaktion von Prof. John Lindley weiter, bis sie 1848 erlosch.

John Curtis (1791–1862) war ursprünglich entomologischer Zeichner, kam dann aber nach dem Ausscheiden von Edwards zu den Tafeln für Curtis. Er stammte aus Norwich und fertigte in seinen Jugendjahren Zeichnungen und Stiche für die Horticultural Society, die Linnean Society wie auch für das *Botanical Magazine*.

Robert Kaye Greville (1794–1866) war Autor mehrerer botanischer Bücher, einschließlich der »Icones Plantarum« (mit W. J. Hooker). Für das *Botanical Magazine* zeichnete er die Tafeln 2615 und 2926.

William Herbert (1778–1847) wurde in London geboren. Er wurde Dekan von Manchester und gehörte zu den führenden Gärtnern und Naturphilosophen seiner Zeit. Für das *Botanical Magazine* trug er 61 Tafeln und für das »Botanical Register« 45 Tafeln bei.

William Jackson Hooker (1785–1865) stammte aus Norwich in Norfolk. Er wurde 1820 Professor der Botanik in Glasgow und 1841 zum Direktor der Königlichen Botanischen Gärten in Kew berufen. Er schrieb und redigierte das *Botanical Magazine* von 1827 bis 1865. Während der ersten zehn Jahre war er zugleich auch Illustrator; er schuf 64 Orchideentafeln. Zu den Veröffentlichungen dieses vielseitigen und produktiven Mannes gehört »Century of Orchidaceaus Plants« (1849).

Thomas Nicholson (1799–1877) stammte aus Dumfriesshire in Schottland. Als Schiffsarzt und Amateur-Naturforscher war er für einige Zeit in Antigua stationiert. Er versorgte William Hooker mit Pflanzen und Zeichnungen, von denen zwei im *Botanical Magazine* erschienen sind.

Mary Harrison (1788–1875) kam aus Liverpool. Sie heiratete den Orchideenzüchter Richard Harrison, der Pflanzen von Henry und William Harrison aus Rio de Janeiro erhielt; einige von diesen wurden von Mary für das *Botanical Magazine* gezeichnet.

Franz Andreas Bauer (1758–1840) stammte aus Felsberg in Österreich und war der ältere Bruder des gleichermaßen bekannten Ferdinand Bauer. Die Brüder Bauer werden von vielen Kennern als die besten botanischen Illustratoren aller Zeiten angesehen. Für sein mit John Lindley herausgegebenes Buch »Illustrations of Orchidaceous Plants« (1830–1838) fertigte Franz die detaillierten

Zeichnungen. Im *Botanical Magazine* stammen die Tafeln 3172, 3377 und 3378 (alles Orchideen) von ihm. Man kann es nur bedauern, daß er nicht mehr Beiträge geleistet hat. Die meisten seiner Originale befinden sich im Londoner British Museum (Nat. Hist.), einige wenige auch in Kew.

Mrs. Chas. Horsefall (tätig 1830) ist im *Botanical Magazine* mit fünf Tafeln vertreten; Tafel 3534 stellt eine Orchidee dar.

Maria Curtis (tätig in den Dreißigerjahren des 19. Jahrhunderts) zeichnete zwei Tafeln für das *Botanical Magazine*; Tafel 3412 ist eine Orchidee.

Walter Hood Fitch (1817–1892) stammte aus Glasgow. Niemand hat mehr Tafeln für das *Botanical Magazine* gezeichnet als er. Darüber hinaus produzierte er fast 500 Tafeln für Hookers »Icones Plantarum«, die Illustrationen für Elves »Monograph of the Genus Lilium«, J.D. Hookers »Rhododendrons of the Sikkim Himalaya and Illustrations of Himalayan Plants«. Alle Originale seiner Orchideenzeichnungen befinden sich in Kew.

James McNab (1810–1878) stammte aus Richmond in Surrey und war der Sohn von W. MacNab, dem er in seiner Position als Kurator des Königlichen Botanischen Gartens in Edinburgh nachfolgte. Für das *Botanical Magazine* zeichnete er mehrere Tafeln; eine davon (3518) ist eine Orchidee.

Miss Moss (tätig in den Dreißigerjahren des vorigen Jahrhunderts). Sie war möglicherweise die Tochter von John Moss, der eine außerordentliche Orchideensammlung in der Nähe von Liverpool hatte. Ihr Beitrag zum *Magazine* ist die Tafel 3573.

Mrs. Augusta Innes Withers (c. 1793–1860). Sie wurde 1830 von Königin Adelaide als Blumenmalerin angestellt. Neben Pflanzen für das *Botanical Magazine* malte sie auch Illustrationen für James Batemans monumentales Werk »Orchidaceae of Mexico and Guatemala« (1837–1843).

William Beattie Booth (c. 1804–1874) stammte aus Scone in Perthshire, Schottland. Von 1824 bis 1830 arbeitete er als Gärtner für die Horticultural Society am London-Garten in Chiswick; später wurde er stellvertretender Verwaltungssekretär dieser Gesellschaft. Er fertigte Zeichnungen für das *Botanical Magazine* wie auch für das »Botanical Register«. Ihm zu Ehren ist *Epidendrum boothianum* benannt.

M. Norbury zeichnet für Tafel 3819 verantwortlich.

Mrs. E.C. Wrigley malte Tafel 6144.

John Nugent Fitch (1840–1927) war der Neffe von Walter Hood Fitch und stammte ebenfalls aus Glasgow. Für das *Botanical Magazine* lithographierte er seit 1878 nahezu 2500 Tafeln. Er illustrierte auch das »Orchis Album« von R. Warner und B.S. Williams (1882–1894).

Lady Harriet Thiselton-Dyer (1854–1945), die Tochter von Sir Joseph Hooker, stammte aus Hitcham in Suffolk. Sie heiratete T.W. Thiselton-Dyer, der später die Nachfolge von Hooker als Direktor von Kew und als Redakteur des *Botanical Magazine* antrat. W.H. Fitch unterrichtete sie im Zeichnen, sie arbeitete zwischen 1878 und 1906 für das *Botanical Magazine*.

Maltilda Smith (1854–1926) wurde in Bombay geboren. Sie war eine Kusine von Sir Joseph Hooker und arbeitete als Chefzeichnerin für das *Botanical Magazine* von 1888 bis 1921. Aus ihrer Hand stammen mehr als 2300 Tafeln.

J.L. Macfarlane (1836–c. 1913), ein Illustrator und Lithograph, zeichnete die Tafel 7576.

Lilian Snelling (1879–1972) stammte aus St. Mary Cray in Kent. Sie arbeitete am Königlichen Botanischen Garten in Edinburgh von 1916 bis 1921 und danach in Kew. Ihre Tafeln zierten das *Botanical Magazine* von 1922 bis 1952.

A. Kellet zeichnete die Tafel 8979.

William Edward Trevithick (1900–1958) stammte aus Kells in der Grafschaft Meath in Irland. Er trat 1920 als Gärtner in die Dienste von Kew, und wurde dort 1923 in das Herbarium versetzt. Sein Beitrag zum *Botanical Magazine* bestand aus einigen Tafeln; außerdem fertigte er Strichzeichnungen für die »Flora of West Tropical Africa« und für John Hutchinsons »Families of Flowering Plants«.

Otto Stapf (1857–1933) wurde in Ischl in Österreich geboren. Er war Kustos des Herbariums in Kew von 1909 bis 1922 und Redakteur des *Botanical Magazine* von Band 148 bis 156. Die Tafel 9117 wird ihm, gemeinsam mit Lilian Snelling, zugeschrieben.

Stella Ross-Craig (geb. 1906) stammt aus Aldershot in Hampshire. Von 1929 bis 1960 arbeitete sie als Illustratorin für die Royal Horticultural Society und auch als Mitarbeiterin in Kew. Nicht nur ihre Aquarelle sind von hoher Qualität, sondern auch ihre Strichzeichnungen. Die besten Beispiele findet man in ihren »Drawings of British Plants« (1948–1974).

Mary Grierson (geb. 1912) wurde in Bangor in Nordwales geboren. Nach Jahren als freischaffende Illustratorin wurde sie als Zeichnerin in Kew fest angestellt. Sie lieferte die Tafeln für das von Peter Francis Hunt geschriebene Oktavwerk »Orchidaceae«.

Ann Webster (geb. 1930) stammt aus London. Sie arbeitete als Hauptillustratorin für das *Botanical Magazine* von 1951 bis 1958; aber sie zeichnete nur wenige Orchideen.

E. Margaret Stones (geb. 1920) wurde in Colnac in Victoria (Australien) geboren. Sie kam 1951 nach England. In den Jahren von 1958 bis 1980 war sie die Hauptillustratorin des *Botanical Magazine*. Zu den vielen Werken, die sie illustriert hat, gehört die sechsbändige »Endemic Flora of Tasmania«.

Joanna Lowe (geb. 1945) stammt aus Fulmer Chase in Buckinghamshire. Sie trat 1973 die Nachfolge von Mary Grierson in Kew an, arbeitet aber seit 1978 wieder freischaffend.

Christabel King (geb. 1950) war Zeichnerin für das *Botanical Magazine* von 1975 bis 1980: heute arbeitet sie wieder freischaffend. Die zwölf Tafeln von *Pleione* im Band 183 stammen von ihr.

Pandora Sellars (geb. 1936) ist freischaffende Zeichnerin. Sie wurde wiederholt beauftragt, für das *Botanical Magazine* zu arbeiten, neuerdings auch für das »Kew Magazine«.

PUBLIKATIONSDATEN

der Bände des Botanical Magazine

Band	Serie	Band	Inhalt und Datum
1			1–33 (1787), 34–36 (1788)
2			37–69 (1788), 70–72 (1789)
3			73–105 (1789), 106–108 (1790)
4			109–141 (1790), 142–144 (1791)
5			145–177 (1791), 178–180 (1792)
6			181–213 (1792), 214–216 (1793)
7			217–249 (1793), 250–252 (1794)
8			253–285 (1794), 286–288 (1795)
9			289–321 (1795), 322–324 (1796)
10			325–357 (1796), 358–360 (1797)
11			361–393 (1797), 394–396 (1798)
12			397–429 (1798), 430–432 (1799)
13			433–465 (1799), 466–468 (1800)
14			469–501 (1800), 502–504 (1801)
15			505–544 (1801), 545–548 (1802)
16			549–596 (1802)
17			597–612 (1802), 613–644 (1803)
18			645–692 (1803)
19			693–708 (1803), 709–739 (1804)
20			740–786 (1804)
21			787–801 (1804), 802–832 (1805)
22			833–880 (1805)
23			881–895 (1805), 896–923 (1806)
24			923*–966 (1806)
25			967–982 (1806), 983–1013 (1807)
26			1014–1059 (1807)
27			1060–1073 (1807), 1074–1101 (1808)
28			1102–1147 (1808)
29			1148–1162 (1808, 1163–1191 (1809)
30			1192–1236 (1809)
31			1237–1251 (1809), 1252–1282 (1810)
32			1283–1328 (1810)
33			1329–1344 (1810), 1345–1373 (1811)
34			1374–1418 (1811)
35			1419–1432 (1811), 1433–1459 (1812)
36			1460–1501 (1812)
37			1502–1517 (1812), 1518–1547 (1813)
38			1548–1591 (1813)
39			1592–1605 (1813), 1606–1635 (1814)
40			1636–1681 (1814)
41			1682–1695 (1814), 1696–1725 (1815)
42			1726–1770 (1815)
43	new	1	1771–1786 (1815), 1787–1859 (1816)
44	new	2	1860–1873 (1816), 1874–1941 (1817)
45	new	3	1942–1954 (1817), 1955–2022 (1818)
46	new	4	2023–2035 (1818), 2036–2104 (1819)
47	new	5	2105–2118 (1819), 2119–2188 (1820)
48	new	6	2189–2202 (1820), 2203–2272 (1821)
49	new	7	2273–2286 (1821), 2287–2355 (1822)
50	new	8	2356–2369 (1822), 2370–2440 (1823)
51	new	9	2441–2454 (1823), 2455–2522 (1824)
52	new	10	2523–2536 (1824), 2537–2606 (1825)
53	new	11	2607–2620 (1826), 2621–2704 (1826)
54	new	1	2705–2790 (1827)
55	new	2	2791–2875 (1828)
56	new	3	2876–2955 (1829)
57	new	4	2956–3038 (1830)
58	new	5	3039–3122 (1831)
59	new	6	3123–3205 (1832)
60	new	7	3206–3289 (1833)
61	new	8	3290–3373 (1834)
62	new	9	3374–3457 (1835)
63	new	10	3458–3541 (1836)
64	new	11	3542–3625 (1837)
65	new	12	3626–3698 (1838), 3699–3710 (1839)
66	new	13	3711–3770 (1839), 3771–3794 (1840)
67	new	14	3795–3842 (1840), 3843–3879 (1841)
68	new	15	3880–3915 (1841), 3916–3963 (1842)
69	new	16	3964–3987 (1842), 3988–4047 (1843)
70	new	17	4048–4059 (1843), 4060–4131 (1844)
71	iii	1	4132–4202 (1845)
72	iii	2	4203–4274 (1846)
73	iii	3	4275–4344 (1847)
74	iii	4	4345–4416 (1848)
75	iii	5	4417–4485 (1849)
76	iii	6	4486–4553 (1850)
77	iii	7	4554–4622 (1851)
78	iii	8	4623–4688 (1852)
79	iii	9	4689–4757 (1853)
80	iii	10	4758–4824 (1854)
81	iii	11	4825–4890 (1855)
82	iii	12	4891–4957 (1856)
83	iii	13	4958–5024 (1857)
84	iii	14	5025–5090 (1858)
85	iii	15	5091–5156 (1859)
86	iii	16	5157–5222 (1860)
87	iii	17	5223–5288 (1861)
88	iii	18	5289–5353 (1862)
89	iii	19	5354–5419 (1863)
90	iii	20	5420–5485 (1864)
91	iii	21	5486–5551 (1865)
92	iii	22	5552–5617 (1866)
93	iii	23	5618–5682 (1867)
94	iii	24	5683–5747 (1868)
95	iii	25	5748–5812 (1869)
96	iii	26	5813–5877 (1870)
97	iii	27	5878–5942 (1871)
98	iii	28	5943–6008 (1872)
99	iii	29	6009–6073 (1873)
100	iii	30	6074–6139 (1874)
101	iii	31	6140–6205 (1875)
102	iii	32	6206–6271 (1876)
103	iii	33	6272–6336 (1877)
104	iii	34	6337–6402 (1878)
105	iii	35	6403–6468 (1879)
106	iii	36	6469–6533 (1880)
107	iii	37	6534–6599 (1881)
108	iii	38	6600–6664 (1882)
109	iii	39	6665–6730 (1883)
110	iii	40	6731–6792 (1884)
111	iii	41	6793–6852 (1885)
112	iii	42	6853–6912 (1886)
113	iii	43	6913–6972 (1887)
114	iii	44	6973–7032 (1888)
115	iii	45	7033–7092 (1889)
116	iii	46	7093–7152 (1890)
117	iii	47	7153–7211 (1891)
118	iii	48	7212–7271 (1892)
119	iii	49	7272–7331 (1893)
120	iii	50	7332–7391 (1894)
121	iii	51	7392–7451 (1895)
122	iii	52	7452–7511 (1896)
123	iii	53	7512–7571 (1897)
124	iii	54	7572–7631 (1898)
125	iii	55	7632–7691 (1899)
126	iii	56	7692–7751 (1900)

Band	Serie	Band	Inhalt und Datum
127	iii	57	7752–7811 (1901)
128	iii	58	7812–7871 (1902)
129	iii	59	7872–7931 (1903)
130	iii	60	7932–7991 (1904)
131	iv	1	7992–8051 (1905)
132	iv	2	8052–8111 (1906)
133	iv	3	8112–8171 (1907)
134	iv	4	8172–8231 (1908)
135	iv	5	8232–8291 (1909)
136	iv	6	8292–8351 (1910)
137	iv	7	8352–8411 (1911)
138	iv	8	8412–8471 (1912)
139	iv	9	8472–8531 (1913)
140	iv	10	8532–8591 (1914)
141	iv	11	8592–8641 (1915)
142	iv	12	8642–8691 (1916)
143	iv	13	8692–8741 (1917)
144	iv	14	8742–8785 (1918)
145	iv	15	8786–8829 (1919)
146	iv	16	8830–8873 (1920)
147	"1938"		8874–8933 (1938)
148	"1922"		8934–8945 (1922), 8946–8977 (1923)
149	"1923"		8978–8989 (1923), 8990–9023 (1924)
150	"1924"		9024–9034 (1924), 9035–9069 (1925)
151	"1925"		9070–9081 (1925), 9082–9115 (1926)
152	"1926"		9116–9126 (1927), 9127–9161 (1928)
153	"1927"		9162–9183 (1929), 9184–9204 (1930)
154	"1928"		9205–9226 (1930), 9227–9248 (1931)
155	"1929"		9249–9259 (1931), 9260–9292 (1932)
156			9293–9336 (1933)
157			9337–9380 (1934)
158			9381–9424 (1935)
159			9425–9468 (1936)
160			9469–9501 (1937), 9502–9512 (1938)
161			9513–9545 (1938), 9546–9556 (1939)
162			9557–9589 (1939), 9590–9600 (1940)
163			9601–9611 (1940), 9612–9622 (1942), 9623–9633 (1941), 9634–9644 (1942)
164			9645–9655 (1943), 9656–9666 (1944), 9667–9677 (1946), 9678–9688 (1948)

Band	Serie	Band	Inhalt und Datum
165	N.S.	1	1–44, 1948
166	N.S.	2	45–88, 1949
167	N.S.	3	89–132, 1950
168	N.S.	4	133–175, 1951
169	N.S.	5	176–219, 1952–1953
170	N.S.	6	220–263, 1954–1955
171	N.S.	7	264–307, 1956–1957
172	N.S.	8	308–351, 1958–1959
173	N.S.	9	352–395b, 1960–1962
174	N.S.	10	396–439, 1962–1963
175	N.S.	11	440–483, 1964–1965
176	N.S.	12	484–527, 1966–1968
177	N.S.	13	528–571, 1969–1970
178	N.S.	14	572–615, 1970–1972
179	N.S.	15	616–659, 1972–1973
180	N.S.	16	660–703, 1974–1975
181	N.S.	17	704–747, 1976–1977
182	N.S.	18	748–791, 1978–1979
183	N.S.	19	792–836, 1980–1981
184	N.S.	20	837–882, 1982–1983

LITERATURVERZEICHNIS

Spezialliteratur nach Regionen

Europa und Mittlerer Osten

Camus, E.G.: Monographie des Orchidées. Lechevalier, Paris 1908.

Danesch, O. und E.: Orchideen Europas. Hallwag, Bern 1962.

Danesch, O. und E.: Orchideen Europas: Südeuropa. Hallwag, Bern 1969.

Danesch, O. und E.: Orchideen Europas. Oprhys-Hybriden. Hallwag, Bern 1972.

Davies, P., and J., and Huxley, A.: Wild Orchids of Britain and Europe. Chatto and Windus, London 1983.

Delforge, P. et Tyteca, D.: Guide des Orchidées d'Europe. Duculot, Paris 1984.

Godfery, M.J.: British Orchidaceae. Cambridge U.P., Cambridge 1933.

Keller, G. und Schlechter, R.: Monographie und Iconographie der Orchideen Europas und des Mittelmeergebietes, 1–45: Fedde, Repertorium, Sonderbeiheft A, Berlin 1925–1943.

Landwehr, J.: Wilde Orchideeën van Europa, 2 vols. Natuurmonumenten, Nederland 1977.

Nelson, E.: Gestaltwandel und Artbildung erörtert am Beispiel der Orchidaceen Europas und der Mittelmeerländer, insbesondere der Gattung Ophrys. E. Nelson, Chernex-Montreux 1962.

Nelson, E.: Monographie und Ikonographie der Orchidaceen-Gattungen Serapias, Aceras, Loroglossum, Barlia. E. Nelson, Chernex-Montreux 1968.

Nelson, E.: Monographie und Ikonographie der Orchidaceen-Gattung Dactylorhiza. Speich, Zürich 1976.

Nelson, E., und Fischer, H.: Die Orchideen Deutschlands und der angrenzenden Gebiete. Frisch, Berlin 1931.

Reichenbach, H.G.: Orchideae. In: Flora Germanica Recensitae. Hofmeister, Leipzig 1851.

Renz, J.: Orchidaceae. In: K.H. Rechinger: Flora Iranica, No. 126. Akad. Druck- und Verlagsanstalt, Graz 1978.

Summerhayes, V.S.: Wild Orchids of Britain, 2nd ed. Collins, London 1968.

Sundermann, H.: Europäische und mediterrane Orchideen. 2. Aufl. Brücke, Hannover 1975.

Die Orchidee (1949 →). Herausgeber: Deutsche Orchideen-Gesellschaft. Brücke-Verlag, Kurt Schmersow, Hildesheim. Many articles on orchids of Europe and the Middle East. Viele Artikel über Orchideen Europas und des Mittleren Ostens.

Japan, China und Zentralasien

Garay, L., and Sweet, H.: Orchids of Southern Ryukyu Islands. Botanical Museum, Harvard Univ., Cambridge, Mass. 1974.

Hu, S.Y.: The Orchidaceae of China. In: Quart. J. Taiwan Museum, 1971 →.

Hu, S.Y.: The Genera of Orchidaceae in Hongkong. The Chinese U.P., Hongkong 1977.

Kraenzlin, F.: Orchidacearum Sibiriae Enumeratio. Fedde, Repertorium, Beihefte 65, 1931.

Lin, T.-P.: Native Orchids of Taiwan. 2 vols. Taipei, Taiwan 1975 →.

Maekwa, F.: The Wild Orchids of Japan in colour. Tokyo 1971.

Schlechter, R.:Orchideologiae Sino-Japonicae Prodromus. Fedde, Repertorium, Beihefte 4, 1919.

Indien und Burma

Banerji, M.L., and Pradhan, P.: The Orchids of Nepal Himalaya. J. Cramer, Vaduz 1984.

Bose, T.K., and Bhattacharjee, S.K.: Orchids of India. Nayo Prokash, Calcutta 1980.

Duthie, J.F.: The Orchids of the North-Western Himalaya. Annals of the Royal Botanic Garden, Calcutta, 9, 1906.

Grant, B.: The Orchids of Burma. Rangoon 1895.

Hooker, J.D.: Orchideae. Flora of British India, 5, L. Reeve and Co., London 1890.

Hooker, J.D.: A Century of Indian Orchids. Annals of the Royal Botanic Garden, Calcutta, 5, 1895.

King, G., and Pantling, R.: The Orchids of the Sikkim-Himalaya. Annals of the Royal Botanic Garden, Calcutta, 8, 1898.

Pradhan, U.C.: Indian Orchids: Guide to Identification and Culture. 2 vols. Kalimpong 1976–1979.

Südost-Asien und Indonesien

Ames, O., and Schweinfurth, C.: The Orchids of Mount Kinabalu, British North Borneo. Orchidaceae, 6, Merrymount Press, Boston 1920.

Backer, C.A.: Beknopte Flora van Java – Orchidaceae 1–3. Rijksherbarium, Leiden 1952.

Bennett, K.S.: The Tropical Asiatic Slipper Orchids, Genus Paphiopedilum. Angus and Robertson, North Ryde 1984.

Gagnepain, F., et Guillaumin, A.: Orchidacées. Flore Générale de L'Indo-Chine, 2, Masson, Paris 1932.

Holttum, R.E.: Orchids of Malaya, ed. 3. In: A Revised Flora of Malaya. Government Printing Office, Singapore 1964.

Schlechter, R.: Blütenanalysen neuer Orchideen IV. Indische und malesische Orchideen. Fedde, Repertorium, Beihefte 74, 1934.

Seidenfaden, G.: Contribution to a Revision of the Orchid Flora of Cambodia, Laos and Vietnam, 1. A Preliminary Enumeration. Fredensborg, Denmark 1975.

Seidenfaden, G.: Orchid Genera in Thailand. Dansk Botanisk Arkiv 1975 →.

Seidenfaden G., and Smitinand, T.: Orchids of Thailand, 1–4. The Siam Society, Bangkok 1959–1964.

Seidenfaden, G.: Orchid Genera in Thailand X. Trichotosia and Eria. Opera Botanica, No. 62, 1982.

Smith, J.J.: Icones Bogorienses – Orchidées. E.J. Brill, Leiden 1903.

Smith, J.J.: Die Orchideen von Ambon. Landsdrukkerij, Batavia 1905.

Smith, J.J.: Die Orchideen von Java. In: Flora von Buitenzorg, 6, 1905.

Smith, J.J.: Die Orchideen von Java, 1–8. In: Bulletin du Departement de l'Agriculture aux Indes Néerlandaises. In: Bulletin du Jardin Botanique de Buitenzorg, 1905–1924.

Smith, J.J.: Orchidaceae Buruenses. In: Bulletin du Jardin Botanique de Buitenzorg 9, 1928.

Smith, J.J.: Orchidaceae Seranenses. In: Bulletin du Jardin Botanique de Buitenzorg 10, 1928.

Smith, J.J.: Icones Orchidacearum Malayensium, 1–2. In: Bulletin du Jardin Botanique de Buitenzorg, 1930–1938.

Smith, J.J.: On a Collection of Orchidaceae from Central Borneo. Bulletin du Jardin Botanique de Buitenzorg, 11, 1931.

Smith, J.J.: Enumeration of the Orchidaceae of Sumatra and Neighbouring Islands. Fedde, Repertorium, 32, 1933.

Philippinen

Ames, O.: Notes on Philippine Orchids. The Philippine Journal of Science 4, 1909.

Ames, O.: Orchidaceae 1–3, 5–7. Several articles on Philippine orchids 1905–1922.

Ames, O.: Schedulae Orchidianae. Several new species of Philippine orchids described, 1922–1930.

Ames, O.: Enumeration of Philippine Apostasiaceae and Orchidaceae. In: Enumeration of Philippine Flowering Plants. Manila, Philippines 1925.

Ames, O., and Quisumbing, E.: New or Noteworthy Philippine Orchids, 1–6. The Philippine Journal of Science 44–59, 1931–1936.

Valmayor, H.: Orchidiana Philippiana. 2 vols. Samhwa Printing Co. (S. Korea), 1984.

Philippine Orchid Review (1948–1959). Many articles on orchids of the Philippines.

Neuguinea

Millar, A.: Orchids of Papua New Guinea. Australian National U.P., Canberra 1978.
Schlechter, R.: Die Orchidaceen von Deutsch-Neuguinea. Fedde, Repertorium, Beihefte 1 und 21, 1914–1928.
Smith, J.J.: Die Orchideen von Niederländisch-Neu-Guinea. In: Résultats de l'expédition scientifique Néerlandaise à la Nouvelle Guinée. E.J. Brill, Leiden 1909–1934.
Van Bodegom, J.: Enige Orchideeën van West Nieuw Guinea. Enschede, Nederland 1973.
Van Royen, P.: The Orchids of the High Montains of New Guinea. J. Cramer, Vaduz 1980.

Australien

Dockrill, A.W.: Australasian Sarcanthinae. The Australian Native Orchid Society, Sydney 1967.
Dockrill, A.W.: Australian Indigenous Orchids I. The Epiphytes; the Tropical Terrestrial Species. Halstead Press, Sydney 1969.
Firth, M.J.: Native Orchids of Tasmania. C.L. Richmond, Devonport, Tasmania 1965.
Fitzgerald, R.D.: Australian Orchids. Sydney 1875–1894.
Nichols, W.H.: Orchids of Australia. T. Nelson, Melbourne, Australia 1969.
Orchadian. Numerous articles on native species, ab 1963 →.

Pazifische Inseln

Guillaumin, A.: Orchidacées. In: Flore analytique et synoptique de la Nouvelle-Calédonie. Paris 1948.
Hallé, N.: Flore de la Nouvelle-Calédonie et Dépendances, 8. Orchidacées. Muséum National d'Histoire Naturelle, Paris 1977.
Hunt, P.F.: Orchids of the Solomon Islands. Philosophical Transactions of the Royal Society of London 255, 1969.
Johns, J., and Mollay, B.: Native Orchids of New Zealand, 1984.
Kraenzlin, F.: Neu-Caledonische Orchideen. Vierteljahresschrift der Naturforschenden Gesellschaft, Zürich, 74, 1929.
Moore, L.B., and Edgar, E.: Orchidaceae. In: Flora of New Zealand, 2. Wellington, N.Z. 1970.
Parham, J.W.: Orchidaceae. In: Plants of the Fiji Islands. Suva, Fiji 1972.
Seemann, B.: Orchideae. In: Flora Vitiensis. L. Reeve and Co., London 1865–1873.

Tropisches Afrika

Cribb, P.J., and Stewart, J.: Additions to the Orchid Flora of Tropical Africa. Kew Bulletin vol. 40, No. 2, 1985.
Morris, B.: Epiphytic Orchids of Malaŵi. The Society of Malawi, Blantyre 1970.
Piers, F.: Orchids of East Africa. 2nd ed. Cramer, Lehre 1968.
Rolfe, R.A.: Flora of Tropical Africa, 7: Orchidaceae. L. Reeve and Co., London 1897.
Schlechter, R.: Orchidaceae Stolzianae. In: Engler, A.: Botanische Jahrbücher, 1915.
Schlechter, R.: Versuch einer natürlichen Neuordnung der afrikanischen angraekoiden Orchidaceen. Bot. Centralblatt, Beihefte 36 (2), 1918.
Stewart, J.: Orchidaceae. In: Agnew, K.: Upland Kenya Wild Flowers. Oxford U.P. 1974.
Stewart, J., and Campbell, R.: Orchids of Tropical Africa. W.H. Allen, London 1970.
Summerhayes, V.S.: Numerous articles on the taxonomy of tropical African orchids. In: Kew Bulletin, 1927–1966.
Summerhayes, V.S.: Several articles on African orchids. Botanical Leaflets of Harvard University, 1942–1945.
Summerhayes, V.S.: Flora of West Tropical Africa. Orchidaceae, 2nd ed., London 1968.
Summerhayes, V.S.: Flora of Tropical East Africa, Orchidaceae pt. I. London 1968.
Williamson, G.: The Orchids of South Central Africa. Dent, London 1977.

Südafrika

Ball, J.S.: Southern African Epiphytic Orchids. Conservation Press, Johannesburg 1978.
Bolus, H.: Orchids of South Africa. W. Wesley and Son, London 1893–1913.
Compton, R.H.: The Flora of Swaziland. Journal of South African Botany, Supp. vol. 11, 1976.
Hall, A.V.: Studies of the South African species of Eulophia. Journal of South African Botany, Supp. vol. 5, 1965.
Harrison, E.R.: Epiphytic Orchids of Southern Africa. Durban 1972.
Jacot Guillarmod, A.: Flora of Lesotho. J. Cramer, Lehre 1972.
Kraenzlin, F.: Orchidacearum Genera et Species. I. Mayer und Müller, Berlin 1898.
Rolfe, R.A.: Flora Capensis, Orchidaceae. L. Reeve and Co., London 1913.
Schelpe, E.A.: An Introduction to the South African Orchids. MacDonald, London 1966.
Schlechter, R.: Contributions to South African orchidology. Annals of the Transvaal Museum 10, 1924.
Sölch, A.: Orchidaceae. In: Prodromus einer Flora von Südwestafrika. J. Cramer, Lehre 1972.
Stewart, J., and Hennessy, E.F.: Orchids of Africa. Macmillan South Africa, Johannesburg 1981.
South African Orchid Journal (1970 →). Many articles on South African orchids.

Madagaskar und benachbarte Inseln

Perrier de la Bâthie, H.: Flore de Madagascar, Orchidacées. Tananarive 1939–1941.
Richard, A.: Orchidées des Iles de France et de Bourbon. Paris 1828.
Schlechter, R.: Orchidaceae de Madagascar – Orchidaceae Perrierianae Madagascarienses, 1913.
Thouars, A. du Petit: Orchidées des Iles Australes de l'Afrique. Paris 1913.
Adansonia (1960 →). Numerous articles on Madagascan orchids.

Nordamerika

Correll, D.S.: Native Orchids of North America. Stanford U.P., California 1950.
Luer, C.: The Native Orchids of Florida. New York Botanical Garden, 1972.
Luer, C.: The Native Orchids of the United States and Canada. New York Botanical Garden, 1975.

Mittelamerika

Ames, O., and Correll, D.S.: Orchids of Guatemala. In: Fieldiana, 1952–1953.
Bateman, J.: The Orchidaceae of Mexico and Guatemala, 1837–1843.
Dressler, R.L., and Pollard, G.E.: The Genus Encyclia in Mexico. Associacion Mexicana de Orquideologia, Mexico 1976.
Hamer, F.: Las Orquideas de El Salvador. Min. de Educacion, San Salvador 1974.
Hamer, F.: Orchids of Nicaragua. In: Icones Plantarum Tropicarum. Sarasota (Fla.), Fasc. 7–9, 11 and 12, 1982–84.
Schlechter, R.: Beiträge zur Orchideenkunde von Zentralamerika. Fedde, Repertorium, Beihefte 17, 4–95, und 19, 3–307, 1922–1923.
Williams, L.O.: The Orchidaceae of Mexico. Ceiba 2, 1–321, 1951.
Williams, L.O.: An Enumeration of the Orchidaceae of Central America, British Honduras and Panama. Ceiba 5, 1–256, 1956.
Williams, L.O., and Allen, P.H.: Orchidaceae. In: Woodson, R.E., and Schery, R.W.: Flora of Panama. Ann. Missouri Bot. Garden, 1946–1949.
Williams, O., and Allen, P.: Orchids of Panama with Checklist from R. Dressler. Missouri Botanic Garden 1980.

Antillen, Kanarische Inseln

Acuna Gate, J.: Catalogo Descriptivo de las Orquideas Cubanas. Estacion Experimental Agronomica, Boletin 60, Havana, Cuba 1938.
Cogniaux, A.: Orchidaceae. In: Urban, I.: Symbolae Antillanae, 6, 1909–1910.
Fawcett, W., and Rendle, A.B.: Orchidaceae. In: Flora of Jamaica, Vol. 1. British Museum, London 1910.
Garay, L., and Sweet, H.: Orchideae. In: Howard, R.A.: Flora of the Lesser Antilles. Arnold Arboretum, Harvard University, Jamaica Plain, Mass. 1974.
Schultes, R.E.: Native Orchids of Trinidad. Pergamon Press, Oxford 1960.

Südamerika

Braem, G.J.: Cattleya. Brücke Verlag, Hildesheim 1983.
Cogniaux, A.: Orchidaceae. In: Martius, Flora Brasiliensis, Leipzig 1893–1906.
Correa, M.N.: Orchidaceae. In: Flora Patagonica 8, 1970.
Dodson, C.H., and P.M.: Orchids of Ecuador. In: Icones Plantarum Tropicarum. Sarasota (Fla.), Fasc. 1–4, 5 and 10, 1980–84.
Dunsterville, G.C.K.: Die Welt der Orchideen. Lectura Verlag, Caracas 1962.
Dunsterville, G.C.K., and Garay, L.: Venezuelan Orchids Illustrated, 1–6, 1959–1976.
Dunsterville, G.C.K., and Garay, L.: Orchids of Venezuela – an Illustrated Field Guide. Botanical Museum, Harvard University, Cambridge, Mass. 1979.

Foldats, E.: Orchidaceae. In: Flora de Venezuela, 15. Instituto Botanico, Caracas 1969–1970.
Fowlie, J. A.: The Brazilian Bifoliate Cattleyas and Their Color Varieties. Day Printing Corp., Pomona (Calif.) 1977.
Hoehne, F. C.: Flora Brasilica – Orchidaceas. São Paulo 1940–1953.
Hoehne, F. C.: Iconografia de Orchidaceas do Brasil. São Paulo 1949.
Pabst, G., und Dungs, F.: Orchidaceae Brasilienses, 2 Bände. Brücke-Verlag, Kurt Schmersow, Hildesheim 1975–1977.
Rodrigues, J. Barbosa: Genera et Species Orchidearum Novarum. Fleiuss, Rio de Janeiro 1877.
Schlechter, R.: Mehrere längere Artikel über südamerikanische Arten und Gattungen. In: Fedde, Repertorium, Beihefte. 1919–1929.
Schlechter, R., and Hoehne, F. C.: Contribuicöes ao Conhecimento das Orquidáceas do Brasil. In: Anexos das Memorias do Instituto de Butantan; et in: Archivos de Botanico do Estado de São Paulo, 1921–1922.
Schweinfurth, C.: Orchids of Peru. In: Fieldiana 1958–1961; Ergänzungen in Fieldiana, Chicago 1970.
Vásquez, Ch., R., and Dodson, C. H.: Orchids of Bolivia. In: Icones Plantarum Tropicarum. Sarasota (Fla.), Fasc. 6, 1982.
Williams, L. O.: Las Orquideas del Noroeste Argentino. Lilloa 4, 1939.
Zimmermann, W.: Orchidaceae Novae Brasilienses. Bibliotheca Botanica, Fasc. 109, 1934.
American Orchid Society Bulletin (1932 →). Many articles on South American orchids.
Bradea (1969 →). Many articles on Brazilian orchids.
Orchid Digest (1937 →). Many articles on South American orchids.
Orquidea (1938–73). Many articles on Brazilian orchids.
Orquideologia (1966 →). Articles mainly on Colombian orchids.

Allgemeine Literatur

Arditti, J.: Orchid Biology, Reviews and Perspectives. Cornell U. P., Ithaca, London 1977.
Bateman, J.: Second Century of Orchidaceous Plants. L. Reeve and Co., London 1867.
Bateman, J.: A Monograph of Odontoglossum. L. Reeve and Co., London 1874.
Bauer, F., and Lindley, J.: Illustrations of Orchidaceous Plants. J. Ridgway and Sons, London 1830–1838.
Bechtel, H.: Orchideen im Heim. Landbuch Verlag, Hannover 1969.
Bechtel, H.: Exotische Orchideen. Franckh, Stuttgart 1971.
Bechtel, H.: Wunderbare und geheimnisvolle Welt der exotischen Orchideen. Bertelsmann, Gütersloh 1977.
Bechtel, H., Cribb, P., and Launert, E.: Orchideenatlas. Ulmer, Stuttgart 1980.
Bechtel, H., Cribb, P., and Launert, E.: The Manual of Cultivated Orchid Species. Blandford Press, West St. Poole 1981.
Bentham, G., and Hooker, J. D.: Orchideae. In: Genera Plantarum 3. L. Reeve and Co., London 1883.
Blume, C. L.: Collection des Orchidées. Sulpke, Amsterdam 1858.
Burgeff, H.: Mycorrhiza of Orchids. In Withner, C.: The Orchids – Scientific Studies, 361–396, 1959.
Cogniaux, A., et Goossens, A.: Dictionnaire Iconographique des Orchidées. 1–17, Brussels 1896.
Cribb, P. J.: A Revision of Dendrobium sect. Latouria. Kew Bulletin, vol. 38, No. 2, 1983.
Dressler, R.: Classification of the Orchid Family in Proceedings of the 7th World Orchid Congress. 259–278, Medellin, Colombia 1974.
Dressler, R., and Dodson, C.: Classification and Phylogeny in the Orchidaceae. Annals of the Missouri Botanic Garden 47, 25–67, 1960.
Dunsterville, G. C. K.: A letter to orchid conservationists. Amer. Orchid Soc. Bull. 44, 883–885, 1975.
Ebel, F.: Schöne und seltsame Welt der Orchideen. Wasmuth, Tübingen 1971.
Fast, G.: Orchideenkultur. Ulmer, Stuttgart 1980.
Fowlie, J. A.: The Genus Lycaste. Day Printing Corp., Pomona (Calif.) 1970.
Garay, L.: On the Origin of the Orchidaceae. Botanical Museum Leaflets of Harvard University 19 (3), 57–96, 1960.
Garay, L.: On the Origin of the Orchidaceae, 2. Journal of the Arnold Arboretum 52, 202–215, 1972.
Graham, R., and Roy, R.: Slipper Orchids. Croom Helm, London 1982.
Hagsater, E.: Can there be a different view of orchids and their conservation. Amer. Orchid Soc. Bull. 45, 18–21, 1976.
Hawkes, A. D.: Encyclopaedia of Cultivated Orchids. Faber and Faber, London 1965.
Hirmer, M.: Wunderwelt der Orchideen. Hirmer, München 1974.
Hooker, W. J.: A Century of Orchidaceous Plants. Reeve, Bentham and Reeve, London 1849.
Hunt, D. R.: Orchids from Curtis's Botanical Magazine. Curwen Books, London 1981.
Hunt, P.-F.: Conservation of orchids. Orchid Rev. 76, 320–327, 1968.
International Orchid Commission: Handbook of Orchid Nomenclature, ed. 3, London 1985.
I. U. C. N.: Convention on International Trade. In: Endangered Species of Wild Fauna and Flora. Morges, (CH) 1973.
Johanson, D.: The ecology of vascular epiphytes in West Africa. Acta Phytogeographia Suecica 59, 1–129, 1974.
Linden, J.: Pescatorea. Gand 1860.
Linden, J.: Lindenia. Gand 1885–1901.
Lindley, J.: Genera and Species of Orchidaceous Plants. Ridgways, London 1830–1840.
Lindley, J.: Sertum Orchidacearum. 1838–1842.
Lindley, J.: Folia Orchidacea. J. Matthews, London 1852–1859.
Luer, C. A.: Icones Pleurothallidinarum. Selbyana, vol. 3, Nos. 1–4, 1976–77.
Luer, C. A.: Thesaurus Masdevalliarum. Helga Königer Verlag, München 1983 →.
Melville, R.: Red Data Book, Vol. 5: Angiospermae, 1970.
Reichenbach, H. G.: Xenia Orchidacea. A. Brockhaus, Leipzig 1854–1900.
Reichenbach, H. G.: Orchides. In: Walpers, Annales Botanices 6, 1864.
Reinekka, M. A.: A History of the Orchid. Univ. of Miami Press, Florida 1972.
Richter, W.: Orchideen pflegen, vermehren und züchten. Neumann-Neudamm, Melsungen 1969.
Rolfe, R. A., and Hurst, C.: Orchid Stud. Book. F. Leslie and Co., Kew 1909.
Sander, D.: Orchideen und Orchideen-Pflege. Schmersow, Hildesheim 1969.
Sander, F.: Reichenbachia. St. Albans 1888–1894.
Sander, F.: Sander's Orchid Guide. St. Albans 1901.
Sanford, W. W.: The Ecology of orchids. In: Withner, C.: The Orchids, Scientific Studies, 1–100, 1974.
Schlechter, F.: Das System der Orchidaceen. Notizblatt des Botanischen Gartens und Museums, Berlin, 9, 563–591, 1926.
Schlechter, R.: Die Orchideen. 2. Aufl. Parey, Berlin 1927.
Schlechter, R.: Die Orchideen. 3. Aufl. (F. G. Brieger, R. Maatsch, K. Senghas). Parey, Berlin und Hamburg. In Lieferungen ab 1970.
Schultes, R. E., and Pease, A.: Generic Names of Orchids. Academic Press, New York, London 1963.
Schuster, C.: Orchidacearum Iconum Index. Fedde, Repertorium, Beiheft 60, 1974.
Schweinfurth, C.: The Classification of orchids. In: Withner, C.: The Orchids, a Scientific Survey, 15–43, 1959.
Stein, B.: Stein's Orchideenbuch Original Ed. 1892, Brücke Verlag, Hildesheim 1980.
Stafleu, F. A., and Cowan, R. S.: Taxonomic Literature, vols. 1–5. Utrecht 1976.
Stafleu, F. A.: Taxonomic Literature A–Z. Utrecht 1967.
Summerhayes, V. S.: The Wild Orchids of Britain, ed. 2. Collins, London 1968.
Sweet, H.: The Genus Phalaenopsis. Day Printing Corp., Ponoma (Calif.) 1980.
Van der Pijl, L., and Dodson, C.: Orchid Flowers – their pollination and evolution. University of Miami Press 1965.
Van Royen, P.: The Genus Corybas. J. Cramer, Vaduz 1983.
Veitch, J.: A Manual of Orchidaceous Plants. J. Veitch and Sons, Chelsea 1887–1894.
Warner, R.: Select Orchidaceous Plants. Lovell Reeve and Co., London 1862–1878.
Warner, R., and Williams, B. S.: The Orchid Album. B. S. Williams, London 1882–1897.
Withner, C.: The Orchids – a scientific survey. Ronald, New York 1959.
Withner, C.: The Orchids – scientific studies. Wiley-Interscience, New York 1974.
Woolward, F. H.: The Genus Masdevallia. Original Ed. 1896. Lyne and Son, London 1978.
Zander, Handwörterbuch der Pflanzennamen. Von F. Encke, G. Buchheim und S. Seybold. Ulmer, Stuttgart 1984.
Draft Index of Author Abbreviations compiled at The Herbarium, Royal Botanic Gardens. Kew 1980.
The European Garden Flora, Vol. 2 Monocotyledons part 2: Juncaceae to Orchidaceae. Cambridge Univ. Press, Cambridge 1984.
Krypto. F. Flück-Wirth. Spezialkatalog/Special Catalogue No. 6 Febr., Teufen 1985.
Index Kewensis. Kumulierte Microfiche-Ausgabe. Mindata Microform System. 1–484, 1983.

ORCHIDEENTAFELN

alphabetisch nach Gattungen geordnet

8678 Acacallis cyanea Lindl.

4492 Acanthephippium javanicum Blume

4203 *Acineta barkeri* (Bateman) Lindl.

7143 *Acineta chrysantha* (Morren) Lindl. & Paxton

M.S. del, J.N. Fitch lith.

Vincent Brooks Day & Son Ltd imp

L. Reeve & Co London.

8392 *Acineta moorei* Rolfe

4156 *Acineta superba* var. *fulva* (Hook.) Schltr.

5435 Ada aurantiaca Lindl.
5624 Aerangis citrata (Thouars) Schltr.

4159 Aerangis biloba (Lindl.) Schltr.
7204 Aerangis fastuosa (Rchb. f.) Schltr.

7442

M. S. del, J.N. Fitch lith.

Vincent Brooks, Day & Son Imp.

L. Reeve & C° London.

7442 Aerangis kotschyana (Rchb. f.) Schltr.

6693 Aerangis modesta (Hook. f.) Schltr.
4427 Aerides crispa Lindl.

6034 Aeranthes arachnites (Thouars) Lindl.
6728 Aerides emerici Rchb. f.

9274 Aerides jarckiana Schltr.
4049 Aerides multiflora Roxb.

5681 Aerides huttonii (Hook.f.) Veitch
4139 Aerides odorata Lour.

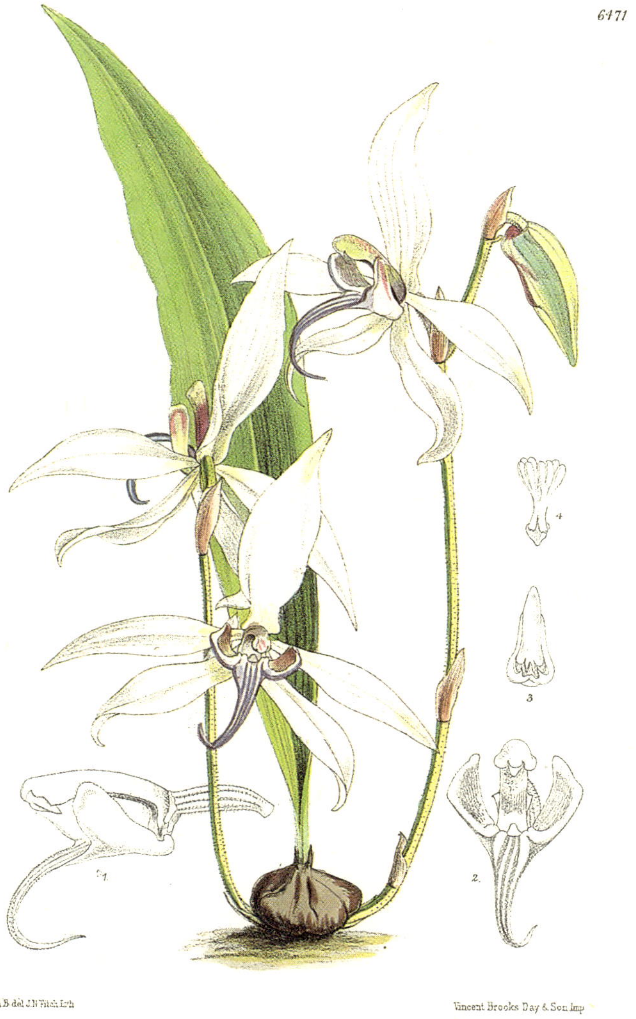

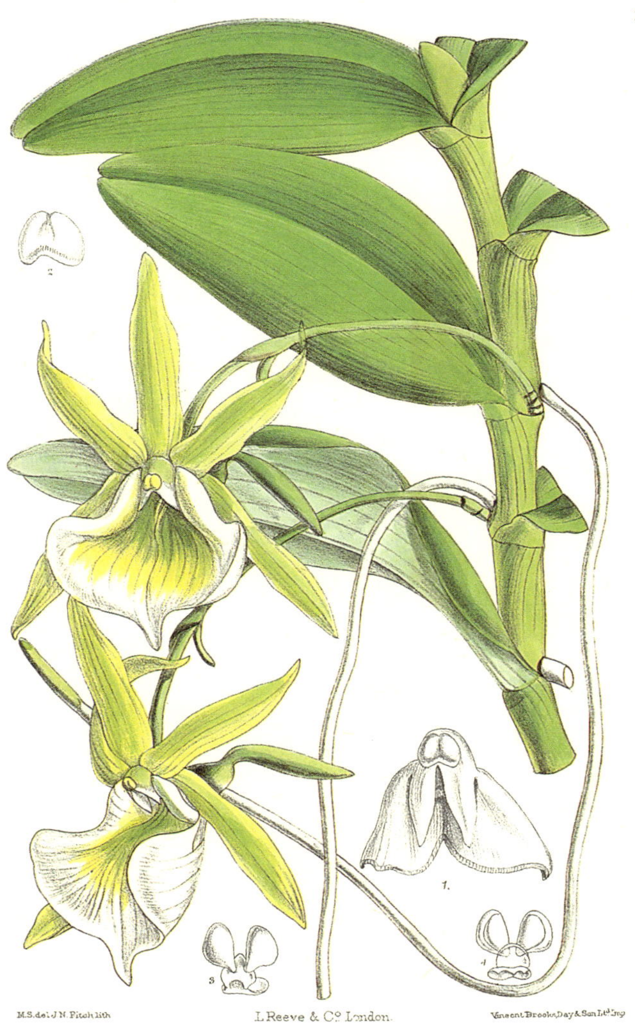

6471 Ancistrochilus thomsonianus (Rchb. f.) Rolfe
5170 Angraecum eburneum Bory

4145 Angraecum distichum Lindl.
7813 Angraecum eichlerianum Kraenzlin

Fitch, del. et lith.

F. Reeve, imp.

4761 Angraecum eburneum Bory

8153 Angraecum infundibulare Lindl.
6723 Angraecum scottianum Rchb. f.

7061 Angraecum ramosum Thouars
5113 Angraecum sesquipedale Thouars

9381.

L. Snelling del. et lith.

9381 Anguloa brevilabris Rolfe

8700

M.S. del. J.N. Fitch lith.

Vincent Brooks Day & Son Ltd imp.

L. Reeve & Co London.

8700 *Anguloa cliftonii* Rolfe

5384 *Anguloa brevilabris* var. *sanguinea* Lindl.
4807 *Anguloa uniflora* Ruiz Lopez & Pavón

4313 *Anguloa clowesii* Lindl.
9553 *Ania hookeriana* (King & Pantl.) Tang & Wang ex Summerh.

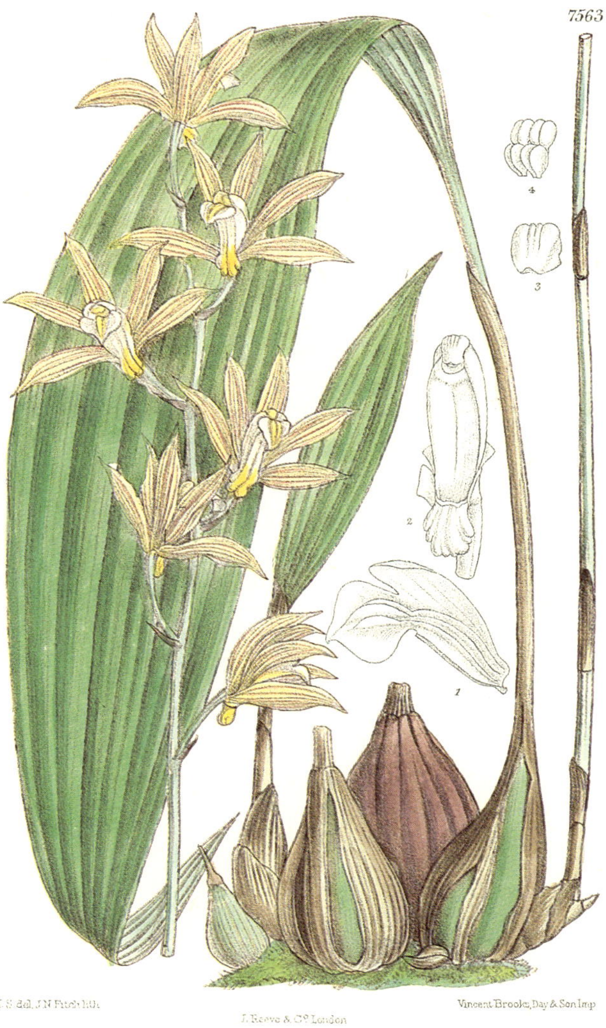

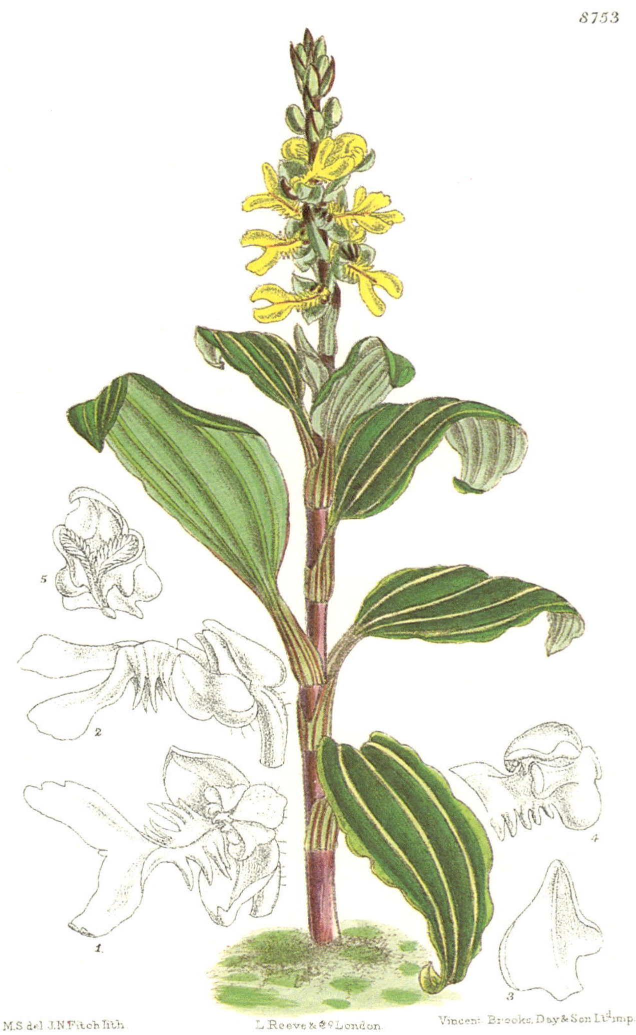

7563 Ania penangiana (Hook. f.) Summerh.
3793 Anneliesia candida (Lindl.) Brieger & Lueckel

4669 Ania viridifusca (Hook.) Tang & Wang ex Summerh.
8753 Anoectochilus lanceolatus Lindl.

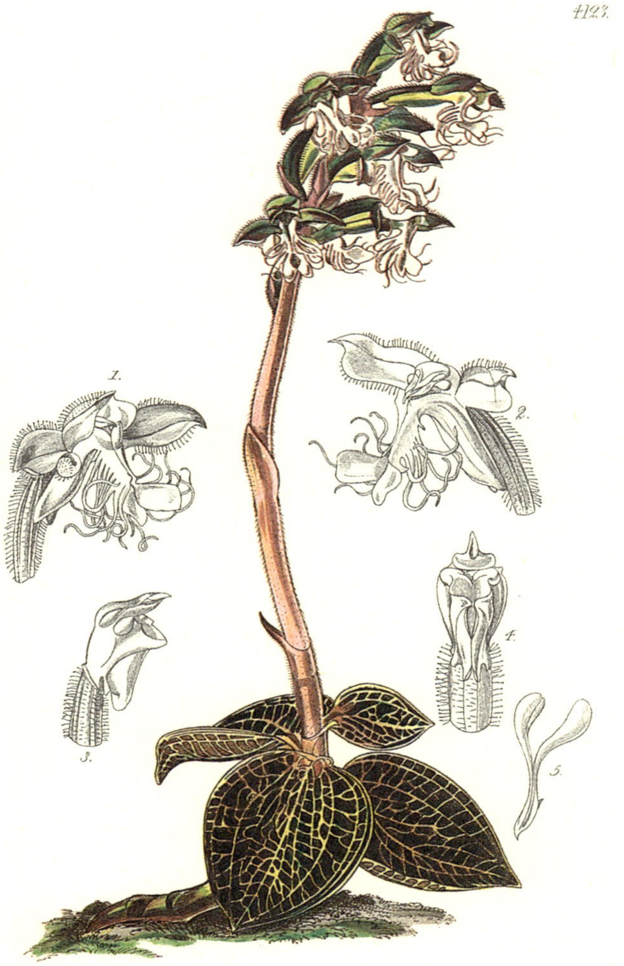

4123 Anoectochilus reinwardtii Blume
5208 Anoectochilus setaceus Blume

9529 Anoectochilus roxburghii (Wallich) Lindl.
3975 Apatostelis ciliaris (Lindl.) Garay

W. Fitch del. et lith.

Vincent Brooks Imp.

4965 *Ansellia africana* Lindl.

M S. del J.N. Fitch lith.

Vincent Brooks, Day & Son Ltd. Imp

L. Reeve & Co. London

8062 *Arachnis annamensis* (Rolfe) J. J. Smith

2204 Arethusa bulbosa L.
7284 Arundina graminifolia (D. Don) Hochr.

6022 Arpophyllum giganteum Hartweg ex Lindl.
7909 Asarca sinuata (Lindl.) Lindl.

5595 Ascocentrum ampullaceum (Roxb.) Schltr.
6222 Ascocentrum hendersonianum (Rchb. f.) Schltr.

5326 Ascocentrum curvifolium (Lindl.) Schltr.
8121 Ascocentrum rubescens (Rolfe) P. Hunt

3962 Aspasia epidendroides Lindl.
6098 Barkeria lindleyana Bateman ex Lindl.

3679 Aspasia variegata Lindl.
3951 Barkeria skinneri (Bateman ex Lindl.) Rich. & Galeotti

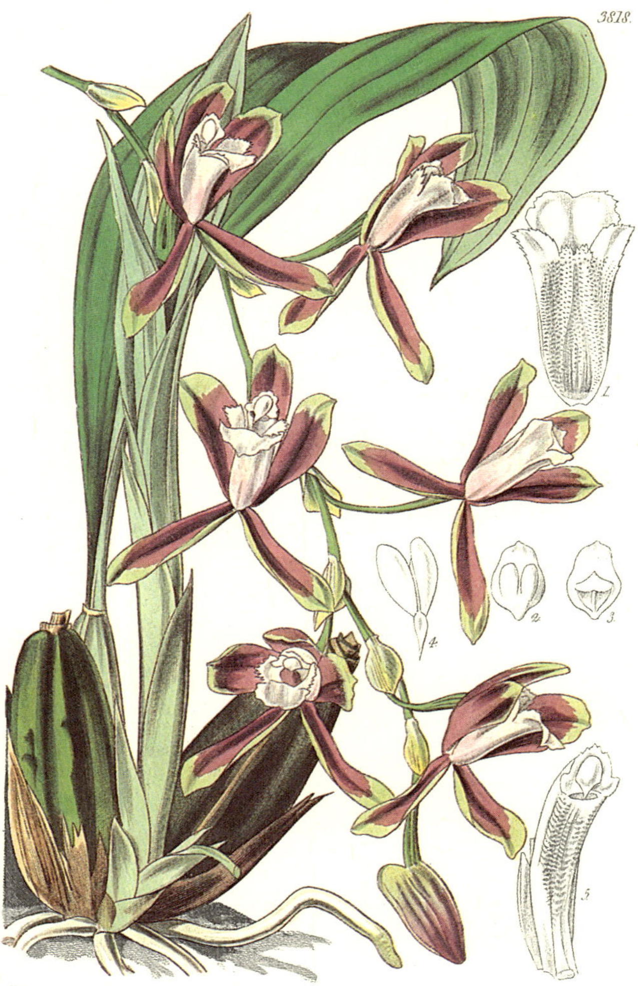

4094 Barkeria spectabilis Bateman ex Lindl.
3818 Batemania colleyi Lindl.

7450 Bartholina burmanniana (L.) Ker-Gawler
2026 Beadlea elata (Sw.) Small ex Britton

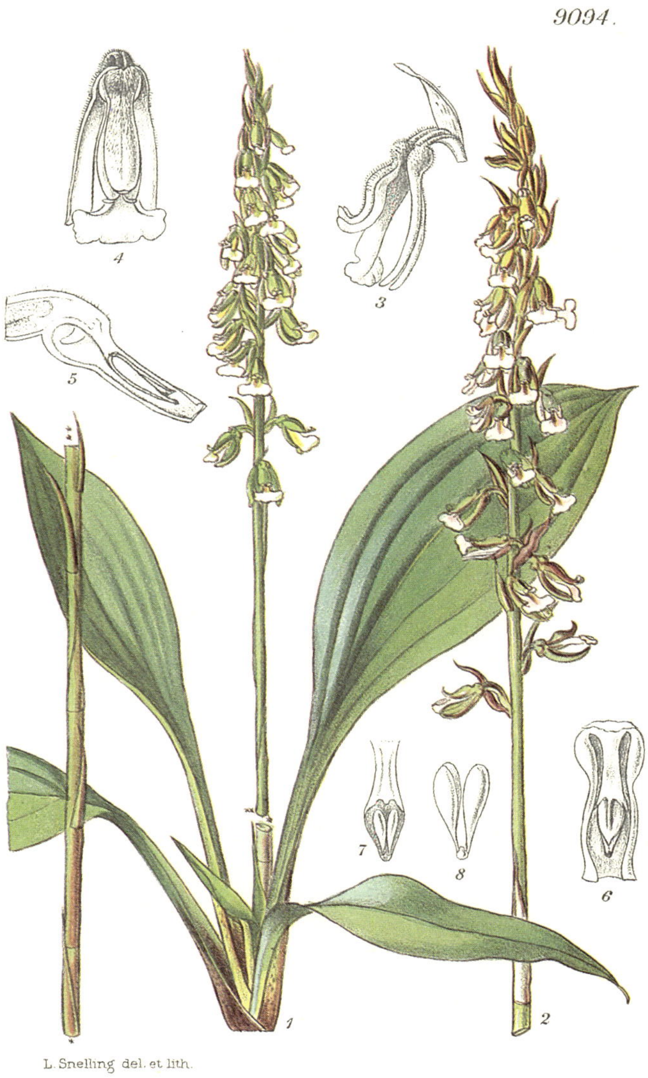

9094 Beadlea elata (Sw.) Small ex Britton
2927 Bifrenaria harrisoniae (Hook.) Rchb. f.

3629 Bifrenaria aureo-fulva (Hook.) Lindl.
2789 Bifrenaria racemosa (Hook.) Lindl.

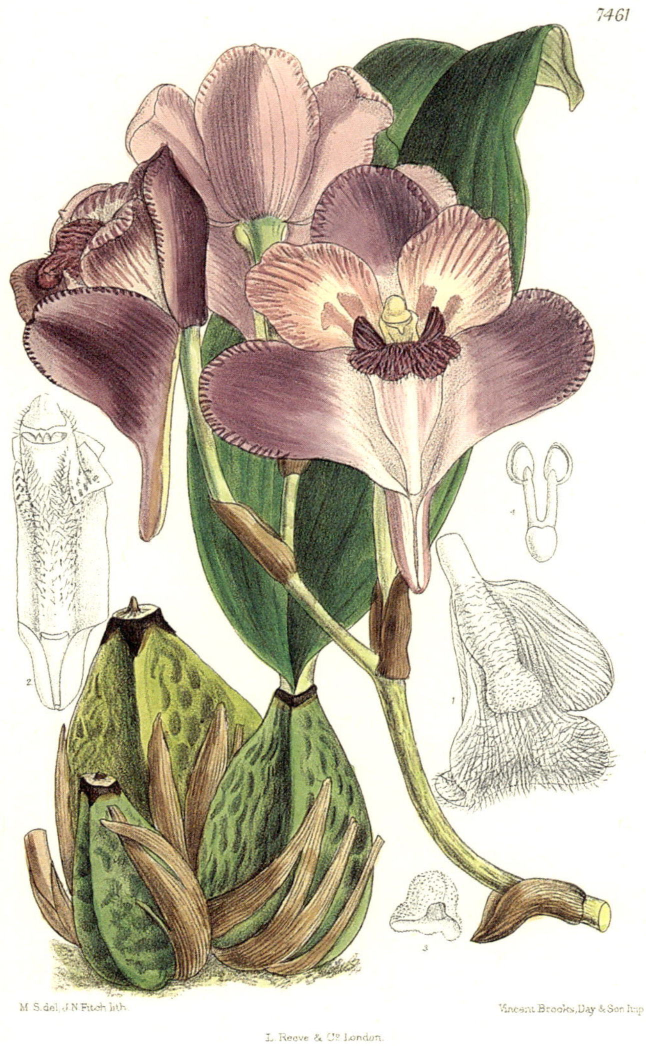

7461 Bifrenaria tyrianthina (Lodd.) Rchb. f.
3736 Bletia parkinsonii Hook.

5646 Bletia catenulata Ruiz Lopez & Pavón
3518 Bletia patula Hook.

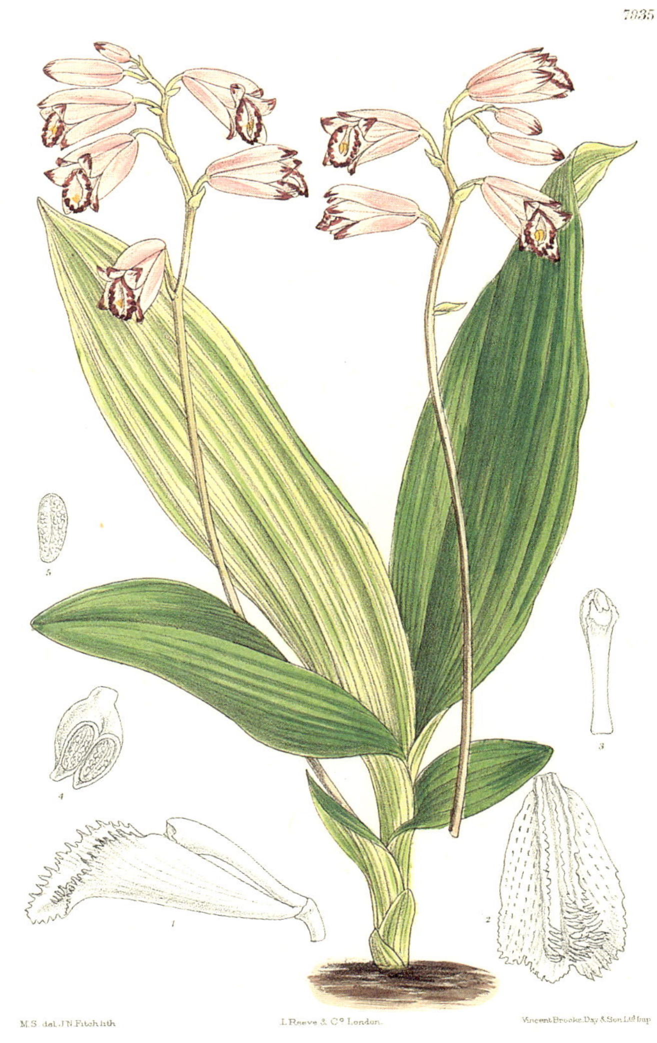

930 Bletia purpurea (Lam.) DC.
3319 Bletia purpurea (Lam.) DC.

3217 Bletia purpurea (Lam.) DC.
7935 Bletilla sinensis (Rolfe) Schltr.

1492 Bletilla striata (Thunb.) Rchb. f.

6331 Bollea lalindei (Linden) Rchb. f.

M.S. del. J.N. Fitch, lith. L. Reeve & Co. London Vincent Brooks, Day & Son Ltd imp

6458 Bollea coelestis (Rchb. f.) Rchb. f.

N. 2926.

Dr Greville del.

Pub. by S. Curtis, Walworth Aug. 1 1829.

Swan Sc

2926 Bonatea speciosa (L.f.) Willd.

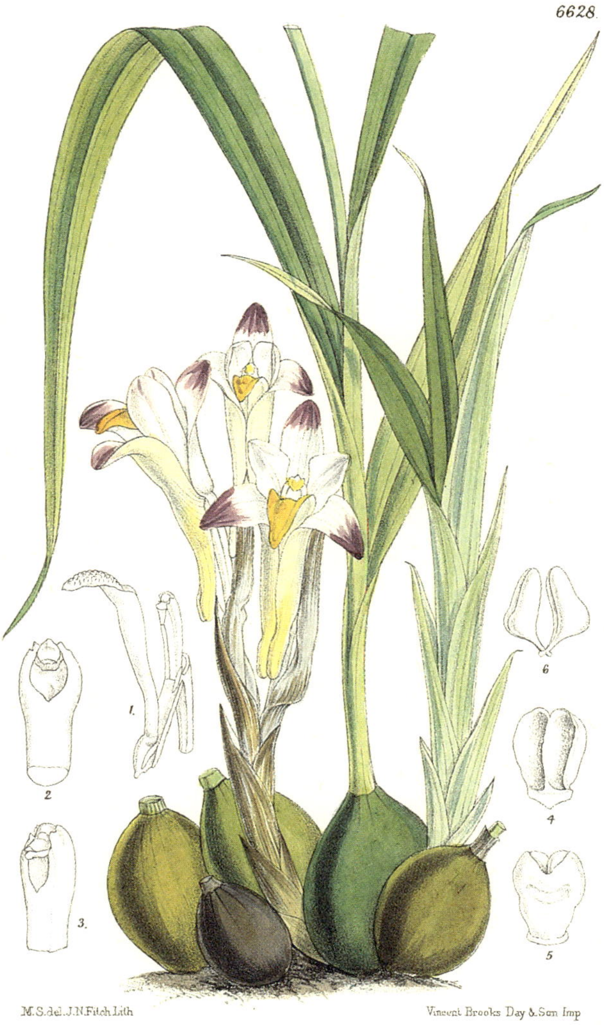

6628 Bothriochilus bellus Lemaire
4734 Brassavola acaulis Lindl.

5875 Brachycorythis macrantha (Lindl.) Summerh.
543 Brassavola cucullata (L.) R.Br.

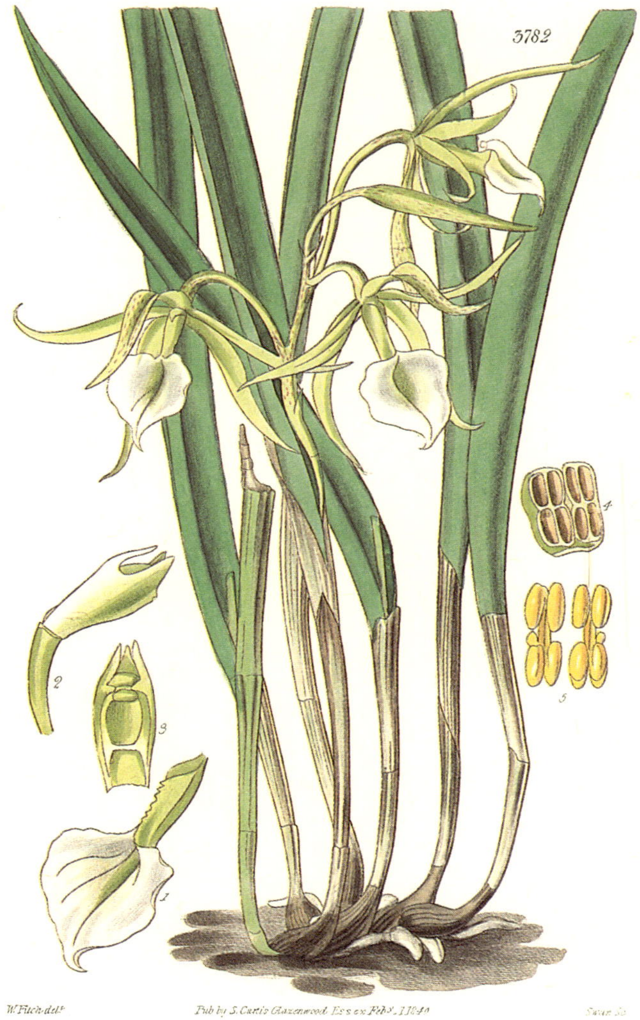

3722 Brassavola cucullata (L.) R. Br.
4021 Brassavola nodosa (L.) Lindl.

3782 Brassavola nodosa (L.) Lindl.
3229 Brassavola subulifolia Lindl.

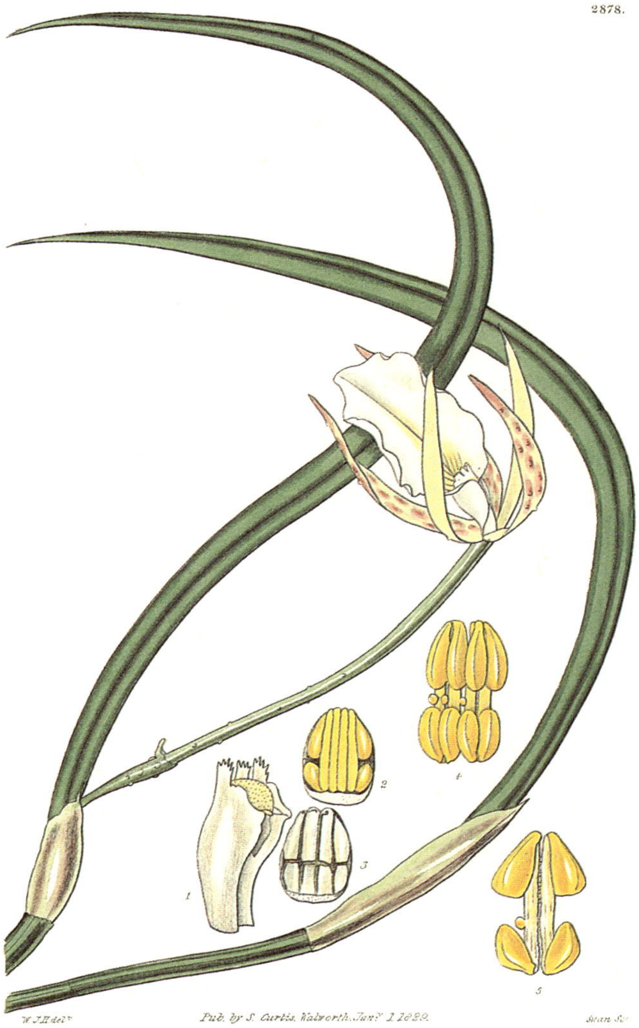

2878 Brassavola tuberculata Hook.
3451 Brassia caudata (L.) Lindl.

3761 Brassavola tuberculata Hook.
3577 Brassia lanceana Lindl.

5748 Brassia arcuigera Rchb. f.

3794 Brassia bidens Lindl.
4003 Brassia maculata R.Br.

1691 Brassia maculata R.Br.
5449 × Brassocattleya lindleyana Rolfe

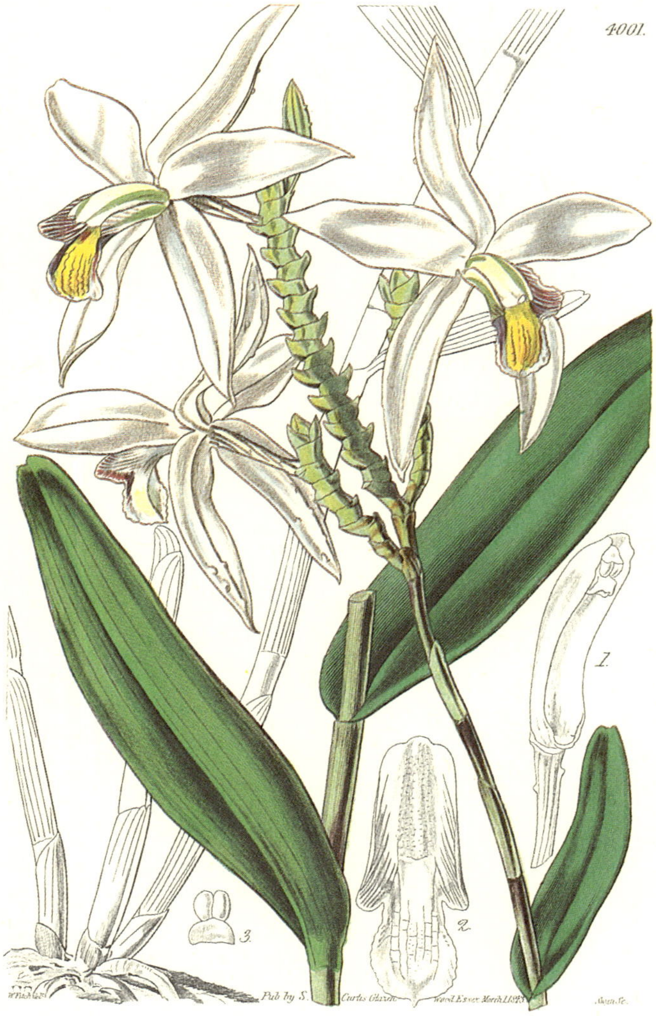

4001 Bromheadia finlaysoniana (Lindl.) Rchb. f.
3536 Broughtonia sanguinea (Sw.) R.Br.

3076 Broughtonia sanguinea (Sw.) R.Br.
7309 Brownleea coerulea Harvey ex Lindl.

8281 Bulbophyllum auratum (Lindl.) Rchb. f.
5288 Bulbophyllum barbigerum Lindl.

7938 Bulbophyllum auricomum Lindl.
4088 Bulbophyllum calamarium Lindl.

M.S. del. J.N. Fitch, Lith. Vincent Brooks Day & Son Imp.

6567 Bulbophyllum beccarii Rchb. f.

8321 Bulbophyllum biflorum Teijsm. & Binnend.

8187 Bulbophyllum binnendijkii J. J. Smith

5316 Bulbophyllum careyanum (Hook.) Sprengel
8000 Bulbophyllum coriophorum Ridley

7283 Bulbophyllum comosum Collett & Hemsley
8792 Bulbophyllum coriophorum Ridley

7554 *Bulbophyllum corolliferum* J. J. Smith
8668 *Bulbophyllum corolliferum* J. J. Smith

4166 *Bulbophyllum crassipes* Hook. f.

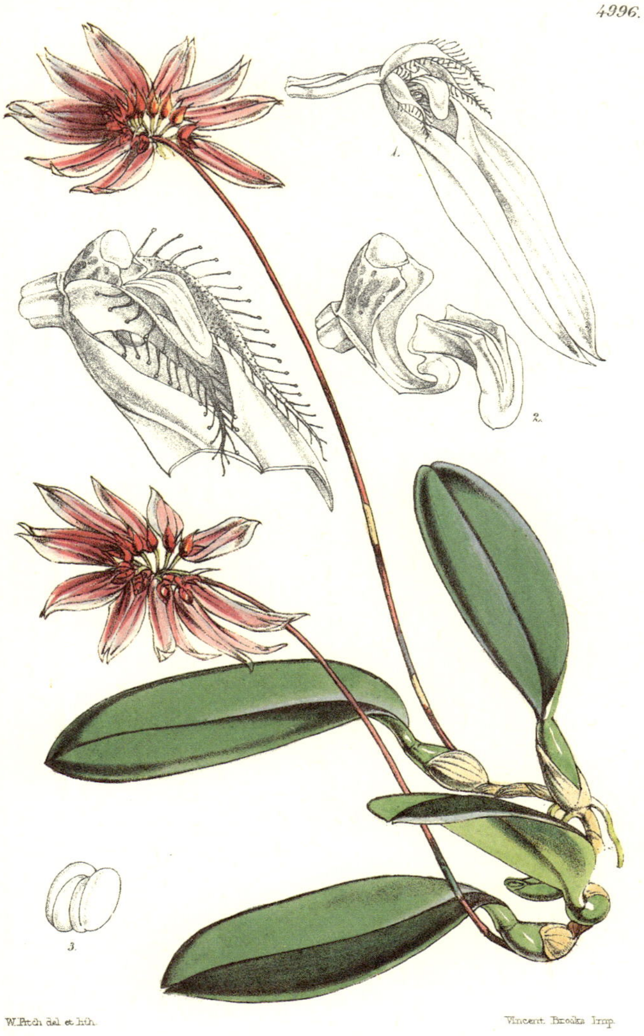

4996 Bulbophyllum cumingii (Lindl.) Rchb. f.
9408 Bulbophyllum elassonotum Summerh.

6119 Bulbophyllum dayanum Rchb. f.
8088 Bulbophyllum ericssonii Kraenzlin

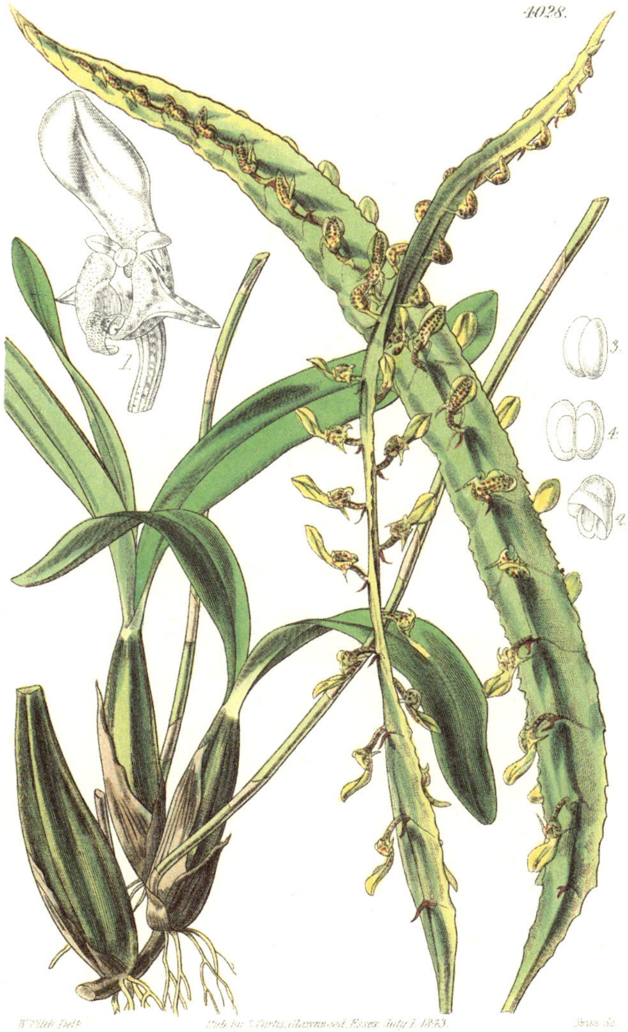

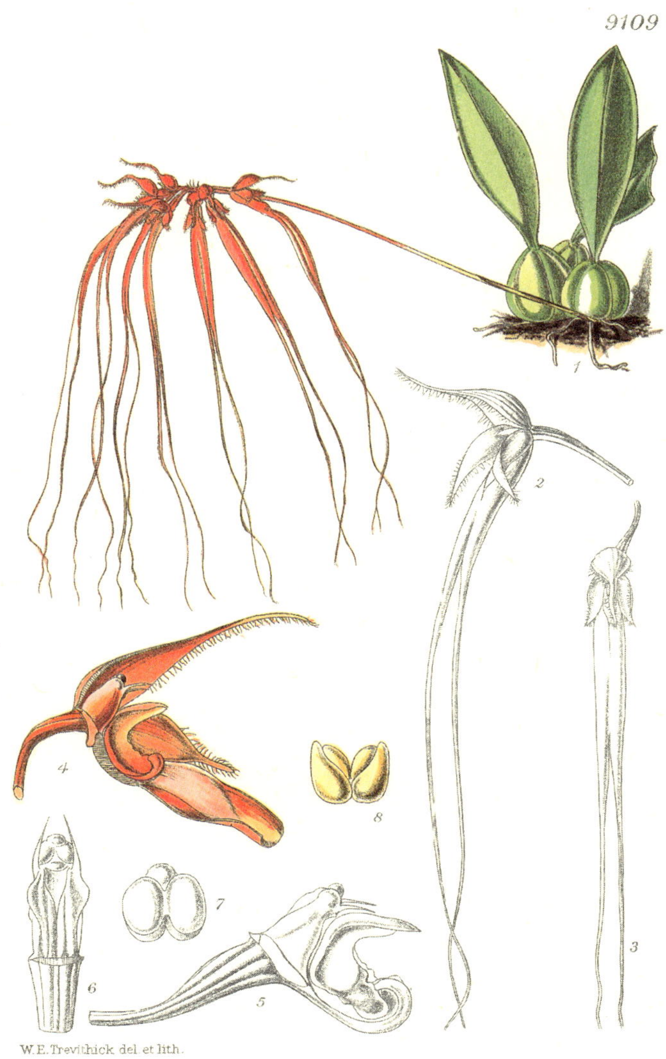

4028 Bulbophyllum falcatum Rchb. f.
4391 Bulbophyllum fimbriatum (Lindl.) Rchb. f.

8933 Bulbophyllum farreri (W. Smith) Seidenf.
9109 Bulbophyllum flaviflorum (Liu & Su) Seidenf.

M.S.del, J.N.Fitch lith

Vincent Brooks Day & Son Ltd Imp

L. Reeve & Co. London

7787 *Bulbophyllum grandiflorum* Blume

8600

M.S. del. J.N. Fitch lith. L. Reeve & Co London Vincent Brooks, Day & Son Ltd imp

4267

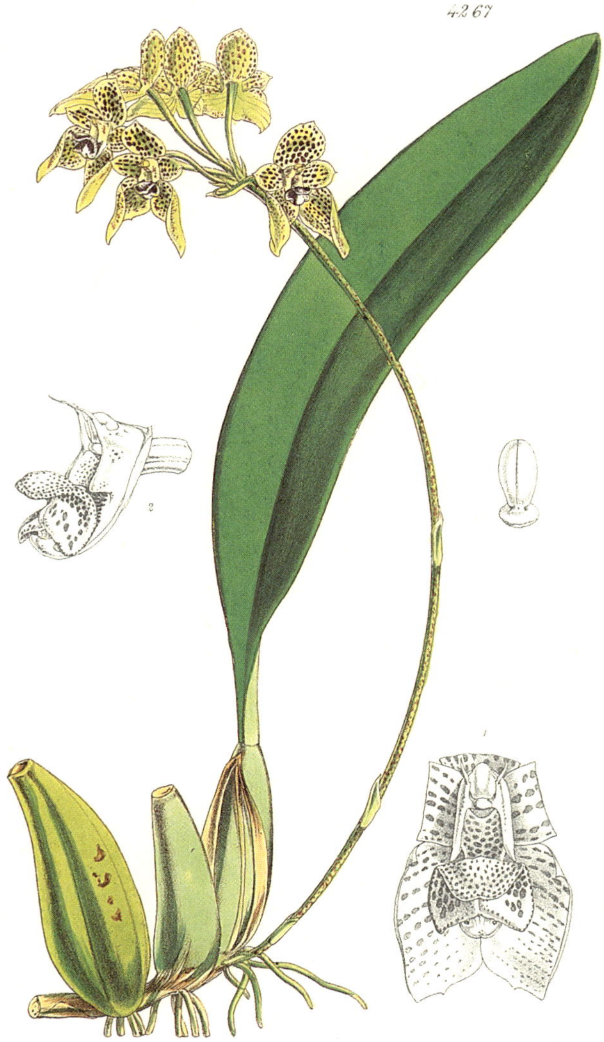

Fitch del. et lith. Reeve imp

8785

M.S. del. J.N. Fitch lith. L. Reeve & Co London Vincent Brooks, Day & Son Ltd imp

8600 Bulbophyllum fletcherianum Rolfe
4267 Bulbophyllum guttulatum Wallich ex Hook. f.

8785 Bulbophyllum hamelinii Rolfe

7557

M. S. del, J. N. Fitch lith.

Vincent Brooks, Day & Son Imp.

L Reeve & C° London.

7557 Bulbophyllum graveolens (Bailey) J.J. Smith

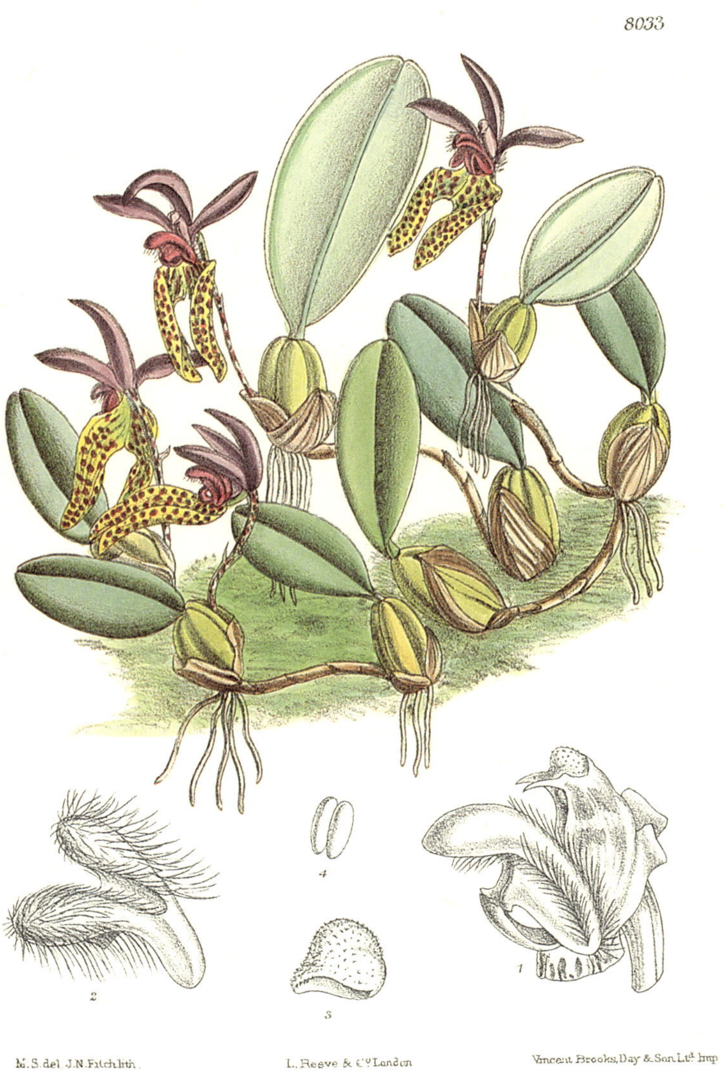

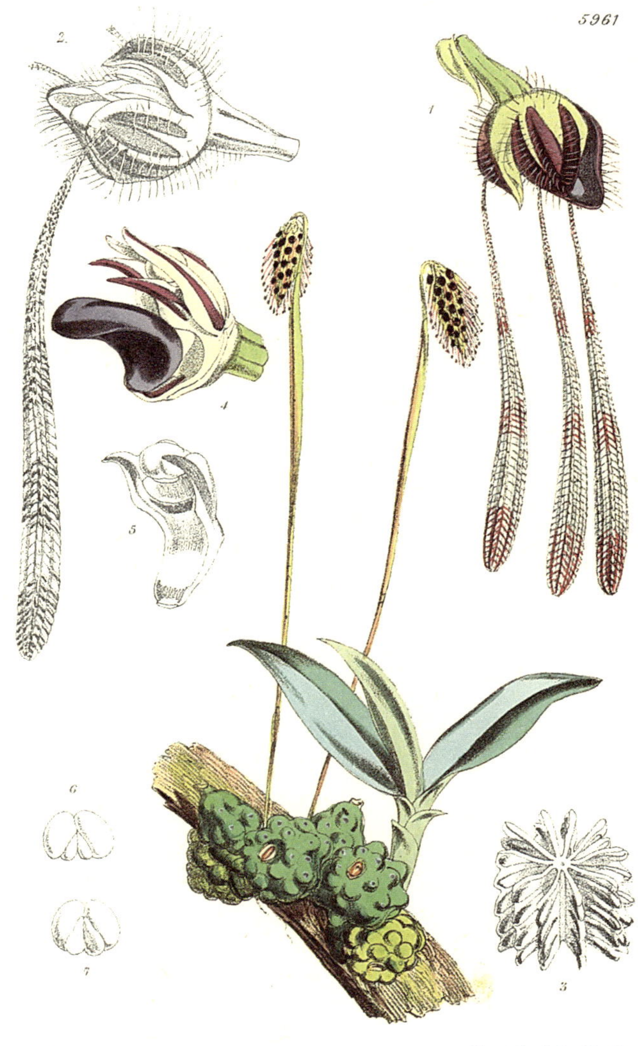

4753 Bulbophyllum helenae (Kuntze) J.J. Smith
8033 Bulbophyllum lasiochilum Parish & Rchb. f.

7869 Bulbophyllum hookeri (Duthie) J.J. Smith
5961 Bulbophyllum lemniscatum Parish ex Hook. f.

9631 *Bulbophyllum leopardinum* Lindl.
8723 *Bulbophyllum lilacinum* Ridley

7811 *Bulbophyllum leucorrhachis* (Rolfe) Schltr.
4532 *Bulbophyllum lobbii* Lindl.

7214 Bulbophyllum longiflorum Thouars
4422 Bulbophyllum macraei (Lindl.) Rchb. f.

8366 Bulbophyllum longissimum (Ridley) Ridley
7208 Bulbophyllum macranthum Lindl.

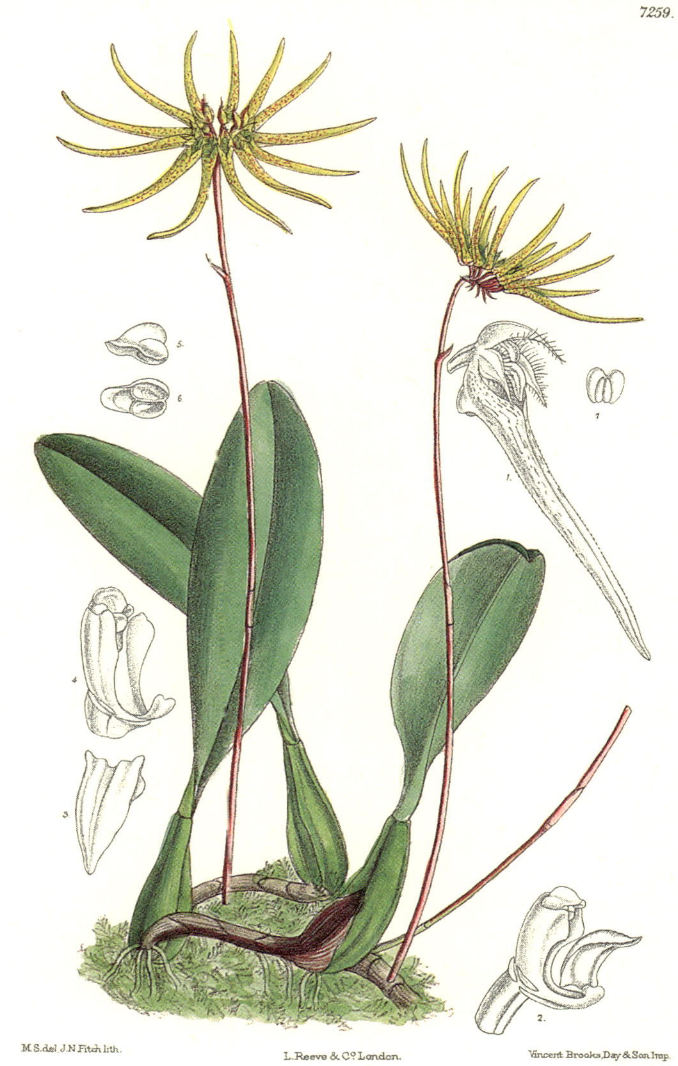

8842 Bulbophyllum macrobulbum J.J. Smith
4334 Bulbophyllum malachadenia Cogn.

7259 Bulbophyllum makoyanum (Rchb. f.) Ridley
8531 Bulbophyllum mastersianum (Rolfe) J.J. Smith

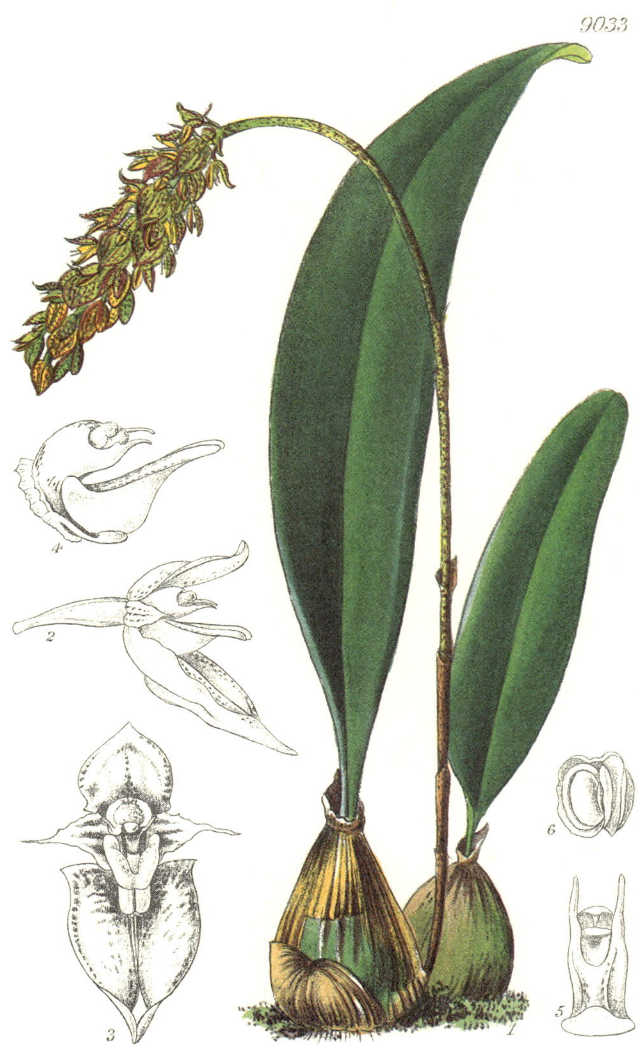

5936 Bulbophyllum maximum (Lindl.) Rchb. f.
7314 Bulbophyllum melanorrhachis Rchb. f.

4977 Bulbophyllum medusea (Lindl.) Rchb. f.
9033 Bulbophyllum morphologorum Kraenzlin

5050 Bulbophyllum neilgherrense Wight
9459 Bulbophyllum orthoglossum Kraenzlin

7229 Bulbophyllum ornatissimum (Rchb.f.) J.J. Smith
4418 Bulbophyllum othonis (Kuntze) J.J. Smith

9299 Bulbophyllum patens King
7286 Bulbophyllum pechei Rchb. f.

5329 Bulbophyllum pavimentatum Lindl.
6802 Bulbophyllum picturatum (Lodd.) Rchb. f.

7946 Bulbophyllum platyrhachis (Rolfe) Schltr.
8273 Bulbophyllum purpureorhachis (De Wild.) Schltr.

5408 Bulbophyllum psittacoglossum Rchb. f.
8199 Bulbophyllum putidum (Teijsm. & Binnend.) J.J. Smith

5605.

W. Fitch, del. et lith. Vincent Brooks Imp.

5309.

W Fitch del. et lith. Vincent Brooks, Imp.

8761

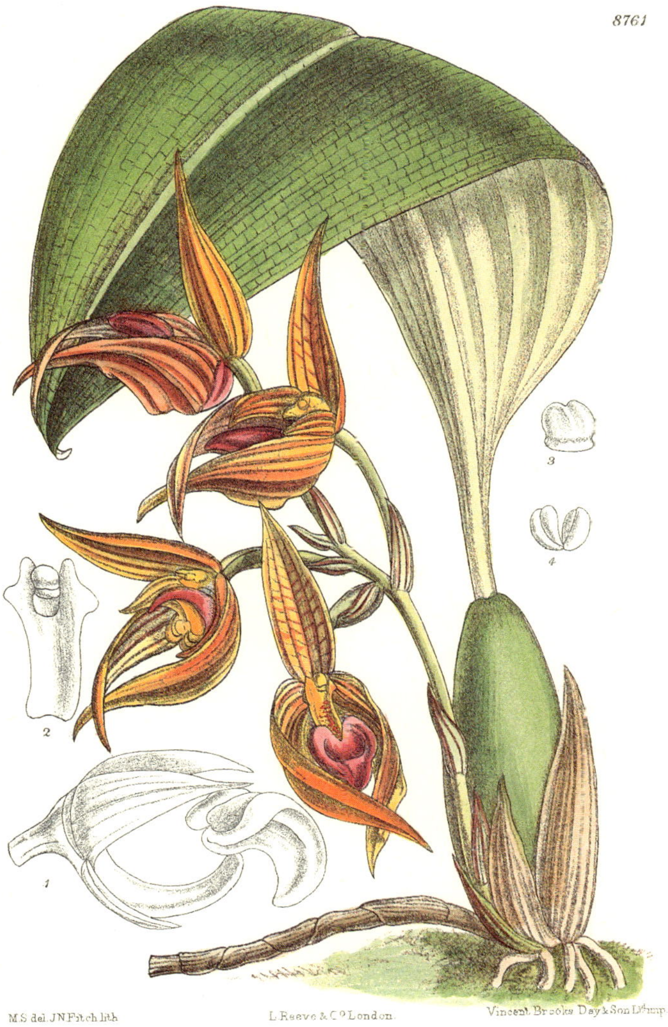

M.S. del. J.N. Fitch lith. L. Reeve & Co London. Vincent Brooks Day & Son Ltd Imp.

8954

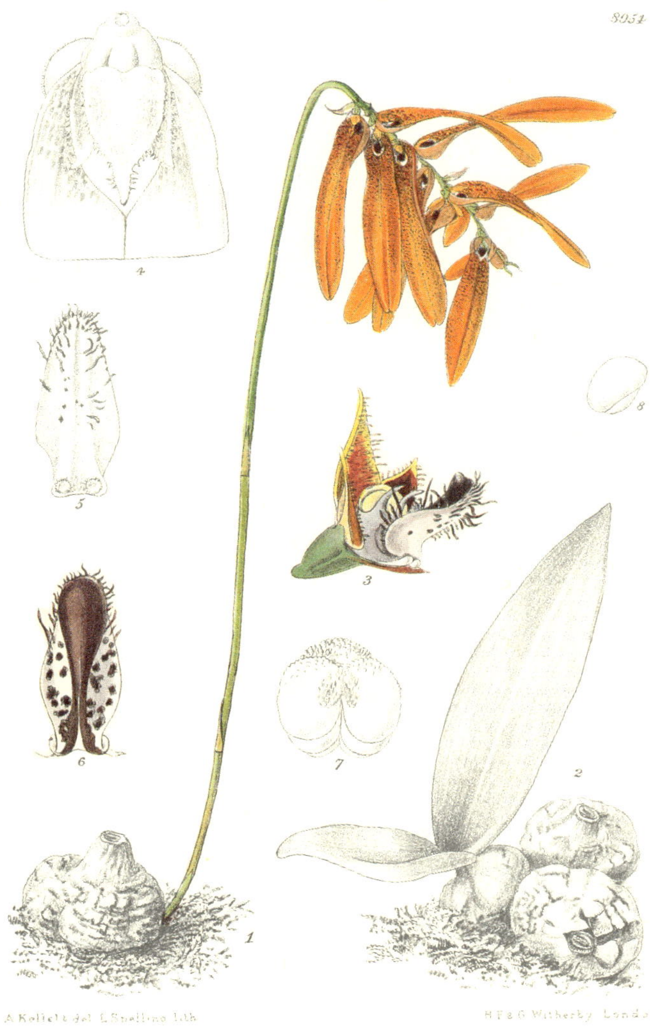

A. Kellett del. L. Snelling lith. H.F. & G. Witherby London.

5605 Bulbophyllum reticulatum Bateman
8761 Bulbophyllum sociale Rolfe

5309 Bulbophyllum rhizophorae Lindl.
8954 Bulbophyllum tripudians Parish & Rchb. f.

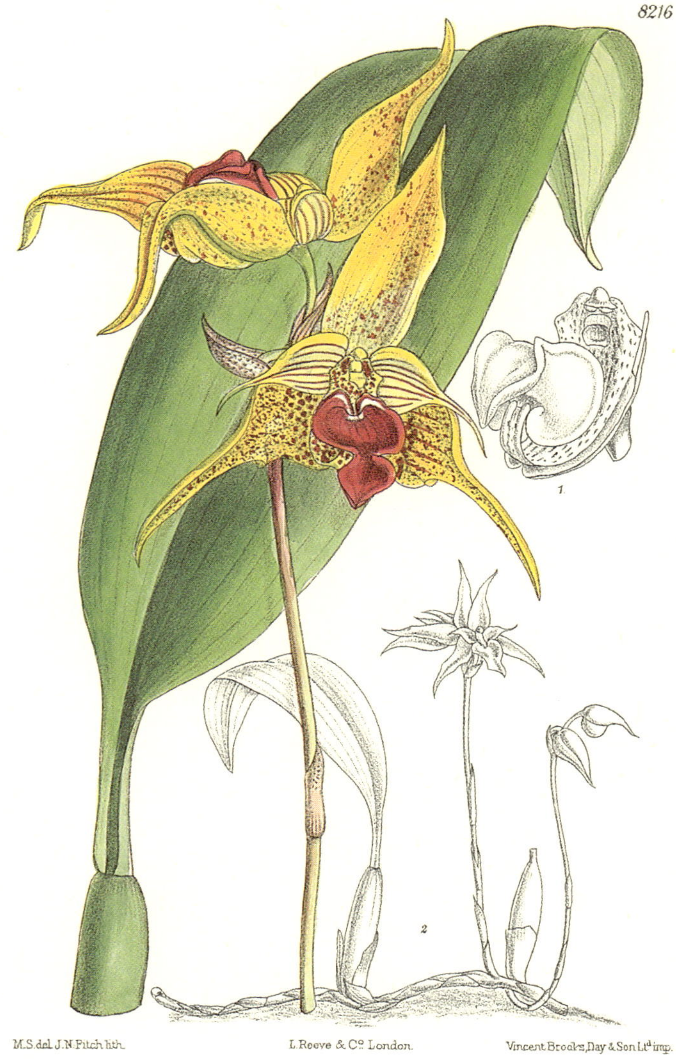

8943 Bulbophyllum triste Rchb. f.
8327 Bulbophyllum virescens J.J. Smith

8216 Bulbophyllum uniflorum (Blume) Hassk.

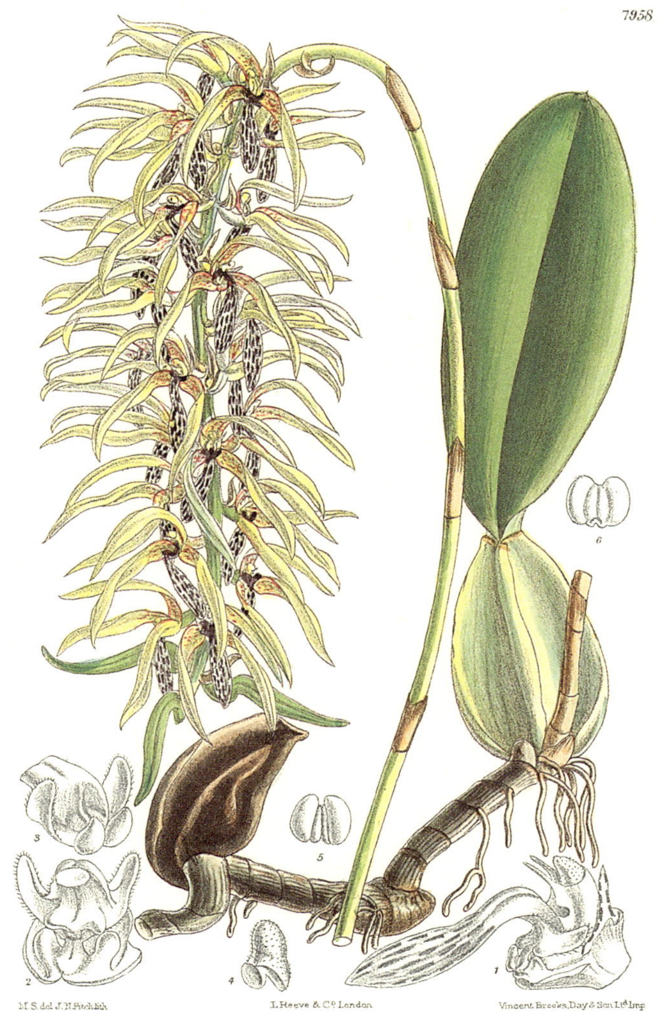

4237 Bulbophyllum weberi Ames
7198 Bulbophyllum wendlandianum (Kraenzlin) Dammer

7958 Bulbophyllum weddelii (Lindl.) Rchb. f.
7630 A: Caladenia catenata (Smith) Druce, B.: Caladenia carnea R.Br.

5042 Calanthe × dominii Lindl.
4541 Calanthe masuca (D. Don) Lindl.

7780 Calanthe madagascariensis Rolfe
6104 Calanthe pulchra (Blume) Lindl.

9648 Calanthe reflexa Maxim.
7026 Calanthe striata (Thunb.) Lindl.

5312 Calanthe rosea (Lindl.) Benth.
6844 Calanthe sylvatica (Thouars) Lindl.

N. 2615.

2615 Calanthe triplicata (Willem.) Ames

8803 Calanthe tricarinata Lindl.
4671 Calanthe vestita Lindl.

5375 Calanthe × veitchii Lindl.
3187 Calochilus campestris R.Br.

116 Calopogon tuberosus (L.) Britton, Sterns & Pogg.
5202 Catasetum atratum Lindl.

2763 Calypso bulbosa var. americana (R.Br.) Luer
3802 Catasetum barbatum Lindl.

3514 Catasetum barbatum Lindl.

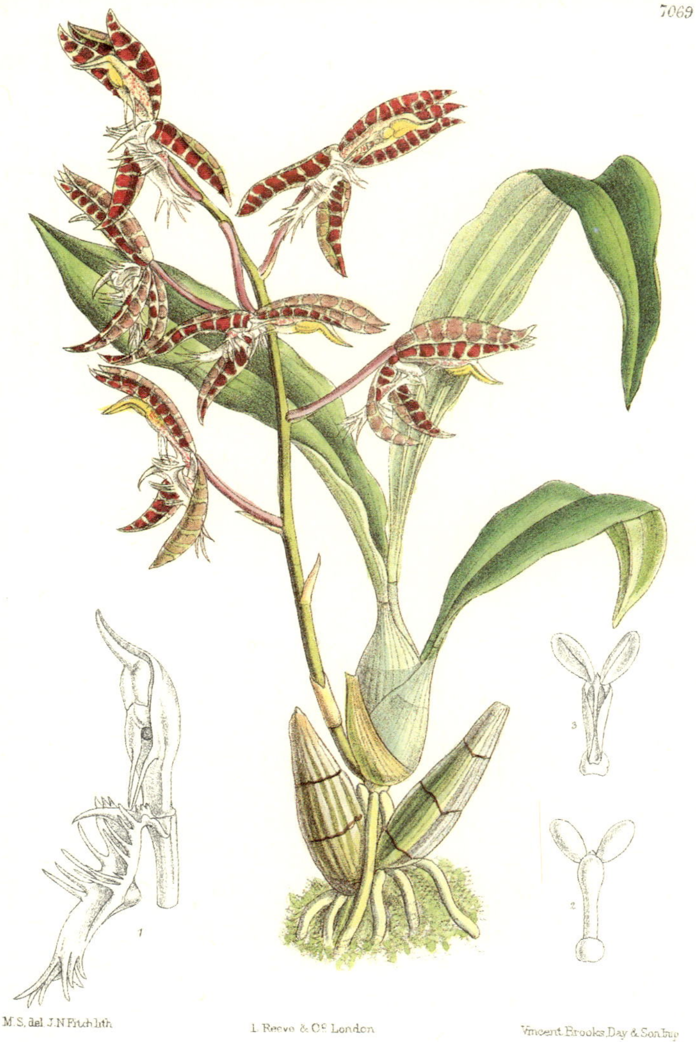

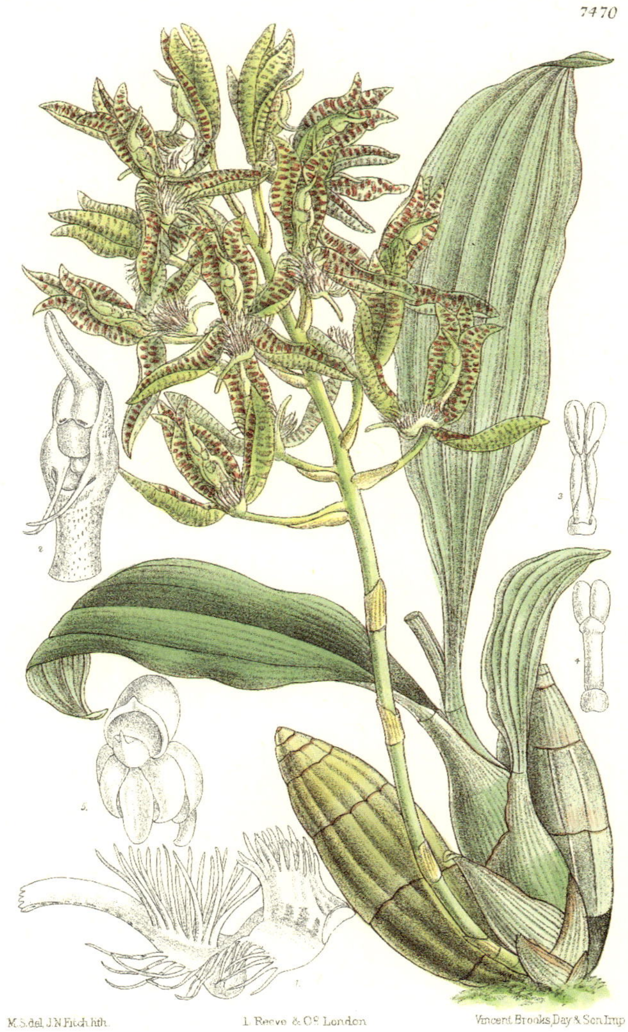

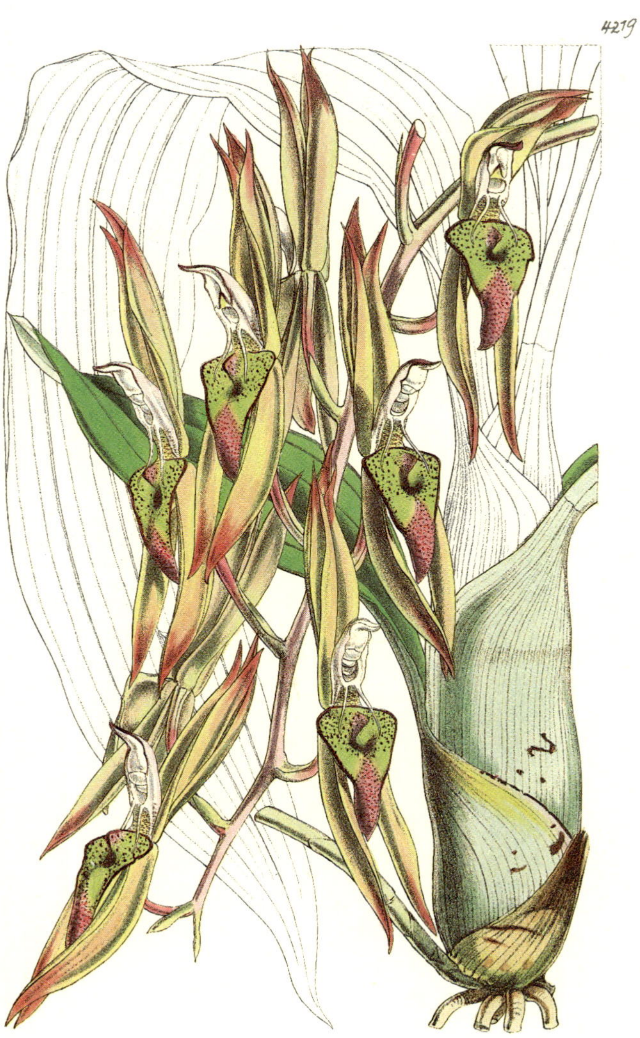

7069 Catasetum barbatum Lindl.
4219 Catasetum callosum Lindl.

7470 Catasetum barbatum Lindl.
6648 Catasetum callosum Lindl.

3262 Catasetum cernuum (Lindl.) Rchb. f.
3923 Catasetum deltoideum (Lindl.) Mutel

5399 Catasetum cernuum (Lindl.) Rchb. f.
3708 Catasetum discolor var. fimbriatum Rchb. f.

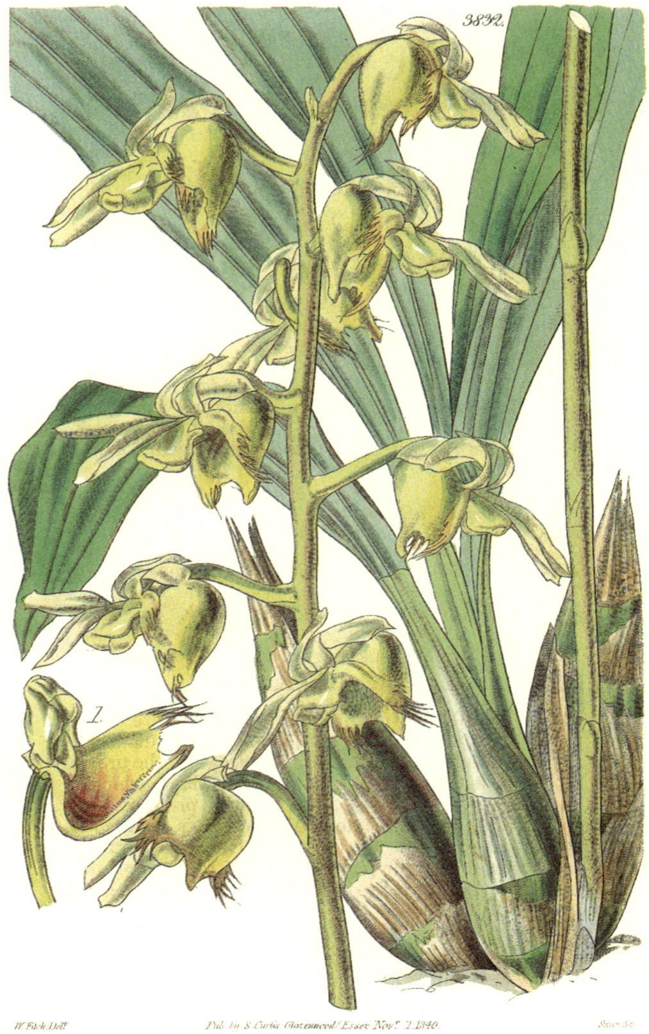

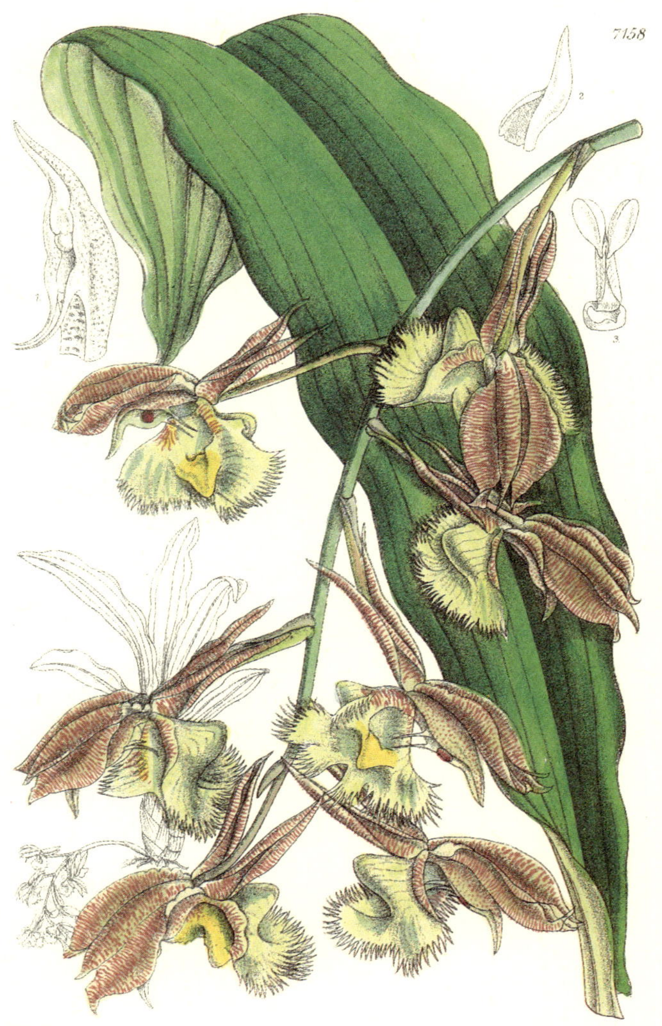

3796 Catasetum discolor var. roseo-album (Hook.) Mansf.
3601 Catasetum discolor var. viridiflorum Cogn.

3832 Catasetum discolor var. roseo-album (Hook.) Mansf.
7158 Catasetum fimbriatum (Morren) Lindl.

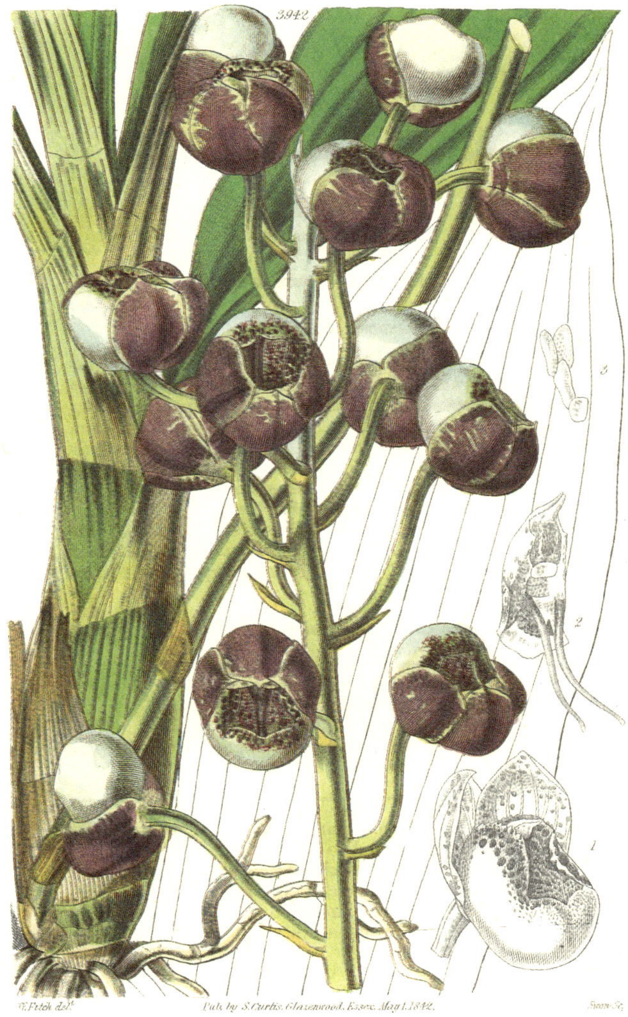

8093 Catasetum galeritum Rchb. f.
3823 Catasetum integerrimum Hook.

3942 Catasetum globiflorum Hook.
3937 Catasetum integerrimum Hook.

3819 Catasetum longifolium Lindl.

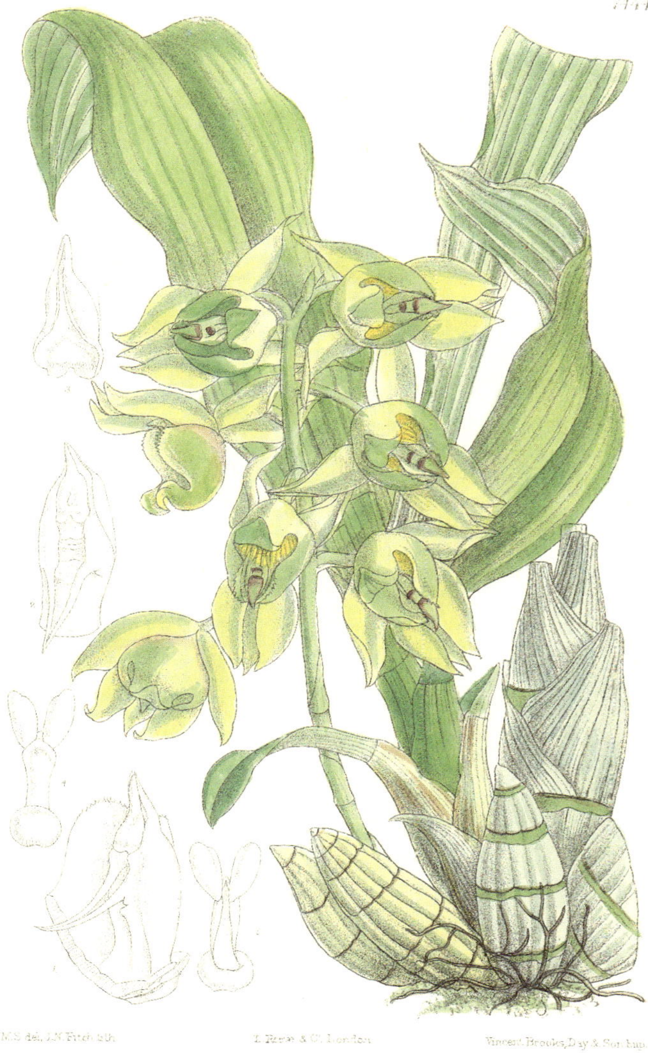

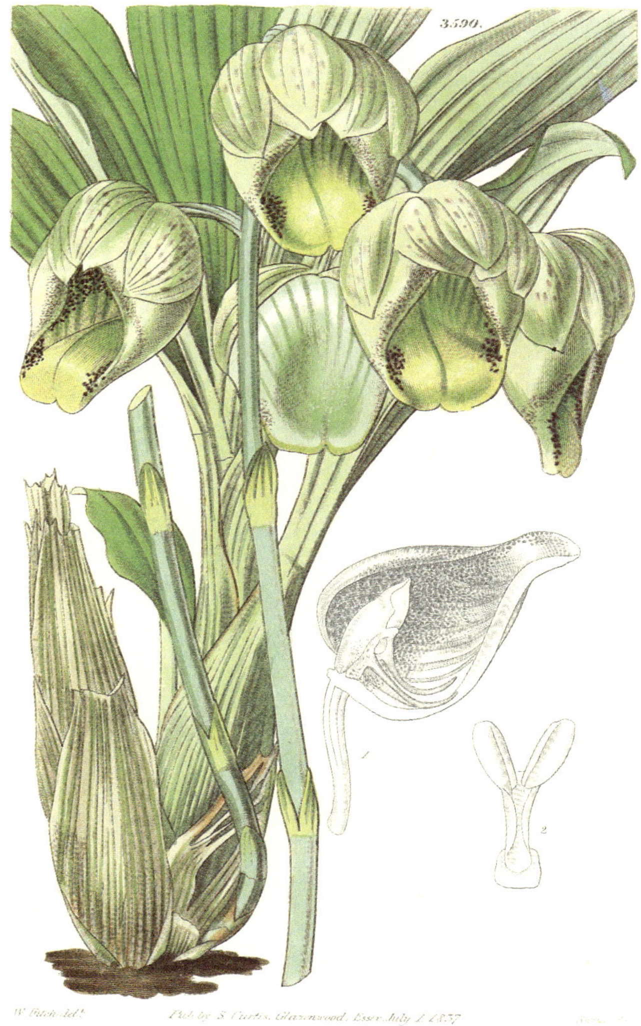

7444 Catasetum lemosii Rolfe
3929 Catasetum luridum (Link) Lindl.

3590 Catasetum luridum (Link) Lindl.
3329 Catasetum macrocarpum Rich. ex Kunth

2559 Catasetum macrocarpum Rich. ex Kunth

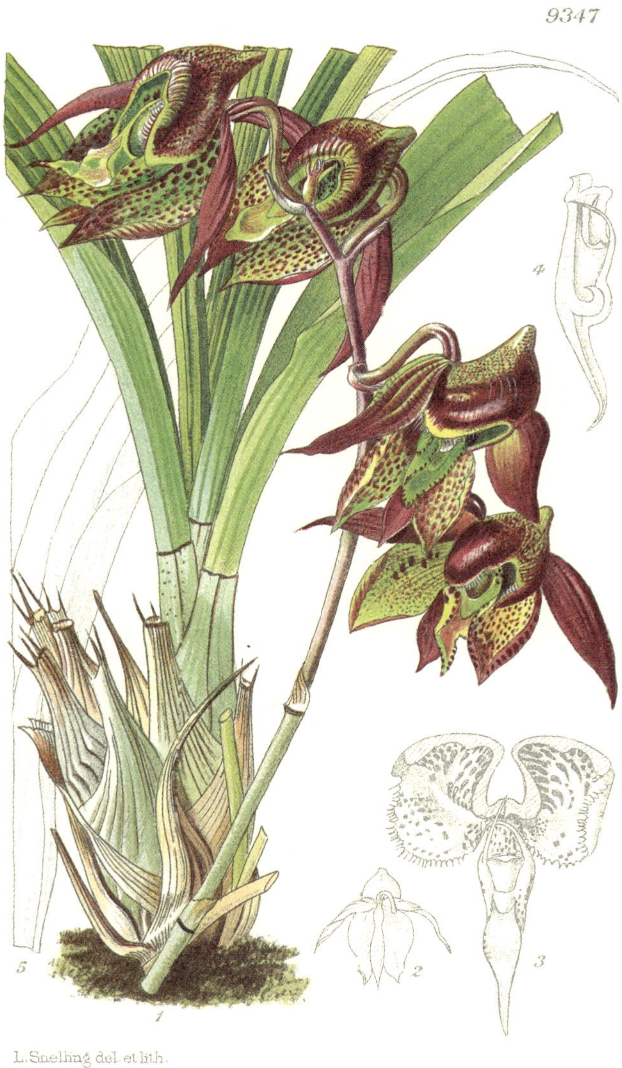

9347 *Catasetum maculatum* Kunth
6998 *Catasetum pileatum* Rchb. f.

8514 *Catasetum microglossum* Rolfe

3388 Catasetum purum Nees

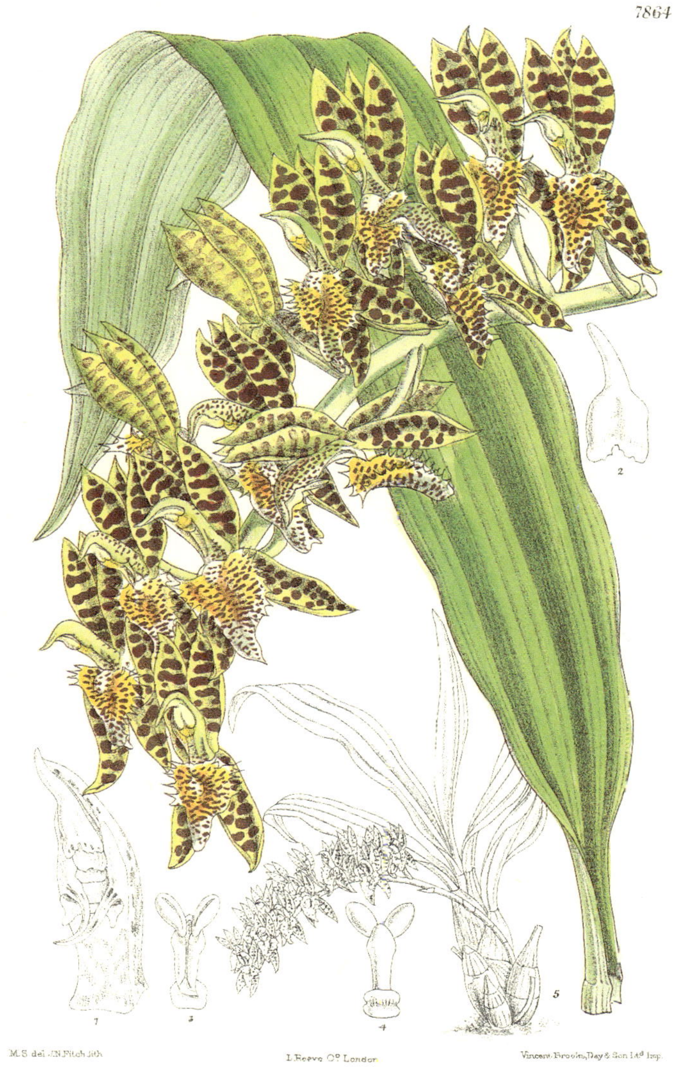

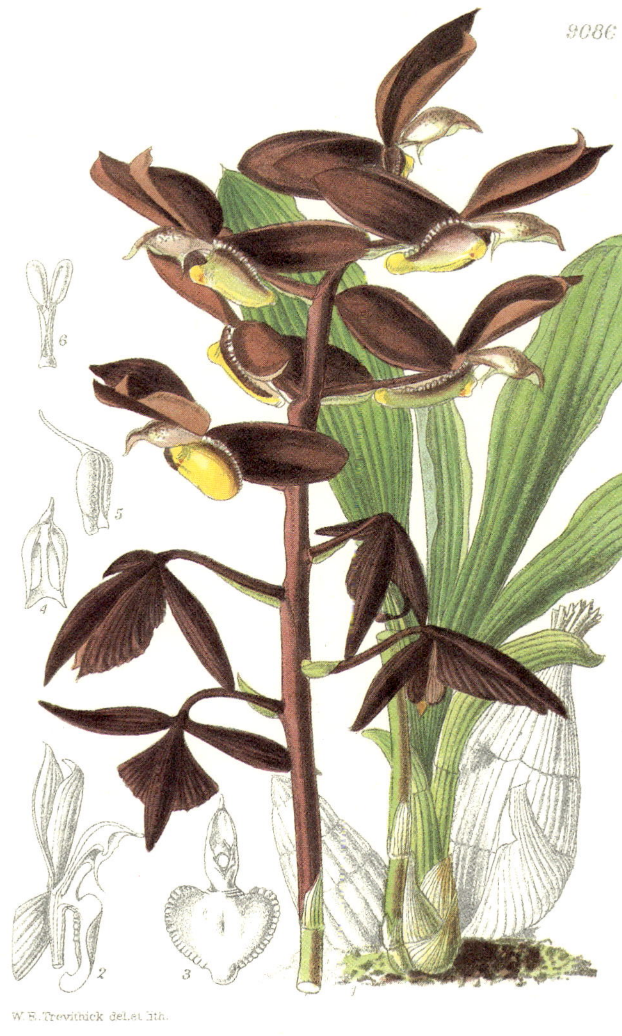

7864 Catasetum quadridens Rolfe
9086 Catasetum tenebrosum Kraenzlin

4792 Catasetum sanguineum Lindl.
4017 Catasetum viridiflavum Hook.

M. S. del, J. N. Fitch lith.

L Reeve & Co London

Vincent Brooks, Day & Son Ltd Imp.

8007 *Catasetum saccatum* var. *christyanum* (Rchb. f.) Mansf.

5683 Cattleya amethystoglossa Linden & Rchb.f. ex Linden

5039 Cattleya acklandiae Lindl.
4916 Cattleya deckeri Klotzsch

4909 Cattleya bicolor Lindl.
7543 Cattleya elongata Barb. Rodr.

W. Fitch, del. et lith.

Vincent Brooks, Imp.

5618 *Cattleya dowiana* Bateman

5048.

W. Fitch del. et lith. Vincent Brooks Imp.

5048 *Cattleya granulosa* Lindl.

3265 Cattleya forbesii Lindl.
2851 Cattleya intermedia Graham ex Hook.
4085 Cattleya harrisoniana Bateman ex Lindl.
3998 Cattleya labiata Lindl.

M. S. del, J. N. Fitch lith.

Vincent Brooks, Day & Son Imp

L Reeve C° London.

7287 Cattleya iricolor Rchb. f.

7133 Cattleya lawrenceana Rchb. f.
8377 Cattleya rex O'Brien

5032 Cattleya luteola Lindl.

3693 Cattleya leopoldii Verschaff. ex Lemaire

4902

Fitch del. et lith. Vincent Brooks Imp.

4902 *Cattleya maxima* Lindl.

3669 Cattleya mossiae Hook.

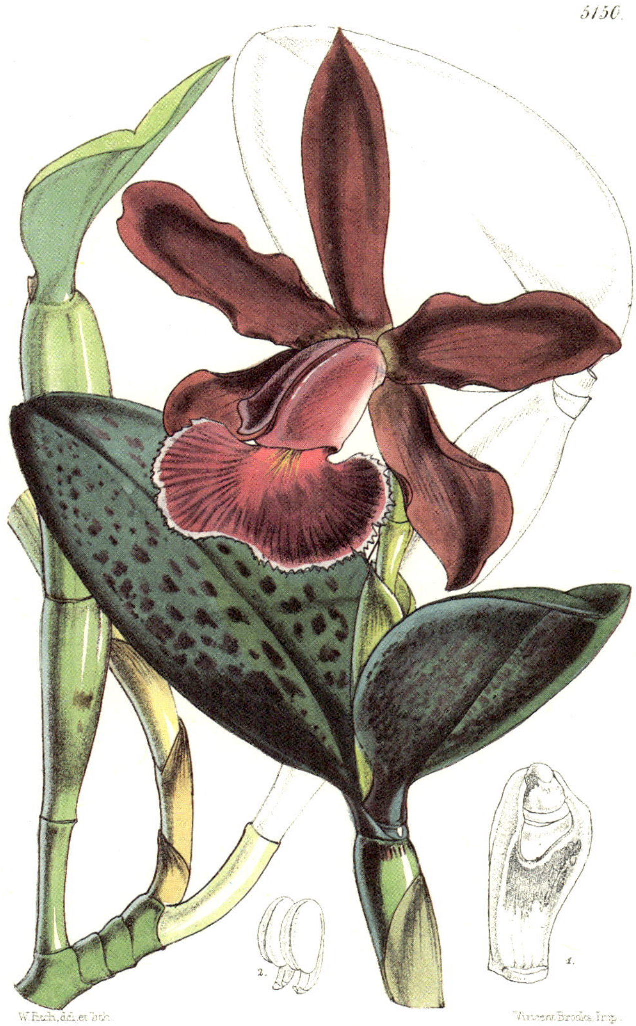

5150 Cattleya schilleriana Rchb. f.
5504 Cattleya trianae Linden & Rchb. f.

4270 Cattleya skinneri Bateman
4083 Cattleya violacea (Kunth) Rolfe

M. S. del, J. N. Fitch lith.　　L. Reeve & C.o London　　Vincent Brooks, Day & Son Lt.d Imp.

7727 Cattleya × whitei Rchb. f.

3332 Caularthron bicornutum (Hook.) Raf.

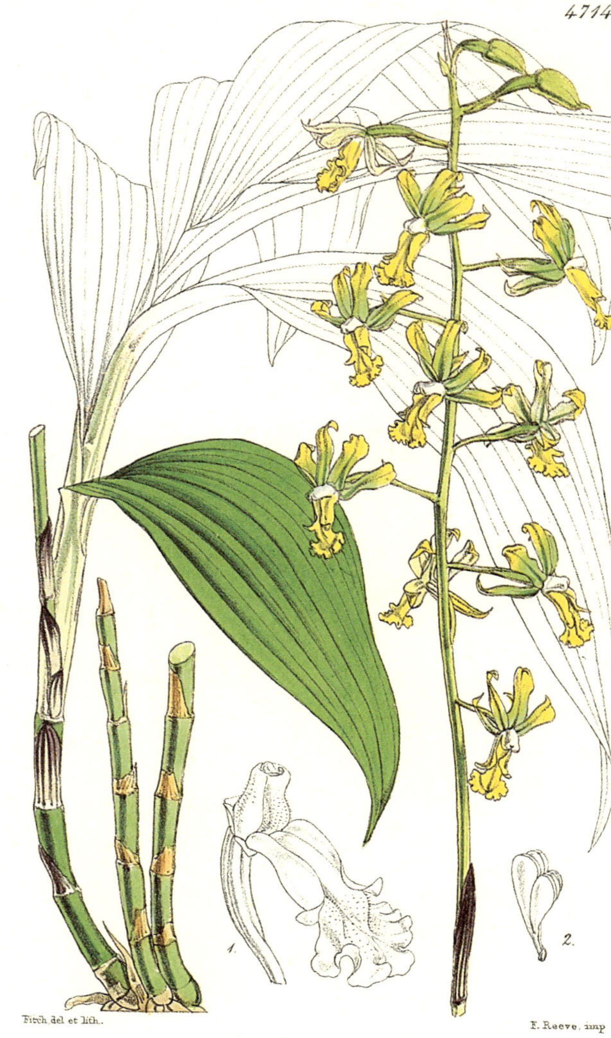

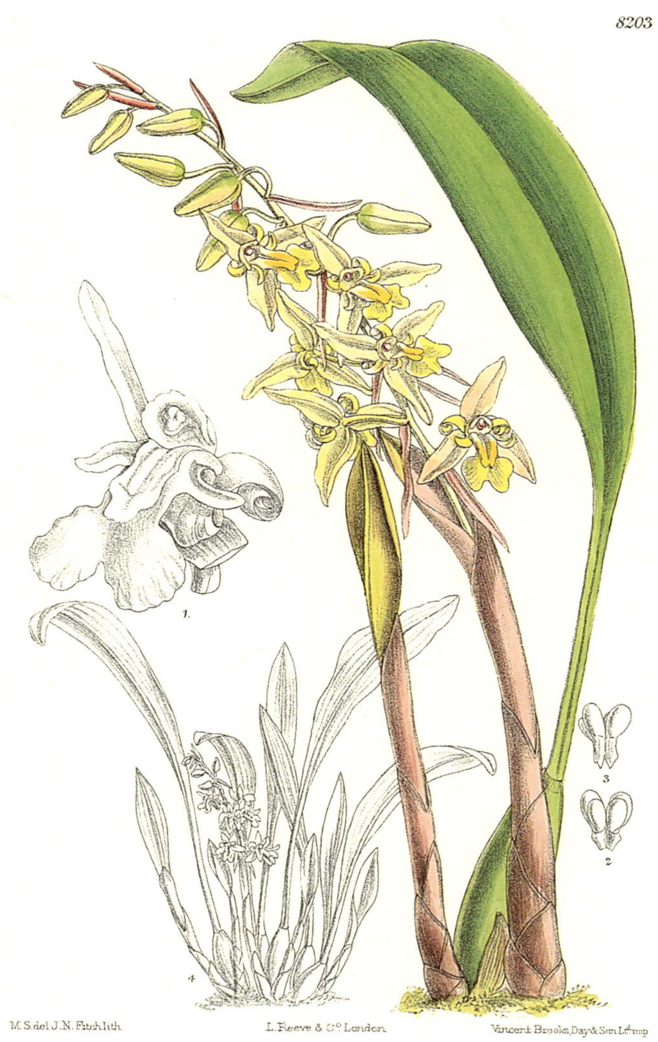

5718 Centropetalum hartwegii (Rchb. f.) Kraenzlin
8203 Chelonistele perakensis (Rolfe) Ridley

4714 Cephalantheropsis gracilis (Lindl.) S. Y. Hu
9046 Chelonistele pusilla (Ridley) Ridley

2956 *Chloraea bletioides* Lindl.

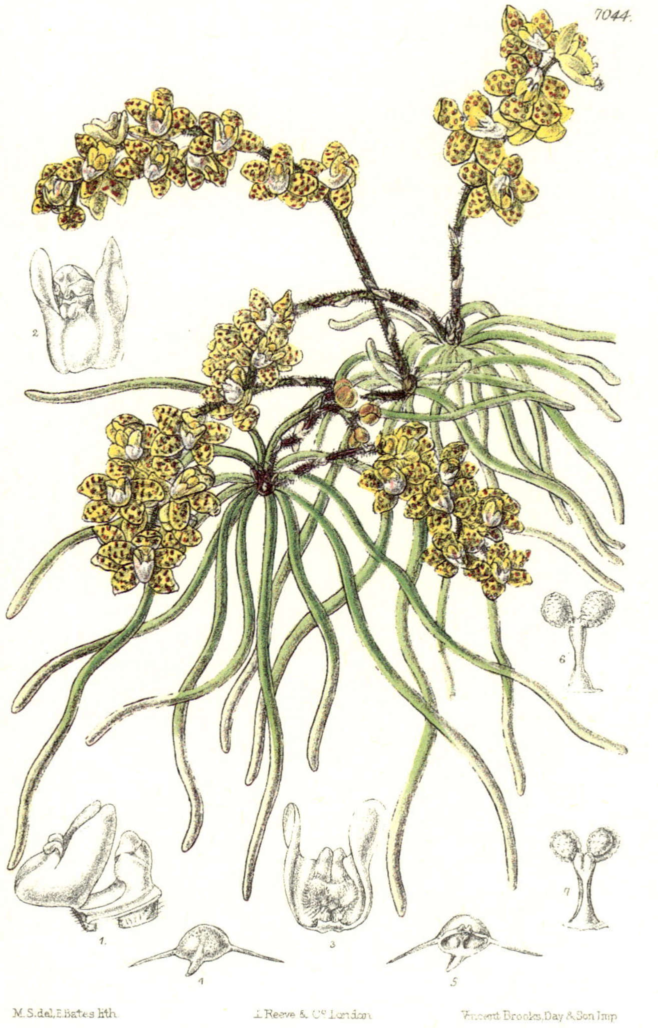

7044 Chiloschista lunifera (Rchb. f.) J. J. Smith
8100 Chloraea virescens (Willd.) Lindl.

7955 Chloraea crispa Lindl.
7601 Chusua monophylla (Collett & Hemsley) P. Hunt

3617 Chysis aurea Lindl.
5265 Chysis limminghei Linden & Rchb. f.

5186 Chysis bractescens Lindl.
4576 Chysis maculata (Hook) Fowl.

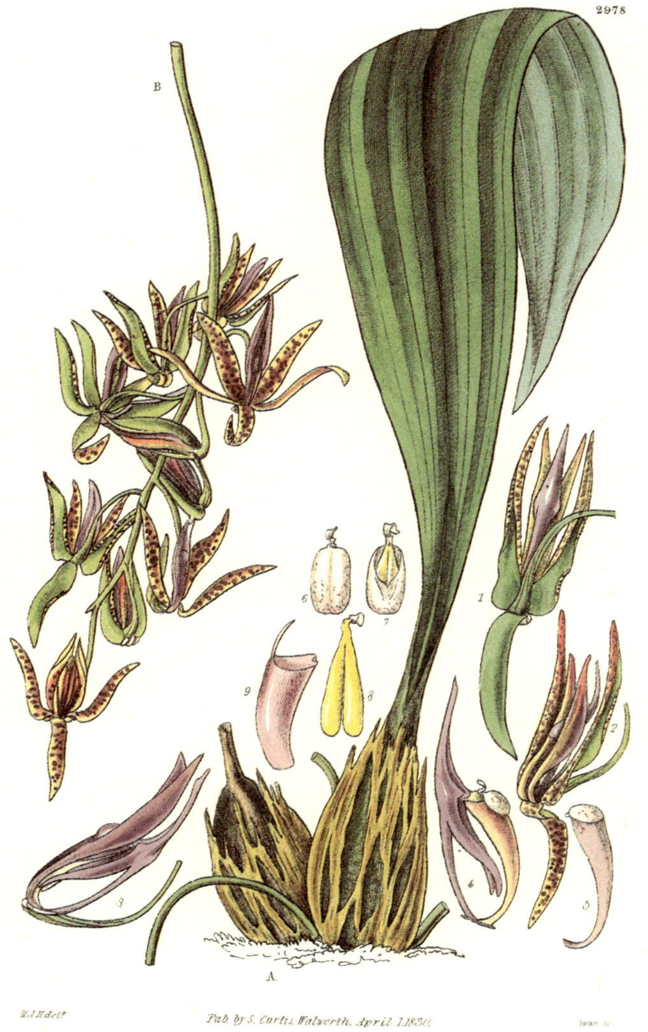

2978 Cirrhaea dependens (Lodd.) Rchb.f.
4639 Cleisostoma filiforme (Lindl.) Garay

3726 Cirrhaea saccata Lindl.
5217 Cleisostoma parishii (Hook.f.) Garay

3571 Cleisostoma simondii (Gagnepain) Seidenf.
9619 Clowesia warczewiczii (Lindl.) Dodson

3777 Clowesia russelliana (Hook.) Dodson
4830 Cochleanthes discolor (Lindl.) R. Schultes & Garay

3585 Cochleanthes flabelliformis (Sw.) R. Schultes & Garay
6084 Cochlioda rosea (Lindl.) Benth.

7474 Cochlioda noezliana (Mast.) Rolfe
6001 Cochlioda vulcanica (Rchb.f.) Benth. & Hook.f. ex veitch

4712 Coelia macrostachya Lindl.
8582 Coelogyne brachyptera Rchb. f.

6955 Coelogyne corymbosa Lindl.

M.S.del. J.N.Fitch lith.

Vincent Brooks, Day & Son Ltd. imp.

L. Reeve & Co. London.

8477 Coelogyne cristata Lindl.

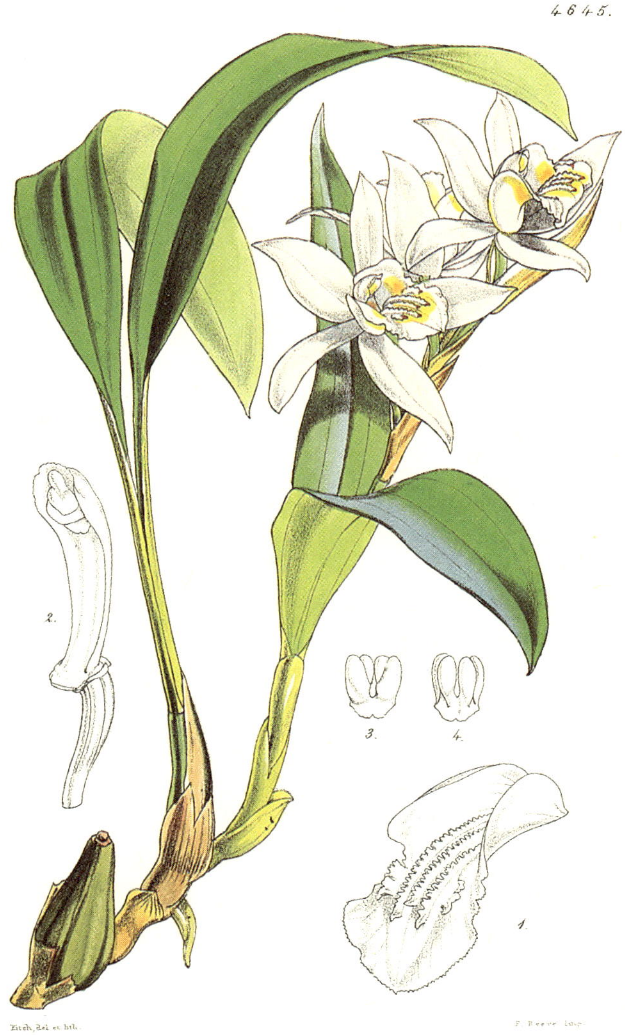

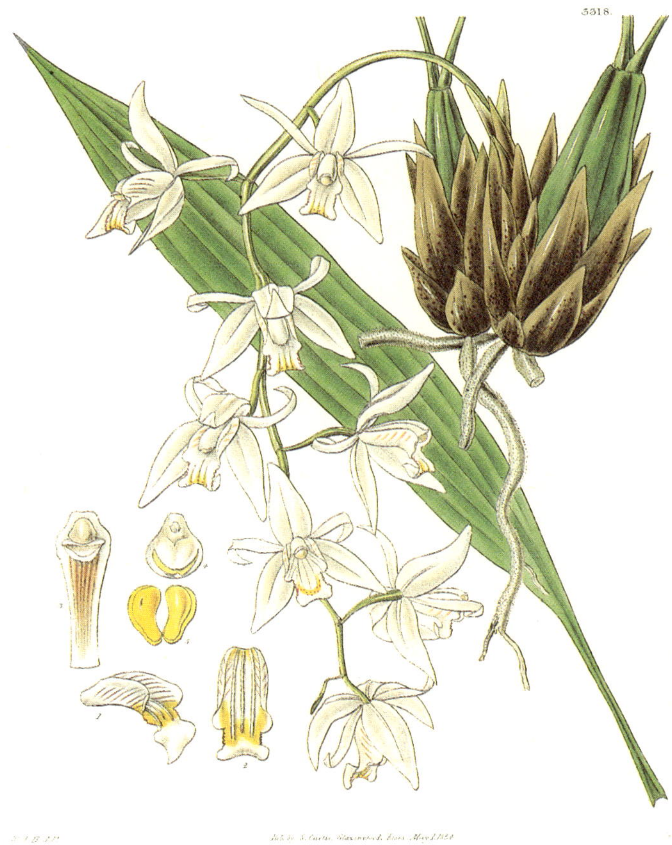

4645 Coelogyne cumingii Lindl.
9563 Coelogyne flexuosa Rolfe

3318 Coelogyne flaccida Lindl.
4440 Coelogyne fuliginosa Hook.

5494 Coelogyne fuscescens var. brunnea (Lindl.) Lindl.
8856 Coelogyne integerrima Ames

5001 Coelogyne holochila P. Hunt & Summerh.
8164 Coelogyne lawrenceana Rolfe

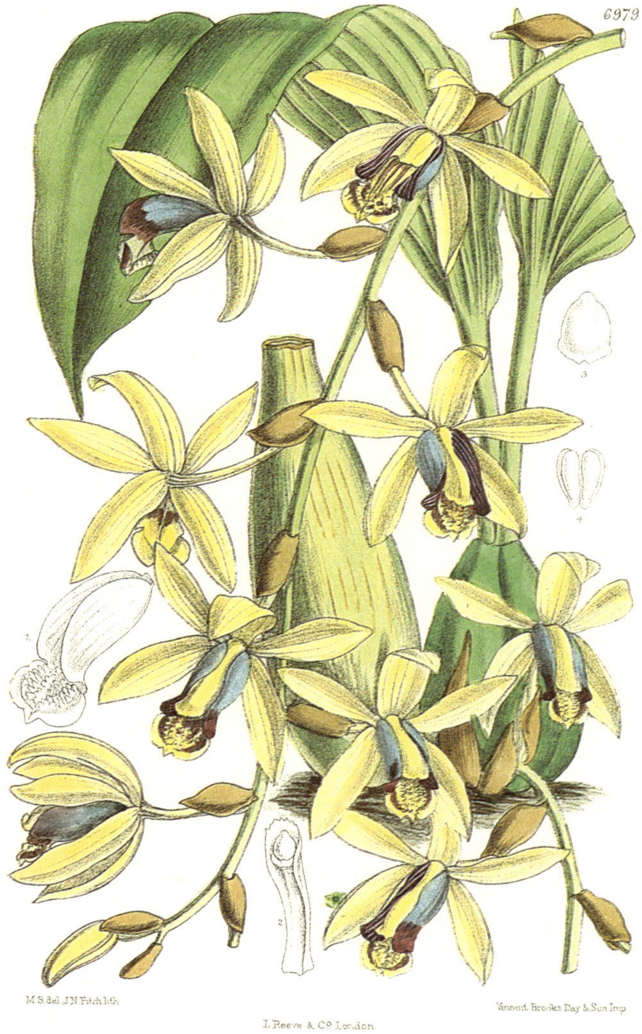

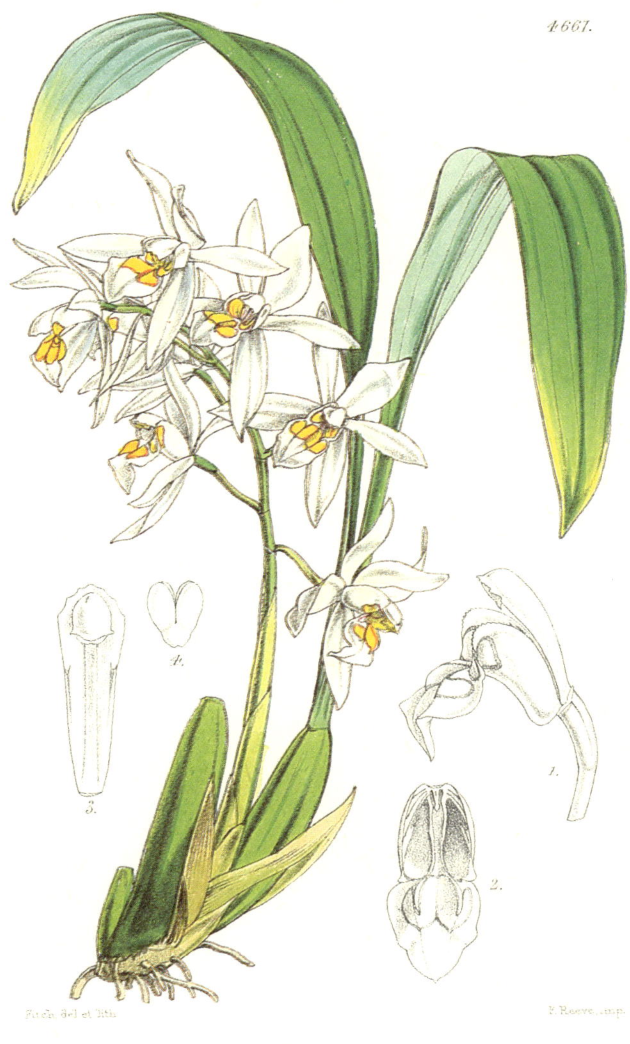

5958 Coelogyne lentiginosa Lindl.
5601 Coelogyne nervosa A. Rich.

6979 Coelogyne massangeana Rchb. f.
4661 Coelogyne nitida (Wallich ex Don) Lindl.

8297 *Coelogyne mooreana* Sander ex Rolfe

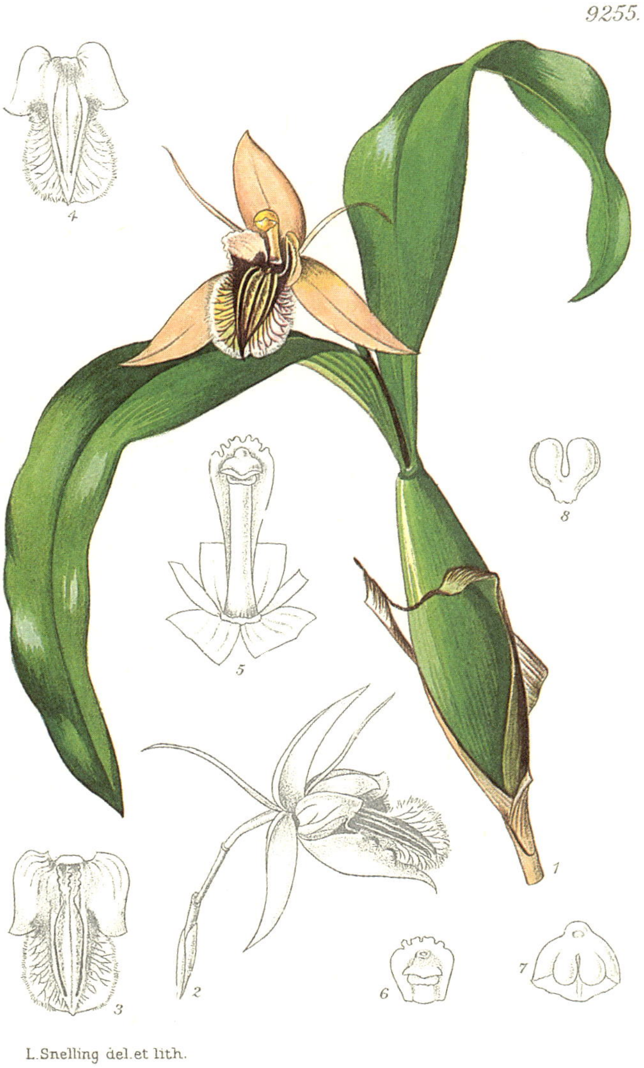

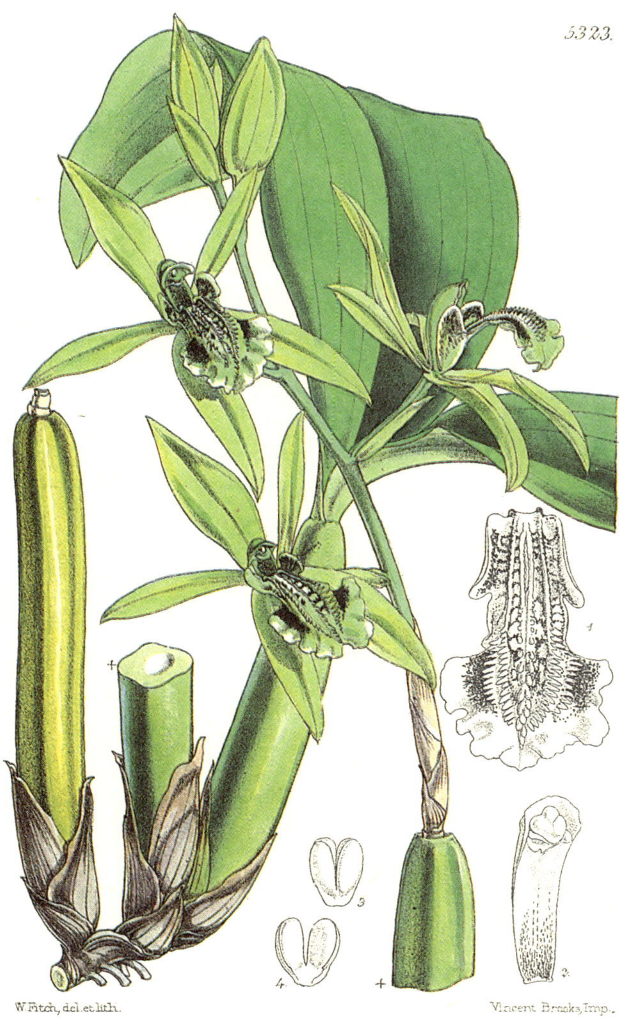

9255 Coelogyne ovalis Lindl.
5323 Coelogyne parishii Hook.

5084 Coelogyne pandurata Lindl.
5767 Coelogyne punctulata Lindl.

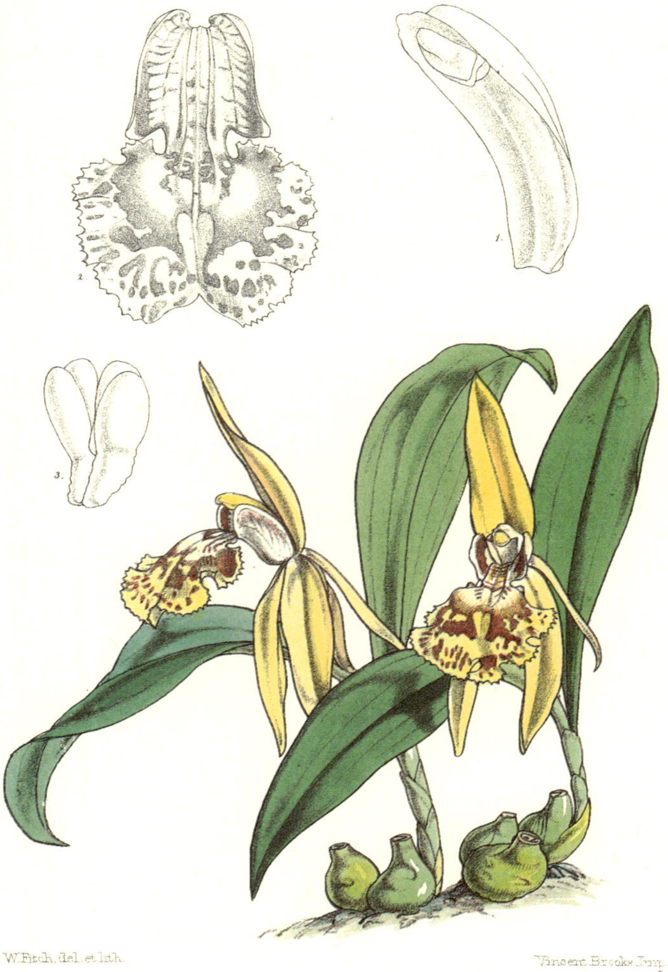

5072 Coelogyne schilleriana Rchb. f.
9539 Coelogyne speciosa var. alba hort.

4889 Coelogyne speciosa (Blume) Lindl.
4785 Coelogyne testacea Lindl.

M.S. del. J.N.Fitch lith.

Vincent Brooks, Day & Son Imp.

L. Reeve & C° London.

7602 Coelogyne swaniana Rolfe

5462 Coelogyne trifida Rchb. f.
7764 Coelogyne veitchii Rolfe

7176 Coelogyne trinervis Lindl.
7006 Coelogyne viscosa Rchb. f.

M.S. del. J.N.Fitch lith.

Vincent Brooks, Day & Son Lt.d imp

L Reeve & Co. London.

8262 Coelogyne venusta Rolfe

4980 Comparettia falcata Poepping & Endl.
7692 Coryanthes macrantha (Hook.) Hook.
6679 Comparettia macroplectron Rchb. f. & Triana

W. J. H. del.   Pub. by S. Curtis, Walworth, Aug. 1. 1827.   Swan Sc.

2755 Coryanthes speciosa (Hook.) Hook.

3102 Coryanthes speciosa (Hook.) Hook.

3747 Coryanthes speciosa (Hook.) Hook.

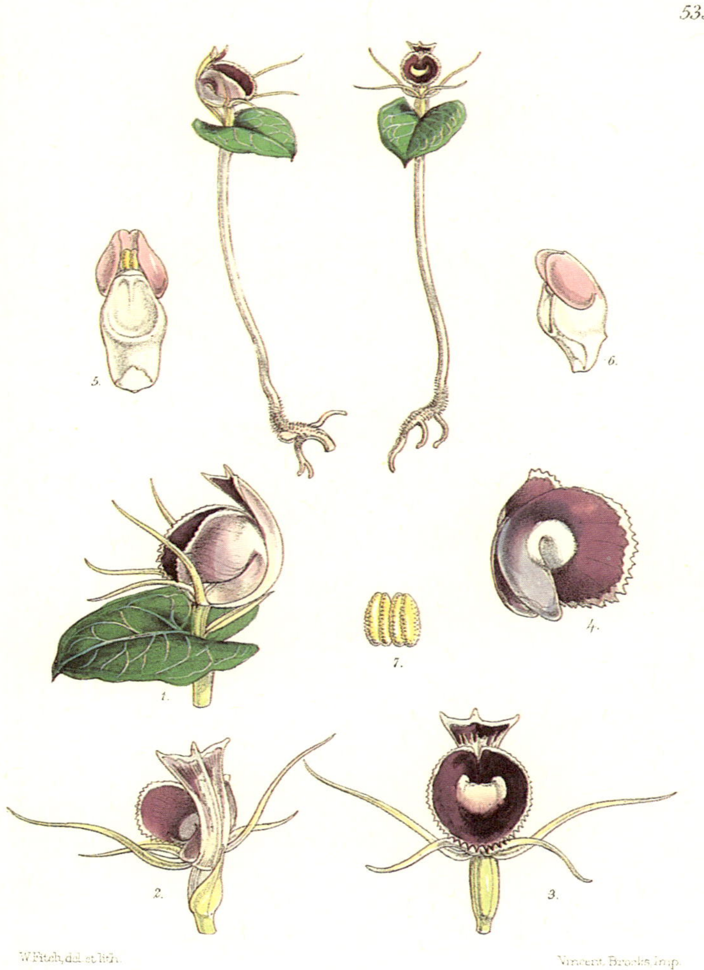

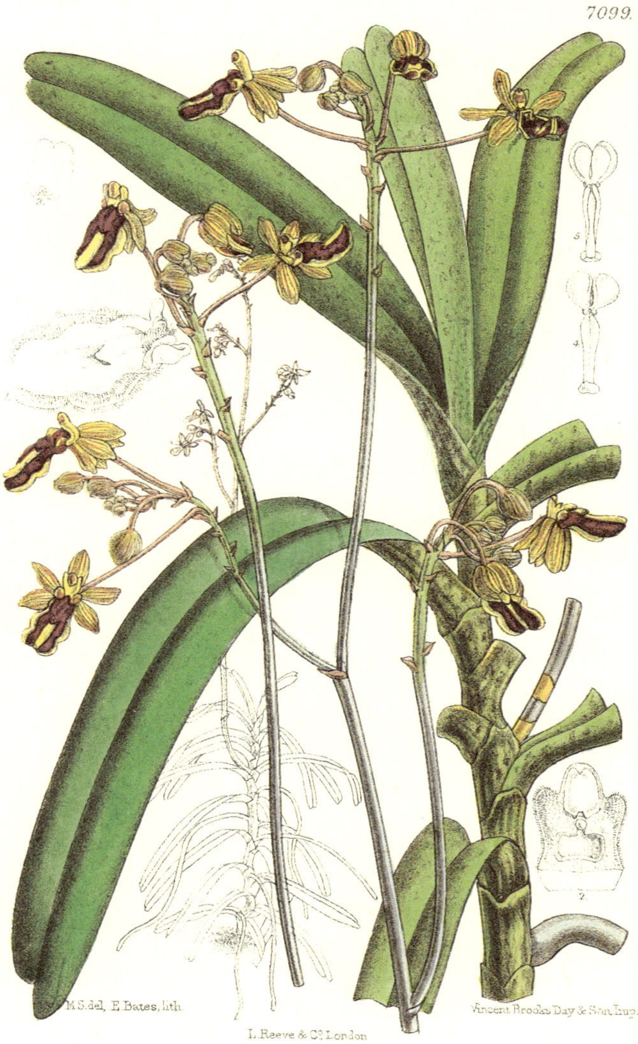

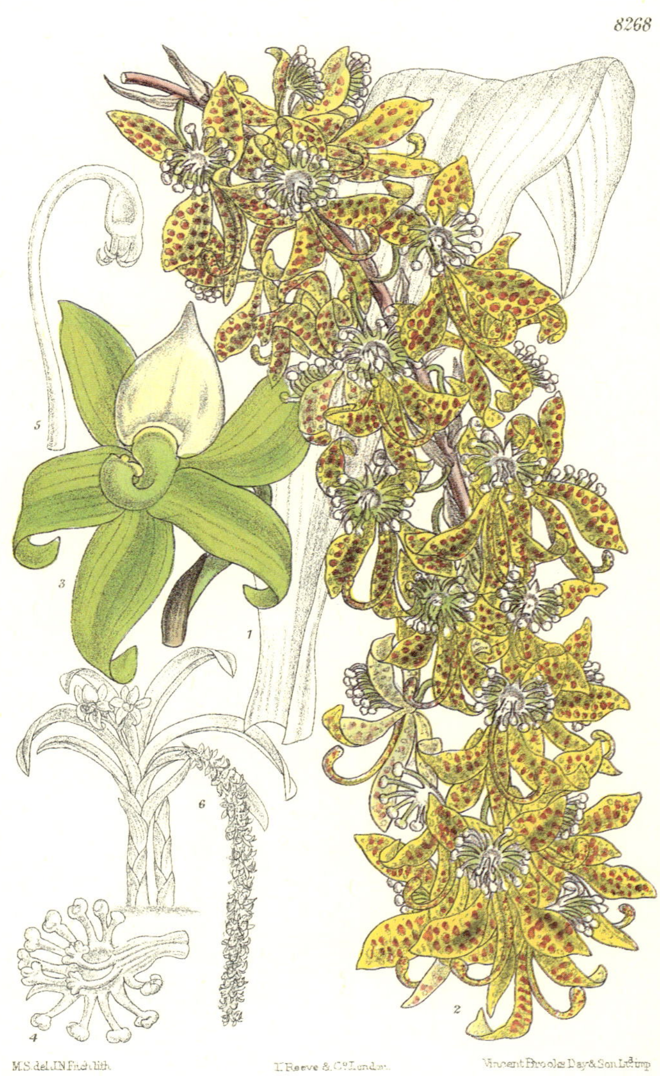

5357 Corybas limbatus (Hook.) Rchb. f.
5381 Cryptostylis arachnites (Blume) Hassk.

7099 Cottonia peduncularis (Lindl.) Rchb. f. ex Schiller
8268 Cycnoches densiflorum Rolfe

4054 Cycnoches egertonianum Bateman

M. S. del, J. N. Fitch lith.

Vincent Brooks Day & Son Imp

L Reeve & C.o London.

7502 Cycnoches haagii Barb. Rodr.

3855 Cycnoches loddigesii Lindl.

4215 Cycnoches loddigesii Lindl.

9260 Cycnoches egertonianum Bateman

9216 Cymbidiella falcigera (Rchb. f.) Garay

M. S. del. J. N. Fitch lith.
Vincent Brooks Day & Son Ltd Imp
L. Reeve & Co London.

7932 Cymbidiella pardalina (Rchb. f.) Garay

7933 Cymbidiella pardalina (Rchb. f.) Garay
5710 Cymbidium atropurpureum (Hook. f.) Rolfe

587 Cymbidium aloifolium (L.) Sw.
5851 Cymbidium canaliculatum R. Br.

4907 Cymbidium chloranthum Lindl.
9327 Cymbidium devonianum Paxton

7863 Cymbidium dayanum Rchb. f.
5126 Cymbidium eburneum Lindl.

7007 Cymbidium elegans Lindl.
8131 Cymbidium erythrostylum Rolfe

1751 Cymbidium ensifolium (L.) Sw.
4844 Cymbidium iridioides D. Don

8312 Cymbidium insigne Rolfe

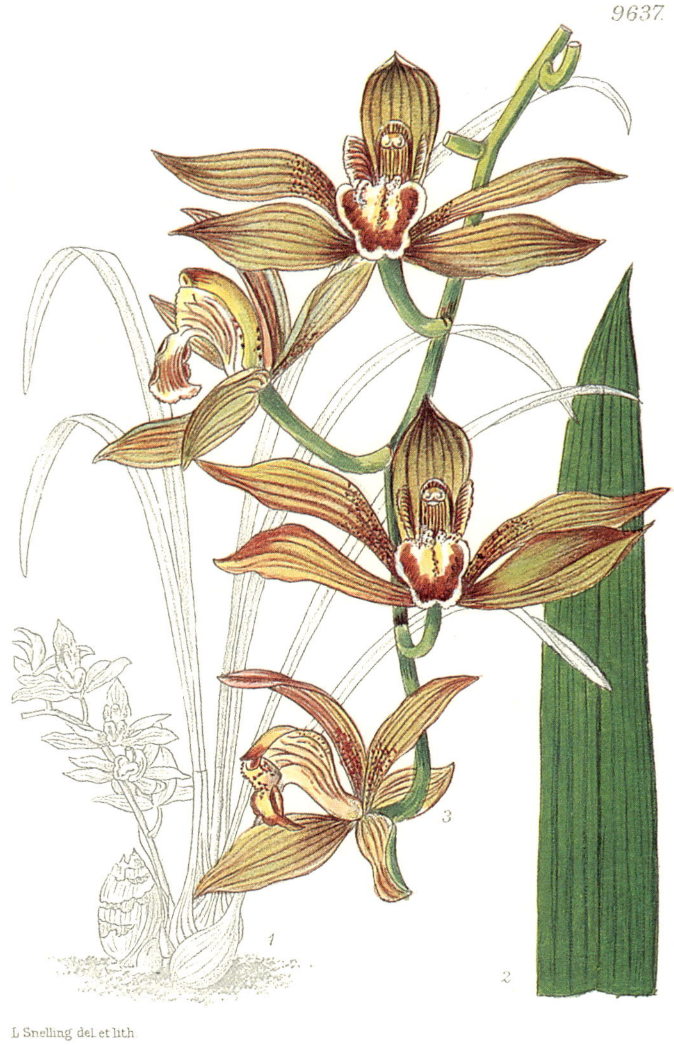

5574 Cymbidium hookerianum Rchb. f.
888 Cymbidium sinense (Andrews) Willd.

9637 Cymbidium schroederi Rolfe
5457 Cymbidium tigrinum Parish ex Hook. f.

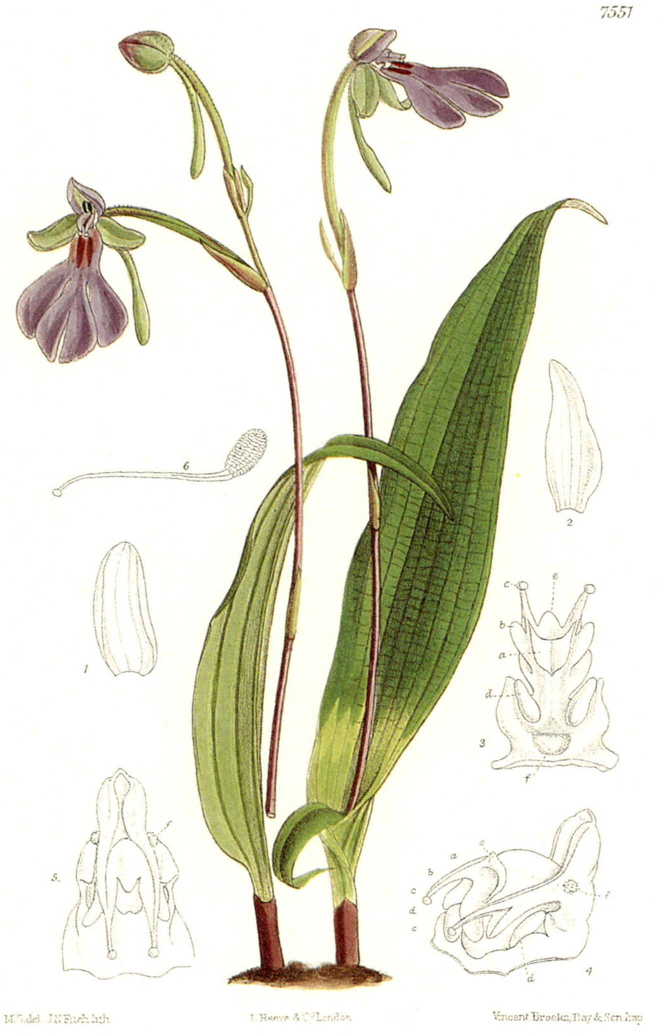

8053 Cynorkis compacta (Rchb. f.) Rolfe
7551 Cynorkis lowiana Rchb. f.

7564 Cynorkis grandiflora Ridley
7845 Cynorkis villosa Rolfe ex Hook. f.

M.S. del. J.N.Fitch lith. Vincent Brooks, Day & Son Ltd Imp.

L. Reeve & Co London.

7852 Cynorkis purpurascens (Sprengel) Thouars

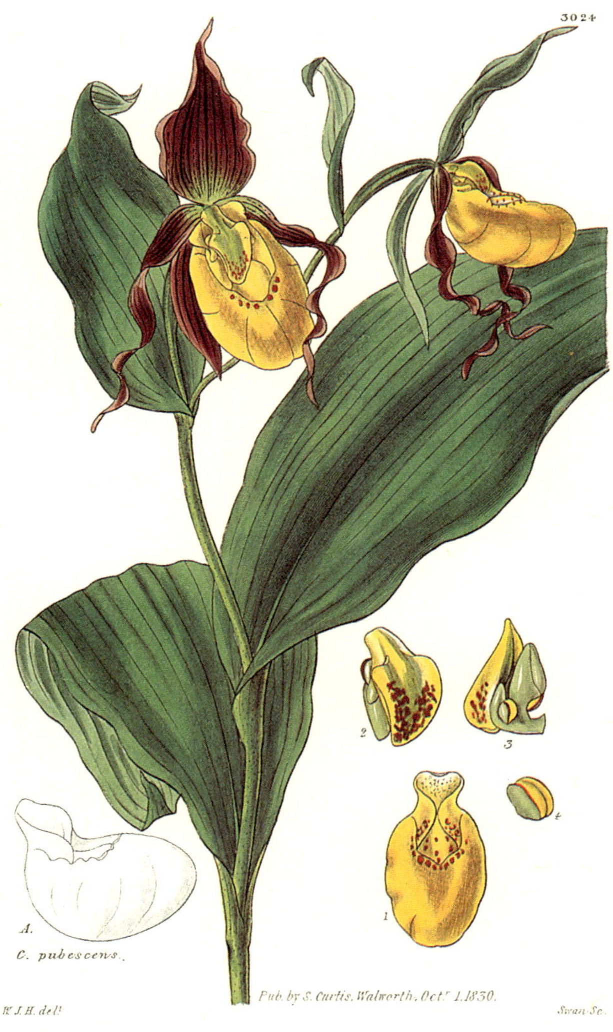

192 Cypripedium acaule Aiton
3024 Cypripedium calceolus var. parviflorum (Salisb.) Fern.

1569 Cypripedium arietinum R. Br.
911 Cypripedium calceolus var. pubescens (Willd.) Correll

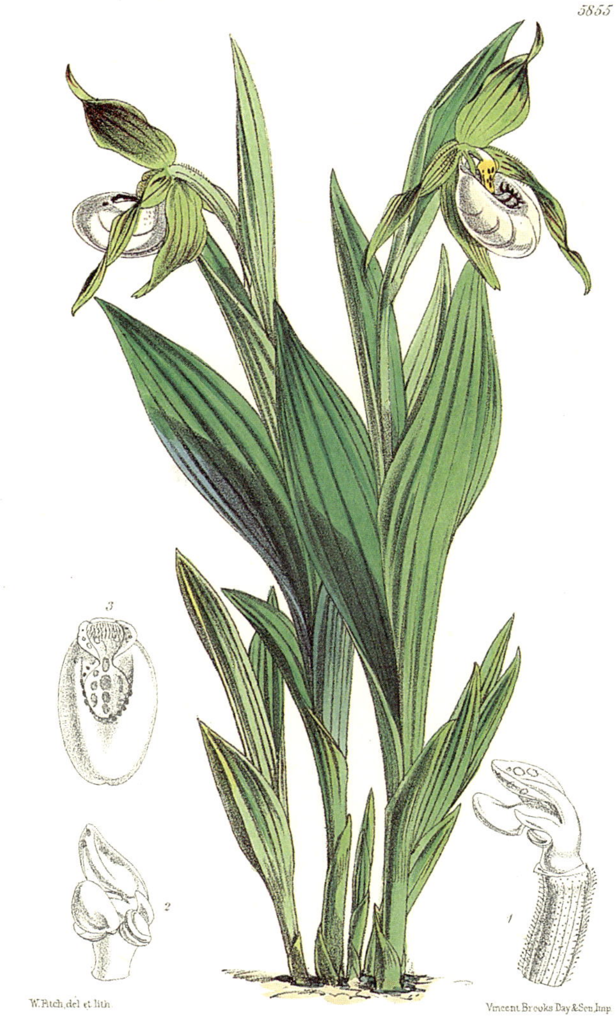

7188 Cypripedium californicum A. Gray
9364 Cypripedium cordigerum D. Don

5855 Cypripedium candidum Muhlenb. ex Willd.
7275 Cypripedium fasciculatum Kellogg ex S. Watson

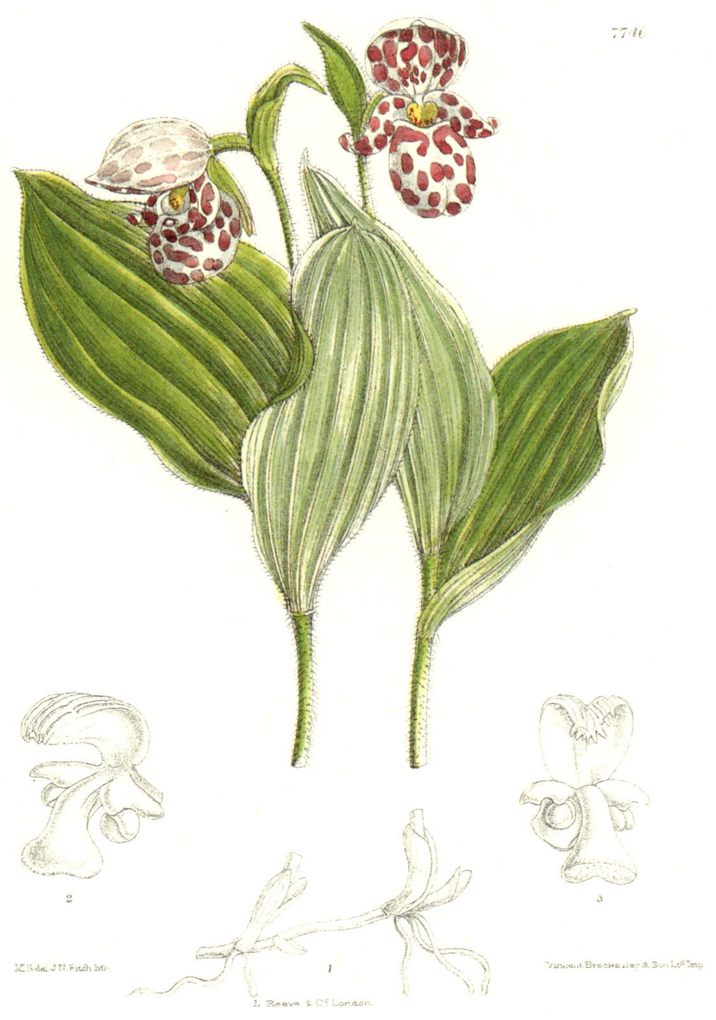

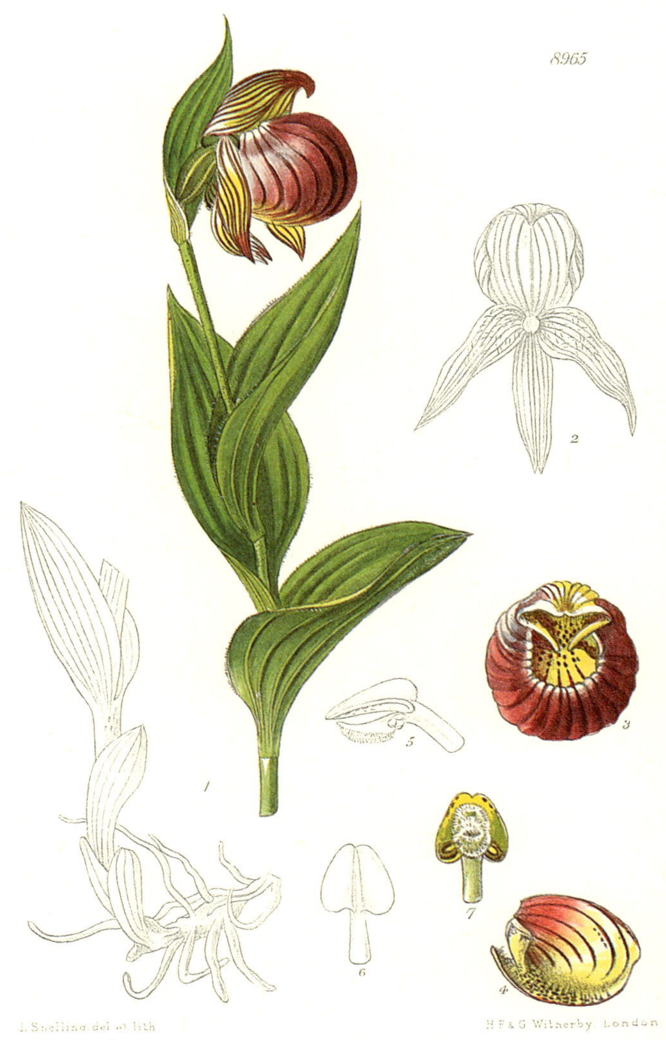

8183 Cypripedium debile Rchb. f.
7746 Cypripedium guttatum Sw.

8965 Cypripedium himalaicum Rolfe apud Hemsley

2938 Cypripedium macranthum Sw.

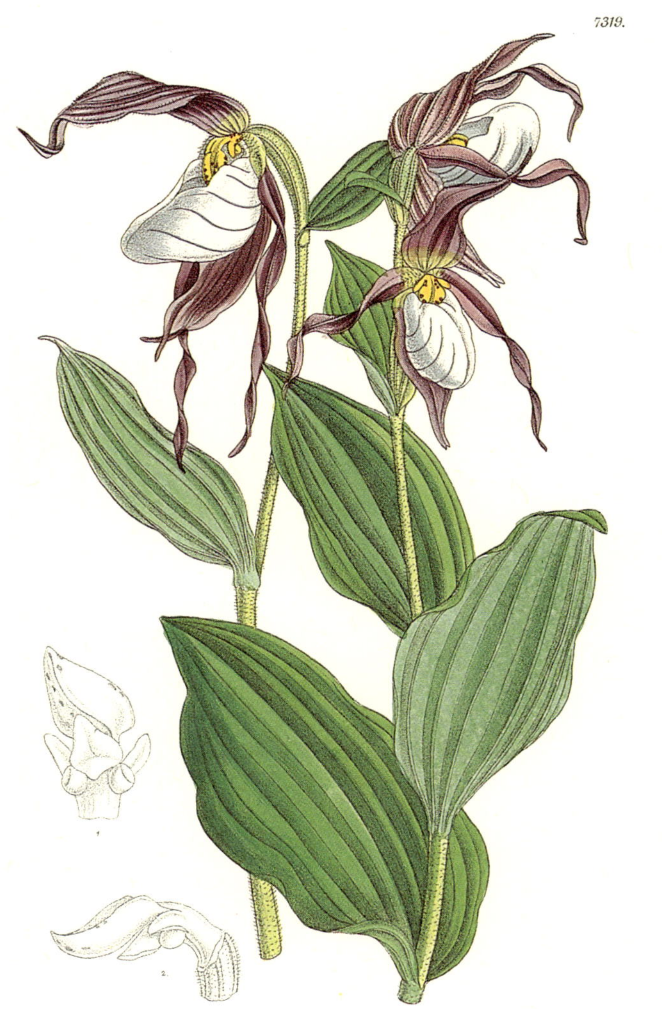

9520 Cypripedium japonicum Thunb.
7319 Cypripedium montanum Douglas ex Lindl.

8386 Cypripedium macranthum var. speciosum (Rolfe) Koidz.
216 Cypripedium reginae Walter

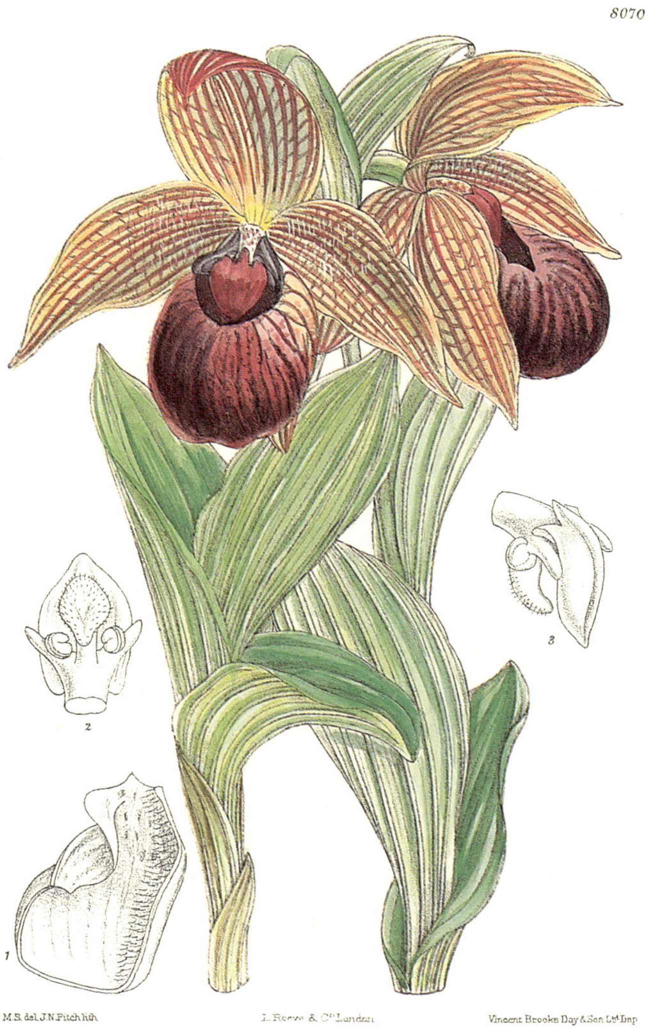

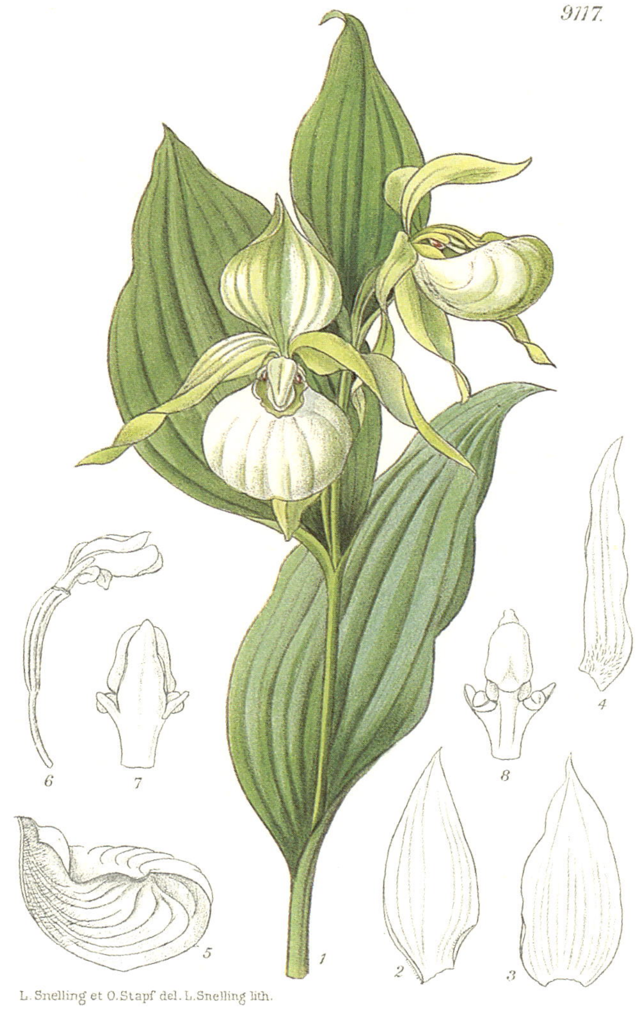

8070 *Cypripedium tibeticum* King ex Rolfe
7807 *Cyrtopodium palmifrons* Rchb. f. & Warm.

9117 *Cypripedium ventricosum album* hort. ex Rolfe

3507 Cyrtopodium punctatum (L.) Lindl.

1800 Cyrtopodium andersonii (Lambert ex Andrews) R. Br.
5589 Cyrtorchis chailluana (Hook. f.) Schltr.

7396 Cyrtopodium virescens Rchb. f. & Warm.
8074 Cyrtorchis hamata (Rolfe) Schltr.

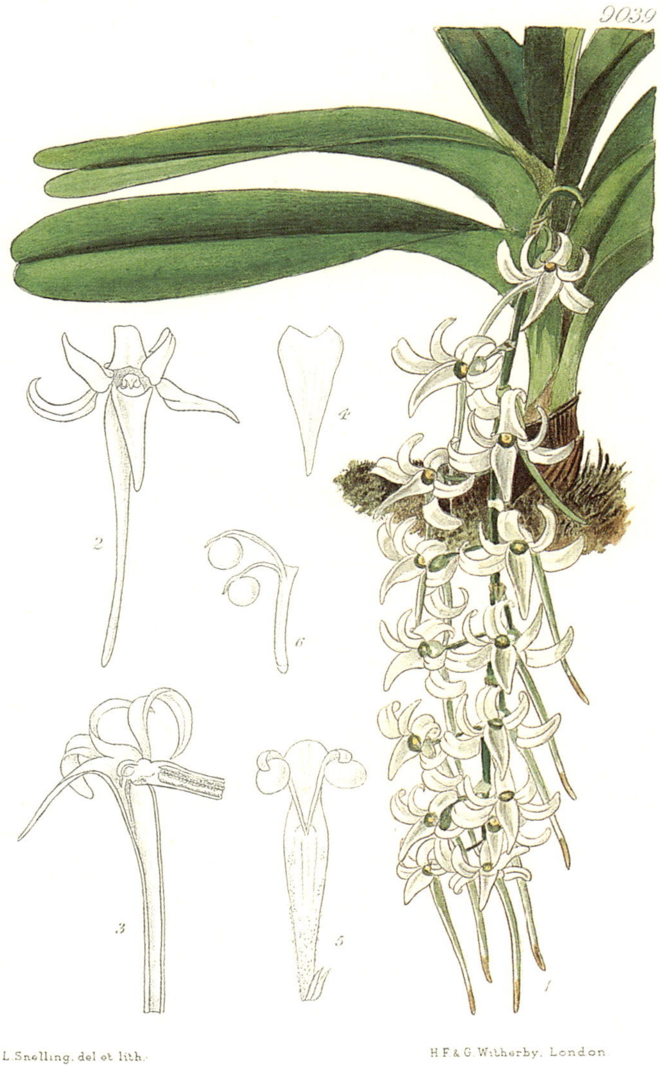

8026 *Cyrtorchis monteiroae* (Rchb. f.) Schltr.
5074 *Dactylorhiza foliosa* (Rchb. f.) Soó

9039 *Cyrtorchis ringens* (Rchb. f.) Summerh.
6784 *Dendrobium aduncum* Lindl.

M.S. del. J.N.Fitch lith.

Vincent Brooks, Day & Son Ltd imp.

L. Reeve & Co. London.

8252 *Dendrobium amabile* (Lour.) O'Brien

2906 Dendrobium aemulum R. Br.
4937 Dendrobium amboinense Hook.

5130 Dendrobium albo-sanguineum Lindl.
5968 Dendrobium amethystoglossum Rchb. f.

3970 Dendrobium anosmum Lindl.

6199 Dendrobium amoenum Wallich ex Lindl.
5470 Dendrobium aphrodite Rchb. f.

3608 Dendrobium anceps Sw.
2242 Dendrobium aphyllum (Roxb.) C. Fischer

2584 Dendrobium aphyllum (Roxb.) C. Fischer
7371 Dendrobium atroviolaceum Rolfe

4640 Dendrobium aqueum Lindl.
5918 Dendrobium barbatulum Lindl.

7985 Dendrobium bellatulum Rolfe
5679 Dendrobium bensoniae Rchb. f.

4898 Dendrobium bigibbum Lindl.

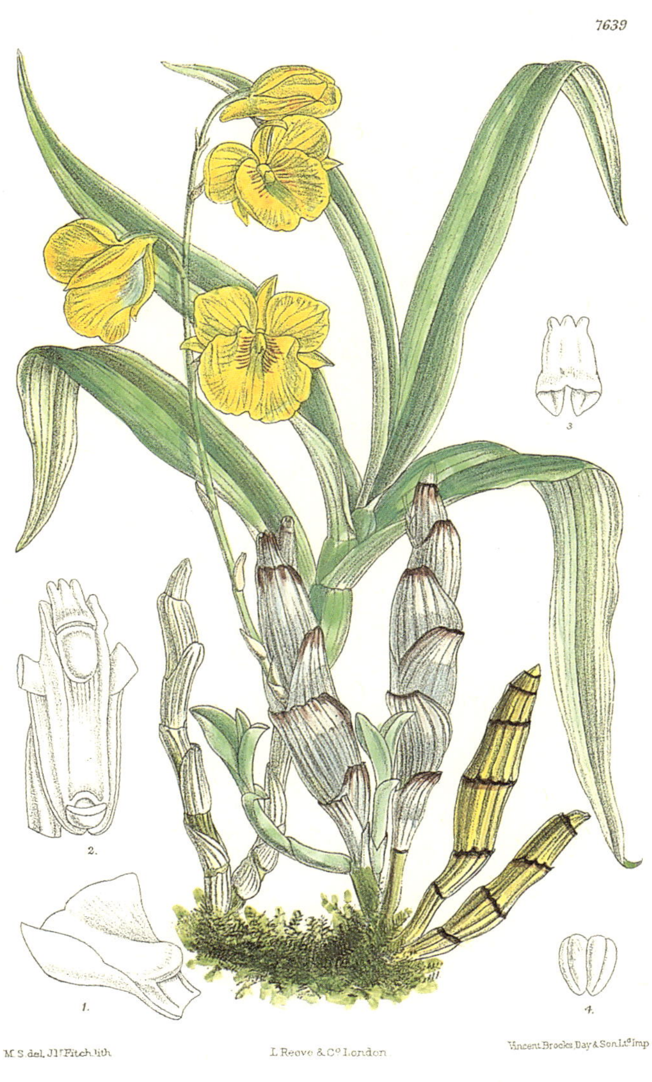

6817 *Dendrobium bigibbum* Lindl.
5537 *Dendrobium canaliculatum* R. Br.

6383 *Dendrobium brymerianum* Rchb. f.
7639 *Dendrobium capillipes* Rchb. f.

6715 Dendrobium cariniferum Rchb. f.
5053 Dendrobium chrysotoxum Lindl.

6007 Dendrobium chrysocrepis Parish & Rchb. f. ex Hook. f.
4993 Dendrobium crepidatum Lindl.

5011 Dendrobium crepidatum Lindl.
4013 Dendrobium crumenatum Sw.

4686 Dendrobium cretaceum Lindl.
6319 Dendrobium crystallinum Rchb. f.

4619 Dendrobium cucumerinum MacLeay ex Lindl.
5430 Dendrobium delacourii Guillaumin

5703 Dendrobium cumulatum Lindl.
3418 Dendrobium densiflorum Wallich ex Lindl.

M.S. del. J.N.Fitch lith.

Vincent Brooks Day & Son Imp

L Reeve & C° London

6993 *Dendrobium denneanum* Kerr

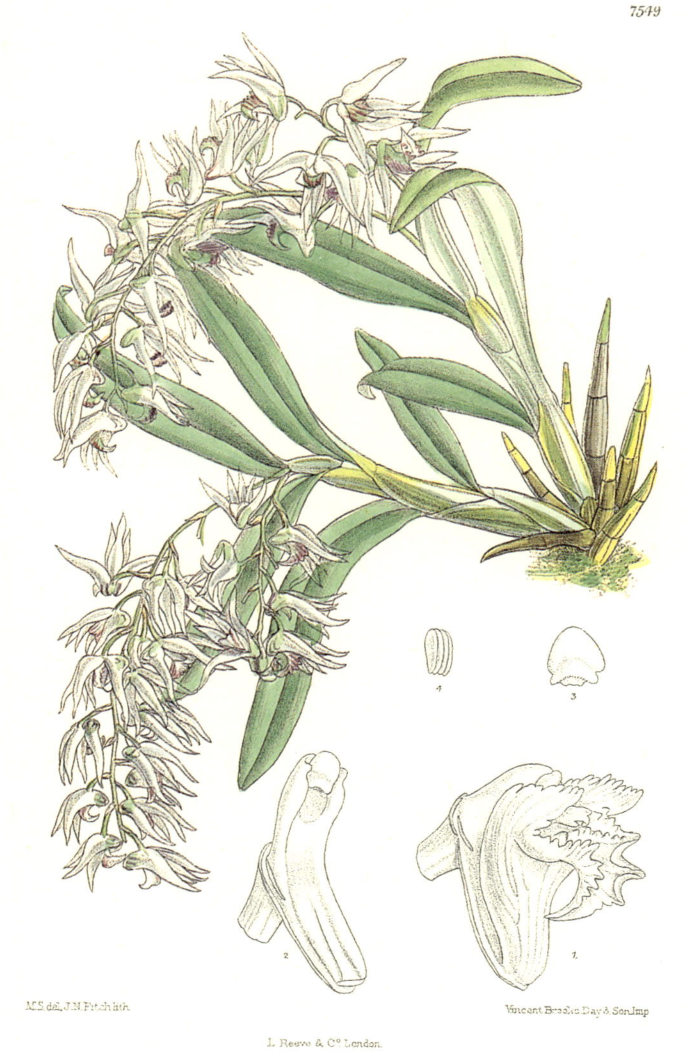

7549 Dendrobium denudans D. Don
5564 Dendrobium dixanthum Rchb. f.

4429 Dendrobium devonianum Paxton
5459 Dendrobium draconis Rchb. f.

4944 Dendrobium falconeri Hook.
4160 Dendrobium fimbriatum Hook.

4659 Dendrobium farmeri Paxton
6438 Dendrobium findlayanum Parish & Rchb. f.

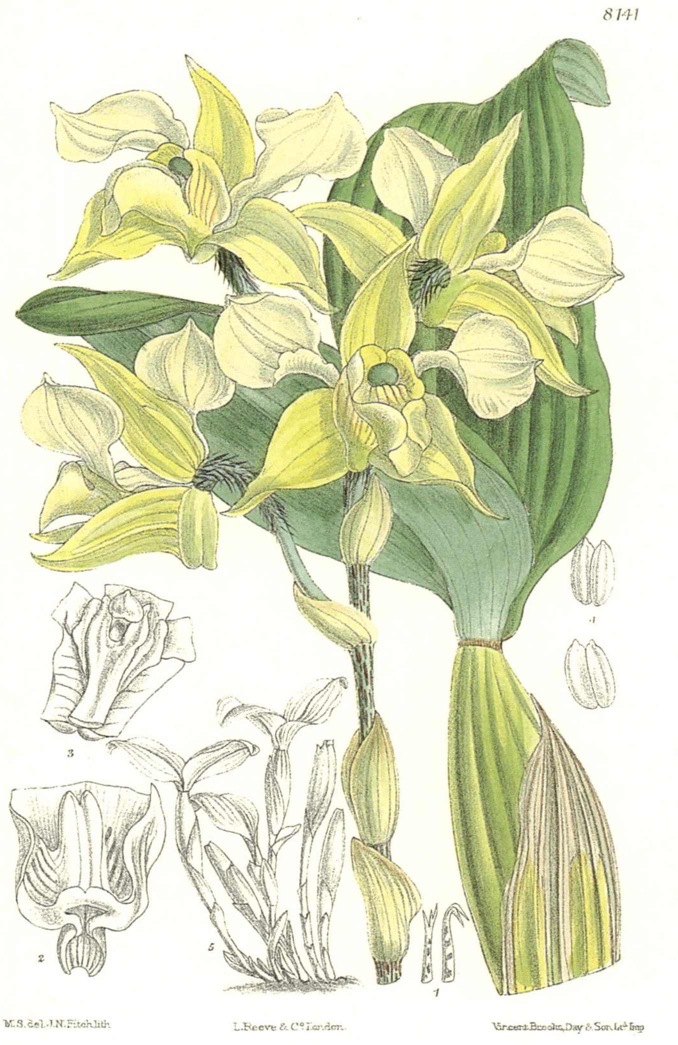

8141 Dendrobium forbesii Ridley
6226 Dendrobium gibsonii Lindl.

5444 Dendrobium fytchianum Bateman
7042 Dendrobium gracilicaule F. Muell.

8452 *Dendrobium gouldii* Rchb. f.

5652.

W. Fitch, del. et lith. Vincent Brooks, Imp.

9428.

S. Ross-Craig del. L. Snelling lith.

5652 Dendrobium gratiosissimum Rchb. f.
9428 Dendrobium hercoglossum Rchb. f.

5451.

W. Fitch, del. et lith. Vincent Brooks, Imp.

4708.

Fitch, del. et lith. F. Reeve, imp.

5451 Dendrobium griffithianum Lindl.
4708 Dendrobium heterocarpum Wallich ex Lindl.

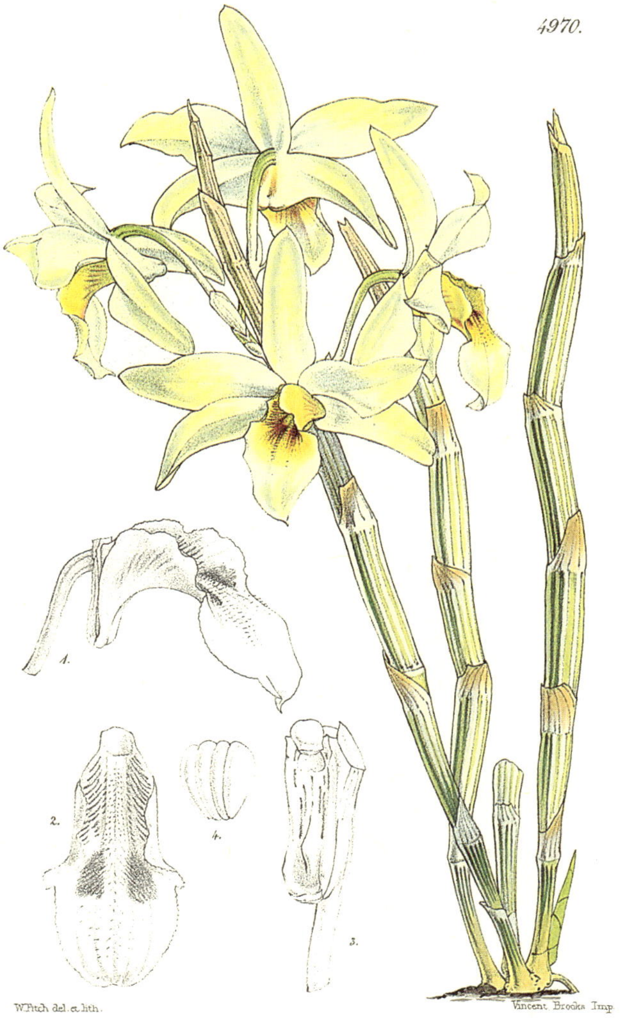

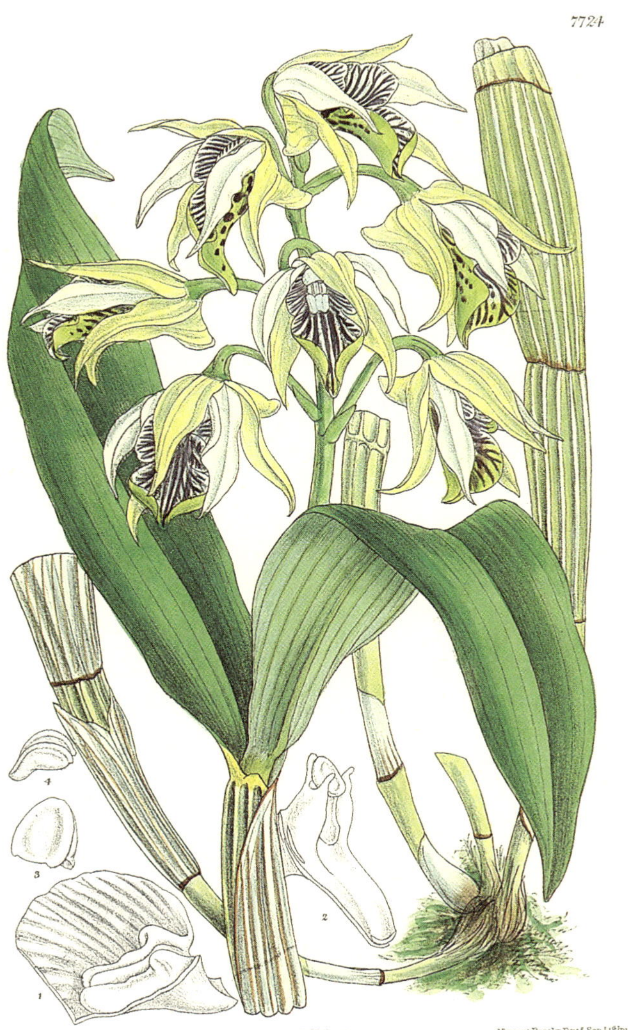

4970 Dendrobium heterocarpum Wallich ex Lindl.
7724 Dendrobium hodgkinsonii Rolfe

7453 Dendrobium hildebrandii Rolfe
6013 Dendrobium hookerianum Lindl.

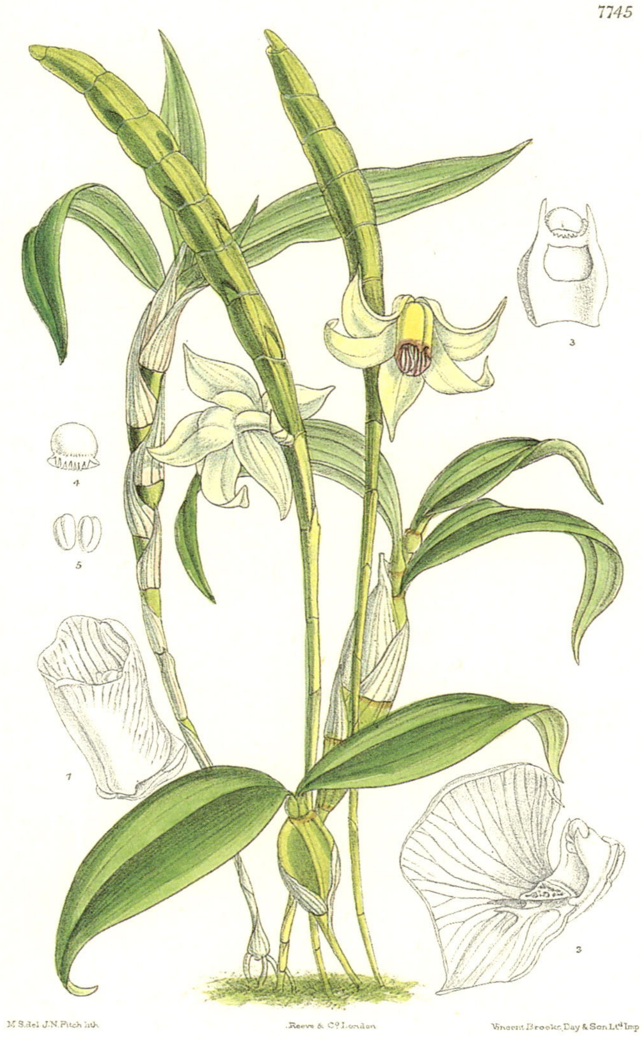

7745 Dendrobium inaequale Rolfe
5540 Dendrobium johannis Rchb. f.

5446 Dendrobium infundibulum Lindl.
4527 Dendrobium kingianum Bidw. ex Lindl.

9011 Dendrobium laevifolium Stapf
7493 Dendrobium leonis (Lindl.) Rchb. f.

5825 Dendrobium lasioglossum Rchb. f.
4153 Dendrobium linawianum Rchb. f.

3643 Dendrobium lindleyi Steudel
6050 Dendrobium lituiflorum Lindl.

5249 Dendrobium linguiforme Sw.
5037 Dendrobium loddigesii Rolfe

5303 Dendrobium lowii Lindl.
4886 Dendrobium maccarthiae Thwaites

5441 Dendrobium luteolum Bateman
5649 Dendrobium macrophyllum A. Rich.

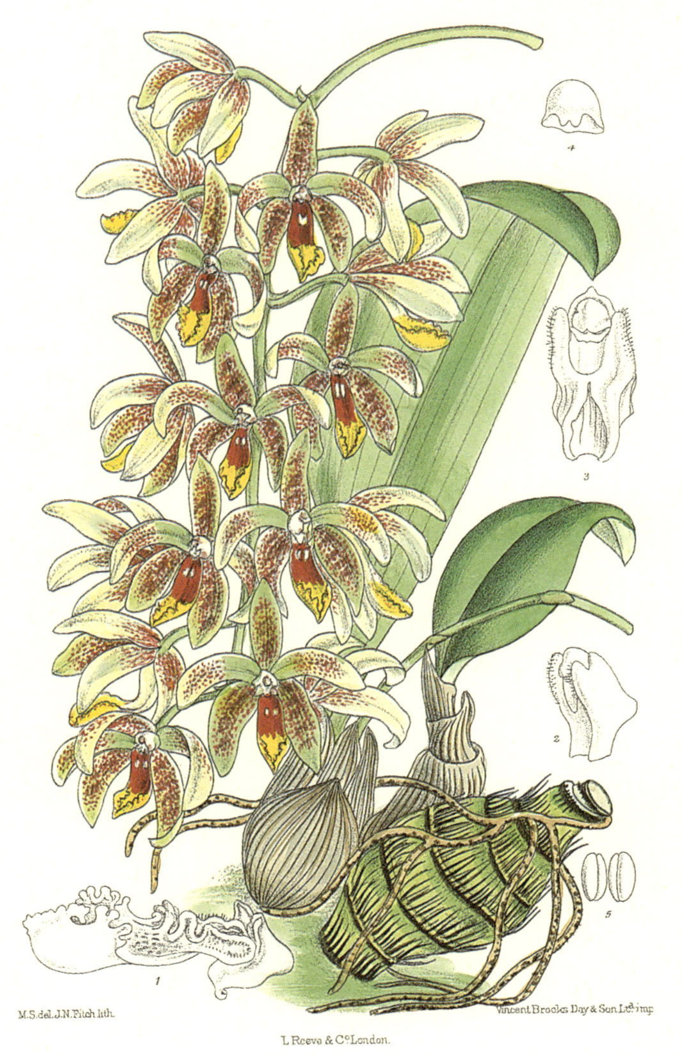

5482 Dendrobium moniliforme (L.) Sw.
5285 Dendrobium mutabile (Blume) Lindl.

8371 Dendrobium munificum (Finet) Hallé
7741 Dendrobium nutans Lindl.

3837 *Dendrobium moschatum* (Buch.-Ham.) Sw.

4450 Dendrobium ochreatum Lindl.
5488 Dendrobium parishii Rchb. f.

8683 Dendrobium palpebrae Lindl.
5766 Dendrobium pendulum Roxb.

5003 Dendrobium primulinum Lindl.
6706 Dendrobium revolutum Lindl.

8003 Dendrobium regium Prain
7900 Dendrobium rhodostictum F. Muell. & Kraenzlin

8351 *Dendrobium sanderae* Rolfe
5515 *Dendrobium scabrilingue* Lindl.

7525 *Dendrobium sarmentosum* Rolfe
8495 *Dendrobium schuetzei* Rolfe

W. J. H. del^t Pub by S. Curtis Glazenwood Essex June 1. 1831. Swan Sc.

3074 Dendrobium speciosum Smith

5261 Dendrobium speciosum var. hillii (Hook.) Bailey

4352 Dendrobium secundum (Blume) Lindl.
6962 Dendrobium sulcatum Lindl.

5520 Dendrobium senile Parish ex Rchb. f.
4711 Dendrobium teretifolium (Sw.) R. Br.

M.S.del. J.N.Fitch lith.

Vincent Brooks, Day & Son Ltd. Imp.

L. Reeve & Co. London.

7747 Dendrobium spectabile (Blume) Miq.

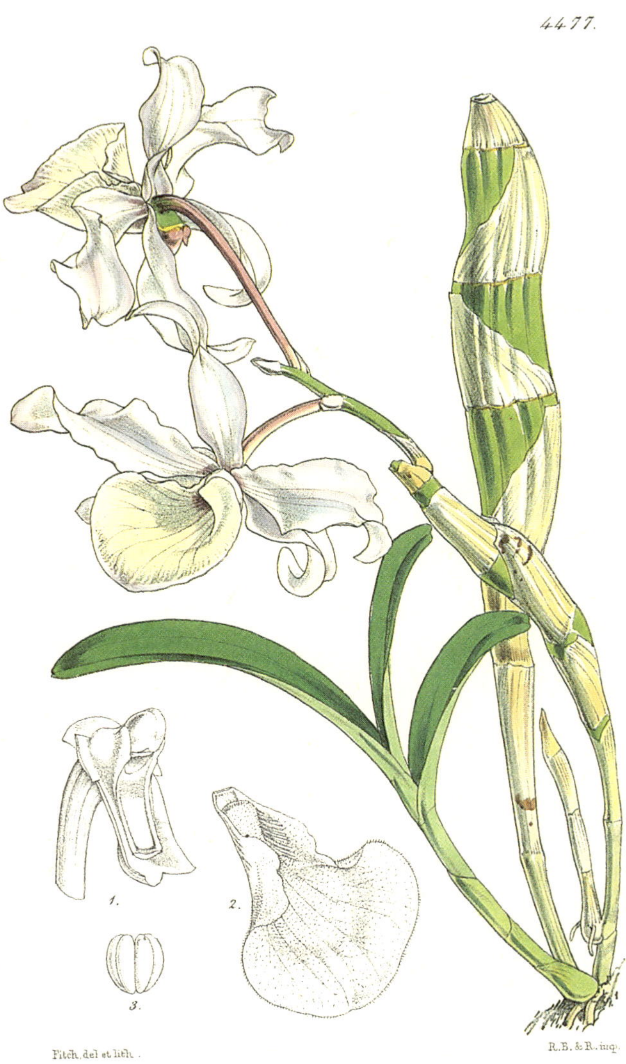

5956 Dendrobium tetragonum Cunn. ex Lindl.
4477 Dendrobium tortile Lindl.

5780 Dendrobium thyrsiflorum Rchb. f. ex André
4663 Dendrobium transparens Wallich

M. S. del. J. N. Fitch lith.

Vincent Brooks, Day & Son Ltd imp

L. Reeve & Co London

8352 Dendrobium tortile var. dartoisianum (De Wild.) O'Brien

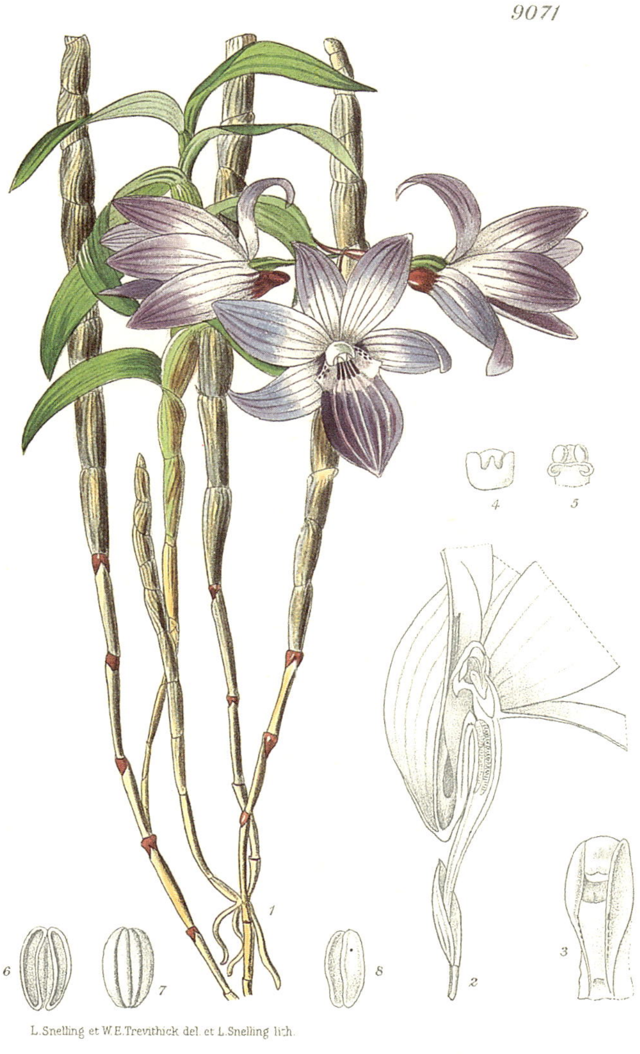

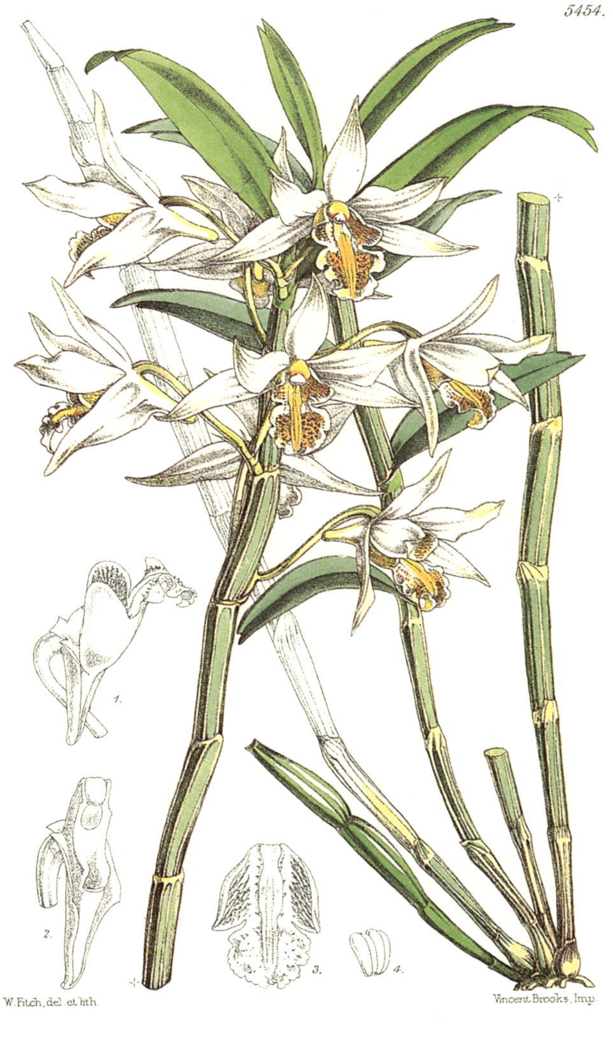

9071 Dendrobium victoriae-reginae Loher
7974 Dendrobium williamsonii Day & Rchb.f.

5058 Dendrobrium wardianum Warner
5454 Dendrobium xanthophlebium Lindl.

4853 Dendrochilum glumaceum Lindl.
4295 Dendrophylax funalis (Sw.) Fawcett

9015 Dendrochilum uncatum Rchb. f.
8014 Diaphananthe bidens (Afzel. ex Sw.) Schltr.

W. Fitch, del. et lith.

Vincent Brooks, Imp.

5475 *Dimorphorchis lowii* (Lindl.) Rolfe

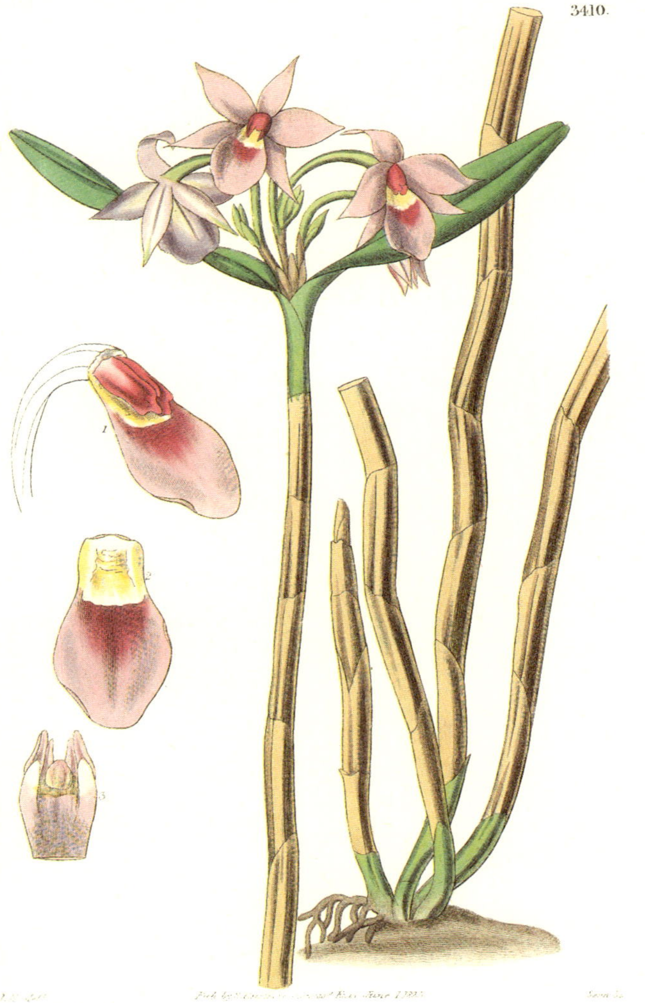

3410 Dimerandra emarginata (G. Meyer) Hoehne
9113 Diplomeris hirsuta Lindl.

4067 Dinema polybulbon (Sw.) Lindl.
7464 Dipodium paludosum (Griffith) Rchb. f.

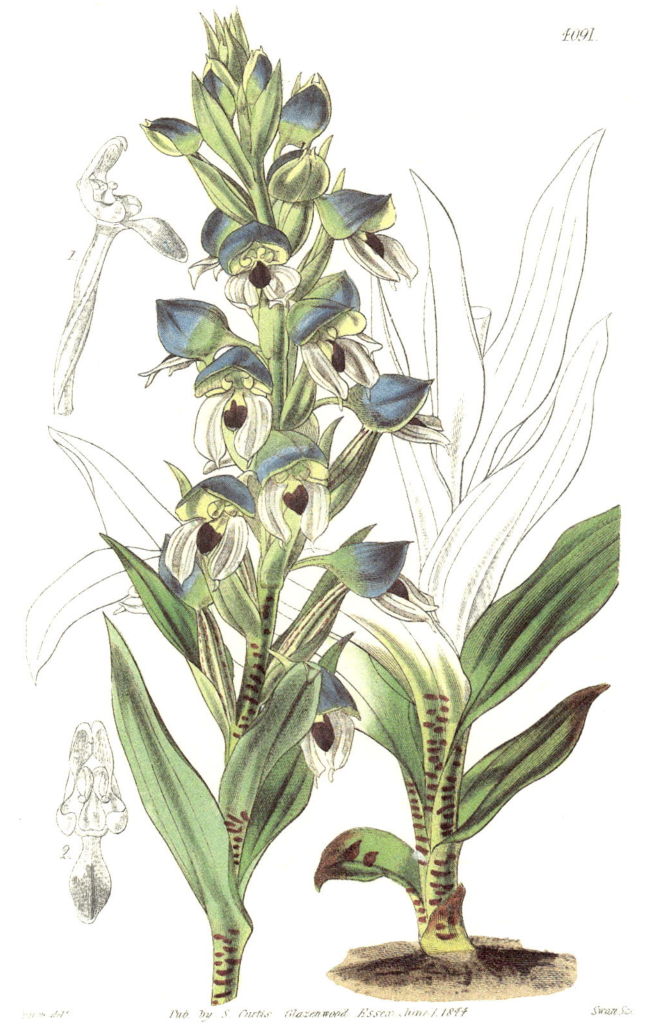

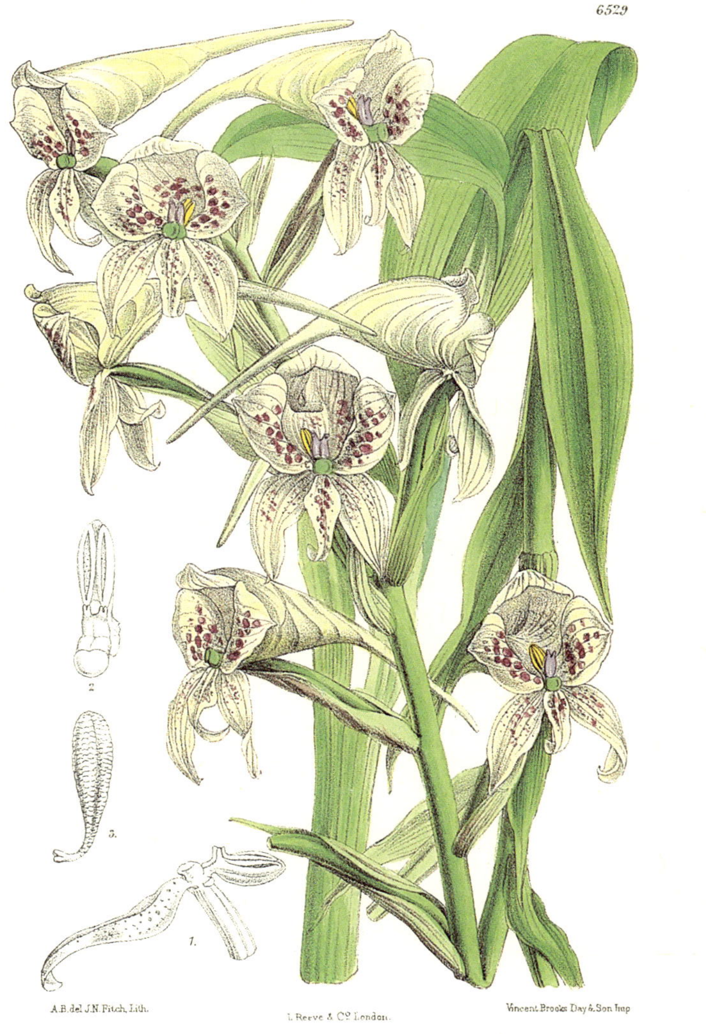

7951 Dipodium pictum (Lindl.) Rchb. f.
4091 Disa cornuta (L.) Sw.

7256 Disa cooperi Rchb. f.
6529 Disa crassicornis Lindl.

7243 Disa incarnata (Lyall ex Lindl.) Lindl.
7021 Disa racemosa L.f.

6532 Disa polygonoides Lindl.
7403 Disa sagittalis (L.f.) Sw.

7206 Disa tripetaloides (L.f.) N.E.Br.
6201 Diuris punctata Smith

4073 Disa uniflora Bergius
3156 Diuris maculata Smith

7196 Doritis pulcherrima Lindl.
6977 Dracula chestertonii (Rchb.f.) Luer

7125 Dracula carderi (Rchb.f.) Luer
6152 Dracula wallisii (Rchb.f.) Luer

5904 Drymoda picta Lindl.
6016 Elleanthus xanthocomus Rchb.f. ex Hook.

5141 Elleanthus caravata (Aublet) Rchb.f.
5403 Eltroplectris calcarata (Sw.) Garay & Sweet

M.S. del. J.N.Fitch lith.

Vincent Brooks, Day & Son Ltd Imp.

L. Reeve & Co London.

7702 Embreea rodigasiana (Claes ex Cogn.) Dodson

3631 Encyclia adenocarpon (Llave & Lex.) Schltr.
4572 Encyclia bractescens (Lindl.) Hoehne

4606 Encyclia adenocaula var. adenocaula (Llave & Lex.) Schltr.
5664 Encyclia brassavolae (Rchb. f.) Dressler

3898 Encyclia alata (Bateman) Schltr.

3765 Encyclia candollei (Lindl.) Schltr.

9243 Encyclia campylostalix (Rchb. f.) Schltr.
3742 Encyclia citrina (Llave & Lex.) Dressler

3557 Encyclia chloroleuca (Hook.) Neumann
572 Encyclia cochleata (L.) Lemée

3534 Encyclia cordigera (Kunth) Dressler
152 Encyclia fragrans (Sw.) Lemée

5491 Encyclia dichroma (Lindl.) Schltr.
1669 Encyclia fragrans (Sw.) Lemée

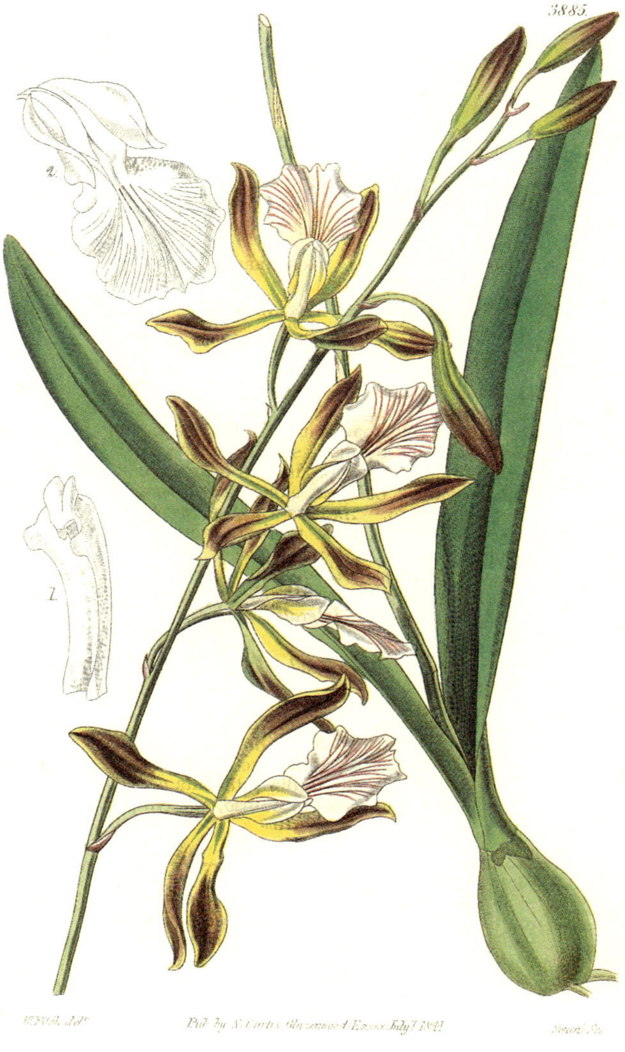

3638 Encyclia livida (Lindl.) Dressler
3013 Encyclia odoratissima (Lindl.) Schltr.

9179 Encyclia mooreana (Rolfe) Schltr.
3885 Encyclia phoenicea (Lindl.) Schltr.

M.S. del, J.N.Fitch lith.

Vincent Brooks Day & Son Ltd Imp

L. Reeve & Co London

7792 Encyclia osmantha (Barb. Rodr.) Schltr.

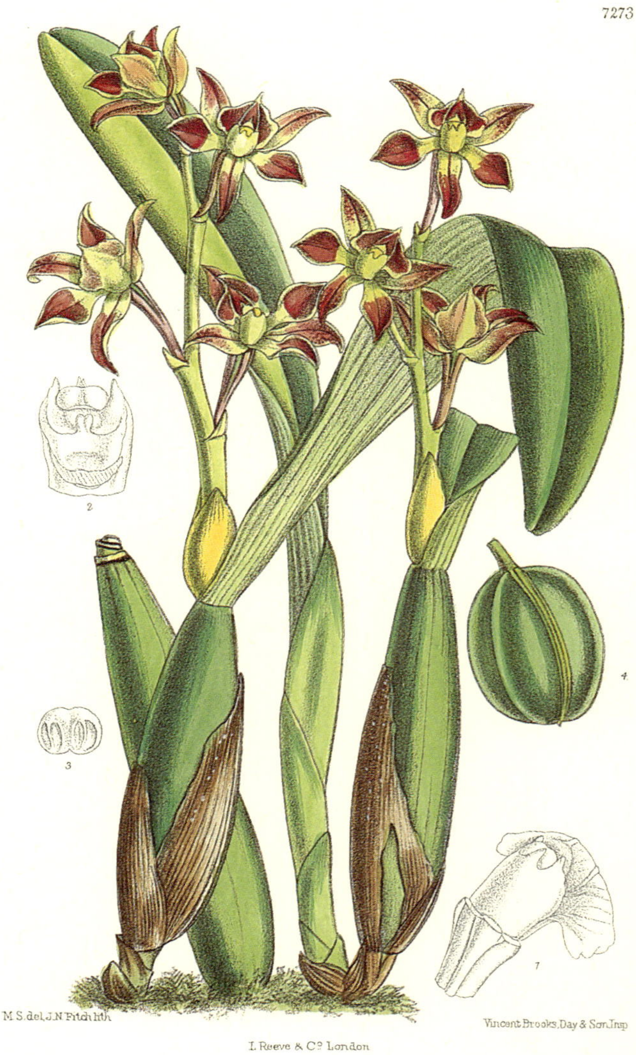

5336 Encyclia prismatocarpa (Rchb. f.) Dressler
3233 Encyclia pygmaea (Hook.) Dressler

8551 Encyclia × profusa (Rolfe) Dressler & Pollard
7273 Encyclia spondiada (Rchb. f.) Dressler

3151.

Mrs Arnold Harrison del^t

Pub by S. Curtis Glazenwood Essex. May 1 1832.

Swan Sc.

3151 Encyclia vespa (Vell.) Dressler

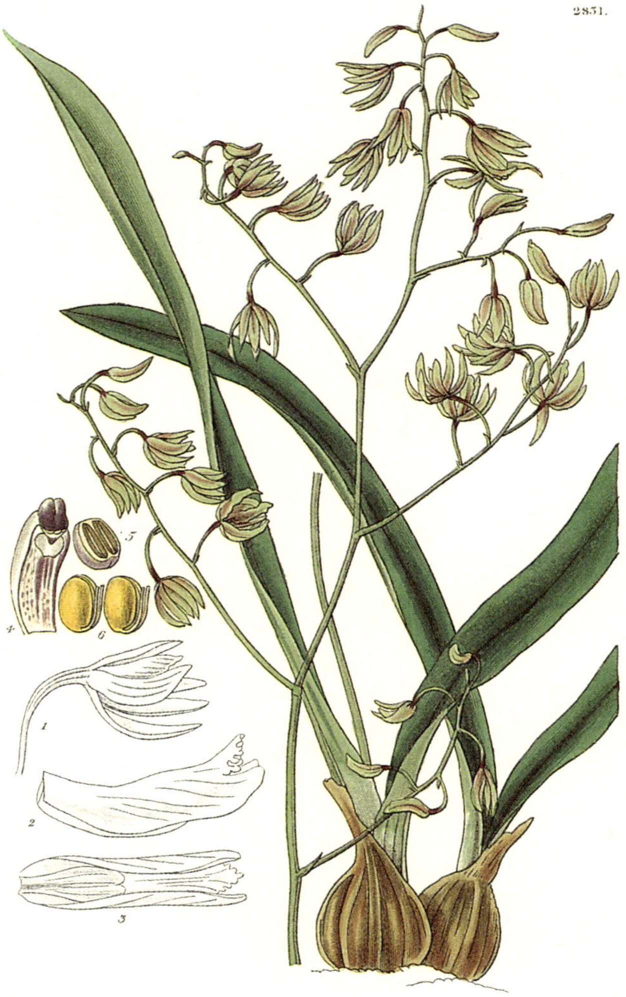

3595 Encyclia vespa (Vell.) Dressler
4107 Encyclia vitellina (Lindl.) Dressler

2831 Encyclia viridiflora Hook.
3298 Epidendrum carpophorum Barb. Rodr.

5656 Epidendrum cnemidophorum Lindl.

463 Epidendrum ciliare L.
5654 Epidendrum cooperianum Bateman

3457 Epidendrum conopseum R.Br.
9477 Epidendrum coriifolium Lindl.

6094 Epidendrum criniferum Rchb. f.
3791 Epidendrum densiflorum Hook.

3637 Epidendrum densiflorum Hook.
2030 Epidendrum difforme Jacq.

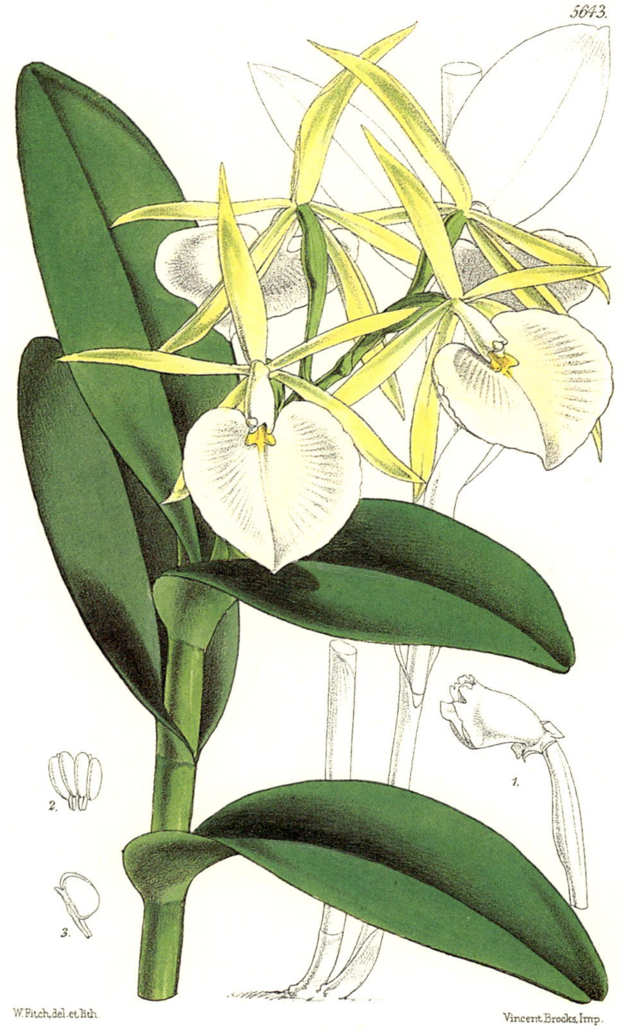

3565 Epidendrum diffusum Sw.
4784 Epidendrum elegans (Knowles & Westc.) Rchb. f.

5643 Epidendrum eburneum Rchb. f.
611 Epidendrum elongatum Jacq.

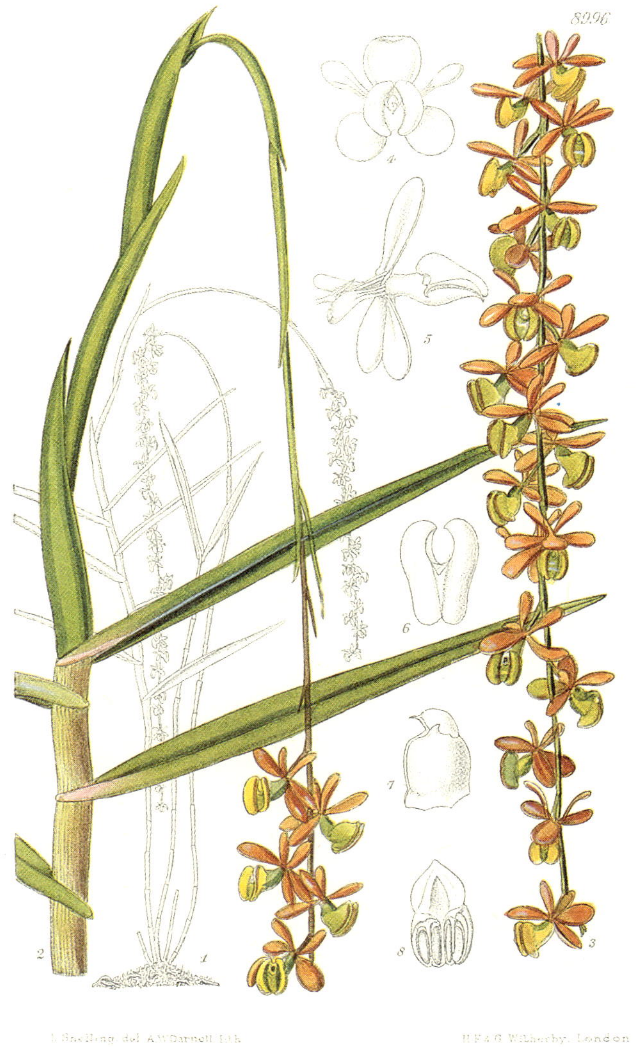

3543 Epidendrum elongatum Jacq.
3209 Epidendrum harrisoniae Hook.

5902 Epidendrum elongatum Jacq.
8996 Epidendrum laucheanum Rolfe ex Bonhof

4165 Epidendrum nocturnum Jacq.
5731 Epidendrum paniculatum Ruiz Lopez & Pavón

2980 Epidendrum pallidiflorum Hook.
3778 Epidendrum parkinsonianum Hook.

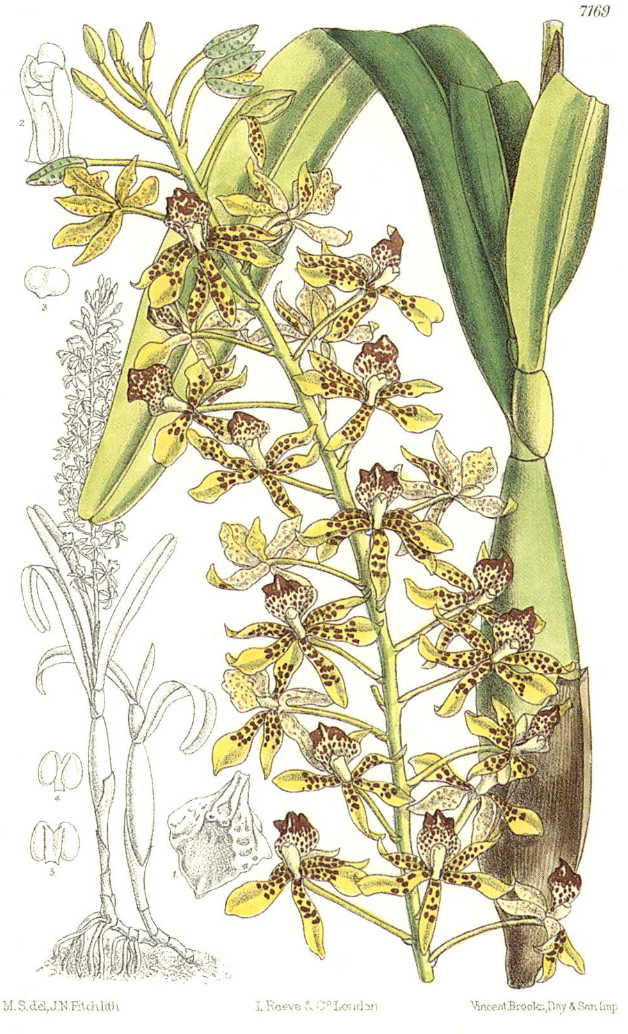

3800 Epidendrum patens Sw.
7169 Epidendrum sceptrum Lindl.

5929 Epidendrum pseudepidendrum Rchb. f.
2844 Epidendrum secundum Jacq.

3666 Epidendrum secundum Jacq.
6145 Epidendrum syringothyrsus Rchb. f.

4759 Epidendrum stamfordianum Bateman
7586 Epidendrum xanthinum Lindl.

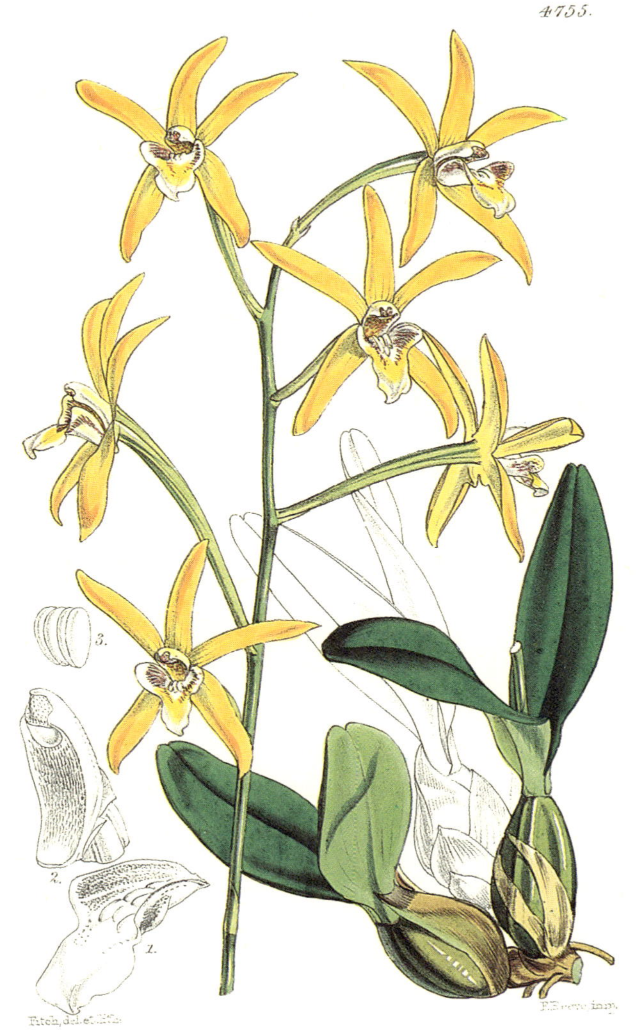

9191 Epigeneium acuminatum (Rolfe) Summerh.
6591 Epigeneium treacherianum (Rchb.f. ex Hook.f.) Summerh.

4755 Epigeneium cymbidioides (Blume) Summerh.
7690 Epipactis gigantea Douglas ex Hook.

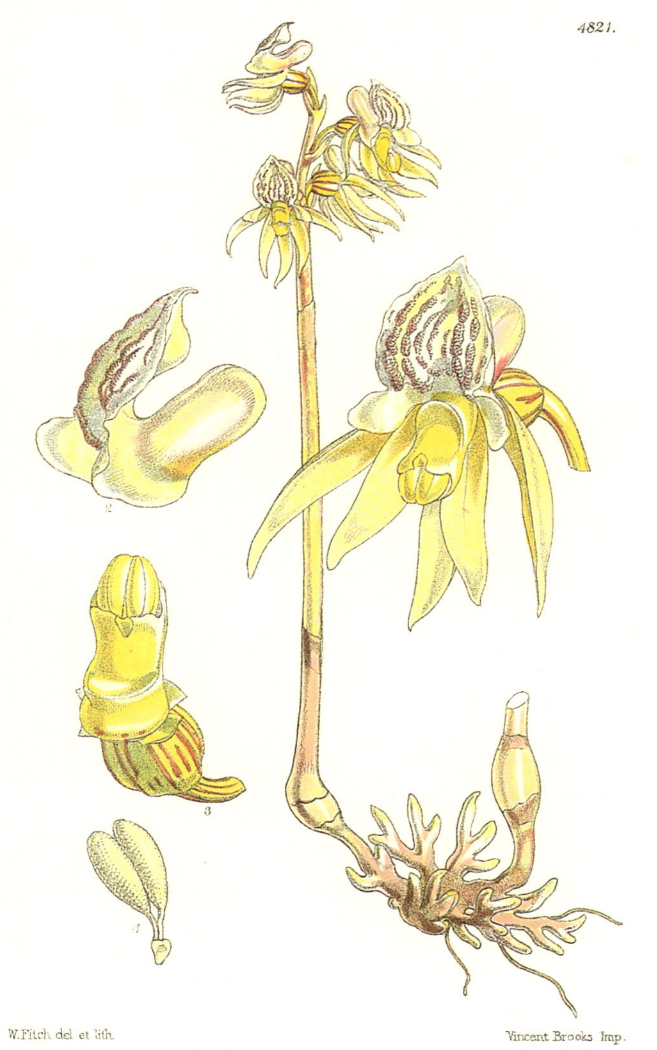

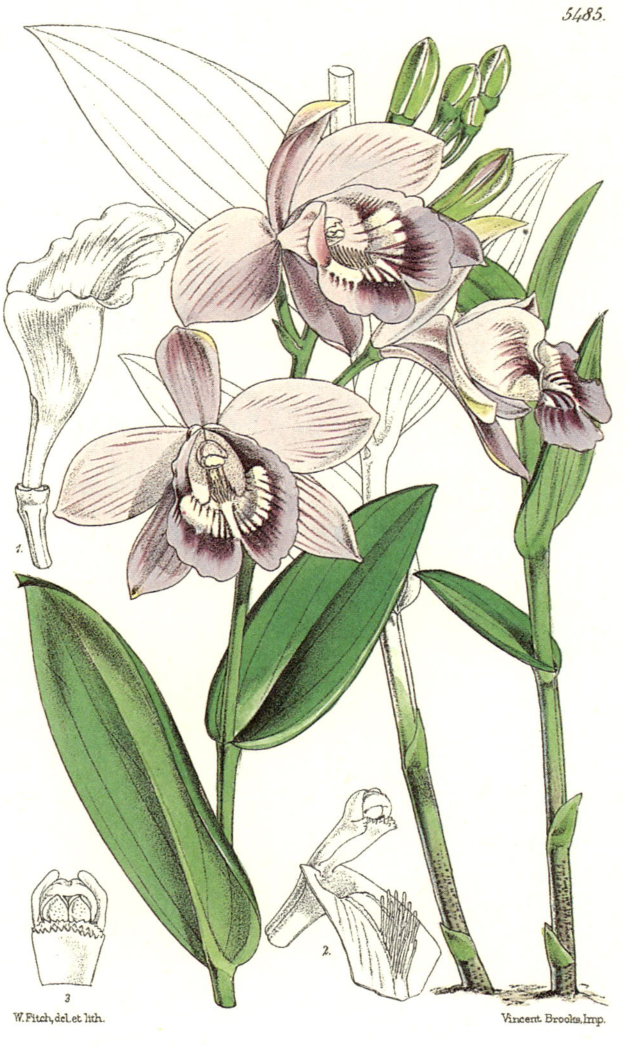

4821 Epipogium aphyllum (F.W. Schmidt) Sw.
9453 Eria amica Rchb. f.

5485 Epistephium williamsii Hook.
4163 Eria bractescens Lindl.

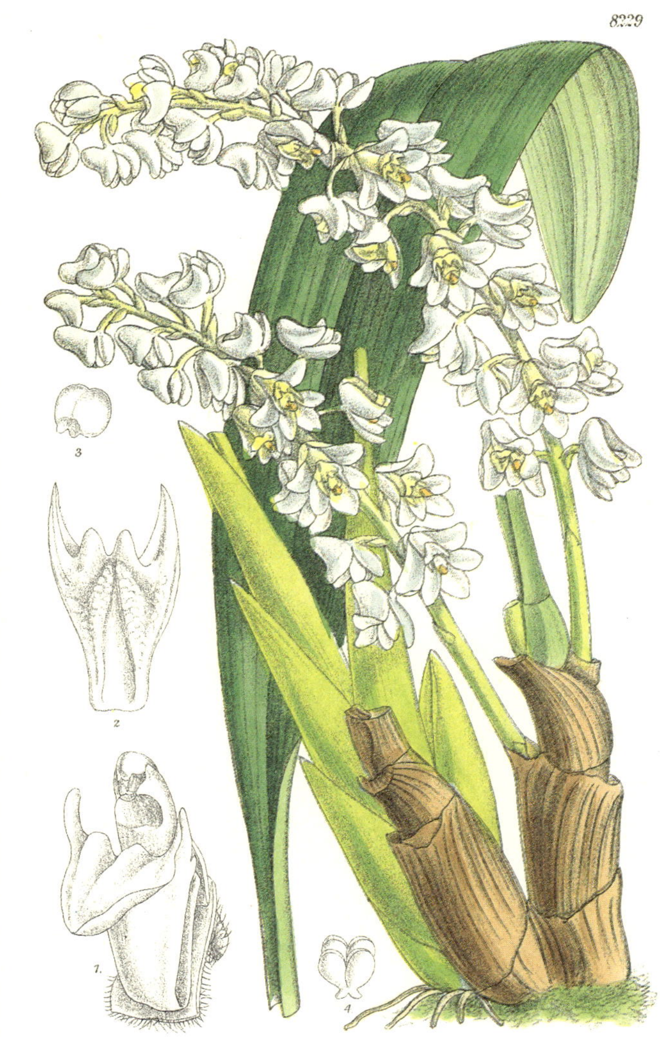

M.S. del. J.N. Fitch lith. L. Reeve & C° London Vincent Brooks, Day & Son Ltd Imp.

M.S. del. J.N. Fitch lith. L. Reeve & C° London. Vincent Brooks, Day & Son Ltd Imp.

M.S. del, J.N. Fitch lith. L. Reeve & C° London. Vincent Brooks, Day & Son Imp.

8229 Eria hyacinthoides (Blume) Lindl.
7605 Eria latibracteata Rolfe

8171 Eria iridifolia Hook. f.

3605 Eria javanica (Sw.) Blume

7238 Eria marginata Rolfe
5391 Eria obesa Lindl.

5415 Eria myristiciformis Hook.
8296 Eria rhodoptera Rchb. f.

M. S. del J. N. Fitch lith.

Vincent Brooks, Day & Son Ltd imp

L. Reeve & Co London

8642 Eria ornata (Blume) Lindl.

8234 Eria rhynchostyloides O'Brien
8662 Eria tomentosa (J. König) Hook. f.

5910 Eria summerhayesiana A. Hawkes & A.H. Heller
5807 Eria vestita (Wallich) Lindl.

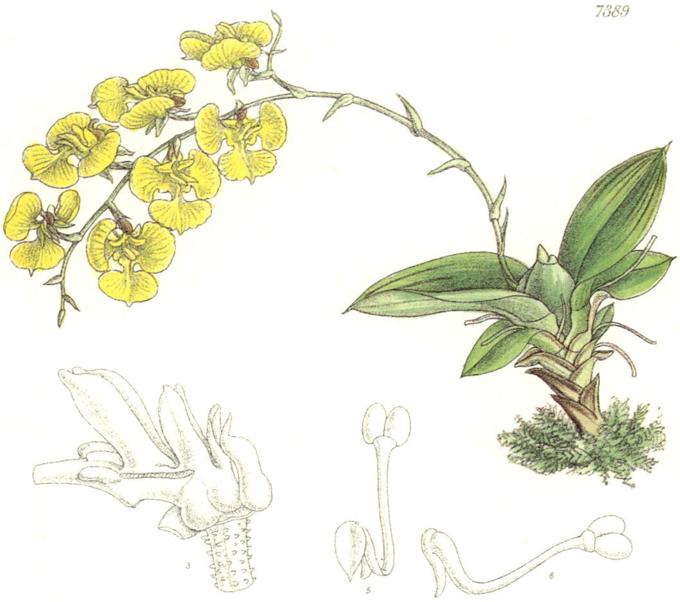

4437 Eriopsis biloba Lindl.
7389 Erycina echinata (Kunth) Lindl.

8462 Eriopsis sceptrum Rchb. f. & Warsc.
7077 Esmeralda clarkei Rchb. f.

W. Fitch, del. et lith.

Vincent Brooks, Day & Son, Imp.

5845 Esmeralda cathcartii (Lindl.) Rchb. f.

M.S. del, R. Morgan lith.

Vincent Brooks, Day & Son Imp.

L. Reeve & C° London

6983 Euanthe sanderiana (Rchb. f.) Schltr.

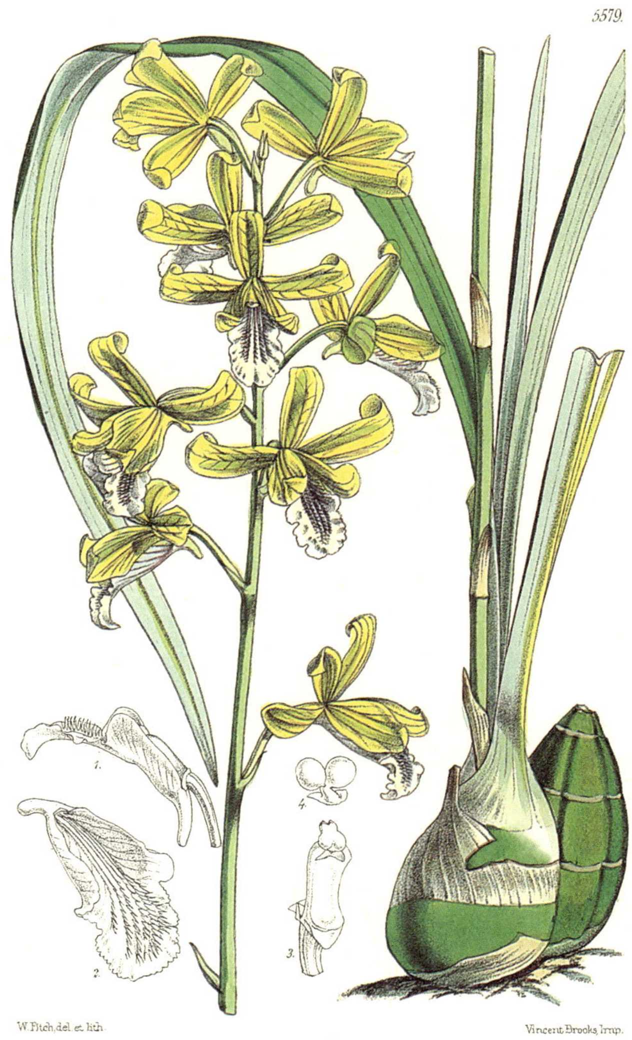

1814 Eulophia alta (L.) Fawcett & Rendle
7921 Eulophia cristata (Sw.) Steudel

8044 Eulophia angolensis (Rchb.f.) Summerh.
5579 Eulophia epidendraea (Retz) Fischer

M. S. del J. N. Fitch lith.

Vincent Brooks, Day & Son Ltd imp

L. Reeve & Co. London

8397 Eulophia cucullata (Sw.) Steudel

5561 Eulophia euglossa (Rchb. f.) Rchb. f.
2467 Eulophia guineensis Lindl.

8470 Eulophia flavopurpurea (Rchb. f.) Rolfe
7546 Eulophia orthoplectra (Rchb. f.) Summerh.

W. Fitch, del et lith.

Vincent Brooks, Imp.

5486 Eulophia horsfallii (Bateman) Summerh.

M.S. del J.N. Fitch lith. L. Reeve & Co. London Vincent Brooks, Day & Son Imp

6858 Eulophia horsfallii (Bateman) Summerh.

M. S. del, J.N. Fitch lith. L. Reeve & C° London Vincent Brooks, Day & Son Ltd Imp

8047 *Eulophia horsfallii* (Bateman) Summerh.

M.S. del. J.N. Fitch lith. L. Reeve & Co. London Vincent Brooks, Day & Son Ltd. Imp.

8057 Eulophia nuda Lindl.

2931 Eulophia streptopetala Lindl.

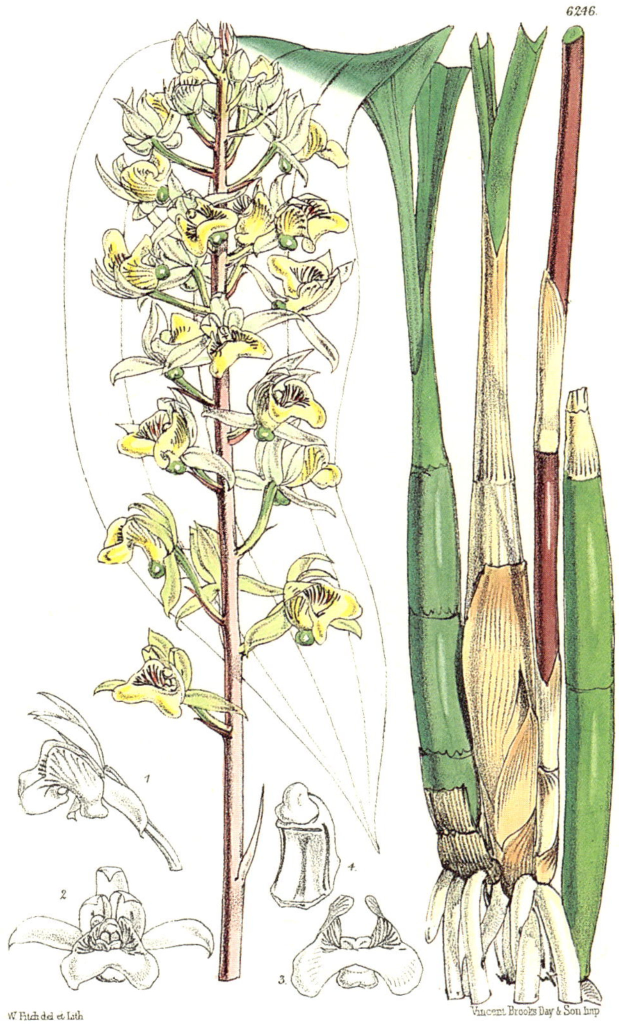

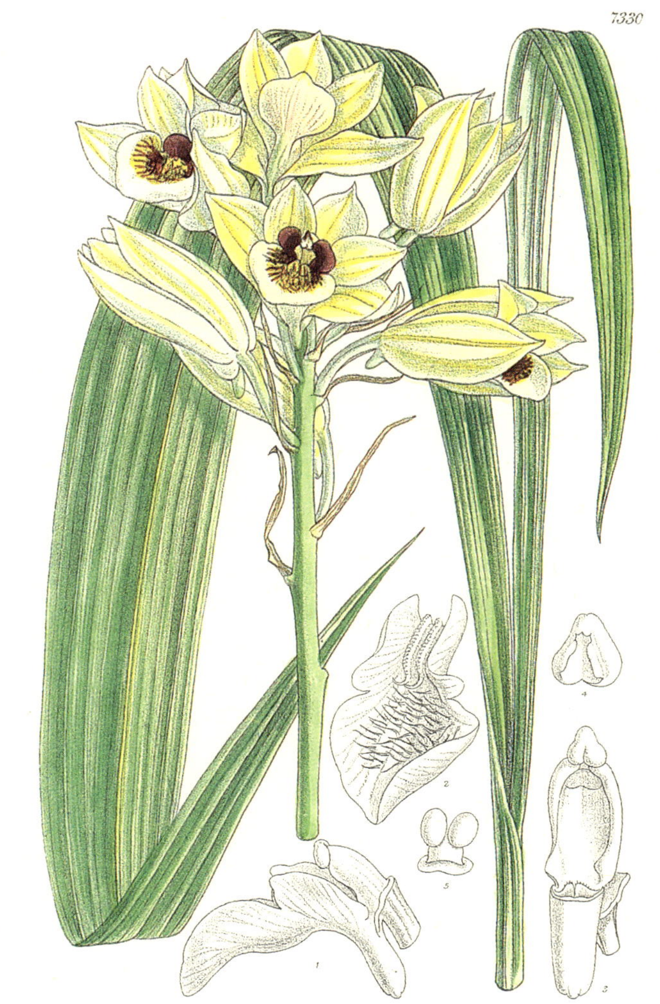

6246 Eulophia pulchra (Thouars) Lindl.
5861 Eulophia streptopetala Lindl.

6161 Eulophia sanguinea (Lindl.) Hook.f.
7330 Eulophia welwitschii (Rchb.f.) Rolfe

M. S. del, J. N. Fitch lith.

Vincent Brooks, Day & Son Imp.

L. Reeve & C° London.

7387 Eulophiella elisabethae Linden & Rolfe

M. S. del. J. N. Fitch lith.

Vincent Brooks Day & Son Ltd Imp.

L. Reeve & Co. London

7612 *Eulophiella roempleriana* (Rchb. f.) Schltr.

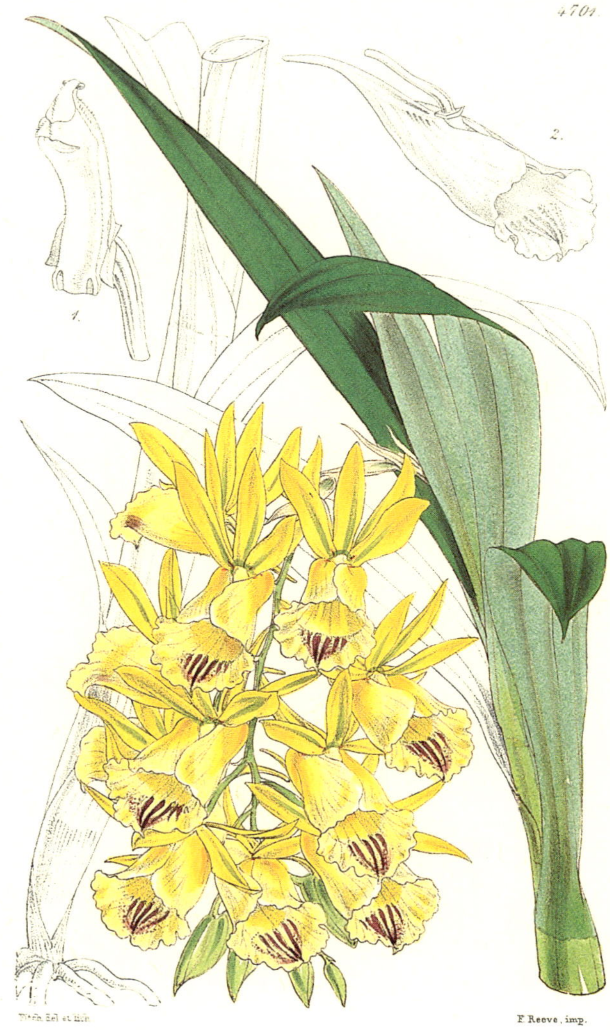

7613 *Eulophiella roempleriana* (Rchb. f.) Schltr.
4610 *Galeandra devoniana* Schomb. ex Lindl.

4701 *Galeandra baueri* Lindl.
4772 *Gastrochilus acutifolius* (Lindl.) Kuntze

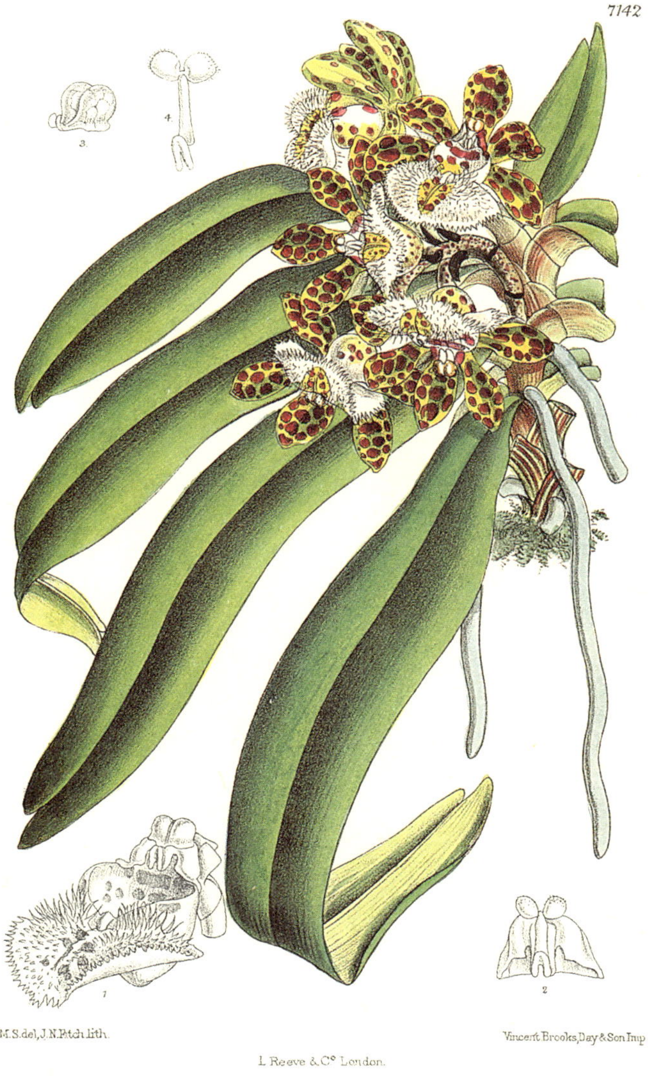

7142 Gastrochilus bellinus (Rchb. f.) Kuntze
3164 Gennaria diphylla (Link) Parl.

5767 Gastrochilus bigibbus (Rchb. f. ex Hook. f.) Kuntze
2195 Geodorum citrinum Jackson

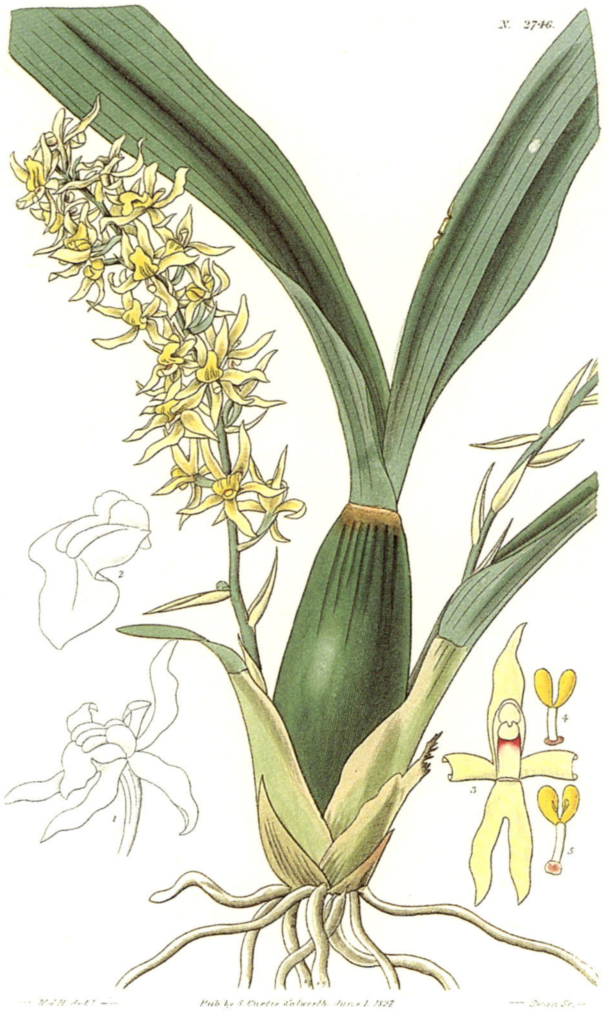

3497 Gomesa barkeri (Hook.) Rolfe
3504 Gomesa planifolia (Lindl.) Klotzsch & Rchb. f.

2746 Gomesa foliosa (Hook.) Klotzsch & Rchb. f.
1748 Gomesa recurva R. Br.

3563 Gongora galeata (Lindl.) Rchb. f.

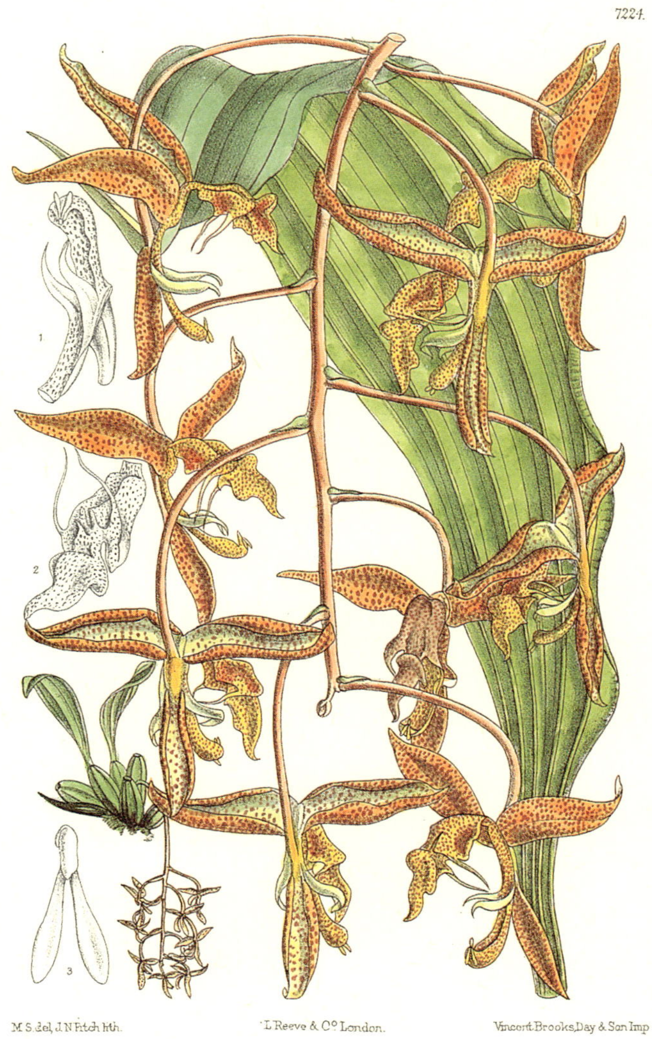

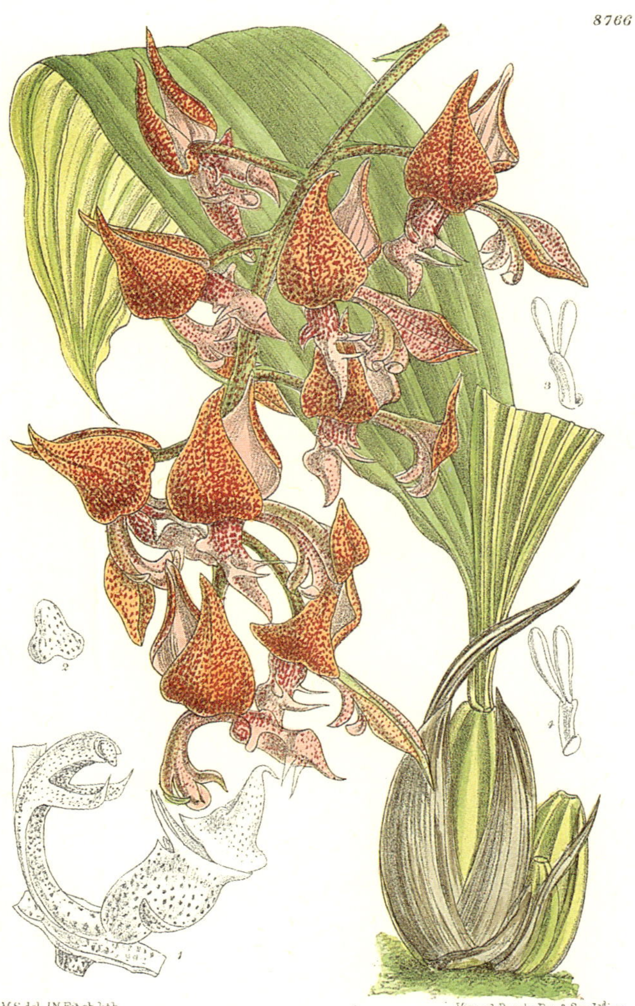

5501 Gongora armeniaca (Lindl.) Rchb. f.
8766 Gongora latisepala Rolfe

7224 Gongora gratulabunda Rchb. f.
6284 Gongora portentosa Linden & Rchb. f.

M. S. del. J. N. Fitch lith. L. Reeve & C° London. Vincent Brooks, Day & Son Lt^d imp.

8562 Gongora grossa Rchb. f.

W. J. H. del.t Pub. by S. Curtis, Glazenwood, Essex, Mar. 1. 1833. Swan Sc.

3220 Gongora quinquenervis Ruiz Lopez & Pavón

3687 Gongora quinquenervis Ruiz Lopez & Pavón

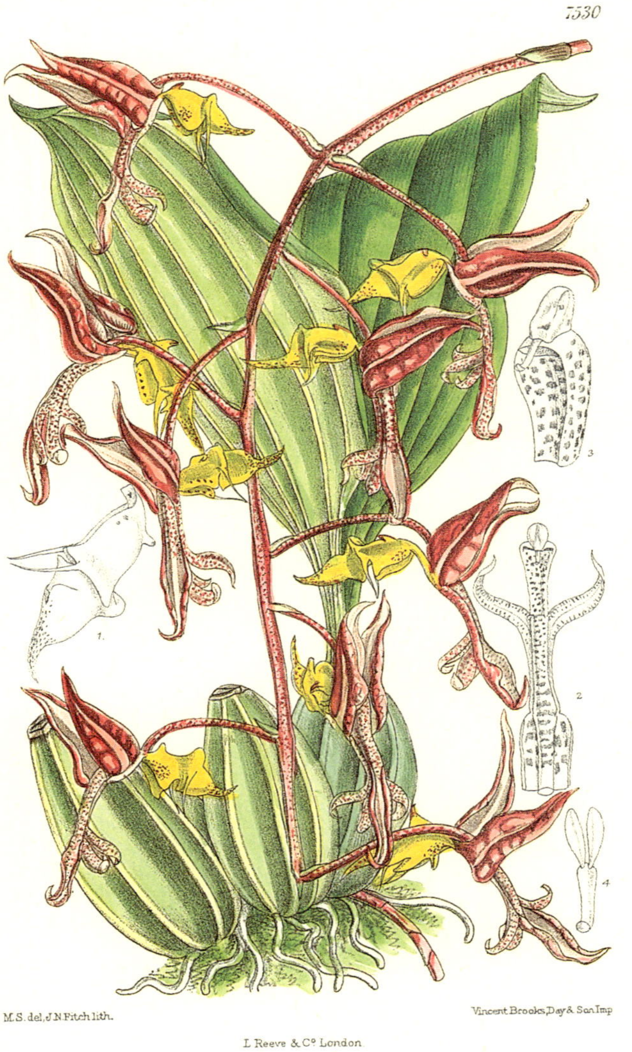

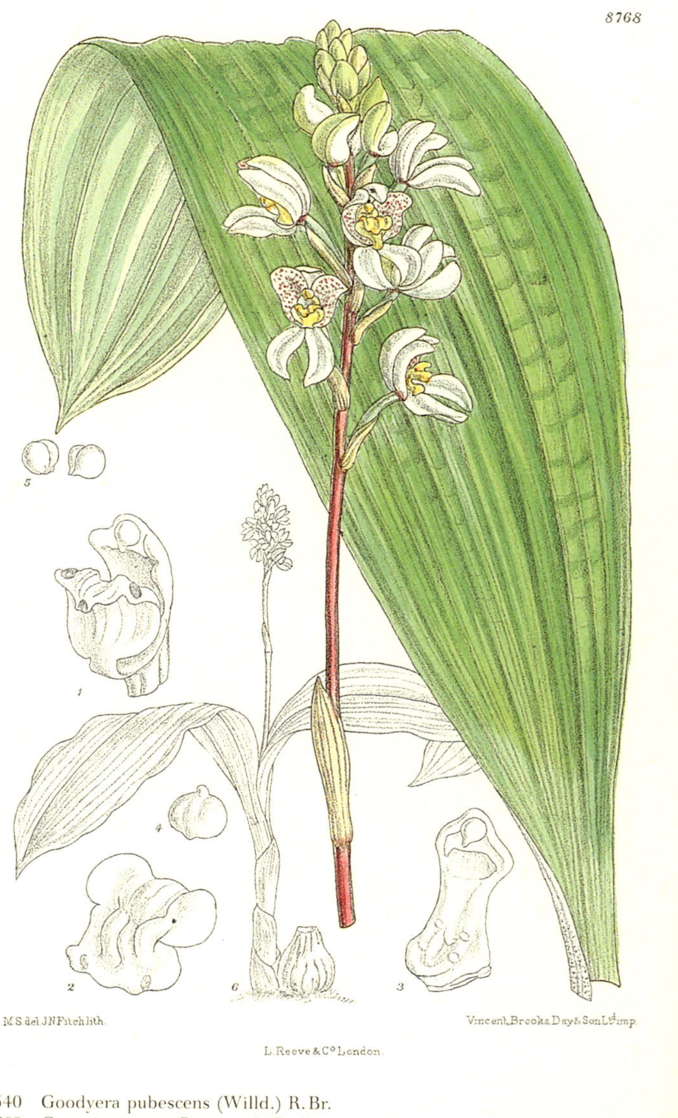

7530 Gongora tricolor Rchb. f.
8794 Govenia superba (Llave & Lex.) Lindl. ex Lodd.

2540 Goodyera pubescens (Willd.) R. Br.
8768 Govenia tingens Poeppig & Endl.

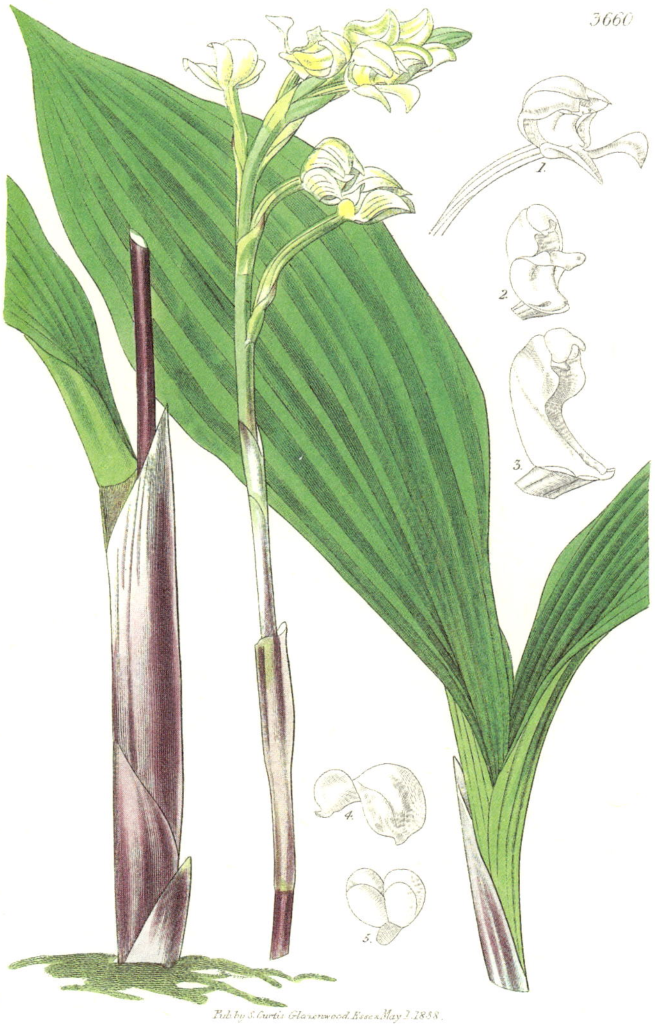

3660 Govenia utriculata (Sw.) Lindl.
5179 Grammangis ellisii (Lindl.) Rchb. f.

4151 Govenia utriculata (Sw.) Lindl.
7507 Grammatophyllum scriptum (L.) Blume

5157 Grammatophyllum speciosum Blume

5676 Grammatophyllum stapeliiflorum (Teijsm. & Binnend.) J.J. Smith
9663 Habenaria dentata (Sw.) Schltr.

7798 Habenaria armatissima Rchb. f.
7478 Habenaria elwesii Hook. f.

2726 Habenaria leptoceras Hook.
2957 Habenaria longicauda Hook.

7228 Habenaria longicalcarata A. Rich.
2947 Habenaria quinqueseta (Michaux) Sw.

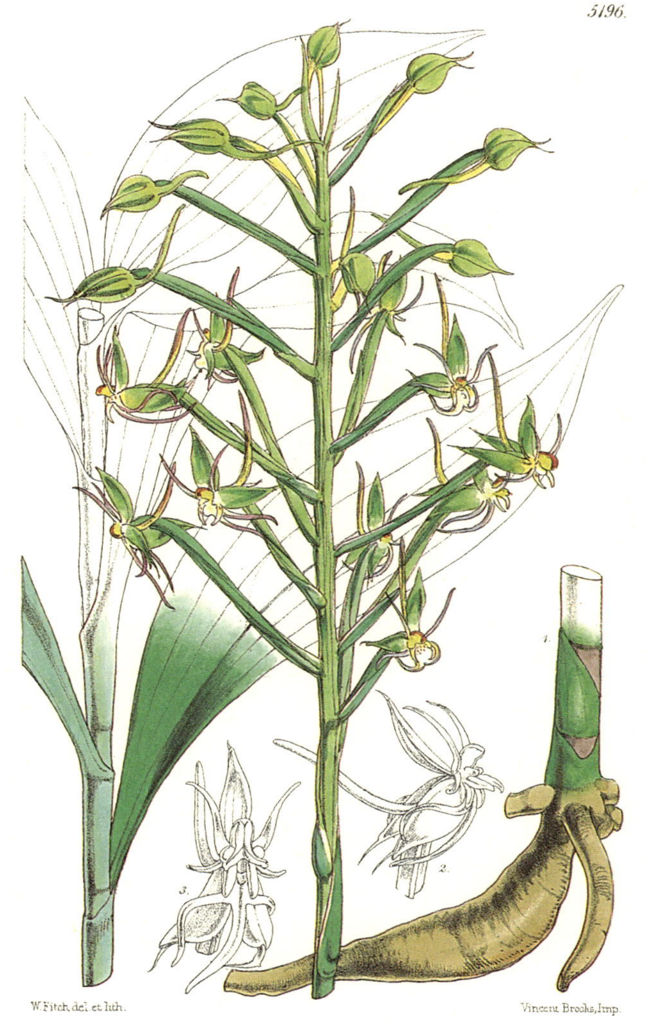

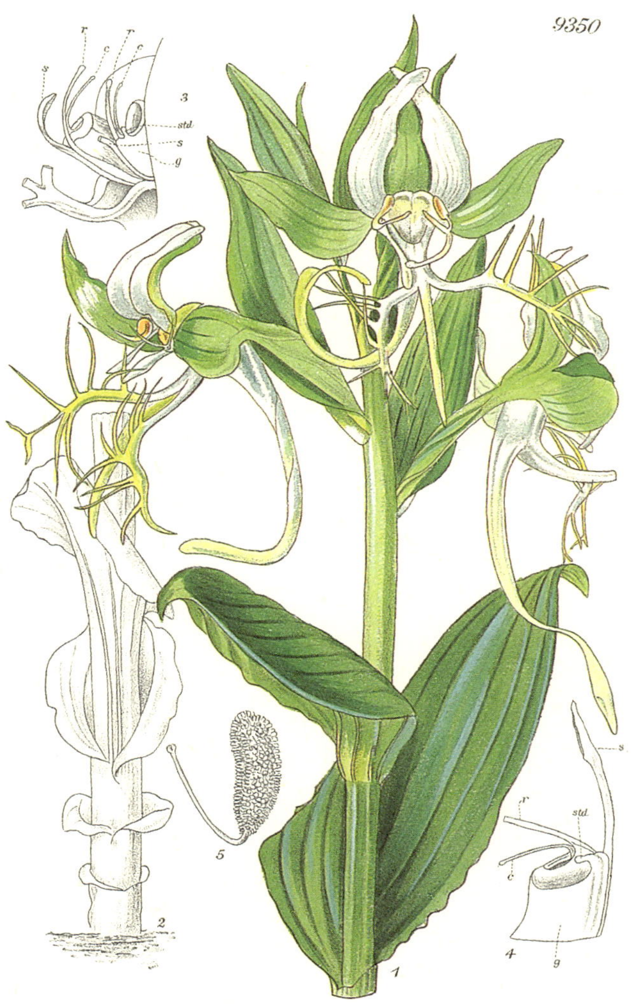

7570 Habenaria rhodocheila Hance
9350 Habenaria splendens Rendle

5196 Habenaria salaccensis Blume

7281 *Helcia sanguinolenta* Lindl.
7521 *Hemipilia amethystina* Rolfe ex Hook. f.

6920 *Hemipilia calophylla* Parish & Rchb. f.

7066 Herschelianthe hians (L. f.) Rauschert
6891 Herschelianthe spathulata (L. f.) Rauschert

8415 Herschelianthe lugens (Bolus) Rauschert
7031 Hexisea bidentata Lindl.

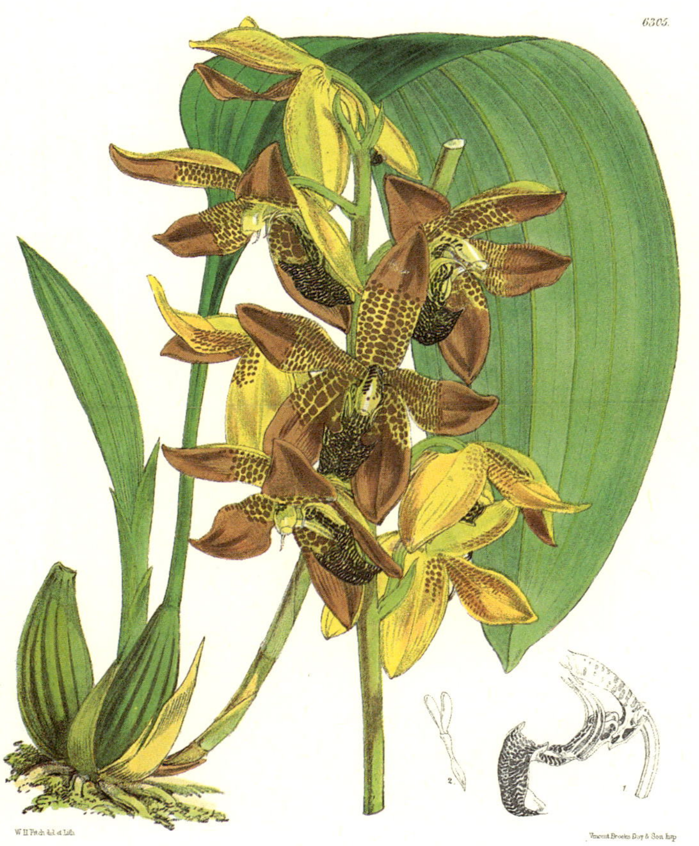

7112 Holcoglossum kimballianum (Rchb. f.) Garay
6305 Houlletia odoratissima Linden ex Lindl. & Paxton

7523 Holothrix orthoceras Rchb. f.
8346 Houlletia sanderi Rolfe

4072.

W. Fitch del.

Pub by S. Curtis Glazenwood Essex March 1. 1844

4072 Houlletia brocklehurstiana Lindl.

7362

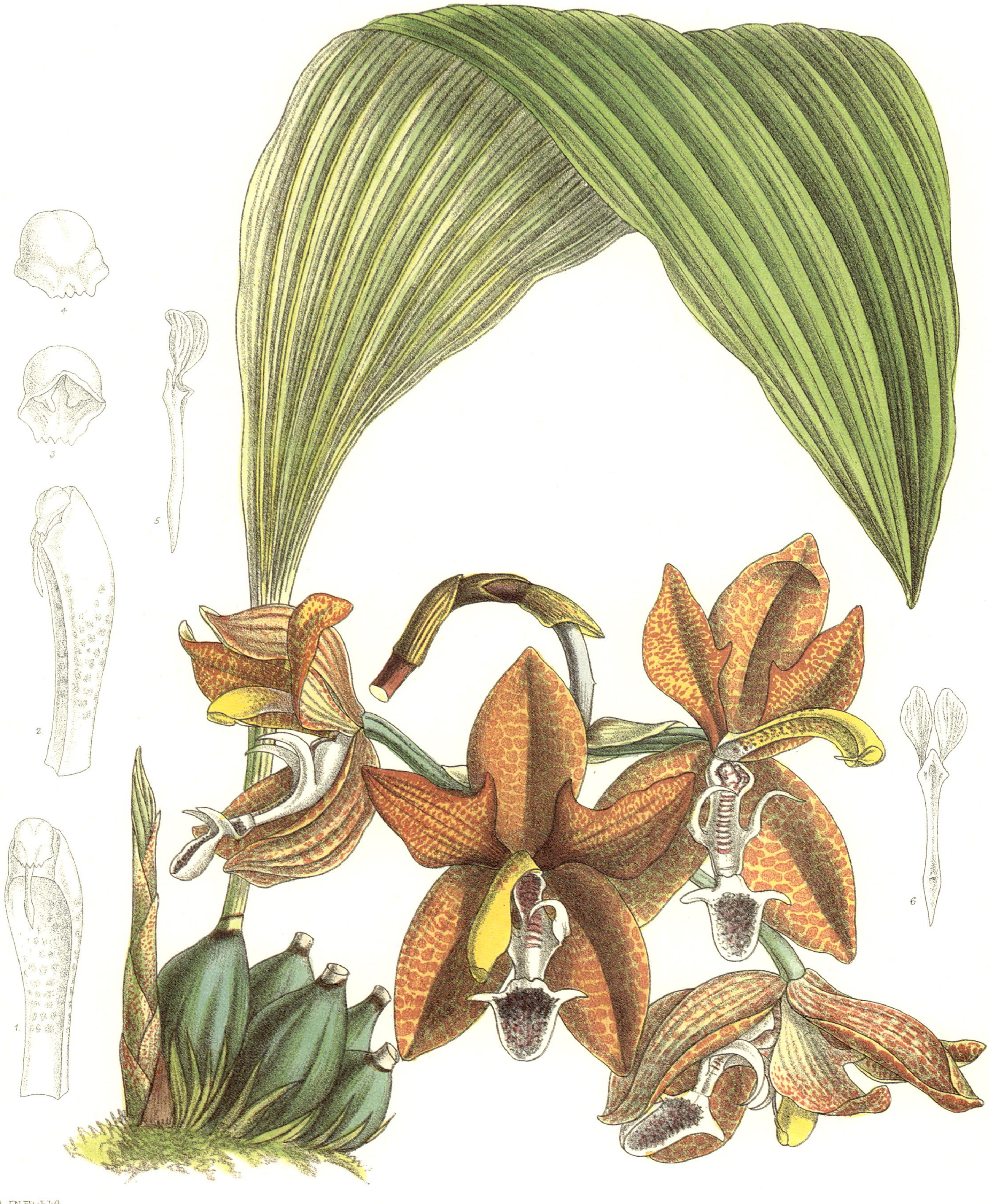

M.S.del, J.N.Fitch lith.

L. Reeve & Co London.

Vincent Brooks, Day & Son Imp.

7362 Houlletia tigrina Linden ex Lindl.

6003 Huntleya burtii (Endres & Rchb. f.) Pfitzer

8689 Huntleya citrina Rolfe

W. Fitch, del. et lith.

Vincent Brooks, Imp.

5541 Ionopsis utricularioides (Sw.) Lindl.

5701 Ipsea speciosa Lindl.
7161 Jumellea fragrans (Thouars) Schltr.

8787 Isabella virginalis Barb. Rodr.
8758 Jumellea saggittata H. Perr.

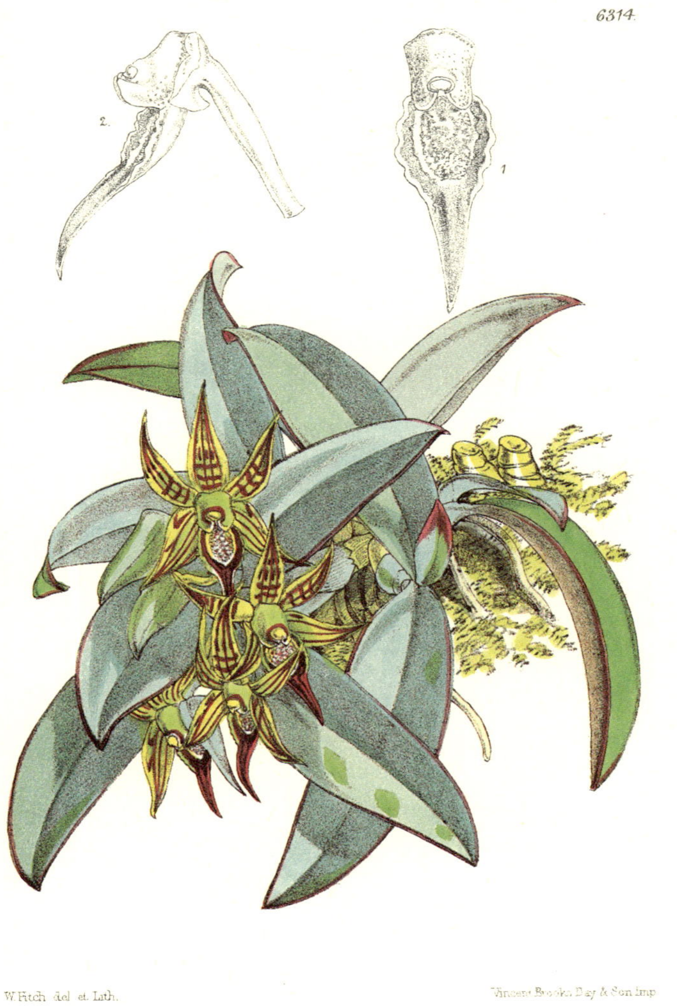

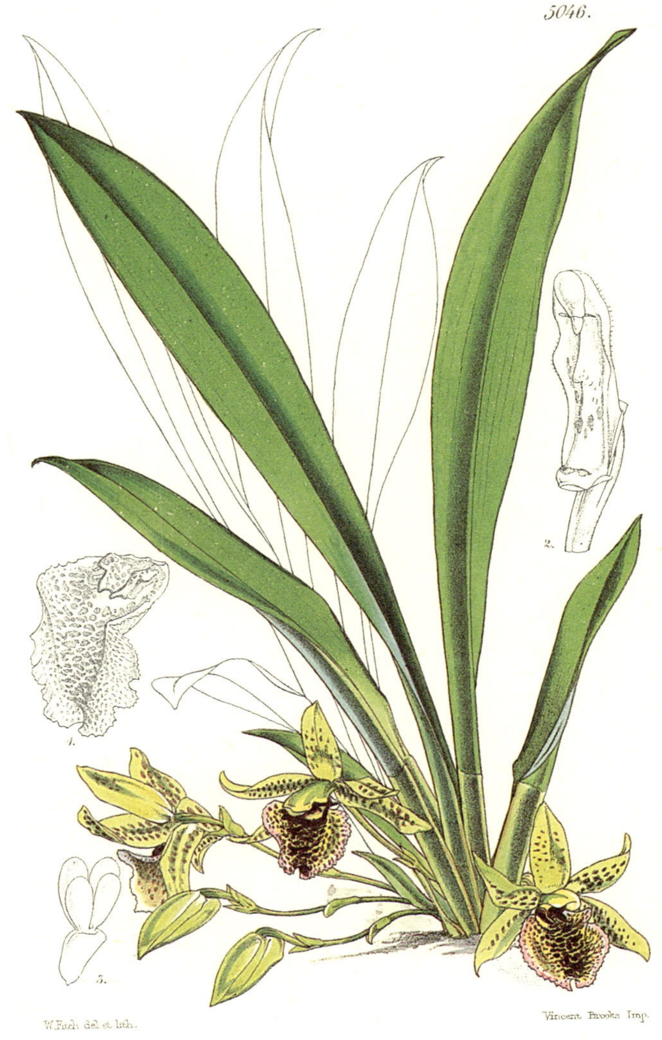

6314 Kalopternix sophronites (Linden & Rchb. f.) Garay & Dunsterv.
6338 Koellensteinia graminea (Lindl.) Rchb. f.

5046 Kefersteinia graminea (Lindl.) Rchb. f.
7270 Koellensteinia inoptera Linden & Rchb. f.

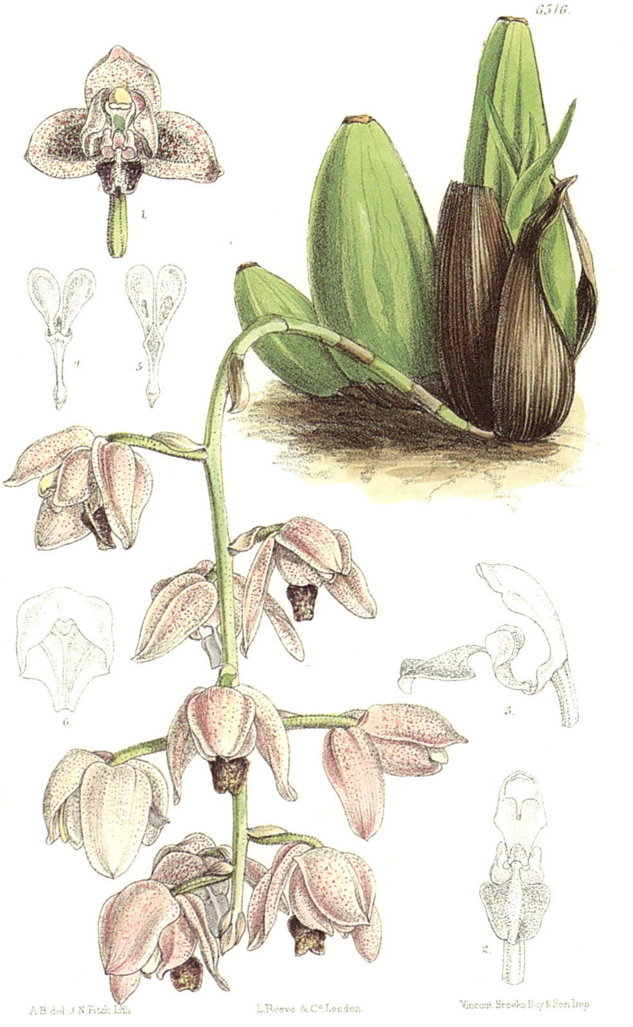

6516 Lacaena spectabilis (Klotzsch) Rchb. f.
3804 Laelia anceps Lindl.

3957 Laelia albida Lindl. & Bateman
3817 Laelia autumnalis Lindl.

3910 Laelia crispa (Lindl.) Rchb. f.

4302 Laelia cinnabarina Bateman ex Lindl.
3810 Laelia furfuracea Lindl.

4700 Laelia elegans (Morren) Rchb. f.
5553 Laelia grandis Lindl.

6038 Laelia jongheana Rchb. f.
3656 Laelia pumila (Hook.) Rchb. f.

7541 Laelia longipes Rchb. f.
5498 Laelia pumila (Hook.) Rchb. f.

3711 Laelia perrinii Lindl.

W. Fitch, del. et lith.

Vincent Brooks, Imp.

5667 Laelia speciosa (Kunth) Schltr.

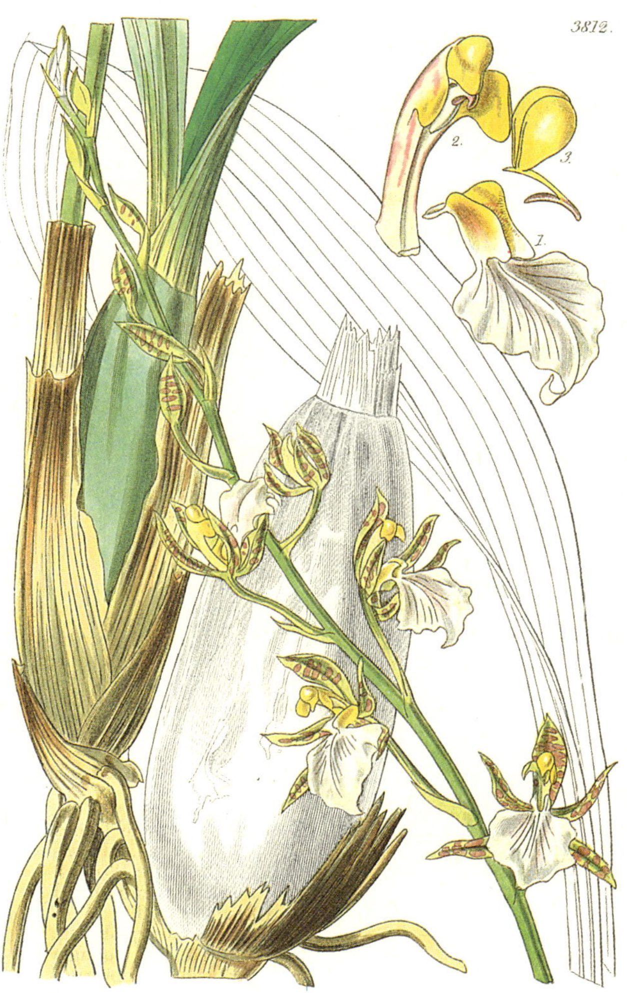

4099 Laelia rubescens Lindl.
5144 Laelia xanthina Lindl. ex Hook.

4905 Laelia rubescens Lindl.
3812 Lemboglossum bictoniense (Bateman ex Lindl.) Halbinger

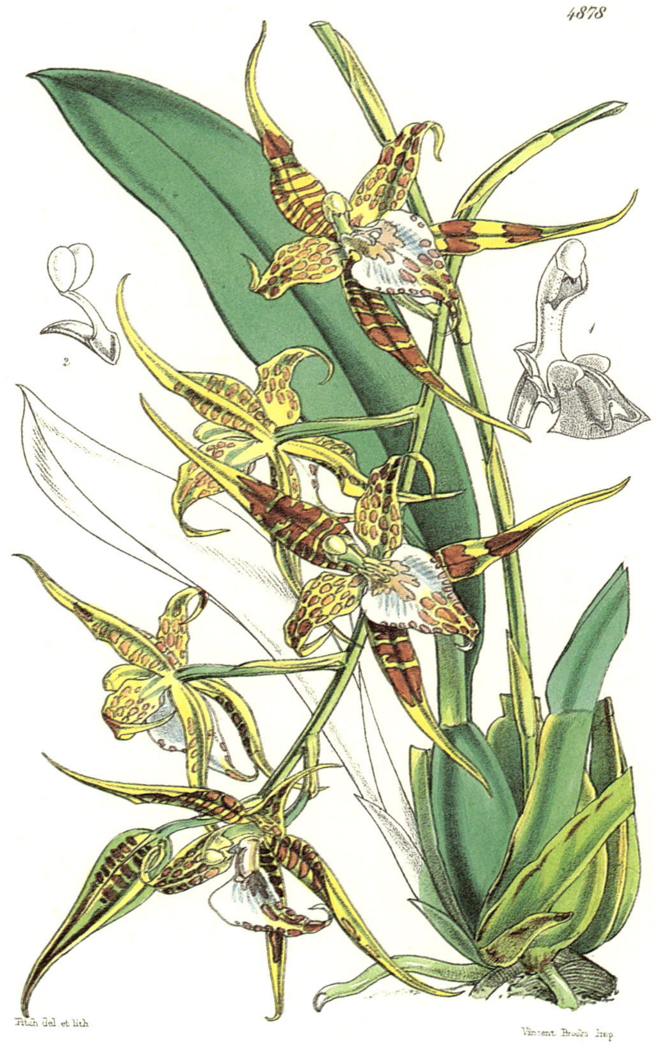

4923 Lemboglossum cervantesii (Llave & Lex.) Halbinger
6455 Lemboglossum maculatum (Llave & Lex.) Halbinger

4878 Lemboglossum cordatum (Lindl.) Halbinger
8718 Lemboglossum majale (Rchb. f.) Halbinger

3845 Leochilus oncidioides Knowles & Westc.
4112 Lepanthes sanguinea Hook.

5259 Lepanthes calodictyon Hook.
3734 Leptotes bicolor Lindl.

5949 Leucohyle subulata (Sw.) Schltr.
2004 Liparis lilifolia (L.) L.C. Rich. ex Lindl.

8195 Liparis atrosanguinea Ridley
2709 Liparis reflexa (R.Br.) Lindl.

M.S.del J.N.Fitch lith.

Vincent Brooks, Day & Son Ltd imp.

L.Reeve & C° London.

8797 Liparis nigra Seidenf.

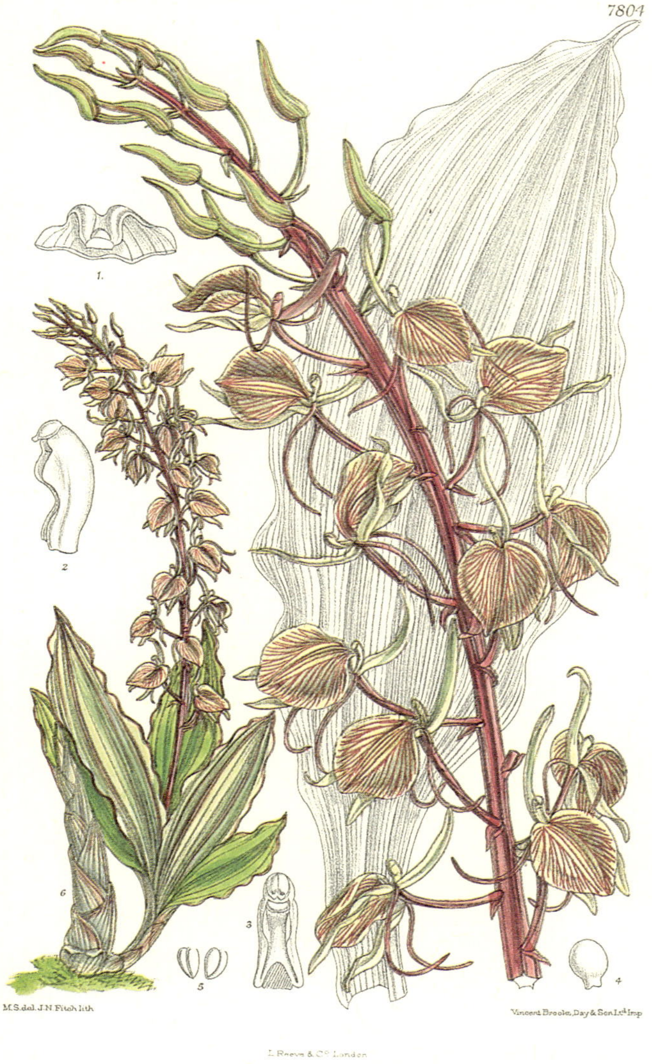

7804 Liparis tricallosa Rchb. f.
5529 Liparis wightiana Thwaites

3770 Liparis walkeriae Graham
4782 Listrostachys pertusa (Lindl.) Rchb. f.

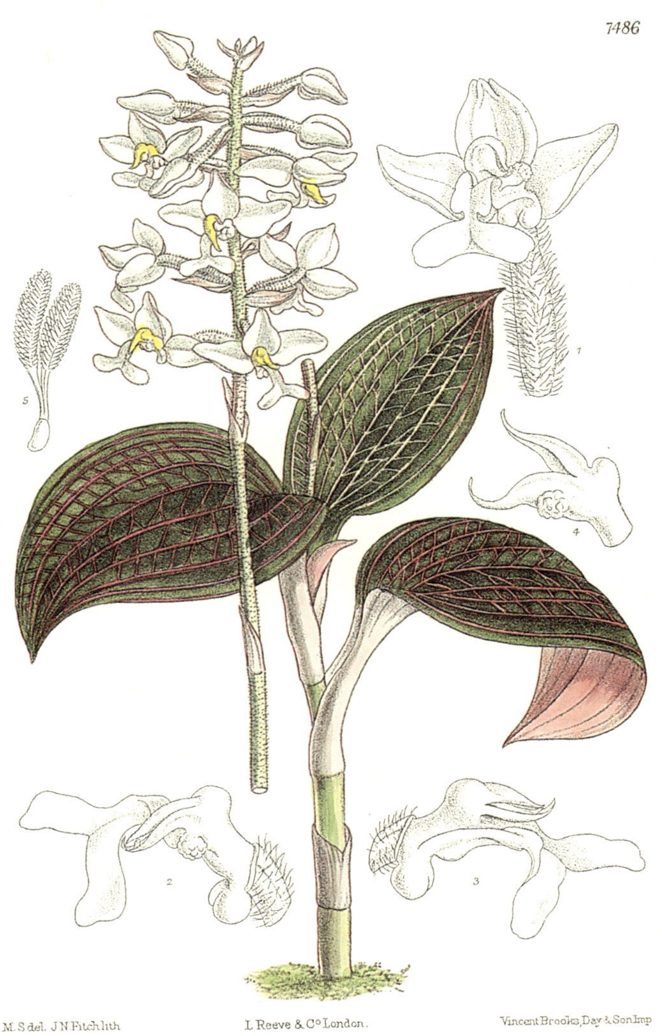

2715 Lockhartia elegans Hook.
2055 Ludisia discolor (Ker Gawler) A. Rich.

5592 Lockhartia oerstedii Rchb. f.
7486 Ludisia discolor (Ker-Gawler) A. Rich.

M.S. del. J. N. Fitch lith.

Vincent Brooks, Day & Son, Imp.

L. Reeve & Co. London.

7123 Lueddemannia pescatorei (Lindl.) Linden & Rchb. f.

3648 Luisia platyglossa Rchb. f.
9231 Lycaste aromatica (Graham ex Hook.) Lindl.

5558 Luisia psyche Rchb. f.
4081 Lycaste barringtoniae (Smith) Lindl.

3395 Lycaste deppei (Lodd.) Lindl.

5706 Lycaste ciliata (Ruiz Lopez & Pavón) Lindl. ex Rchb. f.
4193 Lycaste fulvescens Hook.

8103 Lycaste dyeriana Sander ex Rolfe
6251 Lycaste lasioglossa Rchb. f.

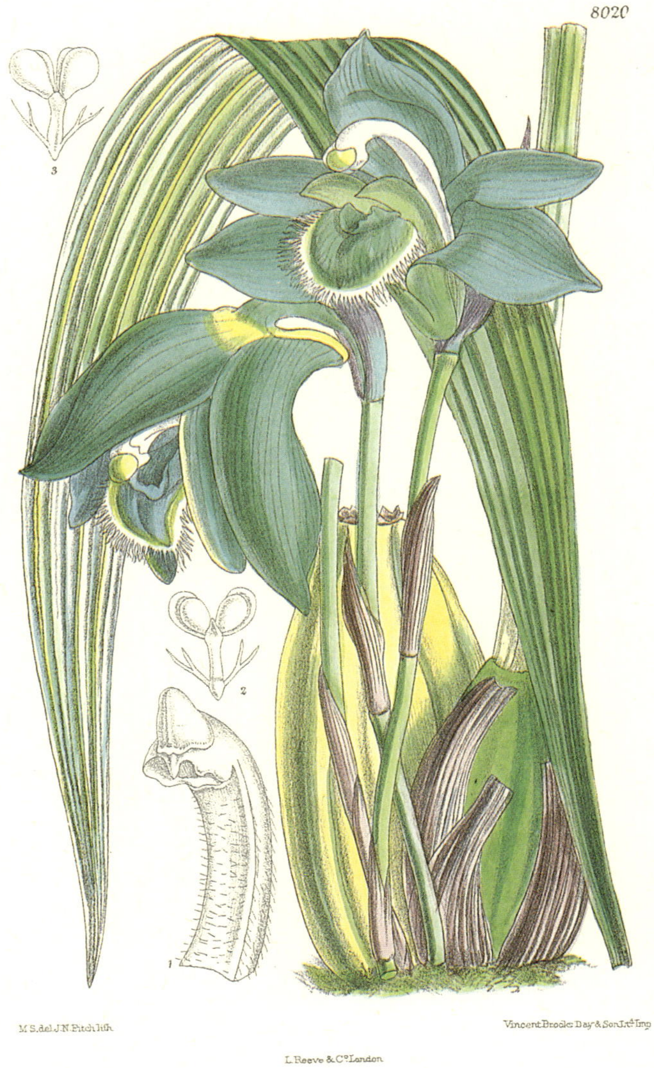

6303 Lycaste linguella Rchb. f.
5616 Lycaste longipetala (Ruiz Lopez & Pavón) Garay

8020 Lycaste locusta Rchb. f.
9400 Lycaste longiscapa Rolfe ex Cooper

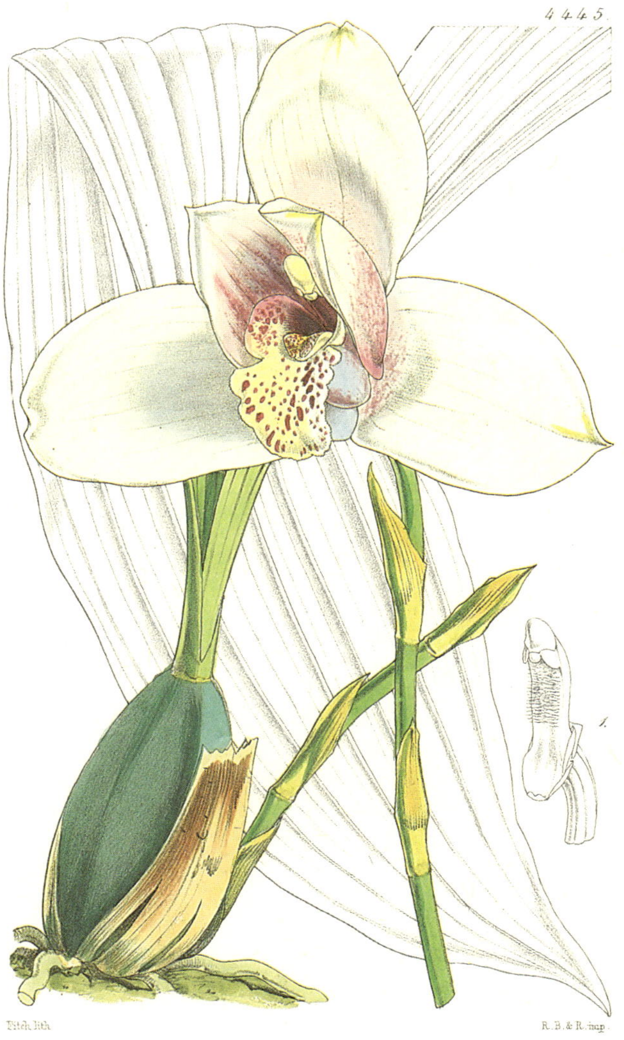

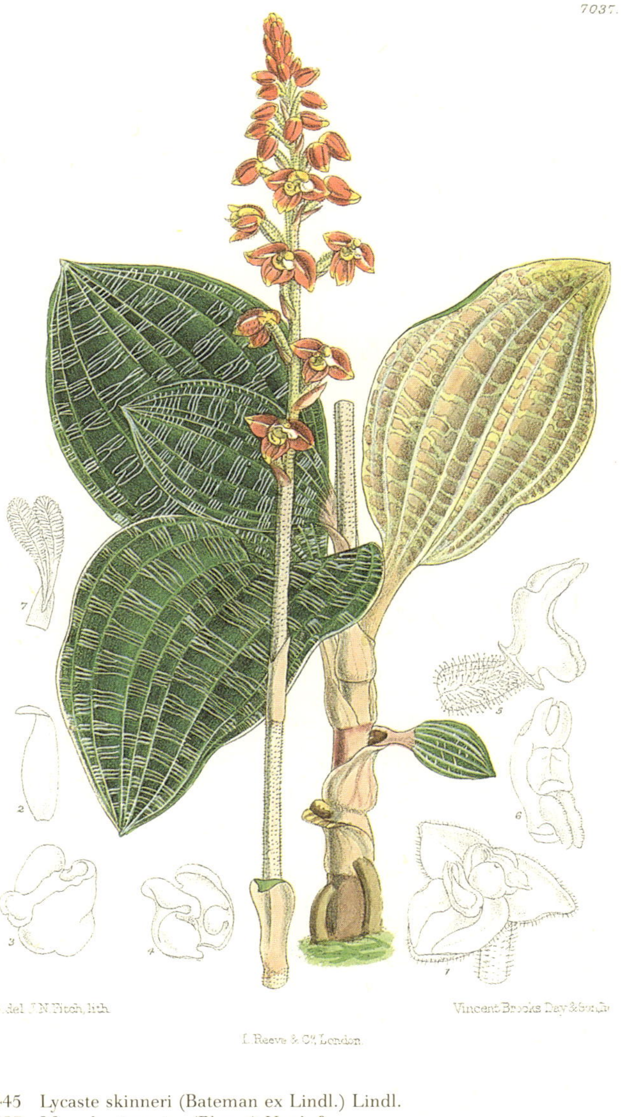

4228 Lycaste macrobulbon (Hook.) Lindl.
3146 Lycaste tetragona (Lindl.) Lindl.

4445 Lycaste skinneri (Bateman ex Lindl.) Lindl.
7037 Macodes javanica (Blume) Hook. f.

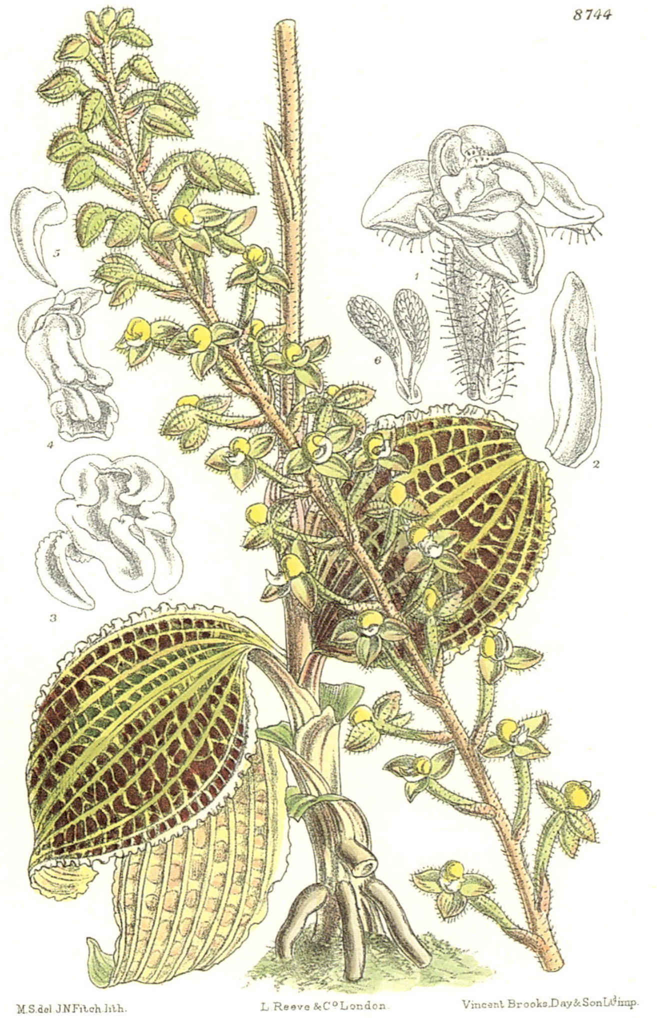

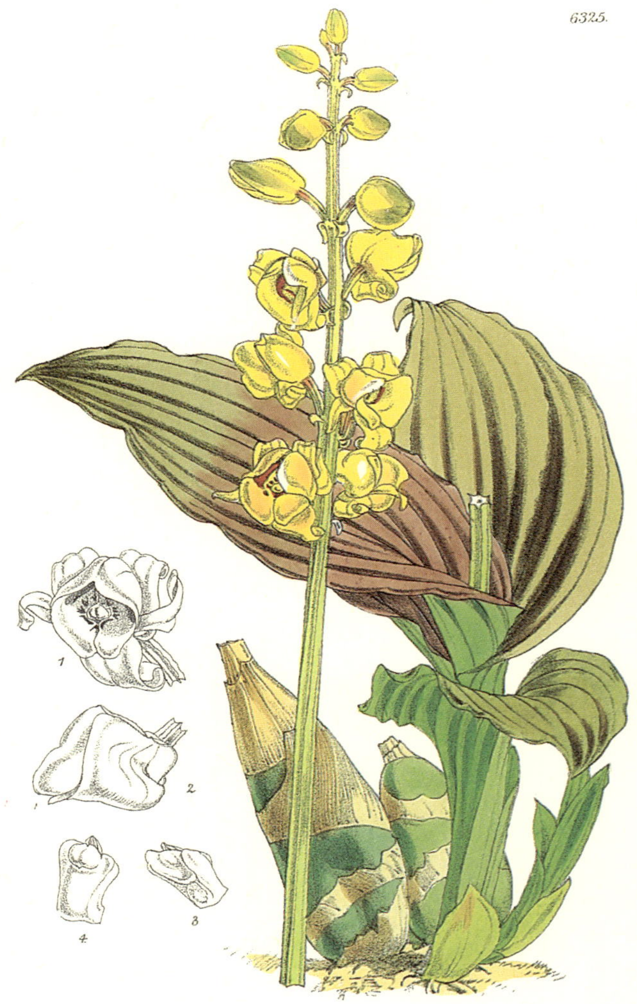

8744 Macodes sanderiana (Kraenzlin) Rolfe
4103 Malaxis excavata (Lindl.) Kuntze

5403 Malaxis discolor (Lindl.) Kuntze
6325 Malaxis josephiana (Rchb. f.) Kuntze

6668 Malaxis metallica (Rchb. f.) Kuntze
6273 Masdevallia attenuata Rchb. f.

7268 Malaxis scottii (Hook. f.) Kuntze
6372 Masdevallia caudata Lindl.

5476 Masdevallia civilis Rchb. f. & Warsc.
7476 Masdevallia corniculata Rchb. f.

5990 Masdevallia coccinea Linden ex Lindl.
6190 Masdevallia davisii Rchb. f.

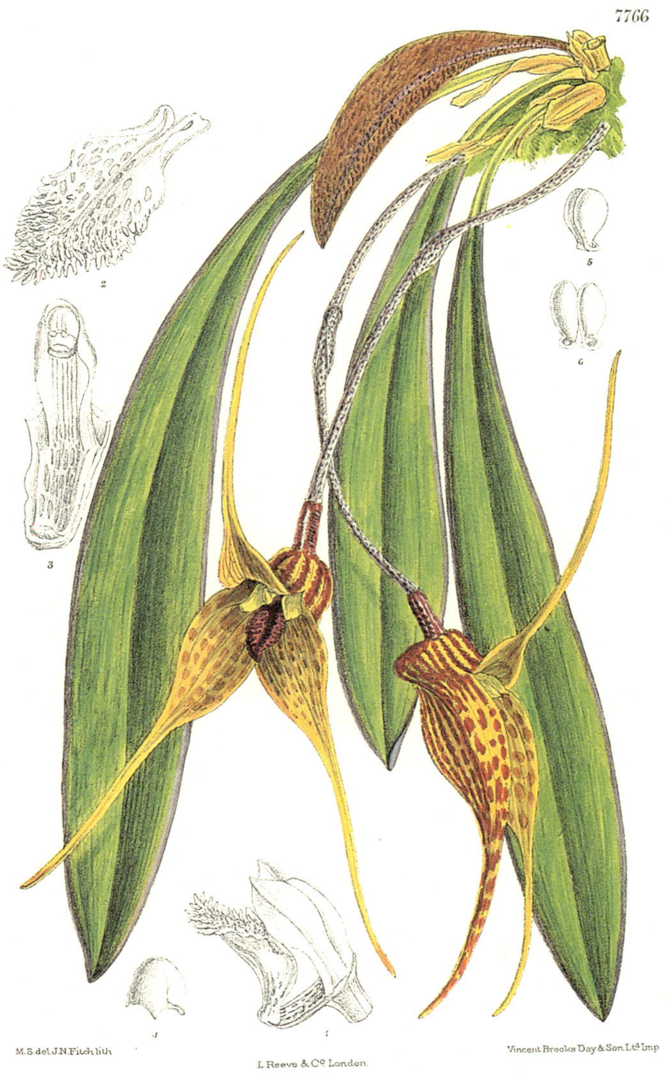

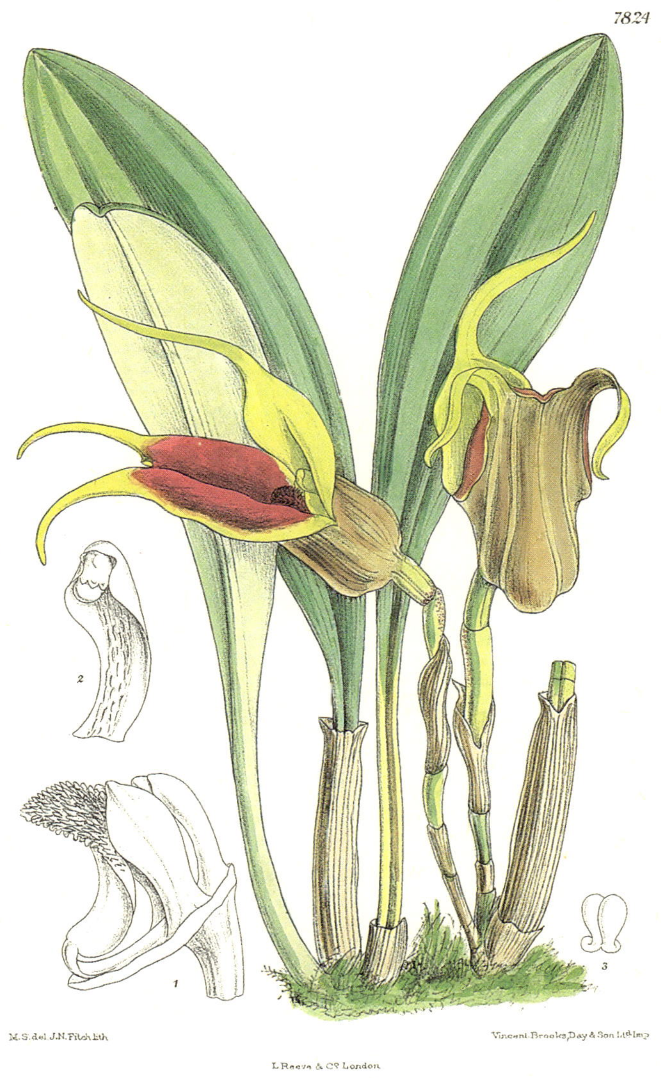

7766 Masdevallia deorsum Rolfe
6208 Masdevallia ephippium Rchb. f.

7824 Masdevallia elephanticeps Rchb. f. & Warsc.
6171 Masdevallia estradae Rchb. f.

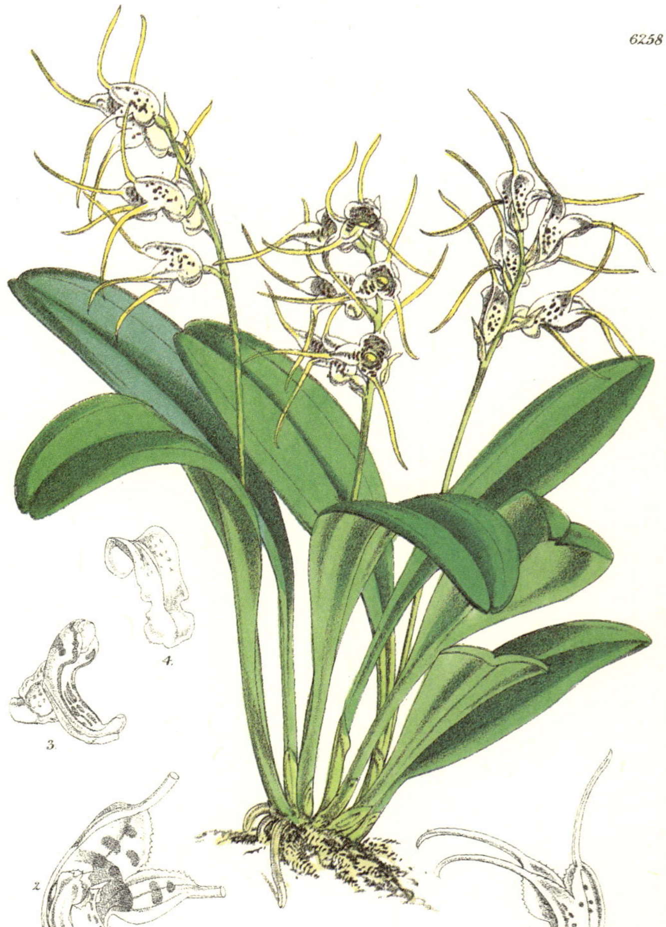

6262 Masdevallia ionocharis Rchb. f.
7164 Masdevallia macrura Rchb. f.

7245 Masdevallia leontoglossa Rchb. f.
6258 Masdevallia melanopus Rchb. f.

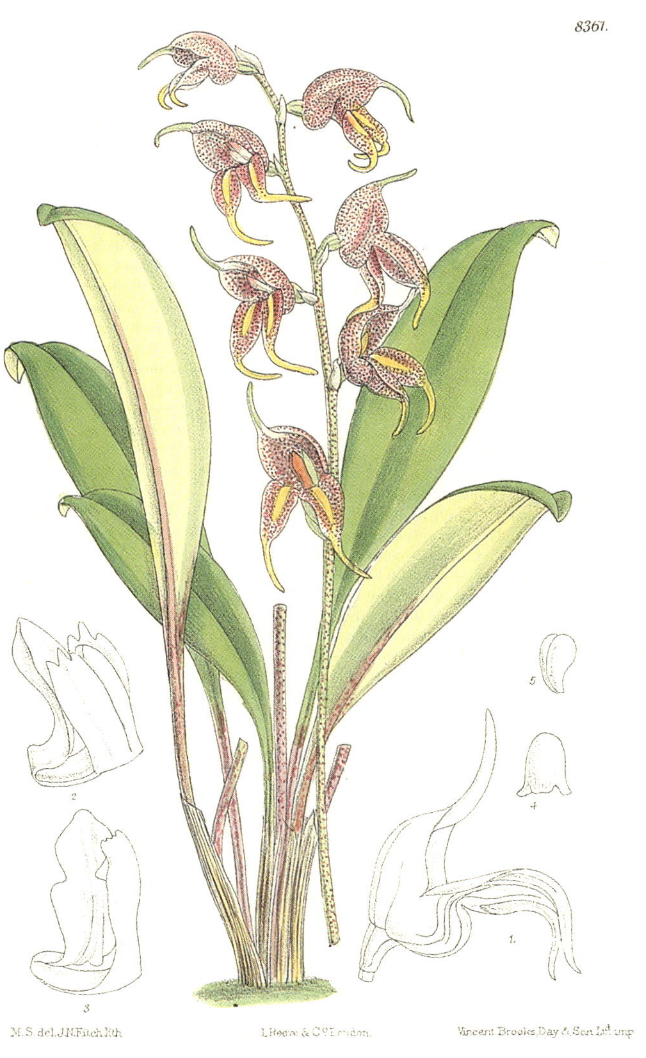

5962 Masdevallia militaris Rchb. f.
8361 Masdevallia pachyura Rchb. f.

7015 Masdevallia mooreana Rchb. f.
6159 Masdevallia peristeria Rchb. f.

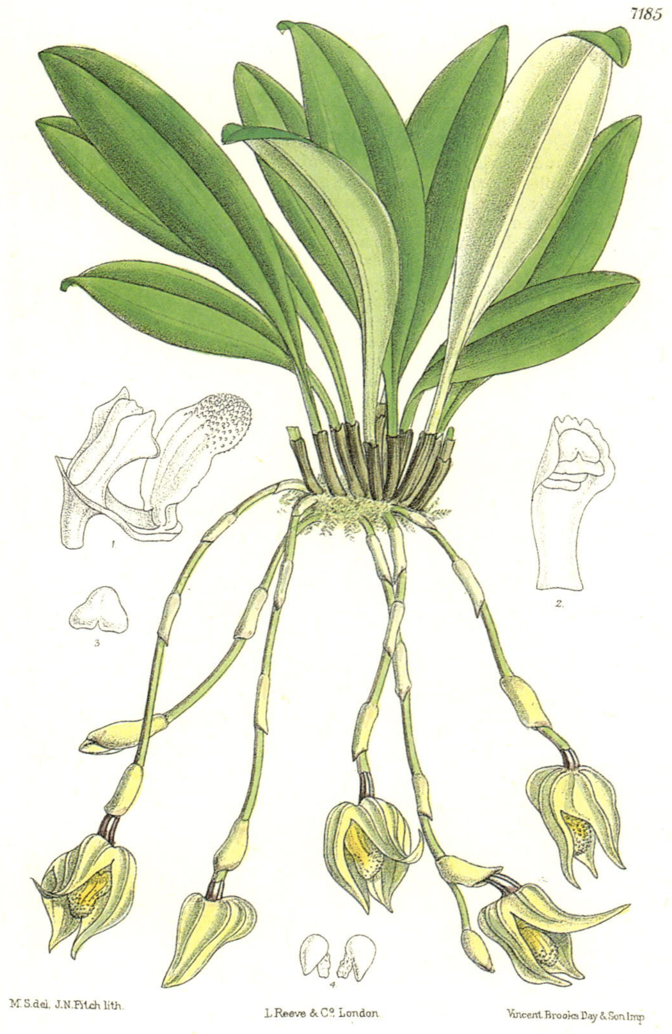

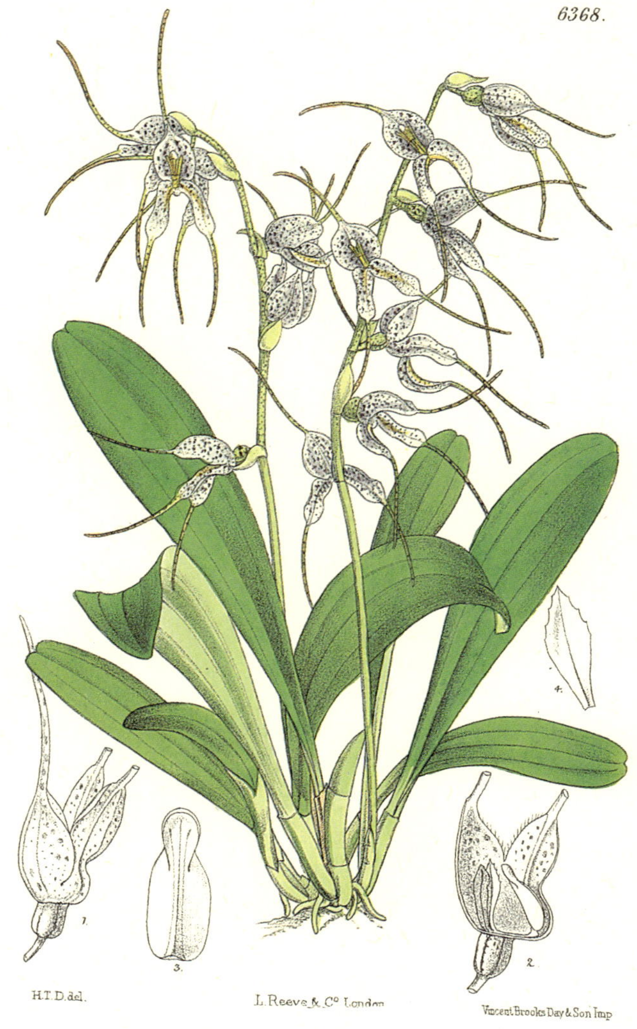

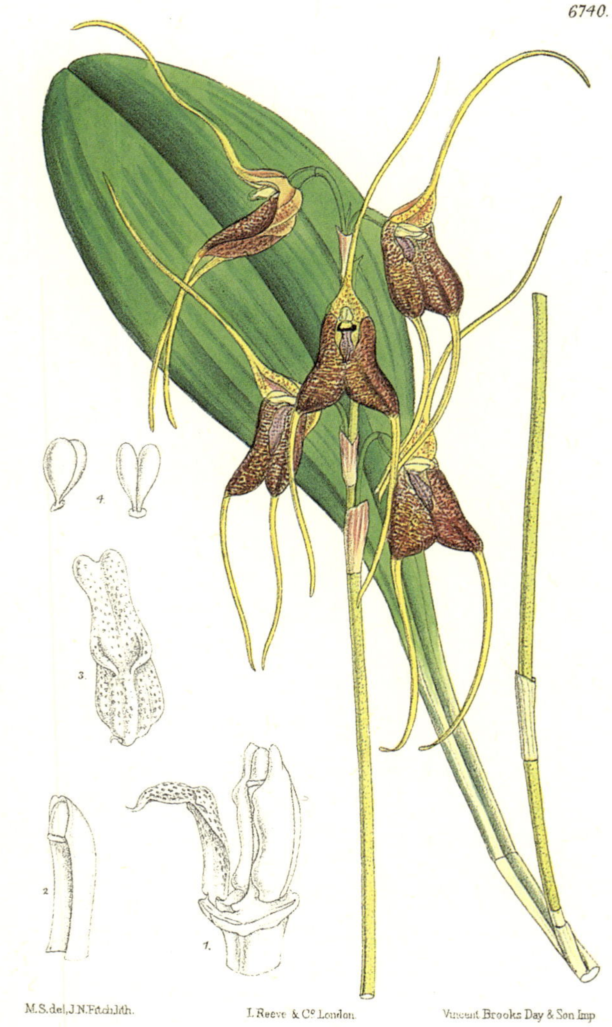

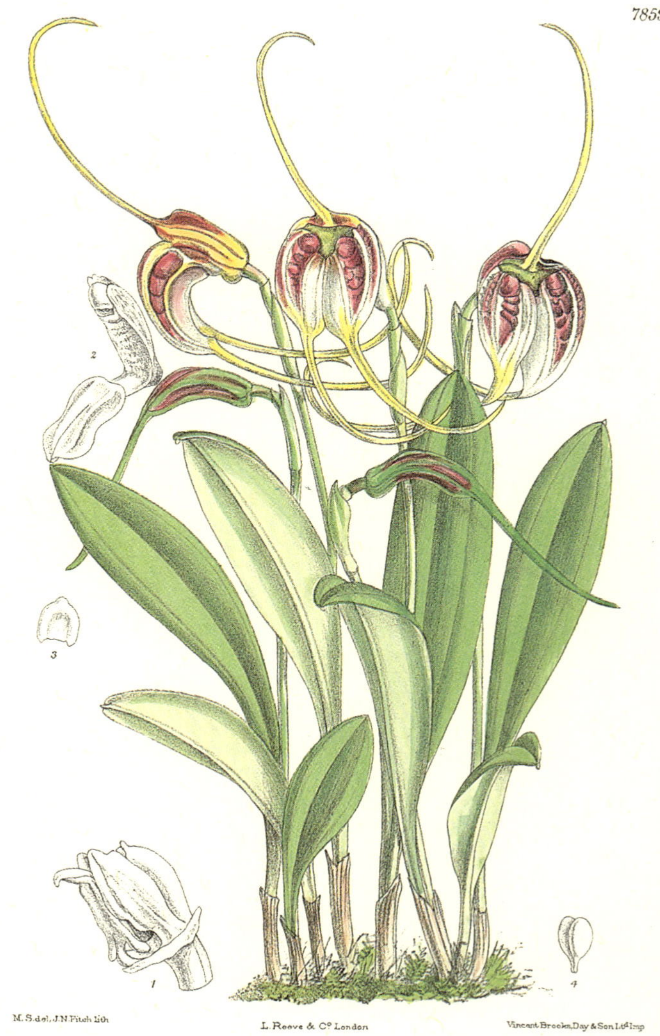

7185 Masdevallia platyglossa Rchb. f.
6740 Masdevallia schlimii Linden ex Lindl.

6368 Masdevallia polysticta Rchb. f.
7859 Masdevallia schroederiana Veitch

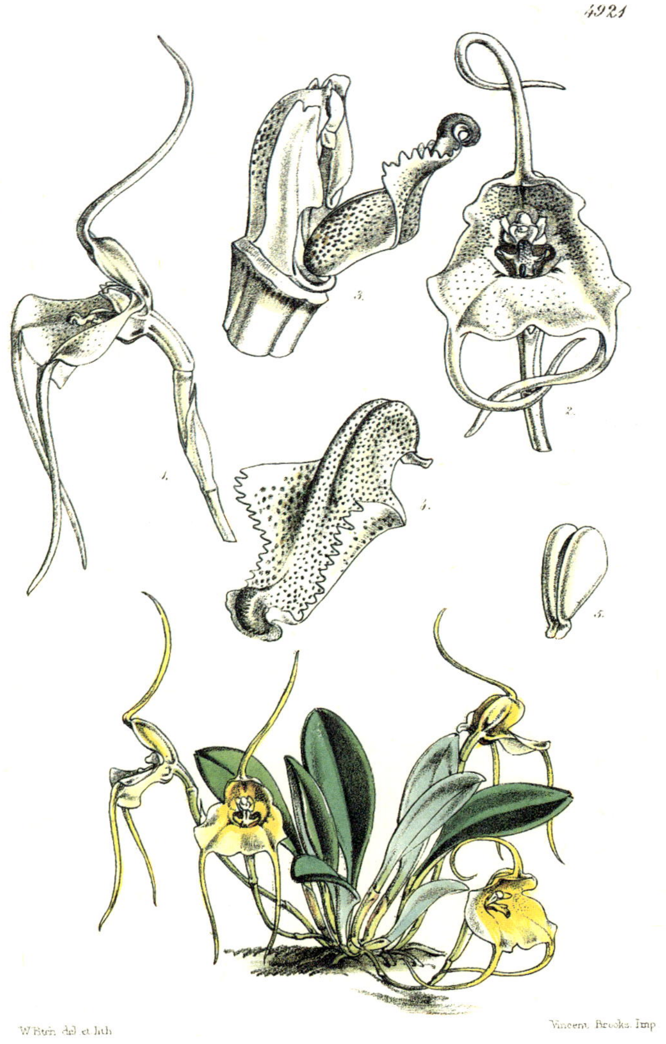

5505 Masdevallia tovarensis Rchb. f.
4921 Masdevallia wageneriana Linden ex Lindl.

5739 Masdevallia veitchiana Rchb. f.
4374 Maxillaria acicularis Herbert ex Lindl.

3966 Maxillaria acutipetala Hook.
4141 Maxillaria camaridii Rchb. f.

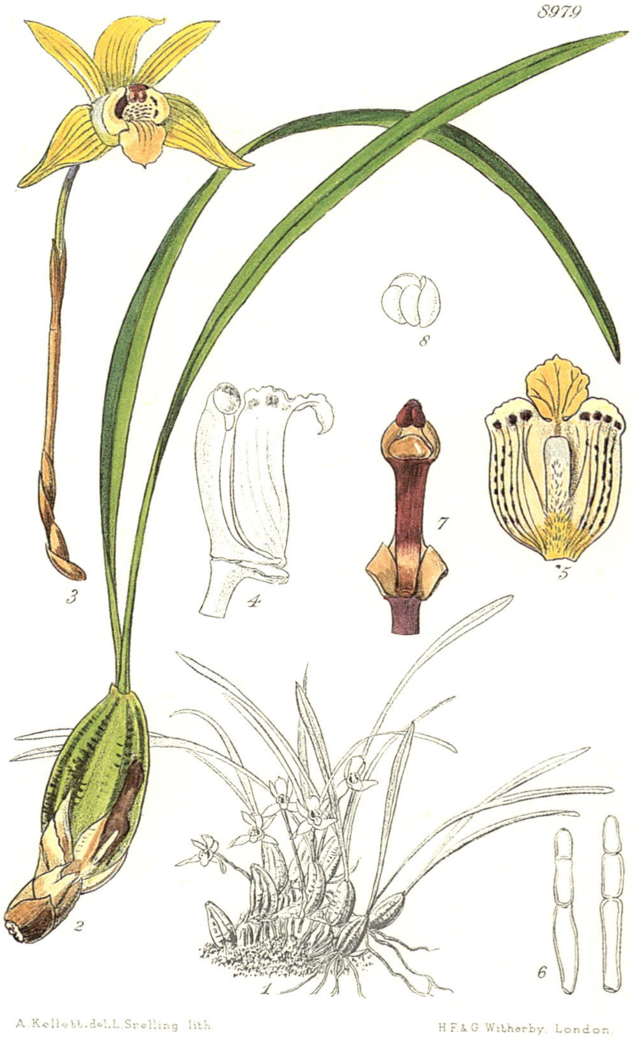

3306 Maxillaria camaridii Rchb. f.
8979 Maxillaria chrysantha Barb. Rodr.

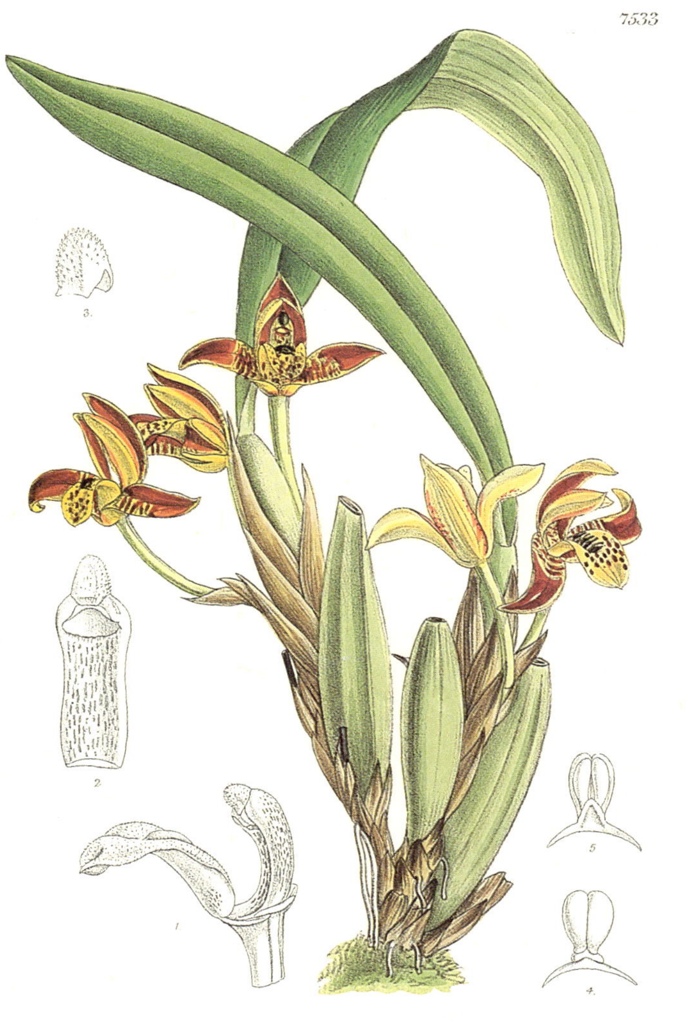

1437 Maxillaria coccinea (Jacq.) L. O. Williams ex Hodge
7533 Maxillaria curtipes Hook.

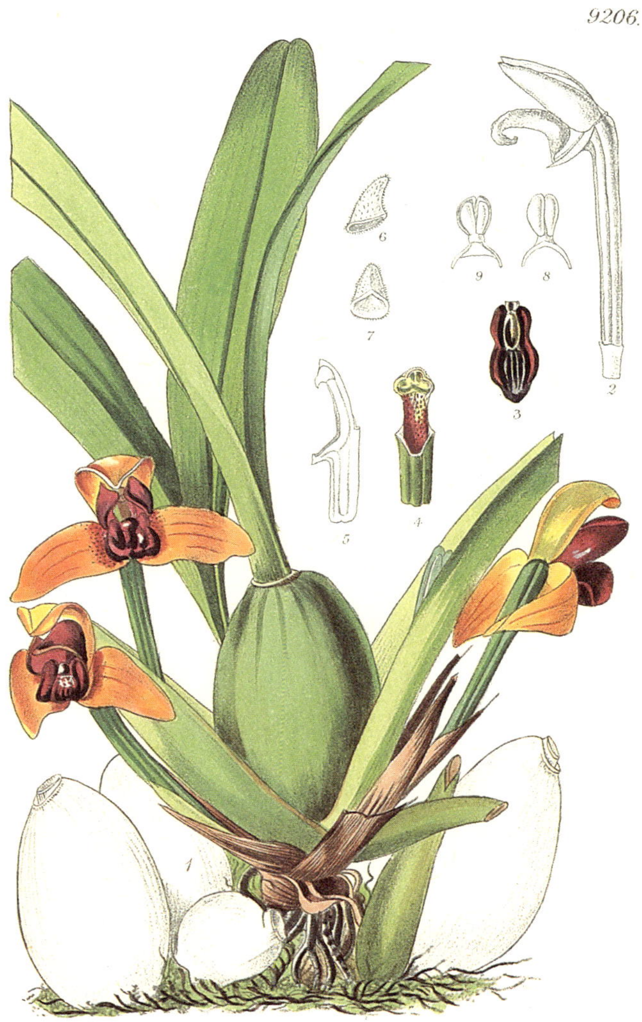

3945 Maxillaria cucullata Lindl.
9206 Maxillaria elatior (Rchb. f.) Rchb. f.

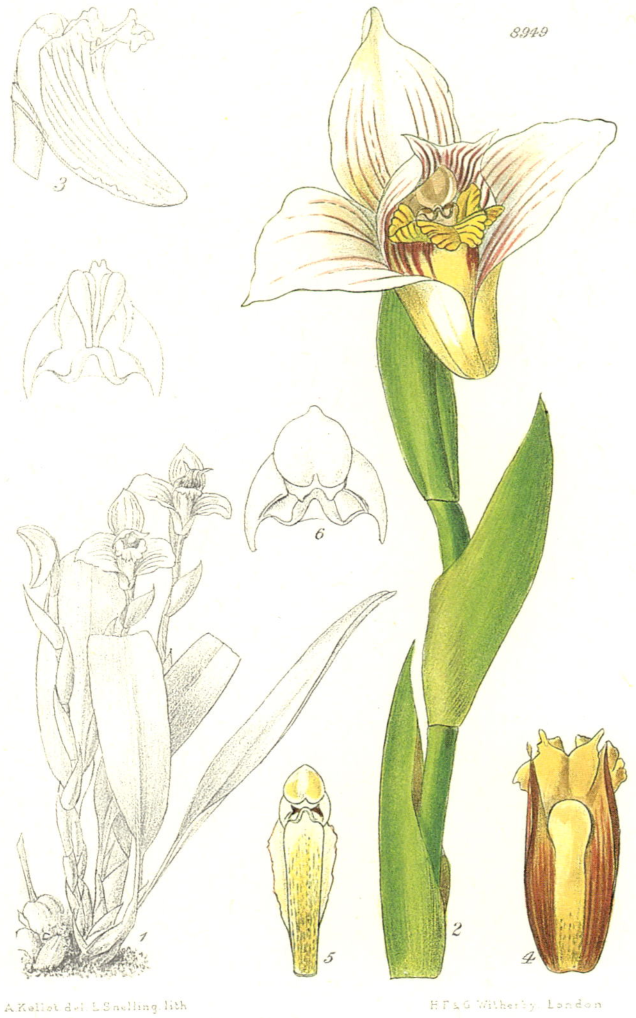

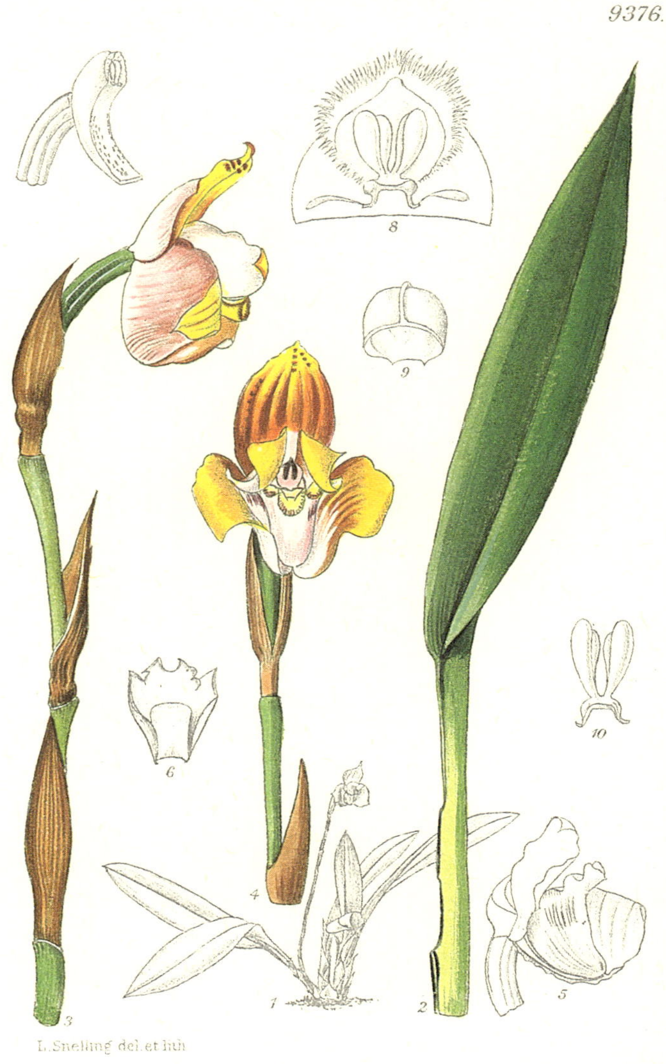

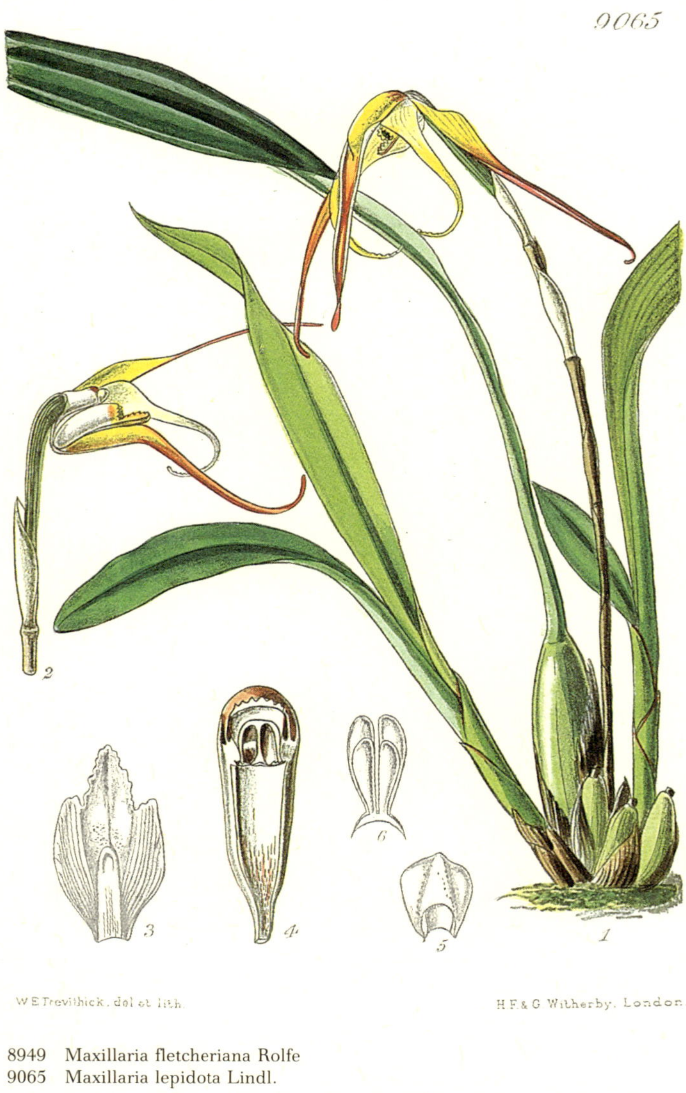

8949 Maxillaria fletcheriana Rolfe
9065 Maxillaria lepidota Lindl.

9376 Maxillaria fucata Rchb. f.
2729 Maxillaria parkeri Hook.

3154 Maxillaria picta Hook.
3613 Maxillaria pumila Hook.

6477 Maxillaria porphyrostele Rchb. f.
7518 Maxillaria sanderiana Rchb. f.

4434 Maxillaria setigera Lindl.
5296 Maxillaria venusta Linden & Rchb. f.

3614 Maxillaria variabilis Bateman ex Lindl.
5567 Mendoncella grandiflora (A. Rich.) A. Hawkes

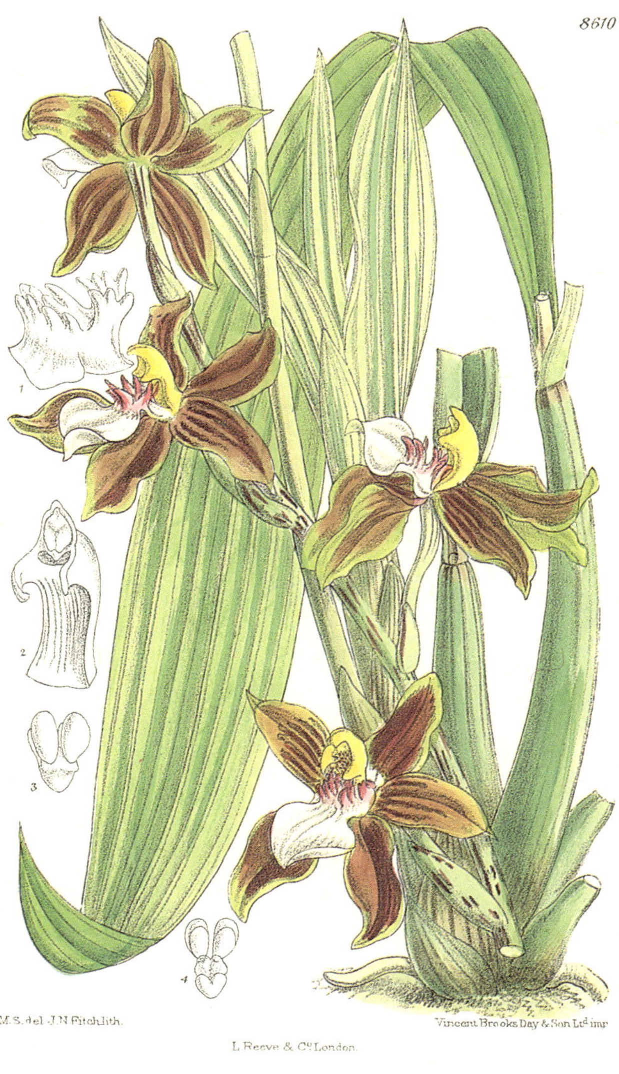

4766 Mendoncella marginata (Garay) Garay
8610 Mendoncella prainiana (Rolfe) Garay

5582 Mendoncella marginata (Garay) Garay
3378 Microtis media R. Br.

3377 Microtis parviflora R. Br.
4109 Miltonia clowesii Lindl.

5572 Miltonia anceps (Klotzsch) Lindl.
5436 Miltonia regnellii Rchb. f.

4204 Miltonia spectabilis Lindl.
6265 Miltonioides laevis (Lindl.) Brieger & Lueckel

4425 Miltonia spectabilis var. moreliana Henfrey
5843 Miltonioides warscewiczii (Rchb.f.) Brieger & Lueckel

6085

W Fitch del et lith

Vincent Brooks Day & Son Imp

6085 Miltoniopsis roezlii (Rchb. f.) Godef.-Leb.

W Fitch, del et lith

Vincent Brooks Day & Son, Imp

6037 Miltoniopsis vexillaria (Rchb. f.) Godef.-Leb.

W Fitch del et Lith

Vincent Brooks Day & Son Imp

6163 *Miltoniopsis warscewiczii* (Rchb. f.) Garay & Dunsterv.

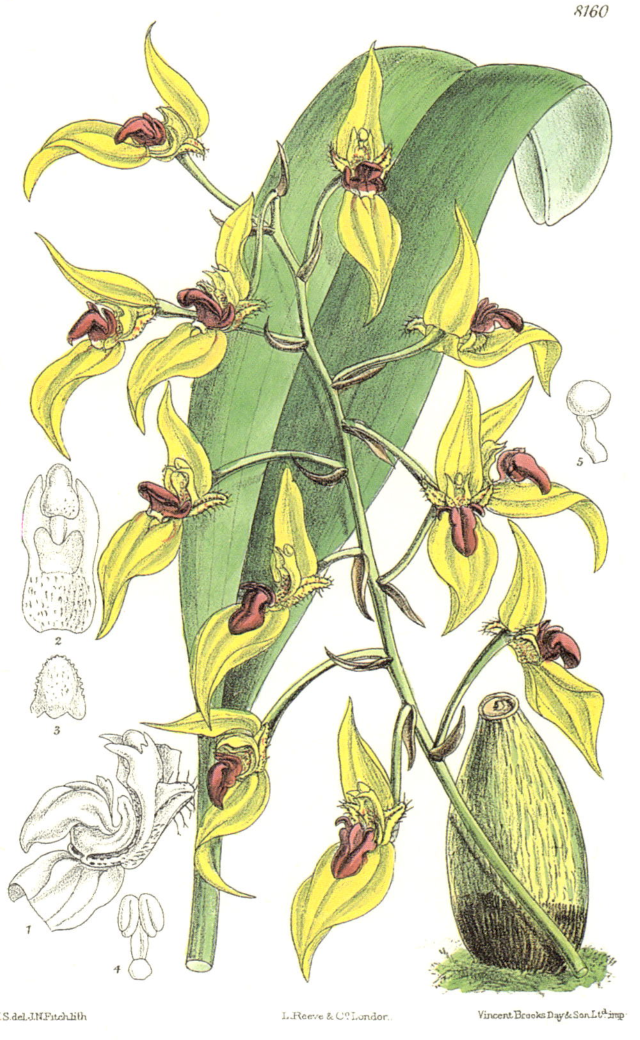

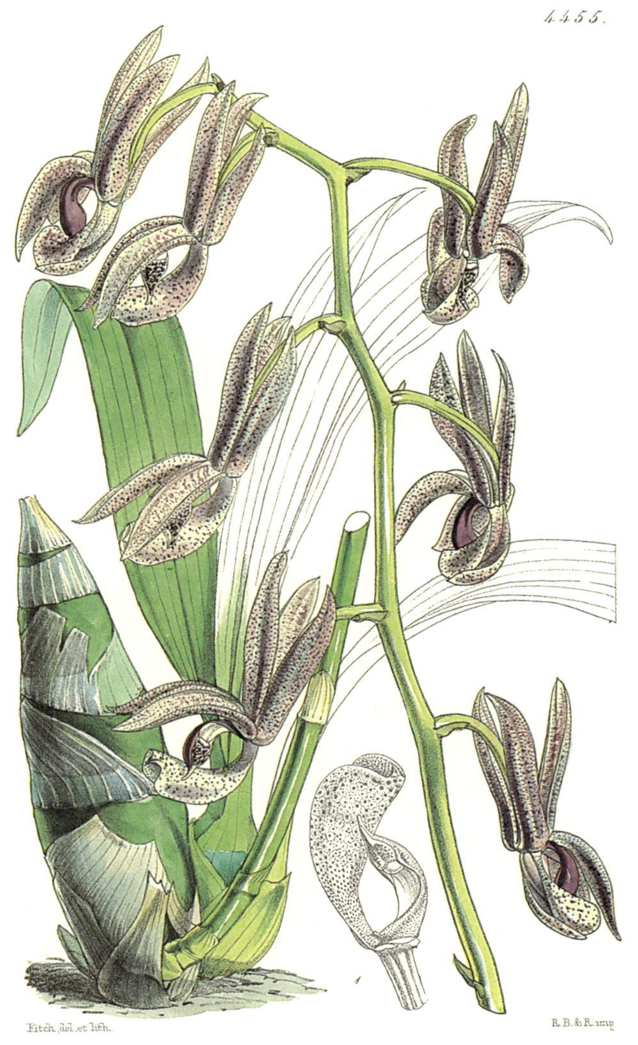

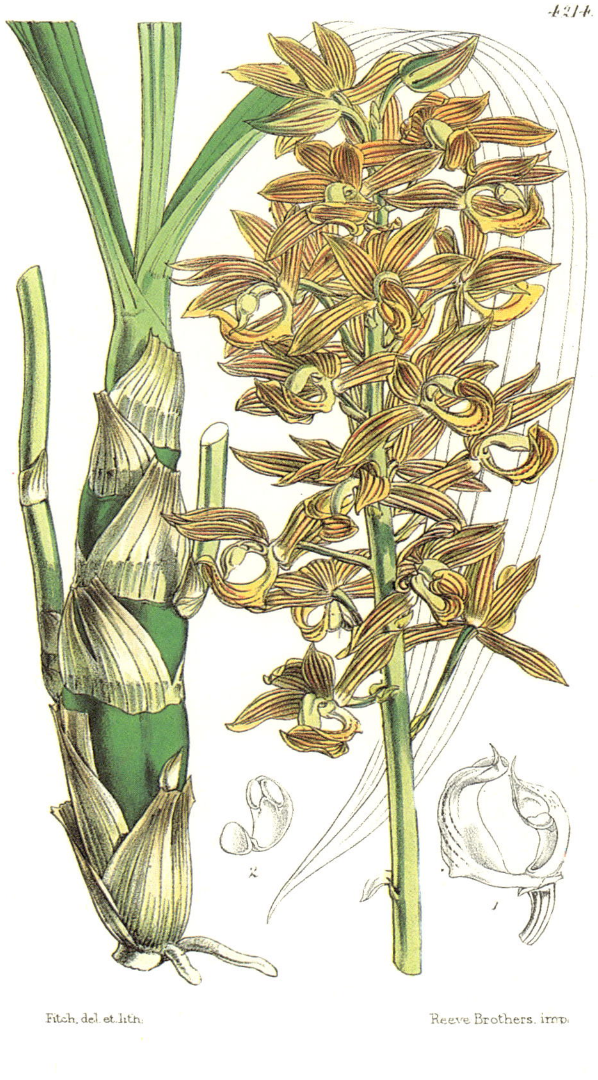

8160 Monomeria dichroma (Rolfe) Schltr.
8041 Mormodes buccinator var. aurantiacum Rolfe

4455 Mormodes buccinator Lindl.
4214 Mormodes cartoni Hook.

5840

W. Fitch, del. et lith.

Vincent Brooks, Day & Son, Imp.

5840 *Mormodes colossus* Rchb. f.

4577 Mormodes hookeri Lemaire
3879 Mormodes maculata var. unicolor (Hook.) L. O. Williams
3900 Mormodes maculata (Klotzsch) L. O. Williams
8390 Mormodes revolutum Rolfe

M.S. del. J.N. Fitch Lith

Vincent Brooks Day & Son Imp

6496 Mormodes ocanae Lindl. & Rchb. f.

W. Fitch, del. et lith.

Vincent Brooks, Day & Son, Imp.

5802 Mormodes uncium Rchb. f.

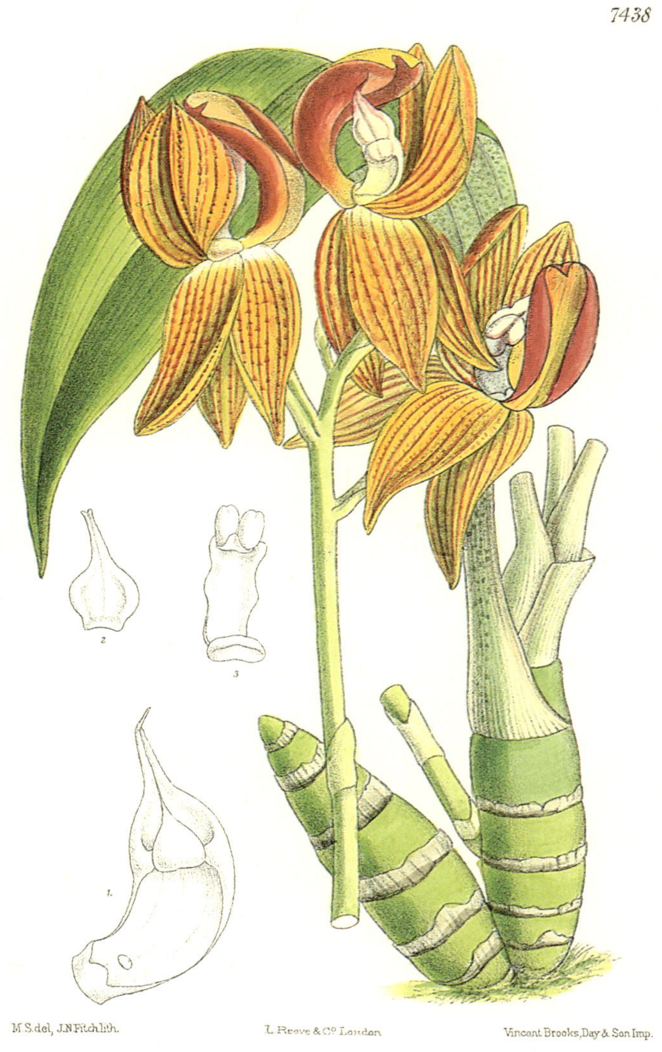

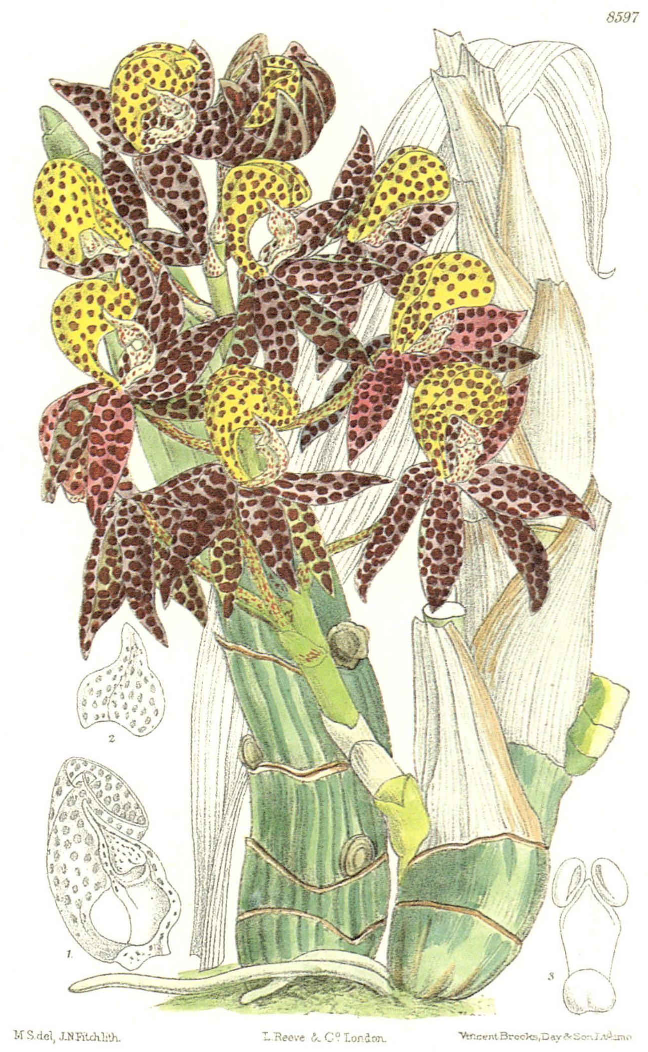

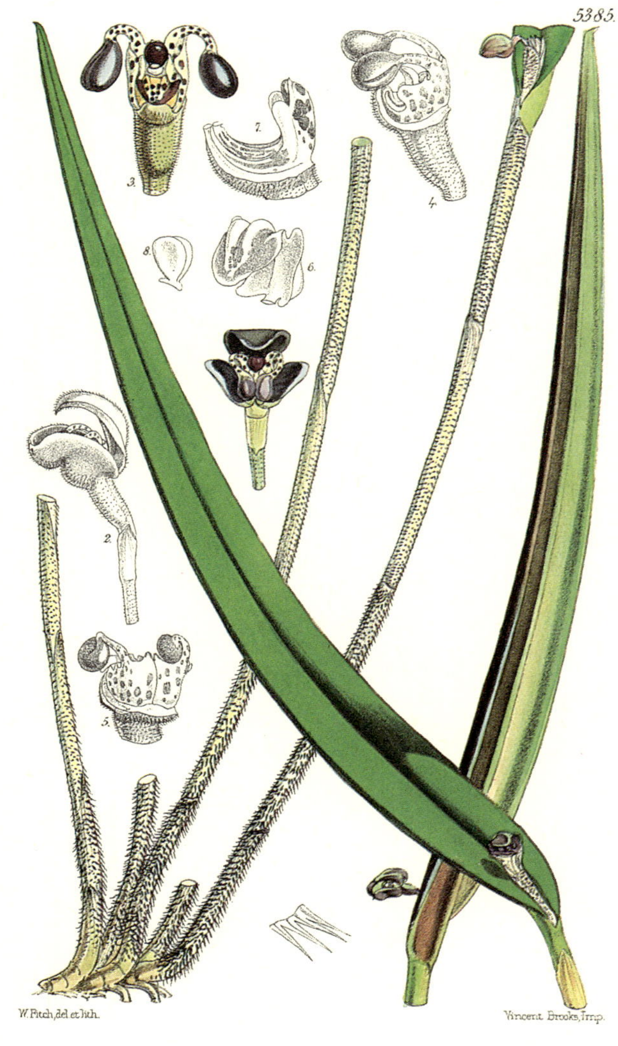

7438 Mormodes rolfeanum Linden
5385 Myoxanthus reymondii (Karsten) Luer

8597 Mormodes tigrinum Barb. Rodr.
4476 Myrmecophila tibicinis (Bateman ex Lindl.) Rolfe

5723 Nanodes medusae Rchb. f.
6683 Neocogniauxia monophylla (Griseb.) Schltr.

7221 Neobenthamia gracilis Rolfe
2097 Neofinetia falcata (Thunb.) Hu

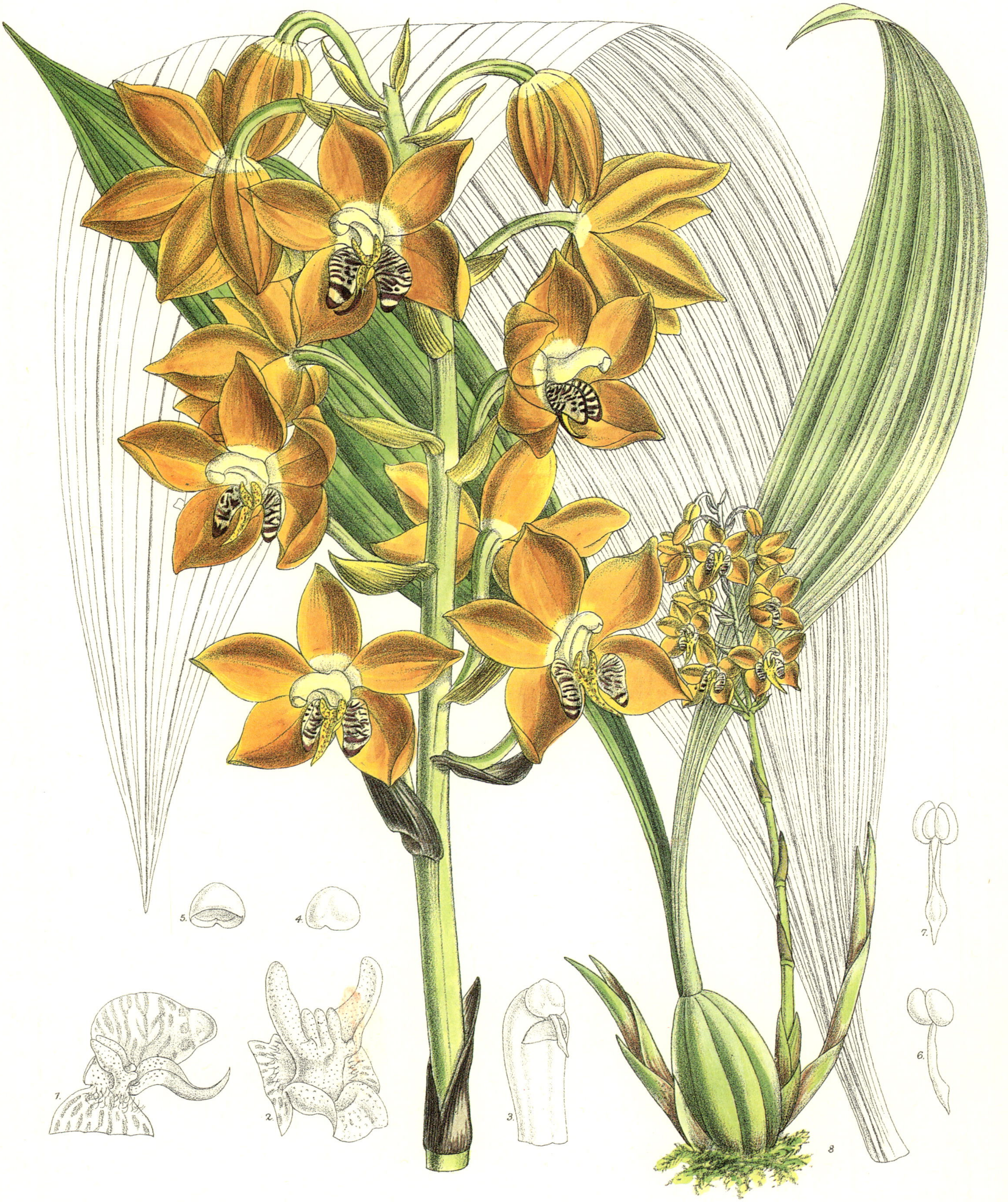

M.S.del, J.N.Fitch, lith.

Vincent Brooks Day & Son, Imp.

L. Reeve & C°. London.

7262 Neomoorea wallisii (Rchb. f.) Schltr.

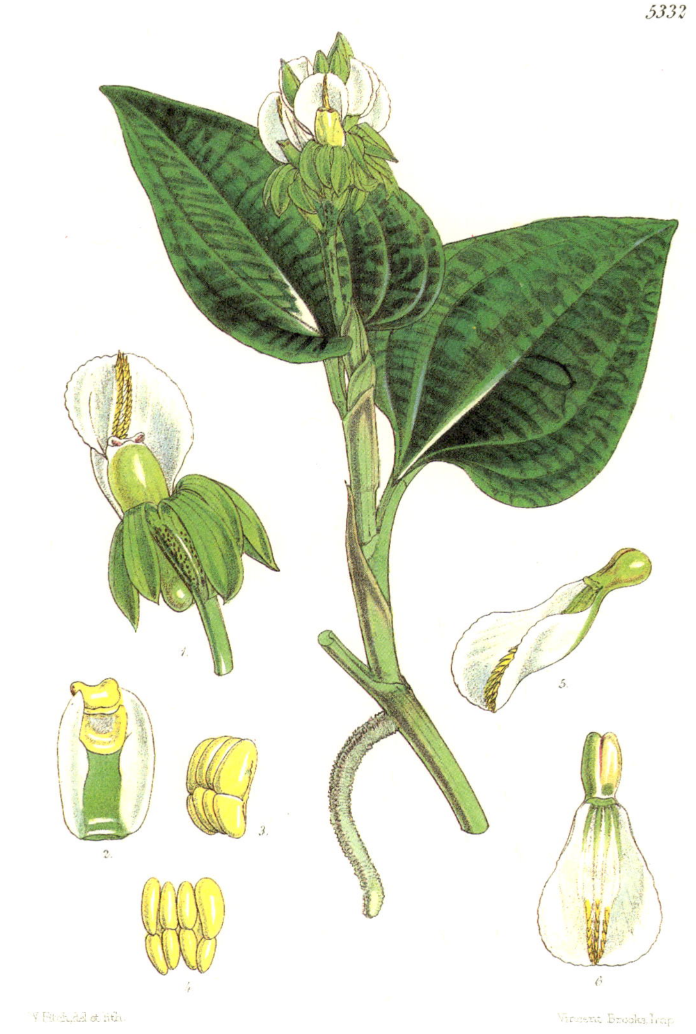

3674 Neogardneria murrayana (Gardner ex Hook.) Garay
5390 Nephelaphyllum scapigerum Hook.

5332 Nephelaphyllum pulchrum Blume
6851 Nervilia fordii (Hance) Schltr.

6125 Nervilia plicata (André) Schltr.
6671 Nervilia gammieana (Hook.f.) Schltr.

7425 Neuwiedia griffithii Rchb.f.

7368

M.S. del. J.N.Fitch lith. L. Reeve & Co London Vincent Brooks, Day & Son Imp.

6311

W. Fitch. del. et lith. Vincent Brooks Day & Son Imp

8306

M.S. del. J.N.Fitch lith. Vincent Brooks, Day & Son Ltd imp. L. Reeve & Co London

5609.

W. Fitch. del. et lith. Vincent Brooks, Imp.

7368 Neuwiedia veratrifolia Blume
8306 Notylia barkeri Lindl.

6311 Notylia albida Klotzsch
5609 Notylia bicolor Lindl.

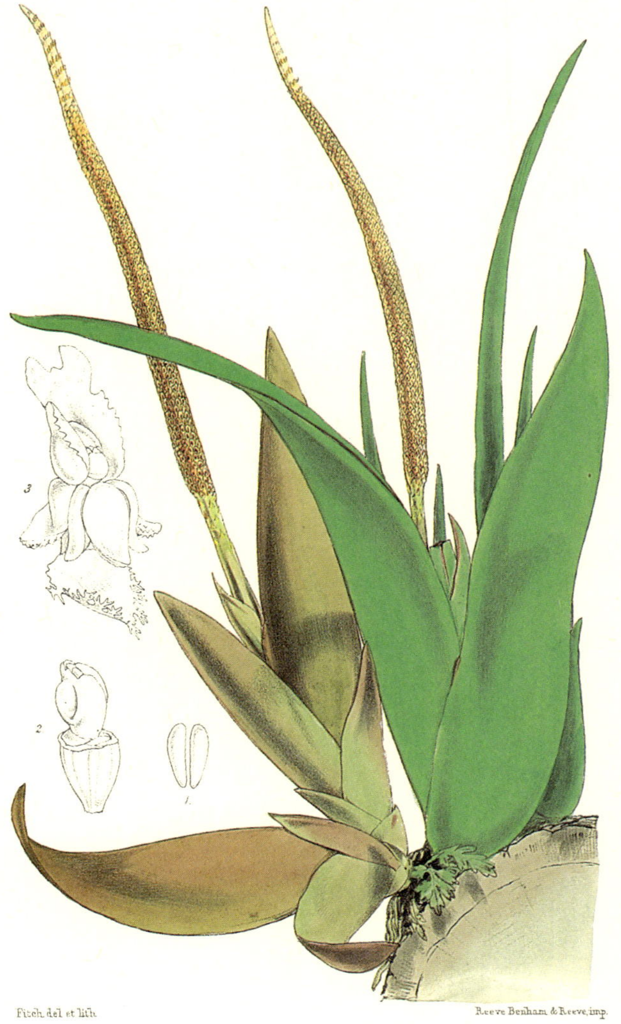

5056 Oberonia acaulis Griffith
2823 Octadesmia montana (Sw.) Benth.

4517 Oberonia iridifolia (Roxb.) Lindl.
2764 Octomeria graminifolia (L.) R. Br.

8133 × Odontioda heatonensis hort.
4919 Odontoglossum cariniferum Rchb. f.

7990 Odontioda × vuylstekeae hort.
6317 Odontoglossum cirrhosum Lindl.

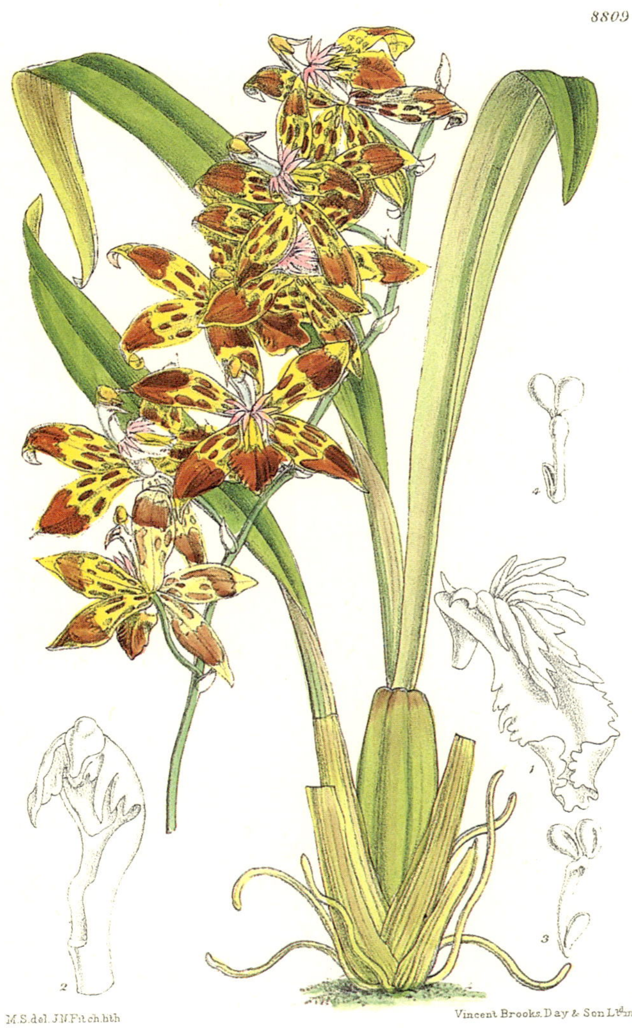

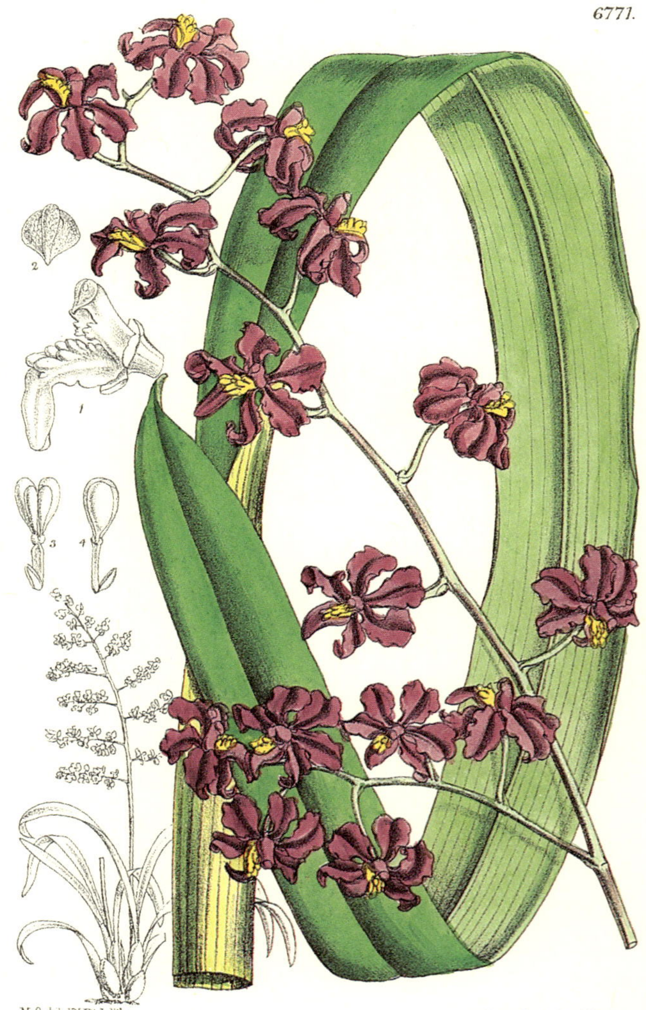

5691 Odontoglossum crispum Lindl.
8809 Odontoglossum cristatum Lindl.

5697 Odontoglossum crispum Lindl.
6771 Odontoglossum edwardii Rchb. f.

6237 Odontoglossum hallii Lindl.
5778 Odontoglossum krameri Rchb. f.

8873 Odontoglossum × humeanum Rchb. f.
6144 Odontoglossum maxillare Lindl. sensu Hook. f.

8142

M.S. del. J.N.Fitch lith.

Vincent Brooks, Day & Son Ltd Imp.

L. Reeve & Co London.

8142 Odontoglossum leeanum Rchb. f.

M.S. del, J.N. Fitch lith.

Vincent Brooks, Day Son Ltd. Imp

L. Reeve & Co. London

8097 Odontoglossum naevium Lindl.

W. Fitch, del et lith.

Vincent Brooks Day & Son, Imp.

5993 Odontoglossum pardinum (Lindl.) Lindl.

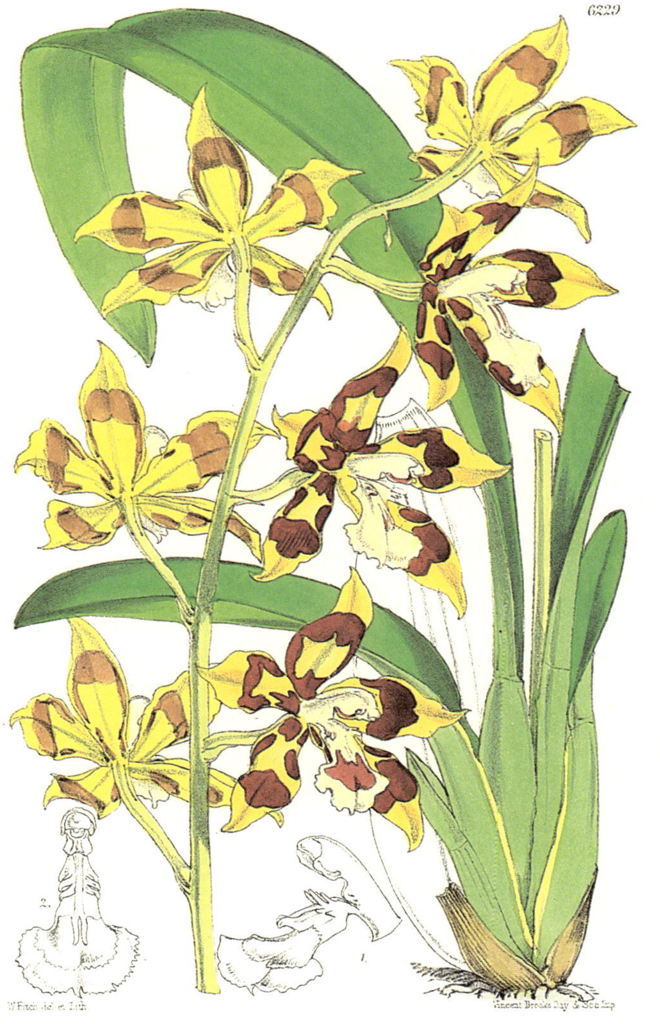

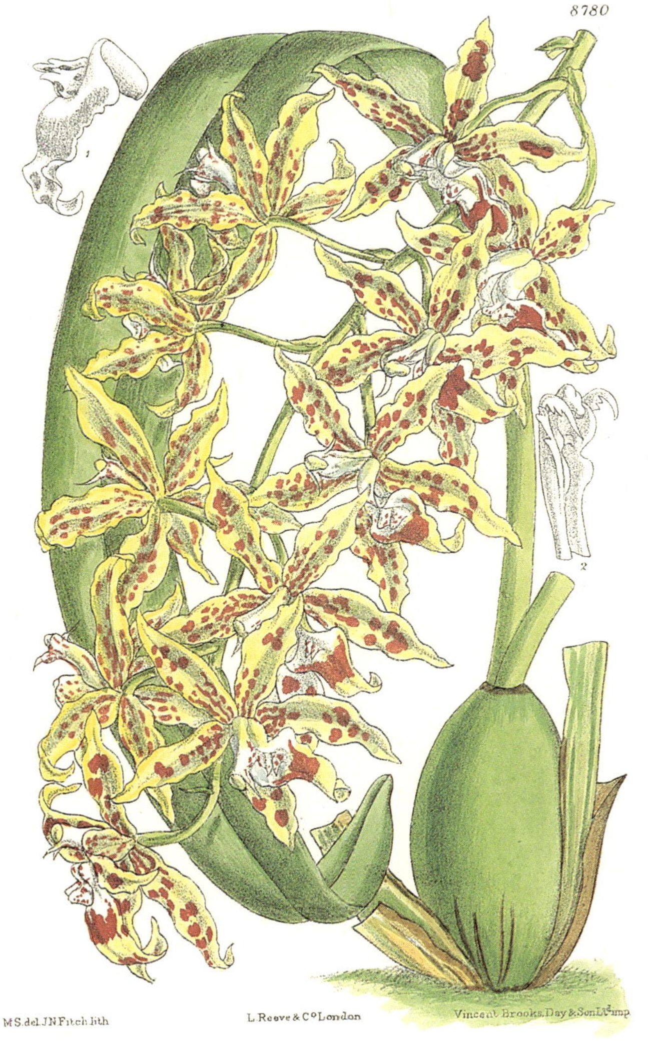

6502 Odontoglossum odoratum Lindl
8780 Odontoglossum × praevisum Rolfe

6229 Odontoglossum praenitens Rchb. f.
8031 Odontoglossum ramulosum Lindl.

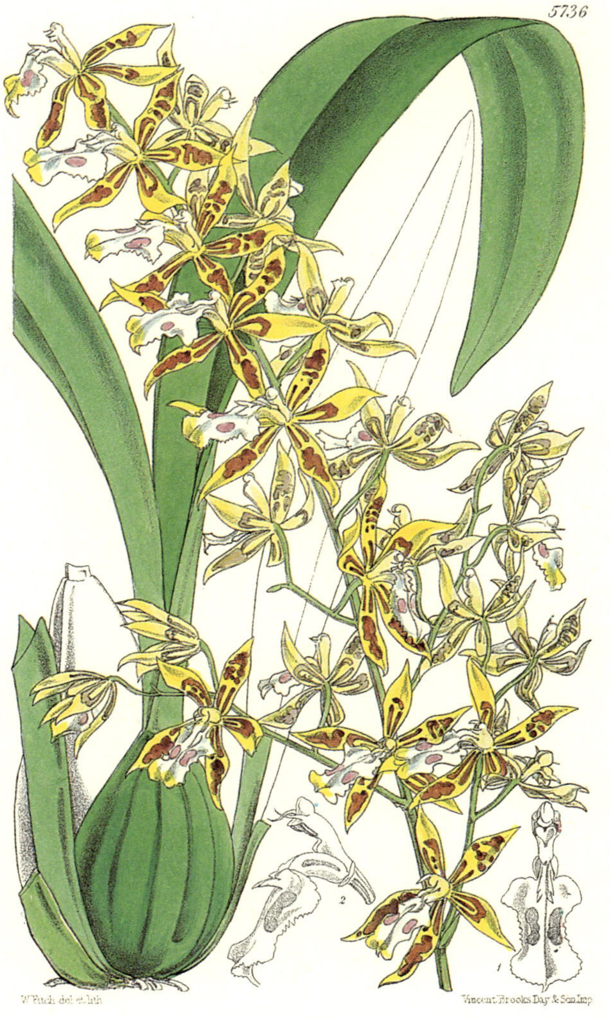

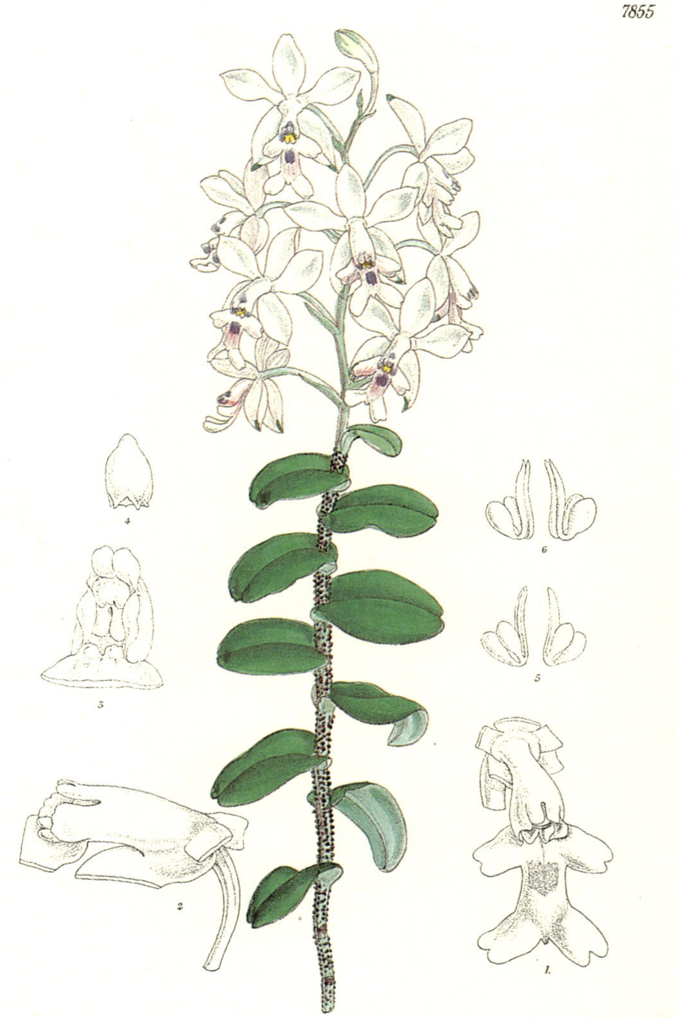

7569 Odontoglossum retusum Lindl.
6029 Odontoglossum tripudians Rchb. f. & Warsc.

5736 Odontoglossum sanderianum Rchb. f.
7855 Oerstedella endresii (Rchb. f.) Hags.

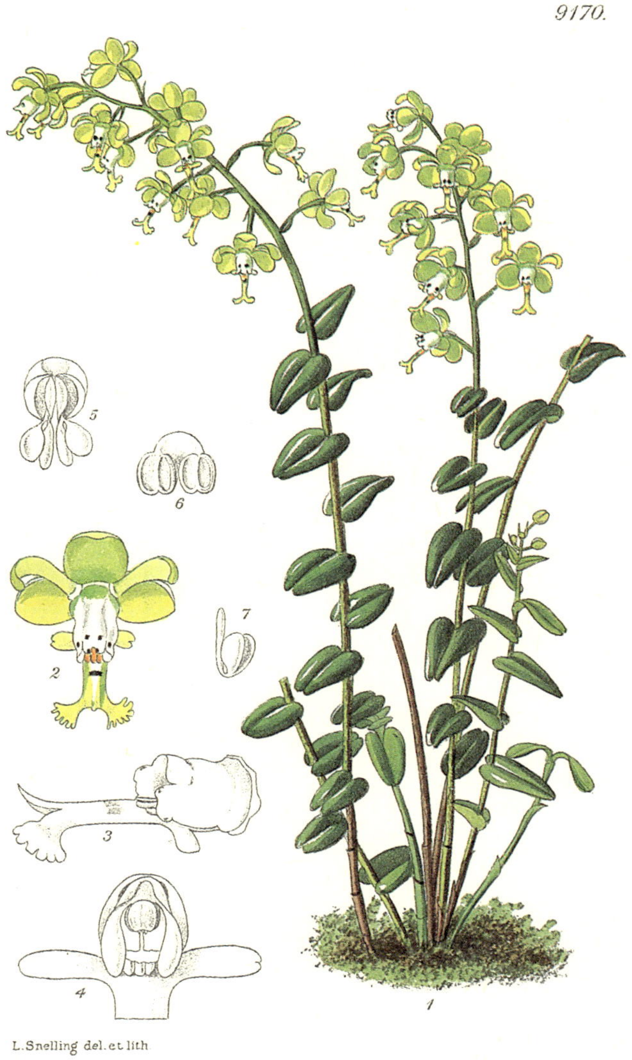

5556 Oerstedella myriantha (Lindl.) Hamer & Garay
3603 Oncidium altissimum (Jacq.) Sw.

9170 Oerstedella pumila (Rolfe) Hags.
4148 Oncidium bicallosum Lindl.

1491 Oncidium bifolium Sims
3806 Oncidium carthagenense (Jacq.) Sw.

777 Oncidium carthagenense (Jacq.) Sw.
3568 Oncidium cebolleta (Jacq.) Sw.

3807 Oncidium cavendishianum Bateman

6278 Oncidium cheirophorum Rchb. f.
4454 Oncidium concolor Hook.

3752 Oncidium concolor Hook.
3499 Oncidium crispum Lodd.

Pub. by S. Curtis, Glazenwood Essex May 1.1836.

Swan Sc.

3486 Oncidium cornigerum Lindl.

5193 Oncidium croesus Rchb. f.
5858 Oncidium cryptocopis Rchb. f.

3926 Oncidium cruciatum Rchb. f.
5708 Oncidium cucullatum Lindl.

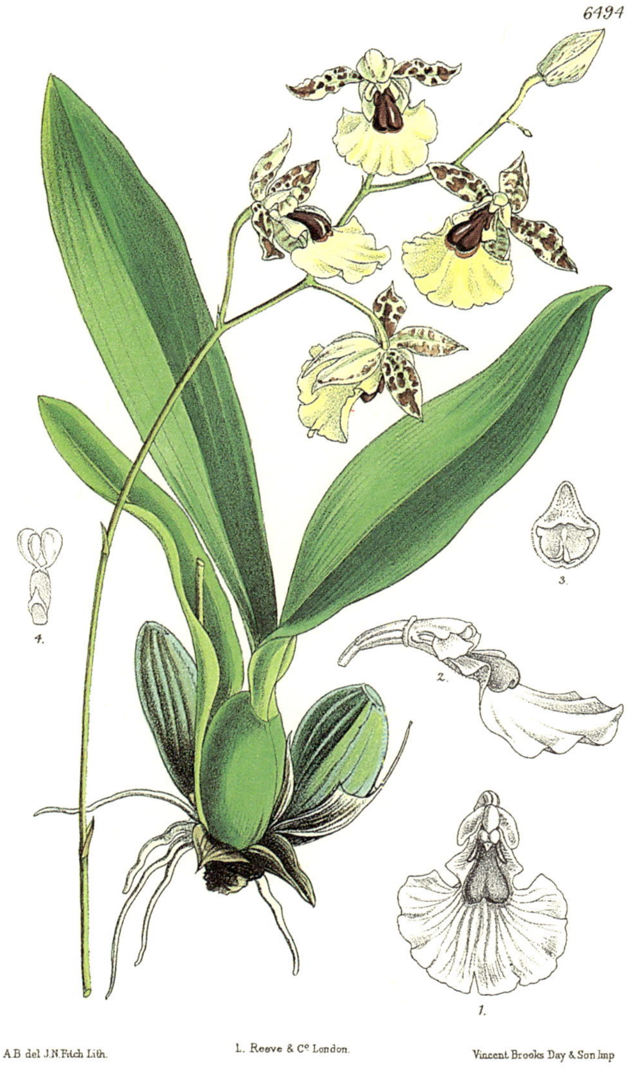

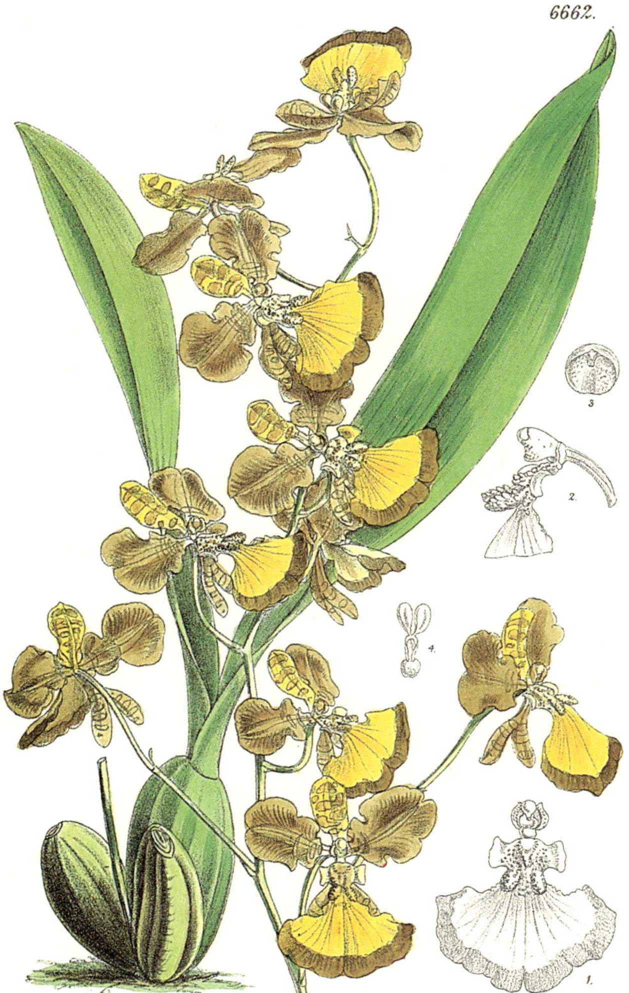

6494 Oncidium dasystyle Rchb. f.
6662 Oncidium gardneri Lindl.

5293 Oncidium excavatum Lindl.
3854 Oncidium graminifolium Lindl.

2203 Oncidium flexuosum Sims

3705 Oncidium forbesii Hook.

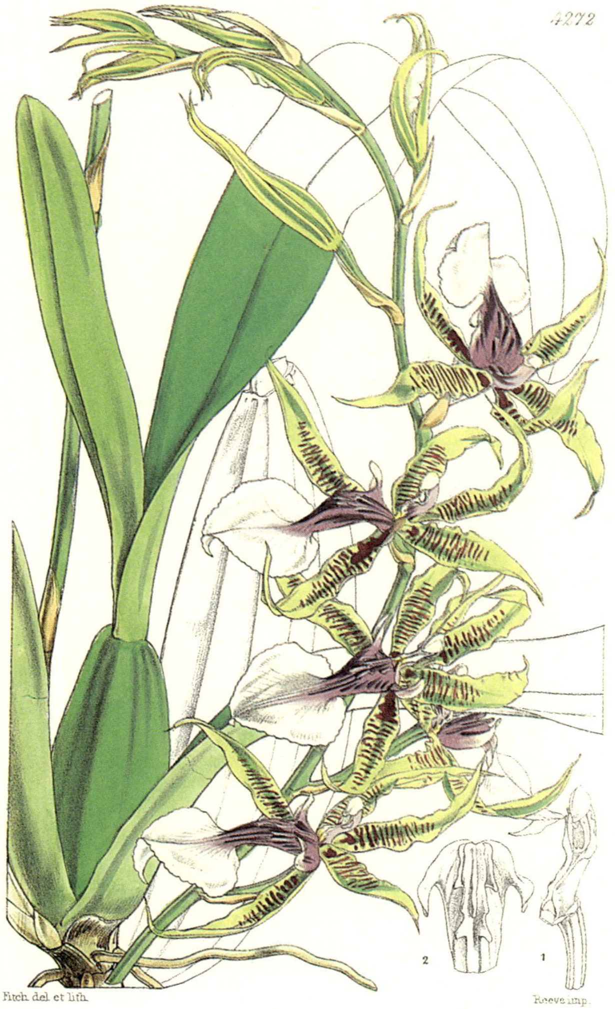

4272 Oncidium hatilabium (Lindl.) Garay & Dunsterv.
4824 Oncidium incurvum Barker ex Lindl.

3712 Oncidium hookeri Rolfe
6982 Oncidium jonesianum Rchb. f.

2990 Oncidium jacquinianum Garay & Stacy

W. Fitch, del et lith.

Vincent Brooks, Day & Son, Imp.

5743 *Oncidium macranthum* Lindl.

3890 Oncidium longicornu Mutel
5725 Oncidium marshallianum Rchb. f.

3836 Oncidium maculatum (Lindl.) Lindl.
6971 Oncidium micropogon Rchb. f.

3880 Oncidium maculatum (Lindl.) Lindl.

3912 Oncidium ornithorhynchum Kunth
2773 Oncidium pulchellum Hook.

5214 Oncidium phymatochilum Lindl.
3581 Oncidium pumilum Lindl.

3109

Mrs Arnold Harrison del^t. Pub. by S. Curtis, Glazenwood Essex Novr. 1. 1831 Swan Sc.

3109 Oncidium pubes Lindl.

W. Fitch, del et lith.

Vincent Brooks, Day & Son Imp.

5878 *Oncidium splendidum* A. Rich. ex Duchartre

5632 *Oncidium serratum* Lindl.
5980 *Oncidium superbiens* Rchb. f.

6254 *Oncidium stramineum* Bateman ex Lindl.
4130 *Oncidium tetrapetalum* (Jacq.) Willd.

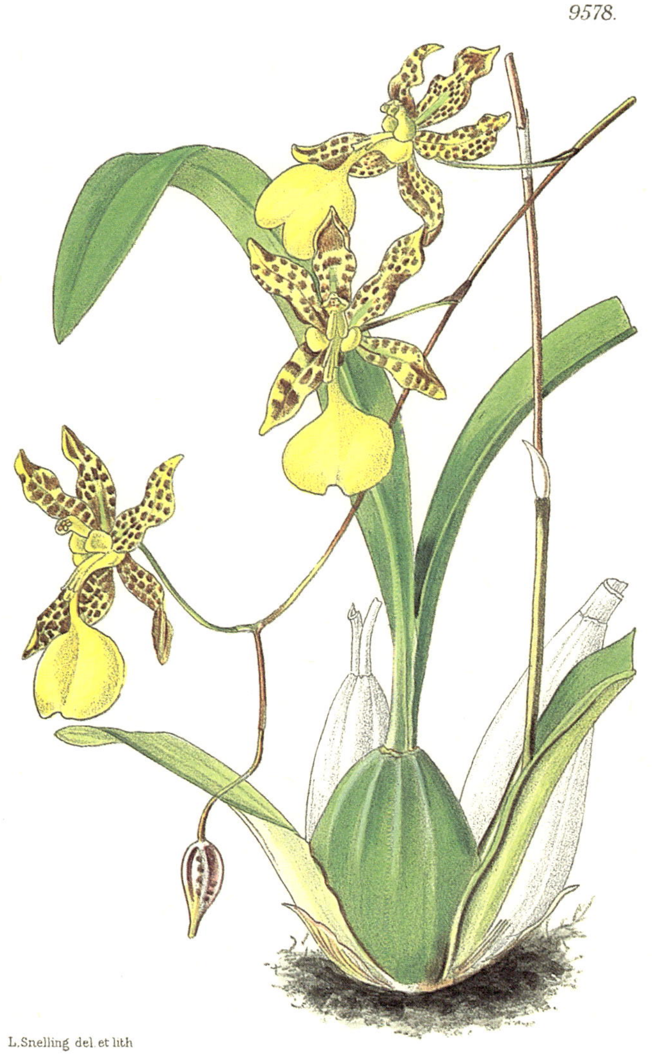

9578 Oncidium tigrinum Llave & Lex.
6322 Oncidium varicosum Lindl.

3393 Oncidium triquetrum (Sw.) R. Br.
5756 Oncidium xanthodon Rchb. f.

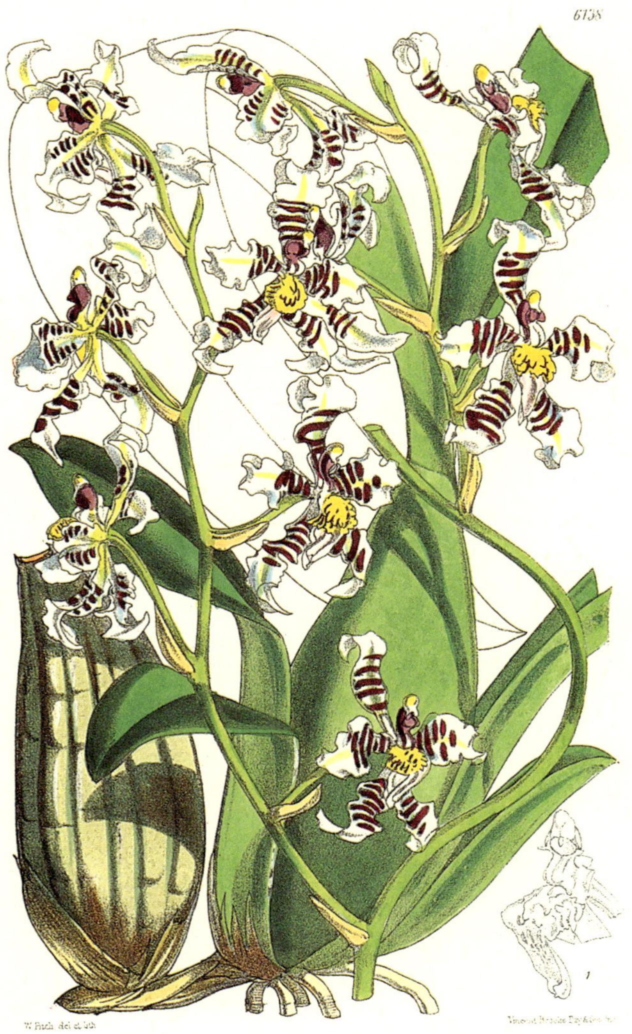

6138 Oncidium zebrinum (Rchb. f.) Rchb. f.
5941 Ophrys lutea (Gouan) Cav.

2516 Ophrys holoserica (Burm. f.) Greuter
5712 Ophrys sphegodes Miller

1930 Ophrys tenthredinifera Willd.
1944 Orchis longicornu Poiret

5844 Ophrys vernixia Brot.
2569 Orchis pallens L.

3426 Orchis simia Lam.
6255 × Orchiserapias barlae Camus

1932 Orchis tridentata Scop.
7385 Ornithochilus difformis (Wallich ex Lindl.) Schltr.

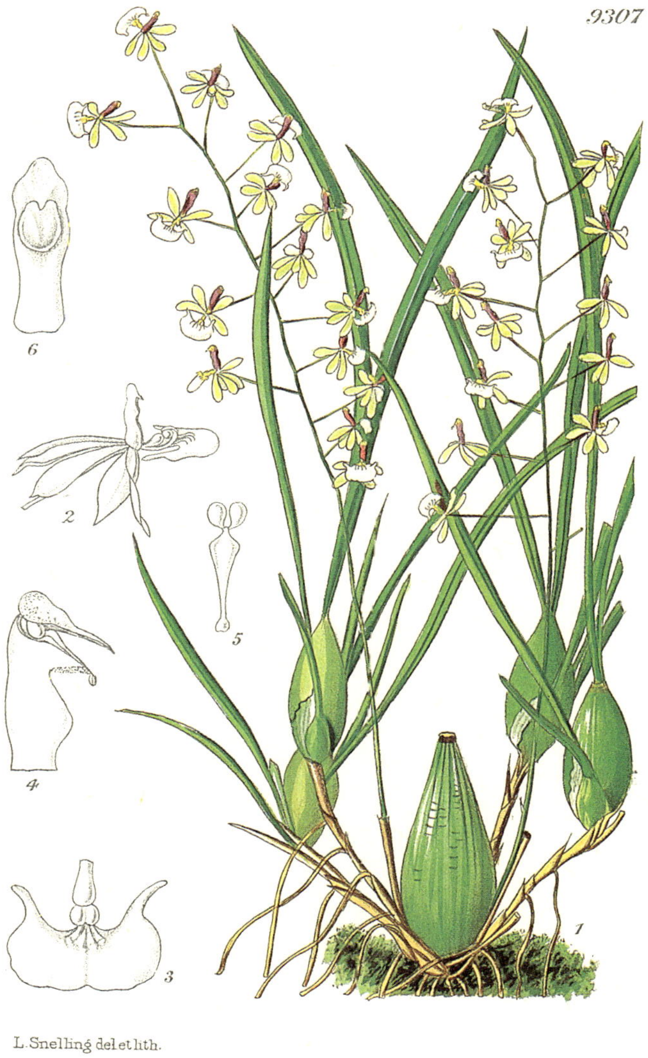

9307 Ornithophora radicans (Rchb.f.) Garay & Pabst.
3921 Otochilus fusca Lindl.

4104 Osmoglossum pulchellum (Bateman ex Lindl.) Schltr.
8725 Otoglossum chiriquense (Rchb.f.) Garay & Dunsterv.

M.S. del. J.N. Fitch lith.

Vincent Brooks, Day & Son Ltd. Imp.

L. Reeve & Co. London

7687 *Otoglossum brevifolium* (Lindl.) Garay & Dunsterv.

5661 Pabstia jugosa (Lindl.) Garay
5546 Palumbina candida (Lindl.) Rchb. f.

3173 Pabstia placanthera (Hook.) Garay
4836 Paphinia cristata (Lindl.) Lindl.

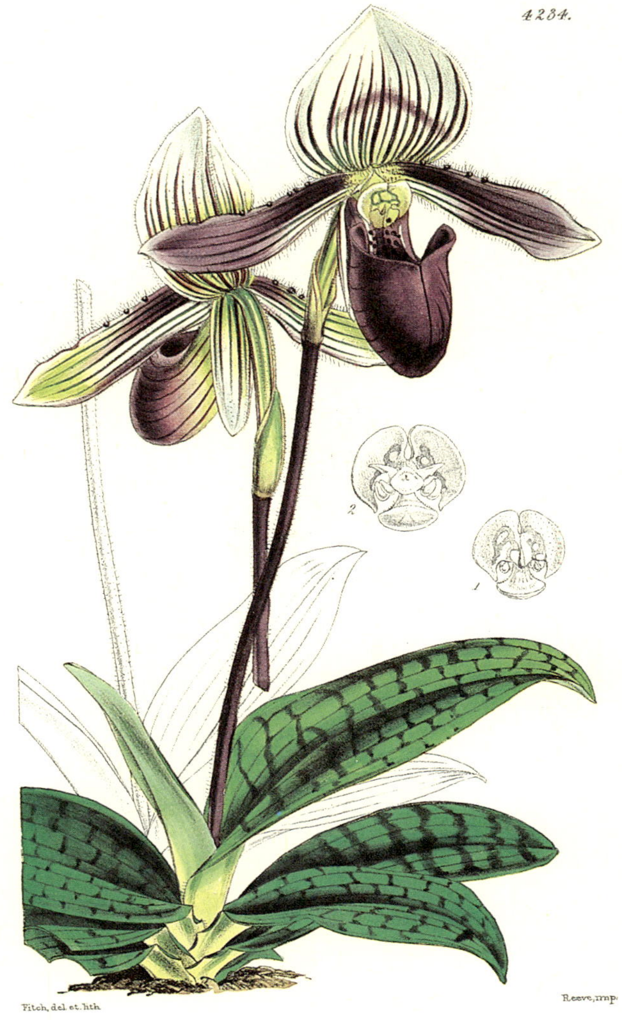

6175 Paphiopedilum argus (Rchb. f.) Stein
9671 Paphiopedilum callosum (Rchb. f.) Stein

4234 Paphiopedilum barbatum (Lindl.) Stein
7578 Paphiopedilum chamberlainianum (Sander ex O'Brien) Stein

7416 *Paphiopedilum charlesworthii* (Rolfe ex Master) Pfitzer
5513 *Paphiopedilum concolor* (Bateman ex Lindl.) Pfitzer

7510 *Paphiopedilum exul* (Ridley) Rolfe

5024

W. Fitch del. et lith. Vincent Brooks Imp.

8084

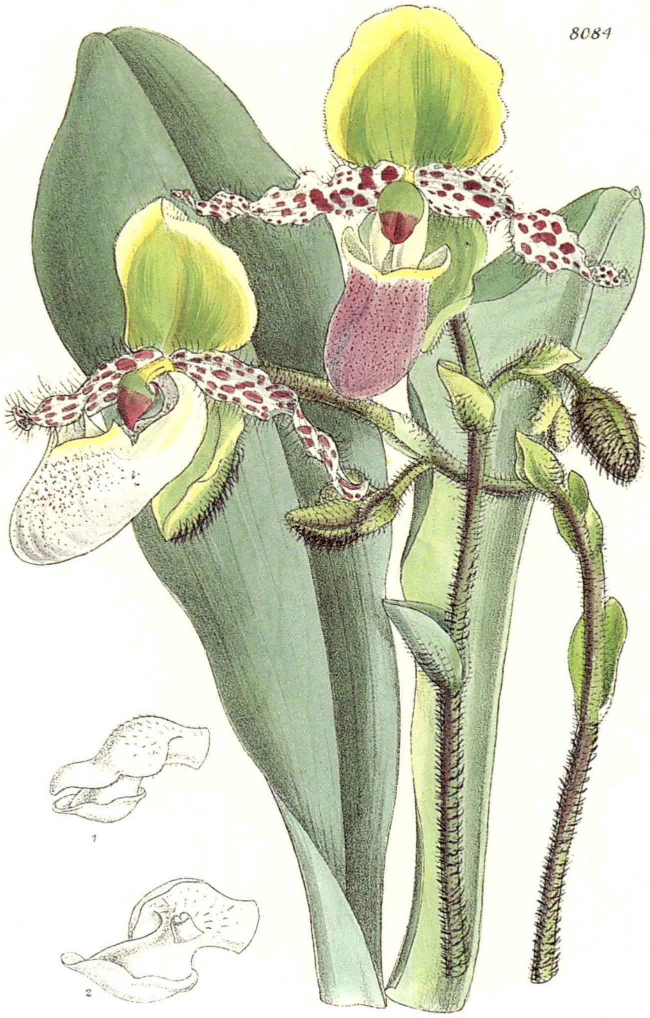

M. S. del. J. N. Fitch lith. L. Reeve & C° London Vincent Brooks, Day & Son Ltd Imp

6876.

M. S. del. J. N. Fitch lith. L. Reeve & C° London Vincent Brooks Day & Son Imp

5024 Paphiopedilum fairrieanum (Lindl.) Stein
6876 Paphiopedilum godefroyae (hort. ex Godef.-Leb.) Stein

8084 Paphiopedilum glaucophyllum J. J. Smith

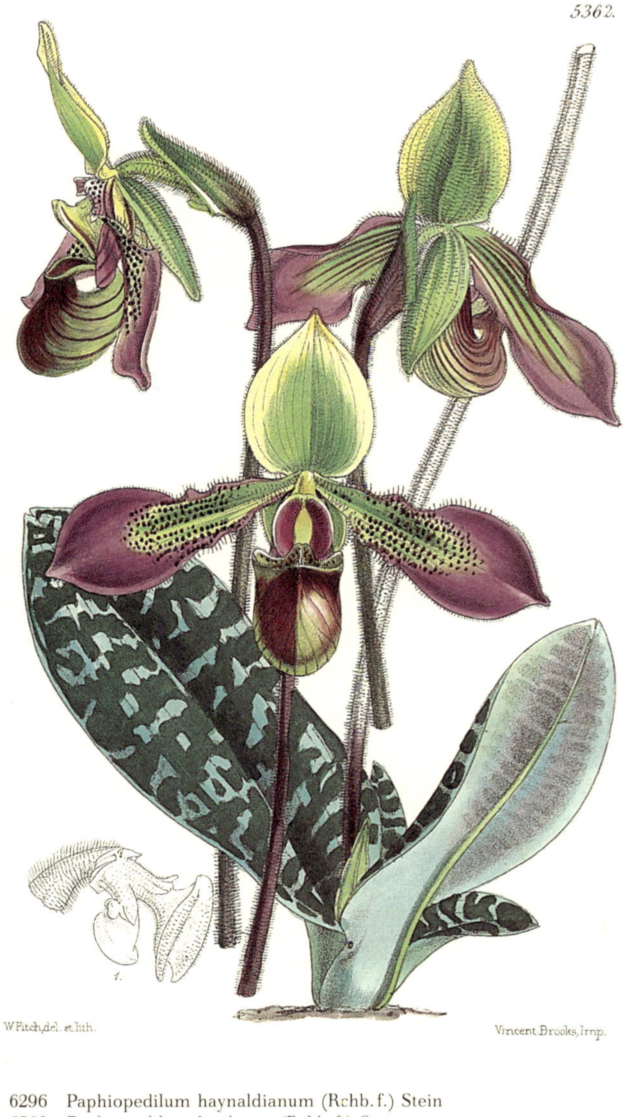

6296 Paphiopedilum haynaldianum (Rchb. f.) Stein
5362 Paphiopedilum hookerae (Rchb. f.) Stein

4990 Paphiopedilum hirsutissimum (Lindl. ex Hook.) Stein
3412 Paphiopedilum insigne (Wallich ex Lindl.) Pfitzer

6432 *Paphiopedilum lawrenceanum* (Rchb. f.) Pfitzer
5922 *Paphiopedilum niveum* (Rchb. f.) Stein

7629 *Paphiopedilum mastersianum* (Rchb. f.) Stein
4901 *Paphiopedilum purpuratum* (Lindl.) Stein

W Fitch del. et lith.

5791 Paphiopedilum parishii (Rchb. f.) Stein

5508.

W. Fitch, del. et lith.

Vincent Brooks, Imp.

5508 Paphiopedilum philippinense (Rchb. f.) Stein

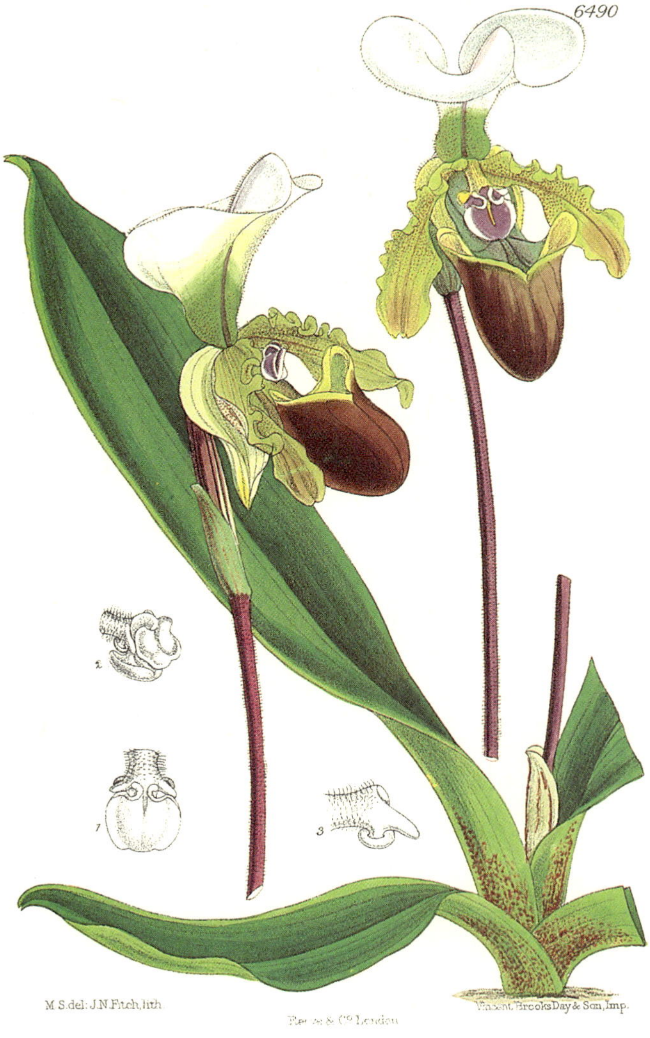

9155 Paphiopedilum robinsonii (Ridley) Ridley
6490 Paphiopedilum spicerianum (Rchb. f.) Pfitzer

7102 Paphiopedilum rothschildianum (Rchb. f.) Stein
2129 Paphipedilum venustum (Wallich ex Sims) Pfitzer

5349 Paphiopedilum stonei (Hook.) Stein

7573

M.S.del J.N.Fitch lith. L. Reeve & Cº London. Vincent Brooks, Day & Son Imp

8126

M.S.del J.N.Fitch lith. L. Reeve & Cº London. Vincent Brooks Day & Son Ltd Imp

9481.

L.Snelling del et lith

4982.

W.Fitch del et lith. Vincent Brooks Imp.

7573 Paphiopedilum victoria-mariae (Sander ex Masters) Rolfe
9481 Paphiopedilum wardii Summerh.

8126 Paphiopedilum villosum (Lindl.) Stein
4982 Papilionanthe vandarum (Rchb.f.) Garay

4114 Papilionanthe teres (Roxb.) Schltr.

9445 Paraphalaenopsis denevei (J. J. Smith) A. Hawkes
9418 Pelexia laxa (Poeppig & Endl.) Lindl.

3374 Pecteilis susannae (L.) Raf.
3116 Peristeria elata Hook.

3479 Peristeria pendula Hook.

3397 Peristylus plantagineus Lindl.
6214 Pescatoria dayana var. rhodacra Rchb. f.

5598 Pescatoria cerina (Lindl. & Paxton) Rchb. f.
3960 Phaius flavus (Blume) Lindl.

N. 27

Pub by S. Curtis. Walworth Feb. 1. 1827.

— Swan Sc —

2719 Phaius flavus (Blume) Lindl.

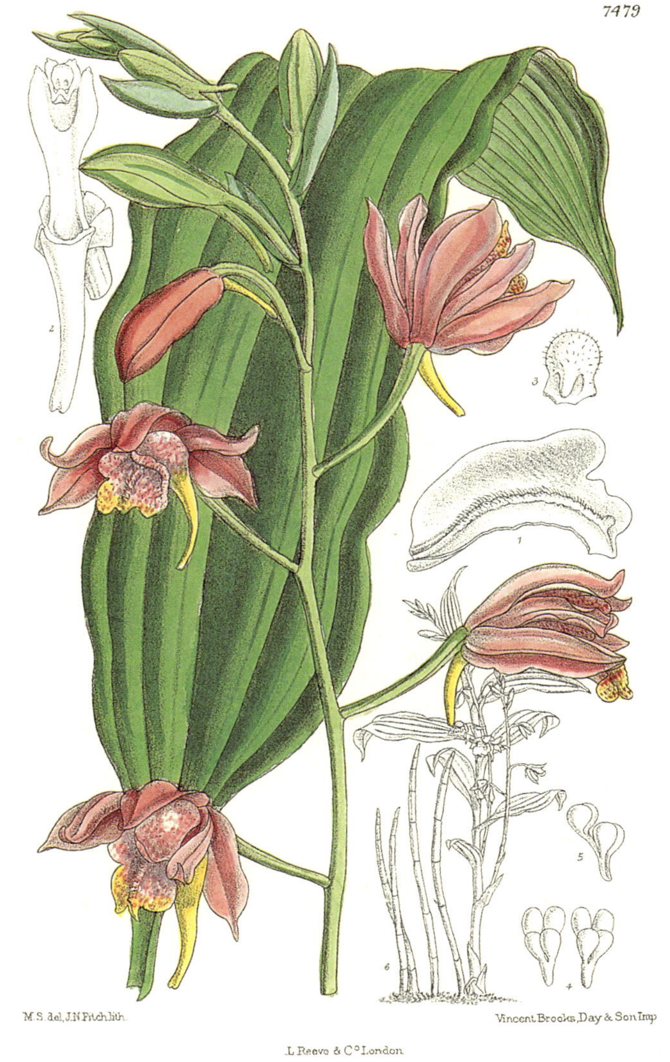

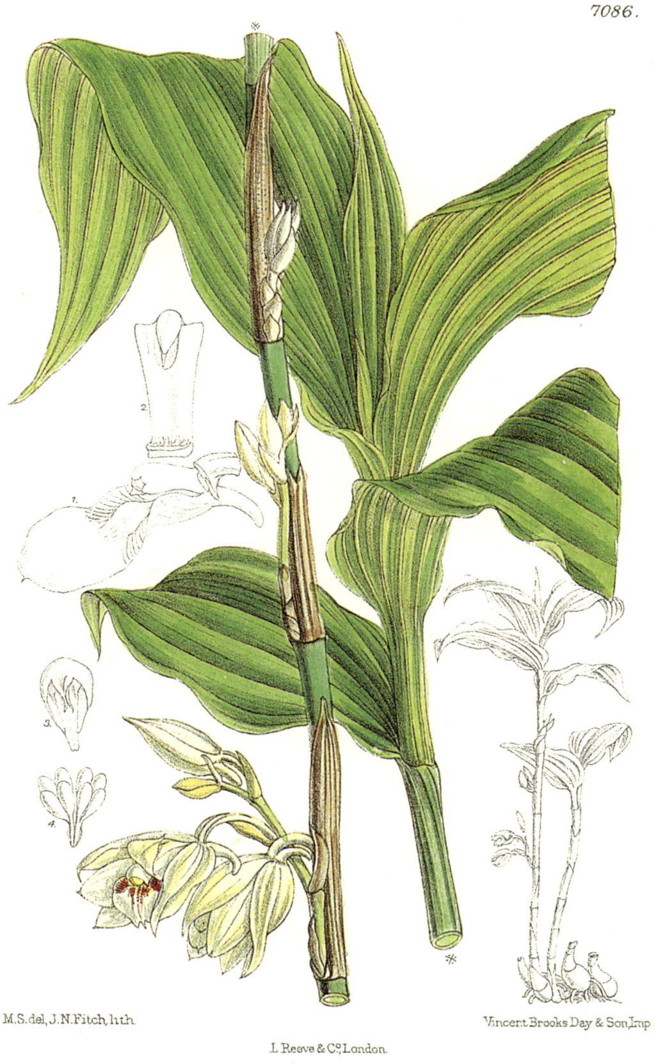

7479 Phaius mishmensis (Lindl.) Rchb. f.
1924 Phaius tankervilleae (Banks) Blume

7086 Phaius pauciflorus (Blume) Blume
4442 Phaius tetragonus (Thouars) Rchb. f.

4078 Phaius tankervilleae (Banks) Blume

W. Fitch, del. et. lith.

Vincent Brooks Day & Son Imp.

6032 Phaius tankervilleae (Banks) Blume

M. S. del, J. N. Fitch, lith.

L. Reeve & Co. London.

Vincent Brooks, Day & Son Imp.

7023 Phaius tankervilleae (Banks) Blume

7307

M S. del, J. N. Fitch lith. L. Reeve & C° London. Vincent Brooks, Day & Son Imp.

7307 *Phaius tuberculosus* (Thouars) Blume

4297

Fitch del. et lith

Reeve imp

4297 Phalaenopsis aphrodite Rchb. f.

5184 Phalaenopsis amabilis (L.) Blume
5212 Phalaenopsis equestris (Schauer) Rchb. f.

5570 Phalaenopsis cornu-cervi (Breda) Blume & Rchb. f.
7885 Phalaenopsis kunsterli Hook. f.

5351.

W. Fitch, del. et lith. Vincent Brooks, Imp.

5523.

W. Fitch, del. et lith. Vincent Brooks, Imp.

6964.

M.S. del, J.N. Fitch, lith. L. Reeve & Co London. Vincent Brooks, Day & Son, Imp.

5815.

W. Fitch, del. et lith. Vincent Brooks, Day & Son, Imp.

5351 Phalaenopsis lowii Rchb. f.
6964 Phalaenopsis mariae Burb. ex Warner & Williams

5523 Phalaenopsis lueddemanniana Rchb. f.
5815 Phalaenopsis parishii Rchb. f.

5530

W. Fitch, del. et lith. Vincent Brooks, Imp.

5530 *Phalaenopsis schilleriana* Rchb. f.

M.S. del. J.N. Fitch Lith

Vincent Brooks Day & Son Imp

6622 *Phalaenopsis stuartiana* Rchb. f.

7321 Phalaenopsis speciosa var. tetraspis (Rchb.f.) Sweet
9198 Phalaenopsis violacea Witte

5527 Phalaenopsis sumatrana Korth. & Rchb.f.
5466 Phragmipedium caricinum (Lindl. & Paxton) Rolfe

5970 *Phragmipedium longifolium* (Rchb. f. & Warsc.) Rolfe

6217 *Phragmipedium roezlii* (Rchb. f.) Garay

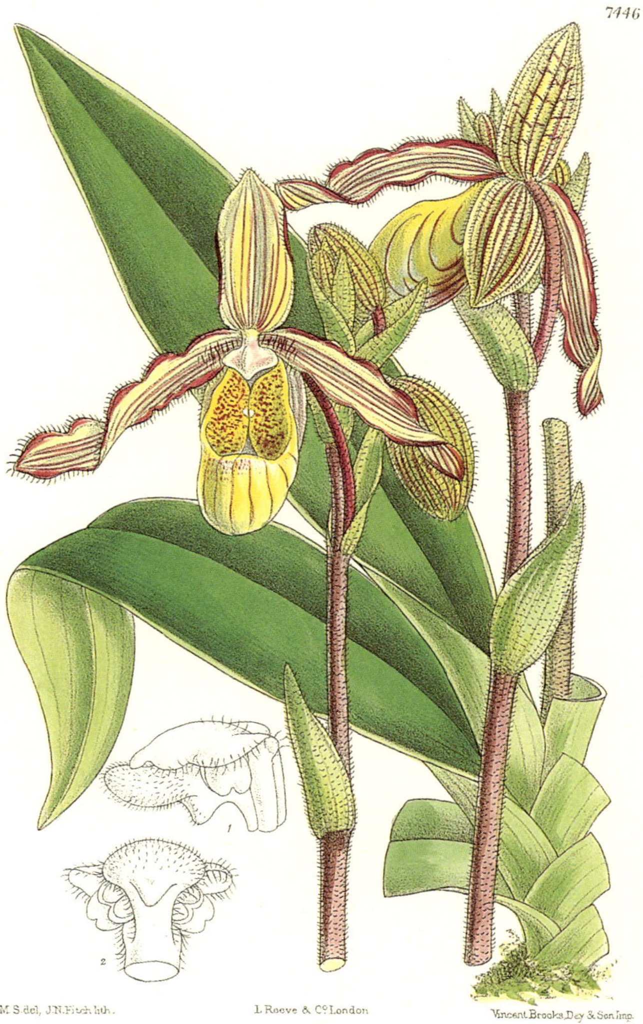

7178 *Phragmipedium klotzscheanum* (Rchb.f. ex Schomb.) Rolfe
5614 *Phragmipedium schlimii* (Rchb.f.) Rolfe

7446 *Phragmipedium sargentianum* (Rolfe) Rolfe
4869 *Physosiphon tubatus* (Lodd.) Rchb.f.

9325 Physosiphon tubatus (Lodd.) Rchb. f.
5305 Platythelys maculata (Hook.) Garay

1668 Platanthera ciliaris (L.) Lindl.
4370 Plectrelminthus caudatus (Lindl.) Summerh.

8106 Pleione bulbocodioides (Franchet) Rolfe
6388 Pleione hookeriana (Lindl.) B.S. Williams

8729 Pleione formosana Hayata
5674 Pleione humilis (Smith) D. Don

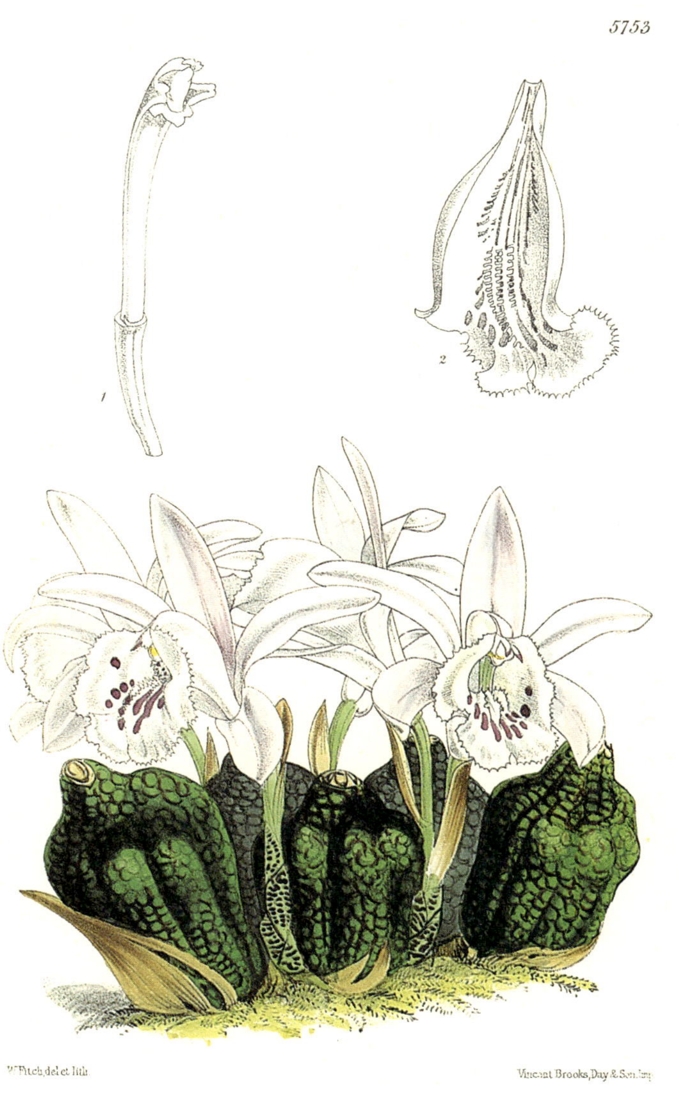

5370 Pleione × lagenaria Lindl.
4496 Pleione praecox (Smith) D. Don

4691 Pleione maculata (Lindl.) Lindl.
5753 Pleione praecox (Smith) D. Don

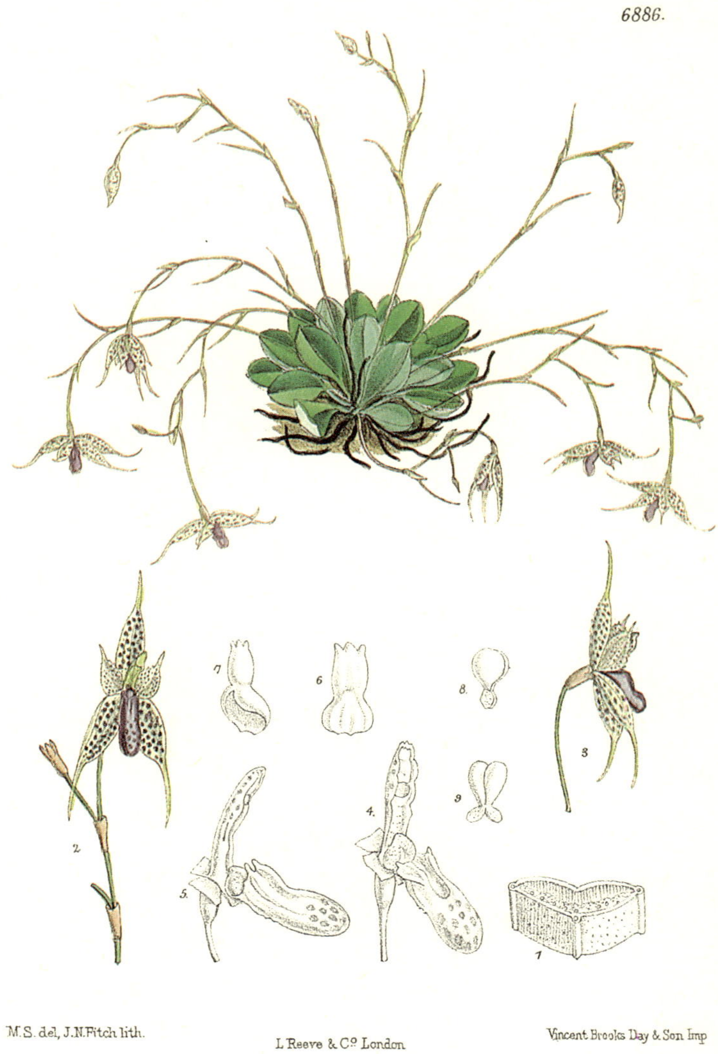

8588 Pleione speciosa Ames & Schltr.
4142 Pleurothallis bicarinata Lindl.

6886 Pleurothallis aristata Hook.
7431 Pleurothallis biserrula Rchb. f.

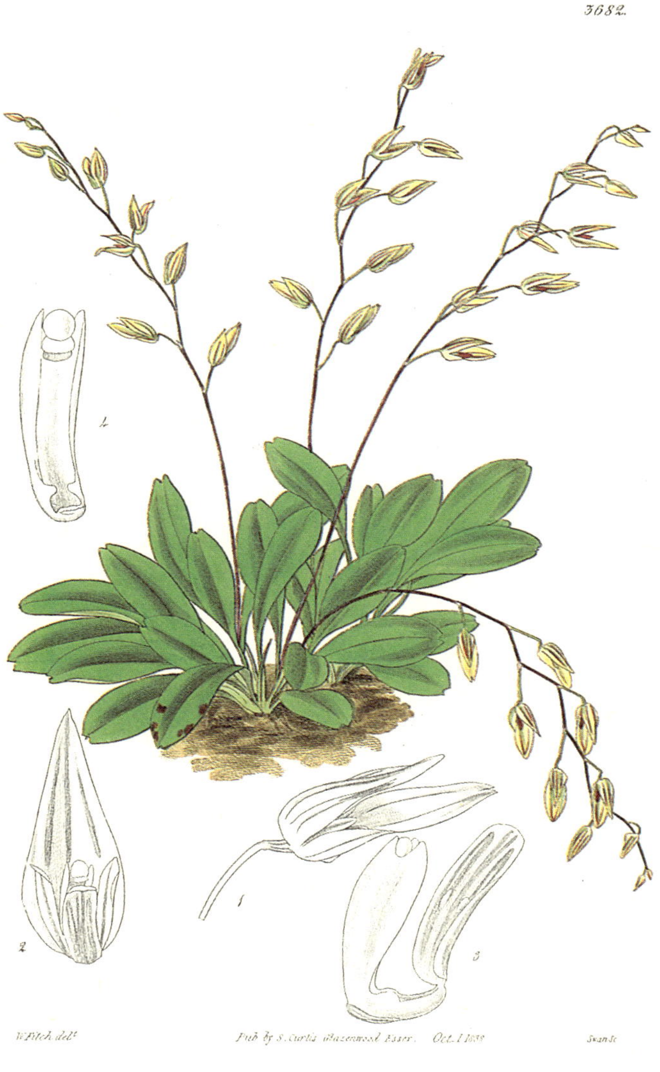

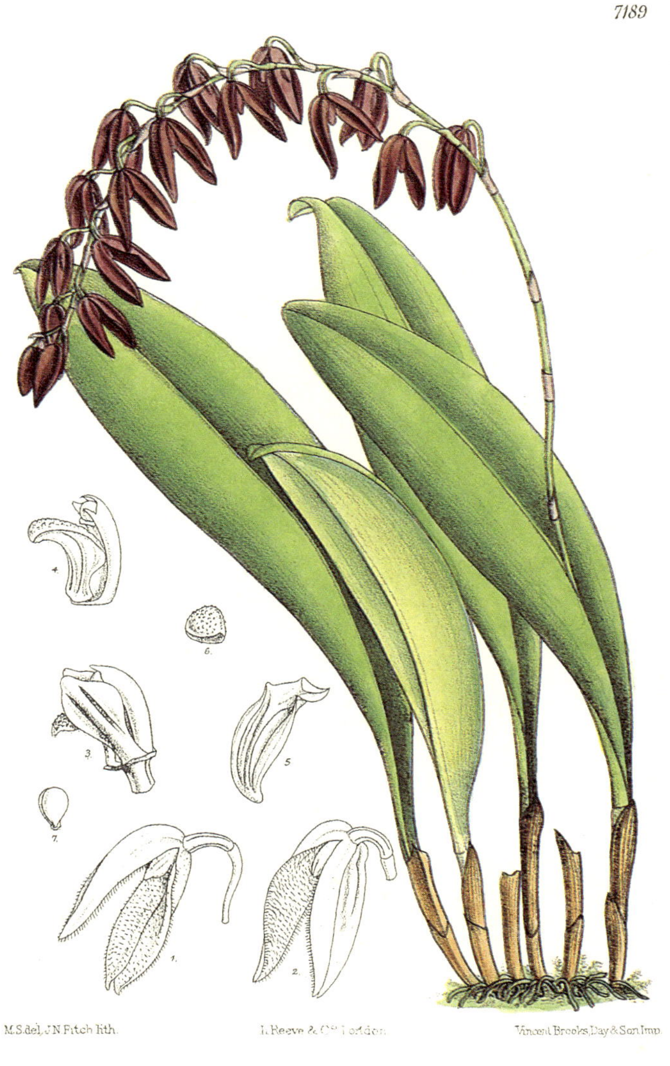

7129 Pleurothallis endotrachys Rchb. f.
3682 Pleurothallis grobyi Bateman ex Lindl.

8853 Pleurothallis grandis Rolfe
7189 Pleurothallis immersa Linden & Rchb. f.

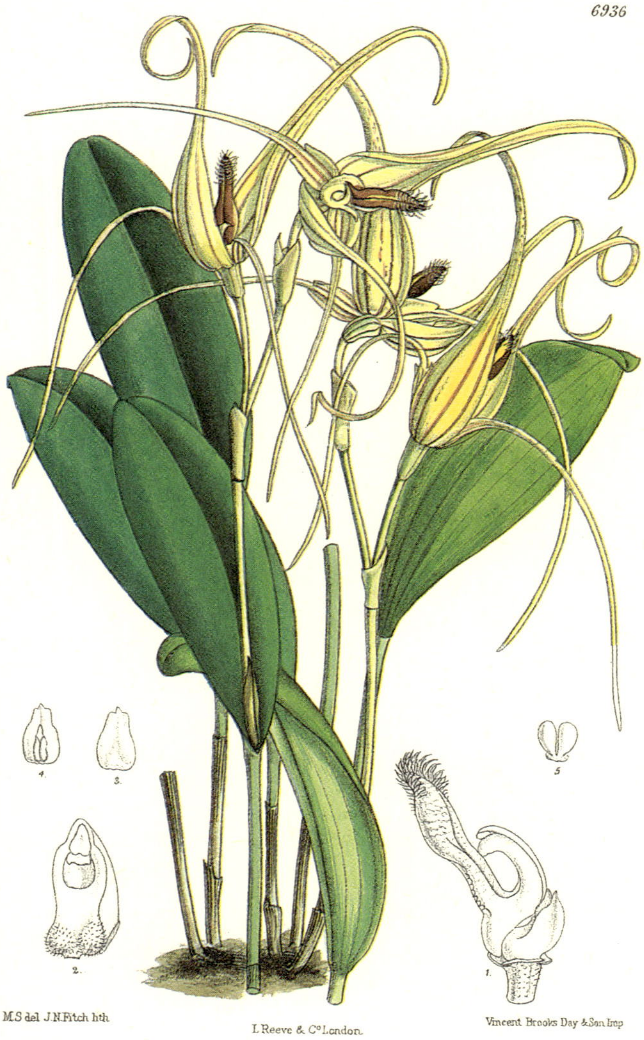

6936 Pleurothallis insignis Rolfe
3897 Pleurothallis pubescens Lindl.

3261 Pleurothallis prolifera Herbert ex Lindl.
8839 Pleurothallis punctulata Rolfe

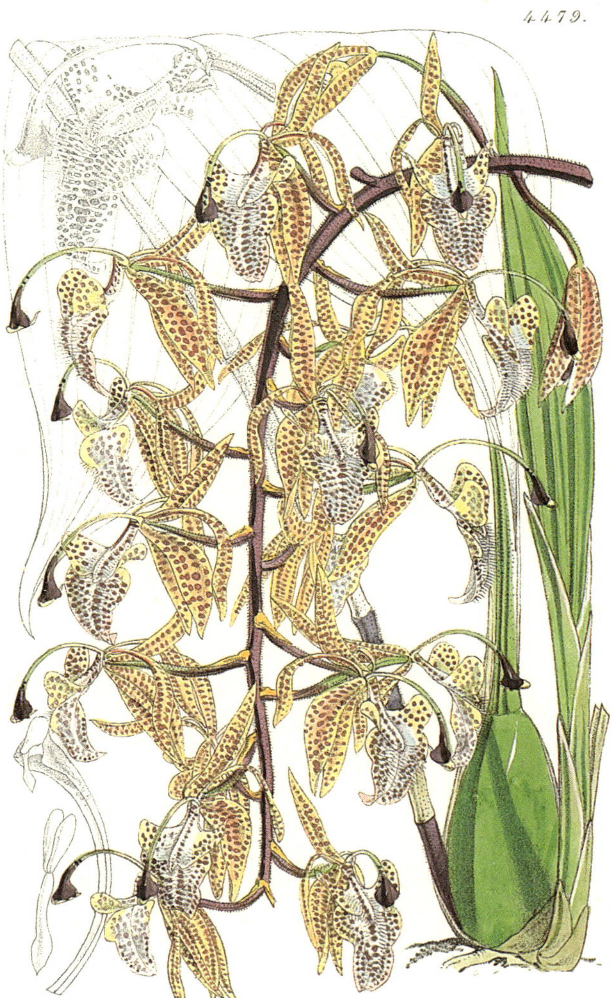

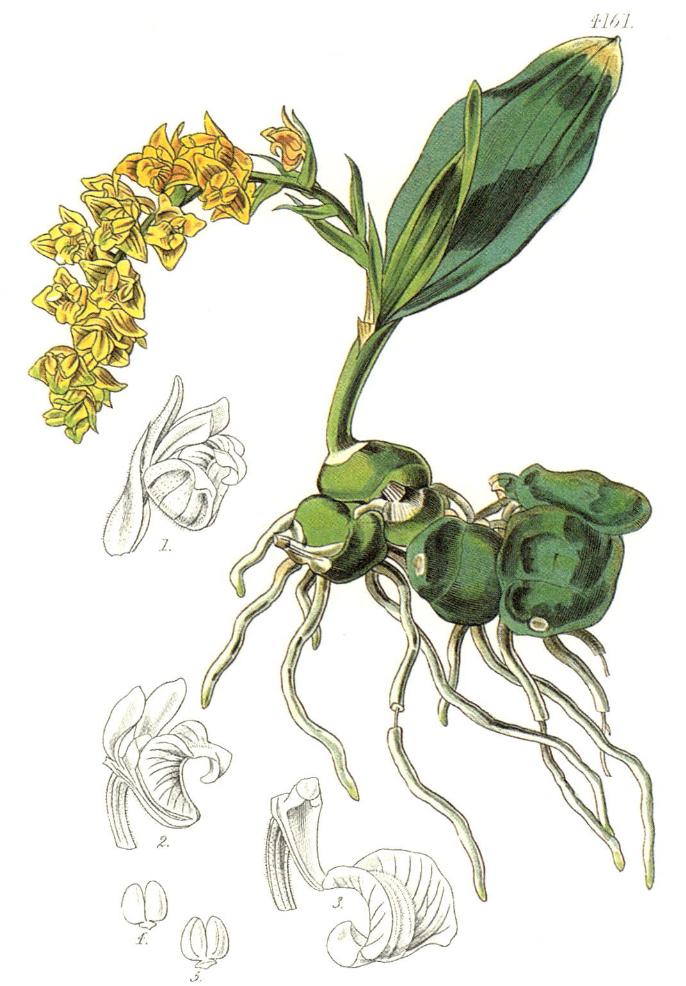

3030 Pleurothallis saurocephala Lodd.
4479 Polycycnis barbata (Lindl.) Rchb. f.

7094 Pleurothallis schiedei Rchb. f.
4161 Polystachya affinis Lindl.

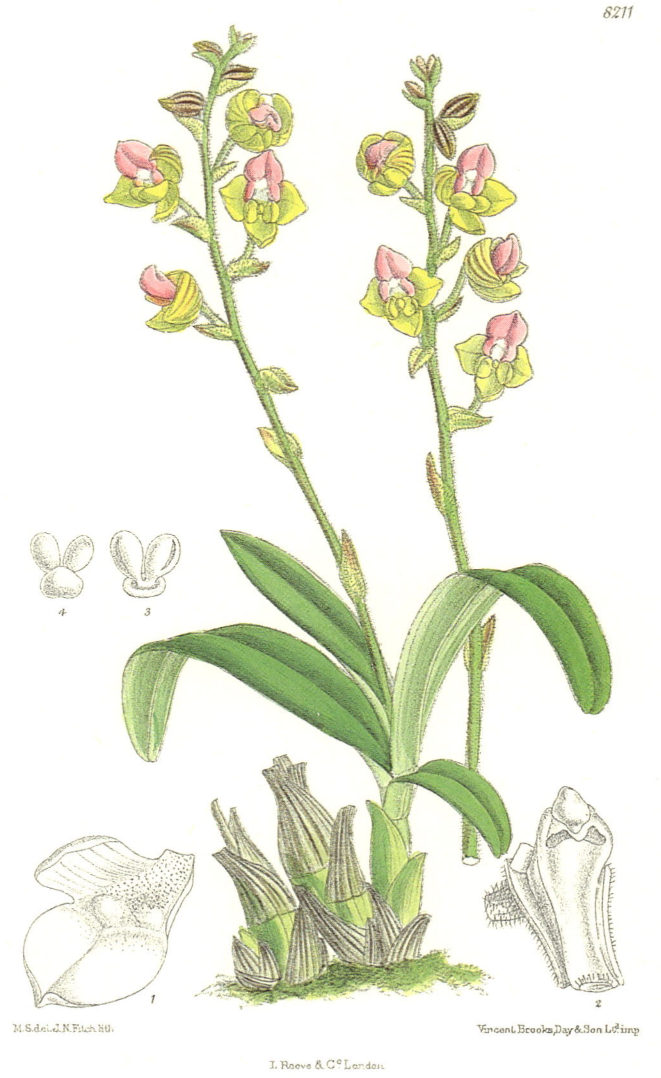

3707 Polystachya galeata (Sw.) Rchb. f.
8618 Polystachya paniculata (Sw.) Rolfe

8211 Polystachya lawrenceana Kraenzlin
8772 Polystachya pobeguinii (Finet) Rolfe

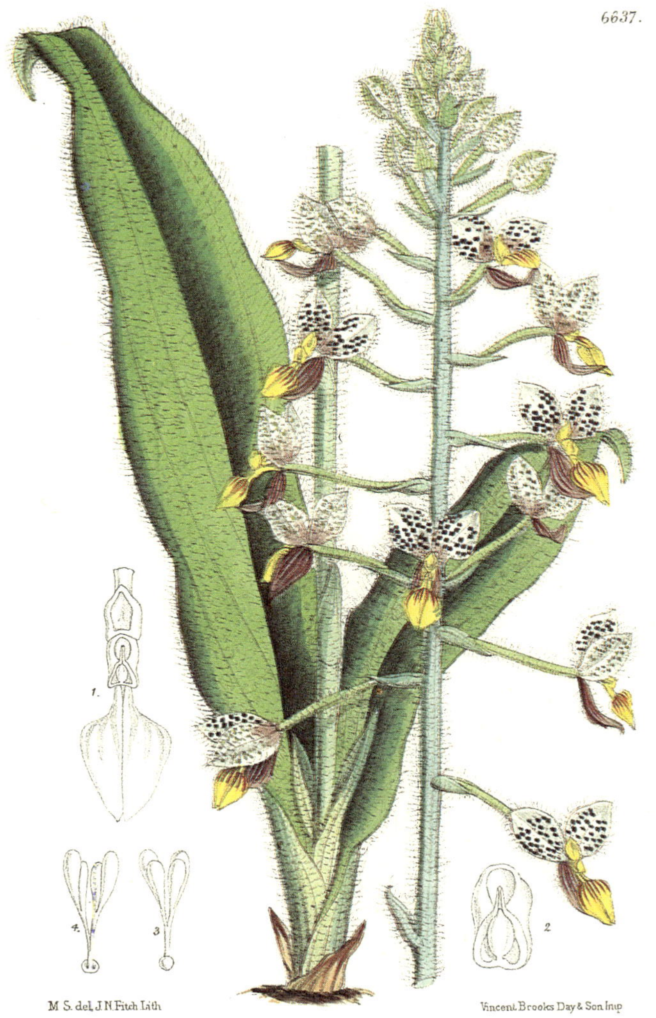

5586 Polystachya pubescens (Lindl.) Rchb. f.
842 Ponthieva racemosa (Walter) C. Mohr.

6637 Ponthieva maculata Lindl.
7329 Porpax meirax (Parish & Rchb. f.) King & Pantl.

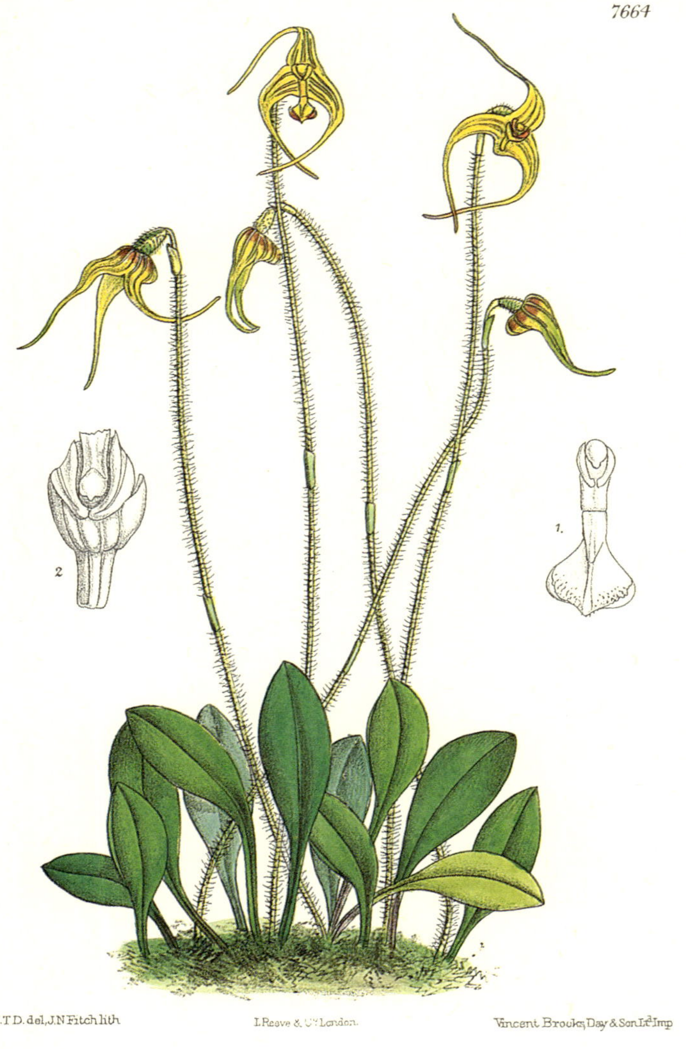

7664 Porroglossum echidnum (Rchb. f.) Garay
3877 Promenaea stapelioides (Link & Otto) Lindl.

8631 Promenaea microptera Rchb. f.
2795 Psychopsis papilio (Lindl.) H. G. Jones

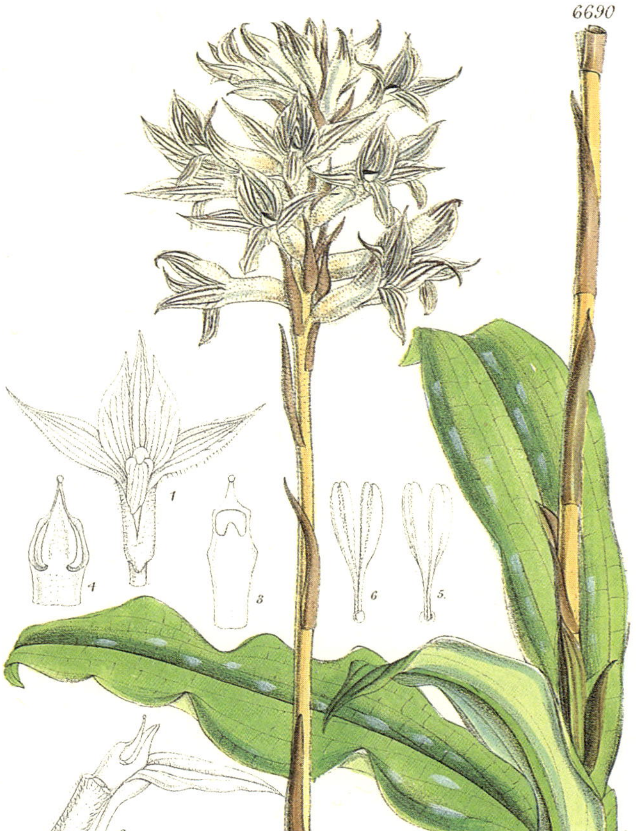

3733 Psychopsis papilio (Lindl.) H. G. Jones
6690 Pteroglossa euphlebia (Olivier ex Rchb.f.) Garay

8374 Psychopsis sanderae (Rolfe) Lueckel & Braem
3401 Pterostylis acuminata R. Br.

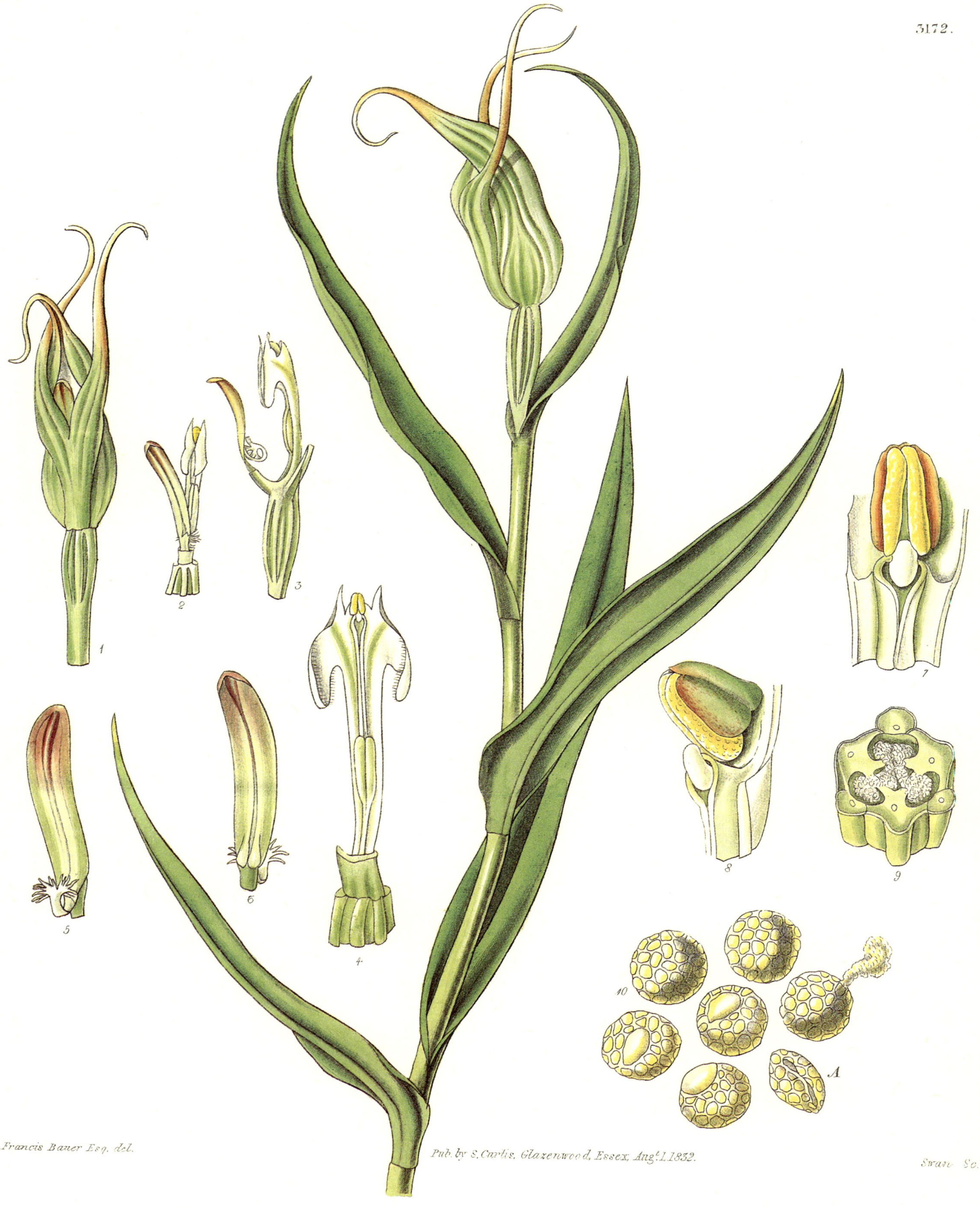

3172 Pterostylis banksii R. Br. ex Cunn.

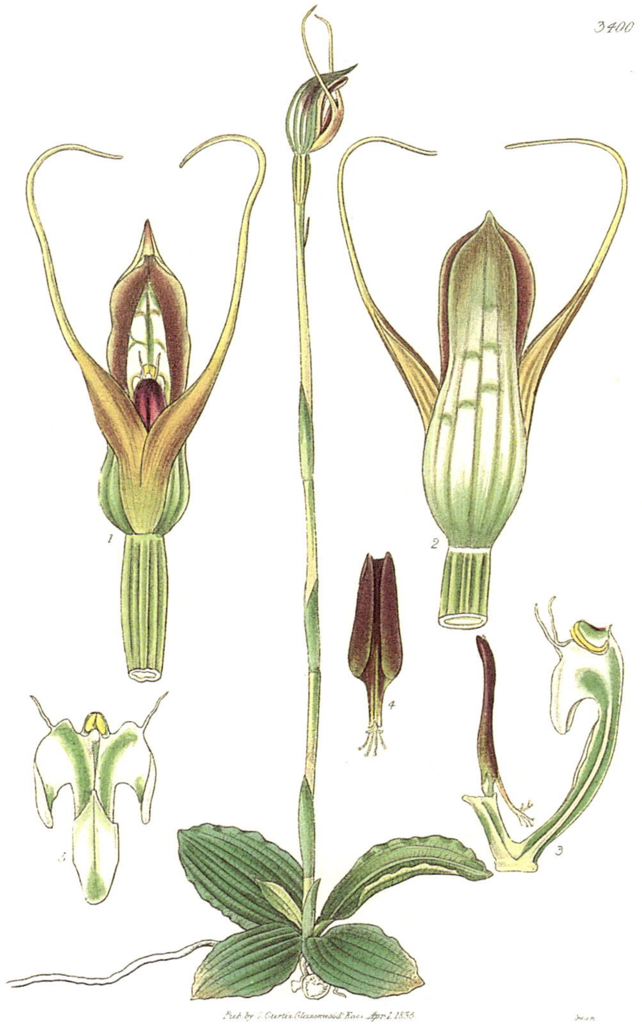

6351 Pterostylis baptistii Fitzg.
3086 Pterostylis curta R. Br.

3400 Pterostylis concinna R. Br.
3085 Pterostylis nutans R. Br.

2997 Renanthera coccinea Lour.

M.S. del. J.N. Fitch lith.

Vincent Brooks, Day & Son Imp.

L. Reeve & C° London.

7537 Renanthera storiei Rchb. f.

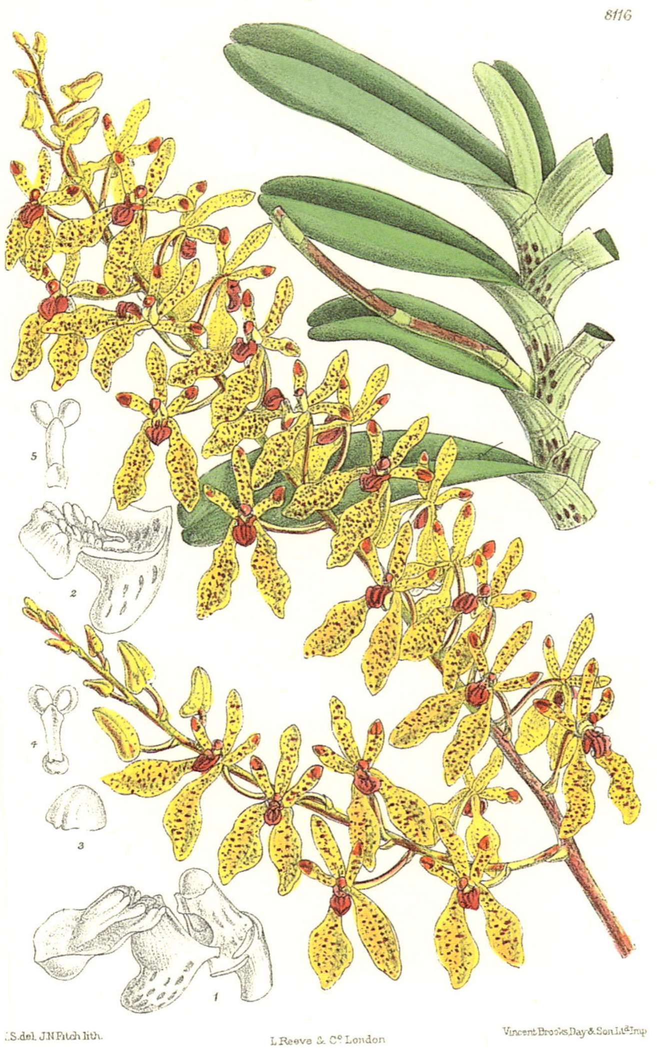

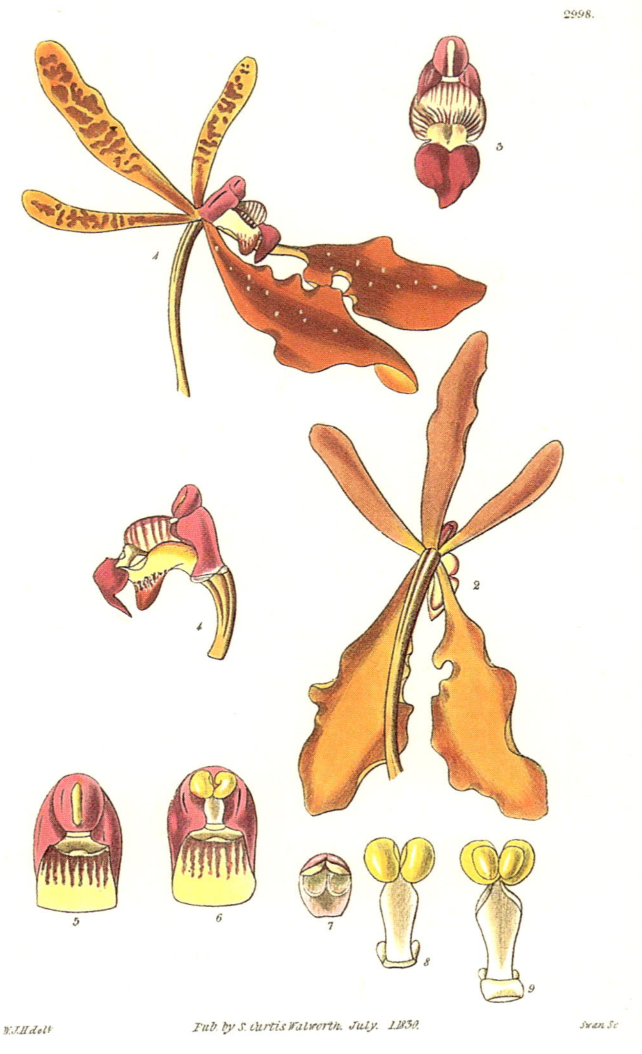

8116 Renanthera annamensis Rolfe
7711 Renanthera imschootiana Rolfe

2998 Renanthera coccinea Lour.
5966 Restrepia elegans Karsten

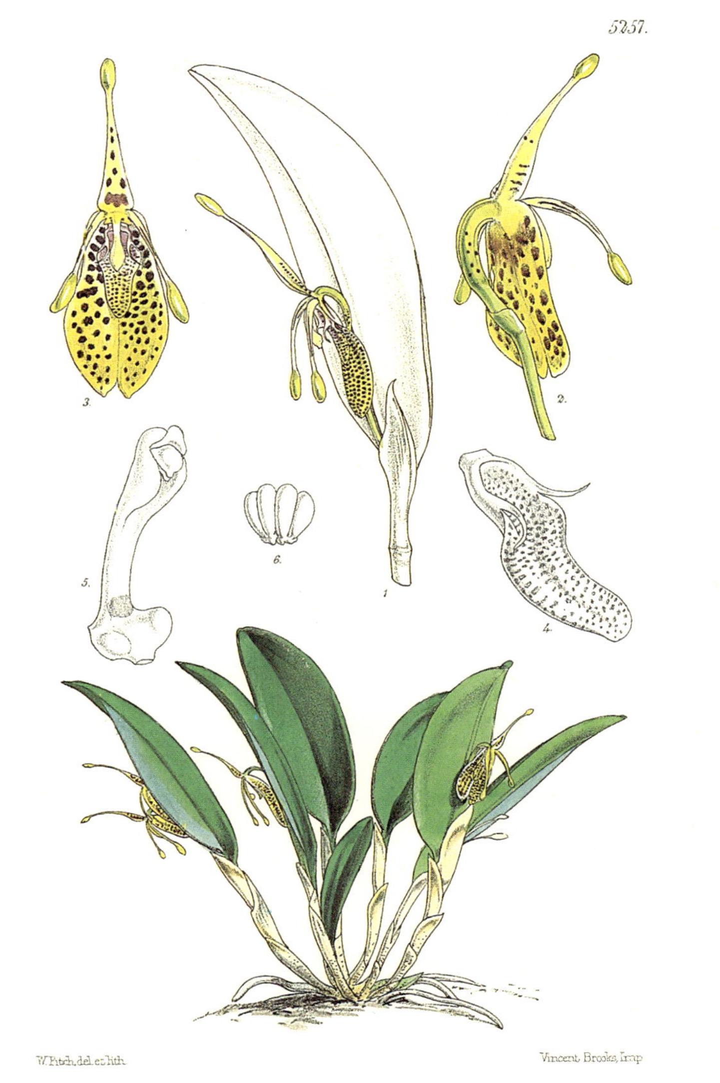

6288 Restrepia guttulata Lindl.
7233 Restrepia striata Rolfe

7930 Restrepia hemsleyana Schltr.
5257 Restrepia xanthophthalma Rchb. f.

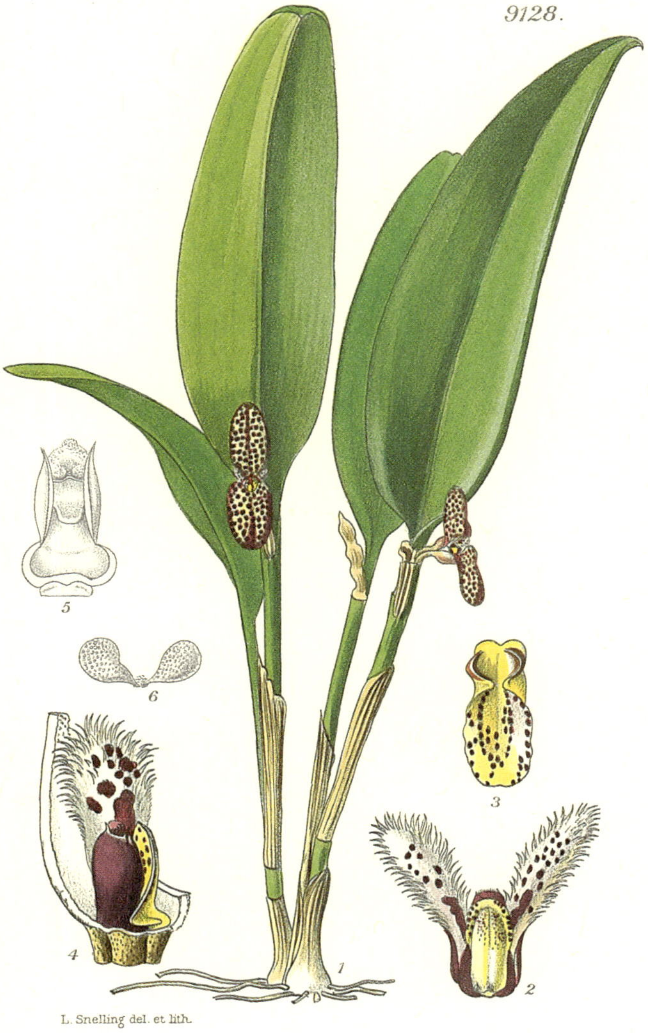

9128 Restrepiella ophiocephala (Lindl.) Garay & Dunsterv.
4033 Rhyncholaelia glauca (Lindl.) Schltr.

4474 Rhyncholaelia digbyana (Lindl.) Schltr.
5433 Rhynchostylis gigantea var. harrisoniana (Hook.) Holttum

W. Fitch, del. et lith.

Vincent Brooks, Imp.

5635 Rhynchostylis gigantea (Lindl.) Ridley

4108 Rhynchostylis retusa (L.) Blume

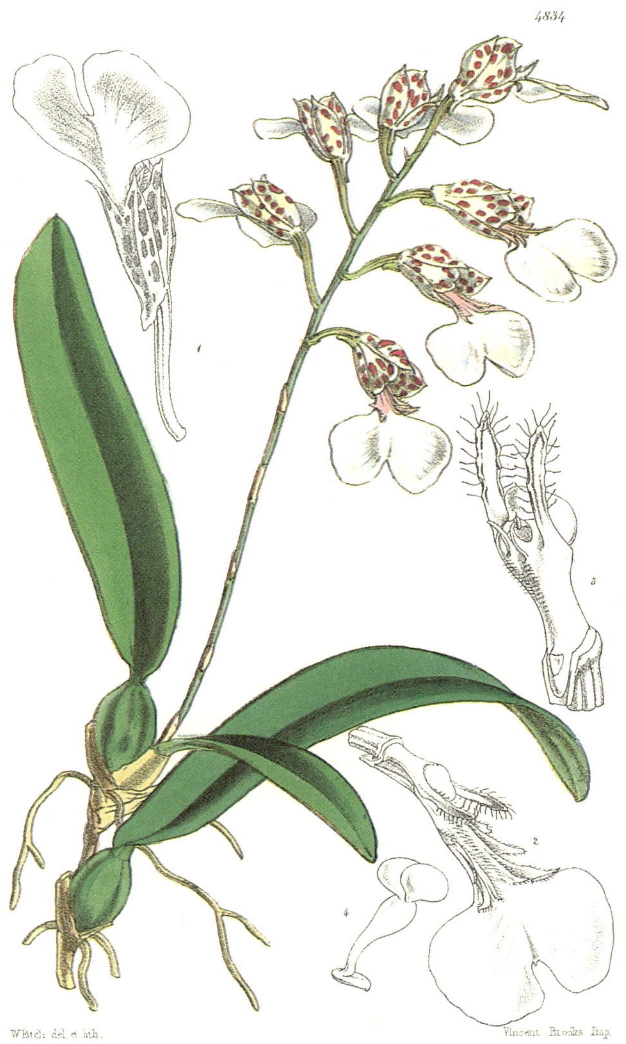

7428 Robiquetia mooreana (Rolfe) J. J. Smith
5419 Rodriguezia decora (Lemaire) Rchb. f.

4834 Rodriguezia decora (Lemaire) Rchb. f.
3524 Rodriguezia lanceolata Ruiz Lopez & Pavón

3955 Rossioglossum grande (Lindl.) Garay & G. C. Kennedy
1036 Sacoila lanceolata (Aublet) Garay

3597 Rudolfiella aurantiaca (Lindl.) Hoehne
2797 Sacoila lanceolata (Aublet) Garay

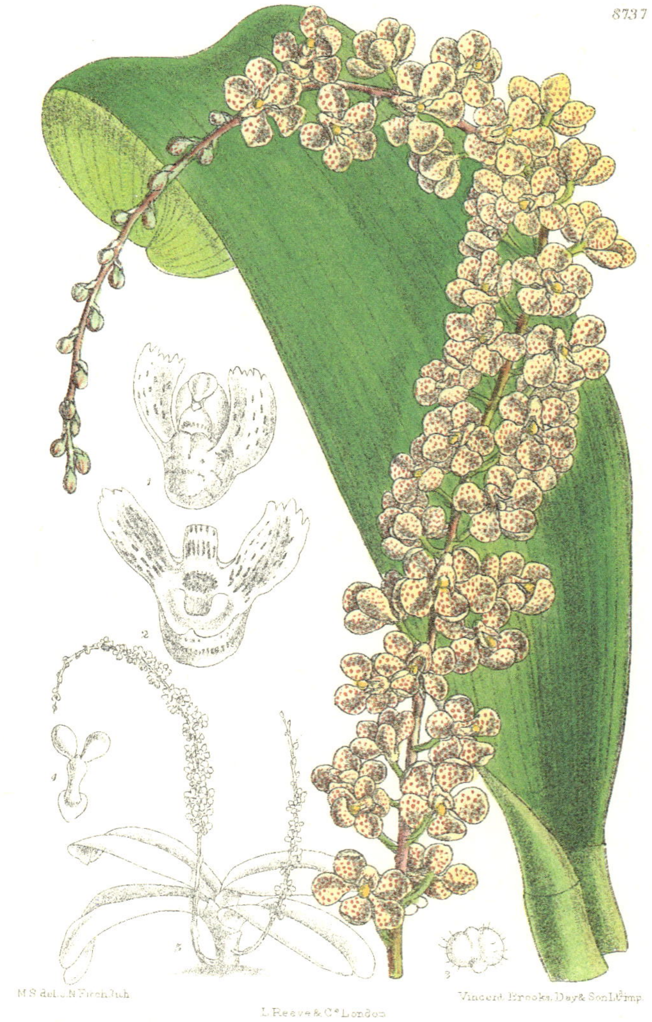

7010 Sarcochilus hartmannii F. Muell.
1562 Sarcoglottis acaulis (Smith) Schltr.

8737 Sarcochilus moorei (Rchb. f.) Schltr.
2730 Sarcoglottis grandiflora (Lindl.) Klotzsch

1512 Satyrium carneum (Dryander) R. Br.
7289 Satyrium coriifolium var. maculatum Hook. f.

2172 Satyrium coriifolium Sw.
6625 Satyrium nepalense D. Don

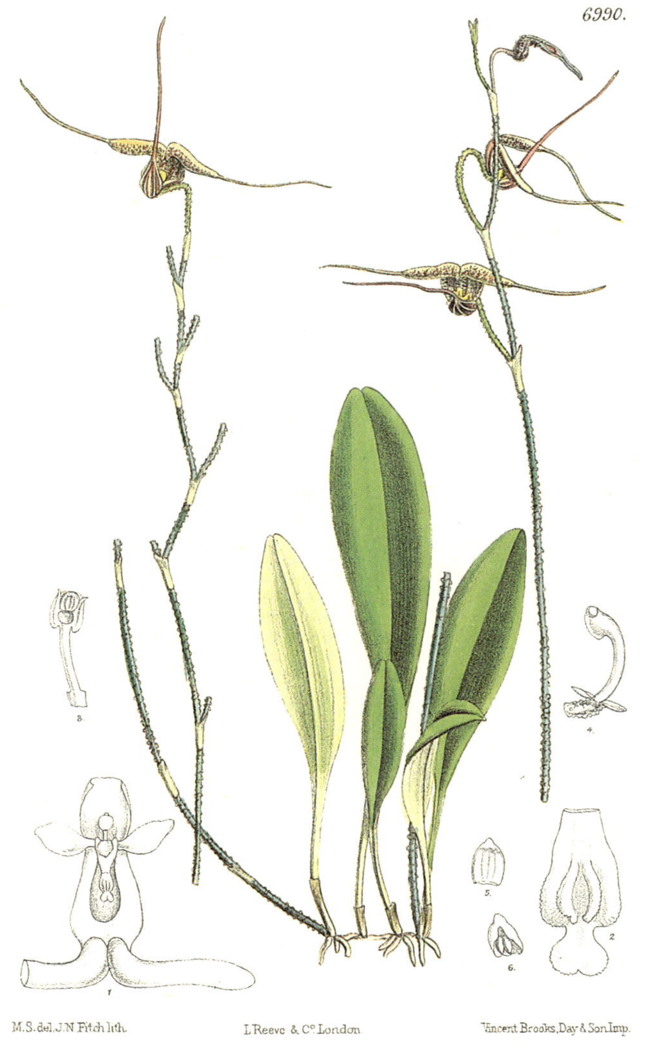

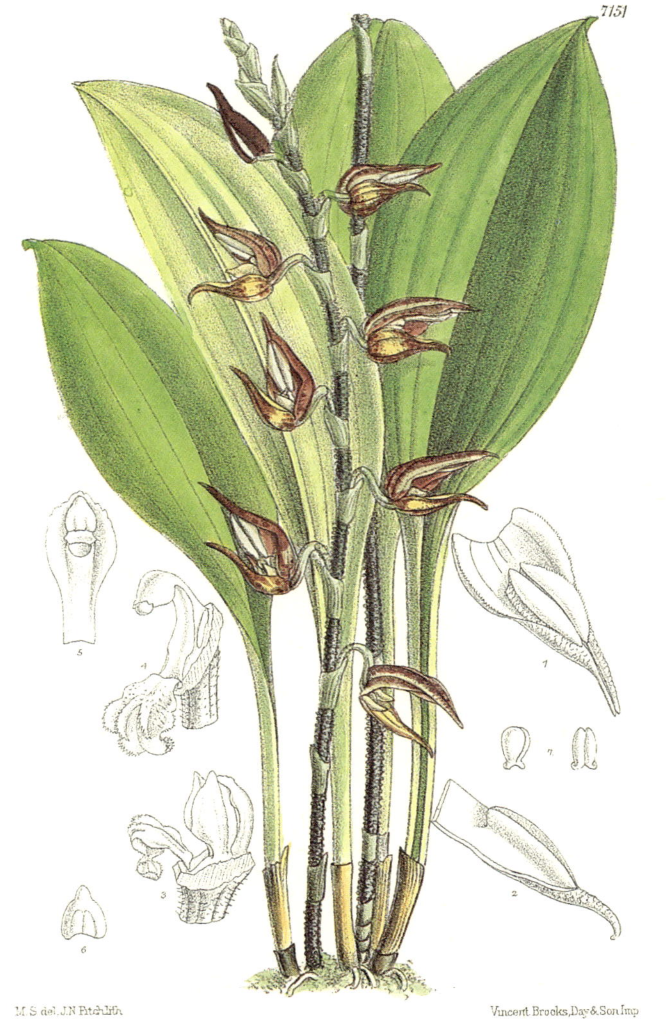

7104 Satyrium princeps Bolus
6990 Scaphosepalum gibberosum (Rchb. f.) Rolfe

7295 Satyrium sphaerocarpum Lindl.
7151 Scaphosepalum pulvinare (Rchb. f.) Rolfe

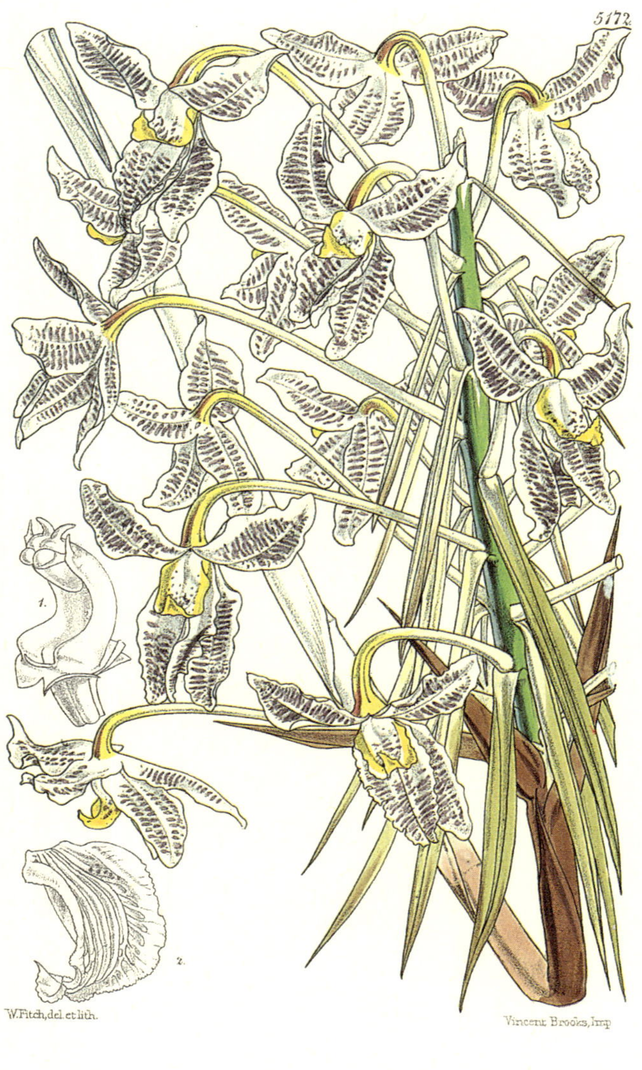

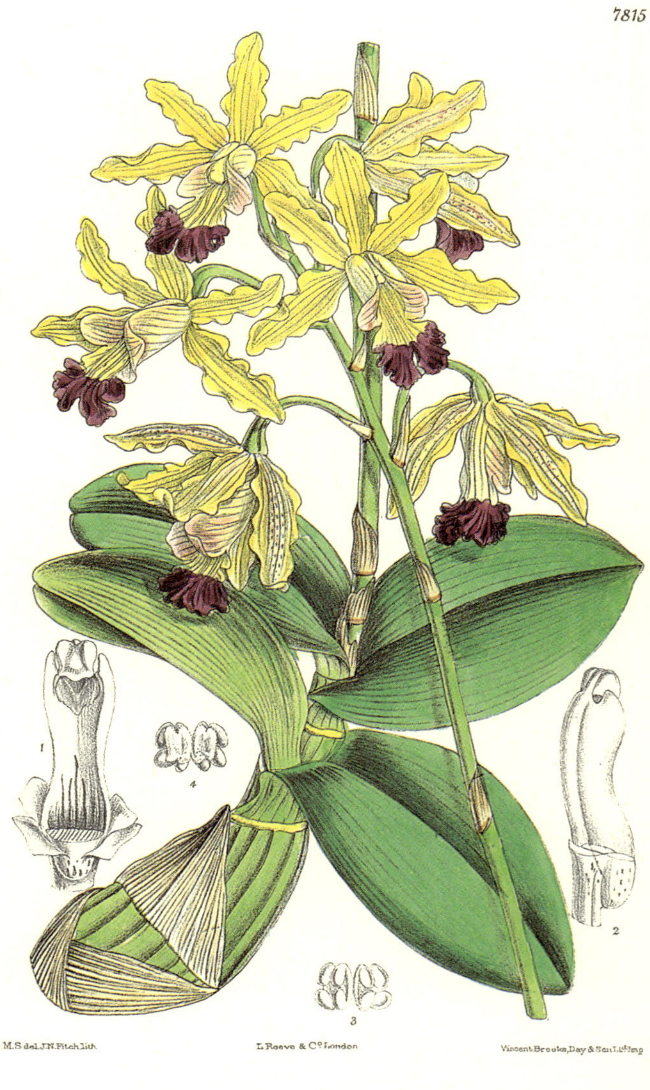

7165 Scaphosepalum punctatum (Rolfe) Rolfe
5172 Schomburgkia lyonsii Lindl.

4071 Scaphyglottis violacea Lindl.
7815 Schomburgkia thomsoniana var. minor Hook. f.

W. Fitch del.t Pub by S. Curtis Glazenwood Essex June 1. 1839. Swan Sc.

3729 Schomburgkia gloriosa Rchb. f.

4090 Schomburgkia superbiens (Lindl.) Rolfe

8427 Schomburgkia undulata Lindl.

4629 Scuticaria hadwenii (Lindl.) hort. ex Hook.
5798 Sedirea japonica (Linden & Rchb. f.) Garay & Sweet

3573 Scuticaria steelei (Hook.) Lindl.
5728 Seidenfadenia mitrata (Rchb. f.) Garay

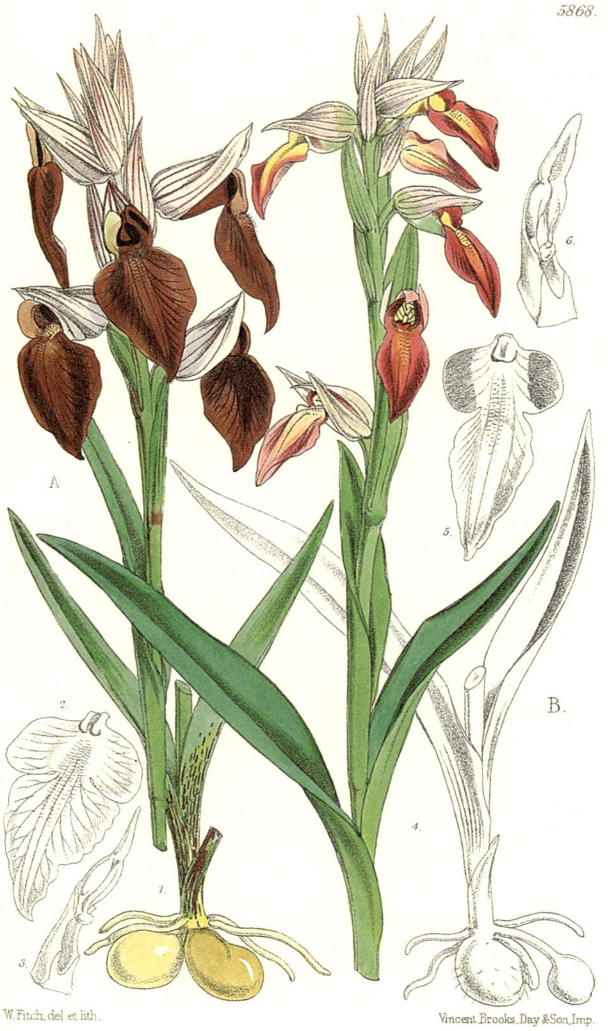

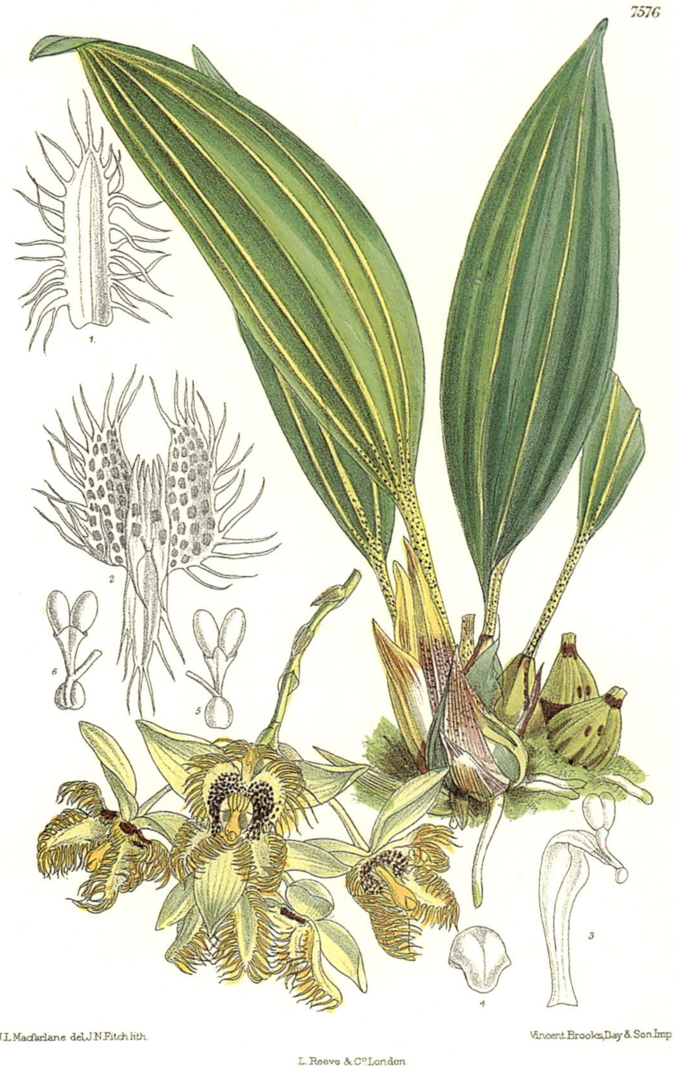

5868 A: Serapias cordigera L., B: Serapias lingua L.
8635 Sievekingia shepheardii Rolfe

7576 Sievekingia reichenbachiana (F. Lehm.) Rolfe
8825 Sigmatostalix guatemalensis Schltr.

M.S.del, J.N.Fitch, lith.

Vincent Brooks Day & Son, Imp.

L. Reeve & C°. London.

7058 Sobralia leucoxantha Rchb. f.

4570 Sobralia decora Bateman
4682 Sobralia macrophylla Rchb. f.

4882 Sobralia fragrans Lindl.
7376 Sobralia sessilis Lindl.

4446 Sobralia macrantha Lindl.

M.S. del, J.N. Fitch lith.   L. Reeve & C° London.   Vincent Brooks, Day & Son Imp.

7332 Sobralia xantholeuca hort. ex Williams

8654 × Sophrolaelia psyche Rolfe
3677 Sophronitis cernua Lindl.

6880 Sophronitella violacea (Lindl.) Schltr.
3709 Sophronitis coccinea (Lindl.) Rchb. f.

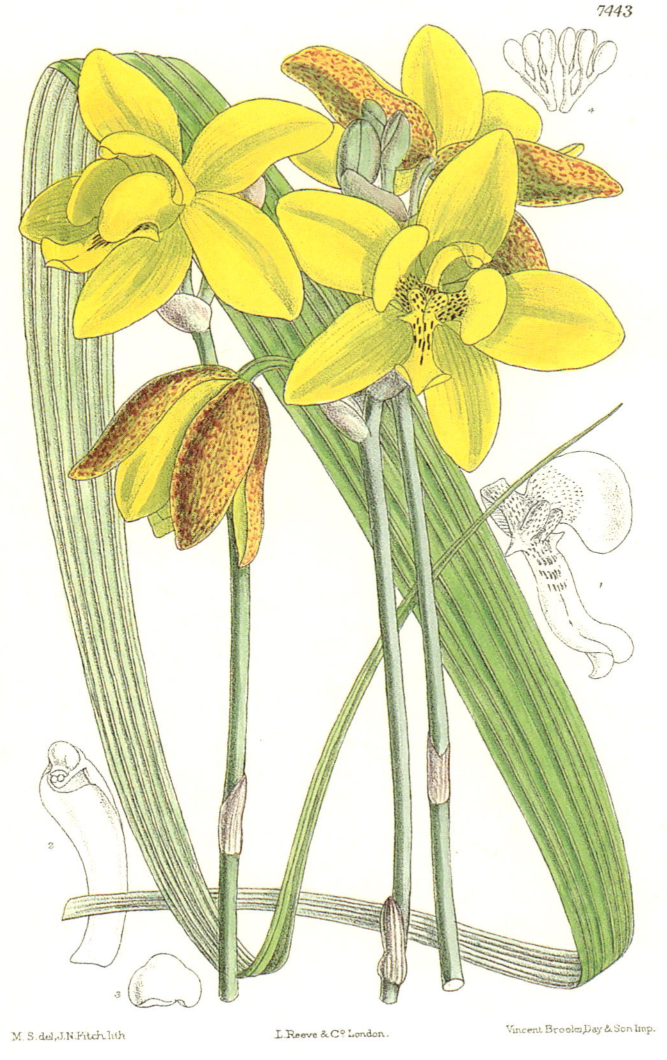

7443 Spathoglottis aurea Lindl.
7964 Spathoglottis hardingiana Parish & Rchb. f.

7366 Spathoglottis gracilis Rolfe ex Hook. f.
7060 Spathoglottis ixioides (Don) Lindl.

M.S. del. J.N. Fitch lith.

Vincent Brooks, Day & Son Imp.

L. Reeve & Cº London.

7013 Spathoglottis plicata Blume

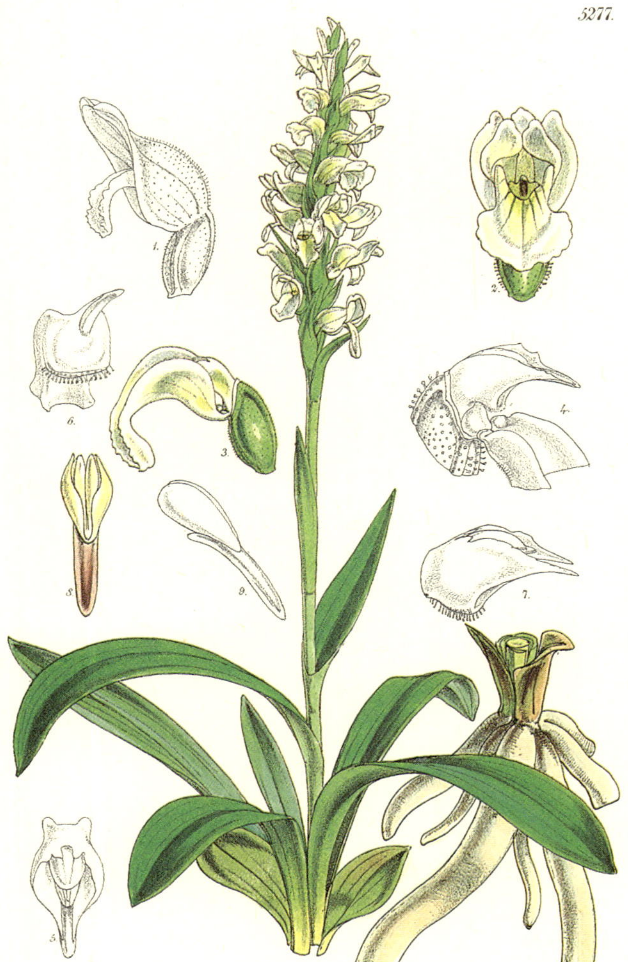

6354 Spathoglottis petri Rchb. f.
5277 Spiranthes cernua (L.) L.C. Rich.

1568 Spiranthes cernua (L.) L.C. Rich.
4885 Stanhopea ecornuta Lemaire

M.S.del J.N.Fitch lith. I. Reeve & C° London. Vincent Brooks, Day & Son L^td imp

8830 *Stanhopea costaricensis* Rchb. f.

M.S. del. J.N. Fitch lith.

Vincent Brooks, Day & Son Ltd imp

L. Reeve & Co. London.

8417 Stanhopea florida Rchb. f.

3359 Stanhopea grandiflora (Lodd.) Lindl.

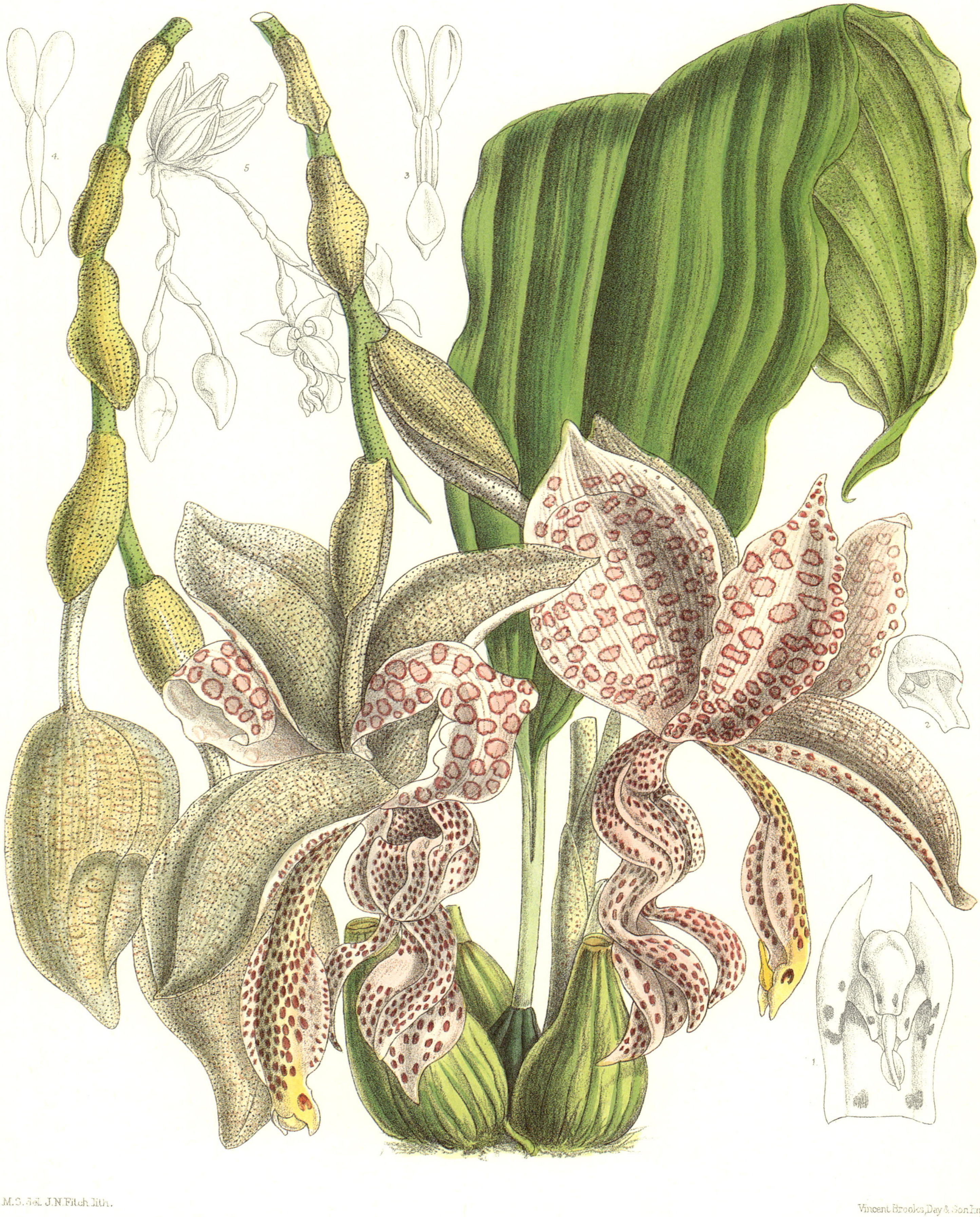

M.S. del. J.N. Fitch lith.

Vincent Brooks, Day & Son Imp.

L. Reeve & C° London.

7452 *Stanhopea haseloviana* Rchb. f.

4197 Stanhopea hernandezii (Kunth) Schltr.

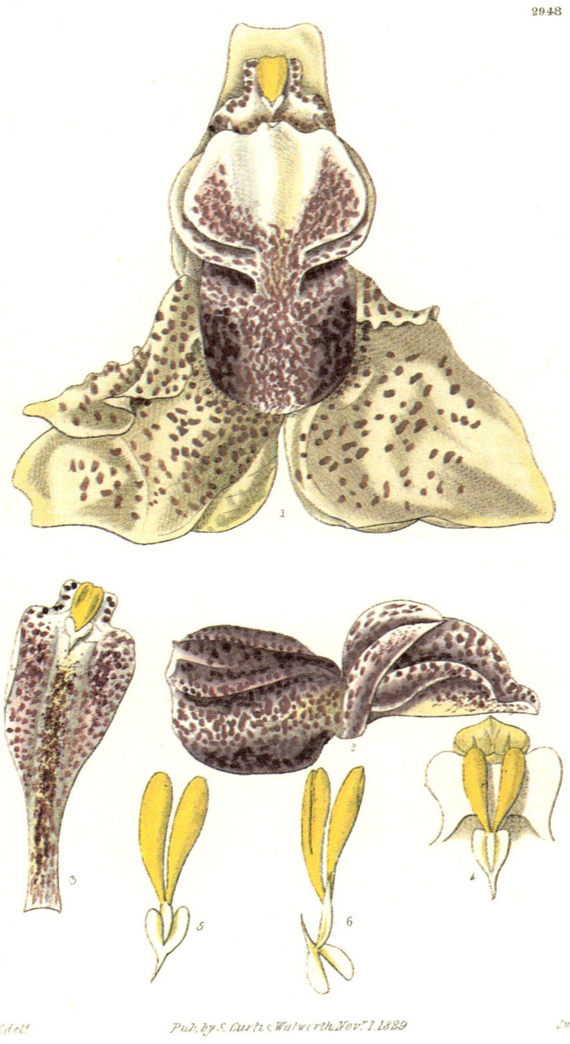

2948 Stanhopea insignis Frost ex Hook.
8517 Stanhopea jenishiana Kramer ex Rchb. f.

2949 Stanhopea insignis Frost ex Hook.

W. Fitch, del et lith.

Vincent Brooks, Imp.

5278 Stanhopea oculata (Lodd.) Lindl.

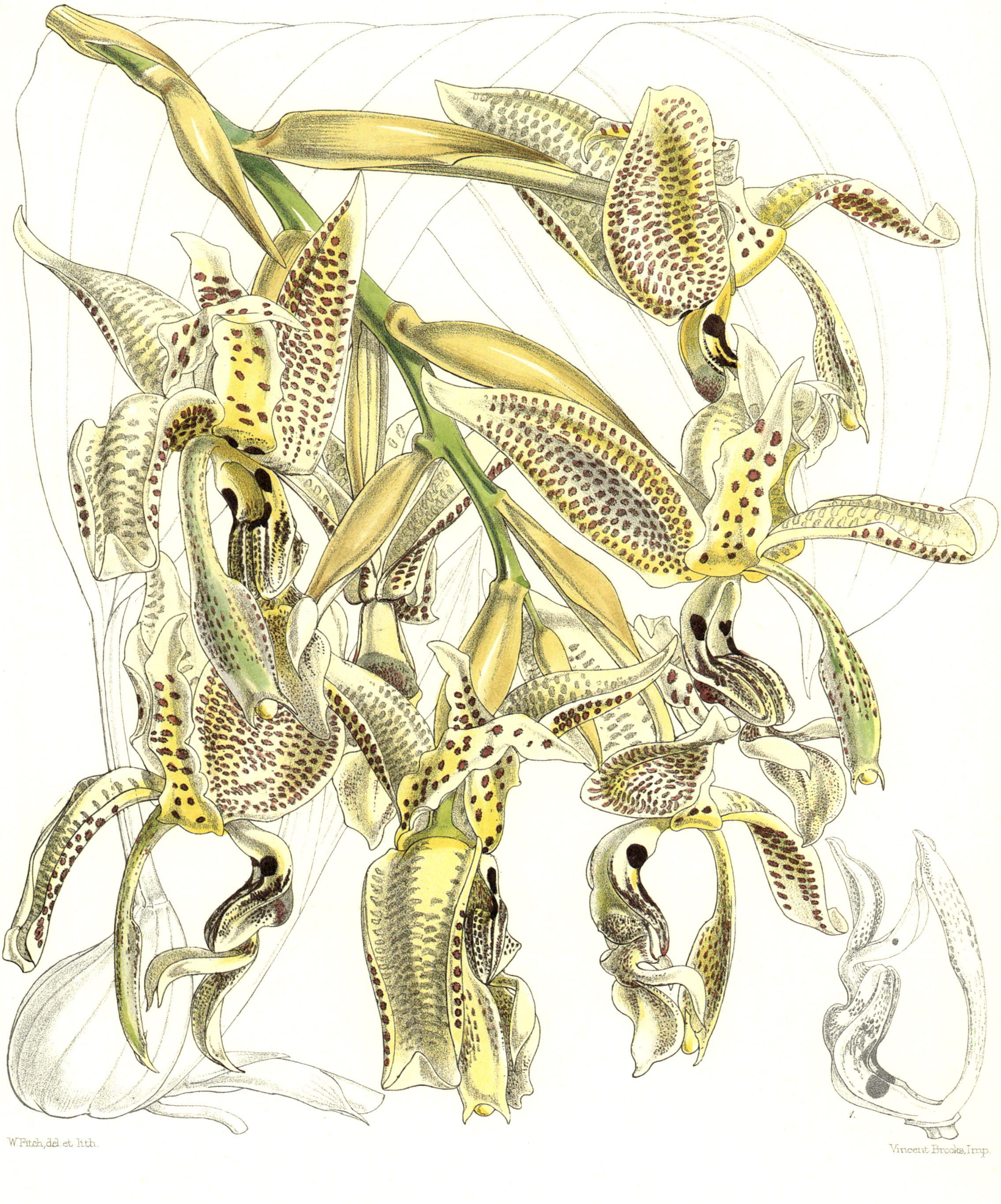

W Fitch, del et lith.

Vincent Brooks, Imp.

5300 Stanhopea oculata (Lodd.) Lindl.

M.S. del, J.N. Fitch lith.

Vincent Brooks Day & Son Ltd imp

L. Reeve & Co London

8507 *Stanhopea tricornis* Lindl.

W. Fitch, del. et lith.

Vincent Brooks, Imp.

5289 Stanhopea wardii Lodd. ex Lindl.

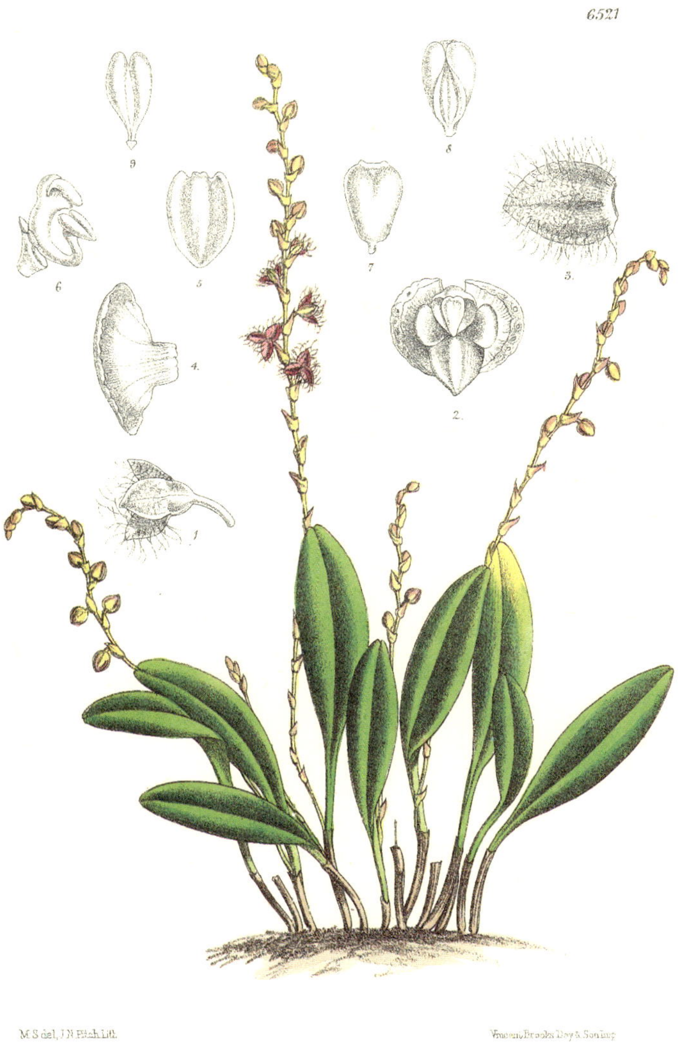

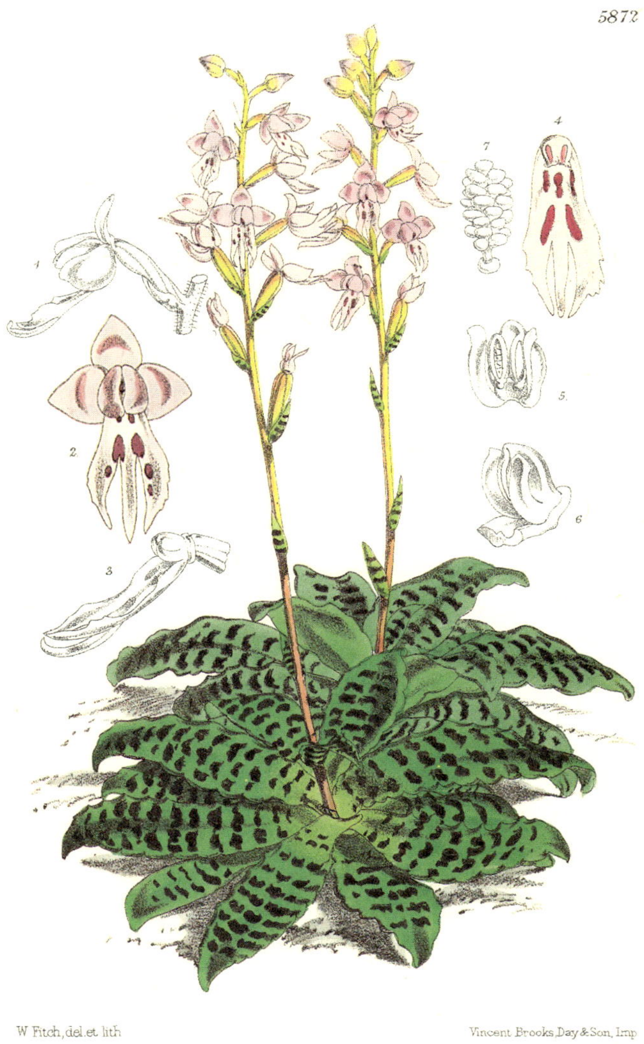

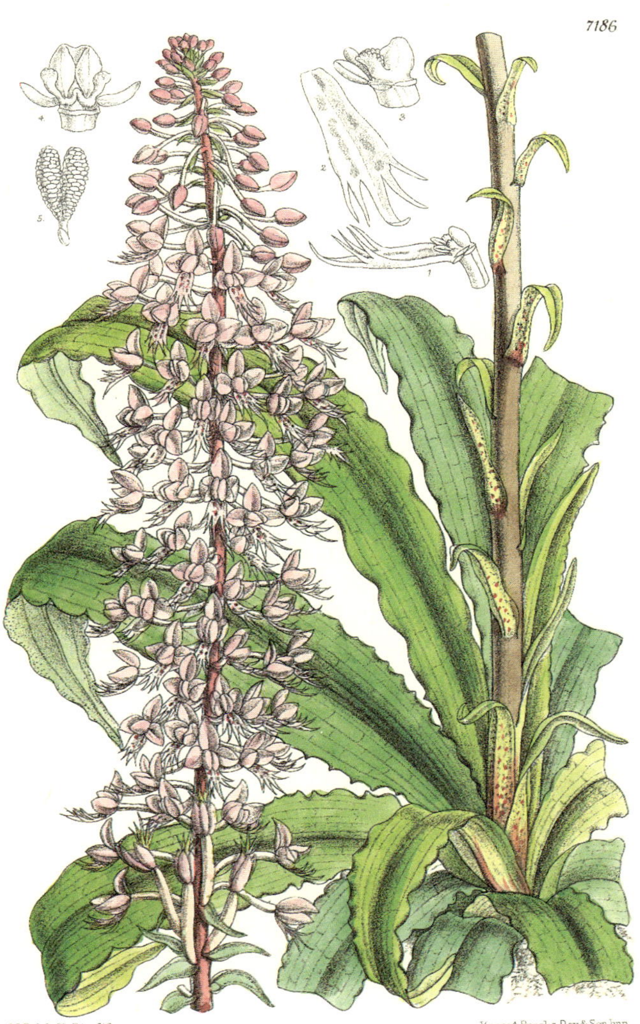

6521 Stelis eublepharis Rchb. f.
7186 Stenoglottis longifolia Hook. f.

5872 Stenoglottis fimbriata Lindl.
1374 Stenorrhynchos speciosum (Jacq.) Rich. ex Sprengel

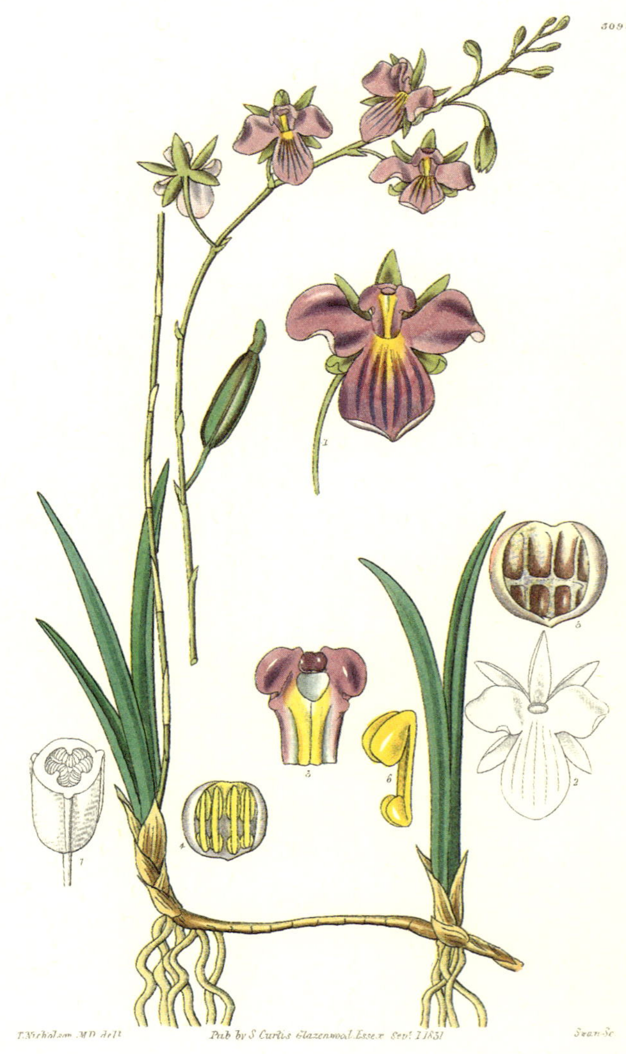

5630 Stereochilus erinaceus (Rchb. f.) Garay
5627 Symphyglossum sanguineum (Rchb. f.) Schltr.

6344 Sunipia paleacea (Lindl.) P. Hunt
3098 Tetramicra canaliculata (Aublet) Urban

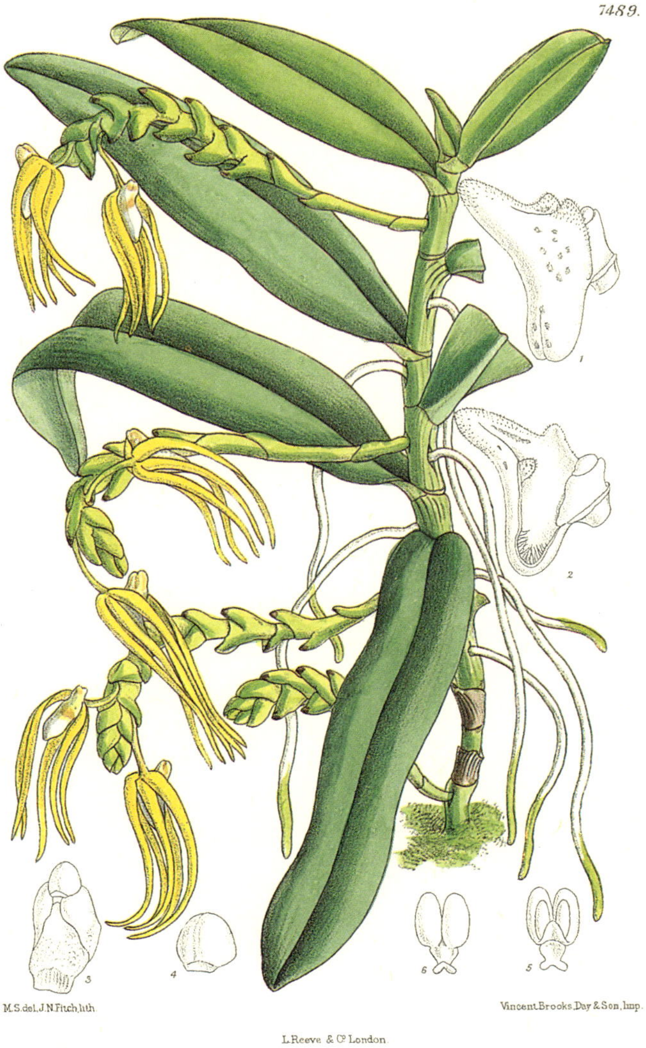

7754 Thrixspermum amplexicaulis (Blume) Rchb. f.
3991 Thunia alba (Lindl.) Rchb. f.

7489 Thrixspermum hainanense (Rolfe) Schltr.
5694 Thunia bensoniae Hook. f.

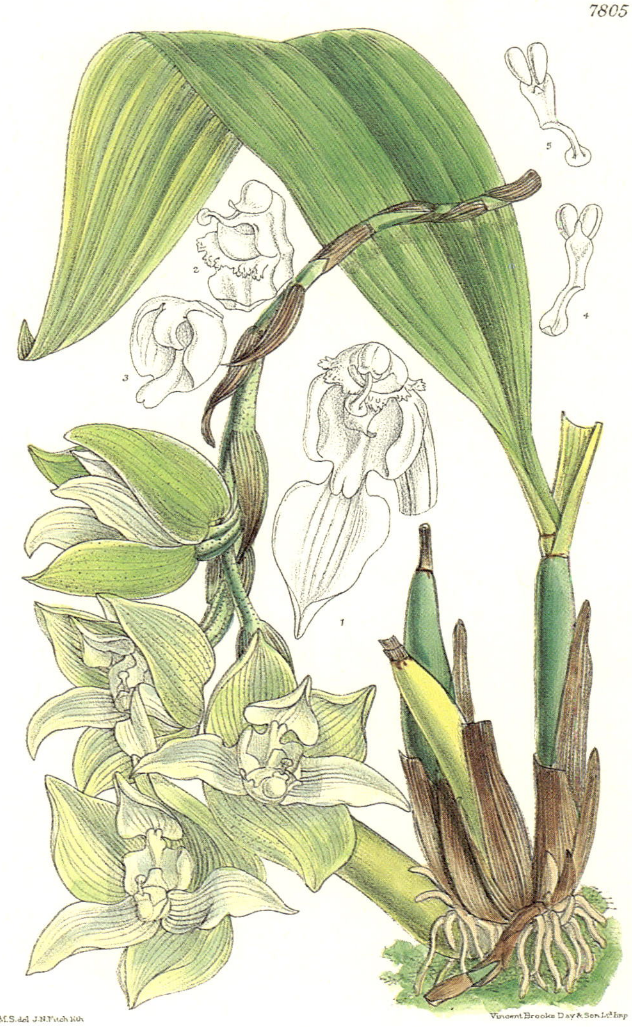

6820 Ticoglossum oerstedii (Rchb. f.) R. Rodriguez ex Halbinger
9150 Trias picta (Parish & Rchb. f.) Parish ex Hemsley

7805 Trevoria chloris F. Lehm.
5688 Trichocentrum albopurpureum Linden & Rchb. f. ex Rchb. f.

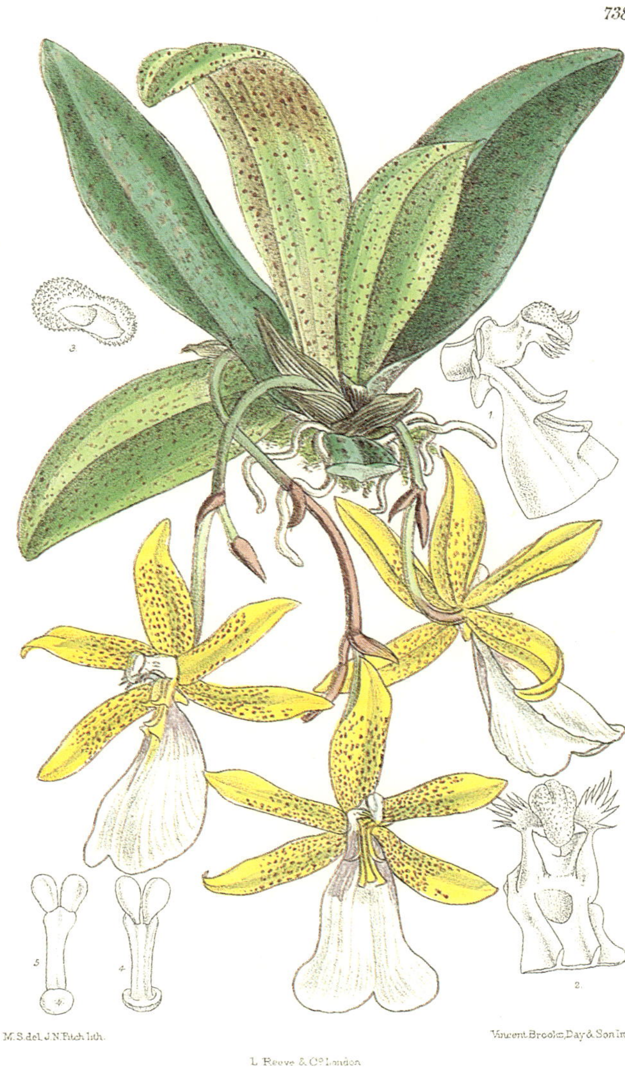

3969 Trichocentrum fuscum Lindl.
5035 Trichopilia fragrans (Lindl.) Rchb. f.

7380 Trichocentrum tigrinum Linden & Rchb. f.
5550 Trichopilia galeottiana A. Rich.

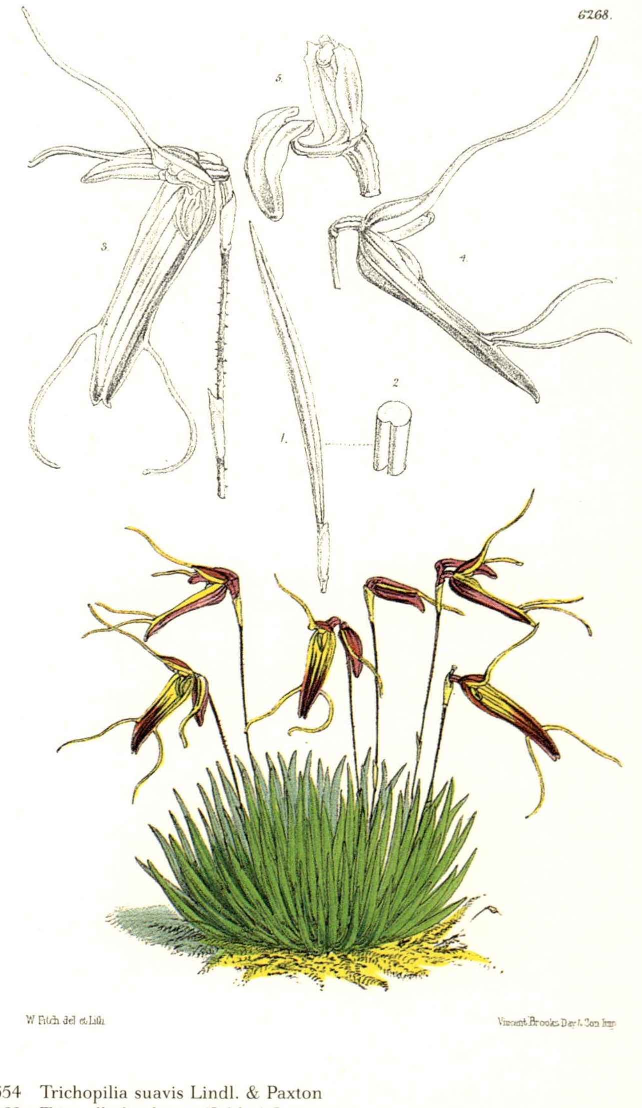

4857 Trichopilia marginata Henfrey
3739 Trichopilia tortilis Lindl.

4654 Trichopilia suavis Lindl. & Paxton
6268 Trisetella huebneri (Schltr.) Luer

7139 Vanda amesiana Rchb. f.
5834 Vanda coerulescens Griffith

5611 Vanda bensonii Bateman
3416 Vanda concolor Blume

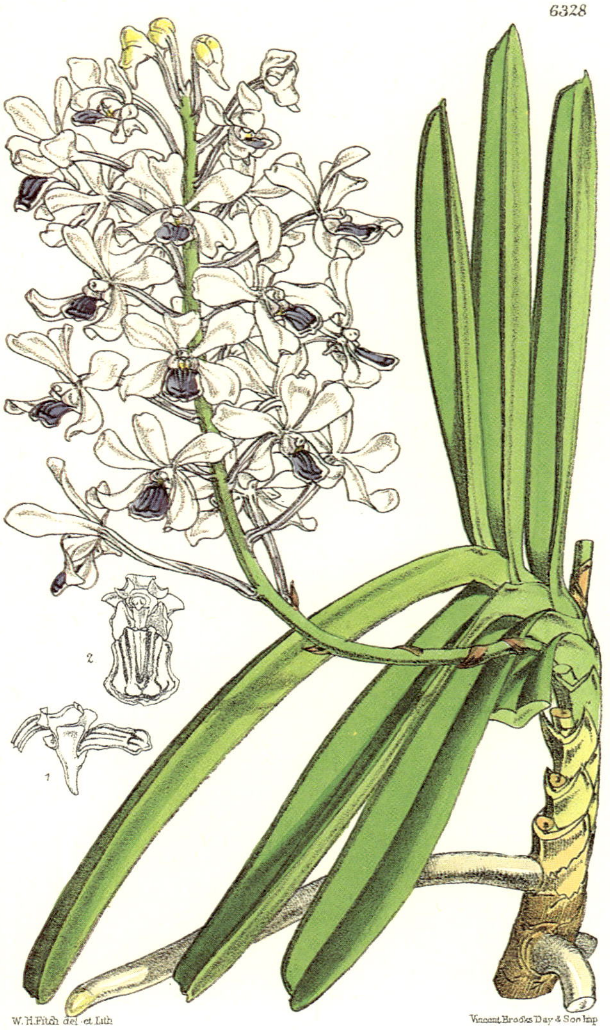

6328 Vanda confusa Rolfe
5811 Vanda denisoniana Benson & Rchb. f.

4304 Vanda cristata Lindl.
8709 Vanda luzonica Loher ex Rolfe

W. Fitch, del, et. lith.

5759 Vanda insignis Blume

6173 Vanda limbata Blume

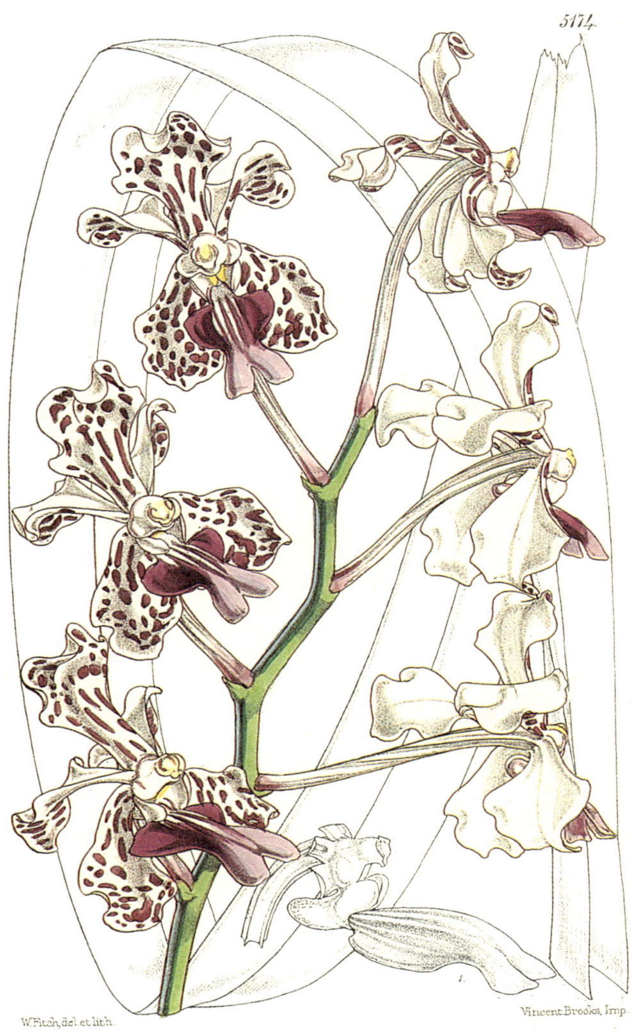

5138 Vanda parviflora Lindl.
4432 Vanda tricolor Lindl.

7968 Vanda pumila Hook. f.
5174 Vanda tricolor var. suavis (Lindl.) Rchb. f.

N 2245

2245 Vanda tessellata (Roxb.) Lodd. ex G. Don

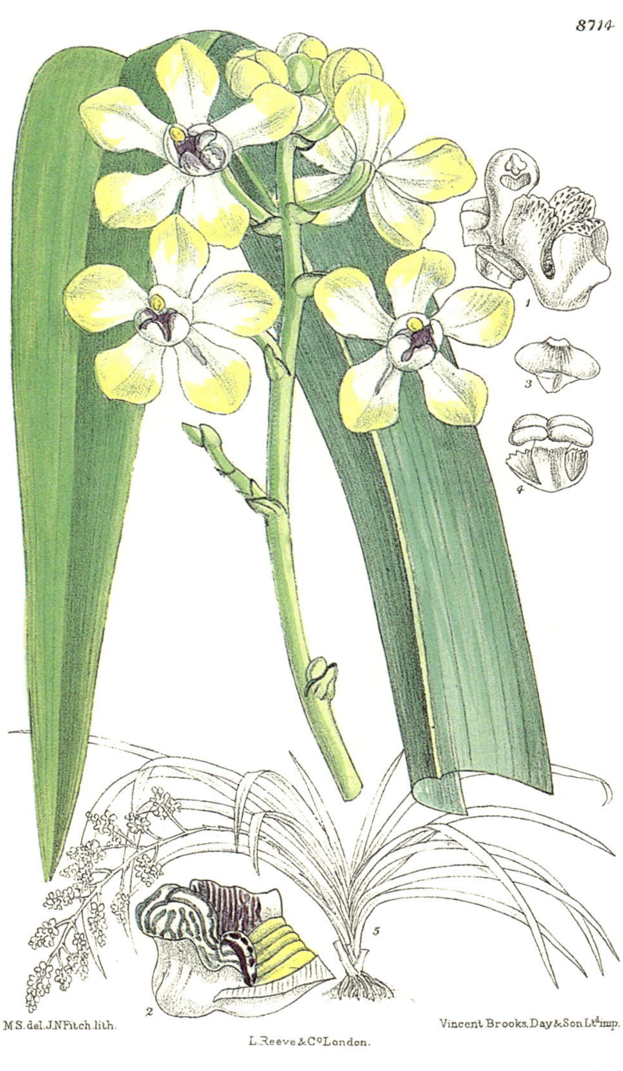

8109 Vanda watsonii Rolfe
8714 Vandopsis imthurnii (Rolfe) P. Hunt

5189 Vandopsis gigantea (Lindl.) Pfitzer
7996 Vanilla humblotii Rchb.f.

M. S. del, J. N. Fitch lith.

Vincent Brooks, Day & Son Imp.

L. Reeve & Co. London

7167 Vanilla planifolia Jackson

4235 Warrea warreana (Lodd. ex Lindl.) C. Schweinf.
2806 Xylobium pallidiflorum (Hook.) Nicholson

7085 Xylobium leontoglossum (Rchb. f.) Rolfe
3981 Xylobium palmifolium (Sw.) Benth. ex Fawcett

2955 Xylobium variegatum (Ruiz Lopez & Pavón) Garay & Dunsterv.

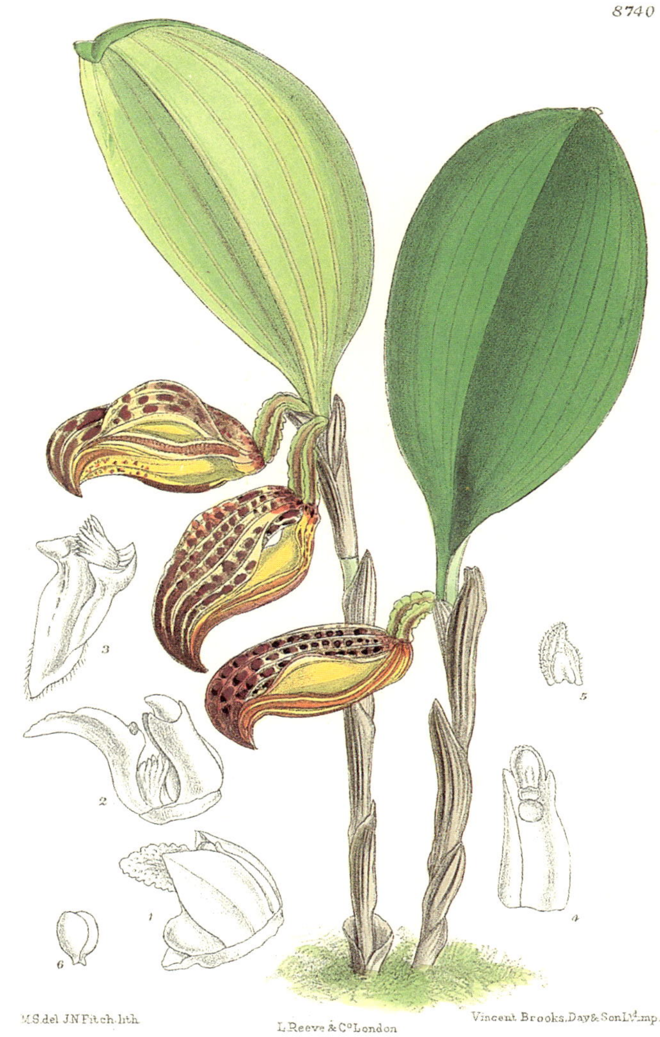

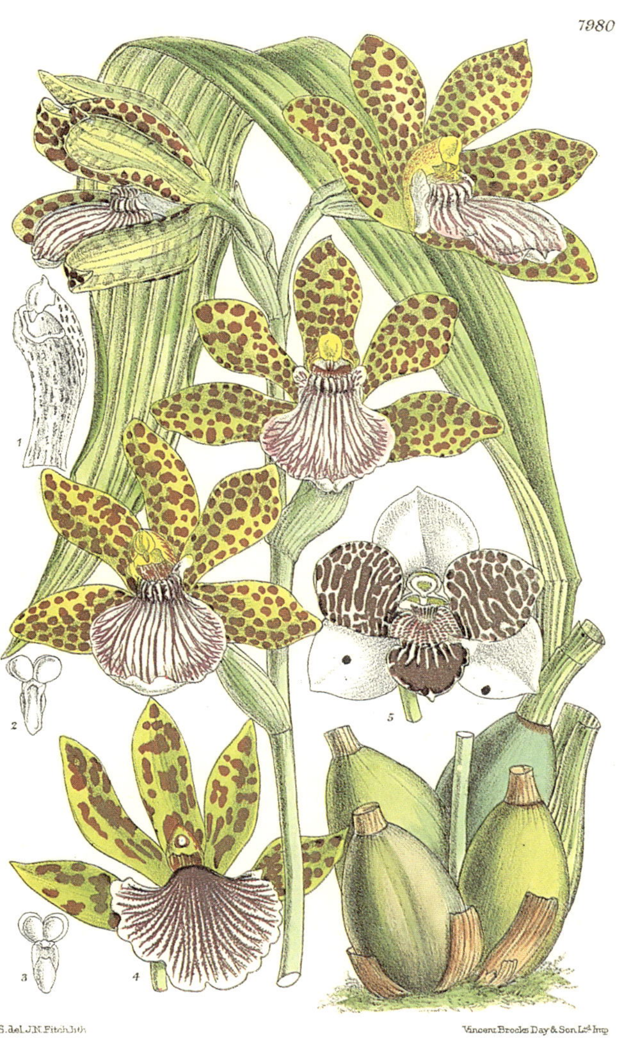

4164 *Zootrophion atropurpureum* (Lindl.) Luer
7980 × *Zygopabstia veitchii* (Rolfe) Dressler

8740 *Zootrophion dayanum* (Rchb. f.) Luer
3402 *Zygopetalum crinitum* Lodd.

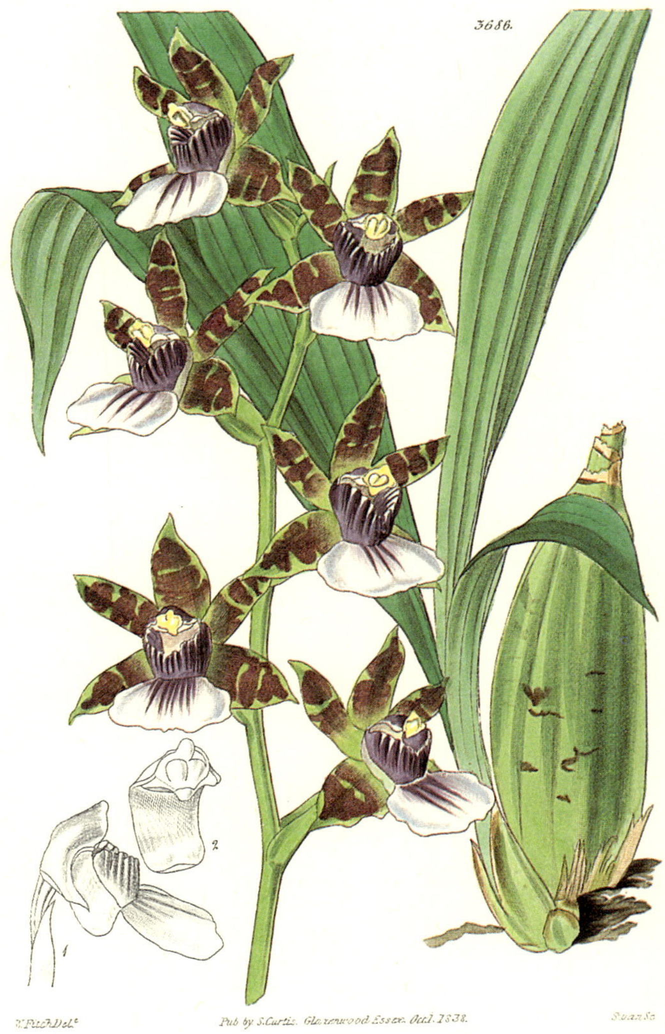

6240 Zygopetalum lamellosum (Rchb. f.) Rchb. f.

3686 Zygopetalum maxillare Lodd.

2748 Zygopetalum mackaii Hook.

W. J. H. delt. Pub. by S. Curtis, Walworth, May 1 1828. Swan Sc.

2819 *Zygosepalum labiosum* (L. C. Rich.) C. Schweinf.

Zeichenerklärung

im Katalog:
o = Überschrift in Curtis's Botanical Magazine
E = epiphytisch
L = lithophytisch
T = terrestrisch (geophytisch)
S = saprophytisch
BM = Curtis's Botanical Magazine

im Register:
* = falsch bestimmte Pflanze
ns = Neue Serie

Von diesem Werk wurde parallel zur vorliegenden deutschen auch eine englische Ausgabe hergestellt, in der sowohl die Tafeln als auch der Katalog und das Register sowie das Literaturverzeichnis identisch sind. Zugunsten eines gemeinschaftlichen Druckes sind die geographischen Vermerke im Katalog in der englischen Form angelegt; sie sind für den deutschsprachigen Leser ebenso verständlich.

KATALOG

Orchideentafeln aus Curtis's Botanical Magazine (1787–1948)

Acacallis cyanea Lindl., Fol. Orch. Acacallis 1, 1853
BM 8678
Venezuela, Colombia, Brazil, Amazonas – E
Aganisia cyanea (Lindl.) Rchb. f., Beitr. zur Orchideenk. 13: t. 4, 1869
Aganisia tricolor N. E. Br., Lindenia 1: 95 t. 45, 1885
Aganisia coerulea Rchb. f., Gard. Chron.: 720, 1886
Kochiophyton negrense Schltr. ex Cogn., Fl. Bras. 3, pt. 6: 574 t. 119, 1906
Kochiophyton coeruleum (Rchb. f.) Hoehne, Comm. Link. Telegr. Matto-Grosso, Annexo 5, pt. 1: 49 t. 39, 1910
Acacallis hoehnei Schltr., Orchis 12: 14, 1918
Acacallis coerulea Schltr., Orchis 12: 14, 1918
o **Acanthephippium javanicum** Blume, Bijdr. 352: 47, 1825
BM 4492
Malaya, Sumatra, Java, Borneo – T
Acineta barkeri (Bateman) Lindl., Bot. Reg. 29: Misc. p. 68, 1843
BM 4203
Mexico – E
o Peristeria barkeri Bateman, Orch. Mex. & Guat.: t. 8, 1838
o **Acineta chrysantha** (Morren) Lindl. & Paxton, Paxt. Flow. Gard. 1: 31, 1850
BM 7143
Costa Rica, Panama – up to 1600 m – E
Neippergia chrysantha Morren, Ann. Soc. Bot. 5: 375 t. 282, 1849
o Acineta densa Lindl. & Paxton, Paxt. Flow. Gard. 1: 91, 1850
Acineta warscewiczii Klotzsch, Allg. Gartenz. 20: 145, 1852
o **Acineta moorei** Rolfe, Bot. Mag.: t. 8392, 1911
BM 8392
S. America, Colombia? – E
Acineta superba (Kunth) Rchb. f. var. **fulva** (Hook.) Schltr., Orchis 2: 28, 1917
BM 4156
Panama, Venezuela, Colombia, Ecuador – E
Anguloa superba Kunth, Nov. Gen. Sp. 1: 343, t. 93, 1815
Peristeria humboldtii Lindl., Bot. Reg. n. s. 6: t. 18, 1843
Acineta humboldtii (Lindl.) Lindl., Bot. Reg.: Misc. 68, 1843
o Peristeria humboldtii var. fulva Hook., Bot. Mag. 71: t. 4156, 1845
Acineta fulva Klotzsch, Allg. Gartenz. 20: 146, 1852
Acineta sulcata Rchb. f., Gard. Chron.: 652, 1879
Acineta callosa Sander, Orch. Rev. 6: 287, 1898
Acineta colmanii hort. ex Gard. Chron.: 173, 1904
o **Ada aurantiaca** Lindl., Fol. Orch. Ada 1, Febr. 1853
BM 5435
Venezuela, Colombia – up to 2700 m – L
Brassia cinnabarina Linden ex Lindl. Fol. Orch. Brassia: 6, 1853
Mesospinidium cinnabarinum (Linden ex Lindl.) Rchb. f., Walp. Ann. 5: 858, 1860
Oncidium cinnabarinum (Linden ex Lindl.) Rchb. f., Walp. Ann. 6: 770, 1863
Mesospinidium aurantiacum (Lindl.) Rchb. f., Walp. Ann. 6: 857, 1864
Ada lehmannii Rolfe, Gard. Chron.: 34, 1891
Aerangis biloba (Lindl.) Schltr., Orchideen: 598, 1914
BM 4159
Senegal, Sierra Leone, Liberia, Ivory Coast, Ghana, Togo, Nigeria, W. Cameroun – E
Angraecum bilobum Lindl., F. T. A. 7: 138, 1840
o Angraecum apiculatum Hook., Bot. Mag.: t. 4159, 1845
Angraecum campyloplectron Rchb. f., Bonpl. 3: 226, 1855
Angorchis biloba (Lindl.) Kuntze, Rev. Gen. 2: 651, 1891
Angorchis campyloplectron (Rchb. f.) Kuntze, Rev. Gen. 2: 651, 1891
Listrostachys biloba (Lindl.) Kraenzlin, Engl. Bot. Jahrb. 22: 28, 1895
Rhaphidorhynchus bilobus (Lindl.) Finet, Bull. Soc. Bot. Fr. 54, 9: 32, 1907
Aerangis campyloplectron (Rchb. f.) Garay, Bot. Mus. Leafl. Harv. Univ. 23 (4): 157, 1972
o **Aerangis citrata** (Thouars) Schltr., Beih. Bot. Centralbl. 34: 2, 334, 1916
BM 5624
Madagascar – E
Angraecum citratum Thouars, Orch. Iles Afr.: t. 61, 1822
Aerobion citratum (Thouars) Sprengel, Syst. Veg. 3: 718, 1826
Angorchis citrata (Thouars) Kuntze, Rev. Gen. 2: 651, 1891
Rhaphidorhynchus citratus (Thouars) Finet, Bull. Soc. Bot. Fr. 54, Mém. 9: 35, 1897
o **Aerangis fastuosa** (Rchb. f.) Schltr., Orchis: 598, 1914
BM 7204
Madagascar – E
Angraecum fastuosum Rchb. f., Gard. Chron. 2: 748, 1881
Angorchis fastuosa (Rchb. f.) Kuntze, Rev. Gen. 2: 651, 1891
Rhaphidorynchus fastuosus (Rchb. f.) Finet, Bull. Soc. Bot. Fr. 54, Mém. 9: 38, 1907
Aerangis kotschyana (Rchb. f.) Schltr., Beih. Bot. Centralbl. 36 (2): 118, 1918
BM 7442
Guinea, Sierra Leone, N. Nigeria, Sudan, Uganda, Kenya, Tanzania, Zaire, Zambia, Mozambique – E
Angraecum kotschyanum Rchb. f., F. T. A. 7: 137, 1864
Angraecum grantii Batemann ex Baker, Trans. Linn. Soc. 29: 153, 1873
o Angraecum kotschyi Rchb. f., Gard. Chron. 2: 456, 1880
Aerangis kotschyi (Rchb. f.) Rchb. f., Otia Bot. Hamb.: 78, 1881
Angraecum semipedale Rendle, J. Linn. Soc. 30: 389, 1895
Rhaphidorhynchus kotschyi (Rchb. f.) Finet, Bull. Soc. Bot. Fr. 9: 36, 1907
Aerangis grantii (Bateman ex Baker) Schltr., Beih. Bot. Centralbl. 36 (2): 116, 1918
Aerangis modesta (Hook. f.) Schltr., Orchis: 600, 1914
BM 6693
Madagascar – 100–1200 m – E
o Angraecum modestum Hook. f., Bot. Mag.: t. 6693, (1883)
Angraecum sanderianum Rchb. f., Gard. Chron. 1: 168, 1888
Angorchis modesta (Hook. f.) Kuntze, Rev. Gen. 2: 651, 1891
Rhaphidorhynchus modestus (Hook. f.) Finet, Bull. Soc. Bot. Fr. 54, Mém. 9: 37 (1), 1907
o **Aeranthes arachnites** (Thouars) Lindl., Bot. Reg.: t. 817, 1824
BM 6034
Madagascar, Réunion – E
Dendrobium arachnites Thouars, Orch. Iles Afr.: t. 87, 1822
o **Aerides crispa** Lindl., Wall. Cat.: 7319, 1832
BM 4427
E. India – E
Aerides brookei Bateman, Bot. Reg.: Misc. 116, 1841
Aerides lindleyana Wight., Ic. Pl. Ind. Or.: 1677, 1851
o **Aerides emericii** Rchb. f., Gard. Chron. 18: 586, 1882
BM 6728
Andaman Is. – E
o **Aerides jarckiana** Schltr., Orchis 9: 53, 1915
BM 9274
Philippines (Luzon) – E
Aerides huttonii (Hook. f.) Veitch, Man. Orch. Pl. 7: 70, 1891
BM 5681
Java, Celebes, Malay Archipelago – E
Aerides thibautiana Rchb. f., Gard. Chron.: 100, 1866
o Saccolabium huttonii Hook. f., Bot. Mag.: t. 5681, 1867
Aerides multiflora Roxb., Corom. Pl. 3: 63 t. 271, 1820
BM 4049
Trop. Himalaya, Sikkim, Assam, Thailand, Kampuchea, Laos, Vietnam, Malaya – E
o Aerides affinis Lindl. ex Wall. Cat.: No. 7316, 1832
Aerides rosea Lodd. ex Paxton, Flow. Gard. 2: 109 t. 60, 1851
Aerides trigona Klotzsch, Allg. Gartenz.: 177, 1855

Aerides lobbii hort. ex Ill. Hort.: t. 559, 1868
Aerides veitchii hort. ex Morren, Belg. Hort.: 291, 1876
Cleisostoma vacherotiana Guillaumin, Bull. Mus. Paris 2 s. 19, 4: 357, 1947
o **Aerides odorata** Lour., Fl. Cochinch.: 525, 1790
BM 4139
India, Nepal, Sikkim, Burma, Thailand, China, Kampuchea, Laos, Vietnam, Malaya, Sumatra, Java, Borneo, Celebes, Philippines - E
Epidendrum aerides Raeusch, Nom. ed. 3: 265, 1797
Limodorum latifolium Thunb. ex Sw., Schrad. J. 2: 234, 1799
Epidendrum odoratum Poiret, Encycl. Suppl. 1: 385, 1811
Aerides odora Salisb., Trans. Hort. Soc. 1: 295, 1812
Aerides cornuta Roxb., Hort. Beng.: 63, 1814
Orxera cornuta Raf., Fl. Tellur. 4: 37, 1836
Aerides virens Lindl., Bot. Reg. 29: Misc. 41, 1843
Aerides suaveolens Blume, Rumph. 4: 53 & 55, 1848 (non Roxb., 1832)
Aerides suavissima Lindl., J. Hort. Soc. 4: 264, 1849
Aerides flavida Lindl., Paxt. Flow. Gard. 2: 101, 1851
Aerides reichenbachii Lindl. ex Rchb. f. Koch & Fint., Wochensschr. 1: 61, 1858
Aerides jucunda Rchb. f., Hamb. Gartenz. 16: 281, 1860
Aerides nobilis Warner, Sel. Orch.: t. 11, 1862
Polytoma odorifera Lour. ex Gomes, Mem. Acad. Sci. Lisb. n. s. 4, 1: 30, 1868
Aerides rohaniana Rchb. f., Gard. Chron.: 206, 1884
Aerides wilsoniana hort. ex Gard. Chron.: 705, 1885
Aerides ballentiniana Rchb. f., Gard. Chron.: 198, 1885
Aerides ortgiesiana Rchb. f., Gard. Chron.: 501, 1885
Aerides micholitzii Rolfe, Orch. Rev. 12: 181, 1904
Ancistrochilus thomsonianus (Rchb. f.) Rolfe, F. T. A. 7: 44, 1897
BM 6471
S. Nigeria, W. Cameroun - E
o Pachystoma thomsonianum Rchb. f., Gard. Chron.: 582, 1879
Ipsea thomsoniana (Rchb. f.) Pfitzer, Nat. Pflanzf. 2, 6: 154, 1888
o **Angraecum distichum** Lindl., Bot. Reg. 21: t. 1781, 1836
BM 4145
Guinea, Sierra Leone, Liberia, Ivory Coast, Ghana, Bénin, Nigeria, W. Cameroun - E
Mystacidium distichum (Lindl.) Pfitzer, F. T. A. 7: 175, 1889
o **Angraecum eburneum** Bory, Voy. 1: 359 t. 19, 1804
BM 4761, BM 5170
E. Africa, Madagascar, Bourbon, Mascarene, Comoros, Seychelles, Aldabra Is. - E, L, T
Limodorum eburneum (Bory) Willd., Sp. Pl. 4: 125, 1805
Angraecum superbum Thouars, Orch. Afr.: t. 62 & 64, 1822
Aerobion superbum (Thouars) Sprengel, Syst. 3: 718, 1826
Angraecum virens Lindl., Bot. Reg.: sub. t. 19, 1847
Angraecum brongniartianum Rchb. f. ex Linden, Pescatorea 1: t. 16, 1854
o Angraecum eburnum var. virens Hook., Bot. Mag.: t. 5170, 1860
Angorchis eburnea (Bory) Kuntze, Rev. Gen.: 651, 1891
Angraecum comorense Kraenzlin, Engl. Bot. Jahrb. 17: 60, 1893
Angraecum gyriamae Rendle, J. Linn. Soc. 30: 388, 1895
Angraecum voeltzkowianum Kraenzlin, Engl. Bot. Jahrb. 36: 116, 1905
o **Angraecum eichlerianum** Kraenzlin, Gartenz. 1: 434 fig. 102, 1882
BM 7813
S. Nigeria, W. Cameroun, Gabon, Zaire, Angola - E
o **Angraecum infundibulare** Lindl., J. Linn. Soc. 6: 136, 1862
BM 8153
S. Nigeria, W. Cameroun, Zaire, Ethiopia, Uganda - E
Mystacidium infundibulare (Lindl.) Rolfe, F. T. A. 7: 170, 1897
Angraecum ramosum Thouars, Orch. Iles Afr.: t. 59, 1822
BM 7061
Madagascar - E
o Angraecum germinyanum Hook. f., Bot. Mag.: t. 7061, 1889
Mystacidium germinyanum (Hook. f.) Rolfe, Orch. Rev.: 47, 1904
Macroplectrum ramosum (Thouars) Finet, Bull. Soc. Bot. Fr. 54, Mém. 9: 20 t. 6, 1907
o **Angraecum scottianum** Rchb. f., Gard. Chron.: 556, 1878
BM 6723
Comoro Is. - 350-600 m - E
Angraecum reichenbachianum Kraenzlin, Xen. Orch. 3: 74 t. 239, 1890
Angorchis scottiana (Rchb. f.) Kuntze, Rev. Gen.: 652, 1891
o **Angraecum sesquipedale** Thouars, Orch. Iles Afr.: t. 66-67, 1822
BM 5113
E. Madagascar - E, L
Aeranthes sesquipedalis (Thouars) Lindl., Bot. Reg.: sub. t. 817, 1824
Macroplectrum sesquipedale (Thouars) Pfitzer, Nat. Pflanzenf. II, 6: 214, 1889
Angorchis sesquipedalis (Thouars) Kuntze, Rev. Gen. 2: 652, 1891
Mystacidium sesquipedale (Thouars) Rolfe, Orch. Rev.: 47, 1904
o **Anguloa brevilabris** Rolfe, Orch. Rev. 23: 292, 1915
BM 9381
Venezuela, Colombia, Ecuador - E
Anguloa ruckeri (hort.) Lindl., Bot. Reg.: t. 41, 1846
Anguloa sagittata Summerh., Kew Bull. 36: 102, 1931
Anguloa brevilabris Rolfe var. **sanguinea** Lindl., Gard. Chron.: 271, 1854
BM 5384
Venezuela, Colombia, Bolivia - E
o Anguloa ruckeri var. sanguinea Lindl., Gard. Chron.: 271, 1854
Anguloa purpurea Linden, Ill. Hort. 28: 120 t. 427, 1881
o **Anguloa cliftonii** Rolfe, Kew Bull.: 160, 1910
BM 8700
Colombia - T
o **Anguloa clowesii** Lindl., Bot. Reg. 30: Misc. p. 26, 1830
BM 4313
Venezuela, Colombia - E
Anguloa clowesii var. flava Rchb. f., Walp. Ann. 1: 784, 1849
Anguloa clowesiana Williams, Orch. Grow. Man.: 33, 1852
Anguloa clowesii var. macrantha Williams, Orch. Grow. Man. ed. 2.: 54, 1862
Anguloa clowesii var. eburnea Veitch, Man. Orch. 9: 100, 1893
o **Anguloa uniflora** Ruiz Lopez & Pavón, Syst. Veg. Fl. Peruv. et Chil. 1: 228, 1798
BM 4807
Colombia, Ecuador, Peru, Bolivia - E, T
Anguloa virginalis Lindl., Gard. Chron.: 392, 1851
Anguloa eburnea Williams, Orch. Grow. Man. ed. 3: 67, 1868
Anguloa turneri Williams, Orch. Grow. Man. ed. 6: 133, 1885
o **Ania hookeriana** (King & Pantl.) Tang & Wang ex Summerh., Bot. Mag.: t. 9553, 1939
BM 9553
Sikkim, N. Thailand - 800-1000 m - T
Tainia hookeriana King & Pantl., J. As. Soc. Beng. 64: pt. 2: 336, 1895
Ascotaina hookeriana (King & Pantl.) Ridley, Mat. Fl. Mal. Pen. Pt. 1: 116, 1907
o **Ania penangiana** (Hook. f.) Summerh., Bot. Mag.: sub. t. 7563, 1897
BM 7563
Malaya, Thailand - T
Tainia penangiana Hook. f., Fl. Brit. Ind. 5: 820, 1890
Ania viridifusca (Hook.) Tang & Wang ex Summerh., Bot. Mag.: t. 9553, 1939
BM 4669
Burma, S. China, Thailand - T
o Calanthe viridifusca Hook., Bot. Mag.: t. 4669, 1852
Tainia viridifusca (Hook.) Benth. & Hook. f., Gen. Pl. 3: 515, 1880
Calanthe eberhardtii Gagnepain, Bull. Soc. Bot. Fr. 79: 162, 1932
Anneliesia candida (Lindl.) Brieger & Lueckel, Die Orchidee 34 (4): 130, 1983
BM 3793
Brazil - E
Miltonia candida Lindl., Bot. Reg. 24: Misc. 29, 1838
o Miltonia candida var. flavescens Hook., Bot. Mag.: t. 3793, 1840
Oncidium candidum (Lindl.) Beer, Prakt. Stud. Orch.: 283, 1854 (nomen illeg.)
Oncidium candidum (Lindl.) Rchb. f., Walp. Ann. 6: 763, 1863 (nomen illeg.)
Anoectochilus lanceolatus Lindl., Gen. Sp. Orch. Pl.: 499, 1840
BM 8733
Sikkim, Assam, China, Vietnam - 1500-2000 m - T
Anoectochilus luteus Lindl., J. Linn. Soc. 1: 179, 1857
o Odontochilus lanceolatus (Lindl.) Blume, Coll. Orch. Arch. Ind.: 80 t. 29 fig. 2 & t. 36 A, 1858
Anoectochilus flavus Benth. & Hook. f., Gen. Pl. 3: 598, 1883
Odontochilus flavus Benth. & Hook. f., Gen. Pl. 3: 598 sphalm. pro. luteo, 1883
Anoectochilus grandiflorus auct. non Lindl.: Seidenfaden & Smitinand: 88 fig. 67, 1959
Anoectochilus clarkei auct. non (Hook. f.) Seidenf. & Smitin., Seidenfaden & Smitinand: 88, 1959
Anoectochilus reinwardtii Blume, Fl. Java Orch. 40: t. 12, 1858
BM 4123
Thailand, Java, Sumatra, Ambon - T
o (Anoectochilus setaceus Blume, Bijdr. 1: 412 fig. 135, 1825, misidentified)
o **Anoectochilus roxburghii** (Wallich) Lindl., Gen. Sp. Orch. Pl.: 499, 1840
BM 9529
India, China, Vietnam, Laos, Thailand - T
Chrysobaphus roxburghii Wallich, Tent. Fl. Nepal. 37: fig. 27, 1826

Anoectochilus lobbianus Planchon, Fl. des Serres s. 1, 5: 519, 1849
Anoectochilus setaceus Schltr., Orchideen: fig. 23-24, 1915 (non Blume)
Anoectochilus siamensis auct. non Schltr., Seidenfaden & Smitinand: fig. 68, 1959
Anoectochilus setaceus Blume, Bijdr. 412: fig. 135, 1825
BM 5208
India, Malaysia, Sumatra, Java, Ambon - up to 1100 m - T
Anoectochilus regalis Blume, Orch. Arch. Ind.: 46, 1858
o Anoectochilus setaceus var. inornatus Hook., Bot. Mag.: t. 5208, 1860
o **Ansellia africana** Lindl., Bot. Reg.: sub. t. 12, 1844
BM 4965
Trop. S.E. Centr. Africa, Liberia, Ivory Coast, Ghana, Nigeria, F. Po, E. Cameroun, Gabon, Zaire, Angola, Uganda, Kenya, Zimbabwe, Mozambique, S. Africa (Natal) - up to 2200 m - E, L
o Ansellia gigantea Rchb.f., Linnaea 20: 673, 1874
Ansellia africana var. nilotica Baker, Trans. Linn. Soc. 29: 154, 1875
Ansellia nilotica (Baker) N.E. Br., Lindenia 2: 36, 1886
Ansellia congoensis Rodigas, Lindenia 2: 36, 1886
Ansellia confusa N.E. Br., Lindenia 2: 36, 1886
Ansellia humilis Bulliard, Cat.: 3, 1891
Ansellia gigantea var. nilotica (Baker) Summerh., Kew Bull.: 462, 1937
Apatostelis ciliaris (Lindl.) Garay, Bot. Mus. Leafl. Harv. Univ. 27: 188, 1979
BM 3975
Mexico, Belize, Guatemala, Honduras, Nicaragua, Costa Rica - up to 1100 m - E
Stelis ciliaris Lindl., Comp. Bot. Mag. 2: 353, 1837
o Stelis atropurpurea Hook., Bot. Mag.: t. 3975, 1842
Stelis micrantha var. atropurpurea (Hook.) Josst., Orchid.: 38, 1851
Stelis confusa Schltr., Beih. Bot. Centralbl. 36 (2): 386, 1918
Stelis jimenezii Schltr., Beih. Bot. Centralbl. 36 (2): 389, 1918
Arachnis annamensis (Rolfe) J. J. Smith, Nat. Tijds. Ned. Ind. 72: 73, 1912
BM 8062
Laos - T
o Arachnanthe annamensis Rolfe, Gard. Chron.: 391, 1905
o **Arethusa bulbosa** L., Sp. Pl. 2: 950, 1753
BM 2204
Canada, USA (Virginia, N. Carolina) - T
Arethusa bulbosa L. forma albiflora Rand & Redf., Fl. Mt. Desert: 152, 1894
Arethusa bulbosa L. forma subcaerulea Rand & Redf., Fl. Mt. Desert: 152, 1894
Arpohyllum giganteum Hartweg ex Lindl., Ann. & Mag. Nat. Hist. 4: 384, 1840
BM 6022
Mexico, Guatemala, El Salvador, Honduras, Costa Rica, Nicaragua, Jamaica, Colombia, Venezuela - 1400-1500 m - E
o Arpophyllum spicatum Llave & Lex., Nov. Veg. Descr. 2, Orch. Opusc.: 20, 1825
Arpophyllum cardinale Lindl. ex Rchb.f., Bonpl. 2: 282, 1854
Arpophyllum squarrosum hort., Donat. Lubbers. Cat. Pl. Rar. San Donato: 15, 1880
Arpophyllum jamaicense Schltr., Fedde Rep. 16: 443, 1920
Arpophyllum stenostachyum Schltr., Fedde Rep. 19: 32, 1923
Arundina graminifolia (D. Don) Hochr., Bull. N.Y. Bot. Gard. 6: 270, 1910
BM 7284
Sri Lanka, India, Nepal, China, Thailand, Malaysia, Sumatra, Java, Borneo, Taiwan - T
Bletia graminifolia D. Don, Prodr. Fl. Nepal.: 29, 1825
Arundina speciosa Blume, Bijdr. 8: 401, 1825
Arundina chinensis Blume, Bijdr. 8: 402, 1825
o Arundina bambusifolia Lindl., Gen. Sp. Orch. Pl.: 125, 1831
Arundina minor Lindl., Gen. Sp. Orch. Pl.: 125, 1831
Cymbidium bambusifolium (Lindl.) Roxb., Fl. Ind. 3: 460, 1832
Arundina densa Lindl., Bot. Reg. 28: Misc. 25, 1842
Cymbidium meyenii Schauer, Nov. Act. Nat. Cur. 14: Suppl. 1: 433, 1843
Arundina affinis Griffith, Notul. 3: 330, 1851
Arundina meyenii (Schauer) Rchb.f., Linnaea 25: 227, 1852
Arundina philippii Rchb.f., Linnaea 25: 227, 1852
Arundina pulchella Teijsm. & Binnend., Nederl. Kruidk. Arch. 3: 400, 1855
Arundina pulchra Miq., J. Bot. Neerl. 1: 30, 1861
Arundina densiflora Hook.f., Fl. Brit. Ind. 5: 857, 1890
Limodorum graminifolium (D. Don) Ham. ex Hook.f., Fl. Brit. Ind. 5: 857, 1890
Donacopsis laotica Gagnepain, Bull. Mus. Hist. Nat. Paris s. 2, 4: 593, 1932 p.pt.
o **Asarca sinuata** (Lindl.) Lindl., Gen. Sp. Orch. Pl.: 408, 1840
BM 7909
Chili - T
Chloraea longibracteata Lindl., Brand. Quart. J. Roy. Inst. n.s. 1: 48, 1827
Gavilea sinuata Lindl. var. a, Gen. Sp. Orch. Pl.: 408, 1840
Asarca berteri Rchb.f., Linnaea 15: 377, 1847
Ascocentrum ampullaceum (Roxb.) Schltr., Fedde Rep. Beih. 1: 975, 1913
BM 5595
N.E. India, Burma, Thailand - 300-900 m - E
Aerides ampullacea Roxb., Fl. Ind. 3: 476, 1832
o Saccolabium ampullaceum (Roxb.) Lindl., Wall. Cat.: 7307, 1832
Cymbidium rubrum Buch.-Ham. ex Wallich, Wall. Cat.: 7307, 1832
Saccolabium rubrum (Buch.-Ham. ex Wallich) Lindl., Gen. Sp. Orch. Pl.: 222, 1833
Ascocentrum curvifolium (Lindl.) Schltr., Fedde Rep. Beih. 1: 975, 1913
BM 5326
N.E. India, Nepal, Assam, Burma, Thailand, Kampuchea, Laos, Vietnam - E
Saccolabium curvifolium Lindl., Gen. Sp. Orch. Pl.: 222, 1833
o Saccolabium miniatum Hook., Bot. Mag.: t. 5326, 1862 (non Lindl.)
Gastrochilus curvifolius (Lindl.) Kuntze, Rev. Gen., 1891
Ascocentrum hendersonianum (Rchb.f.) Schltr., Orchideen: 576, 1914
BM 6222
Borneo - E
o Saccolabium hendersonianum Rchb.f., Gard. Chron.: 356, 1875
Ascocentrum rubescens (Rolfe) P. Hunt, Kew Bull.: 98, 1977
BM 8121
S. Vietnam (Annam) - E
o Saccolabium rubescens Rolfe, Kew Bull.: 114, 1906
Aerides rubescens (Rolfe) Schltr., Orchis 9: 29, 1915
o **Aspasia epidendroides** Lindl., Hook. J. Bot. 1: 6, 1843
BM 3962
Guatemala, Honduras, Nicaragua, El Salvador, Costa Rica, Panama, Colombia - up to 1000 m - E, L
Aspasia fragrans Klotzsch, Ind. Sem. Hort. Bot. Berol.: 12, 1852
Odontoglossum aspasia Rchb.f., Walp. Ann. 6: 851, 1861
o **Aspasia variegata** Lindl., Bot. Reg. 22: t. 1907, 1836
BM 3679
Venezuela, Trinidad, Guyana, Surinam, Brazil - E, L
Aspasia lunata Kraenzlin, Bot. Reg. 22: t. 1907, 1836 (non Lindl.)
Aspasia interrupta Hoffsgg., Verz. Orch. 44, 1844
Aspasia liturata Link ex Rchb.f., Xen. Orch. 1: 83, 1855
Odontoglossum variegatum (Lindl.) Rchb.f., Walp. Ann. 6: 851, 1864
Barkeria lindleyana Bateman ex Lindl., Bot. Reg. 28: Misc. p. 2, 1842
BM 6098
Mexico, Guatemala, Honduras, El Salvador, Costa Rica - up to 3500 m - E, L
o Epidendrum lindleyanum (Bateman ex Lindl.) Rchb. f., Walp. Ann. 6: 375, 1862
Barkeria skinneri (Bateman ex Lindl.) Rich. & Galeotti, Comp. Rend. Acad. Sc. Paris 18: 506, 1844
BM 3951
Mexico, Guatemala - E
o Epidendrum skinneri Bateman ex Lindl., Bot. Reg. 22: t. 1881, 1836
Dothiolophis purpurea Raf., Fl. Tellur. 4: 39, 1838
Barkeria skinneri var. major Paxton, Mag. Bot.: 15, 1849
Barkeria skinneri (Bateman ex Lindl.) Paxton, Mag. Bot.: 15, 1849
Epidendrum fuchsii Regel, Ind. Sem. Hort. Turic.: 4, 1850
Epidendrum skinneri var. superbum Warner, Sel. Orch. Pl. 1: t. 38, 1862-65
Barkeria skinneri var. superba Warner, Sel. Orch. Pl. 1: t. 38, 1862-65
o **Barkeria spectabilis** Bateman ex Lindl., Bot. Reg. 28: Misc. 43, 1842
BM 4094
Mexico, Guatemala, El Salvador, Nicaragua - up to 3500 m - E
Epidendrum spectabile (Bateman ex Lindl.) Rchb.f., Walp. Ann. 6: 375, 1862
Bartholina burmanniana (L.) Ker-Gawler, J. Sci. & Arts 4: 204 t. 6 fig. 2, 1818
BM 7450
S. Africa -T
Orchis burmanniana L., Sp. Pl. ed. 2: 1334, 1763
Orchis pectinata Thunb., Fl. Cap. ed. Schult.: 5, 1794
o Bartholina pectinata (Thunb.) R.Br., Hort. Kew., ed. 2, 5: 194, 1813
Arethusa ciliaris L.f., Suppl. Syst. Veg.: 405, 1871
Bartholina lindleyana Rchb.f., Otia Bot. Hamb. 2 pt. 1: 119, 1881
o **Batemania colleyi** Lindl., Bot. Reg. 20: t. 1714, 1834
BM 3818
Brazil, Guyana, Venezuela, Colombia, Peru, Bolivia - E
Lycaste colleyi hort. ex Planchon, Hart. Donat. Orch.: 16, 1858

Maxillaria colleyi hort. ex Planchon, Hart. Donat. Orch.: 16, 1858
Petronia regia Barb. Rodr., Gen. & Sp. Orch. 1: 107, 1877
Batemania petronia Barb. Rodr., Vellosia 1: 131, 1891
Batemania yauaperyensis Barb. Rodr., Vellosia 1: 131, 1891
Batemania peruviana Rolfe, Kew Bull.: 193, 1895
Beadlea elata (Sw.) Small ex Britton, Brooklyn Bot. Gard. Mem. 1: 38, 1918
BM 2026, BM 9094
USA (Florida), W. Indies, Mexico, C. America, except Panama, S. America to Argentina – T
Satyrium elatum Sw., Prodr. Veg. Ind. Occ.: 119, 1788
Neottia minor Jacq., Coll. 3: 172, 1789
○ Neottia elata (Sw.) Sw., Kongl. Vet. Acad. Handl. 21: 226, 1800
Spiranthes elata (Sw.) Rich., Mém. Mus. Paris 4: 59, 1818
Cyclopogon ovalifolium Presl., Rel. Haenk 1: 93 t. 13, 1827
Spiranthes preslii Lindl., Gen. Sp. Orch. Pl.: 467, 1840
Spiranthes lineata Lindl., Gen. Sp. Orch. Pl.: 471, 1840
Spiranthes comosa Rchb. f., Linnaea 18: 408, 1844
Sarcoglottis elata (Sw.) P. N. Don, Hort. Cantabr. ed. 13: 590, 1845
Gyrostachys ovalifolia (Presl.) Kuntze, Rev. Gen.: 664, 1891
Spiranthes elata var. ovata Cogn., Fl. Bras. 3, 4: 192, 1895
Spiranthes lineata Stuckert, An. Mus. Nac. Buenos Aires 9: 12, 1903 (non Lindl.)
Sauroglossum richardii Ames, Orch. 1: 44, 1905
Spiranthes variegata Kraenzlin, Engl. Bot. Jahrb. 37: 392, 1906
Cyclopogon elatus (Sw.) Schltr., Rep. Sp. Nov. Beih. 6: 53, 1919
○ Spiranthes pamii Braid, Kew Bull.: 204, 1924
Cyclopogon miradorensis Schltr., Fedde Rep. 21: 332, 1925
Bifrenaria aureo-fulva (Hook.) Lindl., Bot. Reg. 30: Misc. 52, 1843
BM 3629
Brazil – E, T
Epidendrum secundum Vell., Enum. Syst. Pl. 29, 1760 (non Jacq.)
○ Maxillaria aureo-fulva Hook., Bot. Mag.: t. 3629, 1838
Maxillaria stenopetala Knowles & Westc., Fl. Cabin. 2: 112, 1838
Stenocoryne aureo-fulva (Hook.) Kraenzlin, Xen. Orch. 3: 142, 1896
Stenocoryne secunda (Vell.) Hoehne, Arq. Bot. Estad. S. Paulo 2: 14, 1944
Bifrenaria secunda (Vell.) Pabst, Orquidea 29: 165, 1967
Bifrenaria harrisoniae (Hook.) Rchb. f., Xen. Orch. 1: 61, 1854
BM 2927
Brazil (Rio de Janeiro) – E
Dendrobium harrisoniae Hook., Exot. Fl.: t. 120, 1825
○ Maxillaria harrisoniae (Hook.) Lindl., Bot. Reg. 11: t. 897, 1825
Colax harrisoniae (Hook.) Lindl., Bot. Reg. 11: t. 897, 1825
Maxillaria spathacea Lindl., Gen. Sp. Orch. Pl.: 151, 1832
Colax grandiflorus Raf., Fl. Tellur. 2: 85, 1836
Stanhopea harrisoniae (Hook.) P. N. Don, Hort. Cantab. ed. 13: 607, 1845
Lycaste harrisoniae (Hook.) G. Don, Append. Hort. Cantab. ex Loud. Encycl. Pl. Suppl. 2: 1468, 1855
Maxillaria pubigera Klotzsch, Allg. Gartenz. 23: 106, 1855
Maxillaria barringtoniae hort. ex Rchb. f., Xen. Orch. 1: 224, 1858 (non Lodd.)
Stenocoryne harrisoniae (Hook.) Kraenzlin, Xen. Orch. 3: 142, 1896
Bifrenaria racemosa (Hook.) Lindl., Bot. Reg. 29: sub. Misc. 67 p. 52, 1843
BM 2789
Brazil (Rio de Janeiro) – E
○ Maxillaria racemosa Hook., Bot. Mag.: t. 2789, 1827
Colax racemosus (Hook.) Sprengel f., Tent.: 29, 1828
Adipe fulva Raf., Fl. Tellur. 2: 101, 1836
Adipe racemosa (Hook.) Raf., Fl. Tellur. 2: 101, 1836
Stenocoryne racemosa (Hook.) Kraenzlin, Xen. Orch. 3: 142, 1896
○ **Bifrenaria tyrianthina** (Lodd.) Rchb. f., Xen. Orch. 1: 61, 1854
BM 7461
Brazil – E
Lycaste tyrianthina Lodd., Cat. ex Hort. Brit. suppl. 3: 582, 1850
Maxillaria tyrianthina hort. ex Baxter, Hort. Brit. Suppl. 3: 582, 1850
Bifrenaria dallemagnei hort. ex Linden, Lindenia 10: 31, 1894
Bletia catenulata Ruiz Lopez & Pavón, Syst. Veg. Fl. Peruv. et Chil. 1: 229, 1798
BM 5646
Colombia, Ecuador, Brazil, Bolivia – T
Bletia sanguinea Poeppig & Endl., Nov. Gen. Sp. Pl. 1: 56 t. 95, 1836
○ Bletia sherrattiana Bateman ex Hook. f., Bot. Mag.: t. 5646, 1867
Regnellia purpurea Barb. Rodr., Gen. & Sp. Orch. 1: 82, 1877
Bletia watsonii hort. ex Orch. Rev. 2: 298, 1894
Bletia rodriguesii Cogn., Fl. Bras. 3, pt. 5: 351 t. 74, 1901
○ **Bletia parkinsonii** Hook., Bot. Mag.: t. 3736, 1839
BM 3736
Mexico – T
○ **Bletia patula** Hook., Bot. Mag.: t. 3518, 1836
BM 3518
S. W. USA, Cuba, W. Indies, Hispaniola – T
Bletia verecunda DC., Mém. Soc. Phys. et Hist. Nat. Genève 9 pt. 1: 100, 1841
Bletia shepherdii Griseb., Cat. Pl. Cub.: 263, 1866 (non Hook.)
Bletia florida Brown, Symb. Ant. 6: 571, 1910. (non R. Br.)
Bletia patula var. alba A. Hawkes, Phytol. 3: 260, 1950
Bletia purpurea (Lam.) DC., Mém. Soc. Phys. Hist. Nat. Genève 9: 97, 1841
BM 930, BM 3217, BM 3319
Mexico to Panama, Venezuela, Colombia, Ecuador, W. Indies – T
○ Limodorum altum Jacq., Hort. Kew. 3: 301, 1789
Limodorum tuberosum Jacq., Coll. 4: 108, 1790 (non L.)
Limodorum purpureum Lam., Encycl. Meth. Bot. 3: 515, 1791
Limodorum verecundum Salisb., Prodr. 9, 1796
Cymbidium floridum Salisb., Prodr. 9, 1796
Limodorum floridum Salisb., Prodr. 9, 1796
Cymbidium verecundum (Salisb.) Sw., Nov. Act. Upsal. 6: 75, 1799
Limodorum trifidum Michaux, Fl. Bor. Amer. 2: 159, 1803
Bletia florida (Salisb.) R. Br., Hort. Kew. ed. 2, 5: 206, 1813
Bletia verecunda (Salisb.) R. Br., Hort. Kew. ed. 2, 5: 206, 1813
Bletia pallida Lodd., Bot. Cab. 7: t. 629, 1822
Thiebautia nervosa Colla, Mém. Soc. Linn. Paris 3: 161 t. 4., 1824
○ Bletia acutipetala Hook., Bot. Mag.: t. 3217, 1833
○ Bletia shepherdii Hook., Bot. Mag.: t. 3319, 1834
Bletia havanensis Lindl., Bot. Reg. 24: Misc. p. 28 no. 35, 1838
Bletia alta (Jacq.) Hitchc., Ann. Rep. Missouri Bot. Gard. 4: 132, 1893
Bletia tuberosa (L.) Ames, Proc. Biol. Soc. Wash. 45: 1, 1932
Bletilla sinensis (Rolfe) Schltr., Fedde Rep. 10: 256, 1911
BM 7933
W. China (Yunnan), Sikkim – T
○ Arethusa sinensis Rolfe, J. Linn. Soc. 36: 46, 1903
Jimensia sinensis (Rolfe) Garay & Schultes, Bot. Mus. Leafl. Harv. Univ. 18, 5: 184, 1958
Bletilla striata (Thunb.) Rchb. f., Bot. Zeit. 36: 75, 1878
BM 1492
E. Tibet, Japan, Okinawa – T
Epidendrum tuberosum Lour., Fl. Cochinch.: 523, 1790
Epidendrum striatum (Thunb.) Thunb., Trans. Linn. Soc. 2: 327, 1794
Cymbidium striatum (Thunb.) Sw., Nov. Act. Upsal. 6: 77, 1797
○ Cymbidium hyacinthinum Smith, Exot. Bot. 1: 117 t. 60, 1804
Limodorum hyacinthinum (Smith) Don, Hort. Cantab. ed. 4: 201, 1807
Gyas humilis Salisb., Trans. Hort. Soc. 1: 300, 1812
Bletia hyacinthina (Smith) R. Br., Hort. Kew. ed. 2., 5: 206, 1813
Jimensia nervosa Raf., Fl. Tellur. 4: 38, 1838
Calanthe gebina Lodd., Orchid. 43: No. 1846, 1844 (nomen)
Bletia gebina (Lodd.) Lindl., J. Hort. Soc. 2: 307, 1847
Bletilla gebina (Lindl.) Rchb. f., Fl. Serres, s. 1, 8: 246, 1853
Bletilla striata var. gebina (Lindl.) Rchb. f., Bot. Zeit. 36: 75, 1878
Bletilla hycinthina Rchb. f., Bot. Zeit. 36: 75, 1878
Bletia striata (Thunb.) Druce, Rep. Bot. Exch. Club Brit. Is. 4: 609, 1917
Bletilla striata var. albomarginata Makino, J. Jap. Bot. 6: 31, 1929
Bletilla striata forma gebina (Lindl.) Ohwi, Bull. Nat. Sci. Mus. Tokyo 33: 70, 1953
Jimensia striata (Thunb.) Garay & Schultes, Bot. Mus. Leafl. Harv. Univ. 18: 184, 1958
○ **Bollea coelestis** (Rchb. f.) Rchb. f., Gard. Chron.: 756, 1876
BM 6458
Colombia, Ecuador – E
Zygopetalum coeleste Rchb. f., Linnaea 41: 5, 1877
Bollea pulvinaris Rchb. f., Linnaea 41: 107, 1877
Zygopetalum pulvinare (Rchb. f.) Rchb. f., Linnaea 41: 107, 1877
○ **Bollea lalindei** (Linden) Rchb. f., Gard. Chron.: 33, 1874
BM 6331
Colombia – E
Batemania lalindei Linden, Cat.: n. 90, 1873
Zygopetalum lalindei (Linden) Rchb. f., Gard. Chron.: 33, 1874
Bollea patini Rchb. f., Gard. Chron.: 33, 1874
Zygopetalum patinii Rchb. f., Gard. Chron.: 34, 1874
○ **Bonatea speciosa** (L. f.) Willd., Sp. Pl. 4: 43, 1805
BM 2926
S. Africa (Cape of Good Hope), Zimbabwe – up to 1500 m – T
Orchis speciosa L. f., Suppl.: 401, 1781
Habenaria bonatea Rchb. f., Otia Bot. Hamb. 2: 101 pt. 1, 1881
Habenaria robusta N. E. Br., Gard. Chron.: 307, 1885
Bothriochilus bellus Lemaire, Ill. Hort. 3: Misc. 30, 1853
BM 6628
Mexico, Guatemala, Honduras – 1500–2000 m – T

Bifrenaria bella Lemaire, Jard. Fleur. 3: t. 325, 1853
o Coelia bella (Lemaire) Rchb.f., Walp. Ann. 6: 218, 1861
Coelia picta Bateman ex Hook., Bot. Mag.: sub.t. 6628, 1882 (nomen)
Brachycorytis macrantha (Lindl.) Summerh., Kew Bull. 9: 236, 1955
BM 5875
Sierra Leone, Liberia, Nigeria, Cameroun – T
Gymnadenia macrantha Lindl., Gen. Sp. Orch. Pl.: 279, 1835
o Eulophia helleborina Hook.f., Bot. Mag.: t. 5875, 1870
Habenaria helleborina (Hook.f.) Nicholson, Dict. Gard. 2: 107, 1885
Platanthera helleborina (Hook.f.) Rolfe, F.T.A. 7: 204, 1898
Phyllomphax helleborina (Hook.f.) Schltr., F.T.W.A. 2: 407, 1919
Phyllomphax macrantha (Lindl.) Summerh., Kew Bull.: 143, 1938
Brassavola acaulis Lindl., Paxt. Flow. Gard. 2: 152, fig. 216, 1851
BM 4734
Guatemala, Costa Rica, Panama – up to 1200 m – E
o Brassavola lineata Hook., Bot. Mag.: t. 4734, 1853
Bletia acaulis (Lindl.) Rchb.f., Walp. Ann. 6: 435, 1861
Bletia lineata (Hook.) Rchb.f., Walp. Ann. 6: 436, 1861
Brassavola cucullata (L.) R.Br., Hort. Kew. ed. 2., 5: 216, 1813
BM 543, BM 3722
Mexico, Guatemala, El Salvador, Honduras, Venezuela, Trinidad, W. Indies – E
o Epidendrum cucullatum L., Sp.Pl. ed. 2: 1350, 1763
Cymbidium cucullatum (L.) Sw., Nov. Act. Upsal. 6: 73, 1799
o Brassavola cuspidata Hook., Bot. Mag.: t. 3722, 1839
Brassavola appendiculata Rich. & Galeotti, Ann. Sci. Nat. s. 3, 3: 23, 1845
Brassavola odoratissima Regel, Gartenfl.: 325 t. 33, 1852
Bletia cucullata (L.) Rchb.f., Walp. Ann. 6: 433, 1862
Brassavola cucullata var. elegans Schltr., Orchis 13: 46, 1919
Brassavola nodosa (L.) Lindl., Gen. Sp. Orch. Pl.: 114, 1831
BM 3782, BM 4021
W. Indies, Mexico to Panama, Venezuela to Peru – E
Epidendrum nodosum L., Sp.Pl.: 953, 1753
Cymbidium nodosum (L.) Sw., Nov. Act. Upsal. 6: 73, 1799
Brassavola grandiflora Lindl., Bot. Reg. 25: Misc.p. 16, 1839
o Brassavola venosa Lindl., Bot. Reg. 26: t. 39, 1840
Brassavola rhopalorrachis Rchb.f., Bot. Zeit. 10: 833, 1852
Bletia nodosa (L.) Rchb.f., Walp. Ann. 6: 437, 1861
Bletia venosa (Lindl.) Rchb.f., Walp. Ann. 6: 438, 1861
Brassavola stricta hort., Gard. Chron.: 505, 1885
Brassavola scaposa Schltr., Orchis 13: 77, 1919
Brassavola nodosa var. rhopalorrachis Schltr., Orchis 13: 77, 1919
Brassavola nodosa var. grandiflora (Lindl.) H. Jones, Am. Orch. Soc. Bull. 41 (6): 595, 1972
o (Brassavola cordata Lindl., Bot. Reg.: t. 1914, 1836; misidentified)
Brassavola subulifolia Lindl., Gen. Sp. Orch. Pl.: 113, 1831
BM 3229
Jamaica – E
Brassavola cordata Lindl., Bot. Reg. 22: t. 1913, 1836
Brassavola sloanei Griseb., Fl. Brit. W. Ind.: 626, 1864
o (Brassavola nodosa Lindl., Gen. Sp. Orch. Pl.: 114, 1831; misidentified)
o **Brassavola tuberculata** Hook., Bot. Mag.: t. 2878, 1829
BM 2878, BM 3761
Brazil, Bolivia – E, L
o Brassavola perrinii Lindl., Bot. Reg. 18: t. 1561, 1832
Brassavola fragrans Lemaire, Jard. Fleur. 3: Misc. 78 & 88, 1853
Bletia perrinii (Lindl.) Rchb.f., Walp. Ann. 6: 436, 1862
Bletia tuberculata (Hook.) Rchb.f., Walp. Ann. 6: 435, 1862
Brassavola gibbsiana Williams, Orch. Grow. Man. ed. 5, 1877
Brassia arcuigera Rchb.f., Gard. Chron.: 388, 1869
BM 5748
Nicaragua to Peru – 500–1200 m – E
o Brassia lawrenciana var. longissima Rchb.f., Gard. Chron.: 1313, 1868
Brassia antherotes Rchb.f., Gard. Chron.: 782, 1879
Brassia longissima (Rchb.f.) Schltr., Orchideen: 496, 1914 (in part)
Brassia longissima (Rchb.f.) Nash, Stand. Cyclop. Hort. 1: 541, 1914
Brassia rhizomatosa Garay & Dunsterv., Venez. Orch. Ill. 3: 46, 1965
Brassia bidens Lindl., Bot. Reg. 30: Misc.p. 6, 1844
BM 3794
Venezuela, Guyana, Brazil, Peru – E, T
o Brassia lanceana var. viridiflora Hook., Bot. Mag.: t. 3794, 1840
Oncidium bidens (Lindl.) Rchb.f., Walp. Ann. 6: 769, 1863
o **Brassia caudata** (L.) Lindl., Bot. Reg. 10: t. 832, 1824
BM 3451
USA (Florida), Jamaica, W. Indies, Mexico to Panama, Venezuela to Bolivia – up to 1200 m – E
Epidendrum caudatum L., Sp.Pl. ed. 2: 1349, 1763
Malaxis caudata (L.) Willd., Sp.Pl. 4: 93, 1805
Oncidium caudatum (L.) Rchb.f., Walp. Ann. 6: 766, 1863
Brassia caudata var. hieroglyphica Rchb.f., Ill. Hort. 27: 20, 1881
Brassia lewisii Rolfe, Orch. Rev. 1: 199, 1893
Brassia longissima var. minor Schltr., Fedde Rep. Beih. 17: 80, 1922
o **Brassia lanceana** Lindl., Bot. Reg. 21: t. 1754, 1835
BM 3577
Panama, Venezuela, Tobago, Guyana, Brazil, Colombia – E
Brassia macrostachya Lindl., Sert. Orch.: t. 6, 1838
Brassia pumila Lindl., Bot. Reg.: 60, 1845
Oncidium suaveolens Rchb.f., Walp. Ann. 6: 765, 1863
o **Brassia maculata** R.Br., Hort. Kew. ed. 2, 5: 215, 1813
BM 1691, BM 4003
Belize, Guatemala, El Salvador, Honduras, Nicaragua, Jamaica, W. Indies – E
Brassia guttata Lindl., Pl. Hartw.: 94, 1842
Oncidium brassia Rchb.f., Walp. Ann. 6: 765, 1842
o Brassia wrayae Skinner, Bot. Mag.: t. 4003, 1843
× **Brassocattleya lindleyana** Rolfe, Gard. Chron.: 437, 1889
BM 5449
Brazil (Bahia) – E
= Brassavola tuberculata Hook. × Cattleya intermedia Graham ex Hook.
o Cattleya lindleyana Rchb.f., Allg. Gartenz.: 118, 1857
Bletia lindleyana Rchb.f., Xen. Orch. 2: 112 t. 135, 1863
Laelia lindleyana hort. ex Bateman, Sec. Cent. Orch.: sub.t. 175, 1867
Bromheadia finlaysoniana (Lindl.) Rchb.f., Walp. Ann. 6: 882, 1864
BM 4001
Thailand, Malaya, Kampuchea, Laos, Sumatra, Borneo, Philippines – E
Grammatophyllum finlaysonianum Lindl., Wall. Cat.: n. 7561, 1832
o Bromheadia palustris Lindl., Bot. Reg. 30: Misc.p. 89, 1841
o **Broughtonia sanguinea** (Sw.) R.Br., Hort. Kew. ed. 2: 217, 1813
BM 3076, BM 3536
Jamaica, Cuba – up to 1000 m – E
Epidendrum nodosum var. β L., Sp.Pl.: 953, 1753
Epidendrum sanguineum Sw., Prodr. Veg. Ind. Occ.: 124, 1788
Dendrobium sanguineum (Sw.) Sw., Nov. Act. Upsal. 6: 82, 1799
o Broughtonia coccinea Hook., Bot. Mag.: t. 3536, 1836
o **Brownleea coerulea** Harvey ex Lindl., J. Bot. 1: 16, 1834–35
BM 7309
S. Africa – 1000–1500 m – T
Brownleea macroceras Sonder, Linnaea 19: 106, 1847
Disa coerulea (Harvey ex Lindl.) Rchb.f., Otia Bot. Hamb. 2: 119, 1881
Brownleea madagascarica Ridley, J. Linn. Soc. 22: 126, 1886
Brownleea nelsoni Rolfe, Fl. Cap. 5, 3: 262, 1913
Brownleea woodii Rolfe, Fl. Cap. 5, 3: 263, 1913
Bulbophyllum auratum (Lindl.) Rchb.f., Walp. Ann. 6: 261, 1861
BM 8281
Malaya, Sumatra, Borneo, Philippines – E
Cirrhopetalum auratum Lindl., Bot. Reg. 26: Misc. 50 no. 107, 1840
Phyllorchis aurata (Lindl.) Kuntze, Rev. Gen.: 675, 1891
Cirrhopetalum borneense Schltr., Bull. Herb. Bois. 2 s. 6: 464, 1906
o Bulbophyllum campanulatum Rolfe, Kew Bull.: 62, 1909
Cirrhopetalum campanulatum (Rolfe) Rolfe, Orch. Rev. 18: 73 fig. 6, 1910
Bulbophyllum borneense (Schltr.) J.J. Smith, Bull. Buitenz. 2 s. 8: 23, 1911
non Bulbophyllum auratum auct. Ames: 139, 1912
o **Bulbophyllum auricomum** Lindl., Gen. Sp. Orch. Pl.: 50, 1830
BM 7938
Burma, Sumatra, Java – E
Dendrobium tripetaloides Roxb., Hort. Beng. 63: 1814 (nomen nudum)
Bulbophyllum foenisecii Parish & Rchb.f., Bot. Zeit. 23: 99, 1865
Phyllorchis auricoma (Lindl.) Kuntze, Rev. Gen. 2: 677, 1891
Bulbophyllum tripetaloides (Roxb.) Schltr., Orchideen: 329, 1914
o **Bulbophyllum barbigerum** Lindl., Bot. Reg. 23: t. 1942, 1837
BM 5288
Sierra Leone, Liberia, Ivory Coast, S. Nigeria, Ghana, W. Cameroun – E
Phyllorchis barbigera (Lindl.) Kuntze, Rev. Gen.: 675, 1891
o **Bulbophyllum beccarii** Rchb.f., Gard. Chron.: 41, 1879
BM 6567
Borneo – E
Phyllorchis beccarii (Rchb.f.) Kuntze, Rev. Gen.: 675, 1891
Bulbophyllum biflorum Teijsm. & Binnend., Nat. Tijds. Ned. Ind. 5: 488, 1853
BM 8321
Thailand, Malaya, Sumatra, Java, Bali, Lombok, N. Borneo, Philippines – E
Phyllorchis biflora (Teijsm. & Binnend.) Kuntze, Rev. Gen. 2: 677, 1891

o Cirrhopetalum biflorum (Teijsm. & Binnend.) J. J. Smith, Ic. Bog. 2: 104 t. 120 B, 1903

Bulbophyllum geminatum Carr, Gard. Bull. Sing. 5, 1–2: 12 pl. 6, 1929

o **Bulbophyllum binnendijkii** J. J. Smith, Fl. Buitenz. 6: 442, 1905

BM 8187

Java, Borneo – E

Cirrhopetalum leopardinum Teijsm. & Binnend., Nat. Tijds. Ned. Ind. 23: 309, 1862

non Bulbophyllum leopardinum Lindl.

o **Bulbophyllum calamarium** Lindl., Bot. Reg. 29: Misc. 70, 1843

BM 4088

Sierra Leone, Liberia, S. Nigeria – E

Phyllorchis calamaria (Lindl.) Kuntze, Rev. Gen.: 675, 1891

Bulbophyllum careyanum (Hook.) Sprengel, Syst. 3: 732, 1826

BM 5316

Nepal, Sikkim, Bhutan, Assam, Burma, Thailand – E

Pleurothallis purpurea D. Don, Prodr.: 33, 1825

Anisopetalon careyanum Hook., Exot. Fl. 2: pl. 149, 1825

Tribrachia purpurea (D. Don) Lindl., Coll. Bot. sub. t. 41 a, 1826

o Bulbophyllum cupreum auct. non Lindl., Hook., Bot. Mag.: t. 5316, 1862

Phyllorchis purpurea (D. Don) Kuntze, Rev. Gen. 2: 676, 1891

non Bulbophyllum careyanum Hook., Bot. Mag.: 4166, 1845

non Bulbophyllum careyanum Seidenfaden & Smitinand: 428 fig. 321, 1961

o **Bulbophyllum comosum** Collett & Hemsley, J. Linn. Soc. 28: 130, 1890

BM 7283

Thailand, Burma – 1500–2000 m – E

Phyllorchis comosa (Collett & Hemsley) Kuntze, Rev. Gen. 2: 677, 1891

non Bulbophyllum comosum auct.: Guillaumin 1961 a: 563; Seidenfaden 1975 b: 13 (B. lemniscatoides).

Bulbophyllum coriophorum Ridley, J. Linn. Soc. 22: 119, 1886

BM 8000, BM 8792

Madagascar – 1000–1600 m – E

Bulbophyllum compactum Kraenzlin, Engl. Jahrb. 17: 48, 1893

o Bulbophyllum crenulatum Rolfe, Bot. Mag.: t. 8000, 1905

o Bulbophyllum robustum Rolfe, Bot. Mag.: sub. t. 8792, 1919

Bulbophyllum mandrakanum Schltr., Fedde Rep. 33: 235, 1925

Bulbophyllum corolliferum J. J. Smith, Bull. Buitenz. 2. s. 25: 80, 1917

BM 7554, BM 8668

Thailand, Malaya, Sumatra, Borneo – E

o Cirrhopetalum concinnum var. purpureum Ridl., J. Linn. Soc. 32: 282, 1896

o Cirrhopetalum curtisii Hook. f., Bot. Mag.: t. 7554, 1897

Bulbophyllum pulchellum var. purpureum Ridley, Mat. Fl. Mal. Pen. 1: 83, 1907

Bulbophyllum curtisii (Hook. f.) Ridley, J. Str. Br. Roy. As. Soc. 59: 308, 1933

Bulbophyllum curtisii var. purpureum J. J. Smith, Fedde Rep. 32: 308, 1933

non Bulbophyllum curtisii Ridley, J. Str. Br. Roy. As. Soc. 39: 76, 1903

Bulbophyllum crassipes Hook. f., Fl. Brit. Ind. 5: 760, 1890

BM 4166

Sikkim, Assam, Burma, Malaya – E

Bulbphyllum careyanum Wall., Syst. 3: 732, 1826 (non Sprengel)

o Bulbophyllum careyanum auct. non (Hook.) Sprengel; Hook., Bot. Mag.: t. 4166, 1845

Phyllorchis crassipes (Hook. f.) Kuntze, Rev. Gen. 2: 677, 1891

non Bulbophyllum crassipes auct.: Gagnepain 1934: 278 (B. rufinum); Seidenfaden 1973 a: 109 (presumably B. laoticum)

Bulbophyllum cumingii (Lindl.) Rchb. f., Walp. Ann. 6: 261, 1861

BM 4996

Philippines – up to 500 m – E

o Cirrhopetalum cumingii Lindl., Bot. Reg. 24: sub. t. 49, 1843

Cirrhopetalum stramineum auct. non Teijsm. & Binnend., Tijdschr. Ned. Ind. 24: 310, 1862

Phyllorchis cumingii (Lindl.) Kuntze, Rev. Gen.: 675, 1891

Cirrhopetalum amesianum Rolfe, Lindenia 7: 55 t. 314, 1891

Bulbophyllum amesianum (Rolfe) J. J. Smith, Bull. Buitenz. s. 2, 8: 22, 1912

Bulbophyllum stramineum Ames, Orchid. 5: 190, 1915

o **Bulbophyllum dayanum** Rchb. f., Gard. Chron.: 434, 1865

BM 6119

Burma, Thailand, Kampuchea – E

Phyllorchis dayana (Rchb. f.) Kuntze, Rev. Gen. 2: 677, 1891

Trias dayanum Grant, Orch. Burma: 55, 1895 (nomen nudum)

Bulbophyllum dyphoniae Tixier, Bull. Mus. Paris 2. s. 39, 6: 1238 fig. 5–9, 1968

o **Bulbophyllum elassonotum** Summerh., Bot. Mag.: t. 9408, 1935

BM 9408

Assam – E

o **Bulbophyllum ericssonii** Kraenzlin, Gard. Chron.: 522, 1893

BM 8088

Malay Archipelago – E

Bulbophyllum falcatum Rchb. f., Walp. Ann. 6: 258, 1861

BM 4028

Sierra Leone, Liberia, Ivory Coast, Togo, S. Nigeria, Uganda – E

Megaclinium falcatum Lindl., Bot. Reg.: t. 989, 1826

Phyllorchis falcata (Rchb. f.) Kuntze, Rev. Gen.: 677, 1891

Megaclinium endotrachys Kraenzlin, Engl. Bot. Jahrb. 36: 115, 1905

Bulbophyllum leptorrhachis Schltr., Engl. Bot. Jahrb. 38: 17, 1905/7

o (Megaclinium maximum Lindl., Gen. Sp. Orch. Pl.: 47, 1830; missidentified)

Bulbophyllum farreri (W. Smith) Seidenf., Dansk Bot. Ark. 29 (1): 212, 1973

BM 8933

Burma – E

o Cirrhopetalum farreri W. Smith, Notes Bot. Gard. Edinb. 23: 196, 1921

Bulbophyllum fimbriatum (Lindl.) Rchb. f., Walp. Ann.: 6, 1861

BM 4391

India – E

o Cirrhopetalum fimbriatum Lindl., Gen. Sp. Orch. Pl., 1839

Cirrhopetalum wallichii J. Graham, Cat. Pl. Bomb.: 205, 1839

Phyllorchis fimbriata (Lindl.) Kuntze, Rev. Gen.: 677, 1891

Bulbophyllum flaviflorum (Liu & Su) Seidenf., Bull. Mus. Paris 3. s. no. 71, Bot. 5: 109, 1972

BM 9109

Vietnam, Laos, China, Taiwan – up to 1000 m – E

o Cirrhopetalum miniatum Rolfe, Kew Bull.: 28, 1913

Cirrhopetalum flaviflorum Liu & Su, Quart. J. Taiwan Mus. 24, 1–2: 174, 1971

Bulbophyllum fletcherianum Rolfe, Orch. Rev. 22: 164, 1914

BM 8600

New Guinea – E

o Cirrhopetalum fletcherianum Rolfe, Bot. Mag.: t. 8600, 1915

o **Bulbophyllum grandiflorum** Blume, Rumph. 4: 42, t. 195 fig. 3 t. 199, 1848

BM 7787

New Guinea, Solomon Is. – E

Phyllorchis grandiflora (Blume) Kuntze, Rev. Gen.: 675, 1891

Bulbophyllum cominsii Rolfe, Kew Bull.: 138, 1895

Bulbophyllum burfordiense hort. ex Hook. f., Bot. Mag.: t. 7787, 1901

Bulbophyllum fritillariiflorum J. J. Smith, Bull. Buitenz. s. 2, 3: 76, 1912

Hyalosema cominsii (Rolfe) Rolfe, Orch. Rev. 27: 130, 1919

Hyalosema grandiflorum (Blume) Rolfe, Orch. Rev. 27: 130, 1919

Bulbophyllum graveolens (Bailey) J. J. Smith, Bull. Buitenz. s. 2, 8: 24, 1912

BM 7557

New Guinea – E

o Cirrhopetalum robustum Rolfe, Orch. Rev. 1: 175, 1893

Cirrhopetalum graveolens Bailey, Bull. Dept. Agr. Queensl. 13: 33, 1896

Bulbophyllum guttulatum Wallich ex Hook. f., Fl. Brit. Ind. 5: 776, 1890

BM 4267

India, Nepal, Sikkim, Bhutan, Assam – E

o Bulbophyllum umbellatum auct. non Lindl. 1830; Lindl., Bot. Reg.: t. 44, 1844

Cirrhopetalum guttulatum (Wallich) Hook. f., Fl. Brit. Ind. 5: 776, 1890

Phyllorchis guttulata (Wallich) Kuntze, Rev. Gen. 2: 677, 1891

o **Bulbophyllum hamelinii** Rolfe, Orch. Rev.: 284, 1902

BM 8785

Madagascar – E

Bulbophyllum helenae (Kuntze) J. J. Smith, Bull. Buitenz. 2. s. 8: 24, 1912

BM 4753

N. E. India, Nepal, Sikkim, Burma, Thailand – 1000–2000 m – E

o Cirrhopetalum cornutum Lindl., Bot. Reg. 24: Misc. 138: 75, 1838

Bulbophyllum cornutum Rchb. f., Walp. Ann. 6: 261, 1861

Phyllorchis helenae Kuntze, Rev. Gen. 2: 676, 1891

Bulbophyllum picturatum auct. non (Lodd.) Rchb. f.; Seidenfaden & Smitinand: 367 fig. 276, 1961

non Bulbophyllum cornutum Rchb. f., Walp. Ann. 6: 247, 1861

Bulbophyllum hookeri (Duthie) J. J. Smith, Bull. Buitenz. 2. s. 8: 25, 1912

BM 7869

W. Himalaya, Nepal, Assam – E

o Cirrhopetalum hookeri Duthie, J. As. Soc. Beng. 71, 2: 38, 1902
Bulbophyllum lasiochilum Parish & Rchb.f., Trans. Linn. Soc. 30: 153, 1874
BM 8033
Burma, Thailand, Malaya - E
Cirrhopetalum lasiochilum (Parish & Rchb.f.) Hook.f., Fl. Brit. Ind. 5: 772, 1890
Phyllorchis lasiochila (Parish & Rchb.f.) Kuntze, Rev. Gen.: 675, 1891
o Cirrhopetalum breviscapum Rolfe, Bot. Mag.: t. 8033, 1905
Bulbophyllum breviscapum (Rolfe) Ridley, Mat. Fl. Mal. Pen. 1: 78, 1907
non Bulbophyllum breviscapum J.J. Smith, Bull. Dept. Agr. Ned. Ind. 39: 2, 1910
o **Bulbophyllum lemniscatum** Parish ex Hook f., Bot. Mag.: t. 5961, 1872
BM 5961
Burma, Thailand - E
Bulbophyllum lemniscatum var. tumidum Parish & Rchb.f., Trans. Linn. Soc. 30: 151, 1874
Phyllorchis lemniscata (Parish ex Hook.f.) Kuntze, Rev. Gen. 2: 677, 1891
non Bulbophyllum lemniscatum auct.; Seidenfaden & Smitinand, Orch. Thailand, pt. 3: 415 fig. 312, 1961
o **Bulbophyllum leopardinum** Lindl., Gen. Sp. Orch. Pl.: 48, 1830
BM 9631
Nepal, Bhutan, Assam, Burma, Thailand - 1500-2000 m - E
Dendrobium leopardinum Wallich, Tent. Fl. Nep. 1: 39 t. 28, 1824
Sarcopodium leopardinum (Wallich) Lindl., Paxt. Flow. Gard. 1: 155, 1850
Phyllorchis leopardina (Wallich) Kuntze, Rev. Gen. 2: 677, 1891
Bulbophyllum leucorhachis (Rolfe) Schltr., Engl. Bot. Jahrb. 38: 17, 1905
BM 7811
Sierra Leone, N. Nigeria, Gabon, Zaire, Uganda - E
o Megaclinium leucorhachis Rolfe, F.T.A. 7: 37, 1891
o **Bulbophyllum lilacinum** Ridley, J. Linn. Soc. 32: 276, 1896
BM 8723
Malaya, Thailand - E
non Bulbophyllum lilacinum auct.; Seidenfaden & Smitinand, Orch. Thailand, pt. 3: 434, 1961; pt. 4/2: 809 fig. 607, 1965
o **Bulbophyllum lobbii** Lindl., Bot. Reg.: sub.t. 29, 1847
BM 4532
Assam, Burma, Kampuchea, Malaya, Sumatra, Java, Bali, Borneo, Philippines - E
Sestochilos uniflorum Breda, Gen. Sp. Orch. Asclep. 29: t. 3, 1827
Sarcopodium lobbii (Lindl.) Lindl., Paxt. Flow. Gard. 1: 155, 1850
Bulbophyllum henshallii Lindl., Gard. Chron.: 422, 1852
Bulbophyllum lobbii var. henshallii (Lindl.) Henfrey, Gard. Mag. Bot. 3: 269, 1852
Bulbophyllum siamense Rchb.f., Gard. Chron.: 572, 1867
Bulbophyllum lobbii var. siamense (Rchb.f.) Rchb.f., Saunders Ref. Bot. 2: t. 116, 1882
Phyllorchis lobbii (Lindl.) Kuntze, Rev. Gen. 2: 677, 1891
Bulbophyllum lobbii var. colosseum hort., Gard. Chron.: 184 fig. 68, 1905
Bulbophyllum lobbii var. breviflorum J.J. Smith, Bull. Dépt. Agr. Ind. Neerl. 15: 18, 1908
Bulbophyllum longiflorum Thouars, Orch. Iles Afr.: t. 3 & t. 98, 1822
BM 7214
Africa, Madagascar, Malay Archipelago, Philippines, Moluccas, New Guinea, Australia, New Caledonia, Fiji, Rarotonga, Tahiti, Guam - E
Epidendrum umbellatum Forster, Ins. Austr. Prod.: 60, 1786
Cymbidium umbellatum (Forster) Sprengel, Pl. Min. Cog. Pugill. 2: 82, 1815
o Cirrhopetalum thouarsii Lindl., Bot. Reg. 10: sub. t. 832, 1824;
Cirrhopetalum umbellatum (Forster) Hook. & Arn., Bot. Beechey Voy.: 71, 1832
Cirrhopetalum clavigerum Fitzg., J. Bot. 21: 204, 1883
Bulbophyllum clavigerum (Fitzg.) F. v. Muell., Syst. Cens. Aust. Pl. Suppl. 1: 3, 1884
Phyllorchis umbellata (Forster) Kuntze, Rev. Gen. 2: 675, 1891
Phyllorchis thouarsii (Lindl.) Kuntze, Rev. Gen. 2: 677, 1891
Phyllorchis clavigera (Fitzg.) Kuntze, Rev. Gen. 2: 677, 1891
Cirrhopetalum thouarsii var. concolor Rolfe, Gard. Chron.: 178, 1892
? Cirrhopetalum layardii F. v. Muell. & Kraenzlin, Oestr. Bot. Zeit. 44: 210, 1894
? Bulbophyllum trisetum Ames, Phil. J. Sci. 7: 142, 1912
? Bulbophyllum layardii (F. v. Muell. & Kraenzlin) J.J. Smith, Bull. Buitenz. 2. s. 8, 1912
Cirrhopetalum kenejianum Schltr., Fedde Rep. Beih. 1: 889, 1913
Cirrhopetalum longiflorum (Thouars) Schltr., Beih. Bot. Centralbl. 33, 2: 420, 1915
Cirrhopetalum africanum Schltr., Engl. Bot. Jahrb. 53: 573, 1915
non Epidendrum umbellatum Sw., Kongl. Vet. Acad. Handl. 21: 241, 1800
non Zygopetalum umbellatum Reinw., Syll. Pl. Nov. 2: 5, 1825/26
non Bulbophyllum umbellatum Lindl., Gen. Sp. Orch. Pl.: 56, 1830
non Bulbophyllum longiflorum Rchb.f., Naves Nov. App.: 235, 1880
non Bulbophyllum longiflorum Ridley, J. Linn. Soc. 32: 268, 1896
non Bulbophyllum clavigerum Perrier, Not. Syst. 14: 153, 1951
Bulbophyllum longissimum (Ridley) Ridley, J. Str. Br. Roy. As. Soc. 59: 194, 1911
BM 8366
Thailand, Malaya - E
o Cirrhopetalum longissimum Ridley, J. Linn. Soc. 32: 280, 1896
Bulbophyllum macraei (Lindl.) Rchb.f., Walp. Ann. 6: 263, 1861
BM 4422
Sri Lanka, India, Japan, Taiwan - E
o Cirrhopetalum macraei Lindl., Gen. Sp. Orch. Pl.: 59, 1830
Cirrhopetalum walkerianum Wight, Ic. 5: t. 1657, 1851
Phyllorchis macraei (Lindl.) Kuntze, Rev. Gen. 2: 677, 1891
Bulbophyllum boninense Makino, Iinuma Somuku Dzusetsu ed. 3, 18: 14 t. 20, 1912
Bulbophyllum uraiense Hayata, Ic. Pl. Form. 4: 50 t. 11, 1914
Cirrhopetalum uraiense (Hayata) Hayata, Ic. Pl. Form 4: 51, 1914
Cirrhopetalum makinoanum Schltr., Fedde Rep. Beih. 4: 254, 1919
Cirrhopetalum boninense (Makino) Makino, Fedde Rep. Beih. 4: 254, 1919
Bulbophyllum makinoanum (Schltr.) Masam., J. Soc. Trop. Agr. 2: 153, 1930
Cirrhopetalum autumnale Fukuyama, Bot. Mag. Tokyo 49: 760, 1935
Bulbophyllum tanegasimense Masam., J. Geobot. Hokuriku 26: 57, 1968
Cirrhopetalum tanegasimense (Masam.) Masam., Col. Ill. Fl. Nip. 8: 268, 1970
non Cirrhopetalum macraei Wight, Ic. t. 1652
o **Bulbophyllum macranthum** Lindl., Bot. Reg. 30: t. 13, 1844
BM 7208
Burma, Vietnam, Sumatra, Bangka - E
Sarcopodium macranthum (Lindl.) Lindl., Paxt. Flow. Gard. 1: 155, 1850
Sarcopodium purpureum Rchb.f., Bonpl. 4: 330, 1856
Phyllorchis macrantha (Lindl.) Kuntze, Rev. Gen. 2: 677, 1891
Bulbophyllum cochinchinense Gagnepain, Bull. Mus. Paris s. 2, 22: 400, 1950
Bulbophyllum patens auct. non King ex Hook.f.; Gagnepain, Fl. Indo-Chine: 119, 1951
o **Bulbophyllum macrobulbum** J.J. Smith, Bull. Dép. Agr. Ind. Néerl.: 39, 1910
BM 8842
New Guinea - E
Bulbophyllum makoyanum (Rchb.f.) Ridley, Mat. Fl. Mal. 1: 81, 1907
BM 7259
Malaya, Borneo, Philippines - E
o Cirrhopetalum makoyanum Rchb.f., Gard. Chron.: 234, 1879
Bulbophyllum malachadenia Cogn., Fl. Bras. 3, 5: 596, 1902
BM 4334
Brazil - E
o Malachadenia clavata Lindl., Bot. Reg. 25: Misc. 67, 1839
Bulbophyllum clavatum (Lindl.) Pfitzer, Nat. Pflanzenfam. 2, 6: 179, 1888 (non Thouars 1822)
Bulbophyllum mastersianum (Rolfe) J.J. Smith, Bull. Buitenz. s. 2, 8: 26, 1912
BM 8531
Borneo, Moluccas - E
o Cirrhopetalum mastersianum Rolfe, Lindenia 6: 33 t. 255, 1890
Bulbophyllum maximum (Lindl.) Rchb.f., Walp. Ann. 6: 259, 1861
BM 5936
Sierra Leone to Zaire, Ethiopia to Zambia, Zimbabwe, Mozambique - E
Megaclinium maximum Lindl., Gen. Sp. Orch. Pl.: 47, 1830
Megaclinium oxypterum Lindl., Bot. Reg. 25: Misc. No. 14, 1839
Bulbophyllum oxypterum (Lindl.) Rchb.f., Walp. Ann. 6: 258, 1861
o Megaclinium purpuratum Lindl., J. Linn. Soc. 6: 128, 1862
Bulbophyllum purpuratum (Lindl.) Lindl., J. Linn. Soc. 6: 123-140, 1862
Phyllorchis maxima (Lindl.) Kuntze, Rev. Gen.: 677, 1891
Phyllorchis oxyptera (Lindl.) Kuntze, Rev. Gen.: 677, 1891
Bulbophyllum nyassanum Schltr., Engl. Bot. Jahrb. 53: 571, 1915
Bulbophyllum medusae (Lindl.) Rchb.f., Walp. Ann. 6: 262, 1861
BM 4977
Thailand, Malaya, Sumatra, Bangka, Sunda Is., Borneo, Philippines - E
o Cirrhopetalum medusae Lindl., Bot. Reg.: t. 12, 1842
Phyllorchis medusae (Lindl.) Kuntze, Rev. Gen.: 675-78, 1891

Bulbophyllum melanorrhachis Rchb.f., Gard. Chron.: 162, 1875
BM 7314
Sierra Leone, Liberia, S. Nigeria – E
o Megaclinium minutum Rolfe, Kew Bull. 73: 5, 1893
Megaclinium millenii Rolfe, F.T.A. 7: 40, 1898
Megaclinium angustum Rolfe, Kew Bull.: 26, 1922
o **Bulbophyllum morphologorum** Kraenzlin, Orchis 2: 89, 1908
BM 9033
Vietnam, Thailand – E
Bulbophyllum dixonii Rolfe, Kew Bull.: 442, 1908
Bulbophyllum cupreum auct. non Lindl.; Gagnepain, Fl. Indo-Chine: 277, 1934
o **Bulbophyllum neilgherrense** Wight, Ic. Pl. Ind. Or. 5: t. 1650, 1851
BM 5050
India (Neilgherries, Malabar), Thailand – E
Phyllorchis nilgherensis (Wight) Kuntze, Rev. Gen.: 677, 1891
Bulbophyllum ornatissimum (Rchb.f.) J.J. Smith, Bull. Buitenz. s. 2, 8: 26, 1912
BM 7229
E. Himalaya, Sikkim, Assam – E
o Cirrhopetalum ornatissimum Rchb.f., Gard. Chron.: 424, 1882
Phyllorchis ornatissima (Rchb.f.) Kuntze, Rev. Gen. 2: 677, 1891
o **Bulbophyllum orthoglossum** Kraenzlin, Gard. Chron.: 326, 1896
BM 9459
Philippines (Sarangani Is., S. Mindanao) – E
Bulbophyllum othonis (Kuntze) J.J. Smith, Bull. Buitenz. s. 2, 8: 26, 1912
BM 4418
Philippines (Manilla) – E
o Cirrhopetalum nutans Lindl., Bot. Reg. 25: Misc. 71, 1839
Bulbophyllum nutans auct. non Thouars; Rchb.f., Walp. Ann. 6: 260, 1861
Phyllorchis othonis Kuntze, Rev. Gen. 2: 677, 1891
o **Bulbophyllum patens** King, Fl. Brit. Ind. 6: 187, 1890
BM 9299
Sumatra, Malaya, Thailand – E
Phyllorchis patens (King) Kuntze, Rev. Gen.: 675, 1891
o **Bulbophyllum pavimentatum** Lindl., J. Linn. Soc. 6: 128, 1862
BM 5329
S. Nigeria, E. Cameroun, Gabon, Zaire – E
Bulbophyllum recurvum Lindl., Gen. Sp. Orch. Pl.: 53, 1830
Phyllorchis pavimenta (Lindl.) Kuntze, Rev. Gen.: 675, 1891
Phyllorchis recurva (Lindl.) Kuntze, Rev. Gen.: 675, 1891
Bulbophyllum dorotheae Rendle, Cat. Talb.: 100, 1913
o **Bulbophyllum pechei** Rchb.f., Gard. Chron.: 676, 1841
BM 7286
Burma – E
Bulbophyllum picturatum (Lodd.) Rchb.f., Walp. Ann. 6: 262, 1861
BM 6802
Assam, Burma, Thailand, Vietnam – 1500–2000 m – E
o Cirrhopetalum picturatum Lodd., Bot. Reg. 46: Misc. 49, 1840
Phyllorchis picturata (Lodd.) Kuntze, Rev. Gen.: 678, 1891
Cirrhopetalum eberhardtii Gagnepain, Bull. Soc. Bot. Fr. 78: 4, 1931
Bulbophyllum platyrhachis (Rolfe) Schltr., Engl. Bot. Jahrb. 38: 15, 1907
BM 7946
Uganda, Tanzania, Malawi – 400–1500 m – E
o Megaclinium platyrhachis Rolfe, F.T.A. 7: 43, 1898 (non De Wild. 1906, non Ridley 1917)
Bulbophyllum psittacoglossum Rchb.f., Bot. Zeit. 21: 237, 1863
BM 5408
Burma – E
o Sarcopodium psittacoglossum (Rchb.f.) Hook., Bot. Mag.: t. 5408, 1863
Phyllorchis psittacoglossa (Rchb.f.) Kuntze, Rev. Gen. 2: 677, 1891
Bulbophyllum purpureorhachis (De Wild.) Schltr., Orchideen: 328, 1914
BM 8273
Ivory Coast, E. Cameroun, Gabon, Zaire – E
Megaclinium bufo Lindl., Bot. Reg.: Misc. 42, 1841
Phyllorchis bufo (Lindl.) Kuntze, Rev. Gen.: 677, 1891
o Megaclinium purpureorhachis De Wild., Not. Pl. Util. Congo: 126, 1903
Bulbophyllum putidum (Teijsm. & Binnend.) J.J. Smith, Bull. Buitenz. 2. s. 8: 27, 1912
BM 8199
Sikkim, Bengal, Laos, S. Vietnam, Malaya, Sumatra, Java, Bangka, Borneo, Philippines – E
Cirrhopetalum putidum Teijsm. & Binnend., Tijdschr. Ned. Ind. 24: 311, 1862
Cirrhopetalum ornatissimum auct. non Rchb.f.; King & Pantl.: 95 t. 122, 1898
Cirrhopetalum appendiculatum Rolfe, Kew Bull.: 148, 1901
Cirrhopetalum fascinator Rolfe, Kew Bull.: 69, 1908
o Bulbophyllum fascinator (Rolfe) Rolfe, Bot. Mag.: t. 8199, 1908
Bulbophyllum appendiculatum (Rolfe) J.J. Smith, Bull. Buitenz. s. 2, 8: 22, 1912
o **Bulbophyllum reticulatum** Bateman, Bot. Mag.: t. 5605, 1866
BM 5605
Borneo – E
Phyllorchis reticulata (Bateman) Kuntze, Rev. Gen. 675, 1891
o **Bulbophyllum rhizophorae** Lindl., J. Linn. Soc. 6: 125, 1862
BM 5309
Sierra Leone, Ivory Coast, Ghana, S. Nigeria, W. Cameroun, Zaire – E
Phyllorchis rhizophorae (Lindl.) Kuntze, Rev. Gen.: 675, 1891
o **Bulbophyllum sociale** Rolfe, Bot. Mag.: t. 8761, 1818
BM 8761
Sumatra – E
Bulbophyllum tripudians Parish & Rchb.f., Trans. Linn. Soc. 30: 154, 1874
BM 8954
Burma, N. Thailand, Laos, S. Vietnam – 1500–2000 m – E
o Cirrhopetalum tripudians (Parish & Rchb.f.) Parish & Rchb.f., Gard. Chron.: 816, 1876
Cirrhopetalum refractum auct. non Zollinger; Hook.f., Fl. Brit. Ind.: 779, 1890
Bulbophyllum refractum auct. non Rchb.f.; Seidenfaden & Smitinand, Orch. Thailand: 363 fig. 272, 1961
o **Bulbophyllum triste** Rchb.f., Walp. Ann. 6: 253, 1861
BM 8943
N.W. Himalaya, India, Nepal, Sikkim, Assam, Bengal, Burma – E
Bulbophyllum alopecurus Rchb.f., Gard. Chron.: 70, 1880
Bulbophyllum micranthum Hook.f., Fl. Brit. Ind. 5: 768, 1890
Phyllorchis alopecurus (Rchb.f.) Kuntze, Rev. Gen. 2: 677, 1891
Phyllorchis micrantha (Hook.f.) Kuntze, Rev. Gen. 2: 677, 1891
Phyllorchis tristis (Rchb.f.) Kuntze, Rev. Gen. 2: 677, 1891
Bulbophyllum mackeeanum Guill., Bull. Mus. Paris 2. s., 34, 1: 95, 1962
non Bulbophyllum micranthum Rodr., Contr. Jard. Bot. Rio de Janeiro fasc. 6 ano 11, 1937
Bulbophyllum uniflorum (Blume) Hassk., Fl. Beibl. 2: 1, 1842
BM 8216
Malaya, Sumatra, Java – E
Ephippium uniflorum Blume, Bijdr.: 309, 1825
Cirrhopetalum compressum Lindl., Bot. Reg.: sub. t. 49. 1843
Sarcopodium reinwardtii Lindl., Fol. Orch. Sarc.: 4, 1853
Bulbophyllum reinwardtii (Lindl.) Rchb.f., Walp. Ann. 6: 246, 1861
Dendrobium grandiflorum Reinw. ex Hook.f., Fl. Brit. Ind.: 755, 1890
Phyllorchis uniflora (Blume) Kuntze, Rev. Gen. 2: 678, 1891
Phyllorchis reinwardtii (Lindl.) Kuntze, Rev. Gen. 2: 678, 1891
o Bulbophyllum galbinum Ridley, J. Linn. Soc. 32: 267, 1896
non Cirrhopetalum uniflorum Schltr., Engl. Bot. Jahrb. 59: 81, 1906
o **Bulbophyllum virescens** J.J. Smith, Bull. Buitenz. 7: 3, 1900
BM 8327
Java, Ambon – E
Bulbopyhllum weberi Ames, Phil. J. Sci. 7: 128 & 142, 1912
BM 4237
Philippines – up to 1500 m – E
o Cirrhopetalum thouarsii auct. non. Lindl. 1830, Lindl.; Bot. Reg. 24: t. 11, 1839
Bulbophyllum longiflorum auct. non Thouars; Rchb.f., Walp. Ann. 6: 260, 1861
Cirrhopetalum weberi (Ames) Senghas, Orchideen 1: 775, 1983
Bulbophyllum baucoense Ames, Orchid. 5: 166, 1915
o **Bulbophyllum weddelii** (Lindl.) Rchb.f., Walp. Ann. 6: 251, 1861
BM 7958
Brazil – E
Didactyle weddelii Lindl., Fol. Orch. Didact.: 2, 1852
Xiphizusa weddelii Rchb.f., Bot. Z. 10: 919, 1852 (nom. tant.)
Phyllorchis weddelii (Lindl.) Kuntze, Rev. Gen. 1: 678, 1891
Bulbophyllum wendlandianum (Kraenzlin) Dammer, Orchis 1: 87, 1907
BM 7198
Burma, Thailand – E
o Cirrhopetalum collettii Hook.f., Fl. Brit. Ind. 5: 773, 1890
Cirrhopetalum wendlandianum Kraenzlin, Gard. Chron.: 612, 1891
Cirrhopetalum proliferum hort., Kew Handl. Orch.: 57, 1896 (nomen nudum)
Bulbophyllum collettii auct. non King & Pantl., Seidenfaden & Smitinand: 354 fig. 265, 1961
o **Caladenia carnea** R.Br., Prodr. Fl. Nov. Holl.: 324, 1810
BM 7630 B
Australia (S.E. Queensland, E. New South Wales), New Zealand, New Caledonia – T

Caladenia catenata (Smith) Druce, Rep. Bot. Exch. Cl. Brit. Isles: Suppl. 2, 1916
BM 7630 A
Australia (S.E. Queensland, E. New South Wales), New Zealand, New Caledonia – T
Arethusa catenata Smith, Exotic Bot. 2: 89 t. 104, 1804
Caladenia alba R.Br., Prodr. 323, 1810
o Caladenia carnea var. alba Benth., Fl. Austral. 6: 387, 1873
Calanthe × dominii Lindl., Gard. Chron.: 4, 1858
BM 5042
o = Calanthe masuca Lindl. × Calanthe furcata Lindl.
o **Calanthe madagascariensis** Rolfe, Kew Bull.: 84, 1906
BM 7780
Madagascar – 1000–1500 m – T
o **Calanthe masuca** (D. Don) Lindl., Wall. Cat.: No. 7337, 1832
BM 4541
Sri Lanka, Trop. Asia, Taiwan, Java, Sumatra, Borneo – T
Bletia masuca D. Don, Prod. Fl. Nepal.: 30, 1825
Zoduba masuca (D. Don) Buch.-Ham., Prodr. Fl. Nepal: 30, 1825
Calanthe versicolor Lindl., Ser. Orch.: t. 42, 1838
Calanthe emarginata Lindl., Ic. Pl. 3: t. 918, 1845
Calanthe wightii Rchb.f., Walp. Ann. 6: 932, 1861
Alismorchis masuca (D. Don) Kuntze, Rev. Gen. 2: 650, 1891
Calanthe pulchra (Blume) Lindl., Gen. Sp. Orch. Pl.: 250, 1833
BM 6104
Malaya, Sumatra, Java, Borneo, Philippines – up to 1000 m – T, E
Amblyglottis pulchra Blume, Bijrd.: 371, 1825
Styloglossum nervosum Breda, Gen. Sp. Orch. Asclep.: t. 7, 1827
o Calanthe curculigoides Lindl., Gen. Sp. Orch. Pl.: 251, 1833
Alismorchis pulchra (Blume) Kuntze, Rev. Gen.: 650, 1891
Calanthe curantigoides Kuntze, Rev. Gen.: 650, 1891
o **Calanthe reflexa** Maxim., Bull. Acad. Petersb. 18: 68, 1873
BM 9648
Japan, W. China – T
Calanthe puberula Lindl., Gen. Sp. Orch. Pl.: 252, 1833
Alismorchis reflexa (Maxim.) Kuntze, Rev. Gen.: 650, 1891
Paracalanthe reflexa (Maxim.) Kudô, J. Soc. Trop. Agr. Taiwan 2: 235, 1930
Calanthe okushirrensis Miyabe & Tatew., Trans. Nat. Hist. Soc. 14: 190, 1936
Calanthe reflexa var. okushirrensis (Miyabe & Tatew.) Ohwi, Orch. Flow. 2: 86, 1971
Calanthe puberula var. reflexa (Maxim.) Hiroe, Orch. Flow. 2: 86, 1971
Calanthe rosea (Lindl.) Benth., J. Linn. Soc. 18: 309, 1880
BM 5312
Thailand, Burma – T
o Limatodes rosea Lindl., Paxt. Flow. Gard. 3: 35 t. 81, 1852
Alismorchis rosea (Lindl.) Kuntze, Rev. Gen.: 650, 1891
o **Calanthe striata** (Thunb.) Lindl., Gen. Sp. Orch. Pl.: 251, 1833
BM 7026
Japan, Ryukyu Is. – T
Limodorum striatum Thunb., Fl. Jap.: 28, 1784
Calanthe discolor Lindl., Sert. Orch. sub.t. 9, 1838
Calanthe bicolor Lindl., Sert Orch.: sub.t. 9, 1838
Calanthe lurida Decne, Rev. Hort. s. 4, 4: 381, 1855
Calanthe sieboldii Decne ex Regel, Ind. Sem. Hort. Petrop.: 80, 1868
Calanthe discolor var. viridialba Maxim., Bull. Acad. Petersb. 8: 642, 1872
Alismorchis discolor (Lindl.) Kuntze, Rev. Gen. 2: 650, 1891
Alismorchis discolor var. kanashiroi Fukuyama, Trans. Nat. Hist. Soc. Formosa 32: 271, 1942
Calanthe amamiana Fukuyama, Act. Phytotax. & Geobot. 14: 134, 1952
Calanthe discolor forma viridialba (Maxim.) Honda, Nom. Pl. Jap.: 364, 1957
Calanthe discolor var. amamiana (Kukuyama) Masam., Sci. Rep. Kanazawa Univ. 9: 136, 1964
Calanthe tokunoshimensis Hatusima & Ida, J. Geobot. 17: 98, 1969
Calanthe discolor var. divaricatipetala Ida, J. Geobot. 17: 98, 1969
Calanthe amamiana var. latilabella Ida, J. Geobot. 17: 98, 1969
Calanthe tokumoshimensis forma latilabella (Ida) Hatusima, Fl. of the Ryukyus: 862, 1971
Calanthe sylvatica (Thouars) Lindl., Gen. Sp. Orch. Pl.: 250, 1833
BM 6844
Trop. & S. Africa, Madagascar, Mauritius, Réunion – 700–1200 m – T
Centrosis sylvatica Thouars, Orch. Iles Afr.: t. 35 & 36, 1822
o Calanthe natalensis Rchb.f., Bonpl. 4: 322, 1856
Calanthe corymbosa Lindl., J. Linn. Soc. 6: 129, 1862
Calanthe delphinioides Kraenzlin, Engl. Bot. Jahrb. 17: 55, 1893
Calanthe volkensii Rolfe, F.T.A. 7: 46, 1896
Calanthe warpurii Rolfe, Kew Bull.: 85, 1906
Calanthe stolzii Schltr., Engl. Bot. Jahrb. 53: 569, 1915
Calanthe neglecta Schltr., Engl. Bot. Jahrb.: 570, 1915
Calanthe schliebenii Mansf., Notizbl. Bot. Gart. Berlin 11: 808, 1933
o **Calanthe tricarinata** Lindl., Gen. Sp. Orch. Pl.: 252, 1833
BM 8803
Himalaya (Kashmir to Bhutan), W. China, Japan – 1800–2000 m – T
Calanthe pantlingii Schltr., Fedde Rep. Beih. 4: 240, 1919
Calanthe triplicata (Willem.) Ames, Phil. J. Sci. Bot. 2: 326 fig. 14 c, 1907
BM 2615
Sri Lanka, E. India, S.E. Asia, Indonesia, Japan, Fiji, Australia, Guam – T
Orchis triplicata Willem., Usteri Ann. Bot. 6 pt. 12: 52, 1796
o Limodorum veratrifolium Willd., Sp. Pl. 4: 122, 1805
Limodorum ventricosum Steudel, Nomencl. 1.: 481, 1821
Calanthe veratrifolia (Willd.) R.Br., Bot. Reg. 9: t. 720, 1823
Ambyglottis veratrifolia (Willd.) Blume, Bijdr. 8: 370, 1825
Calanthe furcata Bateman ex Lindl., Bot. Reg. 24: Misc. p. 28, 1838
Calanthe perottetii A. Rich., Ann. Sci. Nat. s. 2, 15: 68, 1841
Calanthe comosa Rchb.f., Linnaea 19: 374, 1846
Calanthe odora Griffith, Notul. 3: 365, 1851
Alismorchis japonica Kuntze, Rev. Gen.: 650, 1851
Alismorchis pleiochroma Kuntze, Rev. Gen.: 650, 1851
Alismorchis textorii Kuntze, Rev. Gen.: 650, 1851
Calanthe gracillima Lindl., Fol. Orch. Calanthe: 26, 1854
Calanthe catiligera Rchb.f., Bonpl. 5: 37, 1857
Calanthe textori (Kuntze) Miq., Prol. Fl. Jap.: 136, 1867
Calanthe japonica (Kuntze) Blume ex Miq., Prol. Fl. Jap.: 137, 1867
Calanthe pleiochroma (Kuntze) Rchb.f., Gard. Chron.: 938, 1871
Calanthe violacea Decne. ex Maxim., Mel. Biol. 8: 646, 1873
? Calanthe angraeciflora Rchb.f., Linnaea 41: 75, 1877
Alismorchis veratrifolia (Willd.) Kuntze, Rev. Gen. Pl. 2: 650, 1891
Alismorchis gracillima (Lindl.) Kuntze, Rev. Gen. Pl. 2: 650, 1891
Alismorchis diploxiphion (Hook.f.) Kuntze, Rev. Gen. Pl. 2: 650, 1891
Alismorchis odora (Griffith) Kuntze, Rev. Gen. Pl. 2: 650, 1891
Alismorchis furcata (Bateman ex Lindl.) Kuntze, Rev. Gen. Pl. 2: 650, 1891
Calanthe celebica Rolfe, Kew Bull.: 129, 1899
Calanthe matsumurana Schltr., Fedde Rep. 2: 168, 1906
Calanthe okinawensis Hayata, Mat. Fl. Form.: 331, 1911
Calanthe orthocentron Schltr., Fedde Rep. Beih. 1: 380, 1912
Calanthe veratrifolia var. kennyi Bail., Queensl. Agr. J. 28: 276, 1912
Calanthe veratrifolia var. dupliciloba J.J. Smith, Bull. Buitenz. 3. s. 5: 69, 1922
? Calanthe pubescens Ridley, Kew Bull.: 117, 1923
Calanthe veratrifolia var. incurvicalcar J.J. Smith, Bull. Buitenz. 3. s. 11 (2): 115,1931
Calanthe veratrifolia var. densissima J.J. Smith, Bull, Buitenz. 3. s. 11 (2): 116, 1931
Calanthe veratrifolia var. lancipetala J.J. Smith, Bull. Buitenz. 3. s. 11 (1): 74, 1931
Calanthe veratrifolia var. timorensis J.J. Smith, Fedde Rep. 35: 110, 1934
Calanthe furcata forma albo-lineata Nakajima, J. Geobot. 17: 81, 1969
Calanthe furcata forma albo-marginata Nakajima, J. Geobot. 17: 55, 1969
Calanthe triplicata forma albo-lineata (Nak.) Hatusima, Fl. of the Ryukyus: 862, 1971
o **Calanthe × veitchii** Lindl., Gard. Chron.: 1016, 1859
BM 5375
= Calanthe rosea Benth. × Calanthe vestita Lindl.
o **Calanthe vestita** Lindl., Gen. Sp. Orch. Pl.: 250, 1833
BM 4671
Burma, S. Vietnam, Malaya, Sumatra, Bangka, Java, Borneo, Celebes – T
Cyteris griffithii Wight, Ic. 5: t. 1751, 1852
Preptanthe vestita (Lindl.) Rchb.f., Fl. Serres 8: 245, 1852
Amblyglottis pilosa De Vriese ex Lindl., Fol. Orch. Calanthe: 11, 1854
Preptanthe villosa Rchb.f., Bonpl. 5: 42, 1857
Calanthe pilosa (De Vriese) Miq., Fl. Bat. 3: 711, 1859
Calanthe regnieri Rchb.f., Gard. Chron.: 274, 1883
Calanthe turneri Rchb.f., Gard. Chron.: 274, 1883
Calanthe grandiflora Rolfe, Orch. Rev. 9: 141, 1901
Calanthe padangensis Schltr. ex Mansf., Fedde Rep. Beih. 74, 4: t. 54 fig. 214, 1934
o **Calochilus campestris** R.Br., Prodr. Fl. Nov. Holl.: 320, 1810
BM 3187
E. Australia, New Zealand – T
Calochilus cupreus R. Rogers, Trans. Roy. Soc. 42: 24 t. 2, 1918

Calopogon tuberosus (L.) Britton, Sterns & Pogg., Prel. Cat. N.Y.: 52, 1888
BM 116
USA (Virginia) – T
o Limodorum tuberosum L., Sp. Pl. 2: 950, 1753
Limodorum pulchellum Salisb., Prodr. 8: 1796
Calopogon pulchellus (Salisb.) R.Br., Hort. Kew. ed. 2. 5: 204, 1813
Cathea tuberosa (L.) Morong, Bull. Torrey Club 20: 34 & 121, 1893
Limodorum simpsonii Small, Fl. SE. U.S.: 322, 1903
Calopogon pulchellus var. simpsonii (Small) Ames, Contr. Orch. S. Fla.: 18, 1904
Limodorum tuberosum var. nanum Nieuwland, Am. Midl. Nat. 3: 130, 1913
Calopogon pulchellus var. latifolius (St. John) Fernald, Rhodora 48: 188, 1946
Calypso bulbosa (L.) Ames var. **americana** (R.Br.) Luer, Nat. Orch. USA, Canada excluding Florida: 336, 1975
BM 2763
N. America – T
Cypripedium bulbosum L., Sp. Pl.: 951, 1753
Cymbidium boreale Sw., Nov. Act. Upsal. 6: 76, 1799
Limodorum boreale (Sw.) Sw., Neues J. 1: 85, 1805
o Calypso borealis (Sw.) Salisb., Parad. Lond.: 89, 1807
Cytherea borealis (Sw.) Salisb., Trans. Hort. Soc. 1: 301, 1812
Calypso americana R.Br., Hort. Kew ed. 2. 5: 208, 1813
Orchidium boreale (Sw.) Sw., Svensk. Bot.: t. 518, 1816
Orchidium americanum (R.Br.) Steudel, Nom. Bot. ed. 2. 2: 222, 1841
Calypso bulbosa (L.) Oakes, Thomp., Hist. of. V. t. 1: 200, 1842
Cytherea bulbosa (L.) House, Bull. Torrey Club 32: 382, 1905
o **Catasetum atratum** Lindl., Bot. Reg. 24: Misc. 114, t. 63, 1838
BM 5202
Brazil – E
Catasetum adnatum Steudel, Nom. Bot. ed. 2. I: 311, 1841
Catasetum mentosum Lemaire, Jard. Fleur. 3: Misc. 65, 1852/53
Catasetum pallidum Klotzsch, Allg. Gartenz. 23: 217, 1855
Catasetum barbatum Lindl., Bot. Reg. 30: Misc. 38, 1844
BM 3514, BM 3802, BM 7069, BM 7470
Venezuela, Guyana, Surinam, Brazil, Colombia, Ecuador, Peru, Bolivia – E, T
o Myanthus barbatus Lindl., Bot Reg. 21: t. 1778, 1835
Monachanthus viridis Schomb., Trans. Linn. Soc. 17: 551 t. 29, 1837
Catasetum proboscideum Lindl., Bot. Reg. 25: Misc. p. 86, 1839
Catasetum spinosum Lindl., Bot. Reg. 26: Misc. p. 65, 1840
o Myanthus spinosus (Lindl.) Hook., Bot. Mag.: t. 3802, 1840
Catasetum barbatum var. proboscideum Lindl., Bot. Reg. 27: t. 5 fig. 3, 1841
Catasetum lanciferum Lindl., Bot. Reg. 25: t. 5 fig. 5, 1841
Catasetum cristatum var. spinosum Hook., Cent. Orch. 46: t. 54, 1846
Catasetum cristatum var. spinigerum Hook., Cent. Orch. 46: t. 54, 1846
Catasetum rivularium Barb. Rodr., Gen. & Sp. Orch. 1: 130, 1877
Catasetum crinitum Lind. & Rchb.f., Ill. Hort. 28: Misc. p. 80, 1881
o Catasetum garnettianum Rolfe, Gard. Chron.: 692, 1888
Catasetum tridentatum Pfitzer, Nat. Pflanzenf. 2: 6: 160 fig. 163, 1888
Catasetum barbatum var. spinosum Rolfe, Lindenia 7: 23, 1891
Catasetum macrocarpum Stein, Orchideenb.: fig. 36, 1892
o Catasetum randii Rolfe, Kew Bull.: 394, 1894
Catasetum comosum Cogn., J. Orch. 6: 266, 1895
Catasetum appendiculatum Schltr., Beih. Bot. Centralbl. 42, pt. 2: 115, 1925
Catasetum brachybulbon Schltr., Beih. Bot. Centralbl. 42, pt. 2: 116, 1925
Catasetum polydactylon Schltr., Beih. Bot. Centralbl. 42, pt. 2: 122, 1925
Catasetum buchtienii Kraenzlin, Fedde Rep. 25: 27, 1928
Catasetum barbatum var. barbatum Mansf., Fedde Rep. 31: 116, 1932
o **Catasetum callosum** Lindl., Bot. Reg. 26: Misc. p. 77 No. 183, 1840
BM 4219, BM 6648
Venezuela, Colombia, Peru, Brazil, Guyana – E
o Catasetum callosum var. grandiflorum Hook., Bot. Mag.: t. 4219, 1846
Catasetum lansbergii Lindl., Paxt. Flow. Gard. 1: 156, 1850
Catasetum callosum var. crenatum Regel, Gartenfl. 2: 273, 1853
Catasetum carunculatum Rchb.f. & Warsc., Allg. Gartenz. 22: 174, 1854
Myanthus grandiflorus Beer, Prakt. Orch.: 272, 1854
Catasetum fuliginosum Rolfe, Gard. Chron.: 473, 1887 (non Lindl.)
Catasetum darwinianum Rolfe, Gard. Chron.: 394, 1889
Catasetum arachnoideum Ames, Am. Gard.: 741, 1898
Catasetum callosum var. carunculatum (Rchb.f. & Warsc.) Mansf., Fedde Rep. 31: 114, 1932
Catasetum callosum var. eucallosum Mansf., Fedde Rep. 31: 114, 1932
o **Catasetum cernuum** (Lindl.) Rchb.f., Walp. Ann. 6: 670, 1863
BM 3262, BM 5399
Trinidad, Venezuela, N. Brazil – E
Myanthus cernuus Lindl., Bot. Reg. 18: sub. t. 1538, 1832
Monachanthus viridis Lindl., Bot. Reg. 18: sub. t. 1538, 1832
o Catasetum trifidum Hook., Bot. Mag.: t. 3262, 1833
Catasetum viride (Lindl.) Lindl., Bot. Reg. 27: Misc. p. 79, 1841
Catasetum deltoideum (Lindl.) Mutel, Prem. Mém. sur Orch., 1838
BM 3923
Guyana – E
o Myanthus deltoideus Lindl., Bot. Reg. 22: t. 1896, 1836
Catasetum discolor Lindl. var. **fimbriatum** Rchb.f., Saund. Ref. Bot. 2: t. 83, 1869
BM 3708
Brazil – E
o Monachanthus fimbriatus Gardner ex Hook., Bot. Mag.: t. 3708, 1839
Monachanthus bushnanii var. fimbriatum Rchb.f., Saund. Ref. Bot. 2: t. 83, 1869 & sub. t. 137, 1872
Catasetum gardneri Schltr., Orchis 8: 84, 1914
Catasetum discolor Lindl. var. **roseo-album** (Hook.) Mansf., Fedde Rep. 30: 264, 1932
BM 3796, BM 3832
Brazil, Venezuela – E, T
o Monachanthus roseo-albus Hook., Bot. Mag.: t. 3796, 1840
Catasetum roseo-album (Hook.) Lindl., Bot. Reg. 26: 65, 1840
o Monachanthus bushnanii Hook., Bot. Mag.: t. 3832, 1841
Catasetum ciliatum Barb. Rodr., Gen. & Sp. Orch. 1: 130, 1877
Monachanthus bushnanii var. vinosum Cogn., J. Orch. 5: 240 252, 1894
Catasetum discolor Lindl. var. **viridiflorum** Cogn., Fl. Bras. 3, pt. 5: 445, 1902
BM 3601 a+b
Brazil – E
o Monochanthus discolor var. viridiflorus Hook., Bot. Mag. 64: t. 3601, fig. B, 1837
o Monochanthus discolor var. bushnanii Hook., Bot. Mag. 64: t. 3601, fig. A, 1837
o **Catasetum fimbriatum** (Morren) Lindl., Paxt. Flow. Gard. 1: 124, 1850
BM 7158
Venezuela, Guyana, Brazil, Paraguay, Argentina, Bolivia – E
Myanthus fimbriatus Morren, Ann. Soc. Hort. Gard. 4: 453, 1848
Catasetum fimbriatum var. fissum Rchb.f., Gard. Chron.: 498, 1881
Catasetum fimbriatum var. viridulum Rchb.f., G. Chron.: 272, 1887
Catasetum fimbriatum var. cogniauxii Linden, J. Orch. 6: 282, 1895
Catasetum fimbriatum var. callosum Linden, J. Orch. 6: 283, 1895
Catasetum cogniauxii Linden, J. Orch. 11: 223, 1900
Catasetum fimbriatum var. aurantiacum Porsch, Denschr. Akad. Wien 79: 35, 1906
Catsetum fimbriatum var. brevipetalum Porsch, Denkschr. Akad. Wien 79: 35, 1906
Catasetum fimbriatum var. micranthum Porsch, Denkschr. Akad. Wien 79: 35, 1906
Catasetum ornithorrhynchus Porsch, Denkschr. Akad. Wien 79: 35, 1906
Catasetum pflanzii Schltr., Fedde Rep. 11: 45, 1912
Catasetum wredeanum Schltr., Orchis 9: 14, 1915
Catasetum inconstans Hoehne, Comm. L. T. Estr. M. Gr. Amazonas 5: 57, 1915
Catasetum fimbriatum var. subtropicale Hauman, Ann. Mus. Nac. Buenos Aires 29: 380, 1917
Catasetum fimbriatum var. morrenianus Mansf., Fed. Rep. 31: 108, 1932
Catasetum fimbriatum var. ornithorrhynchum Mansf., Fedde Rep. 31: 109, 1932
Catasetum galeritum Rchb.f., Gard. Chron.: 616, 1886
BM 8093
Brazil – E
o Catasetum galeritum var. pachyglossum Rchb. f., G. Chron.: 73, 1889
Catasetum galeritum var. galeritum (Rchb.f.) Mansf., Fedde Rep. 31: 104, 1932
o **Catasetum globiflorum** Hook., Bot. Mag.: t. 3942, 1842
BM 3942
Brazil – E
Catasetum globiferum Beer, Prakt. Stud. Orch.: 205, 1854
o **Catasetum integerrimum** Hook., Bot. Mag.: t. 3823, 1840
BM 3823 a+b, BM 3937
Mexico, Belize, Guatemala, Honduras, El Salvador, Nicaragua, Costa Rica – E
Catasetum maculatum auct. non Kunth; Bateman, Orch. Mex. & Guat. 2, 1837
Catasetum integerrimum var. purpurascens Hook., Bot. Mag.: sub. t. 3823, 1840
Catasetum integerrimum var. viridiflorum Hook., Bot. Mag.: sub. t. 3823, 1840

o Catasetum wailesii Hook., Bot. Mag.: t. 3937, 1842
Catasetum rostratum Klinge, Act. Hort. Petrop. 17, 1: 134, 1899
Catasetum brenesii Schltr., Fedde Rep. Beih. 19: 136 & 225, 1923
o **Catasetum lemosii** Rolfe, Kew Bull. 1894: 393, Addit. S. 4: 78, 1894
BM 7444
Brazil, Amazonas - E
Catasetum roseum Barb. Rodr., Gen. & Sp. Orch. 1: 128, 1877 (non Rchb.f., 1872)
Catasetum longifolium Lindl., Bot. Reg. 25: Misc.p. 94, 1839
BM 3819
Brazil, Venezuela, Guyana, Surinam - E
o Monachanthus longifolius (Lindl.) Hook., Bot. Mag.: t. 3819, 1840
o **Catasetum luridum** (Link) Lindl., Gen. Sp. Orch. Pl.: 156, 1832
BM 3590, BM 3929
Brazil - E
Anguloa lurida Link, Verhandl. Gartenb. Königl. Preuss. Staat. 1: 289 t. 6, 1824
Epidendrum olare Vell., Fl. Flum. Ic. 9: t. 5, 1827
Catasetum craniomorphum Hoffsgg. ex Heynh., Nom. Bot. 2: 126, 1840 (nomen tantum)
Catachaetum lituratum Hoffsgg., Verz. Orch.: 45, 1842
Catachaetum squalidum Hoffsgg., Verz. Orch.: 46, 1842
o Catasetum abruptum Hook., Bot. Mag.: t. 3929, 1842
Catasetum macrocarpum Rich. ex. Kunth, Syn. Pl. Aequin. 1: 331, 1822
BM 2559, BM 3329
Trinidad, Venezuela, Guyana, Surinam, Brazil - 500–1100 m - E
Catasetum claveringii Lindl. ex van Jeel, Bot Reg. 10: t. 840, 1824
o Catasetum tridentatum Hook., Exot. Fl. 2: t. 90, 91, 1825
Catasetum floribundum Hook., Exot. Fl. 2: t. 151, 1825
Monachanthus viridis Lindl., Bot. Reg. 21: t. 1752, 1836
Catachaetum claveringii (Lindl. ex Van Jeel) Hoffsgg., Verz. Orch.: 38, 1842
Catachaetum floribundum (Hook.) Hoffsgg., Verz. Orch.: 38, 1842
Catasetum tricolor hort. ex Planchon, Hort. Donat. 25, 1858
Catasetum linguiferum Schltr., Beih. Bot. Centralbl. 42, pt. 2: 120, 1925
o **Catasetum maculatum** Kunth, Syn. Pl. Aequin 1: 331, 1822
BM 9347
Guatemala, Nicaragua, Costa Rica, Panama - E
Catasetum oerstedii Rchb.f., Bonpl. 3: 218, 1855
o **Catasetum microglossum** Rolfe, Bot. Mag.: t. 8514, 1913
BM 8514
Colombia, Ecuador, Peru - E
Catasetum pileatum Rchb.f., Gard. Chron.: 492, 1882
BM 6998
Venezuela, Trinidad, Brazil, Amazonas, Colombia, Ecuador - E
o Catasetum bungerothii N.E.Br., Lindenia 2: 21 t. 57, 1886
o **Catasetum purum** Nees, Pl. Hort. Bonn. Ic. 1: t. 1, 1824
BM 3388
Brazil - E
Catasetum semiapertum Hook., Exot. Fl. 3: t. 213, 1826
Catasetum inapertum Steudel, Nom. Bot. ed. 2.1: 311, 1840
Catachaetum purum (Nees) Hoffsgg., Verz. Orch.: 38, 1842
Catachaetum semiapertum (Hook.) Hoffsgg., Verz. Orch.: 38, 1842
o **Catasetum quadridens** Rolfe, Kew Bull.: 149, 1901
BM 7864
Brazil - E
Catasetum saccatum Lindl. var. **christyanum** (Rchb.f.) Mansf., Fedde Rep. 30: 272, 1932
BM 8007
Guyana, Brazil, Ecuador, Peru, Bolivia - E
Catasetum incurvum Klotzsch, Allg. Gartenz. 22: 178, 1854
Catasetum secundum Klotzsch, Allg. Gartenz. 22: 178, 1854
Catasetum baraquinianum Lemaire, Ill. Hort. 9: Misc.p. 81 & 90, 1862
o Catasetum christyanum Rchb.f., Gard. Chron.: 588, 1882
Catasetum christyanum var. obscurum Rchb.f., Gard. Chron.: 649, 1884
Catasetum stupendum Cogn., J. Orch. 6: 13, 1895
Catasetum cruciatum Schltr., Orchis 10: 183, 1916
Catasetum colossus Schltr., Bot. Centralbl. 42: 118, 1925
Catasetum sanguineum Lindl., Paxt. Flow. Gard. 2: 168 fig. 225, 1852
BM 4792
Costa Rica, Venezuela, Colombia, Ecuador - up to 1000 m - E
o Catasetum naso Hook., Bot. Mag.: t. 4792, 1854 (non Lindl.)
Catasetum sanguineum var. integrale Rchb.f., Gard. Chron.: 214, 1887
o **Catasetum tenebrosum** Kraenzlin, Gard. Chron.: 229, 1910
BM 9086
Ecuador, Peru - up to 1000 m - E

o **Catasetum viridiflavum** Hook., Bot. Mag.: t. 4017, 1843
BM 4017
S. America, Panama - E
Catasetum serratum Lindl., Bot. Reg. n.s. 10: post. t. 24, 1847
o **Cattleya acklandiae** Lindl., Bot. Reg. 26: t. 48, 1840
BM 5039
Brazil (Bahia) - E
Epidendrum acklandiae (Lindl.) Rchb.f., Walp. Ann. 6: 312, 1861
o **Cattleya amethystoglossa** Linden & Rchb.f., Cat. Pl. Exot.: 26, 1857
BM 5683
Brazil - E, L
Cattleya guttata var. prinzii Rchb.f., Bonpl. 4: 327, 1856
Epidendrum amethystoglossum (Linden & Rchb.f.) Rchb.f., Walp. Ann. 6: 319, 1861
Epidendrum elatius var. prinzii (Rchb.f.) Rchb.f., Xen. Orch. 2: 33, 1862
Cattleya amethystoglossa var. sulphurea Rchb.f., Gard. Chron.: 313, 1866 (ic. tantum)
Cattleya guttata var. keteleerii Houllet, Rev. Hort.: 350, 1875
Cattleya purpurina Barb. Rodr., Gen. & Sp. Orch. 2: 158, 1882
o **Cattleya bicolor** Lindl., Bot. Reg. 22: sub.t. 1919, 1836
BM 4909
Brazil - up to 800 m - E
Epidendrum bicolor (Lindl.) Rchb.f., Walp. Ann. 6: 311, 1861
Cattleya grossi Kraenzlin, Gartenfl. 46: 113 t. 1436, 1897
Cattleya measuresiana (L.O. Williams) Blume, Publ. Cient. Inst. Genét. Univ. S. Paulo No. 2: 26, 1961
Cattleya deckeri Klotzsch, Allg. Gartenz. 23: 81, 1855
BM 4916
Mexico, C. America, W. Indies - E
o Cattleya skinneri var. parviflora Hook., Bot. Mag.: t. 4916, 1856
o Cattleya guatemalensis Moore, Fl. Mag. 1: t. 61, 1861
o **Cattleya dowiana** Bateman, Gard. Chron.: 922, 1866
BM 5618
Costa Rica, Panama, Colombia - E
Cattleya labiata var. dowiana Veitch, Man. Orch. Pl. 2: 16, 1887
o **Cattleya elongata** Barb. Rodr., Gen. & Sp. Orch. 1: 72, 1877
BM 7543
E. Brazil - E, L
? Cattleya nilsonii hort., Gartenfl.: 481, 1889
Cattleya alexandrae Linden & Rolfe, Gard. Chron.: 522, 1892
Cattleya alexandrae var. elegans Rolfe, Lindenia 8: 47 t. 358, 1892
o **Cattleya forbesii** Lindl., Coll. Bot.: sub.t. 37, 1821 ad. 1824
BM 3265
Brazil - E
Epidendrum pauper Vell., Fl. Flum.: t. 13, 1790
Maelenia paradoxa Dumort., l'Hortic. Belg. 2: 198 t. 44, 1834
Cattleya vestalis Hoffsgg., Verz. Orch.: 46, 1843
Cattleya fulva Beer, Prakt. Stud. Orch.: 210, 1854
Cattleya isopetala Beer, Prakt. Stud. Orch.: 211, 1854
Epidendrum forbesii (Lindl.) Rchb.f., Walp. Ann. 6: 316, 1861
Cattleya pauper (Vell.) Stellf., Arq. Mus. Paranaense 4: 357, 1945
o **Cattleya granulosa** Lindl., Bot. Reg. 28: t. 1, 1842
BM 5048
Guatemala, Brazil - E
Epidendrum granulosum (Lindl.) Rchb.f., Walp. Ann. 6: 319, 1861
Cattleya harrisoniana Bateman ex Lindl., Bot. Reg.: sub. t. 1919, 1836
BM 4085
Brazil - E
Cattleya harrisoniae Paxton, Mag. Bot. 4: 247, 1838
Cattleya harrisoniae P.N. Don, Florist' J.: 183, 1840
? Cattleya concolor Drapiez, Hort. Univ. 2: 197, 1841
o Cattleya intermedia var. variegata Hook., Bot. Mag.: t. 4085, 1844
Cattleya papeiansiana Morren, Ann. Gand. 1: 57 t. 5, 1845
Cattleya harrisonii Beer, Prakt. Stud. Orch.: 211, 1854
Epidendrum harrisonianum (Bateman ex Lindl.) Rchb.f., Walp. Ann. 6: 317, 1861
Cattleya loddigesii var. harrisoniae Veitch, Man. Orch. pl. 2: 42, 1887
Cattleya loddigesii var. harrisoniana Rolfe, Gard. Chron.: 746, 1889
o **Cattleya intermedia** Graham ex Hook., Bot. Mag.: t. 2851, 1828
BM 2851
Brazil - E
Cattleya ovata Lindl., Bot. Reg. 22: t. 1919, 1836
Cattleya maritima Lindl., Bot. Reg. 22: sub.t. 1919, 1836
Cattleya loddigesii var. intermedia Lindl., Bot. Reg. 30: sub. t. 5, 1844 (misapplied name)
Cattleya amethystina Morren, Ann. Gand. 4: 217 t. 201, 1848
? Cattleya ianthina hort., Gard. Chron.: 247, 1853 (nomen)
Cattleya loddigesii var. amethystina Lemaire, Jard. Fleur. 4: sub.t. 379, 1853
Epidendrum intermedium (Graham ex Hook.) Rchb.f., Walp. Ann. 6: 318, 1861

Cattleya amabilis Lindl. ex Du Buyss., l'Orchidoph.: 232, 1878
Cattleya aquinii Barb. Rodr., Pl. Nov. Jard. Bot. Rio 1: 23t. 4c., 1891
○ **Cattleya iricolor** Rchb.f., Gard. Chron.: 162, 1874
BM 7287
Ecuador – up to 800 m – E
○ **Cattleya labiata** Lindl., Coll. Bot.: t. 33, 1821–24
BM 3998
Brazil – E
Cattleya perrinii Endl., Harting. Parad. Vindob. 1: t. 10, 1844 (non Lindl.)
Cattleya lemoniana Lindl., Bot. Reg. 32: t. 35, 1846
Cattleya pallida Lindl., Paxt. Flow. Gard. 2: 51 t. 48, 1851
Epidendrum labiatum (Lindl.) Rchb.f., Walp. Ann. 6: 313, 1861
Cattleya regalis hort., Gard. Chron.: 404, 1883
Cattleya nalderiana Rchb.f., Gard. Chron.: 756, 1883
Cattleya labiata var. autumnalis L. Linden, Lindenia 3: 35 t. 112, 1887
Cattleya autumnalis hort., l'Orchidoph.: 122, 1887
Cattleya warocqueana L. Linden, J. Orch. 1: 219, 1890
Cattleya labiata var. warocqueana Rolfe. Gard. Chron.: 735, 1890
Cattleya labiata var. genuina Stein, Orchideenb.: 124, 1892
○ **Cattleya lawrenceana** Rchb.f., Gard. Chron.: 388 & 374–375 fig. 68 & 69, 1885
BM 7133
Venezuela, Guyana, Brazil – E
Cattleya pumila Schomb., Trav. Brit. Guian. 3: 1068, 1848; (non Hook.)
Cattleya leopoldii Verschaff. ex Lemaire, Ill. Hort. 1: Misc. p. 68, 1854
BM 3693
Brazil – E
? Epidendrum elegans Vell., Fl. Flum. Ic. 9: t. 12, 1827
○ Cattleya guttata var. russelliana Hook., Bot. Mag.: t. 3693, 1838
Cattleya tigrina Rich., Portef. Hort. 2: 166, 1848
Cattleya guttata var. leopoldii (Verschaff. ex Lemaire) Lemaire, Ill. Hort. 2: sub. t. 69, 1855
Epidendrum elatius var. leopoldii (Verschaff. ex Lemaire) Rchb. f., Xen. Orch. 2: 33, 1862
Cattleya guttata L. Linden & Rodigas, Lindenia 10: 21 t. 441, 1894 (non Lindl.)
○ **Cattleya luteola** Lindl., Gard. Chron.: 774, 1853
BM 5032
Brazil, Ecuador, Peru, Bolivia – E
Cattleya meyeri Regel, Gartenfl. 5: 116, 1856
Cattleya florida Klotzsch, Allg. Gartenz. 24: 73, 1856
Cattleya epidendroides hort. ex Rchb.f., Xen. Orch. 1: 209, 1856
Epidendrum luteolum (Lindl.) Rchb.f., Walp. Ann. 6: 313, 1861
Cattleya luteola var. roezlii Rchb.f., Gard. Chron.: 782, 1881
Cattleya sulphurea hort. ex Gard. Chron.: 10, 1883
○ **Cattleya maxima** Lindl., Gen. Sp. Orch. Pl.: 116, 1831
BM 4902
Colombia, Ecuador, Brazil, Amazonas – E
Epidendrum maximum (Lindl.) Rchb.f., Walp. Ann. 6: 316, 1861
Cattleya malouana Linden & Rodigas, Ill. Hort. 33: 102, 1886; (nomen nudum)
○ **Cattleya mossiae** Hook., Bot. Mag.: t. 3669, 1838
BM 3669
Venezuela – E
Cattleya labiata var. mossiae (Hook.) Lindl., Bot. Reg. 26: t. 58, 1840
Cattleya labiata var. atropurpurea Paxton, Mag. Bot. 7: 73, 1844
Cattleya labiata var. picta Lindl. & Paxton, Paxt. Flow. Gard. 1: 118, 1850
Cattleya labiata var. candida Lindl. & Paxton, Paxt. Flow. Gard. 1: 118, 1850
Epidendrum labiatum var. mossiae (Hook.) Rchb.f., Walp. Ann. 6: 314, 1861
Epidendrum labiatum var. pictum (Lindl. & Paxton) Rchb.f., Xen. Orch. 2: 30, 1862
Cattleya edithiana Williams, Orch. Grow. Man. ed. 3: 88, 1868
Cattleya carrieri Houllet, Rev. Hort.: 350, 1876
Cattleya aliciae L. Linden, Lindenia 10: 31 t. 494, 1895
○ **Cattleya rex** O'Brien, Gard. Chron.: 684, 1890
BM 8377
Peru, Colombia – E
Cattleya schilleriana Rchb.f., Allg. Gartenz.: 335, 1857
BM 5150
Brazil – E, L
○ Cattleya schilleriana var. concolor Hook., Bot. Mag.: t. 5150, 1859
Epidendrum schillerianum (Rchb.f.) Rchb.f., Walp. Ann. 6: 318, 1861
Cattleya aclandiae var. schilleriana (Rchb.f.) Jennings, Orch.: t. 25, 1875
○ **Cattleya skinneri** Bateman, Orch. Mex. & Guat.: t. 13, 1838
BM 4270
Mexico, Belize, Guatemala, El Salvador, Honduras, Costa Rica – E

Cattleya trianae Linden & Rchb.f., Bot. Zeit. 18: 74, 1860
BM 5504
Colombia – E
Cattleya labiata var. lindigii Karsten, Fl. Columb. 1: t. 49, 1858–66
Epidendrum labiatum var. trianae (Linden & Rchb.f.) Rchb.f., Walp. Ann. 6: 315, 1861
○ Cattleya quadricolor Bateman, Gard. Chron.: 269, 1864
Cattleya bogotensis Linden ex Morren, Belg. Hort. 15: 102, 1865
Cattleya kimballiana L. Linden & Rodigas, Lindenia 2: 85 t. 89, 1887
Cattleya violacea (Kunth) Rolfe, Gard. Chron.: 802, 1889
BM 4083
Venezuela, Guyana, Brazil, Peru – E
Cymbidium violaceum Kunth, Nov. Gen. & Sp. 1: 341, 1815
○ Cattleya superba Schomb. ex Lindl., Sert. Orch.: t. 22, 1838
Cattleya schomburgkii Lodd. ex Lindl., Sert. Orch.: sub. t. 22, 1838
Epidendrum violaceum (Kunth) Rchb.f., Walp. Ann. 6: 318, 1861
Epidendrum superbum (Schomb. ex Lindl.) Rchb.f., Xen. Orch. 2: 32, 1862
○ **Cattleya × whitei** Rchb.f., Gard. Chron.: 586, 1882
BM 7727
Brazil (Bahia) – E
= Cattleya bicornutum Rchb. f. × Cattleya warneri Moore
Cattleya labiata var. whitei (Rchb.f.) Stein, Orchideenb.: 131, 1892
? Cattleya russeliana Mantin, Rev. Hort.: 353, 1897
Caularthron bicornutum (Hook.) Raf., Fl. Tellur. 2: 41, 1836
BM 3332
Brazil, Guyana, Venezuela, Trinidad, Tobago, Colombia – E
○ Epidendrum bicornutum Hook., Bot. Mag.: t. 3332, 1834
Diacrium bicornutum (Hook.) Benth., J. Linn. Soc. 18: 312, 1881
Diacrium amazonicum Schltr., Beih. Bot. Centralbl. 42, pt. 2: 108, 1925
Centropetalum hartwegii (Rchb. f.) Kraenzlin, Pflanzenr. Heft 83: 30, 1923
BM 5718
Peru – E
○ Nasonia punctata Lindl., Pl. Hartw.: 150, 1844
Nasonia hartwegii Rchb.f., Xen. Orch. 1: 97, 1855
Centropetalum punctatum (Lindl.) Kraenzlin, Pflanzenr. Heft 83: 32, 1923
Cephalantheropsis gracilis (Lindl.) S.Y. Hu, Quart. J. Taiwan Mus.: 25, 1972
BM 4714
India, Sikkim, China, Malay Peninsula, Vietnam, Taiwan, Ryukyu Is., Japan, Philippines – T
○ Calanthe gracilis Lindl., Wall. Cat.: 7341, 1832
Limotodes gracilis (Lindl.) Lindl., Fol. Orch.: 1, 1855
Alismorchis gracilis (Lindl.) Kuntze, Rev. Gen.: 650, 1891
Calanthe venusta Schltr., Fedde Rep. Beih. 4: 69, 1919
Paracalanthe venusta (Schltr.) Kudo, J. Soc. Trop. Agric. 2: 236, 1930
Calanthe dolichopoda Fukuyama, Bot. Mag. Tokyo 49: 296, 1935
Phaius longipes (Hook.f.) Holttum, Gard. Bull. Singapore 11: 286, 1947
Cephalantheropsis venusta (Schltr.) S.Y. Hu, Quart. J. Taiwan Mus. 25 (3/4): 213, 1972
Chelonistele perakensis (Rolfe) Ridley, Fl. Mal. Pen. 4: 138, 1924
BM 8203
Malaya, Borneo – E
○ Coelogyne perakensis Rolfe, Bot. Mag.: t. 8203, 1908
○ **Chelonistele pusilla** (Ridley) Ridley, Fl. Mal. Pen. 4: 138, 1924
BM 9046
Malaya – E
Coelogyne pusilla Ridley, J. Linn. Soc. 32: 327, 1896
Coelogyne decipiens Sander, Orch. Guide: 31, 1901
Chiloschista lunifera (Rchb.f.) J.J. Smith, Orch. Java: 553, 1905
BM 7044
N. India, Sikkim, Burma, Thailand – E
Thrixspermum luniferum Rchb.f., Gard. Chron.: 786, 1868
○ Sarcochilus luniferus (Rchb.f.) Benth. ex Hook.f., Bot. Mag.: t. 7044, 1889
Chloraea bletioides Lindl., Quart. J. Sci. Lit. Art. 50, 1827
BM 2956
Chili – T
Chloraea ulanthoides Lindl., Gen. Sp. Orch. Pl.: 404, 1840
Chloraea ulantha Rolfe, Kew Bull.: 278, 1893
Chloraea grandis Kraenzlin, Orchid. 2: 58, 1904
○ (Neottia grandiflora Hook., Bot. Mag.: t. 2956, 1830; misidentified)
(Ulantha grandiflora Hook., Bot. Mag.: t. 2956, 1830; misidentified)
○ **Chloraea crispa** Lindl., Gen. Sp. Orch. Pl.: 401, 1840
BM 7955
Chili – T
Cymbidium luteum Willd., Sp. Pl. 4: 106, 1805
Chloraea cygnaea Philippi, Linnaea 33: 241, 1864
Chloraea spectabilis Philippi, Linnaea 33: 240, 1864/65

Asarca crispa (Lindl.) Kuntze, Rev. Gen. 2: 652, 1891
Asarca cygnaea (Philippi) Kuntze, Rev. Gen. 2: 652, 1891
o **Chloraea virescens** (Willd.) Lindl., Quart. J. Sci. Lit. Art.: 51, 1827
BM 8100
Chili, Argentina - T
Cymbidium virescens Willd., Sp. Pl. 4: 106, 1805
Chloraea incisa Poeppig. Frag. Syn. Pl. Phan.: 17, 1833
Chloraea chrysantha Poeppig & Endl., Frag. Syn. Pl. Chil.: 15, 1833
Chloraea piquichen Lindl., Gen. Sp. Orch. Pl.: 400, 1840
Chloraea odontoglossa A. Rich., Fl. Chil. 5: 455, 1849
Chloraea unguis-cati Rchb. f., Linnaea 22: 864, 1849
Chloraea fimbriata Philippi, Linnaea 29: 49, 1857 (non Poeppig)
Chloraea chlorosticta Philippi, Linnaea 29: 52, 1857
Chloraea patagonica Philippi, Linnaea 33: 245, 1863-65
Chloraea pigichen Kuntze, Rev. Gen. Pl. 2: 652, 1891
Asarca chlorosticta (Philippi) Kuntze, Rev. Gen. Pl. 2: 652, 1891
Asarca odontoglossa (A. Rich.) Kuntze, Rev. Gen. Pl. 2: 652, 1891
Asarca unguis-cati (Rchb. f.) Kuntze, Rev. Gen. Pl. 2: 652, 1891
Asarca incisa (Poeppig) Kuntze, Rev. Gen. Pl. 2: 652, 1891
Asarca fimbriata (Philippi) Kuntze, Rev. Gen. Pl. 2: 652, 1891
Asarca patagonica (Philippi) Kuntze, Rev. Gen. Pl. 2: 652, 1891
Chloraea pleistodactyla Kraenzlin & Speg., An. Mus. Nac. Buenos Aires 7: 167, 1902
Chusua monophylla (Collett & Hemsley) P. Hunt, Kew Bull. 26 (1): 175, 1971
BM 7601
Burma (Shan Hills) - T
Habenaria monophylla Collett & Hemsley, J. Linn. Soc. 28: 134, 1890
o Orchis monophylla (Collett & Hemsley) Rolfe, Orch. Rev. 6: 144, 1898
Peristylus monophyllus (Collett & Hemsley) Kraenzlin, Orch. Gen. Sp. 1: 516, 1898
o **Chysis aurea** Lindl., Bot. Reg. 23: t. 1937, 1837
BM 3617
Mexico, Belize, Costa Rica, Panama, Venezuela, Colombia, Peru - E
o **Chysis bractescens** Lindl., Bot. Reg. 26: Misc. p. 61, 1840
BM 5186
Mexico, Guatemala - E
Thorvaldsenia speciosa Liebm., Bot. Not.: 103, 1844
Chysis aurea var. bractescens (Lindl.) Allen, Am. Orch. Soc. Bull. 24: 665, 1955
Chysis limminghei Linden & Rchb. f., Allg. Gartenz., 1858
BM 5265
C. America - E
o Chysis aurea var. limminghei (Linden & Rchb. f.) Hook., Bot. Mag.: t. 5265, 1861
Chysis maculata (Hook.) Fowl., Orch. Digest 35: No. 3, 1971
BM 4576
Colombia, Panama - E
o Chysis aurea var. maculata Hook., Bot. Mag.: t. 4576, 1851
Chysis costaricensis Schltr., Fedde Rep. Beih. 19: 297, 1923
Cirrhaea dependens (Lodd.) Rchb. f., Walp. Ann. 6: 496, 1863
BM 2978
Brazil - E
Cymbidium dependens Lodd., Bot. Cab. 10: t. 936, 1825
o Gongora viridipurpurea Hook., Bot. Mag.: t. 2978, 1830
Cirrhaea viridipurpurea (Hook.) Lindl., Bot. Reg. 18: sub. t. 1538, 1832
Cirrhaea fusco-lutea Lindl., Bot. Reg. 18: sub. t. 1538, 1832
Cirrhaea warreana Lodd., Bot. Cab.: t. 1999, 1833
Cirrhaea tristis Lindl., Bot. Reg. 22: t. 1889, 1836
Cirrhaea violascens Hoffsgg., Verz. Orch.: 47, 1843
Cirrhaea violaceo-virens Hoffsgg., Verz. Orch.: 47, 1843
Sarcoglossum suaveolens Beer, Prakt. Stud. Orch.: 306, 1854
Cirrhaea hoffmannseggii Heinhold ex Rchb. f., Walp. Ann. 6: 496, 1863
Cirrhaea livida Hoffsgg., Walp. Ann. 6: 497, 1863
Cirrhaea purpurascens Hoffsgg., Walp. Ann. 6: 497, 1863
Cirrhaea russelliana Lodd. ex Rchb. f., Walp. Ann. 6: 497, 1863
Cirrhaea saccata Lindl., Bot. Reg. 25: Misc. p. 72, 1839
BM 3726
Brazil - E
o Cirrhaea fusco-lutea Hook., Bot. Mag.: t. 3726, 1839 (non Lindl.)
Scleropteris flava Scheidw., Allg. Gartenz. 7: 407, 1839
Cleisostoma filiforme (Lindl.) Garay, Bot. Mus. Leafl. Harv. Univ. 23: 171, 1972
BM 4639
Sikkim, Assam, Burma, Vietnam - E
o Sarcanthus filiformis Lindl., Bot. Reg. 28: Misc. 61, 1842
? Saccolabium luisioides Gagnepain, Bull. Mus. Paris 2.s. 22: 5: 629, 1950
non Sarcanthus filiformis Wight, Ic. 5: t. 1684, 1851
Cleisostoma parishii (Hook. f.) Garay, Bot. Mus. Leafl. Harv. Univ. 23: 173, 1972
BM 5217
Burma - E
o Sarcanthus parishii Hook. f., Bot. Mag.: t. 5217, 1860
Cleisostoma simondii (Gagnepain) Seidenf., Dansk Bot. Ark. 29 (3): 66, 1975
BM 3571
Sikkim, Laos, Vietnam, Hainan, Hong Kong - E
Vanda teretifolia Lindl., Coll. Bot.: t. 6, 1821
o Sarcanthus teretifolius (Lindl.) Lindl., Gen. Sp. Orch. Pl.: 324, 1833 (non Rchb. f., 1874)
Sarcanthus appendiculatus auct. non (Lindl.) Benth. & Hook. f.; King & Pantling, Orch. Sikkim Himalaya: 240 t. 318, 1898
Sarcanthus siamensis Rolfe ex Downie, Kew Bull.: 405, 1925
Luisia trichorhiza auct. non (Hook.) Blume; Merrill & Metcalf: 12 p. p., 1945
Vanda simondii Gagnepain, Bull. Mus. Paris 2.s., 22: 628, 1950
Luisia acutilabris Guillaumin, Bull. Mus. Paris 2.s., 32, 2: 188, 1960
Cleisostoma seidenfadenii Garay, Bot. Mus. Leafl. Harv. Univ.: 174, 1972
Cleisostoma teres Garay, Bot. Mus. Leafl. Harv. Univ.: 174, 1972
non Cleisostoma teretifolium Teijsm. & Binnend., Nat. Tijds. Ned. Ind. 27: 20, 1864
non Sarcanthus teretifolius Rchb. f., Trans. Linn. Soc. 30: 136, 1874
non Cleisostoma siamensis Rolfe ex Downie, Kew Bull.: 405, 1925
non Sarcanthus simondianus Gagnepain, 1950
Clowesia russelliana (Hook.) Dodson, Selbyana 1: 136, 1975
BM 3777
Mexico, Guatemala, El Salvador, Honduras, Nicaragua, Panama, Venezuela - E
o Catasetum russellianum Hook., Bot. Mag.: t. 3777, 1840
Catasetum calceolatum Lemaire, Jard. Fleur. 1: Misc. p. 45, 1851
Cycnoches viride Koch, Allg. Gartenz. 25: 291, 1857
Clowesia warczewiczii (Lindl.) Dodson, Selbyana 1: 136, 1975
BM 9619
Mexico to Panama, Venezuela, Guyana, Surinam, Brazil, Colombia, Ecuador - E
o Catasetum warczewiczii Lindl., Paxt. Flow. Gard. 1: 45 fig. 29, 1850
Myanthus warczewiczii (Lindl.) Beer, Prakt. Orch.: 272, 1854
Catasetum scurra Rchb. f., Gard. Chron.: 1003, 1872
Cochleanthes discolor (Lindl.) R. Schultes & Garay, Bot. Mus. Leafl. Harv. Univ. 18: 324, 1959
BM 4830
Cuba, Honduras, Costa Rica, Panama, Venezuela - 1200-1600 m - E
o Warrea discolor Lindl., J. Hort. Soc. Lond. 4: 265, 1849
Warscewiczella discolor (Lindl.) Rchb. f., Bot. Zeit. 10: 636, 1852
Zygopetalum discolor (Lindl.) Rchb. f., Walp. Ann. 6: 653, 1863
Chondrorhyncha discolor (Lindl.) P. Allen, Ann. Mi. Bot. Gard. 36: 87, 1949
Cochleanthes flabelliformis (Sw.) R. Schultes & Garay, Bot. Mus. Leafl. Harv. Univ. 18: 324, 1959
BM 3585
Trop. America, W. Indies, Nicaragua, Venezuela, Brazil - E
Epidendrum flabelliforme Sw., Prodr. Veg. Ind. Occ.: 123, 1788
Cymbidium flabelliforme (Sw.) Sw., Nov. Act. Upsal. 6: 73, 1799
Cochleanthes fragans Raf., Fl. Tellur. 4: 45, 1836
o Zygopetalum cochleare Lindl., Bot. Reg. 22: t. 1857, 1836
Eulophia cochleare (Lindl.) Knight ex Hook., Bot. Mag.: sub. t. 3585, 1837
Zygopetalum cochleatum Paxton, Mag. Bot. 4: 279, 1838
Eulophia cochlearis (Lindl.) Steudel, Nom. ed. 2., 1: 605, 1840
Warscewiczella cochlearis (Lindl.) Rchb. f., Bot. Zeit. 10: 714, 1852
Huntleya imbricata hort. ex Rchb. f., Bot. Zeit. 10: 714, 1852
Zygopetalum flabelliforme (Sw.) Rchb. f., Walp. Ann. 6: 652, 1863
Zygopetalum conchaceum Hoffsgg. ex Rchb. f., Walp. Ann. 6: 652, 1863
Cymbidium flabellifolium (Sw.) Griseb., Fl. Brit. W. Ind.: 629, 1864
Warscewiczella cochleata (Paxton) Barb. Rodr., Struct. Orch.: t. 13 fig. 4, 1883
Zygopetalum gibeziae N. E. Br., Lindenia 4: 79 t. 181, 1888
Warscewiczella gibeziae (N. E. Br.) Stein, Orchideenb.: 595, 1892
Warscewiczella flabelliformis (Sw.) Cogn., Symb. Antill. 4: 182, 1903
o **Cochlioda noezliana** (Mast.) Rolfe, Lindenia 6: 9 t. 266, 1891
BM 7474
Peru, Bolivia - up to 1900 m - E
Odontoglossum noezlianum Mast., Gard. Chron.: 570 & 602, 1890
Cochlioda rosea (Lindl.) Benth., J. Linn. Soc. 18: 327, 1881
BM 6084
Peru, Ecuador - up to 1800 m - E
o Odontoglossum roseum Lindl., Pl. Hartw.: 151, 1844
Mesospinidium roseum (Lindl.) Rchb. f., Gard. Chron.: 393, 1872

Cochlioda vulcanica (Rchb. f.) Benth. & Hook. f. ex Veitch, Man. Orch. Pl. 9: 189, 1893
BM 6001
Peru, Ecuador – 1800–3200 m – E
○ Mesospinidium vulcanicum Rchb. f., Gard. Chron.: 393, 1872
Coelia macrostachya Lindl., Pl. Hartw.: 92, 1842
BM 4712
Mexico, Guatemala, El Salvador, Honduras, Nicaragua, Costa Rica, Panama – T, E
○ Coelia macrostachya var. genuina Rchb. f., Beitr. Orch. Cent. Am.: 41, 1866
Coelia macrostachya var. integrilabia Rchb. f., Beitr. Orch. Cent. Am.: 41, 1866
Bothriochillus macrostachyus (Lindl.) L. Williams, Bot. Mus. Leafl. Harv. Univ. 8: 148, 1940
○ **Coelogyne brachyptera** Rchb. f., Gard. Chron.: 6, 1881
BM 8582
Burma, Laos, Kampuchea, Vietnam – E
Coelogyne parishii var. brachyptera (Rchb. f.) Pfitzer & Kraenzlin, Pflanzenr. Heft 32: 78, 1907
Coelogyne virescens Rolfe, Kew Bull.: 70, 1908
Coelogyne parishii auct. non Hook. f., Gagnepain, Fl. Indo-Chine: 312, 1934
○ **Coelogyne corymbosa** Lindl., Fol. Orch.: 7, 1854
BM 6955
N. E. India, Sikkim, Bhutan – 1500–2000 m – E
○ **Coelogyne cristata** Lindl., Coll. Bot.: t. 33, 1821
BM 8477
N. E. India, Sikkim – 1000–2000 m – E
Cymbidium speciosissimum D. Don, Prodr. Fl. Nepal.: 35, 1825
○ **Coelogyne cumingii** Lindl., Bot. Reg. 26: Misc. 187: 76, 1840
BM 4645
Laos, Malaya, Sumatra, Riau Arch., Borneo – E
Pleione cumingii (Lindl.) Kuntze, Rev. Gen. 2: 680, 1891
○ **Coelogyne flaccida** Lindl., Gen. Sp. Orch. Pl.: 39, 1830
BM 3318
Nepal, Sikkim, Burma, China (Yunnan), Laos – 1000–1600 m – E
Coelogyne flexuosa Rolfe, Kew Bull.: 209, 1892
BM 9563
Sumatra, Java, Bali – E
Coelogyne bimaculata Ridley, Linn. Soc. 32: 327, 1896
○ Ptychogyne flexuosa (Rolfe) Pfitzer & Kraenzlin, Pflanzenr. Heft 32: 18, 1907
Ptychogyne bimaculata Pfitzer & Kraenzlin, Pflanzenr. Heft 32: 20, 1907
○ **Coelogyne fuliginosa** Hook., Bot. Mag.: t. 4440, 1849
BM 4440
India, Burma, ? Java – 1200–2200 m – E
? Coelogyne longeciliata Teijsm. & Binnend., Nat. Tijds. Ned. Ind. 27: 16, 1864
Coelogyne ovalis auct. non Lindl., Rchb. f., Trans. Linn. Soc. 30: 136, 1874
Coelogyne fimbriata auct. non Lindl., Parish, Mason, Burmah: 196, 1883
Pleione fuliginosa (Hook.) Kuntze, Rev. Gen. 2: 680, 1891
○ **Coelogyne fuscescens** Lindl. var. **brunnea** (Lindl.) Lindl., Fol. Orch. Coel.: 11, 1854 (nomen tantum)
BM 5494
Burma, Laos, Thailand, Vietnam – 1000–1500 m – E
Coelogyne fuscescens Lindl., Bot. Reg.: Misc. p. 1, 1844
Coelogyne brunnea Lindl., Gard. Chron.: 71, 1848
Coelogyne holochila P. Hunt & Summerh., Kew Bull. 20: 52, 1966
BM 5001
India, Burma – E
○ Coelogyne elata Hook., Bot. Mag.: t. 5001, 1857 (non Lindl.)
○ **Coelogyne integerrima** Ames, Philipp. J. Sci. 4: 665, 1909
BM 8856
Philippines – up to 2400 m – E
○ **Coelogyne lawrenceana** Rolfe, Gard. Chron.: 227, 1905
BM 8164
Vietnam – E
Coelogyne fleuryi Gagnepain, Bull. Mus. Hist. Nat. Paris s. 2, 2: 424, 1930
○ **Coelogyne lentiginosa** Lindl., Fol. Orch. Coel.: 3, 1854
BM 5958
Burma, Thailand, Vietnam – E
○ **Coelogyne massangeana** Rchb. f., Gard. Chron.: 684, 1878
BM 6979
Thailand, Malaya, Sumatra, Java – E
Pleione massangeana (Rchb. f.) Kuntze, Rev. Gen. 2: 680, 1891
Coelogyne densiflora Ridley, J. Str. Br. Roy. As. Soc. 39: 89, 1903
Coelogyne dayana var. massangeana (Rchb. f.) Ridley, Mat. Fl. Mal. Pen.: 127, 1907
Coelogyne cymbidioides Ridley, J. Linn. Soc. 38: 329, 1908
Coelogyne tomentosa var. cymbidioides Ridley, J. Linn. Soc. 38: 329, 1908
Coelogyne tomentosa var. massangeana (Rchb. f.) Ridley, Fl. Mal. Pen. 4: 130, 1924
○ **Coelogyne mooreana** Sander ex Rolfe, Kew Bull.: 129, 1907
BM 8297
Thailand, Laos, Kampuchea, Vietnam – E
Coelogyne nervosa A. Rich., Ann. Sci. Nat. 2 s. 15: 16, 1841
BM 5601
India – E
Coelogyne glandulosa Lindl., Fol. Orch. Coel.: 6, 1854
○ Coelogyne corrugata Wight, Ic. Pl. Ind. Or. 5: t. 1639, 1853
Coelogyne nitida (Wallich ex Don) Lindl., Coll. Bot.: sub. t. 33, 1822
BM 4661
N. W. Himalaya, Nepal, Sikkim, Bhutan, Burma, China (Yunnan), Thailand, Laos – 1200–2200 m – E
Cymbidium nitidum Wallich ex Don, Prod. Fl. Nepal.: 35, 1825 (non Roxb. 1832)
○ Coelogyne ochracea Lindl., Bot. Reg.: t. 69, 1846
? Coelogyne goweri Rchb. f., Gard. Chron.: 443, 1869
Coelogyne ochracea ssp. conferta Parish & Rchb. f., Trans. Linn. Soc. 30: 146 t. 30, 1874
Coelogyne conferta hort., Gard. Chron. 1: 314, 1875
? Pleione goweri (Rchb. f.) Kuntze, Rev. Gen. 2: 680, 1891
Coelogyne ochracea var. foliata (Rchb. f.) Pfitzer & Kraenzlin, Pflanzenr. Heft 32: 57, 1907
Coelogyne punctulata var. conferta (Parish & Rchb. f.) Tang & Wang, Act. Phytotax. Peking 1: 78, 1951
○ **Coelogyne ovalis** Lindl., Bot. Reg. 24: 91 Misc. 171, 1838
BM 9255
W. Himalaya, Nepal, Sikkim, Assam, Manipur, Burma, China (Tibet, Yunnan) – 800–1900 m – E
Coelogyne pilosissima Planchon, Hort. Donat. Orch.: 104, 1854
Coelogyne triplicatula Rchb. f., Bot. Zeit. 53: 415, 1864
Broughtonia linearis Wallich ex Hook. f., Fl. Brit. Ind. 5: 836, 1890
non Coelogyne ovalis Rchb. f., Trans. Linn. Soc. 30: 136 1874 (C. fuliginosa)
non Coelogyne ovalis Pfitzer & Kraenzlin, Pflanzenr. Heft 32: 34 53 fig. 17, 1907 (C. fimbriata)
○ **Coelogyne pandurata** Lindl., Fol. Orch. Coel.: 3, 1854
BM 5084
Malaya, Sumatra, Borneo – E
○ **Coelogyne parishii** Hook. f., Bot. Mag.: t. 5323, 1862
BM 5323
Burma – E
Coelogyne punctulata Lindl., Coll. Bot.: sub. t. 33, 1821
BM 3767
Nepal, Assam, Burma, W. China – E
Cymbidium nitidum Roxb., Hort. Beng.: 63, 1814 (nomen nudum)
○ Coelogyne ocellata (Wallich ex Lindl.) Lindl., Gen. Sp. Orch. Pl.: 40, 1830
Coelogyne nitida (Roxb.) Hook. f., Fl. Brit. Ind. 5: 837, 1890
○ **Coelogyne schilleriana** Rchb. f., Allg. Gartenz.: 189, 1858
BM 5072
Burma – E
Pleione schilleriana (Rchb. f.) Pfitzer & Kraenzlin, Pflanzenr. Heft 32: 123, 1907
○ **Coelogyne speciosa** (Blume) Lindl., Gen. Sp. Orch. Pl.: 39, 1830
BM 4889
Malaya, Sumatra, Java, Borneo – E
Chelonanthera speciosa Blume, Bijdr.: 384 t. 51, 1825
○ **Coelogyne speciosa** (Blume) Lindl. var. **alba** hort., Bot. Mag.: 9539, 1838
BM 9539
Malaya, Sumatra, Java, Borneo – E
○ **Coelogyne swaniana** Rolfe, Kew Bull.: 183, 1894
BM 7602
Malaya, Sumatra, Borneo, Philippines – E
Coelogyne quadrangularis Ridley, J. Linn. Soc. 32: 323, 1896
○ **Coelogyne testacea** Lindl., Bot. Reg.: Misc. 34, 1842
BM 4785
Singapore, Malaya, Sumatra – E
Coelogyne trifida Rchb. f., Hamb. Gartenz.: 546, 1863
BM 5462
Sri Lanka, India, Burma, N. W. Malaya – E
○ Coelogyne odoratissima Bateman, Bot. Mag.: t. 5462, 1864 (non Lindl.)
Coelogyne trinervis Lindl., Gen. Spec. Orch. Pl. 41, 1830
BM 7176
Burma, Laos, Kampuchea, Vietnam, Thailand, Malaya, Java, Moluccas? – E

Coelogyne cinnamomea Teijsm. & Binnend., Nat. Tijds. Ned. Ind. 24: 306, 1862
Coelogyne rhodeana Rchb.f., Gard. Chron.: 1901, 1867
o Coelogyne rossiana Rchb.f., Gard. Chron.: 808, 1884
Coelogyne angustifolia Ridley, J. Linn. Soc. 32: 322, 1896
Coelogyne pachybulbon Ridley, J. Linn. Soc. 32: 324, 1896
Coelogyne cinnamomea var. angustifolia (Ridley) Pfitzer & Kraenzlin, Pflanzenr. Heft 32: 49, 1907
? Coelogyne wettsteinianua Schltr., Oester. Bot. Zeit. 69: 124, 1920
o **Coelogyne veitchii** Rolfe, Kew Bull.: 282, 1895
BM 7764
New Guinea - E
o **Coelogyne venusta** Rolfe, Gard. Chron.: 259, 1904
BM 8262
S.W. China - E
Coelogyne viscosa Rchb.f., Allg. Gartenz. 24, 28: 218, 1856
BM 7006
India, Burma, Vietnam, Malaya - E
o Coelogyne graminifolia Parish & Rchb.f., Trans. Linn. Soc. 30: 146, 1874
o **Comparettia falcata** Poeppig & Endl., Nov. Gen. Sp.Pl. 1: 42 t. 73, 1836
BM 4980
W. Indies, Mexico, Guatemala, Honduras, Costa Rica, Panama, S. America - 700-1500 m - E
Comparettia rosea Lindl., Bot. Reg. 26: Misc.p. 78, 1840
o **Comparettia macroplectron** Rchb.f. & Triana, Gard. Chron.: 524, 1878
BM 6679
Colombia - E
o **Coryanthes macrantha** (Hook.) Hook., Bot. Mag.: sub.t. 3102, 1831
BM 7692
Trinidad, Venezuela, Guyana, Brazil, Colombia, Peru - E
Gongora macrantha Hook., Bot. Reg.: Misc. 2: 151 t. 80, 1831
Panstrepis paradoxa Raf., Fl. Tellur. 4: 41, 1836 (nomen illeg.)
Coryanthes speciosa (Hook.) Hook., Bot. Mag.: sub.t. 3102, 1831
BM 2755, BM 3102, BM 3747
Guatemala, Honduras, Costa Rica, Panama, Trinidad, Venezuela, Guyana, Brazil, Colombia, Peru - E
o Gongora speciosa Hook., Bot. Mag.: t. 2755, 1827
Epidendrum galeatum Vell., Fl. Flum. Ic. 9: t. 3, 1827
o Coryanthes maculata Hook., Bot. Mag.: t. 3102, 1831
Coryanthes speciosa var. alba Lindl., Bot. Reg. 26: Misc.p. 42, 1840
o Coryanthes maculata var. parkeri Hook., Bot. Mag.: t. 3747, 1840
Coryanthes speciosa var. vitellina Morren, Ann. Gand.. 2: 15, 1846
Coryanthes eximia Gérard, Portef. Hort. 1: 357, 1847
Coryanthes albertinae Karsten, Ausw. Neu. Gew. Venez. 5: t. 1, 1848
Coryanthes maculata var. albertinae Lindl., Fol. Orch. Coryanthes: 2, 1852
Coryanthes barkeri Beer, Prakt. Stud. Orch.: 222, 1854
Coryanthes parkeri (Hook.) Seemann, Hort. Parad. Vindob. 19: t. 32 fig. 1, 1860
Coryanthes picturata Rchb.f., Bot. Zeit. 22: 332, 1864
Coryanthes splendens Barb. Rodr., Gen. & Sp. Orch. 1: 103, 1877
Coryanthes maculata var. vitrina Rolfe, Orch. Rev. 3: 240, 1895
Coryanthes maculata var. fournieri André, Rev. Hort. 71: 429, 1899
Coryanthes maculata var. speciosa (Hook.) André, Rev. Hort. 71: 429, 1899
Coryanthes speciosa var. eximia (Gérard) Cogn., Fl. Bras. 3, pt. 5: 513, 1902
Coryanthes maculata var. splendens (Barb. Rodr.) Cogn., Fl. Bras. 3, pt. 5: 513, 1902
Coryanthes hunteriana Schltr., Fedde Rep. Beih. 17: 63, 1922
Coryanthes powellii Schltr., Fedde Rep. Beih. 17: 64, 1922
Corybas limbatus (Hook.) Rchb.f., Beitr. Syst. Pfl.: 67, 1871
BM 5357
Java - T
o Coryanthes limbata Hook., Bot. Mag.: t. 5357, 1863
Corybas limbatus (Hook.) Kuntze, Rev. Gen. 2: 65, 1891
Cottonia peduncularis (Lindl.) Rchb.f. ex Schiller, Cat. Orch. Samml.: 22, 1857
BM 7099
India, Sri Lanka - E
Vanda peduncularis Lindl., Gen. Sp. Orch. Pl.: 216, 1833
o Cottonia macrostachya Wight, Ic.: t. 1755, 1851
Cryptostylis arachnites (Blume) Hassk., Cat. Bog.: 48, 1844
BM 5381
Sri Lanka, N.E. India, Thailand, Kampuchea, Vietnam, Malaya, Sumatra, Java, Borneo to New Caledonia - T
o Zosterostylis arachnites Blume, Bijdr.: 419 t. 32, 1825
Zosterostylis zeylanica Lindl., Gen. Sp. Orch. Pl.: 446, 1840
Zosterostylis walkerae Wight, Ic.: t. 1748, 1851
Cryptostylis alismifolia F. Muell., South Sc. Rec. 1: 172, 1881
Cryptostylis papuana Schltr., Schum. & Lauterb. Nachtr.: 82, 1905
Cryptostylis vitiensis Schltr., Fedde Rep.: 16, 1906
Cryptostylis stenochila Schltr., Engl. Bot. Jahrb. 39: 49, 1906
Cryptostylis fulva Schltr., Fedde Rep. Beih. 1: 26 fig. 39, 1911
Cryptostylis philippinensis Schltr., Engl. Bot. Jahrb. 58: 54, 1922
Cryptostylis zeylanica (Lindl.) Schltr., Engl. Bot. Jahrb. 58: 54, 1922
non Cryptostylis arachnites J.J. Smith, Fl. Buitenz. 6: 59 fig. 37, 1905
o **Cycnoches densiflorum** Rolfe, Kew Bull.: 63, 1909
BM 8268
Colombia - E
o **Cycnoches egertonianum** Bateman, Orch. Mex. & Guat.: t. 40, 1843
BM 4054, BM 9260
Belize, Guatemala, El Salvador, Honduras, Costa Rica, Peru - E
Cycnoches ventricosum Bateman, Orch. Mex. & Guat.: t. 5, 1837
o Cycnoches ventricosum var. egertonianum (Bateman) Hook., Bot. Mag.: t. 4054, 1844
Cycnoches stelliferum Lodd., Cat. Orch.: 25, 1844 (nomen nudum)
Cycnoches egertonianum var. viride Lindl., Bot. Reg. 32: t. 46, 1846
Cycnoches glanduliferum Rich. & Galeotti ex Hemsl., Gard. Chron.: 268, 1879
Cycnoches rossianum Rolfe, Gard. Chron.: 456, 1891
Cycnoches peruvianum Rolfe, Lindenia 7: 29 t. 301, 1891
Cycnoches guttulatum Schltr., Fedde Rep. Beih. 17: 56, 1922
Cycnoches pachydactylon Schltr., Fedde Rep. Beih. 17: 57, 1922
Cycnoches stenodactylon Schltr., Fedde Rep. Beih. 17: 59, 1922
Cycnoches amparoanum Schltr., Fedde Rep. Beih. 19: 48, 1923
Cycnoches pauciflorum Schltr., Fedde Rep. Beih. 19: 137, 1923
o **Cycnoches haagii** Barb. Rodr., Gen. & Sp. Orch. 2: 221, 1881
BM 7502
Venezuela, Colombia, Peru, Bolivia, Brazil - E
Cycnoches versicolor Rchb.f., Gard. Chron.: 596, 1888
o **Cycnoches loddigesii** Lindl., Gen. Sp. Orch. Pl.: 154, 1832
BM 3855, BM 4215
Venezuela, Colombia, Brazil, Guyana - E
Cycnoches cucullata Lindl., Bot. Reg. 23: 1951, 1837
o Cycnoches loddigesii var. leucochilum Hook., Bot. Mag.: t. 3855, 1841
Cymbidiella falcigera (Rchb.f.) Garay, Orch. Digest 40 (5): 192, 1976
BM 9216
E. Madagascar, Comoro Is. - E
Grammangis falcigera Rchb.f., Flora 68: 541, 1885
o Cymbidium humblotii Rolfe, Gard. Chron.: 8, 1892
Caloglossum humblotii (Rolfe) Schltr., Fedde Rep. 15: 213, 1918
Cymbidiella magnificum Schltr., Fedde Rep. 15: 214, 1918
Cymbidiella humblotii (Rolfe) Rolfe, Orch. Rev. 26: 58, 1918
Cymbidiella pardalina (Rchb.f.) Garay, Orch. Digest 40 (5): 192, 1976
BM 7932, BM 7933
E. Madagascar - E
Grammangis pardalina Rchb.f., Flora 68: 541, 1885
o Cymbidium rhodochilum Rolfe, Bot. Mag.: t. 7932/33, 1904
Cymbidiella rhodochila (Rolfe) Rolfe, Orch. Rev. 26: 58, 1918
Cymbidium aloifolium (L.) Sw., Nov. Act. Upsal. 6: 73, 1799
BM 387
Sri Lanka, India, Sikkim, S. China, Hong Kong, Burma, Thailand, Malaya, Andaman Is., Sumatra, Java, Borneo, Taiwan - E
Epidendrum aloifolium L., Sp.Pl.: 953, 1753
Epidendrum pendulum Roxb., Pl. Coast Coromandel 1: 35 t. 44, 1795
o Epidendrum aloides Curtis, Bot. Mag.: t. 387, 1797
Cymbidium pendulum (Roxb.) Sw., Nov. Act. Upsal. 6: 73, 1799
Aerides borassii Buch. - Ham. ex J.E. Smith, Rees, Cyclop. 39: Addend. Aerides 8, 1819
Cymbidium wallichii Lindl., Gen. Sp. Orch. Pl.: 165, 1833
Cymbidium erectum Wight, Ic. Pl. Ind. Or. 5: 21 t. 1753, 1852
Cymbidium mannii Rchb.f., Flora 55: 274, 1872
Cymbidium simulans Rolfe, Orch. Rev. 25: 175, 1917
Cymbidium intermedium H.G. Jones, Reinwardtia 9: 71, 1974
Cymbidium atropurpureum (Hook.f.) Rolfe, Orch. Rev. 11: 190, 1903
BM 5710
Malaya, Sumatra, Java, Borneo, Philippines - E
o Cymbidium pendulum var. atropurpureum Hook.f., Bot. Mag.: 5710, 1865
Cymbidium pendulum sensu Vidal, Phan. Cunn. Phil. 150, 1885 (non Sw.)
Cymbidium finlaysonianum var. atropurpureum (Hook.f.) Veitch, Man. Orch. Pl. 2: 16, 1894
o **Cymbidium canaliculatum** R. Br., Prodr. Fl. Nov. Holl.: 331, 1810
BM 5851
N.E. Australia - E
Cymbidium hillii F. Muell., Regel Gartenfl.: 138, 1879
Cymbidium sparkesii Rendle, J. Bot. Lond. 36: 221, 1898
Cymbidium canaliculatum var. sparkesii (Rendle) F.M. Bailey, Compreh. Cat. Qd. Pls.: 845, 1913

o **Cymbidium chloranthum** Lindl., Bot. Reg. 29: 68, 1843
BM 4907
Malaya, Sumatra, Java, Borneo – E
Cambidium variciferum Rchb. f., Bonpl. 4: 324, 1856
Cymbidium sanguineolentum Teijsm. & Binnend., Tijdschr. Ned. Ind. 24: 14, 1862
Cymbidium sanguineum Teijsm. & Binnend., Cat. Hort. Bog.: 51, 1866
Cymbidium pulchellum Schltr., Fedde Rep. 8: 570, 1910
Cymbidium dayanum Rchb. f., Gard. Chron.: 710, 1869
BM 7863
Assam, Thailand, Malaya, Sumatra, Celebes, Borneo, Philippines – E
Cymbidium leachianum Rchb. f., Gard. Chron.: 106, 1878
Cymbidium eburneum var. dayana (Rchb. f.) Hook. f., Fl. Brit. Ind. 6: 12, 1891
Cymbidium pulcherrimum Sander, Gard. Chron.: 712, 1891
o Cymbidium simonsianum King & Pantl., J. As. Soc. Beng. 64 (2): 338, 1895
Cymbidium acutum Ridley, J. Linn. Soc. 32: 334, 1896
Cymbidium alborubens Makino, Bot. Mag. Tokyo 16: 11, 1902
Cymbidium simonsianum forma vernale Makino, Iinuma Somoku-Dzusetzu ed. 3, 4 (18): 1186, 1912
Cymbidium marginatum Makino, Iinuma Somoku-Dzusetzu ed. 3, 4: 1183, 1912
Cymbidium sutepense Rolfe ex Downie, Kew Bull.: 382, 1925
Cymbidium poilanei Gagnepain, Bull. Mus. Paris s. 2, 3: 681, 1931
Cymbidium dayanum var. austro-japonicum Tuy., Nakai Ic. Pl. Asiae Orient. 4: 363 t. 118, 1941
Cymbidium eburneum var. austro-japonicum (Tuy.) Hiroe, Orchid Flow. 2: 96, 1971
o **Cymbidium devonianum** Paxton, Mag. Bot. 10: 97, 1843
BM 9327
Nepal to Bhutan, Assam (Khasia) – 1500–2000 m – E, L
Cymbidium sikkimense Hook. f., Fl. Brit. Ind. 6: 9, 1890
o **Cymbidium eburneum** Lindl., Bot. Reg.: t. 67, 1847
BM 5126
Nepal, Sikkim, Assam (Khasia), Burma, China – 300–1000 m – E
Cymbidium syringodorum Griffith, Notul. 3: 338, 1851
Cymbidium eburneum var. williamsianum Rchb. f., Gard. Chron.: 530, 1881
Cymbidium eburneum var. philbrickierum Rchb. f., Gard. Chron.: 285, 1886
Cyperorchis eburnea (Lindl.) Schltr., Fedde Rep. 20: 107, 1924
Cymbidium elegans Lindl., Gen. Sp. Orch. Pl.: 163, 1833
BM 7007
Nepal, Sikkim, N. E. India, Burma, China, Taiwan – 1200–1500 m – E
o Cyperorchis elegans (Lindl.) Blume, Rumph. 4: 47, 1848
Cymbidium densiflorum Griffith, Notul. 3: 337, 1851
Grammatophyllum elegans (Lindl.) Rchb. f., Walp. Ann. 3: 1028, 1853
Cymbidium elegans var. obcordatum Rchb. f., Gard. Chron.: 41, 1880
Cymbidium elegans var. lutescens Hook. f., Fl. Brit. Ind. 6: 15, 1891
Arethusantha bletioides Finet, Bull. Soc. Bot. Fr. 44: 179, 1897
Cyperorchis elegans var. blumei hort., J. Hort. s. 3, 54: 71, 1907
o **Cymbidium ensifolium** (L.) Sw., Nov. Act. Upsal. 6: 77, 1799
BM 1751
N. India, Sikkim, Thailand, Kampuchea, Laos, Vietnam, Malaya, Sumatra, Java, Borneo, New Guinea, China, Hong Kong, Taiwan, Ryukyu Is., Japan – E
Epidendrum ensifolium L., Sp. Pl.: 954, 1753
Limodorum ensatum Thunb., Fl. Jap.: 29, 1784
Epidendrum sinense Redouté, Liliac. 2: t. 113, 1805
Cymbidium xiphiifolium Lindl., Bot. Reg. 7: t. 529, 1821
Cymbidium haematodes Lindl., Gen. Sp. Orch. Pl.: 162, 1833
Cymbidium ensifolium var. estriatum Lindl., Bot. Reg. 23: t. 1976, 1837
Cymbidium ensifolium var. striatum Lindl., Bot. Reg. 23: t. 1976, 1837
Jensoa ensata (Thunb.) Raf., Fl. Tellur. 4: 38, 1838
Cymbidium estriatum (Lindl.) Steudel, Nom. Bot. 2: 460, 1840
Cymbidium ecristatum (Lindl.) ex Steudel, Nom. Bot. 2: 460, 1840 (nomen nudum)
Cymbidium micans Schauer, Nov. Act. Nat. Cur. 19 Suppl. 1: 433, 1843
Cymbidium ensifolium var. haematodes (Lindl.) Trimen, Cat.: 89, 1885
Cymbidium munronianum King & Pantl., J. As. Soc. Beng. 64: 338, 1895
Cymbidium ensifolium sensu J. J. Smith, Die Orch. Java: 478, 1905 (non Sw.)
Cymbidium albo-marginatum Makino, Iinuma, Sömoku-Dzusetzu ed. 3: 4 (18): 1183, 1912
Cymbidium ensifolium forma flaccidior Makino, Iinuma Sömoku-Dzusetzu ed. 3, 4 (18): 1179 t. 2, 1912
Cymbidium koran Makino, Iinuma Sömoku-Dzusetzu ed. 3: 1179 t. 3, 1912
Cymbidium niveo-marginatum Makino, Iinuma Sömoku-Dzusetzu ed. 3: 1183, 1912
Cymbidium shimaran Makino, Iinuma Somoku-Dzusetzu ed. 3., 4: 1183, 1912
Cymbidium yakibaran Makino, Iinuma Somoku-Dzusetzu ed. 3, 4: 1181, 1912
Cymbidium yakibaran var. albo-marginatum Makino, Iinuma Somoku-Dzusetzu ed. 3, 4: 1182, 1912
Cymbidium yakibaran var. niveo-marginatum Makino, Iinuma Somoku-Dzusetzu ed. 3, 4: 1182, 1912
Cymbidium arrogans Hayata, Ic. Pl. Form. 4: 76, 1914
Cymbidium misericors Hayata, Ic. Pl. Form. 4: 79, 1914
Cymbidium rubigemmum Hayata, Ic. Pl. Form. 6: 81, 1916
Cymbidium sundaicum Schltr., Fedde Rep. Beih. 4: 266, 1919
Cymbidium sundaicum var. estriata Schltr., Fedde Rep. Beih. 4: 266, 1919
Cymbidium munronianum sensu Ridley, Fl. Mal. Pen. 4: 46, 1924 (non King & Pantl.)
Cymbidium siamense Rolfe ex Downie, Kew Bull.: 382, 1925
Cymbidium ensifolium var. munronianum Tang & Wang, Act. Phytotax. Sin. 1: 91, 1951
Cymbidium munronianum sensu Holttum, Fl. Malaya 1: 515, 1953
Cymbidium ensifolium var. susin Yen, Ic. Cymb. Amoy. D–b 1, 1964
Cymbidium ensifolium var. misericors (Hayata) T. P. Lin, Nat. Orch. of Taiwan 2: 105, 1977
Cymbidium gyokuchin var. arrogans (Hayata) Ying, Coll. Ill. Ind. Orch. Taiwan 1: 126, 1977
Cymbidium kanran var. misericors (Hayata) Ying, Coll. Ill. Ind. Orch. Taiwan: 440, 1977
Cymbidium ensifolium var. rubigenmum (Hayata) Liu & Su, Fl. Taiwan 5: 940, 1978
Cymbidium ensifolium var. yakibaran (Makino) Wu & Chen, Act. Phytotax. Sin. 18: 296, 1980
o **Cymbidium erythrostylum** Rolfe, Gard. Chron.: 427, 1905
BM 8131
Kampuchea, Laos, Vietnam – T
Cyperorchis erythrostyla (Rolfe) Schltr., Fedde Rep. 20: 427, 1905
Cymbidium erythrostylum var. magnificum hort. ex Gard. Chron.: 81, suppl. fig., 1931
o **Cymbidium hookerianum** Rchb. f., Gard. Chron.: 7, 1866
BM 5574
Tibet, Sikkim, Nepal, E. Bhutan – 1600–2100 m – E
Cymbidium grandiflorum Griffith, Notul. 3: 342, 1851
Cymbidium grandiflorum var. punctulatum Cogn., J. Orch. 4: 76, 1893
Cymbidium giganteum var. hookerianum (Rchb. f.) Bois., Orchid: 119, 1893
Cyperorchis grandiflora (Griffith) Schltr., Fedde Rep. 20: 107, 1924
Cymbidium hookerianum var. hookerianum (Rchb. f.) Wu & Chen, Act. Phytotax. 18: 302, 1980
o **Cymbidium insigne** Rolfe, Gard. Chron.: 387, 1904
BM 8312
Thailand, Kampuchea, Laos, Vietnam – E, T
Cymbidium sanderi O'Brien, Gard. Chron.: 115 fig. 49, 1905
Cymbidium sanderi var. sanderi (O'Brien) hort., J. Hort. s. 3, 58: 415 + fig., 1909
Cymbidium insigne var. album hort. ex Gard. Chron.: 101 fig. 35, 1917
Cyperorchis insignis (Rolfe) Schltr., Fedde Rep. 20: 108, 1924
Cymbidium iridioides D. Don, Prodr. Fl. Nepal: 36, 1825
BM 4844
Himalaya (Kumaon to Bhutan), Assam (Khasia), N. Burma – 1000–2000 m – E
o Cymbidium giganteum Wallich ex Lindl., Gen. Sp. Orch. Pl.: 163, 1833
Limodorum longifolium Buch.-Ham. ex Lindl., Gen. Sp. Orch. Pl.: 163, 1833
Iridorchis gigantea (Wallich ex Lindl.) Blume, Coll. Orch. Arch. Ind. Jap.: 91 t. 26, 1858
Cyperorchis gigantea (Wallich ex Lindl.) Schltr., Fedde Rep. 20: 107, 1924
o **Cymbidium schroederi** Rolfe, Gard. Chron.: 243, 1905
BM 9637
Kampuchea, Laos, Vietnam – E
Cyperorchis schroederi (Rolfe) Schltr., Fedde Rep. 20: 108, 1924
Cymbidium sinense (Andrews) Willd., Sp. Pl. ed. 4: 111, 1805
BM 888

N. India, Sri Lanka, China, Hong Kong, Taiwan, Ryukyu Is. – T
○ Epidendrum sinense Andrews, Bot. Rep. 3: t. 216, 1802
Cymbidium fragrans Salisb., Trans. Hort. Soc. 1: 298, 1812
Cymbidium chinense Heynh., Nom. Bot. 2: 179, 1840
Cymbidium hoosai Makino, Bot. Mag. Tokyo 16: 23, 1902
Cymbidium albojucundissimum Hayata, Ic. Pl. Form. 4: 74, 1914
Cymbidium sinense var. margicoloratum Hayata, Ic. Pl. Form. 6: 82, 1916
Cymbidium sinense forma margicoloratum (Hayata) Fuk., Short Fl. Form.: 287, 1936
Cymbidium sinense forma albojucundissimum (Hayata) Fuk., Trans. Nat. Hist. Soc. Form. 22: 415
Cymbidium sinense var. albojucundissimum (Hayata) Masam., Trop. Hort. 3: 31, 1933
Cymbidium sinense var. bellum Yen, Ic. Cymb. Amoy. E–a 1, 1964
Cymbidium sinense var. album Yen, Ic. Cymb. Amoy. F–a 1, 1964
○ **Cymbidium tigrinum** Parish ex Hook. f., Bot. Mag.: t. 5457, 1864
BM 5457
Thailand, Burma – 2000 m – L
Cyperorchis tigrina (Parish ex Hook. f.) Schltr., Fedde Rep. 20: 108, 1924
Cymbidium evrardii Guillaumin, Bull. Soc. Bot. Fr. 77: 339, 1930
○ **Cynorkis compacta** (Rchb. f.) Rolfe, Bot. Mag.: t. 8053, 1906
BM 8053
S. Africa (Natal) – up to 1000 m – L, T
Cynosorchis compacta Rchb. f., Flora 71: 149, 1888
○ **Cynorkis grandiflora** Ridley, J. Linn. Soc. 20: 332, 1883
BM 7564
Madagascar – T, L, E
Cynosorchis uniflora Lindl., Gen. Sp. Orch. Pl.: 331, 1835
Gymnadenia uniflora (Lindl.) Steudel, Nom. ed. 2, 1: 712, 1846
Cynorkis lowiana Rchb. f., Flora 150, 1888
BM 7551
Madagascar, Mascarene Is. – L, E
○ Cynosorchis purpurascens Hook. f., Bot. Mag.: t. 7551, 1897 (non Thouars)
○ **Cynorkis purpurascens** (Sprengel) Thouars, Orch. Iles Afr.: t. 15, 1822
BM 7852
Madagascar, Mascarene Is. – up to 500 m – L, E
Orchis purpurascens Sprengel, Syst. 2: 687, 1826
Gymnadenia purpurascens (Sprengel) A. Rich., Orch. Iles France & Bourbon: 29, 1828
Cynosorchis calanthoides Kraenzlin, Abh. Nat. Ver. Bremen 7: 260, 1882
Cynosorchis purpurascens var. praecox Schltr., Ann. Mus. Col. Marseille s. 3, 1: 40, 1913
Cynosorchis praecox Schltr., Fedde Rep. 33: 65, 1925
○ **Cynorkis villosa** Rolfe ex Hook. f., Bot. Mag.: t. 7845, 1905
BM 7845
Madagascar – L
○ **Cypripedium acaule** Aiton, Hort. Kew 3: 303, 1789
BM 192
N. E. America, Canada – T
Cypripedium humile Salisb., Trans. Linn. Soc. 1: 79, pl. 3, 1793
Cypripedium acaule var. album Ballif., Lindenia 4: 96, 1888 (nomen nudum)
Cypripedium acaule forma albiflorum Rand & Redfield, Fl. Mt. Desert I: 154, 1894
Fissipes acaulis (Aiton) Small, Fl. SE. U. S.: 311, 1903
Fissipes hirsuta Farw., Drugg. Circular 61: 230, 1917
Cypripedium hirsutum (Farw.) Miller, Drugg. Circular 61: 230, 1917
○ **Cypripedium arietinum** R. Br., Hort. Kew. ed. 2. 5: 222, 1813
BM 1569
N. America, Canada, China, N. Burma – T
Criosanthes borealis Raf., Am. Mo. Mag.: 268, 1818
Arietinum americanum Beck, Bot. N. Mid. U. S.: 352, 1833
Criosanthes parviflora Raf., Fl. Tellur. 2: 46, 1837
Criosanthes plectrochilus Franchet, Bull. Soc. Bot. Fr. 32: 27, 1885
Criosanthes arietina (R. Br.) House, Bull. Torrey Club 32: 374, 1905
Cypripedium calceolus L. var. **parviflorum** (Salisb.) Fern., Rhodora 48: 4, 1946
BM 3024
N. E. America – T
○ Cypripedium parviflorum Salisb., Trans. Linn. Soc. 1: 77 pl. 2 fig. 2, 1791
Cypripedium luteum Aiton ex Raf., Med. Fl. 1: 140 pl. 30, 1828
Cypripedium luteum var. parviflorum (Salisb.) Raf., Med. Fl. 1: 142, 1828
Cypripedium bifidum Raf., Atl. J. 1: 178, 1833
Cypripedium hirsutum var. parviflorum (Salisb.) Rolfe, Orch. Rev. 15: 184, 1907
Calceolus parviflorus (Salisb.) Nieuwl., Am. Midl. Nat. 3: 118, 1913
Cypripedium bulbosum var. parviflorum (Salisb.) Farw., Rep. Mich. Acad. Sc. 15: 170, 1913
Cypripedium calceolus L. var. **pubescens** (Willd.) Correll, Bot. Mus. Leafl. Harw. Univ. 7 (1): 14, 1938
BM 911
N. America –T
Cypripedium calceolus L., Sp. Pl. 2: 951, 1753
○ Cypripedium flavescens A. DC., Liliac. 1: 20, 1802
Cypripedium pubescens Willd., Hort. Berol. 1: pl. 13, 1804
Cypripedium parviflorum Sims., Bot. Mag.: t. 911, 1806 (non Salisb.)
Cypripedium luteum var. pubescens (Willd.) Raf., Med. Fl. 1: 142, 1828
Cypripedium luteum var. glabrum Raf., Med. Fl. 1: 142, 1828
Cypripedium luteum var. maculatum Raf., Med. Fl. 1: 142, 1828
Cypripedium luteum var. biflorum Raf., Med. Fl. 1: 142, 1828
Cypripedium luteum var. concolor Raf., Med. Fl. 1: 142, 1828
Cypripedium luteum var. angustifolium Raf., Med. Fl. 1: 142, 1828
Cypripedium furcatum Raf., Herb. Raf.: 76, 1833
Cypripedium assurgens Raf., Herb. Raf.: 76, 1833
Cypripedium aureum Raf., Herb. Raf.: 76, 1833
Cypripedium undatum Raf., Herb. Raf.: 77, 1833
Cypripedium hirsutum Miller, Mem. Torrey Bot. Club 5: 121, 1894
Cypripedium veganum Cockerell & Barker., Proc. Biol. Soc. Wash. 4: 178, 1901
Cypripedium parviflorum var. pubescens (Willd.) Knight, Rhodora 8: 93, 1906
Cypripedium bulbosum Miller, Rep. Mich. Acad. Sci. 15: 170, 1913
Cypripedium bulbosum var. flavescens (A. DC.) Farw., Rep. Mich. Acad. Sci. 15: 170, 1913
Calceolus hirsutus (Miller) Nieuwl., Am. Midl. Nat. 3: 118, 1913
Cypripedium makasin Farw., Rep. Mich. Acad. Sci. 20: 198, 1918
Cypripedium pubescens var. makasin Farw., Rep. Mich. Acad. Sci. 20: 198, 1918
○ **Cypripedium californicum** A. Gray, Proc. Am. Acad. 7: 389, 1868
BM 7188
USA (California) – T
○ **Cypripedium candidum** Muhlenb. ex Willd., Sp. Pl. 4: 142, 1805
BM 5855
USA (Pennsylvania), Canada – T
Calceolus candidus (Muhlenb. ex Willd.) Nieuwl., Am. Midl. Nat. 3: 117, 1913
○ **Cypripedium cordigerum** D. Don, Prodr. Fl. Nep.: 37, 1825
BM 9364
Kashmir, Nepal, Bhutan – T
○ **Cypripedium debile** Rchb. f., Xen. Orch. 2: 223, 1874
BM 8183
China, Japan – T
Cypripedium cardiophyllum Franchet & Savat., Enum. Pl. Jap. 2: 39, 1877
Cypripedium fasciculatum Kellogg ex S. Watson, Proc. Am. Acad. 17: 380, 1882
BM 7275
N. W. America – T
Cypripedium pusillum Rolfe, Kew Bull.: 211, 1892
○ Cypripedium fasciculatum var. pusillum (Rolfe) Hook. f., Bot. Mag.: t. 7275, 1893
Cypripedium knightae Nelson, Bot. Gaz. 42: 48, 1906
○ **Cypripedium guttatum** Sw., Kongl. Vet. Acad. Handl. 21: 251, 1800
BM 7746
N. Eur. to E. Siberia, USA (Alaska), Canada, – up to 4500 m – T
Cypripedium orientale Sprengel, Syst. 3: 746, 1826
○ **Cypripedium himalaicum** Rolfe apud Hemsley, J. Linn. Soc. Bot. 29: 319, 1892
BM 8965
S. E. Tibet, Nepal to Bhutan –T
Cypripedium macranthon auct. non Sw.; Hook. f., Fl. Brit. Ind. 6: 170, 1890
Cypripedium macranthon var. himalaicum (Rolfe) Kraenzlin, Orch. Gen. Sp. 1: 26, 1897
○ **Cypripedium japonicum** Thunb., Fl. Jap.: 30, 1784
BM 9520
Japan, China – T
○ **Cypripedium macranthum** Sw., Kongl. Vet. Acad. Handl.: 251, 1800
BM 2938
Siberia, N. Mongolia, N. W. China, Korea, Japan – T
Cypripedium macranthos var. vulgare Sw., Act. Holm.: 251, 1800
Cypripedium thunbergii Blume, Coll. Orch. Arch. Ind. Jap.: 169, 1859
Cypripedium macranthum Sw. var. **speciosum** (Rolfe) Koidz., Jap. Bot. Mag. 40: 336, No. 474, 1926
BM 8386
Japan – T
Cypripedium atsmori Morren, Belg. Hort. 1: 171, t. 1, 1851

Cypripedium calceolus var. atsmori (Morren) Pfitzer, Pflanzenr. Heft 12: 37, 1903
Cypripedium thunbergii Matsum., Ind. Pl. Jap. 2: 242, 1905 (non Blume)
○ Cypripedium speciosum Rolfe, Kew Bull.: 207, 1911
○ **Cypripedium montanum** Douglas ex Lindl., Gen. Sp. Orch. Pl.: 528, 1840
BM 7319
W. N. America – T
Cypripedium occidentale S. Watson, Proc. Am. Acad. 2: 147, 1876
Cypripedium reginae Walter, Fl. Carol.: 222, 1788
BM 216
N. America, Canada – T
Cypripedium calceolus var. L., Sp. Pl. 2: 951, 1753
○ Cypripedium album Aiton, Hort. Kew 3: 303, 1789
Cypripedium spectabile Salisb., Trans. Linn. Soc. 1: 78 pl. 3. fig. 3, 1791
Cypripedium canadensis Michaux, Fl. Bor. Am. 2: 161, 1803
Cypripedium hirsutum Miller, Bull. Torrey Club 32: 375, 1905
Cypripedium reginae var. album Rolfe, Orch. Rev. 19: 208, 1911
Calceolus reginae (Walter) Nieuwl., Am. Midl. Nat. 3: 117, 1913
Cypripedium hirsutum forma album (Rolfe) R. Hoffm., Proc. Boston Soc. Nat. Hist. 36: 246, 1922
○ **Cypripedium tibeticum** King ex Rolfe, J. Linn. Soc. 29: 320, 1893
BM 8070
E. Tibet, W. China – T
Cypripedium macranthon var. ventricosa Hook. f., Fl. Brit. Ind. 6: 170, 1891 (non Sw. nec Carrière)
Cypripedium macranthos var. tibeticum (King ex Rolfe) Kraenzlin, Orch. Gen. Sp. 1: 26, 1897
Cypripedium ventricosum Sweet var. **album** hort. ex Rolfe, Orch. rev. 25: 124, 1917
BM 9117
Siberia – T
Cypripedium ventricosum Sweet, Brit. Fl. Gard. 4: t. 1, 1838 (non Sw.)
Cypripedium macranthon var. ventricosum (Sweet) Rchb. f., Ic. Pl. Germ. 14: 169 t. 145, 1851
Cypripedium macranthon Rchb. f., Garden 11: 30 c. ic. col., 1877
Cypripedium macranthos var. ventricosa (Sweet) Carrière, Rev. Hort.: 310, 1877
Cypripedium macranthon album hort. ex Rolfe, Orch. Rev. 24: 175, 1916
○ Cypripedium manchuricum var. virescens Stapf, Bot. Mag.: t. 9117, 1927
○ **Cyrtopodium andersonii** (Lambert ex Andrews) R. Br., Hort. Kew ed. 2, 5: 216, 1813
BM 1800
W. Indies, Trinidad, Brazil, Guyana, Colombia – T
Cymbidium andersonii Lambert ex Andrews, Bot. Repos. 10: 651, 1811
○ **Cyrtopodium palmifrons** Rchb. f. & Warm. ex Rchb. f., Otia Bot. Hamb. Fasc. 2: 88, 1881
BM 7807
Brazil, Argentina – E
○ **Cyrtopodium punctatum** (L.) Lindl., Gen. Sp. Orch. Pl.: 188, 1833
BM 3507
USA (Florida), Mexico to Panama, W. Indies, S. America to Argentina – T, E
Epidendrum punctatum L., Syst. Nat. 2: 1246, 1760
Cymbidium trinerve Meyer, Prim. Fl. Essequeb.: 258, 1818
Epidendrum gigas Vell., Fl. Flum. Ic. 9: t. 20, 1827
Cyrtopodium willmorei Knowles & Westc., Fl. Cabin. 1: t. 4, 1837
Oncidium palmophilum Martius Herb. ex Lindl., Sert. Orch.: sub. t. 12, 1838
Cyrtopodium speciosissimum hort. ex Du Buysson, l'Orchidoph. 299, 1873
Cyrtopodium tigrinum Linden, Ill. Hort. 28: 95, 1881 (nomen tantum)
Cyrtopodium saintlegerianum Rchb. f., Flora 68: 301, 1885
Cyrtopodium punctatum var. saint legerianum (Rchb. f.) Stein, Orchideenb.: 181, 1892
○ **Cyrtopodium virescens** Rchb. f. & Warm. ex Rchb. f., Otia Bot. Hamb. Fasc. 2: 89, 1881
BM 7396
Paraguay, Brazil – T, E
Cyrtorchis chailluana (Hook. f.) Schltr., Orchideen: 596, 1914
BM 5589
S. Nigeria, Cameroun, Gabon, Zaire, Uganda – E
○ Angraecum chailluanum Hook. f., Cat.: t. 147, 1866
Listrostachys chailluana (Hook. f.) Rchb. f., F. T. A. 7: 153, 1883
Cyrtorchis hamata (Rolfe) Schltr., Orchideen: 596, 1914
BM 8074
Ghana, Nigeria – E
○ Listrostachys hamata Rolfe, Bot. Mag.: t. 8074, 1906
Cyrtorchis monteiroae (Rchb. f.) Schltr., Orchideen: 596, 1914
BM 8026
Sierra Leone, Liberia, Ghana, S. Nigeria, Cameroun, Zaire, Principe Is., Gabon, Uganda, Angola – E
○ Listrostachys monteiroae Rchb. f., F. T. A. 7: 156, 1877
Angraecum aschersonii Kraenzlin, Mitth. Deutsch. Schutzgeb. 2: 160, 1889
Cyrtorchis ringens (Rchb. f.) Summerh., Kew Bull. 12: 87, 1958
BM 9039
Senegal, Sierra Leone, Liberia, Ivory Coast, Ghana, S. Nigeria, W. Cameroun, Sao Tomé, Zaire, Burundi, Uganda, Tanzania – E
Listrostachys ringens Rchb. f., Gard. Chron.: 266, 1878
Angraecum bistortum Rolfe, Kew Bull.: 65, 1893
Listrostachys bistorta (Rolfe) Rolfe, F. T. A. 7: 155, 1897
Listrostachys hookeri Rolfe, F. T. A. 7: 154, 1897
Listrostachys ignotii Kraenzlin, Engl. Bot. Jahrb. 51: 395, 1914
○ Cyrtorchis bistorta (Rolfe) Schltr., F. W. T. A. 1, 2: 460, 1918
Dactylorhiza foliosa (Rchb. f.) Soó, Nom. Nov. Gen. Dactyl.: 7, 1962
BM 5074
Madeira – 900–1000 m – T
○ Orchis foliosa Sol. ex Lowe, Trans. Cambridge Phil. Soc. 4: 13, 1831 (nomen illeg.)
Orchis latifolia var. foliosa Rchb. f., Ic. Fl. Germ. 13/14: 60, 1851
Orchis orientalis subsp. foliosa (Rchb. f.) Klinge, Act. Hort. Petrop.: 189, 1898
Orchis maderensis Summerh., Kew Bull.: 123, 1947
Dactylorchis foliosa (Rchb. f.) Vermeulen, Stud. Dactylorch.: 69, 1947
○ **Dendrobium aduncum** Lindl., Bot. Reg. 1842: Misc. 62 t. 15, 1846
BM 6784
Burma, Sikkim, Kampuchea, Laos, Vietnam – E
Callista adunca (Lindl.) Kuntze, Rev. Gen.: 653–655, 1891
○ **Dendrobium aemulum** R. Br., Prod. Fl. Nov. Holl.: 333, 1810
BM 2906
Australia (New South Wales, Queensland) – E
Tropilis aemula (R. Br.) Raf., Fl. Tellur. 2: 95, 1837
Callista aemulum (R. Br.) Kuntze, Rev. Gen.: 654, 1891
Dendrocoryne aemulum (R. Br.) Brieger, Orchideen ed. 3: 724, 1981
○ **Dendrobium albo-sanguineum** Lindl., Paxt. Flow. Gard. 2: 93 t. 57, 1851
BM 5130
Burma, Thailand – E
Dendrobium atro-sanguineum (Lindl.) Morren & Voss., Ind. Bibl. Hort. Belge: 166, 1887
Callista albosanguinea (Lindl.) Kuntze, Rev. Gen., 1891
Dendrobium amabile (Lour.) O'Brien, Gard. Chron.: 393, 1909
BM 8252
N. Vietnam – E
Callista amabilis Lour., Fl. Coch. Chin.: 519, 1790
Epidendrum callista Raeusch., Nomencl. ed. 3: 265, 1797
○ Dendrobium bronckartii De Wild., Gard. Chron.: 380, 1906
○ **Dendrobium amboinense** Hook., Bot. Mag.: t. 4937, 1856
BM 4937
Malaya (Amboina) – E
Callista amboinensis (Hook.) Kuntze, Rev. Gen., 1891
Euphlebium amboinense (Hook.) Brieger, Orchideen ed. 3: 772, 1981
○ **Dendrobium amethystoglossum** Rchb. f., Gard. Chron.: 109, 1872
BM 5968
Philippines – up to 1400 m – E
Callista amethystoglossa (Rchb. f.) Kuntze, Rev. Gen., 1891
○ **Dendrobium amoenum** Wallich ex Lindl., Gen. Sp. Orch. Pl.: 78, 1830
BM 6199
Nepal to Bhutan, Burma, Thailand, Kampuchea, Laos, Vietnam, W. China, Malaya – E
Dendrobium egertoniae Lindl., Bot. Reg.: t. 36, 1847
Dendrobium mesochlorum Lindl., Bot. Reg.: t. 36, 1847
Callista amoena (Wallich ex Lindl.) Kuntze, Rev. Gen., 1891
Dendrobium anceps Sw., Kongl. Vet. Acad. Handl. 21: 246, 1800
BM 3608
Nepal, Sikkim, Assam, Burma, Thailand, Kampuchea, Laos, Vietnam – E
○ Aporum anceps (Sw.) Lindl., Gen. & Sp. Orch.: 70, 1830
Callista anceps (Sw.) Kuntze, Rev. Gen., 1891
Dendrobium anosmum Lindl., Bot. Reg. 21: Misc. 41, 1844
BM 3970
Malaysia, Laos, Vietnam, Philippines (Manilla), New Guinea – E
○ Dendrobium macrophyllum Lindl., Bot. Reg.: Misc. 36, 1839 (non A. Rich.)
Dendrobium macranthum Hook., Bot. Mag.: t. 3970, 1843
Dendrobium superbum Rchb. f., Walp. Ann. 6: 282, 1861
Dendrobium scortechinii Hook. f., Fl. Brit. Ind. 5: 741, 1890

Callista macrophylla (Lindl.) Kuntze, Rev. Gen.: 653, 1891
Callista anosma (Lindl.) Kuntze, Rev. Gen.: 653, 1891
Callista scortechinii (Hook.f.) Kuntze, Rev. Gen.: 653, 1891
Dendrobium leucorhodum Schltr., Fedde Rep. Beih. 1: 499, 1912
Dendrobium aphrodite Rchb.f., Bot. Zeit. 20: 246, 1862
BM 5470
Burma, Thailand – E
○ Dendrobium nodatum Lindl., Gard. Chron.: 177, 1862
Callista aphrodite (Rchb.f.) Kuntze, Rev. Gen., 1891
Dendrobium aphyllum (Roxb.) C. Fischer, Gamble Fl. Presid. Madras 3: 1416, 1928
BM 2242, BM 2584
Nepal to Bhutan, Burma, Thailand, Kampuchea, Laos, Vietnam, W. China, Malaya – E
Limodorum aphyllum Roxb., Pl. Coromandel 1: 34 t. 41, 1795
Cymbidium aphyllum (Roxb.) Sw., Nov. Act. Upsal. 6: 73, 1799
○ Dendrobium pierrardii (Roxb.) Fischer, Hort. Beng. 63: 1814
○ Dendrobium cucullatum R.Br., Bot. Reg. 7: t. 548, 1821
Callista aphylla (Roxb.) Kuntze, Rev. Gen., 1891
Dendrobium madrasense Hawkes, Orquidea 25: 102, 1963
○ **Dendrobium aqueum** Lindl., Bot. Reg.: Misc. 6 t. 54, 1843
BM 4640
India – E
Dendrobium album Wight, Ic. pl. t. 1645, 1852
Callista aquea (Lindl.) Kuntze, Rev. Gen., 1891
○ **Dendrobium atroviolaceum** Rolfe, Gard. Chron.: 463 & 512, 1890
BM 7371
New Guinea – E
Latourorchis atroviolacea (Rolfe) Brieger, Orchideen ed. 3, 1: 727, 1981
Sayeria atroviolacea (Rolfe) Rauschert, Fedde Rep. 94: 466, 1983
○ **Dendrobium barbatulum** Lindl., Gen. Sp. Orch. Pl.: 84, 1830
BM 5918
India – E
Callista barbatula (Lindl.) Kuntze, Rev. Gen., 1891
○ **Dendrobium bellatulum** Rolfe, J. Linn. Soc. 36: 10, 1903
BM 7985
Burma, Thailand, Kampuchea, Laos, Vietnam, China – 900–1500 m – E
○ **Dendrobium bensoniae** Rchb.f., Bot. Zeit. 25: 230, 1867
BM 5679
Burma, Thailand – E
Callista bensoniae (Rchb.f.) Kuntze, Rev. Gen., 1891
○ **Dendrobium bigibbum** Lindl., Paxt. Flow. Gard. 3: 25 fig. 245, 1852
BM 4898, BM 6817
Australia (N. Queensland to Cape York Peninsular), New Guinea – E
Dendrobium sumneri F. Muell., Fragm. Phyt. Aust. 6: 94, 1867
○ Dendrobium phalaenopsis Fitzg., Gard. Chron.: 38, 1880
Callista bigibba (Lindl.) Kuntze, Rev. Gen., 1891
Callista sumneri (F. Muell.) Kuntze, Rev. Gen., 1891
Callista phalaenopsis (Fitzg.) Kuntze, Rev. Gen., 1891
Dendrobium schroederianum hort. ex Gentil, Pl. Cult. Serres Jard. Bot. Brux.: 73, 1907
○ **Dendrobium brymerianum** Rchb.f., Gard. Chron.: 323, 1875
BM 6383
Burma, Thailand, Laos – E
Callista brymeriana (Rchb.f.) Kuntze, Rev. Gen., 1891
Dendrobium canaliculatum R.Br., Prod. Fl. Nov. Holl.: 333, 1810
BM 5537
N. Australia – E
○ Dendrobium tattonianum Bateman ex Rchb. f., Gard. Chron.: 890, 1865
Callista tattoniana (Bateman ex Rchb.f.) Kuntze, Rev. Gen., 1891
Callista canaliculata (R.Br.) Kuntze, Rev. Gen., 1891
○ **Dendrobium capillipes** Rchb.f., Gard. Chron.: 997, 1867
BM 7639
Burma, Thailand, China – 800–1200 m – E
Callista capillipes (Rchb.f.) Kuntze, Rev. Gen., 1891
Dendrobium cariniferum Rchb.f., Gard. Chron.: 611, 1869
BM 6715
N.E. India, Burma, Thailand – E
○ Dendrobium cariniferum var. wattii Hook., Bot. Mag.: t. 6715, 1883
Callista carinifera (Rchb.f.) Kuntze, Rev. Gen., 1891
○ **Dendrobium chrysocrepis** Parish & Rchb.f. ex Hook.f., Bot. Mag.: t. 6007, 1872
BM 6007
Burma – E
Callista chrysocrepis (Parish & Rchb.f.) Kuntze, Rev. Gen., 1891
○ **Dendrobium chrysotoxum** Lindl., Bot. Reg.: t. 19 & 36, 1847
BM 5053
Burma, China (Yunnan), Laos, Thailand, Vietnam – E
Dendrobium suavissimum Rchb.f., Gard. Chron.: 406, 1874
Dendrobium chrysotoxum var. suavissimum (Rchb.f.) Veitch, Man. Orch. Pl. 3: 30, 1888
Callista chrysotoxa (Lindl.) Kuntze, Rev. Gen., 1891
Callista suavissima (Rchb.f.) Kuntze, Rev. Gen., 1891
○ **Dendrobium crepidatum** Lindl., Paxt. Flow. Gard. 1: 63 fig. 45, 1850
BM 4993, BM 5011
S. India, Nepal, Sikkim, Assam, Thail., Laos – up to 1100 m – E
Dendrochilum roseum Dalz., Hook. Kew J. 4: 291, 1852
Dendrobium lawanum Lindl., J. Linn. Soc. 3: 10, 1859
Callista crepidata (Lindl.) Kuntze, Rev. Gen., 1891
○ **Dendrobium cretaceum** Lindl., Bot. Reg.: t. 62, 1847
BM 4686
Himalaya, Assam, Burma – E
Callista cretacea (Lindl.) Kuntze, Rev. Gen., 1891
○ **Dendrobium crumenatum** Sw., Schrad. J. Bot. 2: 237, 1799
BM 4013
India, China, Thailand, Malaysia, Indonesia, Philippines, New Guinea – E
Angraecum crumenatum Rumph., Herb. Amb. 6: t. 47 2, 1750
Epidendrum caninum Burm. f., Fl. Ind.: 189, 1768
Onychium crumenatum (Sw.) Blume, Bijdr.: 328, 1825
Callista crumenata Kuntze, Rev. Gen., 1891
Dendrobium caninum (Burm. f.) Merr., Philipp. J. Sci.: 19, 1921
Dendrobium kwashotense Hayata, Ic. Pl. Formosa 4: 41, 1944
Aporum crumenatum (Sw.) Brieger, Schlechter Orchideen 1: 671, 1981
○ **Dendrobium crystallinum** Rchb.f., Gard. Chron.: 572, 1868
BM 6319
N.E. India, Sikkim, Burma, Laos, Kampuchea, Vietnam – E
Callista crystallina (Rchb.f.) Kuntze, Rev. Gen., 1891
○ **Dendrobium cucumerinum** MacLeay ex Lindl., Bot. Reg. 28: Misc. 58, 1842
BM 4619
Australia – E
Callista cucumerina (MacLeay ex Lindl.) Kuntze, Rev. Gen., 1891
Dockrillia cucumerina (MacLeay & Lindl.) Brieger, Schlechter Orchideen 1: 745, 1981
○ **Dendrobium cumulatum** Lindl., Gard. Chron.: 756, 1855
BM 5703
N.E. India, Sikkim, N. Burma – E
Callista cumulata (Lindl.) Kuntze, Rev. Gen., 1891
Dendrobium delacourii Guillaumin, Bull. Mus. Paris: 522, 1924
BM 5430
Burma, Thailand, Laos, Kampuchea, Vietnam – 800–1300 m – E
○ Dendrobium ciliatum Parish ex Hook., Bot. Mag.: t. 5430, 1864 (non Pers., Syn. 2: 523, 1807)
Callista ciliata (Parish ex Hook.) Kuntze, Rev. Gen., 1891
Dendrobium ciliferum Bakh. f., Blumea 12: 68, 1963
Dendrobium denneanum Kerr, J. Siam Soc. Nat. Hist. suppl. 9: 229, 1933
BM 6993
Himalaya (Kumaun to Nepal), Assam (Khasia) – 1000–2000 m – E
○ Dendrobium clavatum Wallich ex Lindl., Paxt. Flow. Gard. 2: 104 fig. 189, 1851
Callista clavata (Wallich ex Lindl.) Kuntze, Rev. Gen., 1891
○ **Dendrobium densiflorum** Wallich ex Lindl., Pl. As. Rar. 1: 34, 1830
BM 3418
Nepal, Assam, Burma, N. Thail., Laos, Vietnam – up to 1500 m – E
Dendrobium schroederi hort., Flor. Mag. 9: t. 502, 1870
Callista densiflora (Wallich ex Lindl.) Kuntze, Rev. Gen., 1891
○ **Dendrobium denudans** D. Don, Prod. Fl. Nepal.: 34, 1825
BM 7549
Himalaya (Gahrwal to Sikkim) – 900–2000 m – E
Callista denudans (D. Don) Kuntze, Rev. Gen., 1891
○ **Dendrobium devonianum** Paxton, Mag. Bot. 8: 169, 1840
BM 4429
Assam, China, Burma, Thailand, Kampuchea, Laos, Vietnam – E
Callista devoniana (Paxton) Kuntze, Rev. Gen., 1891
○ **Dendrobium dixanthum** Rchb.f., Gard. Chron.: 674, 1865
BM 5564
Thailand, Burma – E
Dendrobium moulmeinense Parish ex Hook.f., Fl. Brit. Ind.: 746, 1890
Callista dixantha (Rchb.f.) Kuntze, Rev. Gen., 1891
Callista moulmeinensis (Parish ex Hook.f.) Kuntze, Rev. Gen., 1891
Dendrobium draconis Rchb.f., Bot. Zeit.: 214, 1862
BM 5459
Burma, Thailand, Kampuchea, Laos, Vietnam – E
○ Dendrobium eburneum Rchb.f. ex Bateman, Bot. Mag.: t. 5459, 1864
Dendrobium andersonii J. Scott., J. Agr. Hort. Soc. Ind. n.s. 3,: 117, 1872
Callista draconis (Rchb.f.) Kuntze, Rev. Gen., 1891

○ **Dendrobium falconeri** Hook., Bot. Mag.: t. 4944, 1856
BM 4944
Assam, Burma, Thailand – up to 1200 m – E
Callista falconeri (Hook.) Kuntze, Rev. Gen., 1891
○ **Dendrobium farmeri** Paxton, Mag. Bot. 15: 241 c.t. 1849
BM 4659
Sikkim, W. Nepal, E. Assam, Burma, Thailand, Malaya – E
Dendrobium densiflorum var. alba Regel, Gartenflora 17: t. 595, 1868
Dendrobium densiflorum var. farmeri (Paxton) Regel, Gartenflora 23: t. 788, 1874
Dendrobium farmeri var. parviflora Regel, Gartenflora 23: t. 67, 1874
Dendrobium thyrsiflorum Regel, Gartenflora 29: t. 1021, 1880
Callista farmeri (Paxton) Kuntze, Rev. Gen., 1891
Dendrobium fimbriatum Hook., Exot. Fl.: t. 71, 1823
BM 4160
India, Nepal, Sikkim, Burma, Thailand, Kampuchea, Laos, Vietnam – E
○ Dendrobium fimbriatum var. oculata Hook., Bot. Mag.: t. 4160, 1845
Callista fimbriata (Hook.) Kuntze, Rev. Gen., 1891
○ **Dendrobium findlayanum** Parish & Rchb. f., Trans. Linn. Soc. 30: 149, 1877
BM 6438
Burma, Thailand – E
Callista findlayana (Parish & Rchb. f.) Kuntze, Rev. Gen., 1891
Dendrobium forbesii Ridley, J. Linn. Soc. 24: 323, 1886
BM 8141
New Guinea – 900–1500 m – E
○ Dendrobium ashworthiae O'Brien, Gard. Chron.: t. 36, 1901
Dendrobium forbesii var. praestans Schltr., Fedde Rep. Beih. 1: 497, 1912
? Dendrobium eustachyum Schltr., Engl., Bot. Jahrb. 58: 100, 1922
Latourorchis forbesii (Ridley) Brieger, Schlechter Orchideen 1: 727, 1981
Sayeria forbesii (Ridley) Rauschert, Fedde Rep. 94: 467, 1983
Dendrobium fytchianum Bateman, Gard. Chron.: 100, 1864
BM 5444
Burma, Malaya – E
○ Dendrobium barbatulum Bateman, Bot. Mag.: t. 5444, 1864 (non Lindl.)
Callista fytchiana (Bateman) Kuntze, Rev. Gen., 1891
Dendrobium gibsonii Lindl., Paxt. Mag. Bot. 5: 169, 1838
BM 6226
Nepal to Bhutan, Assam, Burma – 800–1500 m – E
○ Dendrobium fuscatum Lindl., J. Linn. Soc. 3: 8, 1859
Callista gibsonii (Lindl.) Kuntze, Rev. Gen., 1891
Dendrobium gouldii Rchb. f., Gard. Chron.: 901, 1867
BM 8452
New Ireland, Bougainville, Solomon Is. – up to 400 m – E
Dendrobium undulatum var. woodfordianum Maiden, Proc. Linn. Soc. N.S.W. 24: 652, 1899
○ Dendrobium imthurnii Rolfe, Bot. Mag.: t. 8452, 1912
Dendrobium woodfordianum (Maiden) Schltr., Fedde Rep. Beih. 1: 545, 1912
Callista gouldii (Rchb. f.) Kuntze, Rev. Gen., 1891
○ **Dendrobium gracilicaule** F. Muell., Fragm. Phyt. Austral. 1: 179, 1859
BM 7042
E. Australia – E
Dendrobium elongatum Cunn., Bot. Reg. 25: Misc. 33, 1839 (non Lindl.)
Dendrobium brisbanense Rchb. f., Walp. Ann. 6: 299, 1861
Dendrobium fellowsii F. Muell., Fragm. Phyt. Austral. 7: 63, 1870
Callista gracilicaulis (F. Muell.) Kuntze, Rev. Gen.: 654, 1891
Dendrobium jonesii Rendle, J. Bot. Lond. 39: 197, 1901
Tropilis gracilicaulis (F. Muell.) Butzin, Willdenowia 12 (2): 250, 1982
Dendrobium gratiosissimum Rchb. f., Bot. Zeit. 23: 99, 1865
BM 5652
Burma, Thailand – E
○ Dendrobium bullerianum Bateman, Bot. Mag.: t. 5652, 1867
Dendrobium boxallii Rchb. f., Gard. Chron.: 315, 1874
Callista boxallii (Rchb. f.) Kuntze, Rev. Gen.: 653–55, 1891
Dendrobium griffithianum Lindl., Bot. Reg.: sub. t. 1756, 1886
BM 5451
Burma – E
○ Dendrobium farmeri var. aureo-flava Hook., Bot. Mag.: t. 5451, 1864
Callista griffithiana (Lindl.) Kuntze, Rev. Gen., 1891
○ **Dendrobium hercoglossum** Rchb. f., Gard. Chron.: 487, 1886
BM 9428
Thailand, Vietnam, Malaya, Philippines – E
Dendrobium linguella Rchb. f., Gard. Chron.: 552, 1882
Callista hercoglossa (Rchb. f.) Kuntze, Rev. Gen.: 654, 1891
Dendrobium vexans Dammer, Orchis 4: 87, 1910
Callista vexans (Dammer) Kraenzlin, Pflanzenr. Heft 45: 365, 1910

○ **Dendrobium heterocarpum** Wallich ex Lindl., Gen. Sp. Orch. Pl.: 78, 1830
BM 4708, BM 4970
Sri Lanka, S. India, Sikkim, Assam, Burma, Thailand, Java, Philippines – E
Dendrobium aureum Lindl., Gen. Sp. Orch. Pl.: 77, 1830
Dendrobium aureum var. pallida Lindl., Bot. Reg.: t. 20, 1839
Dendrobium rhombeum Lindl., Bot. Reg.: t. 17, 1843
○ Dendrobium heterocarpum var. henshallii Hook., Bot. Mag.: t. 4708, 1853 & t. 4970, 1857
Dendrobium aureum var. philippinensis Rchb. f., Gard. Chron.: 72, 1880
Dendrobium atractodes Ridley, J. Bot. 23: 123, 1885
Callista aurea Kuntze, Rev. Gen.: 653, 1891
Callista heterocarpa (Wallich ex Lindl.) Kuntze, Rev. Gen.: 653–655, 1891
Dendrobium minahassae Kraenzlin, Pflanzenr. Heft 45: 107 fig. 5, 1910
○ **Dendrobium hildebrandii** Rolfe, Kew Bull.: 182, 1894
BM 7453
Thailand, Burma – E
○ **Dendrobium hodgkinsonii** Rolfe, Kew Bull.: 32, 1906
BM 7724
New Guinea – E
Sayeria hodgkinsonii (Rolfe) Rauschert, Fedde Rep. 94: (7/8): 467, 1983
○ **Dendrobium hookerianum** Lindl., J. Linn. Soc. 3, 1859
BM 6013
Sikkim, Assam – 1300–2000 m – E
Dendrobium chrysotis Rchb. f., Gard. Chron.: 1311, 1870
Callista hookeriana (Lindl.) Kuntze, Rev. Gen., 1891
○ **Dendrobium inaequale** Rolfe, Kew Bull.: 147, 1901
BM 7745
New Guinea – 400–900 m – E
Euphlebium inaequale (Rolfe) Rauschert, Fedde Rep. 94: 447, 1983
○ **Dendrobium infundibulum** Lindl., J. Linn. Soc. 3: 16, 1859
BM 5446
Burma, Thailand – 1000–2100 m – E
Callista infundibula (Lindl.) Kuntze, Rev. Gen.: 653–55, 1891
Dendrobium moulmeinense hort. Low. ex Warn. & Will., Orch. Alb. 10: t. 448, 1893
○ **Dendrobium johannis** Rchb. f., Gard. Chron.: 890, 1865
BM 5540
N.E. Australia, S. New Guinea – E
Callista johannis (Rchb. f.) Kuntze, Rev. Gen., 1891
○ **Dendrobium kingianum** Bidw. ex Lindl., Bot. Reg. 30: Misc. 11, 1844
BM 4527
Australia (S.E. Queensland, N. New South Wales) – E
Callista kingiana (Bidw.) Kuntze, Rev. Gen.: 635–653, 1891
Dendrocoryne kingianum (Bidw.) Brieger, Schlechter Orchideen ed. 3, 1: 724, 1981
Tropilis kingiana (Bidw.) Butzin, Willdenowia 12 (2): 250, 1982
○ **Dendrobium laevifolium** Stapf, Bot. Mag.: t. 9011, 1924
BM 9011
New Guinea, Louisiade Arch., Solomon Is. – E
○ **Dendrobium lasioglossum** Rchb. f., Gard. Chron.: 682, 1868
BM 5825
Burma – E
Callista lasioglossa (Rchb. f.) Kuntze, Rev. Gen., 1891
○ **Dendrobium leonis** (Lindl.) Rchb. f., Walp. Ann. 6: 280, 1861
BM 7493
Borneo, Sumatra, Malaya, Thailand – E
Aporum leonis Lindl., Bot. Reg.: Misc. 59, 1840
Callista leonis (Lindl.) Kuntze, Rev. Gen., 1891
Dendrobium linawianum Rchb. f., Walp. Ann. 6: 284, 1861
BM 4153
China, Japon – E
Callista linawiana (Rchb. f.) Kuntze, Rev. Gen., 1891
Dendrobium alboviride Hayata, Ic. Pl. Form. 9: 108 fig. 36, 1920
○ (Dendrobium moniliforme Sw., Act. Holm: 243, 1800; misidentified)
Dendrobium lindleyi Steudel, Nom. 1, 490, 1840
BM 3643
India, Assam, Burma, S. China, Kampuchea, Laos, Vietnam, Malaya – E
○ Dendrobium aggregatum Roxb., Hort. Beng.: 63, 1814
Dendrobium jenkinsii Wallich ex Lindl., Bot. Reg. 25: t. 37, 1839
Callista aggregata (Roxb.) Kuntze, Rev. Gen., 1891
Callista jenkinsii (Wallich ex Lindl.) Kuntze, Rev. Gen.: 653–55, 1891
○ **Dendrobium linguiforme** Sw., Kongl. Vet. Akad. Handl. 21: 247, 1800
BM 5249
Australia (Queensland, New South Wales, Cape York), – E
Callista linguiformis (Sw.) Kuntze, Rev. Gen.: 653, 1891

Dockrillia linguiformis (Sw.) Brieger, Schlechter Orchideen ed. 3, 1: 746, 1981
Dendrobium lituiflorum Lindl., Gard. Chron.: 372, 1856
BM 6050
N.E. India, Burma, Thailand – E
Dendrobium hanburyanum Rchb. f., Bonpl. 4: 329, 1856
Callista lituiflora (Lindl.) Kuntze, Rev. Gen., 1891
Dendrobium loddigesii Rolfe, Gard. Chron.: 155, 1887
BM 5037
S. China, Hainan, Laos – E
Dendrobium pulchellum Lodd., Bot. Cabin.: t. 1935, 1833 (non Roxb., Lindl. & Rchb. f.)
Dendrobium seidelianum Rchb. f., Gard. World, 1887
Callista loddigesii (Rolfe) Kuntze, Rev. Gen., 1891
Dendrobium lowii Lindl., Gard. Chron.: 1046, 1861
BM 5303
Borneo – up to 900 m – E
Callista lowii (Lindl.) Kuntze, Rev. Gen., 1891
Dendrobium luteolum Bateman, Gard. Chron.: 269, 1864
BM 5441
E. Himalaya, Burma, Thailand, Malaya – E
Callista luteola (Bateman) Kuntze, Rev. Gen., 1891
Dendrobium maccarthiae Thwaites, Bot. Mag.: t. 4886, 1855
BM 4886
Sri Lanka – E
Callista maccarthiae (Thwaites) Kuntze, Rev. Gen., 1891
Dendrobium macrophyllum A. Rich., Sert. Astrolab: 22 t. 9, 1834
BM 5649
New Guinea, Java, Philippines, Palau, Solomon Is., Vanuatu, New Caledonia, Fiji, Samoa – E
Dendrobium veitchianum Lindl., Bot. Reg.: t. 25, 1847
Dendrobium ferox Hassk., Retzia 1: 1, 1855
Dendrobium sarcostoma Teijsm. & Binnend. ex Miq., Fl. Ind. Bot. 3: 637, 1855 (nomen nudum)
Dendrobium macrophyllum var. veitchianum (Lindl.) Hook. f., Bot. Mag.: t. 5649, 1867
Callista veitchiana (Lindl.) Kuntze, Rev. Gen., 1891
Callista macrophylla (A. Rich.) Kuntze, Rev. Gen., 1891
Dendrobium brachythecum F. Muell. & Kraenzlin, Oester. Bot. Zeit. 44: 161, 1894
Dendrobium ternatense J. J. Smith, Bull. Dép. Agr. Ind. Neerl. 22: 26, 1909
Dendrobium psyche Kraenzlin, Pflanzenr. Heft 45: 246, 1910
Dendrobium tomohonense Kraenzlin, Pflanzenr. Heft 45: 244, 1910
Dendrobium musciferum Schltr., Fedde, Rep. Beih. 1: 494, 1914
Latourorchis macrophylla (A. Rich.) Brieger, Schlechter Orchideen ed. 3, 1: 727, 1981
Latourorchis muscifera (Schltr.) Brieger, Schlechter Orchideen ed. 3, 1: 727, 1981
Dendrobium moniliforme (L.) Sw., Nov. Act. Upsal. 6: 85, 1799
BM 5482
China, Japan, Yakusima, Taiwan, Korea – 800–2500 m – E
Epidendrum moniliforme L., Sp. Pl.: 954, 1753
Epidendrum moniliferum Panzer, Pflanzensyst. 10: 122, 1983
Epidendrum monile Thunb., Fl. Jap.: 30, 1784
Limodorum monile (Thunb.) Thunb., Trans. Linn. Soc. 2: 327, 1794
Onychium japonicum Blume, Bijdr. 7: 328, 1825
Dendrobium catenatum Lindl., Gen. & Sp. Orch. Pl.: 84, 1830
Dendrobium japonicum (Blume) Lindl., Gen. & Sp. Orch. Pl.: 89, 1830
Ormostema albiflora Raf., Fl. Tellur. 4: 38, 1838
Ormostema purpurea Raf., Fl. Tellur. 4: 38, 1838
Dendrobium castum Bateman ex Hook. f., Bot. Mag.: t. 5482, 1864
Callista japonica (Blume) Kuntze, Rev. Gen. 2: 654, 1891
Callista moniliformis (L.) Kuntze, Rev. Gen. 2: 654, 1891
Dendrobium zonatum Rolfe, J. Linn. Soc. 36: 13, 1903
Dendrobium monile (Thunb.) Kraenzlin, Pflanzenr. Heft 45: 50 fig. 2, 1910
Dendrobium heisnanense Hayata, Ic. Pl. Form. 4: 40 fig. 13c, 1914
Dendrobium moschatum (Buch.-Ham.) Sw., Neues J. Bot. 1 (1): 94, 1805
BM 3837
Himalaya (Kumaun to Bhutan), India, Burma, Laos, Thailand – E
Epidendrum moschatum Buch.-Ham., Symes Embassy to Ava: 478, 1800
Cymbidium moschatum (Buch.-Ham.) Willd., Sp. Pl. 4: 98, 1805
Dendrobium calceolaria Carey ex Hook., Exot. Fl. 3: t. 184, 1825/26
Dendrobium cupreum Herbert, Bot. Reg.: t. 1779, 1836
Callista moschata (Buch.-Ham.) Kuntze, Rev. Gen., 1891
Callista calceola Kuntze, Rev. Gen., 1891
Dendrobium munificum (Finet) Hallé, Fl. N. Calédonie: 140 pl. 1 & 66, 1977
BM 8371
New Caledonia – E
Dendrobium muricatum var. munificum Finet, Bull. Soc. Bot. Fr. 50: 378, t. 14, 7–8, 1903
Inobulbon munificum (Finet) Kraenzlin, Pflanzenr. Heft 45: 319 fig. 29, 1910
Dendrobium mutabile (Blume) Lindl., Gen. Sp. Orch. Pl.: 86, 1830
BM 5285
Sunda Is., Sumatra, Java, Ryukyu Is. – E
Onychium mutabile Blume, Bijdr.: 324, 1825
Onychium rigidum Blume, Bijdr.: 324, 1825
Dendrobium rigidum (Blume) Lindl., Gen. Sp. Orch. Pl.: 86, 1830
Dendrobium firmum Steudel, Nom. 2, ed. 2, 1: 490, 1840
Dendrobium sclerophyllum Lindl., Bot. Reg.: Misc. 58, 1844
Dendrobium triadenium Lindl., Bot. Reg.: t. 1, 1847
Dendrobium rigescens Miq., Fl. Ned. Ind. 3: 639, 1856
Callista mutabilis Kuntze, Rev. Gen.: 653–655, 1891
Callista rigida Kuntze, Rev. Gen.: 653–655, 1891
Callista rigescens (Miq.) Kuntze, Rev. Gen.: 653–655, 1891
Dendrobium nutans Lindl., Gen. Sp. Orch. Pl.: 90, 1830
BM 7741
India, Sri Lanka – E
Dendrobium villosulum Lindl., Paxt. Flow. Gard. 2: 106, c. xyl. 1852 (non Wallich)
Dendrobium jerdonianum Wight, Ic.: t. 1644, 1855
Callista nutans (Lindl.) Kuntze, Rev. Gen. 2: 655, 1891
Callista jerdoniana (Wight) Kuntze, Rev. Gen., 1891
Callista villosula (Lindl.) Kuntze, Rev. Gen., 1891
Dendrobium nutantiflorum Hawkes & A. H. Heller, Lloydia 20: 122, 1957
Dendrobium ochreatum Lindl., Wall. Cat.: n. 7410, 1828
BM 4450
E. India, Thailand – E
Dendrobium cambridgeanum Paxton, Mag. Bot. 6: t. 265, 1839
Callista ochreata (Lindl.) Kuntze, Rev. Gen., 1891
Dendrobium palpebrae Lindl., J. Hort. Soc. 5: 33, 1849
BM 8683
Burma, China (Yunnan), Thailand – E
Callista palpebrae (Lindl.) Kuntze, Rev. Gen., 1891
Dendrobium parishii Rchb. f., Bot. Zeit. 21: 277, 1863
BM 5488
Burma, China (Yunnan), Thailand, Laos, Kampuchea, Vietnam – E
Callista parishii (Rchb. f.) Kuntze, Rev. Gen., 1891
Dendrobium pendulum Roxb., Hort. Beng.: 63, 1814
BM 5766
Assam, Burma, Thailand – up to 900 m – E
Dendrobium crassinode Benson & Rchb. f., Gard. Chron.: 164, 1869
Callista pendula (Roxb.) Kuntze, Rev. Gen., 1891
Callista crassinodis (Benson & Rchb. f.) Kuntze, Rev. Gen., 1891
Dendrobium primulinum Lindl., Gard. Chron.: 400, 1858
BM 5003
India, Nepal, Sikkim, Burma, China, Thailand, Vietnam, Malaya – E
Dendrobium nobile var. pallidiflorum Hook., Bot. Mag.: t. 5003, 1857
Callista primulina (Lindl.) Kuntze, Rev. Gen., 1891
Dendrobium regium Prain, J. As. Soc. Beng. 71: 80, 1902
BM 8003
India – E
Dendrobium revolutum Lindl., Bot. Reg.: Misc. 51, 1840
BM 6706
Burma, Thailand, Kampuchea, Laos, Vietnam, Malaya, Borneo – E
Dendrobium refractum Teijsm. & Binnend., Tijdschr. Ned. Ind. 24: 315, 1862
Callista revoluta (Lindl.) Kuntze, Rev. Gen., 1891
Dendrobium tonkinensis De Wild., Tribune Hort. 1: 21, 1906
Dendrobium rhodostictum F. Muell. & Kraenzlin, Oester. Bot. Zeit. 44: 300, 1894
BM 7900
New Guinea, Solomon Is. – up to 1200 m – E
Dendrobium madonnae Rolfe, Kew Bull.: 32, 1906
Dendrobium sanderae Rolfe, Gard. Chron.: 374, 1909
BM 8351
S.E. Asia, Philippines – 1000–1700 m – E
Dendrobium sarmentosum Rolfe, Orch. Rev. 4: 72, 1896
BM 7525
N.W. Malaya – E
Dendrobium fragans hort. ex Hook. f., Bot. Mag.: t. 7525, 1897
Dendrobium scabrilingue Lindl., J. Linn. Soc. 3: 25, 1859
BM 5515
Thailand, Burma – E

o Dendrobium hedyosmum Bateman ex Hook. f., Bot. Mag.: t. 5515, 1865
Callista scabrilinguis (Lindl.) Kuntze, Rev. Gen., 1891
o **Dendrobium schuetzei** Rolfe, Orch. Rev. 19: 224, 1911
BM 8495
Philippines - E
o **Dendrobium secundum** (Blume) Lindl., Gen. Sp. Orch. Pl.: 81, 1830
BM 4352
Burma, Thailand, Kampuchea, Laos, Vietnam, Malaysia, Philippines, Sumatra, Java, Borneo - E
Pedilonum secundum Blume, Bijdr.: 322, 1825
Dendrobium bursigerum Lindl., J. Linn. Soc. 3: 16, 1859
Callista bursigera (Lindl.) Kuntze, Rev. Gen.: 653-655, 1891
Callista secunda (Blume) Kuntze, Rev. Gen.: 653-655, 1891
o **Dendrobium senile** Parish ex Rchb.f., Gard. Chron.: 434, 1865
BM 5520
Burma, Thailand, Laos - E
Callista senilis (Parish ex Rchb.f.) Kuntze, Rev. Gen., 1891
o **Dendrobium speciosum** Smith, Exot. Bot. 1: 17, 1804/5
BM 3074
E. Australia - E
Callista speciosa (Smith) Kuntze, Rev. Gen.: 2: 655, 1891
Dendrocoryne speciosum (Smith) Brieger, Schlechter Orchideen ed. 3, 1: 724, 1981
Tropilis speciosa (Smith) Butzin, Willdenowia 12 (2): 250, 1981
Dendrobium speciosum Smith var. **hillii** (Hook.) Bailey, Syn. Qd. Fl.: 509, 1883
BM 5261
Australia (New South Wales, Queensland) - E
o Dendrobium hillii Hook., Bot. Mag.: t. 5261, 1861
o **Dendrobium spectabile** (Blume) Miq., Fl. Ind. Bat. 3: 645, 1855
BM 7747
New Guinea, Solomon Is. - up to 1100 m - E
Latourea spectabilis Blume, Rumph. 4: 41 t. 195, 1850
Dendrobium tigrinum Rolfe ex Hemsley, Am. Bot. 5: 507, 1891
Callista spectabilis (Blume) Kuntze, Rev. Gen., 1891
Latourorchis spectabile (Blume) Brieger, Schlechter Orchideen ed. 3, 1: 727, 1981
Sayeria spectabilis (Blume) Rauschert, Fedde Rep. 94: 468, 1983
o **Dendrobium sulcatum** Lindl., Bot. Reg.: t. 65, 1838
BM 6962
Sikkim, Burma, Vietnam - E
Callista sulcata (Lindl.) Kuntze, Rev. Gen., 1891
o **Dendrobium teretifolium** (Sw.) R.Br., Prodr. Fl. Nov. Holl.: 333, 1810
BM 4711
Australia (Queensland, New South Wales), New Guinea - E
Epidendrum teretifolium Sw., Prodr. Veg. Ind. Occ.: 122, 1788
Dendrobium calamiforme Lodd., Bot. Reg.: Misc. 9, 1841
Dendrobium fairfaxii F. Muell., Sydney Mail Sept. 21: 360, 1872
Callista fairfaxii (F. Muell.) Kuntze, Rev. Gen., 1891
Callista teretifolia (Sw.) Kuntze, Rev. Gen., 1891
Dockrillia teretifolia (Sw.) Brieger, Schlechter Orchideen ed. 3, 1: 746, 1981
o **Dendrobium tetragonum** Cunn. ex Lindl., Bot. Reg. 25: Misc. 33, 1839
BM 5956
Australia (Queensland, New South Wales) - E
Callista tetragona (Cunn. ex Lindl.) Kuntze, Rev. Gen. 2: 655, 1891
Dendrobium tetragonum var. variabilis P.A. Gilbert, Austral. Orchid. Rev. 2: 20, 1937
Dendrocoryne tetragonum (Cunn. ex Lindl.) Brieger, Schlechter Orchideen ed. 3, 1: 724, 1981
Tropilis tetragona (Cunn. ex Lindl.) Butzin, Willdenowia 12 (2): 250, 1982
Dendrobium thyrsiflorum Rchb.f. ex André, Ill. Hort. 22: 88 t. 207, 1875
BM 5780
Burma, Thailand, Laos - up to 1200 m - E
o (Dendrobium densiflorum var. albo-lutea Hook.f., Bot. Mag.: t. 5780, 1869; misidentified)
o **Dendrobium tortile** Lindl., Gard. Chron.: 797, 1847
BM 4477
Kampuchea, Laos, Vietnam - E
Callista tortilis (Lindl.) Kuntze, Rev. Gen., 1891
Dendrobium tortile Lindl. var. **dartoisianum** (De Wild.) O'Brien, Gard. Chron.: 198, 1907
BM 8352
Kampuchea, Laos, Vietnam - E
o Dendrobium dartoisianum De Wild., Gard. Chron.: 380, 1906
Dendrobium haniffii var. dartoisianum (De Wild.) Hawkes, Orquidea 25: 278, 1963
o **Dendrobium transparens** Wallich, Wall. Cat. 2008-1, 1829
BM 4663
Himalaya (Kumaun to Bhutan), Assam - 800-1300 m - E
Dendrobium henshalli Rchb.f., Bonpl. 3: 226, 1855
Callista transparens (Wallich) Kuntze, Rev. Gen., 1891
o **Dendrobium victoriae-reginae** Loher, Gard. Chron.: 399, 1897
BM 9071
Philippines (Luzon) - 1300-2700 m - E
Dendrobium coeleste Loher, Gard. Chron.: 1, 1897
Dendrobium wardianum Warner, Sel. Orch. 1: t. 19, 1862
BM 5058
Assam, Burma, Thailand - E
Callista wardiana (Warner) Kuntze, Rev. Gen., 1891
o (Dendrobium falconeri var. β Hook., Bot. Mag.: t. 5058, 1858; misidentified)
o **Dendrobium williamsonii** Day & Rchb.f., Gard. Chron.: 78, 1869
BM 7974
N.E. India, Assam, Burma, Thailand - E
Callista williamsonii (Day & Rchb.f.) Kuntze, Rev. Gen., 1891
Dendrobium xanthophlebium Lindl., Gard. Chron.: 196, 1856 & 268, 1857
BM 5454
Burma - up to 1200 m - E
o Dendrobium marginatum Bateman, Bot. Mag.: t. 5454, 1864
Callista xanthophlebia (Lindl.) Kuntze, Rev. Gen., 1891
Callista marginata (Bateman) Kuntze, Rev. Gen., 1891
o **Dendrochilum glumaceum** Lindl., Bot. Reg.: Misc. 23 n. 58, 1841
BM 4853
Philippines (Luzon, Mindanao) - up to 2300 m - E
Platyclinis glumacea (Lindl.) Benth., J. Linn. Soc. 18: 295, 1881
Acoridium glumaceum (Lindl.) Rolfe, Orch. Rev. 12: 220, 1904
o **Dendrochilum uncatum** Rchb.f., Bonpl. 3: 222, 1855
BM 9015
Philippines (Luzon) - 1000-2300 m - E
Platyclinis uncata (Rchb.f.) N.E.Br. ex Williams, Orch. Grow. Man. ed. 7: 680, 1894
Acoridium uncatum (Rchb.f.) Rolfe, Orch. Rev. 12: 220, 1904
Dendrophylax funalis (Sw.) Fawcett, Fl. Pl. Jam.: 40, 1893
BM 4295
W. Indies - E
Epidendrum funale Sw., Prodr. Veg. Ind. Occ.: 126, 1788
Limodorum funale (Sw.) Sw., Nov. Act. Upsal. 6: 79, 1799
Oeceoclades funalis (Sw.) Lindl., Gen. Sp. Orch. Pl.: 237, 1833
o Angraecum funale (Sw.) Lindl., Bot. Reg. 26: t. 68, 1840
Aeranthus funalis (Sw.) Rchb.f., Walp. Ann. 6: 902, 1861
Polyrrhiza funalis (Sw.) Pfitzer, Nat. Pflanzenf. 2, 6: 215 fig. 227, 1889
Diaphananthe bidens (Afzel. ex Sw.) Schltr., Orchideen: 593, 1914
BM 8014
Guinea-Bissau, Guinea, Sierra Leone, Liberia, Ivory Coast, Ghana, S. Nigeria, W. Cameroun, Fernando Po, Gabon, Zaire, C. African Rep., Uganda, Angola - E
Limodorum bidens Afzel. ex. Sw., Kongl. Vet. Acad. Handl.: 243, 1800
Listrostachys ashantensis (Lindl.) Rchb.f., F.T.A. 7: 159, 1895
Mystacidium productum Kraenzlin, F.T.A. 7: 174, 1895
o Listrostachys bidens (Afzel. ex Sw.) Rolfe, F.T.A. 7: 174, 1895
Angraecum bidens (Afzel. ex Sw.) Rendle, Cat.: t. 147, 1913
Dimerandra emarginata (G. Meyer) Hoehne, Boletin de Agricultura, Sao Paulo 34a, pt. 1: 618 t. 9, 1934
BM 3410
Mexico, Guatemala, Honduras, Costa Rica, Panama, Trinidad, Venezuela, Colombia, Ecuador, Peru, Guyana, Surinam, Brazil, Jamaica, W. Indies - E
Oncidium emarginatum G. Meyer, Prim. Fl. Essequeb.: 259, 1818
o Epidendrum stenopetalum Hook., Bot. Mag.: t. 3410, 1835
Epidendrum lamellatum Westc. & Lindl., Bot. Reg. 29: Misc. p. 46, 1843
Isochilus elegans Focke, Tijdsch. Nat. Wetensch. 4: 68, 1851
Epidendrum stenopetalum var. tenuicaule Rchb.f., Otia Bot. Hamb. Fasc. 1: 12, 1878
Telipogon buenaventurae Kraenzlin, Ann. Nat. Hist. Mus. Wien 33: 35, 1919
Epidendrum rimbachii Schltr., Fedde Rep. Beih. 8: 167, 1921
Dimerandra stenopetala (Hook.) Schltr., Fedde Rep. Beih. 17: 44, 1922
Dimerandra rimbachii (Schltr.) Schltr., Fedde Rep. Beih. 17: 44, 1922
Dimerandra isthmi Schltr., Fedde Rep. Beih. 17: 44, 1922
Dimorphorchis lowii (Lindl.) Rolfe. Orch. Rev. 27: 149, 1919
BM 5475
Borneo - E
Vanda lowii Lindl., Gard. Chron.: 239, 1847
o Renanthera lowii (Lindl.) Rchb.f., Xen. Orch. 1: 89, 1855
Renanthera rohaniana Rchb.f., Xen Orch. 1: 89, 1855
Arachnanthe lowii (Lindl.) Benth. & Hook.f., Gen. Pl. 3: 573, 1883
Arachnis lowii (Lindl.) Rchb.f., Bot. Centralbl. 28: 344, 1886

Vandopsis lowii (Lindl.) Schltr., Fedde Rep. 10: 196, 1911
o **Dinema polybulbon** (Sw.) Lindl., Gen. Sp. Orch. Pl.: 111, 1831
BM 4067
Mexico, Guatemala, El Salvador, Honduras, Cuba, Jamaica – 1000–1400 m – E, L
Epidendrum polybulbon Sw., Prodr. Veg. Ind. Occ.: 124, 1788
Bulbophyllum occidentale Sprengel, Syst. Veg. 3: 732, 1826
Epidendrum polybulbon var. luteo-album Miethe, Orchis 8: 33 t. 1, 1914
Encyclia polybulbon (Sw.) Dressler, Brittonia 13: 265, 1961
o **Diplomeris hirsuta** Lindl., Gen. Sp. Orch. Pl.: 330, 1835
BM 9113
Nepal, Sikkim, Bhutan – T
Diplochilus hirsutus (Lindl.) Lindl., Gen. Sp. Orch. Pl.: 330, 1835
o **Dipodium paludosum** (Griffith) Rchb.f., Xen. Orch. 2: 15, 1862
BM 7464
Thailand, Malaya, Vietnam, Sumatra, Borneo, Philippines – T
Grammatophyllum paludosum Griffith, Notul. 3: 344, 1851
Wailesia paludosa (Griffith) Rchb.f., Bonpl. 2: 92, 1854
o **Dipodium pictum** (Lindl.) Rchb.f., Xen. Orch. 2: 15 t. 107, 1862
BM 7951
Malaya – E
Wailesia picta Lindl., J. Hort. Soc. 4: 262, 1849
Grammatophyllum scandens Griffith, Notul. 3: 345, 1849
o **Disa cooperi** Rchb.f., Flora: 328, 1881
BM 7256
S. Africa (Natal) – 1800–2200 m – T
Disa scullyi Bolus, J. Linn. Soc. 22: 70, 1887
Disa thodei Kraenzlin, Orch. Gen. Sp. 1: 796, 1900
o **Disa cornuta** (L.) Sw., Kongl. Vet. Acad. Handl. 21: 210, 1800
BM 4091
S. Africa, Lesotho, Zimbabwe, – 1000–1500 m – T
Orchis cornuta L., Sp.Pl. ed. 2: 1330, 1763
Satyrium cornutum (L.) Thunb., Prodr. Pl. Cap. 5, 1794
Disa macrantha Sw., Kongl. Vet. Acad. Handl. 21: 8, 1800
Disa aemula Bolus, J. Linn. Soc. 22: 69, 1885
Disa crassicornis Lindl., Gen. Sp. Orch. Pl.: 348, 1838
BM 6529
S. Africa – 1000–2500 m – T
o Disa megaceras Hook.f., Bot. Mag.: t. 6529, 1880
Disa macrantha Hemsley, Garden 17: 494, 1880 (non Sw.)
Disa jacottetiae Kraenzlin, Vierteljahrsschr. Nat. Ges. 60: 391, 1915
o **Disa incarnata** (Lyall ex Lindl.) Lindl., Gen. Sp. Orch. Pl.: 348, 1838
BM 7243
Madagascar – 1500–2000 m – T
Habenaria incarnata Lyall ex Lindl., Gen. Sp. Orch. Pl.: 328, 1835
Disa fallax Kraenzlin, Engl. Bot. Jahrb. 17: 64, 1893
o **Disa polygonoides** Lindl., Gen. & Sp. Orch. Pl.: 349, 1838
BM 6532
S. Africa, S. Mozambique – T
Disa natalensis Lindl., J. Bot. 1: 16, 1842
o **Disa racemosa** L.f., Suppl.: 406, 1781
BM 7021
S. Africa – up to 1200 m – T
Satyrium secundum Thunb., Prodr. Pl. Cap.: 4, 1794
Disa secunda (Thunb.) Sw., Kongl. Vet. Acad. Handl. 21: 213, 1800
Disa venosa Sonder, Linnaea 20: 219, 1847 (not Sw.)
o **Disa sagittalis** (L. f.) Sw., Kongl. Vet. Acad. Handl. 21: 212, 1800
BM 7403
S. Africa (Cape Province) – 700–1000 m – T
Orchis sagittalis L.f., Suppl.: 399, 1781
Satyrium sagittale (L.f.) Thunb., Prodr. Pl. Cap.: 5, 1794
Disa attenuata Lindl., Gen. Sp. Orch. Pl.: 351, 1838
o **Disa tripetaloides** (L.f.) N.E.Br., Gard. Chron.: 360, 1889
BM 7206
S. Africa (Cape Province) – 900–1100 m – T
Orchis tripetaloides L.f., Suppl.: 398, 1791
Satyrium excelsum Thunb., Prodr. 5 partly, 1794
Disa venosa Lindl., Gen. Sp. Orch. Pl.: 351, 1838 (non Sw.)
Disa uniflora Bergius, Descr. Pl. Cap. B.Sp.: 348 t. 4 fig. 7, 1767
BM 4073
S. Africa (Cape Province) – 900–1300 m – T
o Disa grandiflora L.f., Suppl.: 406, 1781
Satyrium grandiflora (L.f.) Thunb., Prodr. 4, 1794
Disa uniflora var. superba Moore, Proc. hort. Soc. Lond. 2: 617, 1862
Disa uniflora var. barellii hort., Fl. Mag. 2: t. 104, 1874
Disa uniflora var. psittacina Rchb.f., Gard. Chron. 1: 424, 1879
Disa barelli Puydt, Orchidées: 275 t. 18, 1880
o **Diuris maculata** Smith, Exot. Bot. 1: 57 t. 30, 1804–5
BM 3156
Australia (New South Wales, Queensland) – T
Diuris punctata Smith, Exot. Bot. 1: 13, 1804
BM 6201
Australia (New South Wales) – T
Diuris elongata Sw., Schrad. Neues J. Bot. 1 (1): 59, 1805
o Diuris alba R.Br., Prodr.: 316, 1810 (Diuris punctata var. alba (R.Br.) Dockr.)
Diuris punctata var. punctata forma blakneyae Bailey, Compr. Cat. Queensland: pl. 847 fig. 973a, b et e, 1913
Doritis pulcherrima Lindl., Gen. Sp. Orch. Pl.: 178, 1833
BM 7196
Kampuchea, Laos, Vietnam, Malaya, Sumatra – E, L
o Phalaenopsis esmeralda Rchb.f., Gard. Chron.: 582, 1874
Phalaenopsis antennifera Rchb.f., Gard. Chron.: 398, 1879
Phalaenopsis regnieriana Rchb.f., Gard. Chron.: 746, 1887
Phalaenopsis buyssoniana Rchb.f., Gard. Chron., 1888
Phalaenopsis pulcherrima (Lindl.) J.J. Smith, Fedde Rep. 32: 366, 1923
Dracula carderi (Rchb.f.) Luer, Selbyana 2: 194, 1978
BM 7125
Colombia – E
o Masdevallia carderi Rchb.f., Gard. Chron.: 784, 1883
Dracula chestertonii (Rchb.f.) Luer, Selbyana 2: 194, 1978
BM 6977
Colombia – 1800–2200 m – E, T
o Masdevallia chestertonii Rchb.f., Gard. Chron.: 532, 1883
Masdevallia macrochila Regel, Trudy Imp. S. Petersb. Bot. Sada 11: 307, 1890
Dracula wallisii (Rchb.f.) Luer, Selbyana 2: 198, 1978
BM 6152
Colombia – 1700–2200 m – E, T
Masdevallia wallisii Rchb.f., Gard. Chron. 4: 258, 1875
Masdevallia chimaera W.G. Smith, Gard. Chron.: 40 t. 5, 1875 (non Rchb.f.)
o Masdevallia chimaera Hook.f., Bot. Mag.: t. 6152, 1875 (non Rchb.f.)
Masdevallia chimaera var. wallisii (Rchb.f.) Veitch, Man. Orch. Pl. 5: 31, 1889
o **Drymoda picta** Lindl., Sert. Orch.: t. 8C., 1838
BM 5904
Burma, Thailand – up to 1500 m – E
Elleanthus caravata (Aublet) Rchb.f., Otia Bot. Hamb. pt. 2: 62, 1881
BM 5141
Venezuela, Guyana, Brazil – 500–1300 m – T, E
Serapias caravata Aublet, Pl. Guian. 2: 816, 1775
Cymbidium hirsutum Willd., Sp.Pl. 4: 94, 1805 (nomen illeg.)
Sobralia caravata (Aublet) Lindl., Gen. Sp. Orch. Pl.: 177, 1833
o Evelyna caravata (Aublet) Lindl. ex Hook., Bot. Mag.: t. 5141, 1859
Evelyna lepida Rchb.f., Hamb. Gartenz. 15: 56, 1881
Elleanthus lepidus (Rchb.f.) Rchb.f., Otia Bot. Hamb. pt. 2: 62, 1881
o **Elleanthus xanthocomus** Rchb.f. ex Hook., Bot. Mag.: t. 6016, 1873
BM 6016
Costa Rica, Peru – T
Elleanthus brenesii Schltr., Fedde Rep. 11: 44, 1912
Eltroplectris calcarata (Sw.) Garay & Sweet, J. Arn. Arb. 53: 390 fig. 71, 1972
BM 3403
USA (Florida), Jamaica, Dominican Rep., W. Indies, Colombia, Brazil – T
o Neottia calcarata Sw., Fl. Ind. Occ. 3: 1413, 1804
Pelexia setacea Lindl., Gen. Sp. Orch. Pl. 482, 1840
Centrogenium setaceum (Lindl.) Schltr., Beih. Bot. Centralbl. 37 (2): 453, 1920
Embreea rodigasiana (Claes ex Cogn.) Dodson, Phytol. 46: 389, 1980
BM 7702
Colombia, Ecuador – up to 1200 m – E
o Stanhopea rodigasiana Claes ex Cogn., Chron. Orch.: 134, 1898
Encyclia adenocarpon (Llave & Lex.) Schltr., Orchideen: 207, 1914
BM 3631
Mexico, Guatemala, El Salvador, Honduras, Nicaragua – E
Epidendrum adenocarpon Llave & Lex., Nov. Veg. Descr. 2: 24, 1825
o Epidendrum papillosum Bateman ex Lindl., Bot. Reg. 24: Misc. 7, 1838
? Epidendrum crispatum Knowles & Westc., Fl. Cabin. 2: 79, 1838
Epidendrum adenocarpon var. rosei Ames, Hubb. & Schweinf., Bot. Mus. Leafl. Harv. Univ. 3 (5): 61, 1935
Encyclia adenocaula (Llave & Lex.) Schltr. var. **adenocaula** (Llave & Lex.) Schltr., Beih. Bot. Centralbl. 36 (2): 470, 1918
BM 4606
Mexico – 1000–2000 m – E
Epidendrum adenocaulum Llave & Lex., Nov. Veg. Desc. 22, 1825
Epidendrum nemorale Lindl., J. Bot. 3: 82, 1840
o Epidendrum verrucosum Lindl., Bot. Reg. 30: t. 51, 1844 (non Sw.)
Encyclia nemoralis (Lindl.) Schltr., Orchideen: 210, 1914

Encyclia alata (Bateman) Schltr., Orchideen: 207, 1914
BM 3898
Mexico, Belize, Guatemala, El Salvador, Honduras, Nicaragua, Costa Rica – E
Epidendrum alatum Bateman, Orch. Mex. & Guat.: t. 18, 1840
o Epidendrum calocheilum Hook., Bot. Mag.: t. 3898, 1841
Epidendrum longipetalum Lindl. & Paxton, Paxt. Flow. Gard. 1: 149 t. 30, 1850
Epidendrum formosum Klotzsch, Allg. Gartenz. 21: 201, 1853
Epidendrum alatum var. grandiflorum Regel, Ind. Sem. Hort. Petrop.: 19, 1856
Epidendrum alatum var. longipetalum (Lindl. & Paxton) Regel, Ind. Sem. Hort. Petrop.: 19, 1856
Epidendrum alatum var. viridiflorum Regel, Ind. Sem. Hort. Petrop.: 19, 1856
Encyclia bractescens (Lindl.) Hoehne, Arq. Bot. Estad. S. Paulo n.s. 2: 150, 1952
BM 4572
Bahamas, Mexico, Belize, Guatemala, Brazil – up to 1000 m – E
Epidendrum tripartitum (Vell.) Hoehne, Fl. Flum. 9: t. 7, 1825
Epidendrum bractescens Lindl., Bot. Reg. 26: Misc. p. 58, 1840
Epidendrum aciculare Bateman ex Lindl., Bot. Reg. 27: Misc. 46, 1841
o Epidendrum linearifolium Hook., Bot. Mag.: t. 4572, 1851
Encyclia acicularis (Bateman) Schltr., Fl. Baham.: 92, 1920
Encyclia flava (Lindl.) Porto Brade, Rodriguesia 1 (2): 28, 1935
Encyclia brassavolae (Rchb. f.) Dressler, Brittonia 13: 264, 1961
BM 5664
Mexico, Guatemala, Honduras, Panama – 1200–2500 m – E, L
o Epidendrum brassavolae Rchb. f., Bot. Zeit. 10: 729, 1852
Hormidium brassavolae (Rchb. f.) Brieger, Orchideen ed. 3, 1: 576, 1981
Encyclia campylostalix (Rchb. f.) Schltr., Fedde Rep. Beih. 17: 45, 1922
BM 9243
Guatemala, Costa Rica, Panama – up to 1800 m – E
o Epidendrum campylostalix Rchb. f., Bot. Zeit. 10: 730, 1852
Encyclia candollei (Lindl.) Schltr., Orchideen: 208, 1914
BM 3765
Guatemala, Mexico – 700–1500 m – E
Epidendrum candollei Lindl., Bot. Reg.: 55, 1839
o Epidendrum cepiforme Hook., Bot. Mag.: t. 3765, 1839
Epidendrum flabellatum Lindl., Fol. Orch. Epid.: 6, 1853
Encyclia laxa Schltr., Notizbl. Bot. Gart. Mus. Berlin-Dahlem 7: 277, 1918
Encyclia chloroleuca (Hook.) Neumann, Rev. Hort. s. 2. 4: 138, 1845/46
BM 3557
Guyana, Colombia – E
o Epidendrum chloroleucum Hook., Bot. Mag.: t. 3557, 1837
Epidendrum chloranthum Lindl., Bot. Reg. 24: Misc. p. 25, 1838
Encyclia citrina (Llave & Lex.) Dressler, Brittonia 13: 264, 1961
BM 3742
Mexico – 1300–2200 m – E
Sobralia citrina Llave & Lex., Nov. Veg. Descr. Orch. Opusc. 2: 21, 1825
o Cattleya citrina (Llave & Lex.) Lindl., Coll. Bot.: sub. t. 37, 1826
Cattleya karwinskii C. Martius, Ausgew. Merkw. Pfl. 14: t. 10, 1830
Epidendrum citrinum (Llave & Lex.) Rchb. f., Walp. Ann. 6: 317, 1862
Hormidium citrinum (Llave & Lex.) Brieger, Schlechter Orchideen ed. 3, 1: 576, 1977
Encyclia cochleata (L.) Lemée, Fl. Guyane Française 1: 418, 1955
BM 572
USA (Florida), Mexico to Panama, W. Indies, S. America – 100–2000 m – E
o Epidendrum cochleatum L., Sp. Pl. ed. 2: 1351, 1763
Anacheilium cochleatum (L.) Hoffsgg., Linnaea 16: 229, 1842
Epidendrum cochleatum var. pallidum Lindl., Fol. Orch. Epid.: 41, 1853
Aulizeum cochleatum (L.) Lindl. ex Stein, Orchideenb.: 227, 1892
Phaedrosanthus cochleatus (L.) Kuntze, Lex. Gen. Phanerog.: 429, 1904
Epidendrum cochleatum var. triandrum Ames, Contr. Orch. Fl. S. Fla.: 16, 1904
Epidendrum triandrum (Ames) House, Muhlenbergia 1: 129, 1906
Epidendrum cochleatum var. costaricense Schltr., Fedde Rep. Beih. 19: 118, 1923
Anacheilum cochlaetum var. triandrum (Ames) Small, Man. South-east. Fl.: 392, 1933
Hormidium cochleatum (L.) Brieger, Schlechter Orchideen ed. 3, 1: 569, 1977

Encyclia cordigera (Kunth) Dressler, Taxon 13: 247, 1964
BM 3534, BM 290 n s
Mexico to Panama, W. Indies, Venezuela, Trinidad, Peru – up to 900 m – E
Epidendrum atropurpureum auct. non Willd. 1805
Cymbidium cordigerum Kunth, Nov. Gen. Sp. 1: 341, 1815
Epidendrum atropurpureum Lindl., Gen. Sp. Orch. Pl.: 99, 1831
o Epidendrum macrochilum Hook., Bot. Mag.: t. 3534, 1836
Epidendrum macrochilum var. roseum Bateman, Orch. Mex. & Guat.: t. 17, 1839
Encyclia macrochila (Hook.) Neumann, Rev. Hort. 11, 4: 137, 1845/46
Epidendrum duboisianum Brogn. ex A. Rich., Fl. Cuba Fanerog. 2: 239, 1853
Epidendrum atropurpureum var. roseum (Bateman) Rchb. f., Bonpl. 2: 19, 1854
Epidendrum longipetalum Godefr.-Leb., l'Orchidoph. 12: 257, 1892 (non Rich & Galeotti; Lindl. & Paxton)
Epidendrum atropurpureum var. lionetianum Cogn., Dict. Ic. Orch. Epidendr.: t. 10c, 1903
Encyclia atropurpurea var. leucantha Schltr., Fedde Rep. Beih. 17: 45, 1922
Encyclia atropurpurea var. rhodoglossa Schltr., Fedde Rep. Beih. 17: 45, 1922
Epidendrum atropurpureum var. laciniatum Ames, Hubb. & Schweinf., Bot. Mus. Leafl. Harv. Univ. 3: 63, 1935
Encyclia doeringii Hoehne, Arq. Bot. Estad. S. Paulo 2 (2): 24 t. 11, 1946
Epidendrum doeringii (Hoehne) A. D. Hawkes, Orquidea 18: 170, 1956
o Encyclia atropurpurea var. rosea (Bateman) Summerh., Bot. Mag.: t. 290 n. s., 1957
Encyclia cordigera var. rosea (Bateman) H. G. Jones, Darwiniana 15: 23, 1969
Epidendrum cordigerum (Kunth) Foldats, Bol. Soc. Ven. Cienc. Nat. 28: 234, 1969
Encyclia dichroma (Lindl.) Schltr., Orchideen: 209, 1981
BM 5491
Brazil – E
Epidendrum dichromum Lindl., Bot. Reg. 29: Misc. p. 78, 1843
Epidendrum guesnelianum hort. ex Haneshall, Cult. Orch.: 113, 1845
o Epidendrum guesnelianum var. amabile Bateman, Bot. Mag.: 5491, 1865
Epidendrum guesnelianum var. striatum Rchb. f., Gard. Chron.: 218, 1866
Epidendrum conspicuum Lemaire, Ill. Hort. 16: t. 592, 1869
Epidendrum biflorum Barb. Rodr., Gen. & Sp. Orch. 1: 52, 1877
Epidendrum amabile Godef.-Leb., l'Orchidoph.: 304, 1887 (non L. nec Rchb. f.)
Encyclia fragrans (Sw.) Lemée, Fl. Guyane Fr. 1: 418, 1955
BM 152, BM 1669
Jamaica, W. Indies, Centr.-S. America – 500–1500 m – E
o Epidendrum fragrans Sw., Prodr. Veg. Ind. Occ.: 123, 1788
o Epidendrum cochleatum Curtis, Bot. Mag.: t. 152, 1791 (non L.)
Epidendrum lineatum Salisb., Prodr. 10, 1796
Epidendrum cordatum Vell., Fl. Flum. 9: t. 38, 1827
Epidendrum aemulum Lindl., Bot. Reg. 22: t. 1898, 1836
Epidendrum ionoleucum Hoffsgg. ex Rchb. f., Linnaea 24: 244, 1852
Epidendrum lambda Linden & Rchb. f., Bonpl. 2: 281, 1854
Epidendrum aemulum var. breviaristatum Rchb. f., Linnaea 41: 37, 1876
Epidendrum fragrans var. aemulum Barb. Rodr., Gen. & Sp. Orch. 2: 136, 1881
Epidendrum fragrans var. ionoleucum (Hoffsgg. ex Rchb. f.) Barb. Rodr., Gen. & Sp. Orch. 2: 136, 1881
Epidendrum fragrans var. janeirense Barb. Rodr., Gen. & Sp. Orch. 2: 137, 1881
Epidendrum fragrans var. rivularium Barb. Rodr., Gen. & Sp. Orch. 2: 137, 1881
Epidendrum fragrans var. micranthum Barb. Rodr., Gen. & Sp. Orch. 2: 138, 1881
Epidendrum fragrans var. alticallum Barb. Rodr., Gen. & Sp. Orch. 2: 138, 1881
Epidendrum fragrans var. magnum Stein, Orchideenb.: 230, 1892
Epidendrum vaginatum Sessé & Mociño, Fl. Mex. ed. 2: 201, 1894
Epidendrum fragrans var. breviaristatum (Rchb. f.) Cogn., Fl. Bras. 3 pt. 5: 85, 1898
Epidendrum fragrans var. pachypus Schltr., Fedde Rep. Beih. 17: 32, 1922
Anacheilium fragrans (Sw.) Acuña, Cat. Org. Cuba: 86, 1939
Hormidium fragrans (Sw.) Brieger, Schlechter Orchideen ed. 3, 1: 568, 1977

Encyclia livida (Lindl.) Dressler, Brittonia 13: 265, 1961
BM 3638
Mexico, Guatemala, Costa Rica, Panama, Venezuela, Colombia, Ecuador - up to 1200 m - E
Epidendrum lividum Lindl., Bot. Reg. 24: Misc. p. 51, 1838
o Epidendrum tesselatum Bateman ex Lindl., Bot. Reg. 24: Misc. p. 7, 1838 (non Roxb. 1795)
Epidendrum articulatum Klotzsch, Allg. Gartenz. 6: 297, 1838
Epidendrum condylochilum F. Lehm & Kraenzlin, Engl. Bot. Jahrb. 26: 459, 1899
Epidendrum henricii Schltr., Fedde Rep. 3: 108, 1906
Epidendrum deamii Schltr., Beih. Bot. Centralbl. 36, Abt. 2: 402, 1918
Encyclia tesselata (Lindl.) Schltr., Beih. Bot. Centralbl. 36, Abt. 2: 474, 1918
Epidendrum dasytainia Schltr., Fedde Rep. Beih. 8: 71, 1921
Encyclia deamii (Schltr.) Hoehne, Arq. Bot. Estad., S. Paulo n. s. 2: 151, 1952
Hormidium lividum (Lindl.) Brieger, Schlechter Orchideen ed. 3. 1: 574, 1977
Anacheilium lividum (Lindl.) Pabst, Moutinho & Pinto, Bradea 3 (23), 1981
o **Encyclia mooreana** (Rolfe) Schltr., Orchideen: 210, 1914
BM 9179
El Salvador, Nicaragua, Costa Rica, Panama - E
Epidendrum mooreanum Rolfe, Kew Bull.: 199, 1891
Encyclia tonduziana Schltr., Fedde Rep. Beih. 19: 132, 1923
Encyclia brenesii Schltr., Fedde Rep. Beih. 19: 221, 1923
Epidendrum oncidioides var. mooreanum (Rolfe) Ames Hubb. & C. Schweinf., Bot. Mus. Leafl. Harv. Univ. 3 (7): 106, 1935
Encyclia odoratissima (Lindl.) Schltr., Orchideen: 210 1914
BM 3013
Brazil - E
Macradenia lutescens Lodd., Bot. Cabin.: t. 1556, 1830 (non R. Br.)
o Encyclia patens Hook., Bot. Mag.: t. 3013, 1830 (non Sw. 1799)
Epidendrum odoratissimum Lindl., Bot. Reg. 17: t. 1415, 1831
Epidendrum glutinosum Scheidw., Allg. Gartenz.: 110, 1843
Epidendrum serronianum Barb. Rodr., Gen. & Sp. Orch. 1: 50, 1877
Encyclia serroniana (Barb. Rodr.) Hoehne, Arq. Bot. Estad. S. Paulo n. s. 11: 124, 1952
Encyclia osmantha (Barb. Rodr.) Schltr., Orchideen: 210, 1914
BM 7792
Brazil - E
Epidendrum advenum Rchb. f., Gard. Chron.: 1194, 1872
o Epidendrum osmanthum Barb. Rodr., Gen. & Sp. Orch. 2: 134, 1882
Epidendrum godseffianum Rolfe, Gard. Chron.: 136, 1892
Epidendrum capartianum L. Linden, Lindenia 7: 93 t. 333, 1892
Encyclia advena (Rchb. f.) Porto & Brade, Rodriguesia 1 No. 2: 28, 1935
Encyclia phoenicea (Lindl.) Schltr., Orchideen: 211, 1914
BM 3885
Cuba, probably W. Indies - E
Epidendrum phoeniceum Lindl., Sert. Orch.: t. 46, 1838
o Epidendrum grahamii Hook., Bot. Mag.: t. 3885, 1841
Encyclia prismatocarpa (Rchb. f.) Dressler, Brittonia 13: 264, 1961
BM 5336
C. America, Costa Rica, Panama - 1200-3300 m - E
o Epidendrum prismatocarpum Rchb. f., Bot. Zeit. 10: 729, 1852
Epidendrum ionocentrum Rchb. f., Gard. Chron.: 8, 1883
Hormidium prismatocarpum (Rchb. f.) Brieger, Schlechter Orchideen ed. 3. 1: 574, 1977
Encyclia × profusa (Rolfe) Dressler & Pollard, Phytol. 21: 437, 1971
BM 8551
Mexico - E
= Encyclia ambigua Schltr. × Encyclia ceratistes Schltr.
o Epidendrum profusum Rolfe, Bot. Mag.: t. 8551, 1914
Epidendrum oncidioides var. profusum (Rolfe) Ames Hubb. & C. Schweinf., Bot. Mus. Leafl. Harv. Univ. 3 (7): 107, 1935
Encyclia oncidioides var. profusa (Rolfe) Hoehne, Arq. Bot. Estad. S. Paulo n. s. 2: 154, 1952
Encyclia pygmaea (Hook.) Dressler, Brittonia 13: 265, 1961
BM 3233
Trop. America - E
o Epidendrum pygmaeum Hook., J. Bot. 1: 49 t. 118, 1833
Coelogyne triptera Brongn., Dup. Voy. Coq. Phan.: 201 t. 42, 1834
Epidendrum caespitosum Poeppig & Endl., Nov. Gen. Sp. Pl. 2: 1 t. 101, 1838
Epidendrum uniflorum Lindl., Bot. Reg. 25: Misc. 16, 1839 (non Vell., 1825)
Epidendrum monanthum Steudel, Nom. Bot. ed. 2, 1: 588, 1840
Hormidium uniflorum (Lindl.) Heynh., Nom. Bot. 1: 880, 1841
Hormidium pygmaeum (Hook.) Benth. & Hook. f., Biol. Centr.-Am. Bot. 3: 218, 1883
Aulizeum pygmaeum (Hook.) Lindl. ex Stein, Orchideenb.: 236, 1892
Hormidium tripterum (Brongn.) Cogn., Fl. Bras. 3 (5): 50, 1898
Hormidium pseudopygmaeum Finet, Bull. Herb. Bois. 7: 121, 1899
Microstylis humilis Cogn., Fl. Bras. 3 (6): 550, t. 114, 1906
Hormidium humile (Cogn.) Schltr., Rep. Sp. Nov. 16: 331, 1920
Encyclia triptera (Brongn.) Dressler & Pollard, Phytol. 21: 436, 1971
Encyclia spondiada (Rchb. f.) Dressler, Phytol. 21 (7): 441, 1971
BM 7273
Jamaica, Costa Rica, Panama - up to 1500 m - E, L
o Epidendrum spondiadium Rchb. f., Bot. Zeit. 10: 731, 1852
Epidendrum platycardium Schltr., Fedde Rep. Beih. 17: 36, 1922
Encyclia vespa (Vell.) Dressler, Phytol. 21 (7): 441, 1971
BM 3151, BM 3595
Mexico, C. America, Panama, Venezuela, Guyana, Colombia, Ecuador, Peru, Bolivia, Brazil - E, T
Epidendrum vespa Vell., Fl. Flum. 9: t. 27, 1825
o Epidendrum variegatum Hook., Bot. Mag.: t. 3151, 1832
Epidendrum crassilabium Poeppig & Endl., Nov. Gen. Sp. Pl. 2: 50 t. 102, 1837-38
o Epidendrum coriaceum Parker ex Hook., Bot. Mag.: t. 3595, 1837
Epidendrum tigrinum Linden ex Lindl., Orch. Linden: 9, 1846
Epidendrum pamplonense Rchb. f., Linnaea 22: 837, 1849
Epidendrum coriaceum Focke, Bot. Zeit. 11: 228, 1853 (non Hook.)
Epidendrum pachysepalum Klotzsch, Allg. Gartenz. 23: 274, 1855
Epidendrum leopardinum Rchb. f., Linnaea 41: 112, 1877
Epidendrum christii Rchb. f., Linnaea 41: 112, 1877
Epidendrum longipes Rchb. f., Otia Bot. Hamb.: 10, 1878
Aulizeum variegatum (Hook.) Lindl. ex Stein, Orchideenb.: 241, 1892
Epidendrum feddeanum Kraenzlin, Fedde Rep. 1: 188, 1905
Epidendrum saccharatum Kraenzlin, Orchis 2: 113 t. 17, 1908
Epidendrum rhabdobulbum Schltr., Fedde Rep. Beih. 7: 146, 1920
Epidendrum baculibulbom Schltr., Fedde Rep. Beih. 19: 116, 1923
Epidnedrum rhopalobulbon Schltr., Fedde Rep. Beih. 27: 72, 1924
Hormidium crassilabium (Poeppig & Endl.) Brieger, Schlechter Orchideen ed. 3, 1: 571/72, 1977
Anacheilium vespa (Vell.) Pabst, Moutinho & Pinto, Bradea 3 (23), 1981
o **Encyclia viridiflora** Hook., Bot. Mag.: t. 2831, 1828
BM 2831
Brazil - E
Epidendrum viridiflorum (Hook.) Lindl., Bot. Reg. 28: Misc. p. 30, 1842
Encyclia multiflora Rchb. f., Walp. Ann.: 335, 1862 (non Hook.)
Encyclia vitellina (Lindl.) Dressler, Brittonia 13 (3): 265, 1961
BM 4107
Mexico, Guatemala - 1500-2600 m - E
o Epidendrum vitellinum Lindl., Gen. & Sp. Orch. Pl.: 97, 1831
Epidendrum vitellinum var. majus Veitch, Fl. Mag. 5: 261, 1866
Epidendrum vitellinum var. giganteum Warner, Sel. Orch. Pl. 3: t. 27, 1877-78
Epidendrum vitellinum var. autumnale G. Wilson, Orch. World 4: 27, 1913
Hormidium vitellinum (Lindl.) Brieger, Schlechter Orchideen ed. 3. 1: 574, 1977
Epidendrum carpophorum Barb. Rodr., Gen. & Sp. Orch. 2: 148, 1882
BM 3298
W. Indies, El Salvador, Nicaragua, Venezuela, Trinidad - E, L
Epidendrum nocturnum var. latifolium Lindl., Bot. Reg. 23: t. 1961, 1837
Epidendrum latifolium (Lindl.) Garay & Sweet, J. Arn. Arb. 53: 392, 1972
o (Epidendrum nocturnum Jacq., Enum. Pl. Carib.: 29, 1760; misidentified)
o **Epidendrum ciliare** L., Syst. Nat. ed. 10: 1246, 1759
BM 463
W. Indies, Mexico to Panama, Venezuela to Bolivia, Guyana, Brazil - E
Auliza ciliaris (L.) Salisb., Trans. Hort. Soc. 1: 294, 1812
Epidendrum cuspidatum Lodd., Bot. Cabin. 1: t. 10, 1818
Coilostylis emarginata Raf., Fl. Tellur. 4: 37, 1836 (nomen illeg.)
Epidendrum viscidum Lindl., Bot. Reg.: Misc. 81, 1840
Epidendrum ciliare var. cuspidatum (Lodd.) Lindl., Fol. Orch. Epid.: 30, 1853
Epidendrum ciliare var. viscidum (Lindl.) Lindl., Fol. Orch. Epid.: 30, 1853
Epidendrum luteum hort. ex Planchon, Hort. Don.: 50, 1858
Epidendrum ciliare var. minor hort. ex Stein, Orchideenb.: 226, 1892
Aulizeum ciliare (L.) Lindl. ex Stein, Orchideenb.: 226, 1892
Phaedrosanthus ciliaris (L.) Kuntze, Lex. Gen. Phan.: 429, 1904
Epidendrum ciliare var. squamatum Schnee, Rev. Fac. Agr. 1: 206, 1953

o **Epidendrum cnemidophorum** Lindl., Fol. Orch. Epid.: 53, 1853
BM 5656
Guatemala, Honduras, Nicaragua, Costa Rica – E
Epidendrum affine Rchb.f., Bonpl. 4: 327, 1856
Epidendrum macrobotryum Lindl. ex Rchb.f., Bonpl. 4: 327, 1856
Epidendrum pfavii Rolfe, Kew Bull.: 392, 1894
Encyclia affinis (Rchb.f.) Schltr., Beih. Bot. Centralbl. 36: Abt. 471, 1918
o **Epidendrum conopseum** R.Br., Hort. Kew. ed. 2, 5: 219, 1813
BM 3457
USA (Florida, Texas, N. Carolina), E. Mexico – E
Epidendrum magnoliae Muhlenb., Cat.: 81, 1813
Larnandra magnolia Raf., Neogen.: 4, 1825
Larnandra conopsea (R.Br.) Raf., Fl. Tellur. 2: 40, 1837
Amphiglottis conopsea (R.Br.) Small, Man. SE. Fl.: 391, 1933
Epidendrum conopseum var. mexicanum L.O. Williams, Ceiba 2: 152, 1951
o **Epidendrum cooperianum** Bateman, Bot. Mag.: t. 5654, 1867
BM 5654
Brazil – E
Epidendrum longispathum Barb. Rodr., Orch. Nov. 1: 56, 1877
o **Epidendrum coriifolium** Lindl., J. Hort. Soc. Lond. 6: 218, 1851
BM 9477
Mexico to Panama, Venezuela, Colombia, Ecuador, Peru, Bolivia – E, T
Epidendrum imitans Schltr., Fedde Rep. Beih. 8: 74, 1921
Epidendrum magnibracteatum Ames, Sched. Orch. 1: 16, 1922
Epidendrum coriifolium var. purpurascens Schltr., Fedde Rep. Beih. 17: 31, 1922
Epidendrum fuscopurpureum Schltr., Fedde Rep. Beih. 17: 32, 1922
Epidendrum palmense Ames, Sched. Orch. 2: 33, 1923
Epidendrum subviolascens Schltr., Fedde Rep. Beih. 19: 219, 1923
Epidendrum circinatum Ames, Sched. Orch. 7: 4, 1924
o **Epidendrum criniferum** Rchb.f., Gard. Chron.: 1291, 1871
BM 6094
Nacaragua, Costa Rica, Panama, Peru – E
o **Epidendrum densiflorum** Hook., Bot. Mag.: t. 3791, 1816
BM 3637, BM 3791
Mexico, Guatemala, Honduras, Nicaragua, Costa Rica, Panama, Venezuela to Peru, S. Argentina – E, T
o Epidendrum floribundum Kunth, Nov. Gen. Sp. 1: 353, 1816
Epidendrum floribundum var. lilacinum Rchb.f., Linnaea 22: 840, 1849
Epidendrum polyanthum var. densiflorum (Hook.) Lindl., Fol. Orch. Epid.: 60, 1853
o **Epidendrum difforme** Jacq., Enum. Pl. Carib.: 29, 1760
BM 2030
USA (Florida), Jamaica, W. Indies, Mexico, Trop. America – E
Epidendrum umbellatum Sw., Prodr. Veg. Ind. Occ.: 121, 1788
Epidendrum umbelliferum J. Gmelin, Syst. Veg.: 65, 1791
Caularthron umbellatum (Sw.) Raf., Fl. Tellur. 2: 41, 1837
Epidendrum latilabre Lindl., Bot. Reg. 27: Misc.p. 77, 1841
Epidendrum subumbellatum Hoffsgg., Preis-Verz.: 24, 1842
Epidendrum virens Hoffsgg., Preis-Verz.: 24, 1842
Epidendrum radiatum Hoffsgg., Preis-Verz.: 49, 1843
Epidendrum latilabium Rchb.f., Linnaea 25: 244, 1852
Epidendrum umbellatum var. latilabre (Lindl.) Griseb., Fl. Brit. W. Ind.: 618, 1864
Epidendrum arachnoideum Barb. Rodr., Gen. & Sp. Orch. 1: 60, 1877
Auliza difformis (Jacq.) Small, Fl. Miami: 56, 1913
Epidendrum chlorocorymbos Schltr., Fedde Rep. Beih. 17: 30, 1922
Amphiglottis difformis (Jacq.) Britton, Sci. Surv. Porto Rico & Virgin I. 5: pt. 2: 200, 1924
Epidendrum pseudodifforme Hoehne & Schltr., Fedde Rep. Beih. 35: 71, 1925
Epidendrum curvicolumna Ames, Hubb. & C. Schweinf., Bot. Mus. Leafl. Harv. Univ. 3 (5): 67, 1935
Neolehmannia difformis (Jacq.) Pabst., Bradea 2: 306, 1978
o **Epidendrum diffusum** Sw., Prodr. Veg. Ind. Occ.: 121, 1788
BM 3565
Mexico, Guatemala, W. Indies, Columbia, Guyana, Brazil – E
Seraphyta multiflora Fischer & Meyer, Bull. Acad. Petersb. 7: 24, 1840
Epidendrum tenuiflorum hort. ex Lindl., Fol. Orch. Epid.: 88, 1853
Seraphyta diffusa (Sw.) Pfitzer, Nat. Pflanzenf. 2, 6: 142, 1889
Epidendrum diffusum var. depauperatum Cogn., Fl. Bras. 3: pt. 5: 155, 1898
o **Epidendrum eburneum** Rchb.f., Gard. Chron.: 404, 1867
BM 5643
Nicaragua, Panama – E
Epidendrum leucocardium Schltr., Fedde Rep. 12: 206, 1913

Epidendrum elegans (Knowles & Westc.) Rchb.f., Walp. Ann. 6: 374, 1862
BM 4784
Mexico, Guatemala – E
o Barkeria elegans Knowles & Westc., Fl. Cabin. 2: 7 t. 49, 1838
o **Epidendrum harrisoniae** Hook., Bot. Mag.: t. 3209, 1833
BM 3209
Brazil (Rio de Janeiro) – E
Epidendrum aeridiforme Booth, Bot. Reg. 31: Misc.n. 12, 1845
Epidendrum ammophyllum Barb. Rodr., Gen. & Sp. Orch. 2: 149, 1881
o **Epidendrum elongatum** Jacq., Coll. 3: 260, 1789
BM 611, BM 3543, BM 5902
W. Indies, Trop. S. America – T, E
Epidendrum secundum auct. non Jacq., Enum. Pl. Carib.: 29, 1760
Epidendrum corymbosum Ruiz Lopez & Pavón, Syst. Veg.: 246, 1798
Amphiglottis secunda Salisb., Trans. Hort. Soc. 1: 294, 1812
Epidendrum ellipticum Graham, Edinb. N. Phil. Hourn. 1: 171, 1826
Epidendrum dichotomum Presl, Rel. Haenk. 1: 101, 1827
Epidendrum ellipticum Lodd., Bot. Cab. 18: t. 1276, 1831
o Epidendrum crassifolium Lindl., Gen. Sp. Orch. Pl.: 107, 1831
Epidendrum cochlidium Lindl., Ann. Mag. Nat. Hist. 4: 382, 1840
Epidendrum lindenii Lindl., Bot. Reg. 31: Misc.p. 48, 1845
Epidendrum fastigiatum Lindl., Fol. Orch. Epid.: 71, 1853
Epidendrum brachyphyllum Lindl., Fol. Orch. Epid.: 72, 1853
Epidendrum ansiferum Rchb.f., Bonpl. 2: 111, 1854
Epidendrum gracilicaule Rchb.f. & Warsc., Bonpl. 2: 111, 1854
Epidendrum novogranatense Rchb.f. & Warsc., Bonpl. 2: 111, 1854
Epidendrum xytriophorum Rchb.f. & Warsc., Bonpl. 2: 112, 1854
Epidendrum incisum Rchb.f. & Warsc., Bonpl. 2: 112, 1854
Epidendrum fimbria Rchb.f., Bonpl. 2: 282, 1854
Epidendrum giroudianum Rchb.f., Bonpl. 4: 327, 1856
Epidendrum quitensium Rchb.f., Walp. Ann. 6: 392, 1862
Epidendrum elongatum var. crassifolium (Lindl.) Griseb., Fl. Brit. W. Ind.: 617, 1864
o Epidendrum evectum Hook.f., Bot. Mag.: t. 5902, 1871
Epidendrum expansum Rchb.f., Linnaea 41: 115, 1877
Epidendrum longihastatum Barb. Rodr., Gen. & Sp. Orch. 1: 59, 1877
Epidendrum fastigiatum var. bifidum Rchb.f., Otia Bot. Hamb 1: 13, 1878
Epidendrum arachnoglossum Rchb.f. ex André, Rev. Hort.: 554, 1882
Epidendrum ellipticum Rchb.f., Ber. Deutsch. Bot. Ges. 3: 277, 1885 (non Graham)
Epidendrum herzogii Schltr., Fedde Rep. 12: 489, 1913
Epidendrum antioquiense Schltr., Fedde Rep. Beih. 7: 125, 1920
Epidendrum dolichopus Schltr., Fedde Rep. Beih. 7: 131, 1920
Epidendrum pachyphyllum Schltr., Fedde Rep. Beih. 7: 140, 1920
Epidendrum polyschistum Schltr., Fedde Rep. Beih. 7: 143, 1920
Epidendrum cuzcoense Schltr., Fedde Rep. Beih. 9: 82, 1921
Epidendrum tarmense Schltr., Fedde Rep. Beih. 9: 94, 1921
Epidendrum versicolor Hoehne & Schltr., Arq. Bot. Estad. S. Paulo 1, pt. 3: 245, 1926
Epidendrum coroicoense Schltr., Fedde Rep. 27: 60, 1929
Epidendrum inconstans Ames, Bull. Torrey Club 58: 350, 1931
Epidendrum ellipticum var. freybergense Zimmerm., Bibl. Bot. 109: 5, 1934
Epidendrum bulkeleyi Hawkes, Orquidea 18: 169, 1957
Epidendrum laucheanum Rolfe ex Bonhof, Gartenfl. 41: 183, 1892
BM 8996
Guatemala, Honduras, Costa Rica, Colombia – E
Epidendrum dolichostachyum Schltr., Fedde Rep. 3: 79, 1906
o Epidendrum cristobalense Ames, Sched. Orch. 4: 38, 1923
Epidendrum nocturnum Jacq., Enum. Pl. Carib.: 29, 1760
BM 4165
USA (Florida), Mexico to Panama, W. Indies, Guyana, Ecuador, Peru, Brazil – E
Epidendrum carolinianum Lam., Encycl. 1: 182, 1783
Nyctosma nocturna (Jacq.) Raf., Fl. Tellur. 2: 9, 1837
Epidendrum tridens Poeppig & Endl., Nov. Gen. Sp.Pl. 2: 2, 1838
o Epidendrum longicolle Lindl., Bot. Reg. 24: Misc.p. 34, 1838
Epidendrum discolor A. Rich. & Galeotti, Ann. Sci. Nat. s. 3, 3: 22, 1845
Epidendrum spruceanum Lindl., Fol. Orch. Epid.: 80, 1853
Epidendrum bahiense Rchb.f., Hamb. Gartenz. 15: 53, 1859
Epidendrum nocturnum var. tridens (Poeppig & Endl.) Cogn., Fl. Bras. 3: pt. 5: 136, 1898
Epidendrum buenaventurae F. Lehm. & Kraenzlin, Engl. Bot. Jahrb. 26: 470, 1899
Phaedrosanthus nocturnus (Jacq.) Kuntze, Lex. Gen. Phan.: 429, 1904
Epidendrum nocturnum var. minus Cogn., Bull. Soc. Roy. Belg. 43: 323, 1907
Auliza nocturna (Jacq.) Small, Fl. Miami: 56, 1913

Epidendrum leucarachne Schltr., Fedde Rep. Beih. 7: 136, 1920
Epidendrum tunguraguae Schltr., Fedde Rep. Beih. 8: 87, 1921
Epidendrum oliganthum Schltr., Fedde Rep. Beih. 9: 90, 1921
Epidendrum nocturnum var. panamense Schltr., Fedde Rep. Beih. 17: 36, 1922
Epidendrum nocturnum var. minor Schltr., Fedde Rep. Beih. 27: 69, 1924
Amphiglottis nocturna (Jacq.) Britton, Sci. Surv. Port Rico & Virgin Isl. 5, pt. 2: 200, 1924

o **Epidendrum pallidiflorum** Hook., Bot. Mag.: t. 2980, 1830
BM 2980
W. Indies - E

o **Epidendrum paniculatum** Ruiz Lopez & Pavón, Syst. Veg.: 243, 1798
BM 5731
Mexico, Guatemala, Honduras, Nicaragua, Costa Rica, Panama, Venezuela, Ecuador, Peru, S. Argentina - E, T
Epidendrum rubrocinctum Lindl., Bot. Reg. 29: Misc. p. 9, 1843
Epidendrum laeve Lindl., Bot. Reg. 30: Misc. p. 24, 1844
Epidendrum ornatum Lemaire, Fl. Serres 4: 334 B, 1848
Epidendrum paniculatum var. cuspidatum Lindl., Fol. Orch. Epid.: 56, 1853
Epidendrum paniculatum var. longicrure Lindl., Fol. Orch. Epid.: 56, 1853
Epidendrum floribundum var. convexum Lindl., Fol. Orch. Epid.: 91, 1853
Epidendrum syringaeflorum Warsc. ex Rchb. f., Bonpl. 2: 111, 1854
Epidendrum turialvae Rchb. f., Gard. Chron.: 1678, 1871
Epidendrum resectum Rchb. f., Linnaea 41: 82, 1876
Epidendrum piliferum Rchb. f., Linnaea 41: 82, 1876
Epidendrum falsiloquum Rchb. f., Gard. Chron.: 566, 1885
Epidendrum englerianum F. Lehm. & Kraenzlin, Engl. Bot. Jahrb. 26: 466, 1899
Epidendrum frons-bovis Kraenzlin, Fedde Rep. 1: 181, 1905
Epidendrum ionodesme Schltr., Fedde Rep. Beih. 7: 134, 1920
Epidendrum longicrure Schltr., Fedde Rep. Beih. 7: 137, 1920
Epidendrum macroceras Schltr., Fedde Rep. Beih. 7: 138, 1920
Epidendrum atacazoicum Schltr., Fedde Rep. Beih. 8: 67, 1921
Epidendrum bifalce Schltr., Fedde Rep. Beih. 8: 67, 1921
Epidendrum caloglossum Schltr., Fedde Rep. Beih. 8: 68, 1921
Epidendrum isthmi Schltr., Fedde Rep. Beih. 17: 34, 1922
Epidendrum reflexum Ames & C. Schweinf., Sched. Orch. 8: 49, 1925

o **Epidendrum parkinsonianum** Hook., Bot. Mag.: t. 3778, 1840
BM 3778
Mexico, Guatemala, Honduras, Costa Rica, Panama - E, L
Epidendrum falcatum Lindl., Ann. Nat. Hist. 4: 382, 1840
Epidendrum aloifolium Bateman, Orch. Mex. & Guat.: t. 25, 1840 (non Lindl.)
Auliza parkinsonianum (Hook.) Brieger, Schlechter Orchideen ed. 3, 1: 546, 1977

o **Epidendrum patens** Sw., Nov. Act. Upsal. 6: 68, 1799
BM 3800
Brazil, Colombia - E
Exophya fuscata Raf., Fl. Tellur 11: 63, 1836
Epidendrum sulphuroleucum Barb. Rodr., Gen. & Sp. Orch. 1: 56, 1877

o **Epidendrum pseudepidendrum** Rchb. f., Xen. Orch. 1: 160 t. 53, 1856
BM 5929
C. America, Costa Rica, Panama - up to 1200 m - E
Pseudepidendrum spectabile Rchb. f., Bot. Zeit. 10: 733, 1852
Epidendrum pseudepidendrum var. auritum Rchb. f., Gard. Chron.: 406, 1885
non Epidendrum spectabile Focke nec Rchb. f.

o **Epidendrum sceptrum** Lindl., Orch. Linden: 8, 1846
BM 7169
Venezuela, Colombia, Ecuador - 1500–1700 m - E
Epidendrum macrothyrsodes Rchb. f., Linnaea 41: 113, 1877
Epidendrum sphenoglossum F. Lehm. & Kraenzlin, Engl. Bot. Jahrb. 26: 460, 1899

Epidendrum secundum Jacq., Enum. Syst. Pl.: 29, 1760
BM 2844, BM 3666
Trop. & subtrop. America, Jamaica, St. Vincent, Martinique - E
Epidendrum anceps Jacq., Sel. Stirp. Am.: 224, 1763
Epidendrum secundum Sw., Obs. Bot.: 325, 1791
o Epidendrum fuscatum Smith, Spicil. Bot. 2: 21 t. 23, 1792
Amphiglottis lurida Salisb., Trans. Hort. Soc. 1: 294, 1812
Epidendrum virescens Lodd., Bot. Cab. 19: t. 1867, 1832
Epidendrum musciferum Lindl., Hook. J. Bot. 1: 6, 1834
o Epidendrum viridipurpureum Hook., Bot. Mag.: t. 3666, 1838
Epidendrum galeottianum A. Rich. & Galeotti, Ann. Sci. Nat. s. 3, 3: 21, 1845
Epidendrum ensatum A. Rich. & Galeotti, Ann. Sci. Nat. s. 3, 3: 22, 1845
Epidendrum amphistomum A. Rich., Sagra Hist. Cuba 11: 240, 1850
Epidendrum fuscatum var. virescens (Lodd.) Lindl., Fol. Orch. Epid.: 65, 1853
Epidendrum fuscatum var. viridipurpureum (Hook.) Lindl., Fol. Orch. Epid.: 66, 1853
Epidendrum cearense Barb. Rodr., Gen. & Sp. Orch. 2: 141, 1881
Epidendrum schreineri Barb. Rodr., Gen. & Sp. Orch. 2: 142 1881
Epidendrum anceps var. virescens (Lodd.) Hemsley, Biol. Centr.-Amer. Bot. 3: 225, 1883
Epidendrum anceps var. viridipurpureum (Hook.) Hemsley, Biol. Centr.-Am. Bot. 3: 225, 1883
Epidendrum schenckianum Kraenzlin, Fedde Rep. 7: 114, 1909
Amphiglottis anceps (Jacq.) Britton, Sci. Surv. Porto Rico & Virgin. Is. 5, pt. 2: 200, 1924

o **Epidendrum stamfordianum** Bateman, Orch. Mex. & Guat.: t. 11, 1838
BM 4759
Mexico, C.-America, Guatemala, Panama, W. Indies, Venezuela, Colombia, Brazil - E
Epidendrum basilare Klotzsch, Allg. Gartenz. 11: 193, 1843
Epidendrum cycnostalix Rchb. f., Bot. Zeit. 10: 731, 1852
Epidendrum stamfordianum var. pictum Lemaire, Jard. Fl. 3: t. 251, 1852
Epidendrum stamfordianum var. parviflorum Regel, Ind. Sem. Hort. Petrop.: 19, 1856
Epidendrum cycnostachys Rchb. f. ex Benth., J. Linn. Soc. 18: 314, 1881
Epidendrum stamfordianum var. wallacei Rchb. f., Gard. Chron.: 543, 1887
Epidendrum stamfordianum var. leeanum Rchb. f., Gard. Chron.: 521, 1888
Psilanthemum basilare (Klotzsch) Klotzsch ex Stein, Orchideenb.: 238, 1892
Epidendrum stamfordianum var. lawrenceanum hort. ex Stein, Orchideenb.: 240, 1892
Auliza stamfordiana (Bateman) Brieger, Schlechter Orchideen ed. 3, 1: 548, 1977

o **Epidendrum syringothyrsus** Rchb. f., Xen. Orch. 3: 22, 1878
BM 6145
Bolivia - E

o **Epidendrum xanthinum** Lindl., Bot. Reg. 30: Misc. p. 18, 1844
BM 7586
Brazil - E
Epidendrum ellipticum var. flavum Lindl., Ann. Nat. Hist. 4: 382, 1840

Epigeneium acuminatum (Rolfe) Summerh., Kew Bull.: 260, 1957
BM 9191
Philippines - up to 1500 m - E
Dendrobium acuminatum Rolfe in Ames, Orchid. 1: 86, 1905
Dendrobium lyonii Ames, Orchid. 2: 177, 1908
o Sarcopodium lyonii (Ames) Rolfe, Orch. Rev. 28: 240, 1910
Sarcopodium acuminatum var. lyonii (Ames) Kraenzlin, Orch. Rev. 28: 239, 1910
Sarcopodium acuminatum (Rolfe) Rolfe, Orch. Rev. 18: 239, 1910
Katherinea acuminata (Rolfe) A. Hawkes, Lloydia 19: 94, 1956
Katherinea acuminatum var. lyonii (Ames) A. Hawkes, Lloydia 19: 94, 1956

Epigeneium cymbidioides (Blume) Summerh., Kew Bull.: 260, 1957
BM 4755
Java, Sumatra, Malaya - E
Desmotrichum cymbidioides Blume, Bijdr.: 329 t. 35, 1825
o Dendrobium cymbidioides (Blume) Lindl., Gen. Sp. Orch. Pl.: 77, 1830
Dendrobium triflorum Lindl., Gen. Sp. Prch. Pl.: 77, 1830
Dendrobium marginatum Teijsm. & Binnend., Tijdschr. Ned. Ind. 5: 490, 1853
Sarcopodium triflorum (Lindl.) Rolfe, Orch. Rev. 18: 239, 1910
Sarcopodium cymbidioides (Blume) Rolfe, Orch. Rev. 18: 239, 1910
Katherinea cymbidioides (Blume) A. Hawkes, Lloydia 19: 94, 1956

Epigeneium treacherianum (Rchb. f. ex Hook. f.) Summerh., Kew Bull.: 260, 1957
BM 6591
Borneo - E
o Dendrobium treacherianum Rchb. f. ex Hook. f., Bot. Mag.: t. 6591, 1881
Sarcopodium treacherianum (Rchb. f. ex Hook. f.) Kraenzlin, Orch. Rev. 18: 239, 1910
Katherinea treacherianum (Rchb. f.) A. Hawkes, Lloydia 19: 97, 1956

o **Epipactis gigantea** Douglas ex Hook., Fl. Bor.-Am. 2: 202 pl. 202, 1839
BM 7690
N. W. America, Temp. Asia (Japan, Himalaya) - T
Epipactis royleana Lindl., Ill. Bot. Himal.: 368, 1839
Epipactis americana Lindl., Ann. Mag. Nat. Hist. 1, 4: 385, 1840

Epipactis thunbergii A. Gray, Perry. Exp. Jap. 2: 319, 1857
Cephalanthera royleana (Lindl.) Regel, Act. Hort. Petrop. 6: 490, 1879
Limodorum giganteum (Douglas) Kuntze, Rev. Gen. 2: 672, 1891
Peramium giganteum (Douglas) Coulter, Contr. U.S. Nat. Herb. 2: 424, 1894
Serapias gigantea (Douglas) A.A. Eaton, Proc. Biol. Soc. Wash. 21: 67, 1908
Helleborine gigantea (Douglas) Druce, Bull. Torrey Club 36: 547, 1909
Amesia gigantea (Douglas) Nelson & J.F. Macbride, Bot. Gaz. 56: 472, 1913
Epipogium aphyllum (F.W. Schmidt) Sw., Summer. Veg. Scand.: 32, 1814
BM 4821
Europe to Himalaya – 100–4000 m – S
Satyrium epipogium L., Sp. Pl.: 945, 1753
Epipactis epipogium (L.) All., Auct. Fl. Pedem.: 32, 1785
Orchis aphylla F.W. Schmidt, Mayer, Samml. Phys. Aufs. 1: 240, 1791
Limodorum epipogium (L.) Sw., Nov. Act. Upsal. 6: 80, 1799
o Epipogon (Epipogium) gmelinii L.C. Rich., Orch. Eur. Annot. (Mém. Mus. Hist. Nat. Paris 4: 58, 1818)
Serapias epipogium (L.) Steudel, Nom.: 766, sphalm., 1840
Epipogon epipogium (L.) Karst., Deutsche Fl.: 455, 1880/83
Epipogon epipogon Kerner, Sched. Fl. Austro. Hung. 6: 105, 1893
o **Epistephium williamsii** Hook., Bot. Mag.: t. 5485, 1864
BM 5485
Brazil (Bahia) – T
o **Eria amica** Rchb.f., Xen. Orch. 2: 162 t. 168, 1870
BM 9453
N.W. Himalaya, Nepal, Sikkim, Bhutan, N.E. India, Burma, Laos, Vietnam, Taiwan, China – E
Eria excavata auct. non Lindl. p.p.; Lindley Gen. & Sp. Orch. Pl.: 67, 1830
Eria confusa Hook.f., Ic. Pl.: t. 1850, 1889
Eria andersonii Hook.f., Ic. Pl.: 2069, 1891
Pinalia amica (Rchb.f.) Kuntze, Rev. Gen. 2: 679, 1891
Pinalia confusa (Hook.f.) Kuntze, Rev. Gen. 2: 679, 1891
Eria hypomelana Hayata, Ic. Pl. Form. 4: 54 fig. 22, 1914
Eria pubescens auct. p.p. non Steudel nec Wight; Seidenfaden & Smitinand Orch. Thailand pt. 2: 310, 1960
Eria bractescens Lindl., Bot. Reg. 27: 18, Misc. 46, 1841
BM 4163
India, E. Himalaya, Burma, Kampuchea, Vietnam, Malaya, Indonesia, Philippines, New Guinea – E
o Eria dillwynii Hook., Bot. Mag.: t. 4163, 1845
Eria pulchella Griffith, Notul 3: 297, 1851 (non Lindl.)
Eria littoralis Teijsm. & Binnend., Tidschr. Ned. Ind. 24: 312, 1862
Eria griffithii Rchb.f., Xen. Orch. 2: 163, 1870
Eria affinis auct. non Griffith; Parish, Order Orchid. Burma: 194, 1883
Pinalia pulchella (Griffith) Kuntze, Rev. Gen. 2: 679, 1891
Pinalia bractescens (Lindl.) Kuntze, Rev. Gen. 2: 679, 1891
Dendrobium subterrestre Gagnepain, Bull. Mus. Paris s. 2, 1: 239, 1930
o **Eria hyacinthoides** (Blume) Lindl., Gen. Sp. Orch. Pl.: 66, 1830
BM 8229
Malaya, Sumatra, Java – E
Dendrolirium hyacinthoides Blume, Bijdr.: 346, 1825
Eria endymion Ridley, Linn. Soc. 32: 295, 1896
Eria iridifolia Hook.f., Fl. Brit. Ind. 5: 790, 1890
BM 8171
Malaya, Sumatra, Java, Borneo – E
Mycaranthes latifolia Blume, Bijdr.: 353 pl. 57, 1825
Eria latifolia Rchb.f., Bonpl. 5: 55, 1857 (non Blume)
Pinalia latifolia (Blume) Kuntze, Rev. Gen. 2: 678, 1891
Pinalia iridifolia (Hook.f.) Kuntze, Rev. Gen. 2: 679, 1891
Eria bidens Ridley, J. Linn. Soc. 32: 289, 1896
o Eria longispica Rolfe, Bot. Mag.: t. 8171, 1907
Eria validissima Kraenzlin, Pflanzenr. Heft 50: 39 fig. 7, 1911
Eria javanica (Sw.) Blume, Rumphia 2: 23, 1836
BM 3605
Sikkim, Assam, Burma, Laos, Malaya, Indonesia, New Guinea, Philippines – E
Dendrobium javanicum Sw., Kongl. Vet. Akad. Handl. 21: 247, 1800
o Eria stellata Lindl., Bot. Reg.: t. 904, 1825
Dendrolirium rugosum Blume, Bijdr.: 345, 1825
Octomeria stellata (Lindl.) Sprengel, Syst. 4, 2: 310, 1827
Octomeria vaginata Breda, Gen. Sp. Orch. Asclep.: pl. 5, 1827/29
Eria rugosa (Blume) Lindl., Gen. Sp. Orch. Pl.: 55, 1830
Eria cochleata Lindl., Bot. Reg. 30: Misc. 14, 1844
Eria fragrans Rchb.f., Bot. Zeit. 22: 415, 1864
Eria vaginata (Breda) Benth., J. Linn. Soc. 18: 303, 1881
Eria striolata Rchb.f., Gard. Chron.: 554, 1888
Tainia stellata (Lindl.) Pfitzer, Nat. Pflanzenfam. 2, 6: 133, 1888
Dendrobium perakense Hook.f., Fl. Brit. Ind. 5: 712, 1890
Pinalia fragrans (Rchb.f.) Kuntze, Rev. Gen. 2: 679, 1891
Pinalia rugosa (Blume) Kuntze, Rev. Gen. 2: 679, 1891
Pinalia stellata (Lindl.) Kuntze, Rev. Gen. 2: 679, 1891
Pinalia striolata (Rchb.f.) Kuntze, Rev. Gen. 2: 679, 1891
Sarcopodium perakense (Hook.f.) Kraenzlin, Pflanzenr. Heft 45: 328, 1910
Katherinea perakense (Hook.f.) Hawkes, Lloydia 19: 97, 1956
o **Eria latibracteata** Rolfe, Kew Bull.: 194, 1898
BM 7605
Borneo – E
Eria rolfei J.J. Smith, Bull. Dép. Agr. Ind. Neerl. 22: 34, 1909
o **Eria marginata** Rolfe, Gard. Chron.: 200, 1889
BM 7238
Burma, China – E
Pinalia marginata (Rolfe) Kuntze, Rev. Gen. 2: 679, 1891
o **Eria myristiciformis** Hook., Bot. Mag.: t. 5415, 1863
BM 5415
Burma – E
Pinalia myristiciformis (Hook.) Kuntze, Rev. Gen. 2: 679, 1891
o **Eria obesa** Lindl., Wall. Cat.: No. 1976, 1829 (nomen nudum)
BM 5391
N.E. India, Burma – E
Eria lindleyana Griffith, Notul 3: 300, 1851
Pinalia obesa (Lindl.) Kuntze, Rev. Gen. 2: 679, 1891
Eria prainii Briq., Ann. Cons. et Jard. Bot. Genève 4: 210, 1900
o **Eria ornata** (Blume) Lindl., Gen. Sp. Orch. Pl.: 66, 1830
BM 8642
Thailand, Malaya, Sumatra, Philippines – up to 1500 m – E
Dendrolirium ornatum Blume, Bijdr.: 345, 1825
Eria armeniaca Lindl., Bot. Reg. n.s. 14: t. 42, 1841
Pinalia ornata (Blume) Kuntze, Rev. Gen.: 678/79, 1891
o **Eria rhodoptera** Rchb.f., Gard. Chron.: 586, 1882
BM 8296
Philippines – up to 600 m – E
Eria laucheana Kraenzlin, Gard. Chron.: 809, 1892
Eria bractescens var. latipetala Leav., Phil. J. Sc. 4: 210 & 232 fig. 12, 1909
o **Eria rhynchostyloides** O'Brien, Gard. Chron.: 370, 1907
BM 8234
Java – E
Eria summerhayesiana A. Hawkes & A.H. Heller, Llodyia 20: 132, 1957
BM 5910
Burma, Malaya – E
Dendrobium extinctorium Lindl., Bot. Reg.: sub. t. 1756, 1835
o Eria extinctoria (Lindl.) Oliver, Bot. Mag.: t. 5910, 1871
Eria decipiens Summerh., Kew Bull.: 307, 1929
o **Eria tomentosa** (J. König) Hook.f., Fl. Brit. Ind. 5: 803, 1890
BM 8662
N.E. India, Burma, Laos, Vietnam – E
Epidendrum tomentosum J. König, Retzius Observ. 6: 53, 1791
Eria ornata auct. non (Blume) Lindl., J. Linn. Soc. 3: 48, 1859
Pinalia tomentosa (J. König) Kuntze, Rev. Gen. 2: 679, 1891
Eria fuerstenbergiana Schltr., Orchis 8: 132 pl. 3 fig. 16–25, 1914
o **Eria vestita** (Wallich) Lindl., Bot. Reg. 30: Misc. 76, 1844
BM 5807
India, Malaya, Sumatra, Borneo, Philippines – E
Dendrobium vestitum Wallich, Cat.: 2005, 1829
Trichotosia vestita (Wallich) Kraenzlin, Pflanzenr. Heft 50: 151, 1911
Eriopsis biloba Lindl., Bot. Reg. 33: sub. t. 9, 1847
BM 4437, BM 611 ns
Costa Rica, Panama, Venezuela, Guyana, Brazil, Colombia, Ecuador, Peru – 1000–2500 m – T, E
o Eriopsis rutidobulbon Hook., Bot. Mag.: t. 4437, 1849
Pseuderiopsis schomburgkii Rchb.f., Linnaea 22: 853, 1849
Eriopsis rhytidobulbon Lemaire, Jard. Fleur. 2: Misc. p. 77, 1852
Eriopsis schomburgkii (Rchb.f.) Rchb.f., Bonpl. 3: 67, 1855
Eriopsis fuerstenbergii Kraenzlin, Orchis 2: 62, 1908
Eriopsis werckeleyi Schltr., Fedde Rep. 16: 447, 1920
Eriopsis mesae Kraenzlin, Notizbl. Bot. Mus. Berlin 7: 427, 1920
Eriopsis colombiana Schltr., Fedde Rep. Beih. 27: 172, 1924
Eriopsis grandibulbosa Ames & C. Schweinf., Bull. Torrey Club 58: 350, 1931
Eriopsis sceptrum Rchb.f., & Warsc., Bonpl. 2: 98, 1854
BM 8462
Venezuela, Peru, Brazil – up to 1500 m – E
Eriopsis sprucei Rchb.f., Walp. Ann. 6: 663, 1863
Cyrtopodium yauaperyense Barb. Rodr., Vellozia 1, ed. 2.: 128, 1891
o Eriopsis helenae Kraenzlin, Gard. Chron.: 98, 1897

o **Erycina echinata** (Kunth) Lindl., Fol. Orch. Erycina: 1, 1853
BM 7389
Mexico - E
Oncidium echinatum Kunth, Nov. Gen. Sp. 1: 345 t. 79, 1816
Erycina major Schltr., Beih. Bot. Centralbl. 36, Abt. 2: 418, 1918
Esmeralda cathcartii (Lindl.) Rchb.f., Xen. Orch. 2: 39, 1862
BM 5845
E. Himalaya, Sikkim - 1000-1800 m - T, L
o Vanda cathcartii Lindl., Ill. Him. Pl.: t. 23, 1855
Arachnanthe cathcartii (Lindl.) Benth., Gen. Pl. 3: 573, 1883
Arachnis cathcartii (Lindl.) J.J. Smith, Tijdschr. Ned. Ind. 72: 73, 1912
Esmeralda clarkei Rchb.f., Gard. Chron.: 552, 1886
BM 7077
E. Himalaya, Burma, China, Thailand - 1500-2500 m - E, T
o Arachnanthe clarkei (Rchb.f.) Rolfe, Gard. Chron.: 567, 1888
Vanda clarkei (Rchb.f.) N.E. Br., Kew Bull.: 112, 1888
Esmeralda bella Rchb.f., Gard Chron.: 136, 1888
Arachnis clarkei (Rchb.f.) J.J. Smith, Tijdschr. Ned. Ind. 72: 76, 1912
Arachnis bella (Rchb.f.) J.J. Smith, Tijdschr. Ned. Ind. 72: 76, 1912
Euanthe sanderiana (Rchb.f.) Schltr., Orchideen: 568 fig. 194, 1914
BM 6983
Philippines (Mindanao) - up to 500 m - E
Esmeralda sanderiana Rchb.f., Gard. Chron.: 588, 1882
o Vanda sanderiana Rchb.f., Gard. Chron.: 588, 1882
Eulophia alta (L.) Fawcett & Rendle, Fl. Jam. 1: 112 t. 22 figs. 4-8, 1910
BM 1814
USA (Florida), W. Indies, Mexico to Brazil, W. Africa to Uganda - T
Limodorum altum L., Syst. Nat. ed. 12, 2: 594, 1767
Dendrobium longifolium Kunth, Nov. Gen. Sp. 1: 360, 1816
o Cyrtopodium woodfordii Sims, Bot. Mag.: t. 1814, 1816
Cyrtopera woodfordii (Sims) Lindl., Gen. Sp. Orch. Pl.: 189, 1833
Cyrtopera longifolia (Kunth) Rchb.f., Walp. Ann. 6: 668, 1861
Cyrtopera vellosiana Barb. Rodr., Orch. Nov. 2: 179, 1881
Eulophia woodfordii (Sims) Rolfe, F.T.A. 7: 68, 1897
Platypus papilliferus Small & Nash, Fl. SE. US., 1903
Platypus altus (L.) Small, Fl. SE. US. ed. 2: 329, 1913
Eulophia longifolia (Kunth) Schltr., Orchideen: 347, 1914
Cyrtopera alta (L.) Stéhlé, Bull. Agr. Martinique 8: 155, 1939
Eulophia angolensis (Rchb.f.) Summerh., Kew Bull.: 76, 1958
BM 8044
Ghana, Sao Tomé to Zaire, Uganda to S. Africa - T
Cymbidium angolense (Rchb.f.) Rchb.f., Flora 48: 188, 1865
Lissochilus buchanani Rchb.f., Otia Bot. Hamb. 1: 64, 1878
Lissochilus angolensis Rchb.f., Otia Bot. Hamb. 1: 64, 1878
Eulophia latifolia Rolfe, F.T.A. 7: 50, 1891 publ. 1892
o Lissochilus ugandae Rolfe, Bot. Mag.: t. 8044, 1905
Eulophia ugandae (Rolfe) Rolfe, Kew Bull.: 339, 1913
Eulophia cristata (Sw.) Steudel, Nomen. Bot. ed. 2, 1: 605, 1840
BM 7921
Senegal, Gambia, Guinea-Bissau, Sierra Leone, Ivory Coast, Ghana, Togo, Dahomey, Nigeria, W. Cameroun, C. African Rep., Zaire, Sudan, Ethiopia, Uganda - T
Limodorum cristatum Sw., Neues J. 1: 86, 1805
o Lissochilus purpuratus Lindl., F.T.A. 7: 79, 1862
Lissochilus heudelotii Rchb.f., F.T.A., 1878
Graphorchis cristata (Sw.) Kuntze, Rev. Gen.: 662, 1891
Lissochilus uliginosus Rolfe, Kew Bull.: 340, 1913
Eulophia cucullata (Sw.) Steudel, F.W.T.A.: 2, 3 pt. 1: 249, 1968
BM 8397
Mali, Senegal, Gambia, Guinea-Bissau, Guinea, Sierra Leone, Ivory Coast, Ghana, Togo, Nigeria, Cameroun, Zaire, Angola, Tanzania, Malawi, Zambia - T
Lissochilus dilectus Rchb.f., F.T.A. 7: 83, 1878
o Lissochilus stylites Rchb.f., Otia Bot. Hamb.: 61, 1878
Eulophia dilecta (Rchb.f.) Schltr., Westafr. Kauts.-Exped.: 279, 1900
Eulophia epidendraea (Retz) Fischer, Fl. Pres. Madras 3: 1434, 1928
BM 5579
Sri Lanka, S. India, Burma, Thailand, Laos, Kampuchea, Vietnam, Malaya, Philippines - T
Serapias epidendraea Retz, Obs. 6: 65, 1791
Limodorum virens Roxb., Pl. Corom. 1: 32, 1795
Limodorum epidendroides Willd., Sp.Pl. 4: 124, 1805
o Eulophia virens (Roxb.) R.Br., Bot. Reg. 8: t. 573, 1821
Eulophia graminea Lindl., Gen. Sp. Orch. Pl.: 182, 1833
Eulophia epidendroides (Willd.) Schltr, Orchideen: 346, 1914
o **Eulophia euglossa** (Rchb.f.) Rchb.f., Bot. Mag.: t. 5561, 1866
BM 5561
Sierra Leone, Ivory Coast, Ghana, Nigeria, Cameroun, Gabon, Zaire, Uganda - T
Eulophia dusenii Kraenzlin, F.T.A. 7: 52, 1894
Eulophia flavopurpurea (Rchb. f.) Rolfe, F.T.A. 7: 65, 1897
BM 8470
Ivory Coast, Ghana, Togo, Nigeria, Cameroun, Sudan, Uganda, Malawi, Zambia, Zimbabwe, Mozambique - T
Cyrtopera flavopurpurea Rchb. f., Otia Bot. Hamb. 1: 68, 1879
Lissochilus millsonii Rolfe, F.T.A. 7: 79, 1897
Lissochilus lacteus Kraenzlin, Engl. Bot. Jahrb. 43: 398, 1909
o Lissochilus andersonii Rolfe, Kew Bull.: 159, 1910
Lissochilus johnsonii Rolfe, Kew Bull.: 160, 1910
Eulophia millsonii (Rolfe) Summerh., F.W.T.A. ed. 1, 2: 446, 1936
o **Eulophia guineensis** Lindl., Bot. Reg. 8: t. 686, 1823
BM 2467, BM 267 ns
Gambia, Mali, Guinea, Sierra Leone, Ivory Coast, Ghana, Nigeria, Zaire, Uganda, Tanzania, Angola, Yemen, Oman - T
Eulophia quartiniana A. Rich., Tent. Fl. Abyss. 2: 284, 1851
Saccolabium abyssinicum A. Rich., Tent. Fl. Abyss. 2: t. 81, 1851
Galeandra quartiniana (A. Rich.) Rchb.f., Walp. Ann. 3: 552, 1852-3
Graphorchis guineensis (Lindl.) Kuntze, Rev. Gen.: 22, 1891
Eulophia congoensis Cogn., J. Orch. 6: 155, 1895
Eulophia horsfallii (Bateman) Summerh., F.W.T.A. 2: 446, 1936
BM 5486, BM 6858, BM 8047
Guinea-Bissau, Sierra Leone, Liberia, Ivory Coast, Ghana, Nigeria, Cameroun, Fernando Po, Kenya, Uganda, Tanzania, Malawi, S. Africa (Natal) - T
Lissochilus roseus Lindl., F.T.A. 7: 85, 1843
o Lissochilus horsfallii Bateman, F.T.A. 7: 84, 1865
o Lissochilus sandersonii Rchb.f., Otia Bot. Hamb. 1: 62, 1878
Eulophia porphyroglossa Bolus, J. Linn. Soc. 25: 185 partly, 1890
Lissochilus porphyroglossa (Bolus) Durand & Schinz, Conspect. Fl. Afr. 5: 30, 1898 (non Rchb.f.)
o Lissochilus mahonii Rolfe, Bot. Mag.: t. 8047, 1905
Lissochilus transvaalensis Rolfe, Fl. Cap. 5, 3: 57, 1912
Eulophia mahonii (Rolfe) A. Hawkes, Orch. Rev. 72: 27, 1964
Eulophia sandersonii (Rchb.f.) A. Hawkes, Orch. Rev. 72: 27, 1964
o **Eulophia nuda** Lindl., Gen. Spec. Orch. Pl. 180, 1833
BM 8057
Sri Lanka, India, Nepal, Sikkim, Burma, Thailand, Malaya, Sumatra, Philippines, New Guinea - T
Cyrtopera plicata Lindl. ex Wall., Cat. 246: 7362, 1832 (nomen nudum)
Dipodium plicatum Buch.-Ham. ex Wall., Cat. 246: 7362, 1832
Dipodium roniate Buch.-Ham. ex Wall., Cat. 246: 7362, 1832
Eulophia squalida Lindl., Bot. Reg.: Misc. 77, 1841
Eulophia bicolor Dalz., Hook. J. Bot.: Misc. 3: 343, 1851
Cyrtopera fusca Wight, Ic. Pl. Ind. Or. 5 (1): pl. 1690, 1851
Eulophia fusca (Wight) Blume, Orch. Arch. Ind.: 182, 1858
Cyrtopera mysorensis Lindl., J. Linn. Soc. Bot. 3: 32, 1859
Cyrtopera gardneri Thwaites, Enum. Pl. Zeyl.: 302, 1861
Cyrtopera laxiflora Gardner ex Thwaites, Enum. Pl. Zeyl.: 320, 1861
Cyrtopera nuda (Lindl.) Rchb.f., Fl. 55: 274, 1872
Cyrtopodium fuscum (Blume) Trimen, Cat.: 89, 1885
Graphorchis nuda (Lindl.) Kuntze, Rev. Gen: 662, 1891
Eulophia orthoplectra (Rchb.f.) Summerh., Kew Bull.: 499, 1939
BM 7546
Ghana, Togo, Nigeria, W. Cameroun, Kenya, E. Africa to Zimbabwe - T
Lissochilus orthoplectrus Rchb.f., F.T.A. 7: 95, 1878
o Lissochilus milanjianus Rendle, F.T.A. 7: 98, 1894
Eulophia involuta Summerh., F.W.T.A. 2: 444, 1936
Eulophia pulchra (Thouars) Lindl., Gen. Sp. Orch. Pl.: 182, 1833
BM 6246
Madagascar to Pacific Is. - 200-1000 m - T
Limodorum pulchrum Thouars, Orch. Iles Afr.: t. 43-44, 1822
o Eulophia macrostachya Lindl., Gen. Sp. Orch. Pl.: 182, 1833
Graphorchis pulchra (Thouars) Kuntze, Rev. Gen. Pl.: 662, 1891
Eulophia guamensis Ames, Phil. J. Sc. 9: 12, 1914
Eulophia rouxii Kraenzlin, Sar. & Roux Nova Caled. 1: 82, 1914
Lissochilus pulcher (Thouars) H. Perrier, Fl. Madagascar 49. Fam., 2: 41, 1939 (non Schltr.)
Eulophidium pulchrum (Thouars) Summerh., Bull. Jard. Bot. Et. Brux. 27: 400, 1957
Eulophia sanguinea (Lindl.) Hook.f., Fl. Brit. Ind. 6: 8, 1890
BM 6161
Sri Lanka, Himalaya, Sikkim, Bhutan, Assam - 600-1700 m - T
o Cyrtopera sanguinea Lindl., J. Linn. Soc. 3: 32, 1859
Cyrtopera rufa Thwaites, Enum. Pl. Zeyl.: 302, 1861
Cyrtopodium rufum (Thwaites) Trimen, Cat.: 89, 1885
Eulophia macrorhizon Hook.f., Fl. Brit. India 6: 7, 1890
Graphorchis sanguinea (Lindl.) Kuntze, Rev. Gen.: 662, 1891
o **Eulophia streptopetala** Lindl., Bot. Reg. 12: t. 1002, 1826
BM 2931, BM 5861
S. Africa, Trop. Africa, Yemen - T
Lissochilus parviflorus Lindl., Bot. Mag.: t. 2931, 1829

Lissochilus streptopetalus (Lindl.) Lindl., Gen. Sp. Orch. Pl.: 191, 1833
○ Lissochilus krebsii Rchb.f., Linnaea 20: 685, 1847
Lissochilus paivaeanus Rchb.f., Flora 48: 187, 1865
Lissochilus krebsii var. purpurata Ridley, Gard. Chron.: 102, 1885
Eulophia krebsii var. purpurata (Ridley) Bolus, J. Linn. Soc. 25: 185, 1889
Eulophia krebsii (Rchb.f.) Bolus, J. Linn. Soc. 25, 1889
Lissochilus graefei Kraenzlin, Gard. Chron.: 749, 1892
Eulophia paivaeana (Rchb.f.) Summerh., Kew Bull.: 151, 1953
Eulophia welwitschii (Rchb.f.) Rolfe, Bol. Soc. Bot. 7: 236, 1889
BM 7330
Nigeria, Zaire, E. Africa, S. Africa (Natal) – T
Eulophia bicolor Rchb.f. & Sonder ex Reichb. f., Flora 48: 186, 1865
Orthochilus welwitschii Rchb.f., Flora 48: 186, 1865
○ Eulophia zeyheri Hook.f., Bot. Mag.: t. 7330, 1893
Eulophia milanjiana Rendle, F.T.A. 7: 63, 1895
Eulophia woodii Schltr., Engl. Bot. Jahrb. 20 Beibl. No. 50: 5, 1895
○ **Eulophiella elisabethae** Linden & Rolfe, Lindenia 7: 29 t. 325, 1892
BM 7387, BM 656 ns
Madagascar – E
Eulophiella perrieri Schltr., Orchis 15, 2: 28, 1920
Eulophiella roempleriana (Rchb.f.) Schltr., Orchis 9: 109, 1915
BM 7612, BM 7613
Madagascar – E
Grammatophyllum roemplerianum Rchb.f., Gard. Chron.: 240, 1877
○ Eulophiella petersiana Kraenzlin, Gard. Chron.: 182, 1897
Eulophiella hamelinii Baillon ex Rolfe, Orch. Rev. 8: 197, 1900
○ **Galeandra baueri** Lindl., Bauer & Lindl. Ill. Orch. Pl. Gen.: t. 8, 1832
BM 4701
Mexico to Panama, S. America – E
○ **Galeandra devoniana** Schomb. ex Lindl., Sert. Orch.: t. 37, 1838
BM 4610
Venezuela, Guyana, Brazil – E
Gastrochilus acutifolius (Lindl.) Kuntze, Rev. Gen., 1891
BM 4772
Sikkim, Himalaya – up to 1000 m – E
Aerides umbellata Wallich, Wall. Cat.: 1137, 1829
Saccolabium acutifolium Lindl., Gen. Sp. Orch. Pl.: 223, 1833
○ Saccolabium denticulatum Paxton, Mag. Bot. 7: t. 145, 1834–1849
Gastrochilus bellinus (Rchb.f.) Kuntze, Rev. Gen.: 661, 1891
BM 7142
Thailand, Burma – E
○ Saccolabium bellinum Rchb.f., Gard. Chron.: 174, 1887
Gastrochilus bigibbus (Rchb.f. ex Hook.f.) Kuntze, Rev. Gen.: 661, 1891
BM 5767
Burma, Malay Archipelago – E
○ Saccolabium bigibbum Rchb. f. ex Hook.f., Bot. Mag.: sub.t. 5767, 1869
Gennaria diphylla (Link) Parl., Fl. Ital. 3: 405, 1858
BM 3164
Portugal, N. Africa, W. Mediterranean region, Canary Is. – T
Satyrium diphyllum Link, Schrad. J. Bot. 2: 323, 1799
Orchis cordata Willd., Sp.Pl. 4: 27, 1805
○ Habenaria cordata (Willd.) R.Br., Prodr.: 312, 1809
Gymnadenia diphylla (Link) Link, Handb. 1: 243, 1829
Herminium cordatum (Willd.) Lindl., Bot. Reg.: sub.t. 1499, 1832
Peristylus cordatus (Willd.) Lindl., Gen. Sp. Orch. Pl.: 298, 1835
Digomphotis cordata (Willd.) Raf., Fl. Tellur. 2: 37, 1836
Platanthera diphylla (Link) Rchb.f., Ic. Fl. Germ. 13/14: 128 t. 84, 1851
Orchis cordifolia Munby, Bull. Soc. Bot. Fr. 2: 148, 1855
Coeloglossum cordatum (Willd.) Nyman, Syll. Pl. Nov.: 359, 1865
Habenaria diphylla (Link) Durand & Schinz, Consp. Fl. Afr. 5, 1892 (1895)
Coeloglossum diphyllum (Link) Fiori & Paoli, Fl. Ital. 1: 248, 1898
○ **Geodorum citrinum** Jackson, Bot. Rep.: t. 626, 1810
BM 2195
Burma, Thailand, Malaya – T
Gomesa barkeri (Hook.) Rolfe, Orch. Rev. 9: 166, 1901
BM 3497
Brazil – T
○ Rodriguezia barkeri Hook., Bot. Mag.: t. 3497, 1836
Odontoglossum barkeri (Hook.) Rchb.f., Walp. Ann. 6: 854, 1864
Gomesa foliosa (Hook.) Klotzsch & Rchb.f., Bot. Zeit. 10: 772, 1852
BM 2746
Brazil – E
○ Pleurothallis foliosa Hook., Bot. Mag.: t. 2746, 1827
Rodriguezia suaveolens Lindl., Gen. Sp. Orch. Pl.: 195, 1833
Maturna suaveolens (Lindl.) Raf., Fl. Tellur. 2: 99, 1836
Odontoglossum foliosum (Hook.) Rchb.f., Walp. Ann. 6: 854, 1864
○ **Gomesa planifolia** (Lindl.) Klotzsch & Rchb.f., Bot. Zeit. 10: 772, 1852
BM 3504
Brazil, Argentina, Paraguay – T, E
Gomesa recurva Lodd., Bot. Cab.: tab. 660, 1822 (non R.Br.)
Rodriguezia planifolia Lindl., Trans. Hort. Soc. 7: 67, 1830
Gomesa reclinata Hoffsgg., Verz. Orch.: 52, 1843
Gomesa planifolia var. laxa Regel, Ind. Sem. Hort. Petrop.: 21, 1856
Odontoglossum planifolium (Lindl.) Rchb.f., Walp. Ann. 6: 853, 1864
○ **Gomesa recurva** R.Br., Bot. Mag.: t. 1748, 1815
BM 1748
Brazil – E
Epidendrum inflexum Vell., Fl. Flum. Ic. 9: t. 30, 1827
Rodriguezia recurva (R.Br.) Lindl., Trans. Hort. Soc. 7: 67, 1830
Gomezia densiflora Hoffsgg., Verz. Orch.: 50, 1843
Odontoglossum recurvum (R.Br.) Rchb.f., Walp. Ann. 6: 853, 1864
Gongora armeniaca (Lindl.) Rchb.f., Xen. Orch. 1: 52, 1854
BM 5501
Nicaragua, Costa Rica, Panama – up to 1200 m – E
○ Acropera armeniaca Lindl., Paxt. Flow. Gard. 1: 94 fig. 66, 1850
Acropera cornuta Klotzsch, Allg. Gartenz. 20: 186, 1852
Gongora galeata (Lindl.) Rchb.f., Xen. Orch. 1: 51, 1854
BM 3563
Mexico – E
Maxillaria galeata Lindl. ex Lodd., Bot. Cab. 17: t. 1645, 1831
○ Acropera loddigesii Lindl., Gen. Sp. Orch. Pl.: 172, 1833
Cirrhaea loddigesii (Lindl.) Lindl., Bot. Reg.: t. 1538, 1837
○ **Gongora gratulabunda** Rchb.f., Bot. Zeit. 15: 157, 1857
BM 7224
Colombia – E
○ **Gongora grossa** Rchb.f., Gard. Chron.: 781, 1877
BM 8562
Ecuador – up to 1300 m – E
○ **Gongora latisepala** Rolfe, Bot. Mag.: t. 8766, 1918
BM 8766
Colombia – E
○ **Gongora portentosa** Linden & Rchb.f., Gard. Chron.: 892, 1869
BM 6284
Colombia, Peru – E
Gongora quinquenervis Ruiz Lopez & Pavón, Syst. Veg.: 227, 1798
BM 3220, BM 3687
Mexico, Guatemala, Honduras, Nicaragua, Costa Rica, Panama, S. America – E
○ Gongora atropurpurea Hook., Exot. Fl. 3: t. 178, 1827
○ Gongora maculata Lindl., Bot. Reg. 19: t. 1616, 1833
Gongora nigrita Lindl., Bot. Reg. 25: Misc. p. 59, 1839
Gongora fulva Lindl., Bot. Reg. 25: t. 51, 1839
Gongora bufonia Lindl., Bot. Reg. 27: t. 2, 1841
Gongora maculata var. alba Lindl., Bot. Reg. 27: Misc. p. 48, 1841
Gongora fulva var. vitellina Lindl., Bot. Reg. 27: Misc. 1, 1841
Gongora leucochila Lemaire, Fl. Serres 1: 207, 1845
Gongora odoratissima Lemaire, Fl. Serres 2: 229, 1847
Gongora bufonia var. leucochila (Lemaire) Lindl., Bot. Reg. 33: t. 17, 1847
Gongora boothiana hort. ex Allg. Gartenz. 20: 376, 1852
Gongora jenischii hort. ex Allg. Gartenz. 23: 347, 1853
Gongora retrorsa Rchb.f., Bonpl. 2: 19, 1854
Gongora vitellina hort. ex Xen. Orch. 1: 54, 1854
Gongora histrionica Rchb.f., Bonpl. 2: 92, 1854
Gongora quinquevulneris Beer, Prakt. Orch.: 252, 1854
Gongora quadricornis hort. ex Rchb.f., Xen. Orch. 1: 53, 1854
Gongora shepherdii hort. ex Rchb.f., Xen. Orch. 1: 53, 1854
Gongora odoratissima var. jenischii hort. ex Kramer, Cat. Orch. Senat. Jenisch, 1855
Gongora superflua Rchb.f., Xen. Orch. 2: 169, 1873
Gongora truncata var. alba (Lindl.) Nash, Addisonia 2: t. 46, 1917
Gongora powellii Schltr., Fedde Rep. Beih. 17: 62, 1922
Gongora unicolor Schltr., Fedde Rep. Beih. 19: 229, 1923
Gongora maculata forma odoratissima Dodson, Agentes de Pollinizacion Univ. Nac. Amaz. Peruana: 117, 1965
○ **Gongora tricolor** Rchb.f., Bonpl. 2: 93, 1854
BM 7530
Costa Rica – E
Gongora maculata var. tricolor Lindl., Bot. Reg. 33: t. 69, 1847
Goodyera pubescens (Willd.) R.Br., Hort. Kew ed. 2, 5: 198, 1813
BM 2540
Canada to Florida – T
Neottia pubescens Willd., Sp.Pl. 4: 76, 1805
○ Goodyera pubescens var. minor Lindl., Bot. Mag.: t. 2540, 1825
Orchiodes pubescens (Willd.) Kuntze, Rev. Gen. 2: 675, 1891
Peramium pubescens (Willd.) Salisb., Metasp. Minn. Valley: 171, 1892

Epipactis pubescens (Willd.) A. A. Eaton, Proc. Biol. Soc. Wash. 21: 65, 1908
Epipactis willdenovii House, Muhlenb. 6: 74, 1910
Govenia superba (Llave & Lex.) Lindl. ex Lodd., Bot. Cab. 18: t. 1709, 1831
BM 8794
Mexico to Panama, Venezuela, Colombia – up to 2700 m – T
Maxillaria superba Llave & Lex., Nov. Veg. Descr. 2: 13, 1825
o Govenia lagenophora Lindl., Bot. Reg. 25: Misc. p. 46, 1839
Govenia fasciata Lindl., Bot. Reg. 29: Misc. p. 70, 1843
Govenia sulphurea Rchb. f., Gard. Chron.: 70, 1885
Govenia platyglossa Schltr., Fedde Rep. Beih. 7: 157, 1920
Govenia stictoglossa Schltr., Fedde Rep. Beih. 27: 79, 1924
o **Govenia tingens** Poeppig & Endl., Nov. Gen. Sp. Pl. 2: 5 t. 107, 1837–38
BM 8768
Venezuela, Brazil, Amazonas, Peru, Bolivia, Argentina – 1800–2300 m – T
o **Govenia utriculata** (Sw.) Lindl., Bot. Mag. 65: t. 3660, 1839
BM 3660, BM 4151
C. & S. America, (Mexico to Bolivia, Argentina), W. Indies – T
Limodorum utriculatum Sw., Prodr. Veg. Ind. Occ.: 119, 1788
Cymbidium utriculatum (Sw.) Sw., Nov. Act. Upsal. 6: 75, 1799
Govenia liliacea Lindl., Bot. Reg. 21: t. 1795, 1836
o Govenia gardneri Hook., Bot. Mag.: t. 3660, 1839
Govenia boliviense Rolfe, Mem. Torrey Club 4: 263, 1895
Govenia ernstii Schltr., Fedde Rep. Beih. 6: 43, 1919
Govenia sodiroi Schltr., Fedde Rep. Beih. 8: 91, 1921
Grammangis ellisii (Lindl.) Rchb. f., Hamb. Gartenz. 16: 520, 1860 (non Veitch)
BM 5179
Madagascar – E
o Grammatophyllum ellisii Lindl., Bot. Mag.: t. 5179, 1860
Grammatophyllum scriptum (L.) Blume, Bijdr.: 378, 1825
BM 7507
Philippines, Borneo, Celebes, Moluccas, New Guinea, Solomon Is. – E
Epidendrum scriptum L., Sp. Pl. ed. 2, 2: 1351, 1763
Cymbidium scriptum (L.) Sw., Schrad. J. Bot. 2: 128, 1799
Vanda scripta (L.) Spreng., Syst. 3: 719, 1826
Gabertia scripta (L.) Gaudich, Freyc Voy. Bot.: 425, 1826
Grammatophyllum multiflorum Lindl., Bot. Reg.: Misc. 46, 1838
Grammatophyllum fenzlianum Rchb. f., Sp. Pl. ed. 2, 1867
o Grammatophyllum rumphianum Miq., Ann. Mus. Bot. Ludg. Bat. 4: 219, 1869
Cymbidium goweri F. v. M., Wing South Sci. Rec. Aug., 1883
Grammatophyllum measuresianum Weath., Gard. & Forest 2: 524, 1889
Grammatophyllum seegerianum hort. ex Gard. Chron. 2: 49, 1891
Grammatophyllum guilelmi-secundii Kraenzlin, Gartenfl.: 114, 1894
o **Grammatophyllum speciosum** Blume, Bijdr. 20: 278, 1825
BM 5157
Burma, Thailand, Malaya, Sumatra to Philippines, Moluccas, New Guinea, Solomon Is. – E
Grammatophyllum fastuosum Lindl. & Paxton, Paxt. Flow. Gard. 2: 139, 1852
Pattonia macrantha Wight, Ic.: t. 1750, 1852
Grammatophyllum macranthum (Wight) Rchb. f., Xen. Orch. 2: 16, 1862
Grammatophyllum giganteum Blume ex Rchb. f., Linnaea 41: 107, 1877
Grammatophyllum wallisii Rchb. f., Linnaea 41: 107, 1877
Grammatophyllum sanderianum hort. ex Gard. Chron.: 15, 1893
Grammatophyllum stapeliiflorum (Teijsm. & Binnend.) J. J. Smith, Fl. Buitenz. 6: 487 fig. 369, 1905
BM 5676
Malaya, Sumatra, Java, Celebes – E
Cymbidium stapeliiflorum Teijsm. & Binnend., Nat. Tijdschr. Ned. Ind. 24: 319, 1862
o Cymbidium huttonii Hook. f., Bot. Mag.: t. 5676, 1867
Grammangis stapeliiflora (Teijsm. & Binnend.) Schltr., Engl. Bot. Jahrb. 45: Beibl. 104, 53, 1911
Habenaria armatissima Rchb. f., Otia Bot. Hamb.: 98, 1881
BM 7798
Ethiopia, Kenya, Tanganika – T
o Habenaria lugardii Rolfe, F. T. A. 7: 228, 1898
Habenaria dinteriana Kraenzlin, Vierteljahrsschr. Nat. Ges. 74: 106, 1929
o **Habenaria dentata** (Sw.) Schltr., Fedde Rep. Beih. 4: 125, 1919
BM 9663
W. Himalaya, Nepal, Sikkim, Assam, Burma, S. China, Laos, Kampuchea, Vietnam, Hong Kong, Taiwan, Ryukyu Is., Japan, Philippines – 800–1500 m – T
Orchis dentata Sw., Kongl. Vet. Acad. Handl. 21: 207, 1800
Habenaria geniculata D. Don, Prod. Fl. Nepal.: 25, 1825
Habenaria radiata Sprengel, Syst. 3: 693, 1826
Platanthera geniculata (D. Don) Lindl., Wall. Cat.: 7042, 1832 (nomen nudum)
Platanthera dentata (Sw.) Lindl., Gen. Sp. Orch. Pl.: 296, 1835
Habenaria sp. Griffith, Notul 3: 406 & Ic.: t. 340, 1851
Habenaria miersiana Champ. ex Benth., Kew J. Bot. 7: 37, 1855
Habenaria sieboldiana Miq., Ann. Bot. Mus. Ludg. Bat. 2: 208, 1866
Habenaria geniculata var. yunnanensis Kraenzlin, Orch. Gen. & Sp.: 415, 1901
Habenaria miersiana var. yunnanensis Rolfe, J. Linn. Soc.: 60, 1903
Habenaria tohoensis Hayata, Ic. Pl. Form. 4: 128, 1914
Habenaria finetiana Schltr., Fedde Rep. Beih. 4: 126, 1919
non Habenaria sieboldiana auct.: Miq.: 208, 1867
o **Habenaria elwesii** Hook. f., Bot. Mag.: t. 7478, 1896
BM 7478
E. India – T
o **Habenaria leptoceras** Hook., Bot. Mag.: t. 2726, 1827
BM 2726
Brazil – T
Habenaria armondiana Hoehne, Bol. Mus. Nac. Rio de Janeiro 12 (3–4): 76, 1936
o **Habenaria longicalcarata** A. Rich., Ann. Sc. Nat. 2 s. 2, 15: 71 t. 3, 1841
BM 7228
E. India – T
Bonatea gracilis Lindl., Gen. Sp. Orch. Pl.: 329, 1835
Habenaria decipiens Wight, Ic. 1: tp. 1: 14, 1838
Habenaria longicorniculata Graham, Cat. Pl. Bomb.: 202, 1839 (non Hook.)
Habenaria montana Wight, Ic. Pl. Ind. Or.: t. 1714, 1851
Habenaria gracilis Rchb. f., Flora: 180, 1865 (non Lindl.)
o **Habenaria longicauda** Hook., Bot. Mag.: t. 2957, 1830
BM 2957
Guyana, Brazil – T
Habenaria quinqueseta (Michaux) Sw., Adnot. Bot.: 46, 1829
BM 2947
USA (Carolina, Florida), W. Indies, Mexico to Venezuela, Guyana, Surinam – T
Orchis habenaria L., Syst. ed. 10: 1242, 1758/59
Orchis quinqueseta Michaux, Fl. Bor. Am. 2: 155, 1803
Habenaria macroceratitis Willd., Sp. Pl. 4: 44, 1805
o Habenaria macroceras Sprengel, Syst. 3: 692, 1827
Habenaria macroceratitis var. brevicalcarata Ames, Orchid. 4: 224, 1910
o **Habenaria rhodocheila** Hance, Ann. Sci. Nat. 5 s. 5: 243, 1866
BM 7570
S. China, Thailand, Laos, Vietnam, Malaya, Philippines – T
Habenaria pusilla Rchb. f., Otia Bot. Hamb.: 33, 1878
Habenaria militaris Rchb. f., Gard. Chron.: 518, 1886
Habenaria xanthocheila Ridley, J. Linn. Soc. 32: 411, 1896
Habenaria militaris var. philippinensis Ames, Orch. 2: 40, 1908
o **Habenaria salaccensis** Blume, Bijdr.: 403 fig. 13, 1825
BM 5196
Java – T
o **Habenaria splendens** Rendle, J. Linn. Soc. 30: 395, 1895
BM 9350
Uganda, Kenya, Tanganyika, Ethiopia, Zambia – 1000–2400 m – T
Habenaria macrantha Kraenzlin, Orch. Gen. Sp. 1: 402, 1897 (pro parte non Hochst.)
Helcia sanguinolenta Lindl., Bot. Reg.: Misc. p. 18, 1845
BM 7281
Ecuador, Peru – up to 3000 m – E
o Trichopilia sanguinolenta (Lindl.) Rchb. f., Xen. Orch. 2: 99, 1867
o **Hemipilia amethystina** Rolfe ex Hook. f., Bot. Mag.: t. 7521, 1897
BM 7521
Burma – T
o **Hemipilia calophylla** Parish & Rchb. f., J. Bot. 12: 197, 1874
BM 6920
Burma, China (Yunnan), Thailand – T
Herschelianthe hians (L. f.) Rauschert, Fedde Rep. 94 (7/8): 435, 1983
BM 7066
S. Africa (Cape Town) – 600–1000 m – T
Satyrium hians L. f., Suppl. Pl.: 401, 1782
Limodorum hians (L. f.) Thunb., Prod. 3, 1793
Disa lacera Sw., Vet. Acad. Handl. 31: 212, 1800
Disa hians (L. f.) Sprengel, Linn. Syst. Veg. 3: 698, 1826
Eulophia hians (L. f.) Sprengel, Linn. Syst. Veg. 3: 720, 1826
Disa excelsa sensu Lindl., Gen. Sp. Orch. Pl.: 356, 1838 (Non (Thunb.) Sw.)

o Disa lacera var. multifida N.E.Br., Gard. Chron.: 664, 1888
Herschelia excelsa sensu Rolfe, Fl. Cap. 5, 3: 200, 1913 (non (Thunb.) Rolfe)
Disa outeniquensis Schltr., Ann. Trans. Mus. 10: 246, 1924
Herschelia lacera (Sw.) Fourc., Trans. R. Soc. 21: 81, 1932
Herschelia hians (L.f.) Hall, Fl. Pl. Afr. 42: t. 1674, 1973
Herschelianthe lugens (Bolus) Rauschert, Fedde Rep. 94 (7/8): 435, 1983
BM 8415
S. Africa (Cape Province) – T
o Disa lugens Bolus, J. Linn. Soc. 20: 483, 1884
Herschelia lugens (Bolus) Kraenzlin, Orch. Gen. Pl. 1: 806, 1900
Herschelianthe spathulata (L.f.) Rauschert, Fedde Rep. 94 (7/8): 435, 1983
BM 6891
S. Africa (Cape Province) – 100–1000 m – T
Orchis spathulata L.f., Suppl. Pl.: 398, 1781
Satyrium spathulatum (L.f.) Thunb., Prod. 5, 1794
Disa spathulata (L.f.) Sw., Kongl. Vet. Acad. Handl. 21: 213, 1800
Disa propinqua Sonder, Linnaea 19: 95, 1847
Disa propinqua var. trifida Sonder, Linnaea 19: 96, 1847
o Disa atropurpurea Sonder, Linnaea 19: 96, 1847
Disa spathulata var. atropurpurea (Sonder) Schltr., Engl. Bot. Jahrb. 31: 284, 1901
Herschelia atropurpurea (Sonder) Rolfe, Fl. Cap. 5, 3: 205, 1913
Herschelia spathulata (L.f.) Rolfe, Fl. Cap. 5, 3: 205, 1913
Herschelianthe atropurpurea (Sonder) Rauschert, Fedde Rep. 94 (7/8): 434, 1983
o **Hexisea bidentata** Lindl., Hook., J. Bot. 1: 8, 1834
BM 7031
Mexico to Panama, Guyana, Venezuela, Colombia, Peru – E
Diothonaea imbricata Lindl., Sert. Orch.: t. 40, 1841
Epidendrum oppositifolium Rich. & Galeotti, Ann. Sc. Nat. s. 3, 3: 21, 1845
Diothonaea oppositifolia Rchb.f., Linnaea 22: 842, 1849
Euthonaea oppositifolia Rchb.f., Bot. Zeit. 10: 772, 1852
Euthonaea imbricata (Lindl.) Rchb.f., Bot. Zeit. 10: 772, 1852
Hexisea oppositifolia Rchb.f., Walp. Ann. 6: 470, 1862
Hexisea imbricata (Lindl.) Rchb.f., Walp. Ann. 6: 470, 1862
Hexisea bidentata var. imbricata (Lindl.) C. Schweinf., Bot. Mus. Leafl. Harv. Univ. 15: 106, 1951
Holcoglossum kimballianum (Rchb.f.) Garay, Bot. Mus. Leafl. Harv. Univ. 23 (4): 182, 1972
BM 7112
Burma (Shan States) – up to 1200 m – E
o Vanda kimballiana Rchb. f., Gard. Chron.: 232, 1889
Vanda saprophytica Gagnepain, Bull. Soc. Bot. Fr. 79: 37, 1932
o **Holothrix orthoceras** Rchb.f., Otia Bot. Hamb.: 119, 1881
BM 7523
S. Africa (Cape Province) – 1000–1700 m – T
Tryphia orthoceras Harvey, Thes. Cap. 2: 4 t. 105, 1859–63
o **Houlletia brocklehurstiana** Lindl., Bot. Reg. 27: Misc. 99, 1841
BM 4072
Brazil – E
Maxillaria brocklehurstiana Lindl., Bot. Reg. 27: Misc. 10, 1841
Houlletia stapeliaeflora Brongn., Ann. Sc. Nat. s. 2, 15: 37, 1841
Houlletia odoratissima Linden ex Lindl., & Paxton, Flow. Gard. 3: 172, 1853
BM 6305
Panama, Venezuela, Colombia, Peru, Bolivia, Brazil – 800–1300 m – T, E
o Houlletia picta Linden & Rchb.f., Gartenfl. 2, 1855
Houlletia juruenensis Hoehne, Comm. Linh. Telegr. Mato Grosso Amaz. Annexo 5, Bot. 1: 47, 1910
Houlletia antioquiensis hort. ex Ames & Nash, L.H. Bailey Stand. Cycl. Hort.: 1608, 1915
Houlletia buchtienii Kraenzlin, Fedde Rep. 25: 28, 1928
Houlletia boliviana Schltr., Fedde Rep. 27: 65, 1929
o **Houlletia sanderi** Rolfe, Gard. Chron.: 206, 1910
BM 8346
Ecuador, Peru – up to 1700 m – T
Houlletia tigrina Linden ex Lindl., Paxt. Flow. Gard. 3: 172, 1853
BM 7362
Guatemala, Nicaragua, Costa Rica, Panama, Venezuela, Colombia – up to 1300 m – E
o Houlletia landsbergii Linden & Rchb.f., Gartenfl. 4: 2, 1855
Huntleya burtii (Endres & Rchb.f.) Pfitzer, Nat. Pflanzenf. 2, 6: 205, 1889
BM 6003
Nicaragua, Costa Rica, Panama – up to 1300 m – E
o Batemania burtii Endres & Rchb.f., Gard. Chron.: 1099, 1872
o **Huntleya citrina** Rolfe. Bot. Mag.: t. 8689, 1916
BM 8689
Colombia – E
Ionopsis utricularioides (Sw.) Lindl., Coll. Bot.: t. 39 A, 1821
BM 5541
USA (Florida), W. Indies, Mexico to Brazil, Peru, Paraguay – E
Epidendrum utricularioides Sw., Prodr. Veg. Ind. Occ.: 122, 1788
Dendrobium utricularioides (Sw.) Sw., Nov. Act. Upsal. 6: 38, 1799
Ionopsis pulchella Kunth, Nov. Gen. Sp. 1: 348, t. 83, 1816
Iantha pallidiflora Hook., Exot. Fl. 2: t. 113, 1824
Cybelion pallidiflorum (Hook.) Sprengel, Syst. 3: 721, 1826
Epidendrum crenatum Vell., Fl. Flum. 9: t. 6, 1836
Ionopsis tenera Lindl., Bot. Reg. 22: t. 1904, 1836
o Ionopsis paniculata Lindl., Bot. Reg. 22: sub. t. 1904, 1836
Cybelion utriculariae Sprengel, Nom. Bot. ed. 2, 1: 458, 1840
Cybelion tenerum (Lindl.) Steudel, Nom. Bot. ed. 2, 1: 458, 1840
Ionopsis gardneri Lindl., Paxt. Flow. Gard. 2: 13, 1851
Ionopsis pallidiflora (Hook.) Lindl., Paxt. Flow. Gard. 2: 12, 1851
Ionopsis zonalis Lindl. & Paxton, Paxt. Flow. Gard. 2: 13, 1851
Epidendrum calcaratum Sessé & Mocino, Fl. Mex. ed. 2: 201, 1894
o **Ipsea speciosa** Lindl., Gen. Sp. Orch. Pl.: 124, 1831
BM 5701
Sri Lanka, S. India – T
Pachystoma speciosum (Lindl.) Rchb.f., Bonpl. 3: 250, 1855
Spathoglottis speciosa (Lindl.) U.C. Pradhan, Ind. Orch. 2: 700, 1979
o **Isabelia virginalis** Barb. Rodr., Gen. & Sp. Orch. 1: 76 cum Tab., 1877
BM 8787
Brazil – E
Jumellea fragrans (Thouars) Schltr., Orchideen: 609, 1914
BM 7161
Mascarene Is. – E
o Angraecum fragrans Thouars, Orch. Iles Afr.: t. 54, 1822
Aerobion fragrans (Thouars) Kaempf. ex Sprengel, Syst. 3: 679, 1826
Jumellea saggittata H. Perr, Not. Syst. 7: 52, 1938
BM 8758
Madagascar – E
o Angraecum gracilipes Rolfe, Bot. Mag.: t. 8758, 1918
Kalopternix sophronites (Linden & Rchb.f.) Garay & Dunsterv., Venez. Orch. Ill. 6: 40, 1976
BM 6314
Venezuela, Ecuador, Peru – 1200–2600 m – E
o Epidendrum sophronitis Linden & Rchb.f., Gard. Chron.: 655, 1857
o **Kefersteinia graminea** (Lindl.) Rchb.f., Bot. Zeit. 10: 634, 1852
BM 5046
Venezuela, Colombia, Ecuador, Peru – E
Zygopetalum gramineum Lindl., Bot. Reg. 30: Misc. p. 10, 1844
o **Koellensteinia graminea** (Lindl.) Rchb.f., Walp. Ann. 6: 552, 1863
BM 6338
Venezuela, Colombia, Peru, Bolivia, Brazil, Surinam, Guyana – E
Maxillaria graminea Lindl., Bot. Reg. 21: sub. t. 1802, 1836
Promenaea graminea Lindl., Bot. Reg. 29: Misc. p. 13, 1843
Aganisia graminea (Lindl.) Benth. & Hook.f., J. Linn. Soc. 28: 321, 1880
Koellensteinia ionoptera Linden & Rchb.f., Gard. Chron.: 1431, 1871
BM 7270
Peru – E
o Aganisia ionoptera Nicholson, Dict. Gard. 1: 35, 1885
o **Lacaena spectabilis** (Klotzsch) Rchb.f., Bonpl. 2: 92, 1854
BM 6516
Mexico, Guatemala, El Salvador, Nicaragua, Costa Rica – E
Nauenia spectabilis Klotzsch, Allg. Gartenz.: 193, 1853
Lacaena nicaraguensis L.O. Williams, Fieldiana 31 (1): 41, 1964
o **Laelia albida** Lindl. & Bateman, Bot. Reg. 25: Misc. p. 2. t. 54, 1839
BM 3957
Mexico – 1200–2400 m – E
Laelia discolor Rich. & Galeotti, Ann. Sc. Nat. s. 3, 3: 23, 1845
Cattleya albida (Lindl. & Bateman) Beer, Prakt. Orch.: 208, 1854
Bletia albida (Lindl. & Bateman) Rchb.f., Walp. Ann. 6: 428, 1862
o **Laelia anceps** Lindl., Bot. Reg. 21: t. 1751, 1835
BM 3804
Mexico, Honduras – E, L
Laelia anceps var. barkeriana Lindl., Bot. Reg. 22: t. 1947, 1837
Laelia barkeriana Knowles & Westc., Fl. Cabin: 63, 1837
Amalias anceps (Lindl.) Hoffsgg., Linnaea 16: 228, 1842
Cattleya anceps (Lindl.) Beer, Prakt. Stud. Orch.: 208, 1854
Bletia anceps (Lindl.) Rchb.f., Walp. Ann. 6: 418, 1862
o **Laelia autumnalis** Lindl., Gen. Sp. Orch. Pl.: 115, 1831
BM 3817
Mexio, Guatemala – 1500–2400 m – E, L
Bletia autumnalis (Lindl.) Llave & Lex., Nov. Veg. Descr.: 19, 1825
Cattleya autumnalis (Lindl.) Beer, Prakt. Orch.: 208, 1854
Laelia gouldiana Rchb.f., Gard. Chron.: 41, 1888

○ **Laelia cinnabarina** Bateman ex Lindl., Sert. Orch.: t. 28, 1838
BM 4302
Brazil - E, L
Amalias cinnabarina (Bateman ex Lindl.) Hoffsgg., Verz. Orch.: 37, 1842
Cattleya cinnabarina (Bateman ex Lindl.) Beer, Prakt. Stud. Orch.: 209, 1854
Bletia cinnabarina (Bateman ex Lindl.) Rchb.f., Walp. Ann. 6: 430, 1862
Laelia crispa (Lindl.) Rchb.f., Fl. Serres 9: 102, 1853
BM 3910
Brazil - 750-1100 m - E, L
○ Cattleya crispa Lindl., Bot. Reg. 14: t. 1172, 1828
Bletia crispa (Lindl.) Rchb.f., Walp. Ann. 6: 423, 1862
Laelia elegans (Morren) Rchb.f., Allg. Gartenz. 23: 242, 1855
BM 4700
Brazil - E
○ Cattleya elegans Morren, Ann. Gand. 4: 93, t. 185, 1848
Bletia elegans (Morren) Rchb.f., Walp. Ann. 6: 427, 1862
Laelia gigantea Warner, Proc. Roy. Hort. Soc. 2: 247, 1862
Laelia purpurata var. brysiana Du Buysson, Orchid.: 362, 1878
Laelia devoniensis hort., Fl. Mag. n.s.: sub.t. 437, 1881
Laelia pachystele Rchb.f., Gard. Chron.: 596, 1888
× Laeliocattleya elegans (Morren) Rolfe, Gard. Chron: 619, 1889
× Laeliocattleya pachystele (Rchb.f.) Rolfe ex Williams, Orch. Grow. Man. ed. 7: 459, 1894
× Laeliocattleya lindenii hort., Lindenia. 10: 33 t. 447, 1894
× Laeliocattleya sayana L. Linden, J. Orch. 5: 220, 1894
× Laeliocattleya schulziana L. Linden, Lindenia 11: 21 t. 489, 1895
○ **Laelia furfuracea** Lindl., Bot. Reg. 25: t. 26, 1839
BM 3810
Mexico - 2200-3000 m - E
Cattleya furfuracea (Lindl.) Beer, Prakt. Orch.: 210, 1854
Bletia furfuracea (Lindl.) Rchb.f., Walp. Ann. 6: 428, 1862
○ **Laelia grandis** Lindl., Paxt. Flow. Gard. 1: 60 fig. 38, 1850
BM 5553
Brazil (Bahia) - E
Bletia grandis (Lindl.) Rchb.f., Walp. Ann. 6: 424, 1862
○ **Laelia jongheana** Rchb.f., Flora 55: 158, 1872
BM 6038
Brazil - E
○ **Laelia longipes** Rchb.f., Xen. Orch. 2: 59, 1863
BM 7541
Brazil - L
Bletia longipes Rchb.f., Xen. Orch. 2: 59, 1863
Laelia lucasiana Rolfe, Orch. Rev. 1: 265, 1893
Laelia perrinii Lindl., Bot. Reg. 28: sub.t. 62, 1842
BM 3711
Brazil - E
Cattleya perrinii Lindl., Bot. Reg. 24: t. 2, 1838
○ Cattleya intermedia var. angustifolia Hook., Bot. Mag.: t. 3711, 1839
Cattleya integerrima var. angustifolia Hook., Cen. Orch. 33: t. 30, 1846
Bletia perrinii (Lindl.) Rchb.f., Walp. Ann. 6: 421, 1862
Laelia pumila (Hook.) Rchb.f., Fl. Serres 9: 102, 1853
BM 3656, BM 5498
Brazil - 600-900 m - E
○ Cattleya pumila Hook., Bot. Mag.: t. 3656, 1838
Cattleya marginata Paxton, Mag. Bot. 10: 263, cum t., 1843
Cattleya pinellii Lindl., Bot. Reg. 30: t. 5 fig. 1 & text. n. 9, 1844
Cattleya spectabilis Paxton, the Florist 3, 89 & 91 cum t., 1850
Cattleya pinellii var. marginata Beer, Prakt. Stud. Orch.: 214, 1854
○ Laelia praestans Rchb.f., Allg. Gartenz. 25: 336, 1857
Bletia praestans (Rchb.f.) Rchb.f., Walp. Ann. 6: 425, 1862
Bletia pumila (Hook.) Rchb.f., Walp. Ann. 6: 421, 1862
Laelia rubescens Lindl., Bot. Reg. 26: Misc.p. 17 t. 41, 1840
BM 4099, BM 4905
Mexico, Guatemala, El Salvador, Nicaragua, Costa Rica, Panama - E, L
○ Laelia acuminata Lindl., Bot. Reg. 27: Misc.p. 17 t. 24, 1841
○ Laelia peduncularis Lindl., Bot. Reg. 28: Misc. p. 9, 1842
Laelia pubescens Lemaire, Jard. Fleur. Misc.p. 9, 1852
Laelia violacea Rchb.f., Bonpl. 2: 98, 1854
Cattleya acuminata (Lindl.) Beer, Prakt. Stud. Orch.: 208, 1854
Cattleya peduncularis (Lindl.) Beer, Prakt. Stud. Orch.: 213, 1854
Cattleya rubescens (Lindl.) Beer, Prakt. Stud. Orch.: 214, 1854
Bletia rubescens (Lindl.) Rchb.f., Walp. Ann. 6: 425, 1862
Bletia peduncularis (Lindl.) Rchb.f., Walp. Ann. 6: 426, 1862
Bletia violacea (Rchb.f.) Rchb.f., Walp. Ann. 6: 426, 1862
Bletia acuminata (Lindl.) Rchb.f., Walp. Ann. 6: 427, 1862
Laelia speciosa (Kunth) Schltr., Orchideen: 233, 1914
BM 5667
Mexico - E
Bletia speciosa Kunth, Nov. Gen. & Sp. 1: 342, 1816
? Bletia grandiflora Llave & Lex., Nov. Veg. Descr.: 17, 1825
? Laelia grandiflora Lindl., Gen. Sp. Orch. Pl.: 115, 1831
○ Laelia majalis Lindl., Bot. Reg. 25: Misc.p. 35, 1839
Cattleya grahami Lindl., Gen. Sp. Orch. Pl.: 116, 1841
Cattleya majalis (Lindl.) Beer, Prakt. Stud. Orch.: 212, 1854
Laelia majalis var. alba Dimmock, Am. Gard. 22: 398, 1901
Laelia grandiflora var. alba hort. ex Orch. Rev. 9: 202 & 312, 1901
○ **Laelia xanthina** Lindl. ex Hook., Bot. Mag.: t. 5144, 1859
BM 5144
Brazil (Bahia, Espirito Santo) - E
? Laelia virens Lindl., Bot. Reg. 30: Misc.p. 1, 1844
Bletia xanthina (Lindl. ex Hook.) Rchb.f., Walp. Ann. 6: 425, 1862
Laelia wetmorei Ruschi, Bol. Mus. Biol. Prof. Mello-Leitao, S. Bot. No. 29: 1, 1970
Lemboglossum bictoniense (Bateman ex Lindl.) Halbinger, Orquidea (Méx.) 9 (2): 348, 1984
BM 3812
Mexico, Guatemala, El Salvador - 1500-1800 m - E, T
Cyrtochilum bictoniense Bateman, Orch. Mex. & Guat.: t. 6, 1838
○ Zygopetalum africanum Hook., Bot. Mag.: t. 3812, 1840
Odontoglossum bictoniense (Bateman) Lindl., Bot. Reg. 26: t. 66, 1840
Cymbiglossum bictoniense (Bateman) Halbinger, Orquidea (Méx.) 9 (1), 1983
Lemboglossum cervantesii (Llave & Lex.) Halbinger, Orquidea (Méx.) 9 (2): 348, 1984
BM 4923
Mexico, Guatemala, El Salvador - 1500-3000 m - E
Odontoglossum cervantesii Llave & Lex., Nov. Veg. Descr. 2: 34, 1825
○ Odontoglossum membranaceum Lindl., Sert. Orch.: sub.t. 25, 1838
Odontoglossum cervantesii var. membranaceum Lindl., Fol. Orch. Odontoglossum: 10, 1852
Oncidium cervantesii (Llave & Lex.) Beer, Prakt. Stud. Orch.: 283, 1854
Oncidium membranaceum (Lindl.) Beer, Prakt. Stud. Orch.: 283, 1854
Cymbiglossum cervantesii (Llave & Lex.) Halbinger, Orquidea (Méx.) 9 (1), 1983
Lemboglossum cordatum (Lindl.) Halbinger, Orquidea (Méx.) 9 (2): 349, 1984
BM 4878
Mexico, Guatemala, El Salvador, Honduras, Nicaragua, Costa Rica, Venezuela - up to 2500 m - E
Odontoglossum cordatum Lindl., Bot. Reg. 24: Misc.p. 50, 1838
○ Odontoglossum maculatum Lindl. sensu Hook., Bot. Mag.: t. 4878, 1855
Odontoglossum hookeri Lemaire, Ill. Hort. 3: Misc.p. 41, 1856
Odontoglossum lueddemannii Regel, Gartenfl. 8: 353, 1859
Cymbiglossum cordatum (Lindl.) Halbinger, Orquidea (Méx.) 9 (1), 1983
Lemboglossum maculatum (Llave & Lex.) Halbinger, Orquidea (Méx.) 9 (2): 349, 1984
BM 6455
Mexico, Guatemala - up to 3000 m - E
○ Odontoglossum maculatum Llave & Lex., Nov. Veg. Descr. 2: 35, 1825
Odontoglossum anceps Lemaire, Ill. Hort. 3: Misc. 45, 1825
Brassia oestlundiana L.O. Williams, Ceiba 2 (4): 238, 1951
Cymbiglossum maculatum (Llave & Lex.) Halbinger, Orquidea (Méx.) 9 (1), 1983
Lemboglossum majale (Rchb.f.) Halbinger, Orquidea (Méx.) 9 (2): 349, 1984
BM 8718
Guatemala - up to 2600 m - E
Odontoglossum majale Rchb.f., Flora 69: 550, 1886
○ Odontoglossum platycheilum Weathers, Gard. Chron.: 587 fig. 1892
Cymbiglossum majale (Rchb.f.) Halbinger, Orquidea (Méx.) 9 (1), 1983
Leochilus oncidioides Knowles & Westc., Fl. Cabin. 2: 143, 1838
BM 3843
Mexico, Guatemala, El Salvador, Honduras, Nicaragua, Costa Rica, Panama to Ecuador - E
○ Oncidium macrantherum Hook., Bot. Mag.: t. 3843, 1841
Leochilus scriptus Rchb.f., Xen. Orch. 1: 15 t. 6, 1854
Cryptosaccus scriptus (Rchb.f.) Scheidw., Allg. Gartenz.: 101, 1834
Oncidium scriptum (Rchb.f.) Rchb.f., Walp. Ann. 6: 772, 1863
Leochilus major Schltr., Fedde Rep. Beih. 15: 209, 1918
Leochilus powellii Schltr., Fedde Rep. Beih. 17: 81, 1922
Leochilus retusus Schltr., Fedde Rep. Beih. 19: 256, 1923
○ **Lepanthes calodictyon** Hook., Bot. Mag.: t. 5259, 1861
BM 5259
Colombia, Ecuador - E

○ **Lepanthes sanguinea** Hook., Bot. Mag.: t. 4112, 1844
BM 4112
Jamaica - 800–1400 m - E

Leptotes bicolor Lindl., Bot. Reg. 19: t. 1625, 1833
BM 3734
Brazil (Organ M.), Paraguay - E
Leptotes serrulata Lindl., Sert. Orch.: t. 11, 1838
○ Leptotes bicolor var. glaucophylla Hook., Bot. Mag.: t. 3734, 1840
Leptotes glaucophylla Hoffsgg., Verz. Orch.: 54, 1842
Tetramicra bicolor (Lindl.) Benth., J. Linn. Soc. 18: 314, 1881
Tetramicra serrulata (Lindl.) Benth. & Hook. f., Gen. Plant. 3 (2): 533, 1893

Leucohyle subulata (Sw.) Schltr., Orchideen: 469, 1914
BM 5949
Mexico, Guatemala, Honduras, El Salvador, Costa Rica, Panama, W. Indies, Colombia, Peru - E
Epidendrum subulatum Sw., Prodr. Veg. Ind. Occ.: 123, 1788
Cymbidium subulatum (Sw.) Sw., Nov. Act. Upsal. 6: 73, 1799
○ Trichopilia hymenantha Rchb. f., Bonpl. 2: 90, 1854
Leucohyle warscewiczii Klotzsch, Ind. Sem. Hort. Berol. App., 1854
Trichopilia subulata (Sw.) Rchb. f., Flora 48: 278, 1865
Trichopilia jamaicensis Fawcett & Rendle, J. Bot. 48: 107, 1910

Liparis atrosanguinea Ridley, J. Str. Br. Roy. As. Soc. 39: 71, 1903
BM 8195
Malaya, Vietnam, Sumatra - T
○ Liparis tabularis Rolfe, Kew Bull.: 68, 1908
Liparis conspicua J. J. Smith, Bull. Buitenz. 3 s. 10: 48, 1928
Liparis tixieri Guillaumin, Bull. Mus. Paris 2 s. 33, 4: 434, 1961
Liparis macrantha auct. non Hook. f. nec. Rolfe; Cumberlege, Nat. Hist. Bull. Siam Soc. 20 (3): 163, 1963

Liparis lilifolia (L.) L. C. Rich. ex Lindl., Bot. Reg. 2: Pl. 882, 1825
BM 2004
N. America - T
Ophrys lilifolia L., Sp. Pl. 2: 946, 1753
Ophrys trifolia Walter, Fl. Carol.: 221, 1788
○ Malaxis lilifolia (L.) Sw., Kongl. Vet. Akad. Handl. 21: 235, 1800
Leptorchis lilifolia (L.) Kuntze, Rev. Gen. 2: 671, 1891

Liparis nigra Seidenf., Bot. Tidsskr. 65: 129 fig. 19, 1970
BM 8797
China, Hong Kong, Taiwan - T
○ Liparis macrantha Rolfe, Hemsley Ann. Bot. 9: 156, 1895 (nomen illeg.)
non Liparis macrantha Hook. f., Ic. Pl.: t. 1854, 1889
non Liparis macrantha auct., Cumberlege Nat. Hist. Bull. Siam Soc. 20 (3): 163, 1963

Liparis reflexa (R. Br.) Lindl., Bot. Reg. 11: sub. t. 882, 1825
BM 2709
Australia (S. Queensland, New South Wales) - T
Cymbidium reflexum R. Br., Prodr. Fl. Nov. Holl.: 331, 1810
○ Liparis foliosa Lindl., Bot. Reg.: t. 882, 1825
Sturmia reflexa (R. Br.) F. Muell., Fragm. Phyt. Austr. 2: 72, 1860

○ **Liparis tricallosa** Rchb. f., Gard. Chron.: 684, 1879
BM 7804
Malaya, Sumatra, Borneo, Philippines - T
Liparis venosa Ridley, J. Linn. Soc. 24: 350, 1888
Leptorchis tricallosa (Rchb. f.) Kuntze, Rev. Gen. 2: 671, 1891
Leptorchis venosa (Ridley) Kuntze, Rev. Gen. 2: 671, 1891

○ **Liparis walkeriae** Graham, Edinb. N. Phil. J.: 194, 1836
BM 3770
Sri Lanka, India - T

Liparis wightiana Thwaites, Enum. Pl. Zeyl.: 295, 1861
BM 5529
Sri Lanka, India - T
○ Liparis atropurpurea Wight, Ic.: t. 904, 1844/45
Liparis trimenii Ridley, J. Linn. Soc. 24: 350, 1888
Leptorchis wightiana (Thwaites) Kuntze, Rev. Gen. 2: 671, 1891

Listrostachys pertusa (Lindl.) Rchb. f., Bot. Zeit. 10: 930, 1852
BM 4782
Sierra Leone, Liberia, Ivory Coast, Ghana, S. Nigeria, E. Cameroun, Principe, Gabon, Zaire - E
○ Angraecum pertusum Lindl., Cat. Talb.: 147, 1837
Listrostachys jenischiana Rchb. f., Bot. Zeit. 10: 930, 1852
Listrostachys behnickiana Kraenzlin, Notizbl. Bot. Gart. Berl. 5: 122, 1909

○ **Lockhartia elegans** Hook., Bot. Mag.: t. 2715, 1827
BM 2715
Venezuela, Trinidad, Guyana, Brazil - E
Fernandezia elegans (Hook.) Lodd., Bot. Cab.: t. 1212, 1827
Lockhartia obtusifolia Regel, Ann. Sc. Nat. S. 2, 6: 378, 1856

Lockhartia oerstedii Rchb. f., Bot. Zeit. 10: 767, 1852
BM 5592
Mexico, Guatemala, Honduras, Nicaragua, Costa Rica, Panama - up to 2700 m - E
Lockhartia verrucosa Rchb. f., Hamb. Gartenz. 15: 53, 1859
Lockhartia lamellosa Rchb. f., Hamb. Gartenz. 21: 300, 1865
○ Fernandezia robusta Bateman, Bot. Mag.: t. 5592, 1866
Lockhartia robusta (Bateman) Schltr., Fedde Rep. 3: 82, 1906

Ludisia discolor (Ker-Gawler) A. Rich., Dict. Class. Hist. Nat. 7: 437, 1825
BM 2055, BM 7486
China, Thailand, Vietnam, Malaya - T
○ Goodyera discolor Ker-Gawler, Bot. Reg. 4: t. 271, 1818
Gonogona discolor (Ker-Gawler) Link, Enum. Pl. Hort. Berol. 2: 369, 1822
Myoda rufescens Lindl., Bot. Reg. 19: sub. t. 1618, 1833
Dicrophylla elegans Raf., Fl. Tellur. 4: 39, 1838
Haemaria discolor (Ker-Gawler) Lindl., Gen. Sp. Orch. Pl.: 490, 1840
Neottia discolor (Ker-Gawler) Steudel, Nom. ed. 2, 2: 189, 1841
Ludisia odorata Blume, Coll. Orch. Arch. Ind. Jap.: 114 t. 34 fig. 2, 1858
Ludisia furetii Blume, Coll. Orch. Arch. Ind. Jap.: 114 t. 34 fig. 3, 1858
Anoectochilus dawsonianus Low ex Rchb. f., Gard. Chron.: 1038, 1868
Haemaria discolor var. dawsoniana (Low ex Rchb. f.) Rchb. f., Gard. Chron.: 321, 1872
Haemaria otletae Rolfe, Ill. Hort. 38: 31 t. 524, 1891
○ Haemaria dawsoniana Hook. f., Bot. Mag.: t. 7486, 1896
Haemaria merrillii Ames, Phil. J. Sci. 2: 315, 1907
Haemaria dawsoniana (Low ex Rchb. f.) Hasselb., Bail. Stand. Cycl. Hort. 3: 1426, 1915
Haemaria pauciflora Gagnepain, Bull. Soc. Bot. Fr. 80: 349, 1933
Haemaria petelotii Gagnepain, Bull. Soc. Bot. Fr. 80: 349, 1933
Odontochilus petelotii (Gagnepain) Tang & Wang, Act. Phytotax. Peking 1, 1: 71, 1951
Anoectochilus petelotii (Gagnepain) Seidenf., Contr. Rev. Orch. Fl. Camb. Laos & Vietnam 1: 7, 1975

○ **Lueddemannia pescatorei** (Lindl.) Linden & Rchb. f., Bonpl. 2: 281, 1854
BM 7123
Venezuela, Colombia, Ecuador, Peru - 1000–1300 m - E
Cycnoches pescatorei Lindl., Paxt. Flow. Gard. 1: 123, 1850
Acineta glauca Linden ex Lindl., Paxt. Flow. Gard. 1: 123, 1850
Lueddemannia lehmanni Rchb. f., Gard. Chron.: 685, 1880
Lueddemannia triloba Rolfe, Kew Bull.: 283, 1895
Lueddemannia vyvereana Schltr., Orchis 6: 113, 1912

Luisia platyglossa Rchb. f., Walp. Ann. 6: 622, 1861
BM 3648
Assam, Burma (Moulmein), Andaman Is., Thailand, Laos - E
○ Cymbidium triste sensu Hook., Bot. Mag.: t. 3648, 1839 (non Roxb., 1814)
Luisia brachystachys var. flaveola Parish & Rchb. f., Trans. Linn. Soc. 30: 144, 1875

○ **Luisia psyche** Rchb. f., Bot. Zeit. 21: 98, 1863
BM 5558
Burma, Thailand - E
Cymbidium scarabaeiforme Parish ex Rchb. f., Gard. Chron.: 842, 1865

Lycaste aromatica (Graham ex Hook.) Lindl., Bot. Reg. 29: Misc. p. 16, 1843
BM 9231
Belize, Guatemala, Honduras, Nicaragua - up to 1200 m - E
Maxillaria aromatica Graham ex Hook., Exot. Fl. 3: t. 214, 1826
Colax aromaticus (Graham ex Hook.) Sprengel, Syst. 4 Cur. Post.: 307, 1827
Lycaste aromatica var. maius Kunth, Gard. Chron.: 421, 1926
○ Lycaste suaveolens Summerh., Bot. Mag.: t. 9231, 1931

Lycaste barringtoniae (Smith) Lindl., Bot. Reg.: Misc. p. 43, 1844
BM 4081
Jamaica, Cuba - E
Epidendrum barringtoniae Smith, Ic. Pict.: t. 15, 1793
Dendrobium barringtoniae (Smith) Sw., Nov. Act. Upsal. 6: 82, 1799
Colax barringtoniae (Smith) Lindl. ex Sprengel, Syst. 3: 727, 1826
Maxillaria barringtoniae (Smith) Lodd., Bot. Cabin. 19: t. 1834, 1832
○ (Maxillaria ciliata Ruiz Lopez & Pavón, Fl. Peruv. syst.: 221, 1798; misidentified)

Lycaste ciliata (Ruiz Lopez & Pavón) Lindl. ex Rchb. f., Bonpl. 4: 324, 1856
BM 5706, BM 767 ns
Colombia, Ecuador, Peru, Bolivia - T, E
Maxillaria ciliata Ruiz Lopez & Pavón, Syst. Veg. Fl. Peruv. & Chil. 1: 221, 1798
Dendrobium ciliatum Pers., Syn. 2: 523, 1805 (nomen nudum)
Maxillaria fimbriata Poeppig & Endl., Nov. Gen. Sp. Pl. 1: 38 t. 62 fig. 3, 1836

Maxillaria costata Lindl., Bot. Reg. 24: Misc. 93 No. 175, 1838
Lycaste lanipes Lindl., Gard. Chron.: 212, 1842
Lycaste costata (Lindl.) Lindl., Bot. Reg. 29: Misc. 15 No. 3, 1843
Lycaste fimbriata (Poeppig & Endl.) Cogn., Fl. Bras. 3, pt. 5: 455, 1898
Lycaste lata Rolfe, Kew Bull.: 370, 1910
Misapplied names:
o Lycaste barringtoniae var. grandiflora auct. non (Smith) Lindl., Bot. Mag.: t. 5706, 1868
Lycaste mesochlaena auct. non Rchb. f., Rolfe, Orch. Rev. 1: 72, 1893
Lycaste deppei (Lodd.) Lindl., Bot. Reg. 29: Misc. p. 15, 1843
BM 3395
Mexico, Guatemala, El Salvador, Honduras, Nicaragua - E
o Maxillaria deppei Lodd., Bot. Cabin. 17: t. 1612, 1830
o **Lycaste dyeriana** Sander ex Rolfe, Kew Bull.: 195, 1898
BM 8103
Peru - E
o **Lycaste fulvescens** Hook., Bot. Mag.: t. 4193, 1845
BM 4193
Colombia, Venezuela - 1700-2000 m - L
Lycaste crocea Linden ex Lindl., Orch. Linden.: 21, 1846
Maxillaria fulvescens (Hook.) Beer, Prakt. Stud. Orch.: 265, 1854
o **Lycaste lasioglossa** Rchb. f., Gard. Chron.: 215, 1872
BM 6251
Mexico, Guatemala - 600-1100 m - T
o **Lycaste linguella** Rchb. f., Gard. Chron.: 738, 1871
BM 6303
Peru, Ecuador - up to 2000 m - T
o **Lycaste locusta** Rchb. f., Gard. Chron.: 524, 1879
BM 8020
Peru - 1500-3000 m - E, T
Lycaste longipetala (Ruiz Lopez & Pavón) Garay, Caldasia 8: 524, 1962
BM 5616
Venezuela, Colombia, Ecuador, Peru - 1200-2200 m - E
Maxillaria longipetala Ruiz Lopez & Pavón, Syst. Veg. Fl. Peruv. 1: 220, 1798
Dendrobium longipetalum (Ruiz Lopez & Pavón) Sw., Pers. Syn. Pl. 11: 523, 1807
o Lycaste gigantea Lindl., Bot. Reg. 29: Misc. p. 15, 1843
Maxillaria heynderyexii Morren, Ann. Soc. Bot. Gand. 1: 97 t. 9, 1845
Maxillaria gigantea (Lindl.) Beer, Prakt. Stud. Orch.: 265, 1854
o **Lycaste longiscapa** Rolfe ex Cooper, Orch. Rev. 38: 168, 1930
BM 9400
Ecuador - T
Lycaste macrobulbon (Hook.) Lindl., Paxt. Flow. Gard. 1: 126, 1850
BM 4228
Colombia, Venezuela - 1200-1600 m - E, L
o Maxillaria macrobulbon Hook., Bot. Mag.: t. 4228, 1846
Lycaste pleiochroma Rchb. f., Hamb. Gartenz.: 179, 1860
o **Lycaste skinneri** (Bateman ex Lindl.) Lindl., Bot. Reg. 29: Misc. p. 15-16, 1843
BM 4445
Mexico, Guatemala, Honduras, El Salvador - 1700-1800 m - E
Maxillaria skinneri Bateman ex Lindl., Bot. Reg. 26: Misc. p. 48, 1840
Maxillaria virginalis Scheidw., Bull. Acad. Roy. Sci. Brux. 9: 25, 1842
Lycaste virginalis (Scheidw.) Lindl. & Rodigas, Lindenia 4: 22: sub. t. 153, 1888
Lycaste tetragona (Lindl.) Lindl., Bot. Reg. 29: Misc. p. 64, 1843
BM 3146
Brazil - E
o Maxillaria tetragona Lindl., Bot. Reg. 17: t. 1428, 1831
o **Macodes javanica** (Blume) Hook. f., Bot. Mag.: t. 7037, 1889
BM 7037
Java - T
Argyrorchis javanica Blume, Orch. Arch. Ind. 120: t. 31 & 36, 1858
Macodes petola var. argenteo-reticulata J. J. Smith, Fl. Buitenz.: 104, 1905
o **Macodes sanderiana** (Kraenzlin) Rolfe, Kew Bull.: 47, 1896
BM 8744
Malay Archipelago, New Guinea - 300-800 m - T
Anoectochilus sanderianus Kraenzlin, Gard. Chron.: 484, 1895
Macroclinium bicolor (Lindl.) Dodson, Icones Pl. Trop., in adnot.,: pl. 937, 1984
BM 5609
Mexico, Guatemala, El Salvador, Costa Rica - up to 1700 m - E
o Notylia bicolor Lindl., Benth. Pl. Hartw.: 93, 1842
Malaxis discolor (Lindl.) Kuntze, Rev. Gen.: 673, 1891
BM 5403
Sri Lanka - T
o Microstylis discolor Lindl., Gen. Sp. Orch. Pl.: 20, 1830

Malaxis excavata (Lindl.) Kuntze, Rev. Gen. 2: 673, 1891
BM 4103
Mexico to Brazil, Bolivia, Argentina - T, E
Epidendrum umbellatum Vell., Fl. Flum. 9: t. 23, 1827
o Microstylis excavata Lindl., Bot. Reg. 24: Misc. p. 51, 1838
Microstylis hastilabia Rchb. f., Beitr. Orch. Centr.-Amer.: 101, 1866
Microstylis simillima Rchb. f., Beitr. Orch. Centr.-Amer.: 101, 1866
Cheiropterocephalus sertuliferus Barb. Rodr., Gen. & Sp. Orch. 1: 29, 1877
Malaxis simillima (Rchb. f.) Kuntze, Rev. Gen. 2: 673, 1891
Microstylis quadrangularis Cogn., Fl. Bras. 3, pt. 6: 551, 1906
Microstylis spiralipetala Cogn., Bull. Soc. Roy. Belg. 43: 302, 1906
Microstylis carpinterae Schltr., Beih. Bot. Centralbl. 36, pt. 2: 381, 1918
Microstylis paranaensis Schltr., Fedde Rep. 16: 330, 1920
Microstylis muelleri Schltr., Fedde Rep. 17: 12, 1920
Microstylis ottonis Schltr., Fedde Rep. Beih. 10: 39, 1922
Malaxis carpinterae (Schltr.) Ames, Orchid. 7: 157, 1922
Malaxis lankesteri Ames, Sched. Orch. 4: 7, 1923
Malaxis maxonii Ames, Sched. Orch. 6: 36, 1923
Microstylis sertulifera (Barb. Rodr.) Schltr., Fedde Rep. Beih. 35: 46, 1925
Malaxis uncinata Ames & C. Schweinf., Sched. Orch. 10: 15, 1930
Malaxis josephiana (Rchb. f.) Kuntze, Rev. Gen.: 673, 1891
BM 6325
Sikkim - 500-1000 m - T
o Microstylis josephiana Rchb. f., Bot. Mag.: t. 6325, 1877
Malaxis metallica (Rchb. f.) Kuntze, Rev. Gen.: 673, 1891
BM 6668
Borneo - T
o Microstylis metallica Rchb. f., Gard. Chron.: 750, 1879
Malaxis scottii (Hook. f.) Kuntze, Rev. Gen.: 673, 1891
BM 7268
Sikkim, Burma - 800-900 m - T
Microstylis calophylla Rchb. f., Gard. Chron.: 718, 1879
o Microstylis scottii Hook. f., Fl. Brit. Ind. 5: 687, 1890
o **Masdevallia attenuata** Rchb. f., Gard. Chron.: 834, 1871
BM 6273
Costa Rica, Panama - up to 1400 m - E
Masdevallia laucheana Kraenzlin ex Woolward, Gen. Masdevallia: t. 19, 1896
Masdevallia caudata Lindl., Gen. Sp. Orch. Pl.: 193, 1833
BM 6372
Costa Rica, Venez., Colombia, Ecuador, Peru - up to 2700 m - E
o Masdevallia shuttleworthii Rchb. f., Gard. Chron.: 170, 1875
Masdevallia klabochorum Rchb. f., Gard. Chron.: 720, 1876
Masdevallia shuttleworthii var. xanthocorys Rchb. f., Gard Chron.: 366, 1882
Masdevallia caudata var. shuttleworthii (Rchb. f.) Rchb. f., Gard. Chron.: 200, 1889
Masdevallia caudata var. gudotti Rchb. f., Gard. Chron.: 200, 1889
Masdevallia caudata var. xanthocorys (Rchb. f.) Veitch, Man. Orch. Pl. pt. 5: 29, 1889
o **Masdevallia civilis** Rchb. f. & Warsc., Bonpl. 2: 115, 1854
BM 5476
Venezuela, Colombia, Ecuador, Peru - up to 2500 m - E
Masdevallia rufolutea Lindl. ex Gard. Chron.: 292, 1853 (nomen nudum)
Masdevallia aequiloba Regel, Gartenfl. 9: 82, 1860
Masdevallia macroglossa Rchb. f., Otia Bot. Hamb. 1: 15, 1878
Masdevallia porcelliceps Rchb. f., Gard. Chron.: 10, 1883
Masdevallia fragrans Woolward, Monogr. Masdevallia: t. 18, 1896
Masdevallia sulphurea Kraenzlin, Fedde Rep. 17: 423, 1921
Masdevallia porcelliceps var. sulphurea Kraenzlin, Fedde Rep. Beih. 34: 75, 1925
Masdevallia coccinea Linden ex Lindl., Orch. Linden 5: 26, 1846
BM 5990
C. America, Colombia, Peru - 2400-2800 m - E, L
o Masdevallia lindenii André, Ill. Hort. 17: 226 t. 42, 1870
Masdevallia harryana Rchb. f., Gard. Chron.: 1421, 1871
Masdevallia venusta Schltr., Fedde Rep. Beih. 9: 62, 1921
Masdevallia corniculata Rchb. f., Gard. Chron.: 72, 1878
BM 7476
Colombia - 2500-3000 m - E
Masdevallia inflata Rchb. f., Gard. Chron.: 716, 1881
o Masdevallia corniculata var. inflata Veitch, Man. Orch. pl. 5: 37, 1889
Masdevallia calyptrata Kraenzlin, Notizbl. Bot. Gart. Berl. 1: 83, 1895
o **Masdevallia davisii** Rchb. f., Gard. Chron.: 710, 1874
BM 6190
Peru - up to 3200 m - E, L
o **Masdevallia deorsum** Rolfe, Orch. Rev. 8: 255, 1900
BM 7766
Colombia - E

○ **Masdevallia elephanticeps** Rchb. f. & Warsc., Bonpl. 2: 116, 1854
BM 7824
Colombia – E
Masdevallia elephanticeps var. pachysepala Rchb. f., Bonpl. 2: 383, 1854
Masdevallia gargantua Rchb. f., Gard. Chron.: 516, 1876
cf. Masdevallia mooreana
○ **Masdevallia ephippium** Rchb. f., Bot. Zeit.: 390, 1873
BM 6208
Colombia, Ecuador – 1800–3200 m – E
Masdevallia colibri hort., Burbidge Florist & Pomol.: 3, 1873
Masdevallia trochilus Linden & André, Ill. Hort. 21: 136, t. 180, 1874
Masdevallia acrochordonia Rchb. f., Xen. Orch. 2: 213, 1874
○ **Masdevallia estradae** Rchb. f., Gard. Chron.: 435, 1874
BM 6171
Colombia – 2000–2500 m – E
Masdevallia ludibunda Rchb. f., Gard. Chron.: 179, 1882
○ **Masdevallia ionocharis** Rchb. f., Gard. Chron.: 388, 1875
BM 6262
Peru – 2700–3000 m – E
○ **Masdevallia leontoglossa** Rchb. f., Bonpl. 3: 69, 1855
BM 7245
Venezuela, Colombia, Ecuador, Peru – E
○ **Masdevallia macrura** Rchb. f., Gard. Chron.: 240, 1874
BM 7164
Colombia, Ecuador – 2000–2500 m – E, L
Masdevallia melanopus Rchb. f., Gard. Chron.: 338, 1874 (nomen tantum)
BM 6258
N. Peru – E
Masdevallia xanthodactyla Rchb. f., Gard. Chron.: 552, 1877
○ (Masdevallia polysticta Rchb. f., Gard. Chron.: 338, 1874; misidentified)
Masdevallia militaris Rchb. f., Bonpl. 2: 115 & 283, 1854
BM 5962
Colombia, Venezuela – 3000–3500 m – E, L
○ Masdevallia ignea Rchb. f., Gard. Chron.: 1482, 1871
Masdevallia ignea var. marshalliana Rchb. f., Gard. Chron.: 571, 1872
Masdevallia coccinea Linden, Gartenfl. 25: 193, pl. 870, 1876
Masdevallia ignea var. boddaerti hort., Linden, Ill. Hort. 26: 136, t. 357, 1879
Masdevallia ignea var. stobartiana Rchb. f., Gard. Chron.: 136, 1884
Masdevallia ignea var. massangeana Will., Orch. Alb. 6: pl. 273, 1887
○ **Masdevallia mooreana** Rchb. f., Gard. Chron.: 408, 1884
BM 7015
Venezuela, Colombia – 2000–2500 m – E
Masdevallia sororcula Rchb. f., Gard. Chron.: 713, 1887
cf. Masdevallia elephanticeps
○ **Masdevallia pachyura** Rchb. f., Gard. Chron.: 322, 1874
BM 8361
Ecuador – E
○ **Masdevallia peristeria** Rchb. f., Gard. Chron.: 500, 1874
BM 6159
Colombia, Ecuador – 1800–2200 m – T
○ **Masdevallia platyglossa** Rchb. f., Gard. Chron.: 552, 1882
BM 7185
Colombia – E
○ **Masdevallia polysticta** Rchb. f., Gard. Chron.: 338, 1874
BM 6368
Peru, Ecuador – 2000–2500 m – E
○ **Masdevallia schlimii** Linden ex Lindl., Orch. Linden: 5, 1846
BM 6740
Venezuela, Colombia – 2500–3100 m – E
Masdevallia polyantha Lindl., Orch. Linden: 6, 1846
Masdevallia sceptrum Rchb. f., Bonpl. 2: 283, 1854
Masdevallia urostachya Rchb. f., Gard. Chron.: 765, 1882
Masdevallia schlimii var. polyantha Woolward, Monogr. Masdevallia: t. 47, 1896
Masdevallia schlimii var. sceptrum Woolward, Monogr. Masdevallia: t. 47, 1896
○ **Masdevallia schroederiana** Veitch, Gard. Chron.: 51, 1890 (nomen nudum)
BM 7859
Costa Rica, Peru – E
Masdevallia fulvescens Rolfe, Gard. Chron.: 324 fig. 65, 1890
○ **Masdevallia tovarensis** Rchb. f., Linnaea 22: 818, 1849
BM 5505
Venezuela – E
Masdevallia candida Klotzsch & Karsten ex Rchb. f., Bonpl. 2: 23, 1854 (nomen tantum)
○ **Masdevallia veitchiana** Rchb. f., Gard. Chron.: 814, 1868
BM 5739
Peru – 3400–4000 m – E, L

○ **Masdevallia wageneriana** Linden ex Lindl., Paxt. Flow. Gard. 3: 74 fig. 267, 1852
BM 4921
Venezuela – E
○ **Maxillaria acicularis** Herbert ex Lindl., Bot. Reg. 23: sub. t. 1986, 1837
BM 4374
Brazil – E
○ **Maxillaria acutipetala** Hook., Bot. Mag.: t. 3966, 1842
BM 3966
C. America – E
Maxillaria camaridii Rchb. f., Hamb. Gartenz. 19: 547, 1863
BM 3306, BM 4141, BM 472 ns
Guatemala, Honduras, Costa Rica, Panama, W. Indies, Venezuela, Trinidad, Guyana, Surinam, Brazil, Colombia, Peru, Bolivia – E
Camaridium ochroleucum Lindl., Bot. Reg. 10: t. 84, 1824 (non Lodd., 1833)
○ Cymbidium ochroleucum (Lindl.) Lindl., Gen. & Sp. Orch.: 168, 1833
○ Ornithidium album Hook., Bot. Mag.: t. 3306, 1834
Maxillaria lutescens Scheidw., Allg. Gartenz. 7: 143, 1839
Ornithidium fragrans Rolfe, Kew Bull.: 147, 1894
Camaridium cryptopodanthum Barb. Rodr., Contr. Jard. Bot. Rio 4: 101, 1907
Camaridium affine Schltr., Fedde Rep. Beih. 17: 72, 1922
Camaridium amazonicum Schltr., Beih. Bot. Centralbl. 42, pt. 2: 135, 1925
○ **Maxillaria chrysantha** Barb. Rodr., Gen. & Sp. Orch. 1: 115, 1877
BM 8979
Brazil, Surinam – E
Maxillaria picta Rchb. f., 1853 (non Hook.)
Maxillaria galeottiana Regel, Ann. Sc. Nat. s. 4, 6: 373, 1856
Maxillaria serotina Barb. Rodr. & Regnell, Gen. & Sp. Orch. 2: 203, 1881
Maxillaria regaliana Cogn., Fl. Bras. 3, 6: 47, 1905
Maxillaria coccinea (Jacq.) L. O. Williams ex Hodge, Am. Orch. Soc. Bull. 23: 42, 1954
BM 1437
W. Indies, Venezuela, Colombia – E
Epidendrum coccineum Jacq., Enum. Pl. Carib.: 29, 1760
Epidendrum sessile Sw., Prodr. Veg. Ind. Occ.: 122, 1788
○ Cymbidium coccineum (Jacq.) Sw., Nov. Act. Upsal. 6: 70, 1799
Ornithidium coccineum (Jacq.) Salisb., Trans. Hort. Soc. 1: 293, 1812
Ornithidium vestitum Rchb. f., Ber. Deutsch. Bot. Ges. 3: 276, 1885
○ **Maxillaria cucullata** Lindl., Bot. Reg. 26: t. 12, 1840
BM 3945
Mexico, Belize, Guatemala, El Salvador, Honduras, Costa Rica, Nicaragua, Panama – E
Maxillaria rhombea Lindl., Bot. Reg. 26: sub. t. 12, 1840
Maxillaria meleagris Lindl., Bot. Reg. 30: Misc. 3, 1844
Maxillaria lindeniana A. Rich. & Galeotti, Ann. Sc. Nat. 3, 3: 24, 1845
Maxillaria atrata Rchb. f., Beitr. Orch. Centr. Am. 31: t. 6 figs. 1 1–3, 1866
Maxillaria obscura Lindl. & Rchb. f., Beitr. Orch. Centr. Am. 31, 1866
Maxillaria puncto-striata Rchb. f., Linnaea 41: 28, 1877
Maxillaria praestans Rchb. f., Gard. Chron. 1: 566, 1885
Maxillaria curtipes Hook., Ic. Pl.: t. 384, 1841
BM 7533
Mexico, Guatemala, Honduras, Nicaragua, Costa Rica – up to 3000 m – E
○ Maxillaria houtteana Rchb. f., Hamb. Gartenz. 14: 212, 1858
Camaridium xylobiichilum Kraenzlin, Vidensk. Medd. Nat. Copenhagen 71: 174, 1920
○ **Maxillaria elatior** (Rchb. f.) Rchb. f., Walp. Ann. 6: 532, 1863
BM 9206
Mexico, Guatemala, Honduras, Costa Rica – E
Dicrypta elatior Rchb. f., Linnaea 18: 403, 1844
Maxillaria triangularis Lindl., Bot. Reg. 31: Misc. p. 9, 1845
○ **Maxillaria fletcheriana** Rolfe, Gard. Chron.: 258, 1913
BM 8949
S. Peru, Ecuador, Bolivia – 700–2800 m – E, T
○ **Maxillaria fucata** Rchb. f., Gard. Chron.: 616, 1886
BM 9376
Ecuador – 2200–2800 m – E, T
Maxillaria hubschii Rchb. f., Gard. Chron.: 136, 1888
○ **Maxillaria lepidota** Lindl., Ann. Nat. Hist. 15: 38, 1845
BM 9065
Venezuela, Colombia, Ecuador – 1500–2000 m – E, T
Maxillaria pertusa Lindl. ex Rchb. f., Gard. Chron.: 168, 1878
Maxillaria saxicola Schltr., Fedde Rep. Beih. 24: 94, 1924
○ **Maxillaria parkeri** Hook., Bot. Mag.: t. 2729, 1827
BM 2729
Venezuela, Guyana, Surinam, Brazil, Amazonas, Peru – E
Colax parkeri (Hook.) A. Sprengel, Tent.: 28, 1828

Menadena parkeri (Hook.) Raf., Fl. Tellur. 2: 98, 1836
Maxillaria hirtilabia Lindl., J. Hort. Soc. Lond. 8: 132, 1853
Maxillaria lorifolia Rchb. f., Bonpl. 2: 92, 1854
Maxillaria kegelii Rchb. f., Linnaea 41: 127, 1877
Maxillaria loretoensis C. Schweinf., Am. Orch. Soc. Bull. 13: 92, 1944
○ **Maxillaria picta** Hook., Bot. Mag.: t. 3154, 1832
BM 3154
Brazil – E
? Epidendrum uniflorum Vell., Fl. Flum. Ic. 9: t. 34, 1827
Maxillaria leucocheila Hoffsgg., Verz. Orch.: 53, 1843
Maxillaria kreysigii Kuntze ex Rchb. f., Linnaea 25: 230, 1853
Maxillaria fuscata Klotzsch ex Rchb. f., Walp. Ann. 6: 520, 1863
Maxillaria monoceros Klotzsch ex Rchb. f., Walp. Ann. 6: 520, 1863
Maxillaria rupestris Barb. Rodr., Orch. Nov. 2: 199, 1882
○ **Maxillaria porphyrostele** Rchb. f., Gard. Chron.: 168, 1873
BM 6477
Brazil – E
○ **Maxillaria pumila** Hook., Bot. Mag.: t. 3613, 1837
BM 3613
Brazil, Guyana – E, L
○ **Maxillaria sanderiana** Rchb. f., Sander: Reichenbachia 1: 57 t. 25, 1888
BM 7518
Ecuador, Peru – 1200–2400 m – E, L
Maxillaria setigera Lindl., Bot. Reg. 31: Misc. p. 30, 1845
BM 4434
Guyana, Venezuela, Colombia, Brazil – E
○ Maxillaria leptosepala Hook., Bot. Mag.: t. 4434, 1849
Maxillaria callichroma Rchb. f., Bonpl. 2: 16, 1854
Maxillaria leptosepala var. subintegerrima Regel, Ann. Sci. Nat. s. 4, 6: 374, 1856
Maxillaria caloglossa Rchb. f., Gard. Chron.: 654, 1878
Maxillaria setigera var. angustifolia Klinge, Act. Hort. Petrop. 17: 139, 1898
Maxillaria variabilis Bateman ex Lindl., Bot. Reg. 23: sub. t. 1986, 1837
BM 3614
Mexico, Guatemala, Honduras, El Salvador, Nicaragua, Costa Rica, Panama, Guyana – 1000–2000 m – E
○ Maxillaria henchmanni Hook., Bot. Mag.: t. 3614, 1837
Maxillaria angustifolia Hook., Ic. Pl. 4: t. 348, 1841
Maxillaria lyonii Lindl., Bot. Reg. n. s. 8: Misc. 17, 1845
Maxillaria revoluta Klotzsch, Allg. Gartenz. 20: 186, 1852
Maxillaria chiriquensis Schltr., Fedde Rep. Beih. 17: 68, 1922
Maxillaria panamensis Schltr., Fedde Rep. Beih. 17: 70, 1922
Maxillaria costaricensis Schltr., Fedde Rep. Beih. 19: 232, 1923
○ **Maxillaria venusta** Linden & Rchb. f., Bonpl. 2: 280, 1854
BM 5296
Venezuela, Colombia – 1000–1200 m – E
Maxillaria anatamorum Rchb. f., Bot. Zeit. 10: 935, 1852
Mendoncella grandiflora (A. Rich.) A. Hawkes, Orquidea (Méx.) 25: 7, 1964
BM 5567
Mexico, Guatemala, Costa Rica, Panama, Colombia – E
Galeottia grandiflora A. Rich., Ann. Sci. Nat. s. 3, 3: 25, 1845
○ Batemania grandiflora (A. Rich.) Rchb. f., Bonpl. 4: 323, 1856
Huntleya grandiflorum (A. Rich) Lam., Ill. Hort. 15: Misc. 59, 1868
Zygopetalum grandiflorum (A. Rich) Benth. & Hook., ex Hemsl., Godm. & Salv. Biol. Centr.-Am. Bot. 3: 251, 1883
Mendoncella marginata (Rchb. f.) Garay, Orquideologia 8 (1): 32, 1973
BM 4766, BM 5582
Venezuela, Colombia, Ecuador – E
Warscewiczella marginata Rchb. f., Bot. Zeit. 10: 636, 1852
Warrea marginata Rchb. f., Bot. Zeit. 10: 636, 1852
Huntleya marginata hort. ex Rchb. f., Bot. Zeit. 10: 636, 1852
○ Warrea quadrata Lindl., Gard. Chron.: 647, 1853
○ Warscewiczella velata Rchb. f., Xen. Orch. 1: 60 t. 23, 1854
Zygopetalum velatum (Rchb. f.) Rchb. f., Walp. Ann. 6: 655, 1863
Zygopetalum marginatum (Rchb. f.) Rchb. f., Walp. Ann. 6: 654, 1863
Zygopetalum quadratum (Lindl.) Pfitzer, Vergl. Morph. Orch.: 58, 1881
Chondrorhyncha lipsicombiae Rolfe, Kew Bull.: 133, 1912
Chondrorhyncha marginata (Rchb. f.) P. Allen, Ann. Missouri Bot. Gard. 36: 88, 1949
Cochleanthes marginata (Rchb. f.) R. Schultes & Garay, Bot. Mus. Leafl. Harv. Univ. 18: 326, 1959
Mendoncella prainiana (Rolfe) Garay, Orquideologia 8 (1): 32, 1973
BM 8610
Peru, Venezuela – T
○ Zygopetalum prainianum Rolfe, Kew Bull.: 376, 1914

○ **Microtis media** R. Br., Prodr. Fl. Nov. Holl.: 321, 1810
BM 3378
Australia – T
○ **Microtis parviflora** R. Br., Prodr. Fl. Nov. Holl.: 321, 1810
BM 3377
Australia (New South Wales), New Zealand, New Caledonia – T
○ **Miltonia anceps** (Klotzsch) Lindl., Fol. Orch. Milt.: 3, 1853
BM 5572
Brazil – E
Odontoglossum anceps Klotzsch, Allg. Gartenz.: 250, 1851
Miltonia pinelii hort. ex Rchb. f., Xen. Orch. 1: 56 t. 21, 1854
Oncidium anceps (Klotzsch) Rchb. f., Walp. Ann. 6: 758, 1863
○ **Miltonia clowesii** Lindl., Sert. Orch.: t. 34, 1839
BM 4109
Brazil – E
Odontoglossum clowesii Lindl., Bot. Reg. 25: Misc. 133, 1839
Brassia clowesii (Lindl.) Lindl., Bot. Reg. 30: Misc. p. 7, 1844
Oncidium clowesii (Lindl.) Beer, Prakt. Stud. Orch.: 284, 1854
○ **Miltonia regnellii** Rchb. f., Linnaea 22: 851, 1848
BM 5436
Brazil – 800–1400 m – E
Oncidium regnellii (Rchb. f.) Rchb. f., Walp. Ann. 6: 760, 1863
Miltonia cereola Lemaire, Ill. Hort. 12: t. 546, 1865
○ **Miltonia spectabilis** Lindl., Bot. Reg. 23: sub. t. 1976, 1837
BM 4204
Brazil – E
Macrochilus fryanus Knowles & Westc., Fl. Cabin. 1: 93 t. 45, 1837
Oncidium spectabile (Lindl.) Beer, Prakt. Stud. Orch.: 293, 1854
Miltonia spectabilis Lindl. var. **moreliana** Henfrey, Gard. Mag. Bot. 3: 41, 1851
BM 4425
Brazil – E
Miltonia moreliana hort., Portef. Hort. 1: 195, 1847 (nomen tantum)
○ Miltonia spectabilis var. purpureo-violacea Hook., Bot. Mag.: t. 4425, 1849
Oncidium spectabile var. morelianus Beer, Prakt. Stud. Orch.: 293, 1854
Oncidium spectabile var. purpureo-violacea Beer, Prakt. Stud. Orch.: 293, 1854
Miltonia warneri Nicholson, Dict. Gard.: 369, 1886
Miltonia illustris hort., l'Orchid.: 258, 1892
Miltonioides laevis (Lindl.) Brieger & Lueckel, Die Orchidee 34 (4): 131, 1983
BM 6265
Mexico, Guatemala – E
○ Odontoglossum laeve Lindl., Bot. Reg. 30: t. 39, 1844
Oncidium laeve (Lindl.) Beer, Prakt. Stud. Orch.: 288, 1854
Odontoglossum leucomelas Rchb. f., Bot. Zeit. 22: 415, 1864
Miltonia leucomelas (Rchb. f.) Rolfe, Orch. Rev. 12: 300, 1904
Miltonia laevis (Lindl.) Rolfe, Orch. Rev. 12: 300, 1904
Miltonioides warscewiczii (Rchb. f.) Brieger & Lueckel, Die Orchidee 34 (4): 132, 1983
BM 5843
Costa Rica, Colombia, Ecuador, Peru – E
○ Miltonia warscewiczii Rchb. f., Xen. Orch. 1: 129 & 132, 1856
Oncidium fuscatum Rchb. f., Walp. Ann. 6: 763, 1863
Odontoglossum weltonii hort. ex Gard. Chron. 1: 417, 1870
Oncidium weltonii hort. ex Gartenfl. 25: 339, 1876
Miltoniopsis roezlii (Rchb. f.) Godef.-Leb., Orchidoph. 9: 145, 1889
BM 6085
Panama, Colombia, Ecuador – up to 1200 m – E
○ Odontoglossum roezlii Rchb. f., Xen. Orch. 2: 191 t. 182 I, 1873
Miltonia roezlii (Rchb. f.) Nicholson, Ill. Dict. Gard. 2: 367, 1886
Miltoniopsis vexillaria (Rchb. f.) Godef.-Leb., Orchidoph. 9: 148, 1889
BM 6037
Colombia, Ecuador – 1000–1500 m – E
○ Odontoglossum vexillarium Rchb. f., Gard. Chron.: 901, 1867
Miltonia vexillaria (Rchb. f.) Nicholson, Ill. Dict. Gard. 2: 367, 1886
Miltoniopsis warscewiczii (Rchb. f.) Garay & Dunsterv., Venez. Orch. Ill. 6: 278, 1976
BM 6163
Costa Rica – up to 2600 m – E
○ Odontoglossum warscewiczii Rchb. f., Bot. Zeit. 10: 692, 1852
Odontoglossum warscewiczianum Rchb. f. ex Hemsl., Biol. Centr.-Am. Bot. 3: 277, 1883
Miltonia endresii Nicholson, Ill. Dict. Gard. 2: 368, 1886
Miltonia superba Schltr., Fedde Rep. 3: 249, 1907
Monomeria dichroma (Rolfe) Schltr., Orchideen: 338, 1914
BM 8160
Vietnam, Laos – E
○ Bulbophyllum dichromum Rolfe, Kew Bull.: 128, 1907
Ione dichroma (Rolfe) Gagnepain, Fl. Gen. Indoch. 6: 437, 1934

Mormodes buccinator Lindl., Bot. Reg. 26: Misc. p. 10, 1840
BM 4455
Mexico to Nicaragua, S. America – E
Mormodes amazonicum Brade, Arq. Serv. Florest. Rio de Janeiro 1, No. 1: 44, 1939
○ Mormodes lentiginosa Hook., Bot. Mag.: t. 4455, 1849
Mormodes brachystachya Klotzsch, Ind. Sem. Hort. Berol., 1852
Mormodes flavida Klotzsch, Allg. Gartenz. 20: 113, 1852
Mormodes leucochila Klotzsch, Allg. Gartenz. 21: 289, 1853
Mormodes marmorea Klotzsch, Allg. Gartenz. 21: 290, 1853
Mormodes vitellina Klotzsch, Allg. Gartenz. 21: 290, 1853
Mormodes wagneriana Klotzsch, Allg. Gartenz. 21: 147, 1853
○ **Mormodes buccinator** Lindl. var. **aurantiacum** Rolfe, Ill. Hort. 39: 11 t. 144, 1892
BM 8041
Trop. America, Peru – E
○ **Mormodes cartoni** Hook., Bot. Mag.: t. 4214, 1846
BM 4214
Brazil (Sierra Nevada) – E
○ **Mormodes colossus** Rchb. f., Bot. Zeit. 10: 636, 1852
BM 5840
C. America, Costa Rica, Panama – up to 2300 m – E
Mormodes macranthum Lindl. & Paxton, Paxt. Flow. Gard. 3: 98, 1852
Mormodes wendlandii Rchb. f., Walp. Ann. 6: 581, 1861
Mormodes powellii Schltr., Fedde Rep. Beih. 17: 55, 1922
Mormodes hookeri Lemaire, Jard. Fleur 1: Misc. p. 116, 1851–54
BM 4577
Costa Rica, Panama, Colombia – E
○ Mormodes atropurpureum Hook., Bot. Mag.: t. 4577, 1851 (non Lindl.)
Mormodes barbatum Lindl. & Paxton, Paxt. Flow. Gard. 2: 57, 1851
Mormodes maculata (Klotzsch) L. O. Williams, Ceiba 1: 188, 1950
BM 3900
Mexico – E
Cyclosia maculata Klotzsch, Allg. Gartenz. 6: 306, 1838
○ Mormodes pardina Bateman, Orch. Mex. & Guat.: t. 14, 1838
Mormodes maculata (Klotzsch) L. O. Williams var. **unicolor** (Hook.) L. O. Williams, Ceiba 1: 189, 1950
BM 3879
Mexico – E
○ Mormodes pardina var. unicolor Hook., Bot. Mag.: t. 3879, 1841
○ **Mormodes ocanae** Lindl. & Rchb. f., Walp. Ann. 6: 581, 1861
BM 6496
Colombia – E
○ **Mormodes revolutum** Rolfe, Kew Bull.: 367, 1909
BM 8390
Peru – 700–1300 m – E
○ **Mormodes rolfeanum** Linden, Lindenia 7: 5 t. 289, 1891
BM 7438
Peru – E
○ **Mormodes tigrinum** Barb. Rodr., Gen. & Sp. Orch. 1: 131, 1877
BM 8597
Brazil – E
Mormodes uncium Rchb. f., Gard. Chron.: 892, 1869
BM 5802
Mexico – E
○ Mormodes greenii Hook., Bot. Mag.: t. 5802, 1869
Mormodes incisa Rchb. f., Gard. Chron.: 592, 1879 (nomen)
Myoxanthus reymondii (Karsten) Luer, Selbyana 7 (1): 49, 1982
BM 5385
Venezuela, Colombia – E
Duboisia reymondii Karsten, Allg. Gartenz. 15: 394, 1847
Dubois-reymondia palpigera Karsten, Bot. Zeit. 6: 398, 1848
○ Pleurothallis reymondii (Karsten) Rchb. f., Ann. Bot. Syst. 3: 520, 1852
Humboldtia reymondii (Karsten) Kuntze, Rev. Gen. 2: 668, 1891
Pleurothallis palpigera (Karsten) Schltr., Fedde Rep. Beih. 6: 63, 1919
Myrmecophila tibicinis (Bateman ex Lindl.) Rolfe, Orch. Rev. 25: 51, 1917
BM 4476
Mexico, Belize, Guatemala, Honduras, Nicaragua, Costa Rica – E, L
Epidendrum tibicinis Bateman ex Lindl., Bot. Reg. 24: Misc. p. 8, 1838
Schomburgkia tibicinis (Bateman ex Lindl.) Bateman, Orch. Mex. & Guat.: t. 30, 1841
○ Schomburgkia tibicinis var. grandiflora Hook., Bot. Mag.: t. 4476, 1849
Cattleya tibicinis (Bateman ex Lindl.) Beer, Prakt. Stud. Orch.: 215, 1854
Bletia tibicinis (Bateman ex Lindl.) Rchb. f., Walp. Ann. 6: 429, 1862
Laelia tibicinis (Bateman ex Lindl.) L. Williams, Darwiniana 5: 77, 1941
○ **Nanodes medusae** Rchb. f., Fl. Serres 16: 78, 1867
BM 5723
Ecuador – 1800–2200 m – E
Epidendrum medusae (Rchb. f.) Pfitzer, Nat. Pflanzenf. 6: 145 fig. 142, 1889
Epidendrum medusae (Rchb. f.) Siebert, Gartenfl.: 516, 1900
Epidendrum medusae (Rchb. f.) Schltr., Rep. Sp. Nov. Beih. 8: 137, 1921
Neolehmannia medusae (Rchb. f.) Garay, Orch. Digest 41 (1): 22, 1977
○ **Neobenthamia gracilis** Rolfe, F. T. A. 7: 102, 1898
BM 7221
Tanzania – 450–1800 m – E, L
Polystachya neobenthamia Schltr., Baum Kunene-Sambesi-Exped.: 211, 1903
Polystachya holtzeana Kraenzlin, Engl. Bot. Jahrb.: 51, 392, 1914
Neocogniauxia monophylla (Griseb.) Schltr., Urban; Symb. Antill. 7: 496, 1913
BM 6683
W. Indies – E
Trigonidium monophyllum Griseb., Fl. Brit. W. Ind.: 629, 1864
○ Laelia monophylla (Griseb.) N. E. Br., Gard. Chron.: 782, 1882
Octadesmia monophylla (Griseb.) Benth., Gen. Pl. 3: 526, 1883
Epidendrum brachyglossum Cogn., Fedde Rep. 7: 121, 1909
Neofinetia falcata (Thunb.) Hu, Rhodora 27: 107, 1925
BM 2097
Japan, Korea, Ryukyu Is. – E
Orchis falcata Thunb., Fl. Jap. 26, 1784
○ Limodorum falcatum (Thunb.) Thunb., Mus. Nat. Acad. Upsal. 9: 139, 1791
Oeceoclades falcata (Thunb.) Lindl., Gen. Sp. Orch. Pl.: 237, 1833
Angraecum falcatum (Thunb.) Lindl., Gen. Sp. Orch. Pl.: 237, 1833
Oeceoclades lindleyana Regel, Ind. Sem. Hort. Petrop.: 43, 1865
Oeceoclades lindleyi Regel, Gartenfl. 15: 70, 1866
Aerides thunbergii Miq., Ann. Mus. Bot. Ludg. Bat. 2: 205, 1866
Angorchis falcata (Thunb.) Kuntze, Rev. Gen. 2: 651, 1891
Angraecopsis falcata (Thunb.) Schltr., Orchideen: 601, 1915
Finetia falcata (Thunb.) Schltr., Beih. Bot. Centralbl. 36, Pt. 2: 140, 1918
Nipponorchis falcata (Thunb.) Masam., Mem. Fac. Sc. Agri. Taihoku Univ. 11: 592, 1934
Holcoglossum falcatum (Thunb.) Garay & Sweet, Bot. Mus. Leafl. Harv. Univ. 23: 182, 1972
Neogardneria murrayana (Gardner ex Hook.) Garay, Orquideologia 8 (1): 9 & 33, 1973
BM 3674
Brazil – E
○ Zygopetalum murrayanum Gardner ex Hook., Bot. Mag.: t. 3674, 1838
Eulophia murrayana (Gardner ex Hook.) Steudel, Nom. Bot. ed. 2, 1: 605, 1840
Promenaea florida Rchb. f., Hamb. Gartenz. 19: 12, 1863
Zygopetalum binotii De Wild., Gard. Chron.: 258, 1905
Neogardneria binotii (De Wild.) Hoehne, Arq. Bot. Estad. S. Paulo 2, pt. 4: 73, 1947
Neomoorea wallisii (Rchb. f.) Schltr., Orch. Rev. 32: 355, 1924
BM 7262
Panama, S. America, Colombia – E
Lueddemannia wallisii Rchb. f., Linnaea 41: 109, 1877
○ Moorea irrorata Rolfe, Gard. Chron.: 7, 1890 (non Lemaire)
Neomoorea irrorata (Rolfe) Rolfe, Orch. Rev. 12: 30, 1904
○ **Nephelaphyllum pulchrum** Blume, Bijdr.: 373, 1825
BM 5332
Thailand, Kampuchea, Vietnam, Malaya, Java, Philippines – T
○ **Nephelaphyllum scapigerum** Hook., Bot. Mag.: t. 5390, 1863
BM 5390
Borneo – T
Mischobulbon scapigerum (Hook.) Schltr., Fedde Rep. Beih. 1: 98, 1911
Nervilia fordii (Hance) Schltr., Engl. Bot. Jahrb. 45: 403, 1911
BM 6851
Hong Kong, S. China – T
Pogonia fordii Hance, J. Bot. 23: 247, 1885
○ Pogonia pulchella Hook. f., Bot. Mag.: t. 6851, 1885
Nervilia gammieana (Hook. f.) Schltr., Engl. Bot. Jahrb. 45: 404, 1911
BM 6671
Kashmir, Sikkim – up to 1000 m – T
○ Pogonia gammieana Hook. f., Bot. Mag.: t. 6671, 1883
Nervilia plicata (André) Schltr., Engl. Bot. Jahrb. 45: 403, 1911
BM 6125

Sikkim, Bengal, Burma, China, Laos. Vietnam, Malaya, Java, Philippines, Hong Kong, New Guinea, Australia – T
Arethusa plicata André, Bot. Rep. 5: t. 321, 1803
Cordyla discolor Blume, Bijdr.: 417, 1825
Roptrostemon discolor (Blume) Blume, Fl. Jav. Praef. 6, 1828
Epipactis plicata Roxb., Fl. Ind. 3: 454, 1832
Pogonia plicata (Roxb.) Lindl., Gen. Sp. Orch. Pl.: 415, 1840
○ Pogonia discolor (Blume) Blume, Ann. Mus. Bot. Lugd. Bat. 1: 32, 1849
? Pogonia biflora Wight, Ic. 5, 1: t. 1758, 1851
Pogonia dallachyana F. Muell. ex Benth., Fl. Austr. 6: 310, 1873
Pogonia velutina Parish & Rchb. f., Trans. Linn. Soc. 30: 142, 1874
Pogonia pulchella Parish, Mason: 186 & 201, 1883 (nomen nudum)
Nervilia dallachyana (F. Muell. ex Benth.) Schltr., Engl. Bot. Jahrb. 39: 48, 1907
Pogonia pudica Ames, Orchid. 2: 44 fig., 1908
Nervilia velutina (Parish & Rchb. f.) Schltr., Engl. Bot. Jahrb. 45: 403, 1911
? Nervilia biflora (Wight) Schltr., Engl. Bot. Jahrb. 45: 403, 1911
Nervilia discolor (Blume) Schltr., Engl. Bot. Jahrb. 45: 403, 1911
Nervilia fordii auct. non Hance, Engl. Bot. Jahrb. 45: 403, 1911
Aplostellis velutina (Parish & Rchb. f.) Ridley, Fl. Mal. Pen. 4: 204, 1924
○ **Neuwiedia griffithii** Rchb. f., Xen. Orch. 2: 215, 1874
BM 7425
Malaya, Sumatra, Borneo – T
Neuwiedia veratrifolia Blume, Tijdschr. Nat. Gesch. 1: 142, 1833
BM 7368
Malaya, Sumatra to Philippines – T
○ Neuwiedia lindleyi Rolfe, J. Linn. Soc. 25: 232 t. 48, 1889
○ **Notylia albida** Klotzsch, Allg. Gartenz.: 21, 1851
BM 6311
C. America, Panama – E
Notylia panamensis Ames, Orchid. 7: 112, 1922
Notylia barkeri Lindl., Bot. Reg. 24: Misc. p. 90, 1838
BM 8306
Mexico, Guatemala, Honduras, Nicaragua, Costa Rica, Panama – E
Notylia multiflora Hook., J. Bot. 3: 313 t. 10, 1844 (non Lindl.)
Notylia huegelii Fenzl, Denkschr. Akad. Wien 2: 255, 1850
○ Notylia trisepala Lindl., Paxt. Flow. Gard. 3: 45, 1852–53
Tridachne virens Liebm. ex Lindl. & Paxton, Paxt. Flow. Gard. 3: 45, 1852
Notylia tridachne Lindl. & Paxton, Paxt. Flow. Gard. 3: 45, 1852
Notylia bipartita Rchb. f., Xen. Orch. 1: 47, 1854
Notylia tamaulipensis Rchb. f., Hamb. Gartenz. 16: 281, 1860
Notylia guatemalensis S. Watson, Proc. Am. Acad. 22: 477, 1887 (non Schltr.)
Notylia angustilancea Schltr., Orchis 8: 135 t. 4 figs. 8–13, 1914
Notylia guatemalensis Schltr., Fedde Rep. 15: 208, 1918 (non S. Watson)
Notylia bernoullii Schltr., Beih. Bot. Centralbl. 36, Abt. 2: 502, 1918 (nomen)
Notylia pittieri Schltr., Beih. Bot. Centralbl. 36, Abt. 2: 418, 1918
Notylia turialbae Schltr., Fedde Rep. Beih. 19: 145, 1923
Notylia brenesii Schltr., Fedde Rep. Beih. 19: 249, 1923
Notylia bicolor Lindl. = Macroclinium bicolor (Lindl.) Dodson
BM 5609
○ **Oberonia acaulis** Griffith, Notul. Pl. Asiat. 3: 275–276 fig. 1, 1851
BM 5056
E. Himalaya, Assam, Thailand, Kampuchea, Laos, Vietnam – 1000–1500 m – E
Oberonia myriantha Lindl., Fol. Orch. Oberonia: 4, 1859
Oberonia sikkimensis Lindl., Fol. Orch. Oberonia: 4, 1859
Iridorchis myriantha (Lindl.) Kuntze, Rev. Gen.: 669, 1891
○ **Oberonia iridifolia** (Roxb.) Lindl., Wall. Cat. 53: n. 1948, 1829 (nomen nudum)
BM 4517
Himalaya (Nepal to Bhutan), India, Burma, Thailand, Malaysia, Philippines – E
Cymbidium iridifolium Roxb., Hort. Beng.: 63, 1814 (nomen nudum)
Malaxis iridifolia (Roxb.) Rchb. f., Walp. Ann. 6: 208, 1846
Oberonia denticulata Wight, Ic.: t. 165, 1852
Iridorchis iridiflora (Roxb.) Kuntze, Rev. Gen.: 669, 1891
Octadesmia montana (Sw.) Benth., J. Linn. Soc. 18: 311, 1881
BM 2823
Cuba, Haiti, Dominican Rep., Puerto Rico, Jamaica – 1800–2000 m – E
Epidendrum montanum Sw., Prodr. Veg. Ind. Occ.: 121, 1788
Cymbidium montanum (Sw.) Sw., Nov. Act. Upsal. 6: 72, 1799
Tetramicra montana (Sw.) Griseb., Fl. Brit. W. Ind.: 622, 1824
○ Octomeria serratifolia Hook., Bot. Mag.: t. 2833, 1828
Bletia montana (Sw.) Rchb. f., Walp. Ann. 6: 445, 1862
○ **Octomeria graminifolia** (L.) R. Br., Hort. Kew ed. 2, 5: 211, 1813
BM 2764
W. Indies, Nicaragua – 200–900 m – E
Epidendrum graminifolium L., Sp. Pl. ed. 2: 1363, 1763
Dendrobium graminifolium (L.) Willd., Sp. Pl. 4: 135, 1806
○ × **Odontioda heatonensis** hort., Gard. Chron.: 158, 1906
BM 8133
= Cochlioda sanguinea Benth & Hock. f. × Odontoglossum cirrhosum Lindl.
○ × **Odontioda vuylstekeae** hort., Gard. Chron.: 360, 1904
BM 7990
= Odontoglossum nobile Rchb. f. × Cochlioda noetzliana Rolfe
Odontoglossum cariniferum Rchb. f., Bot. Zeit. 10: 638, 1852
BM 4919
Costa Rica, Panama, Venezuela – 1200–2200 m – E
Oncidium cariniferum (Rchb. f.) Beer, Prakt. Stud. Orch.: 283, 1854
○ Odontoglossum hastilabium var. fuscatum Hook., Bot. Mag.: t. 4919, 1856
○ **Odontoglossum cirrhosum** Lindl., Gen. Sp. Orch. Pl.: 211, 1833
BM 6317
Ecuador, Peru – 1400–2000 m – E
Oncidium cirrhosum (Lindl.) Beer, Prakt. Stud. Orch.: 284, 1854
Odontoglossum crispum Lindl., Ann. & Mag. Nat. Hist. 15: 256, 1845
BM 5691, BM 5697
Colombia – 2250–3000 m – E
Odontoglossum edithiae Warner, Select. Orch. Pl. s. 3: t. 25, 1862
○ Odontoglossum alexandrae Bateman, Gard. Chron.: 1083, 1864
○ Odontoglossum alexandrae var. guttatum Bateman, Bot. Mag.: t. 5697, 1868
Odontoglossum latimaculatum Linden, Lindenia 4: t. 145, 1888
Odontoglossum warocqueanum Linden, Lindenia 4: t. 180, 1888
○ **Odontoglossum cristatum** Lindl., Pl. Hartw.: 152, 1844
BM 8809
Colombia, Ecuador – 1500–2000 m – E, T
Oncidium cristatum (Lindl.) Beer, Prakt. Stud. Orch.: 283, 1854
○ **Odontoglossum edwardii** Rchb. f., Gard. Chron.: 74, 1878
BM 6771
Ecuador – E
Cyrtochilum edwardii (Rchb. f.) Kraenzlin, Notizbl. Bot. Gard. Berl. 63: 99, 1917
○ **Odontoglossum hallii** Lindl., Bot. Reg. 23: sub. t. 1992, 1837
BM 6237
Colombia, Ecuador, Peru – 1500–2800 m – E
Oncidium hallii (Lindl.) Beer, Prakt. Stud. Orch.: 287, 1854
Odontoglossum × chaetostroma Rchb. f., Gard. Chron.: 592, 1883
○ **Odontoglossum** × **humeanum** Rchb. f., Gard. Chron.: 170, 1876
BM 8873
S. Mexico – E
= Odontoglossum maculatum Llave & Lex. × Odontoglossum rossii Lindl.
Odontoglossum × aspersum Rchb. f., Gard. Chron.: 266, 1879
○ **Odontoglossum krameri** Rchb. f., Gard. Chron.: 98, 1868
BM 5778
Costa Rica, Panama – E
○ **Odontoglossum leeanum** Rchb. f., Gard. Chron.: 525, 1882
BM 8142
Colombia – E
Odontoglossum odoratum var. leeanum Veitch, Man. 2: 56, 1894
○ **Odontoglossum maxillare** Lindl. sensu Hook. f., Bot. Mag.: t. 6144, 1875
BM 6144
Mexico – E
○ **Odontoglossum naevium** Lindl., Paxt. Flow. Gard. 1: 87, 1850
BM 8097
Venezuela, Colombia, Ecuador, Guyana – 1000–2000 m – E
Oncidium naevium (Lindl.) Beer, Prakt. Stud. Orch.: 289, 1854
○ **Odontoglossum odoratum** Lindl., Orch. Linden.: 16, 1846
BM 6502
Venezuela, Colombia – 1200–1500 m – E, L
Oncidium odoratum (Lindl.) Beer, Prakt. Stud. Orch.: 290, 1854
Odontoglossum gloriosum Linden & Rchb. f., Bonpl. 2: 278, 1854
Odontoglossum × baphicanthum Rchb. f., Gard. Chron.: 260, 1876
Odontoglossum glonerianum Linden, Lindenia 4: 17 t. 151, 1888
○ **Odontoglossum pardinum** (Lindl.) Lindl., Sert. Orch.: sub. t. 25, 1838
BM 5993
Colombia, Ecuador, Peru – 2400–3500 m – E, T
Cyrtochilum pardinum Lindl., Gen. Sp. Orch. Pl.: 210, 1833
Odontoglossum spathaceum Lindl., Fol. Orch. Odont.: 18, 1852
Oncidium pardinum (Lindl.) Beer, Prakt. Stud. Orch.: 291, 1854
Odontoglossum spilotanthum Linden & Rchb. f., Xen. Orch. 2: 175, 1873

o **Odontoglossum praenitens** Rchb.f., Gard. Chron.: 524, 1875
BM 6229
Colombia, Ecuador – 1800–2200 m – E, T
o **Odontoglossum × praevisum** Rolfe, Orch. Rev.: 176, 1904
BM 8780
Colombia – E
= Odontoglossum gloriosum Lindl. & Rchb.f. × Odontoglossum lindleyana Rchb.f.
o **Odontoglossum ramulosum** Lindl., Fol. Orch. Odontoglossum: 13, 1852
BM 8031
Venezuela, Colombia, Ecuador – 2800–3000 m – E, T
Oncidium ramulosum (Lindl.) Beer, Prakt. Stud. Orch.: 290, 1854
Cyrtochilum ramulosum (Lindl.) Kraenzlin, Pflanzenr. Heft 80: 83, 1922
o **Odontoglossum retusum** Lindl., Pl. Hartw.: 152, 1844
BM 7569
Colombia, Ecuador, Peru – 2500–2800 m – E, T
Oncidium retusum (Lindl.) Beer, Prakt. Stud. Orch.: 290, 1854
Cyrtochilum retusum (Lindl.) Kraenzlin, Notizbl. Bot. Gart. Berl. 7: 99, 1917 (nomen)
Odontoglossum sanderianum Rchb.f., Gard. Chron.: 524, 1881
BM 5736
Venezuela, Colombia, Ecuador – 1800–2200 m – E
o Odontoglossum constrictum Lindl., Bot. Reg.: Misc. p. 17, 1844
Odontoglossum constrictum var. majus Lindl., Fol. Orch. Odont.: 2, 1852
Oncidium constrictum var. majus Beer, Prakt. Stud. Orch.: 275, 1854
o **Odontoglossum tripudians** Rchb.f. & Warsc., Bonpl. 2: 100, 1854
BM 6029
Colombia, Peru – E
Oerstedella endresii (Rchb.f.) Hags., Orquidea (Méx.) 8 (1): 21, 1981
BM 7855
Costa Rica, Panama – up to 1800 m – E
o Epidendrum endresii Rchb. f., Gard. Chron.: 432, 1883
Epidendrum adolphii Schltr., Fedde Rep. 3: 108, 1906
Epidendrum tonduzii Lankaster, Orch. Rev. 32: 163 & 267, 1924
Oerstedella myriantha (Lindl.) Hags., Orquidea (Méx.) 8 (1): 21 fig. 23 III, 1981
BM 5556
Mexico, Guatemala, El Salvador, Honduras – E, T
o Epidendrum myrianthum Lindl., Fol. Orch. Epid.: 59, 1853
Epidendrum myrianthum var. album Rchb.f. ex Williams, Orch. Grow. Man. ed. 7: 387, 1894
Epidendrum verrucosum var. myrianthum (Lindl.) Ames & Correll, Bot. Mus. Leafl. Harv. Univ. 10: 82, 1942
Oerstedella pumila (Rolfe) Hags., Orquidea (Méx.) 8 (1): 24, 1981
BM 9170
C. America, Costa Rica, Panama – E
o Epidendrum pumilum Rolfe, Kew Bull.: 171, 1893
Epidendrum acrochordonium Schltr., Beih. Bot. Centralbl. 36: Abt. 2: 400, 1918
Oncidium altissimum (Jacq.) Sw., Kongl. Vet. Acad. Stockh. 21: 240, 1800
BM 3603
USA (Florida), W. Indies, Mexico to Panama, Venezuela, Colombia, Ecuador, Peru, Guyana, Brazil – E
Epidendrum altissimum Jacq., Enum. Pl. Carib.: 30, 1760
Epidendrum maculatum Aublet, Pl. Guin. 2: 825, 1775
Cymbidium altissimum (Jacq.) Sw., Nov. Act. Upsal. 6: 74, 1799
o Oncidium luridum Lindl., Bot. Reg. 9: t. 727, 1823
Oncidium intermedium Knowles & Westc., Fl. Cabin. 2: 33, 1838
Oncidium luridum var. guttatum Lindl., Bot. Reg. 25: t. 16, 1839
Oncidium boydii hort. ex Lindl., Bot. Reg. 25: sub.t. 16, 1839
Oncidium lindenii Lodd., Cat. Orch. ed. 2: No. 1326, 1842
Oncidium cosymbeforum Morren, Ann. Gand. 5: 333, 1849
Oncidium luridum var. atratum Lindl., J. Hort. Soc. 6: 54, 1851
Oncidium luridum var. olivaceum Lindl., Fol. Orch. Onc.: 41, 1855
Oncidium luridum var. intermedium Lindl., Fol. Orch. Onc.: 41, 1855
Oncidium luridum var. morrenii Lindl., Fol. Orch. Onc.: 41, 1855
Oncidium sanguineum var. auriculatum Regel, Ind. Sem. Hort. Petrop.: 21, 1855
Oncidium guttatum Rchb.f., Walp. Ann. 6: 782, 1863
Oncidium guttatum var. olivaceum Rchb.f., Walp. Ann. 6: 782, 1863
Oncidium guttatum var. intermedium Rchb.f., Walp. Ann. 6: 782, 1863
Oncidium guttatum var. morrenii Rchb.f., Walp. Ann. 6: 782, 1863
Oncidium guttatum var. roseum hort., Ill. Hort. 27: 103, 1880
Oncidium luridum var. dodgsonii Williams, Orch. Grow. Man. ed. 6: 490, 1885
Oncidium guttatum var. dodgsonii Cogn., Fl. Bras. 3, pt. 6: 413, 1906
Oncidium guttatum var. auriculatum Cogn., Fl. Bras. 3, pt. 6: 413, 1906
Oncidium maculatum Urban, Fedde Rep. 15: 306, 1918 (non Lindl., 1842)
o **Oncidium bicallosum** Lindl., Pl. Hartw.: 94, 1842
BM 4148
Mexico, Guatemala, El Salvador – 1500–2200 m – E
o **Oncidium bifolium** Sims, Bot. Mag.: t. 1491, 1812
BM 1491
Uruguay, Argentina, Bolivia – E
Coppensia bifolia (Sims) Dumort., Mém. Acad. Brux. 9: Maelen. 10, in adnot., 1835
Oncidium celsianum A. Rich., Lem., Hort. Univ. 6: 113, 1845
Oncidium batemanianum Griseb., Symb. Fl. Argent.: 337, 1879 (non Knowles & Westc.)
Oncidium carthagenense (Jacq.) Sw., Kongl. Vet. Acad. Handl. 21: 240, 1800
BM 777, BM 3806
USA (Florida), Mexico to Panama, W. Indies, Venezuela, Colombia, Brazil – E
Epidendrum carthagenense Jacq., Select. Stirp. Amer.: 228, 1763
o Epidendrum undulatum Sw., Bot. Mag.: t. 777, 1804
Oncidium undulatum (Sw.) Salisb., Trans. Roy. Soc. 1: 295, 1812 (non Lindl.)
Oncidium panduriferum Kunth, Nov. Gen. & Sp. 1: 346, 1816
Oncidium sanguineum Lindl., Sert. Orch.: t. 27, 1838
Oncidium luridum var. henchmanni Knowles & Westc., Fl. Cabin. 3: t. 97, 1840
o Oncidium huntianum Hook., Bot. Mag.: t. 3806, 1841
Oncidium roseum Lodd., Cat. Orch. ed. 2: no. 1381, 1842
Oncidium henchmanni Lodd., Cat. Orch. ed. 2: no. 1323, 1842
Oncidium oerstedii Rchb.f., Bonpl. 2: 91, 1854
Oncidium carthagenense var. swartzii Lindl., Fol. Orch. Onc.: 40, 1855
Oncidium carthagenense var. oerstedii (Rchb.f.) Lindl., Fol. Orch. Onc.: 40, 1855
Oncidium carthagenense var. sanguineum Lindl., Fol. Orch. Onc.: 40, 1855
Oncidium carthagenense var. klotzschii Lindl., Fol. Orch. Onc.: 40, 1855
Oncidium obsoletum Rich. & Galeotti ex Lindl., Fol. Orch. Onc.: 41, 1855
Oncidium sanguineum var. roseum Regel, Ind. Sem. Hort. Petrop.: 22, 1856
Oncidium carthagenense var. roseum Sander, Orch. Guide: 176, 1901
Oncidium carthagenense var. andreanum Cogn., Fl. Bras. 3, pt. 6: 411, 1906
Oncidium kymatoides Kraenzlin, Pflanzenr. Heft 80: 112, 1922
Oncidium oerstedii var. crispiflorum Schltr., Fedde Rep. Beih. 17: 85, 1922
Oncidium cavendishianum Bateman, Orch. Mex. & Guat.: t. 3, 1837
BM 3807
Mexico, Guatemala, Honduras – E
o Oncidium pachyphyllum Hook., Bot. Mag.: t. 3807, 1840
o **Oncidium cebolleta** (Jacq.) Sw., Kongl. Vet. Acad. Handl. 21: 240, 1800
BM 3568
Trop. America, Mexico, Venezuela, Trinidad, Surinam, Argentina, Paraguay – E
Epidendrum cebolleta Jacq., Enum. Pl. Carib.: 30, 1760
Epidendrum juncifolium L., Sp.Pl. ed. 2: 1351, 1763
Cymbidium juncifolium (L.) Willd., Sp.Pl. ed. 4: 102, 1805
Oncidium juncifolium (L.) Willd., Coll. Bot.: 27, 1821
Oncidium longifolium Lindl., Bot. Reg. 27: Misc. p. 22, 1841
Oncidium brachyphyllum Lindl., Bot. Reg. 28: sub.t. 4, 1842
Oncidium cepula Hoffsgg., Bot. Zeit. 1: 833, 1843
Oncidium sprucei Lindl., Fol. Orch. Onc.: 14, 1855
Oncidium glaziovii Cogn., Fl. Bras. 3, pt. 6: 440, 1906
Oncidium ottonis Rchb.f. ex Kraenzlin, Pflanzenr. Heft. 80: 92, 1922
Oncidium vittii Oppenh., Pflanzenr. Heft 80: 96, 1922
Oncidium humboldtii Schltr., Fedde Rep.: 65, 1931
o **Oncidium cheirophorum** Rchb.f., Bot. Zeit. 10: 695, 1852
BM 6278
Costa Rica, Panama, Colombia, S. America – E
Oncidium dielsianum Kraenzlin, Pflanzenr. Heft 80: 197, 1922
o **Oncidium concolor** Hook., Bot. Mag.: t. 3752, 1839
BM 3752, BM 4454
C. America, Brazil, Argentina – E
o Cyrtochilum citrinum Hook., Bot. Mag.: t. 4454, 1849
Oncidium unguiculatum Klotzsch, Allg. Gartenz. 17: 9, 1849
Oncidium ottonis Schltr., Orchis 8: 61, 1914

○ **Oncidium cornigerum** Lindl., Bot. Reg. 18: t. 1542, 1832
BM 3486
Brazil, Paraguay – E
Oncidium chrysorhapis Rchb.f., Gard. Chron.: 72, 1888
○ **Oncidium crispum** Lodd., Bot. Cab.: t. 1854, 1832 (non Beer)
BM 3499
Brazil – E
Oncidium croesus Rchb.f., Hamb. Gartenz. 13: 314, 1857
BM 5193
Brazil – E
Oncidium janeirense Rchb.f., Bonpl. 2: 90, 1854
○ Oncidium longipes Hook., Bot. Mag.: t. 5193, 1860 (non Lindl.)
Oncidium longipes var. croesus Veitch, Man. Orch. 8: 54, 1892
Oncidium cruciatum Rchb.f., Gard. Chron.: 138, 1878
BM 3926
Brazil – E
○ Oncidium pubes var. flavescens Hook., Bot. Mag.: t. 3926, 1842
Oncidium phantasmaticum Lemaire, Ill. Hort. 4: Misc. 77 cum. ic., 1857
○ **Oncidium cryptocopis** Rchb.f., Gard. Chron.: 827, 1870
BM 5858
Peru, Colombia – E
Cyrtochilum cryptocopis (Rchb.f.) Kraenzlin, Notizbl. Bot. Gart. Berl. 7: 92, in key, 1917 (nomen)
Oncidium cucullatum Lindl., Sert. Orch.: sub.t. 21, 1830
BM 5708
Ecuador – 3000–4000 m – E
○ Oncidium cucullatum var. nubigenum Hook., Bot. Mag.: t. 5708, 1868
○ **Oncidium dasystyle** Rchb. f., Gard. Chron.: 253 & 432, 1873
BM 6494
Brazil – E
○ **Oncidium excavatum** Lindl., Sert. Orch.: sub.t. 25 No. 3, 1838
BM 5293
Peru, Ecuador – 2400–2700 m – T
Oncidium rupestre Lindl., Pl. Hartw.: 151, 1844
Oncidium aurosum Rchb.f., Bonpl. 2: 108, 1854
Oncidium skinneri Lindl., Gard. Chron.: 629, 1855
Oncidium excavatum var. dawsonii Williams, Orch. Grow. Man. ed. 6: 483, 1885
○ **Oncidium flexuosum** Sims, Bot. Mag.: t. 2203, 1821
BM 2203
Brazil, Paraguay, Argentina – E
○ **Oncidium forbesii** Hook., Bot. Mag.: t. 3705, 1839
BM 3705
Brazil – E
Oncidium crispum var. forbesii (Hook.) Burb., Die Orch. Trad. Lebl. ed. 2: 117, 1882
Oncidium crispum var. marginatum hort., Nichols. Dict. Gard. 2: 484, 1886
Oncidium gardneri Lindl., Hook. J. Bot. 2: 662, 1843
BM 6662
Brazil – E
Oncidium flabelliferum Pinel ex Paxt. Mag. Bot. 16: 65 fig. 2, 1849
Oncidium elegantissimum Rchb.f., Gard. Chron. 1: 13, 1877
Oncidium praetextum C.J. Morren, Belg. Hort.: 357 t. 20–21, 1877 (non Rchb.f.)
Oncidium gardnerianum hort., Gard. Chron.: 759, 1880
Oncidium praestans Rchb.f., Gard. Chron.: 296, 1880
Oncidium polletianum Rchb.f., Gard. Chron.: 326, 1886
Oncidium forbesio-dasytyle Rolfe, Orch. Rev. 1: 301, 1893
○ (Oncidium praetextum Rchb.f., Gard. Chron.: 1206, 1873; misidentified)
Oncidium graminifolium Lindl., Sert. Orch.: sub.t. 48, 1840
BM 3854
Mexico, Guatemala, El Salvador, Costa Rica – 1500–2700 m – T, L
Cyrtochilum graminifolium Lindl., Ann. Nat. Hist. 4: 384, 1840
Oncidium filipes Lindl., Sert. Orch.: sub.t. 48, 1840
Cyrtochilum filipes (Lindl.) Lindl., Bot. Reg. 27: t. 59, 1841
○ Oncidium wrayae Hook., Bot. Mag.: t. 3854, 1841
Oncidium graminifolium var. filipes (Lindl.) Lindl., Fol. Orch. Onc.: 32, 1855
Oncidium graminifolium var. wrayae (Hook.) Lindl., Fol. Orch. Onc.: 32, 1855
Oncidium graminifolium var. holochilum Lindl., Fol. Orch. Onc.: 32, 1855
Oncidium hastilabium (Lindl.) Garay & Dunsterv., Venez. Orch. Ill. 6: 302, 1976
BM 4272
Venezuela, Colombia, Peru – up to 1500 m – E
○ Odontoglossum hastilabium Lindl., Orch. Linden: 16, 1846
Oncidium hastilabium Beer, Prakt. Stud. Orch.: 287, 1854

Oncidium hookeri Rolfe, Gard. Chron.: 520, 1887
BM 3712
Brazil – E
○ Oncidium raniferum var. major Hook., Bot. Mag.: t. 3712, 1839
○ **Oncidium incurvum** Barker ex Lindl., Bot. Reg. 26: Misc. p. 75, 1840
BM 4824
Mexico – E
Oncidium alboviolaceum Rich. & Galeotti, Ann. Sci. Nat. s. 3, 3: 27, 1845
Oncidium jacquinianum Garay & Stacy, Bradea 1: 407, 1974
BM 2990
W. Indies – E
Epidendrum altissimum Jacq., Sel. Stirp. Am.: 229 t. 141, 1763 (non Jacq., 1760)
○ (Oncidium altissimum auct. non (Jacq.) Sw., Kongl. Vet. Akad. Handl. 21: 240, 1800; misidentified)
○ **Oncidium jonesianum** Rchb.f., Gard. Chron.: 781, 1883
BM 6982
Paraguay, Argentina, Brazil – E
Oncidium longicornu Mutel, Mémorial de la Scarpe 13. 10. 1838
BM 3890
Brazil – E
Oncidium unicornutum Knowles & Westc., Fl. Cabin. 2: 143, 1838
Oncidium unicorne Lindl., Bot. Reg. 25: Misc. p. 55 No. 76, 1839
○ Oncidium monoceras Hook., Bot. Mag.: t. 3890, 1841
Oncidium gautieri Regel, Ind. Sem. Hort. Petrop.: 80, 1868
○ **Oncidium macranthum** Lindl., Gen. Sp. Orch. Pl.: 205, 1833
BM 5743
Colombia, Ecuador, Peru – 2500–3000 m – E
Oncidium hastiferum hort. ex Gard. Chron.: 492, 1875
Cyrtochilum macranthum (Lindl.) Kraenzlin, Notizbl. Bot. Gard. Berl. 7: 95, in Key 1917 (nomen)
Oncidium maculatum (Lindl.) Lindl., Sert. Orch.: sub.t. 48, 1841
BM 3836, BM 3880
Mexico, Guatemala, El Salvador, Honduras, Nicaragua, Brazil – E
Oncidium funereum Llave & Lex., Nov. Veg. Descr. Fasc. 2: 37, 1825
○ Cyrtochilum maculatum Lindl., Bot. Reg. 24: Misc. p. 30 t. 44, 1838
○ Cyrtochilum maculatum var. ecornutum Hook., Bot. Mag.: t. 3836, 1840
Cyrtochilum grandiflorum Lodd., Orchid.: No. 1585, 1844 (nomen)
Oncidium maculatum var. donianum Rchb.f., Bonpl. 3: 215, 1855
Oncidium maculatum var. psittacium Rchb.f. ex Lindl., Fol. Orch. Onc.: 34, 1855
Oncidium maculatum var. vinosum Lindl., Fol. Orch. Onc.: 34, 1855
Cyrtochilum leucochilum Linden ex Morren, Belg. Hort. 35: 287 t. 21, 1885
Oncidium lintriculus Kraenzlin, Pflanzenr. Heft 80: 282, 1922
Oncidium hintonii L.O. Williams, Amer. Orch. Soc. Bull. 9: 336, 1941
Odontoglossum johnsonorum L.O. Williams, Ceiba 4: 191, 1954
Odontoglossum subcruciforme Heller, Fieldiana 32 (7): 73, 1969
○ **Oncidium marshallianum** Rchb.f., Gard. Chron.: 682, 1868
BM 5725
Brazil – 900–1200 m – E
○ **Oncidium micropogon** Rchb.f., Bonpl. 2: 90, 1854
BM 6971
Brazil – E
Oncidium dentatum Klotzsch, Allg. Gartenz. 23: 234, 1855
Oncidium macropetalum Klotzsch, Allg. Gartenz.: 274, 1855 (non Lindl.)
○ **Oncidium ornithorhynchum** Kunth, Nov. Gen. Sp. Pl. 1: 345 t. 80, 1816
BM 3912
Mexico, Guatemala, El Salvador, Costa Rica – 1500–1700 m – E
○ **Oncidium phymatochilum** Lindl., Gard. Chron.: 139, 1848
BM 5214
Mexico, Guatemala, Brazil – 700–1000 m – E
Oncidium pubes Lindl., Bot. Reg. 12: t. 1007, 1826
BM 3109
Brazil, Paraguay, Argentina – E
Oncidium puber Sprengel, Syst. Veg. Cur. Post. 308, 1827
○ Oncidium bicornutum Hook., Bot. Mag.: t. 3109, 1831
Oncidium pubescens Duchartre, Man. Gen. Pl. 4: 488, 1857
○ **Oncidium pulchellum** Hook., Bot. Mag.: t. 2773, 1827
BM 2773
Brazil, Guyana, Jamaica, Cuba – up to 1200 m – E
Tolumnia pulchella (Hook.) Raf., Fl. Tellur. 2: 101, 1836
Oncidium concavum Moir, Phytol. 17: 432, 1968
○ **Oncidium pumilum** Lindl., Bot. Reg. 11: t. 920, 1825
BM 3581
Brazil, Uruguay, Argentina, Paraguay – E
Epidendrum ligulatum Vell., Fl. Tellur Ic. 9: t. 15, 1827

○ **Oncidium serratum** Lindl., Sert Orch.: sub. t. 48 No. 17, 1842
BM 5632
Ecuador, Peru – 1300–3200 m – E
Oncidium diadema Linden, Cat. No. 20, 1866
Oncidium sanderianum Rolfe, Kew Bull.: 337, 1893
Cyrtochilum serratum (Lindl.) Kraenzlin, Notizbl. Bot. Gart. Berl. 7: 93 in key, 1917 (nomen)
Oncidium splendidum A. Rich. ex Duchartre, J. Soc. Imp. Hort. Paris: 50, 1862
BM 5878
Mexico, Guatemala, Honduras, Nicaragua – E, L
○ (Oncidium tigrinum var. splendidum Hook. f., Bot. Mag.: t. 5878, 1871; misidentified)
○ **Oncidium stramineum** Bateman ex Lindl., Bot. Reg. 24: Misc. p. 29, 1838
BM 6254
Mexico, Brazil – up to 1000 m – E
Oncidium saltator Lemaire, Fl. Serres 3: sub. t. 237, 1847
Oncidium colombae hort. ex Lindl., Fol. Orch. Onc.: 36, 1855 (nomen)
Oncidium lindenii hort. ex Rchb. f. fide Lindl., Fol. Orch. Onc.: 36, 1855
○ **Oncidium superbiens** Rchb. f., Linnaea 22: 843, 1849
BM 5980
Colombia, Venezuela, Ecuador, Peru – up to 1800 m – E
Oncidium aemulum Rchb. f., & Warsc., Bonpl. 2: 102, 1854
Oncidium inferlobum hort. ex Gard. Chron.: 904 in syn., 1872
Oncidium undulatum Warner & B. S. Williams, Orch. Alb. 8: t. 368, 1889 (non (Kunth) Lindl.)
Cyrtochilum aemulum Kraenzlin, Notizbl. Bot. Gart. Berl. 7: 93, in key, 1917 (nomen)
Cyrtochilum superbiens (Rchb. f.) Kraenzlin, Notizbl. Bot. Gart. Berl. 7: 93, in key, 1917 (nomen)
Oncidium tetrapetalum (Jacq.) Willd., Sp. Pl. 4: 112, 1806
BM 4130
Mexico, Jamaica, W. Indies, Colombia – E
Epidendrum tetrapetalum Jacq., Enum. Pl. Carib.: 30, 1760
Cymbidium tetrapetalum (Jacq.) Sw., Nov. Act. Upsal. 6: 74, 1799
Oncidium quadripetalum Sw., Kongl. Vet. Akad. Handl. Stockh. 21: 240, 1800
○ Oncidium tricolor Hook., Bot. Mag.: t. 4130, 1844
Oncidium tigrinum Llave & Lex., Nov. Veg. Descr. Fasc. 2: 36, 1825
BM 9578
Mexico – 2000–3500 m – E
Oncidium barkeri Lindl., Bot. Reg. 27: Misc. p. 81, 1841
Odontoglossum ghiesbreghtianum Rich. & Galeotti, Ann. Sci. Nat. s. 3, 3: 27, 1845
○ Oncidium unguiculatum Lindl., J. Hort. Soc. 1: 303, 1846
Odontoglossum tigrinum (Llave & Lex.) Lindl., Fol. Orch. Odontoglossum: 5, 1852
Oncidium ionosmum Lindl., Gard. Chron.: 726, 1853
Oncidium tigrinum var. unguiculatum Lindl., Fol. Orch. Onc.: 45, 1855
Oncidium tigrinum Hemsley, Biol. Centr.-Am. 3: 286, 1884 (non Llave & Lex.)
○ **Oncidium triquetrum** (Sw.) R. Br., Hort. Kew ed. 2: 216, 1813
BM 3393
Jamaica – E
Epidendrum triquetrum Sw., Prodr. Veg. Ind. Occ.: 122, 1788
Cymbidium triquetrum Sw., Nov. Act. Upsal. 6: 74, 1799
Olgasis triquetra (Sw.) Raf., Fl. Tellur. 2 Teil Cent. 2 Nr. 183: 51, 1836
Oncidium dubium André, Ill. Hort. 20: 184, 1873
Jamaiciella triquetra (Sw.) Bream, Die Orchidee 31 (3): 120, 1980
Oncidium varicosum Lindl., Bot. Reg. 23: sub. t. 1920, 1837
BM 6322
Brazil, Paraguay – 1000–1200 m – E
Oncidium lunaeanum hort., Gard. Chron.: 168, 1850
Oncidium rodgersii hort. ex Bateman, Gard. Chron.: 1317, 1865
○ Oncidium euxanthinum Rchb. f., Gard. Chron.: 1158, 1869
Oncidium geraënse Barb. Rodr., Orch. Nov. 2: 193, 1881
○ **Oncidium xanthodon** Rchb. f., Gard. Chron.: 1338, 1868
BM 5756
Colombia, Ecuador – E
Cyrtochilum xanthodon Kraenzlin (Rchb. f.) Kraenzlin, Notizbl. Bot. Gart. Berl. 7: 94, in key, 1917 (nomen)
○ **Oncidium zebrinum** (Rchb. f.) Rchb. f., Bonpl. 2: 12, 1854
BM 6138
Venezuela – 1200–1600 m – E
Odontoglossum zebrinum Rchb. f., Linnaea 22: 849, 1849
Cyrtochilum zebrinum (Rchb. f.) Kraenzlin, Pflanzenr. Heft 80: 54, 1922

Ophrys holoserica (Burm. f.) Greuter, Boissiera 13: 185, 1967
BM 2516
S. C. Europe Medit. – T
Ophrys insectifera var. arachnites L., Sp. Orch. Pl.: 949, 1753
Orchis fuciflora Crantz, Stirp Austr. ed. 2, 6: 483, 1769
Orchis holoserica Burm. f., Nov. Act. Acad. Leop.-Carol. 4, app.: 237, 1770
Orchis arachnites Scop., Fl. Carn. ed. 2, 2: 194, 1772
○ Ophrys arachnites (Scop.) Reichard, Fl. Moeno-Francof. 2: 89, 1778
Orchis fuciflora (Crantz) Haller ex Schrank, Baier. Fl. 1: 242, 1789
Epipactis arachnites (Scop.) F. W. Schmidt, Mayer Samml. Phys. Aufs. 1: 249, 1791
Arachnites fuciflora (Crantz) F. W. Schmidt, Fl. Boëm 1: 76, 1793
Ophrys fuciflora (Crantz) Sw., Kongl. Vet. Akad. Handl. s. 2, 21: 223, 1800 (nomen nudum)
Ophrys fuciflora (Crantz) Moench, Meth. Suppl.: 311, 1802
○ **Ophrys lutea** (Gouan.) Cav., Ic. 2: 46 t. 160, 1793
BM 5941
S. Europe, N. Afr. Medit., Syria, Palestina – T
Ophrys insectifera var. ε L., Sp. Pl.: 949, 1753
Ophrys sphegodes Miller, Gard. Dict. ed. 8: 8, 1768
BM 5712
W. C. Europe – T
Ophrys aranifera Hudson, Fl. Angl.: 392, 1778
○ Ophrys insectifera var. aranifera Hook. f., Bot. Mag.: t. 5712, 1868
○ **Ophrys tenthredinifera** Willd., Sp. Pl. 4: 67, 1805
BM 1930
S. Europe Medit., N. Africa, Asia Minor – T
Ophrys insectifera var. rosea Desf., Fl. Atl. 2: 321, 1799
Ophrys villosa Desf., Choix Mus. Hist. Paris 10: 225, 1807
Ophrys tenoreana Lindl., Bot. Reg.: t. 1093, 1827
Ophrys vernixia Brot., Fl. Lusit 1: 24, 1804
BM 5844
Portugal, Mediterranean region – T
○ Ophrys speculum Link, Schrad. Diar. Bot. 5, 11: 324, 1799
Ophrys ciliata Biv., Cent. 1: 60, 1806
Orchis longicornu Poiret, Voy. en Barb. 2: 247, 1789
BM 1944
W. Mediterranean region – T
○ Orchis longicornis Smith, Prodr. Fl. Graec. 2: 212, 1816
Orchis morio var. longicornu (Poiret) Knoche, Fl. Balear. 1: 400, 1921
Orchis pallens L., Mantissa 2: 292, 1771
BM 2569
S. C. E. Europe – up to 2000 m – T
○ Orchis sulphurea Sims, Bot. Mag.: t. 2569, 1825
Orchis simia Lam., Fl. Fr. ed. 3: 507, 1779
BM 3426
S. W. Europe – T
○ Orchis tephrosanthos Villars, Fl. Dauphin. 2: 32, 1787
Orchis zoophora Thuill., Fl. Paris 459, 1790
Orchis militaris var. cercopithecus Georgi, Besch. Russ. R. 3, 5: 169, 1800
Orchis militaris Smith, Engl. Bot.: t. 1873, 1808
Orchis tridentata Scop., Fl. Carn. ed. 2, 2: 190, 1772
BM 1932
S. C. Europe – up to 1400 m – T
Orchis variegata All., Fl. Pedam.: 147, 1785
Orchis simia Villars, Fl. Dauph. 2: 33, 1787 (non Lam.)
Orchis cercopitheca Poiret, Lam. Encycl. 4: 593, 1789
○ Orchis acuminata Desf., Fl. Atlant. 2: 318, 1798
Orchis acuminata Chaub. & Bory, Exped. Sc. Morée: 262, 1832 (non Desf.)
Orchis commutata Tod., Orch. Sc.: 24, 1842
Orchis brevilabris Fischer & Meyer, Ann. Sc. Nat. 4 s. 1: 30, 1854
× **Orchiserapias barlae** Camus, J. Bot.: 33, 1892
BM 6255
S. France – T
= Serapias lingua L. × Orchis papilionacea L.
Serapias × barlae K. Richter, Pl. Eur. 1: 276, 1890
○ (Serapias papilionacea × Orchis lingua Barla, Fl. Ill. de Nice et des A. M. 34: t. 22 & t. 4–8, 1858; misidentified)
Ornithochilus difformis (Wallich ex Lindl.) Schltr., Fedde Rep. Beih. 4: 277, 1919
BM 7385
E. India, Nepal, Burma, Thailand, Kampuchea, Laos. Vietnam – 1000–1500 m – E
○ Ornithochilus fuscus Wallich, Gen. Sp. Orch. Pl.: 242, 1833
Aerides difformis Wallich, Gen. Sp. Orch. Pl.: 242, 1833
Aerides hystrix Lindl., J. Linn. Soc. 3: 42, 1859
Ornithochilus eublepharon Hance, J. Bot. 22: 364, 1884

Ornithophora radicans (Rchb.f.) Garay & Pabst., Orquidea Rio de Janeiro 13: 50, 1951
BM 9307
Brazil - E
○ Sigmatostalix radicans Rchb.f., Hamb. Gartenz. 16: 16, 1860
Ornithophora quadricolor Barb. Rodr., Gen. & Sp. Orch. 2, 226, 1882
Osmoglossum pulchellum (Bateman ex Lindl.) Schltr., Orchis 10: 162, 1916
BM 4104
Mexico, Guatemala, El Salvador, Honduras, Nicaragua - E
○ Odontoglossum pulchellum Bateman ex Lindl., Bot. Reg. 27: t. 48, 1841
○ **Otochilus fusca** Lindl., Gen. & Sp. Orch.: 35, 1830
BM 3921
Nepal, Sikkim, Assam (Khasia), Manipur - 1000–1500 m - E
Broughtonia amoena Wallich ex Lindl., Gen. & Sp. Orch.: 35, 1830
Otochilus lancifolia Griffith, Notul. 3: 278, 1851
Coelogyne fusca (Lindl.) Rchb.f., Walp. Ann. 6: 236, 1861
Broughtonia fusca (Lindl.) Wallich ex Hook.f., Fl. Brit. Ind. 5: 844, 1890
Otoglossum brevifolium (Lindl.) Garay & Dunsterv., Venez., Orch. Ill. 6: 41, 1976
BM 7687
Panama, Venezuela, Colombia, Ecuador, Peru - 1700–3000 m - E, T
○ Odontoglossum brevifolium Lindl., Pl. Hartw.: 152, 1844
Odontoglossum coronarium var. miniatum Veitch, Man. Orch. Pl. 1: 23, 1886
Odontoglossum miniatum hort. ex Veitch, Man. Orch. Pl. 1: 23, 1886
Otoglossum chiriquense (Rchb.f.) Garay & Dunsterv., Venez. Orch. Ill. 6: 41, 1976
BM 8725
Costa Rica, Panama - up to 2500 m - E
○ Odontoglossum chiriquense Rchb.f., Bot. Zeit. 10: 692, 1852
Oncidium chiriquense (Rchb.f.) Beer, Prakt. Stud. Orch.: 283, 1854
Odontoglossum coronarium var. chiriquense Veitch, Man. Orch. Pl. 1: 23, 1886
Pabstia jugosa (Lindl.) Garay, Bradea 1 (27): 307, 1973
BM 5661
Brazil - E
Maxillaria jugosa Lindl., Bot. Reg. 27: Misc. p. 51, 1841
○ Colax jugosus (Lindl.) Lindl., Bot. Reg. 29: Misc. p. 51, 1843
Maxillaria viridis var. pluriflora Regel, Ann. Sc. Nat. s. 4, 6: 376, 1856
Lycaste jugosa (Lindl.) Nicholson, Dict. Gard. 2: 304, 1885
Colax viridis var. pluriflora (Regel) Cogn., Fl. Bras. 3, pt. 5: 562, 1902
Zygopetalum jugosum (Lindl.) Schltr., Orchideen: 422, 1914
Pabstia placanthera (Hook.) Garay, Bradea 1 (27): 301, 1973
BM 3173
Brazil - E
○ Maxillaria placanthera Hook., Bot. Mag.: t. 3173, 1832
Colax placanthera (Hook.) Lindl., Bot. Reg. 29: Misc. p. 50, 1843
Maxillaria cyanocheile Hoffsgg., Verz. Orch.: 55, 1843
Maxillaria viridis var. stenosepala Regel, Ann. Sc. Nat. s. 4, 6: 375, 1856
Colax viridis var. placanthera (Hook.) Stein, Orchideenb.: 160, 1892
Zygopetalum placantherum (Hook.) Schltr., Orchideen: 423, 1914
○ **Palumbina candida** (Lindl.) Rchb.f., Walp. Ann. 6: 699, 1863
BM 5546
Mexico, Guatemala - E
Oncidium candidum Lindl., Bot. Reg. 29: Misc. p. 56, 1843
○ **Paphinia cristata** (Lindl.) Lindl., Bot. Reg. 29: Misc. p. 14, 1843
BM 4836
Guatemala, Venezuela, Trinidad, Guyana, Brazil, Colombia - E
Maxillaria cristata Lindl., Bot. Reg. 21: t. 1811, 1836
Lycaste cristata (Lindl.) Benth., Gen. Pl. 3: 548, 1883
Paphiopedilum argus (Rchb.f.) Stein, Orchideenb.: 453, 1892
BM 6175
Philippines (Luzon) - 700–2400 m - T
○ Cypripedium argus Rchb.f., Gard. Chron.: 608, 1873
Cypripedium barbatum var. argus C.J. Morren, Belg. Hort. 25: 57, 1875
Cypripedium pitcherianum Manda, Am. Fl. 3: 178, 1887
Cordula argus (Rchb.f.) Rolfe, Orch. Rev. 20: 2, 1912
Paphiopedilum barbatum (Lindl.) Stein, Orchideenb.: 455, 1892
BM 4234
Malaya, Thailand - 200–1300 m - T
Cypripedium javanicum Reinw. ex Blume, Cat. Gew. Buitenz.: 98, 1823
○ Cypripedium barbatum Lindl., Bot. Reg.: Misc. 53, 1841
Cordula barbata (Lindl.) Rolfe, Orch. Rev. 20: 2, 1912
○ **Paphiopedilum callosum** (Rchb.f.) Stein, Orchideenb.: 457, 1892
BM 9671
Thailand, Kampuchea, Laos, Vietnam - 300–1000 m - T
Cypripedium callosum Rchb.f., Gard. Chron.: 326, 1887
Cypripedium schmidtianum Kraenzlin, Bot. Tidsskr. 24: 13, 1901
Cordula callosa (Rchb.f.) Rolfe, Orch. Rev. 20: 2, 1912
○ **Paphiopedilum chamberlainianum** (Sander ex O'Brien) Stein, Orchideenb.: 461, 1892
BM 7578
Sumatra - 700–2000 m - T
Cypripedium chamberlainianum Sander ex O'Brien, Gard. Chron: 234 fig. 34, 1892
Cordula chamberlainianum (Sander ex O'Brien) Rolfe, Orch. Rev. 20: 2, 1912
Paphiopedilum victoria-regina (Sander) M.W. Wood subsp. chamberlainianum (Sander ex O'Brien) M.W. Wood, Orch. Rev. 84: 135, 1976
Paphiopedilum charlesworthii (Rolfe ex Master) Pfitzer, Engl. Bot. Jahrb. 19: 40, 1894
BM 7416
Burma - up to 1600 m - T
○ Cypripedium charlesworthii Rolfe, Orch. Rev. 1: 303, 1893
Paphiopedilum charlesworthii Rolfe, Orch. Rev. 4: 331, 1896
Cordula charlesworthii (Rolfe ex Master) Rolfe, Orch. Rev. 20: 2, 1912
Paphiopedilum concolor (Bateman ex Lindl.) Pfitzer, Nat. Pflanzenf. 2, 6: 84, 1888
BM 5513
Burma, Thailand, Kampuchea, Laos, Vietnam, S. China - 500–1000 m - T
○ Cypripedium concolor Bateman ex Lindl., Bot. Mag.: t. 5513, 1865
Cordula concolor (Bateman ex Lindl.) Rolfe, Orch. Rev. 20: 2, 1912
Paphiopedilum exul (Ridley) Rolfe, Orch. Rev.: 364, 1896
BM 7510
Thailand - T
Cypripedium insigne var. exul Ridley, Gard. Chron., 1891
○ Cypripedium exul (Ridley) Rolfe, J. Hort., 1892
Cordula exul (Ridley) Rolfe, Orch. Rev. 20: 2, 1912
Paphiopedilum fairrieanum (Lindl.) Stein, Orchideenb.: 467, 1892
BM 5024
Sikkim, Bhutan, Assam - 1300–2000 m - T
○ Cypripedium fairrieanum Lindl., Gard. Chron.: 740, 1857
Cordula fairrieana (Lindl.) Rolfe, Orch. Rev. 20: 2, 1912
○ **Paphiopedilum glaucophyllum** J.J. Smith, Bull. Buitenz. 7: 1, 1900
BM 8084
Java - T
Cypripedium glaucophyllum J.J. Smith, Bull. Buitenz. 7: 1, 1900
Cordula glaucophylla (J.J. Smith) Rolfe, Orch. Rev. 20: 2, 1912
Paphiopedilum victoria-regina (Sander) M.W. Wood subsp. glaucophyllum (J.J. Smith) M.W. Wood, Orch. Rev. 84: 137, 1976
Paphiopedilum godefroyae (hort. ex Godef.-Leb.) Stein, Orchideenb.: 468, 1892
BM 6876
Thailand - T
○ Cypripedium godefroyae hort. ex Godef.-Leb., Orchidoph.: 830–833, 1883
Cypripedium concolor var. godefroyae (Godef.-Leb.) Collett & Hemsley, J. Linn. Soc. 28: 135, 1891
Cypripedium godefroyae var. leucochilum Masters, Gard. Chron. s. 3, 15: 717, 1894
Paphiopedilum godefroyae var. leucochilum (Masters) Hallier, Ann. Jard. Buitenz. 14: 35, 1897
Cordula godefroyae (hort. ex Godef.-Leb.) Rolfe, Orch. Rev. 20: 2, 1912
Paphiopedilum leucochilum Fowlie, Orch. Digest: 5, 1976
Paphiopedilum haynaldianum (Rchb.f.) Stein, Orchideenb.: 470, 1892
BM 6296
Philippines - up to 2000 m - T
○ Cypripedium haynaldianum Rchb.f., Xen. Orch. 2: 222, 1874
Cordula haynaldiana (Rchb.f.) Rolfe, Orch. Rev. 20: 2, 1912
Paphiopedilum hirsutissimum (Lindl. ex Hook.) Stein, Orchideenb.: 470, 1892
BM 4990
Assam, Burma, Thailand, China - 1000–1300 m - E, T
○ Cypripedium hirsutissimum Lindl. ex Hook., Bot. Mag.: t. 4990, 1857
Cordula hirsutissima (Lindl. ex Hook.) Rolfe, Orch. Rev. 20: 2, 1912
Paphiopedilum esquirolei Schltr., Fedde Rep. Beih. 4: 39, 1919
Paphiopedilum chiwuanum Tang & Wang, Acta Phytotax. Sinica 1: 56, 1951
Paphiopedilum hookerae (Rchb.f.) Stein. Orchideenb.: 470, 1892
BM 5362
Borneo - up to 1200 m - T
○ Cypripedium hookerae Rchb.f., Bot. Mag.: t. 5362, 1863
Cordula hookerae (Rchb.f.) Rolfe, Orch. Rev. 20: 2, 1912

Paphiopedilum insigne (Wallich ex Lindl.) Pfitzer, Nat. Pflanzenf. 2, 6: 84, 1889
BM 3412
Nepal, N. E. India - 1300-2000 m - T
o Cypripedium insigne Wallich ex Lindl., Coll. Bot.: t. 32, 1821
Paphiopedilum lawrenceanum (Rchb.f.) Pfitzer, Engl. Bot. Jahrb. 19 (1): 40, 1894
BM 6432
N. Borneo - up to 600 m - T
o Cypripedium lawrenceanum Rchb.f., Gard. Chron.: 748, 1878
Cordula lawrenceana (Rchb.f.) Rolfe, Orch. Rev. 20: 2, 1912
o **Paphiopedilum mastersianum** (Rchb.f.) Stein, Orchideenb.: 477, 1892
BM 7629
Moluccas - T
Cypripedium mastersianum Rchb.f., Gard. Chron.: 102, 1879
Cordula mastersiana (Rchb.f.) Rolfe, Orch. Rev. 20: 2, 1912
Paphiopedilum niveum (Rchb.f.) Stein, Orchideenb.: 478, 1892
BM 5922
Thailand, N. Malaya - T
o Cypripedium niveum Rchb.f., Gard. Chron.: 1038, 1869
Cordula nivea (Rchb.f.) Rolfe, Orch. Rev. 20: 2, 1912
Paphiopedilum parishii (Rchb.f.) Stein, Orchideenb.: 479, 1892
BM 5791
Thailand, Burma, S. China (Yunnan) - 1000-1500 m - E, L
o Cypripedium parishii Rchb.f., Flora 52: 322, 1869
Cordula parishii (Rchb.f.) Rolfe, Orch. Rev. 20: 2, 1912
Paphiopedilum philippinense (Rchb.f.) Stein, Orchideenb.: 480, 1892
BM 5508
Philippines, Borneo - T, E
Cypripedium philippinense Rchb.f., Bonpl.: 335, 1862
o Cypripedium laevigatum Bateman, Bot. Mag.: 5508, 1865
Cypripedium roebellinii Rchb.f., Gard. Chron.: 684, 1883
Paphiopedilum laevigatum (Bateman) Pfitzer, Nat. Pflanzenf. 2, 6: 84, 1883
Selenipedium laevigatum (Bateman) May, Rev. Hort.: 301, 1885
Paphiopedilum roebellinii (Rchb.f.) Pfitzer, Engl. Bot. Jahrb. 19: 41, 1894
Cordula philippinensis (Rchb.f.) Rolfe, Orch. Rev. 20: 2, 1912
Paphiopedilum purpuratum (Lindl.) Stein, Orchideenb.: 481, 1892
BM 4901
S.E. China, Hong Kong - 200-600 m - T
o Cypripedium purpuratum Lindl., Bot. Reg. 33: t. 1991, 1837
Cypripedium sinicum Hance, Fl. Austr. Chin. ex Walp. Ann. 3: 602, 1853
Cordula purpurata (Lindl.) Rolfe, Orch. Rev. 20: 2, 1912
o **Paphiopedilum robinsonii** (Ridley) Ridley, Fl. Mal. Pen.: 232, 1924
BM 9155
Malaya - T
Cypripedium barbatum sensu Ridley, J. Linn. Soc.: 38: 330, 1908
Cypripedium robinsonii Ridley, J. Fed. Mal. Stat. Mus. 6: 183, 1915
Paphiopedilum rothschildianum (Rchb.f.) Stein, Orchideenb.: 482, 1892
BM 7102
Borneo - 600-1000 m - T
o Cypripedium rothschildianum Rchb.f., Gard. Chron.: 457, 1888
Cypripedium neo-guineense Linden, Gard. Chron.: 505, 1888
Cypripedium elliottianum O'Brien, Gard. Chron.: 501 & 532, 1888
Paphiopedilum elliottianum (O'Brien) Pfitzer, Engl. Bot. Jahrb. 19 (1): 40, 1894
Paphiopedilum rothschildianum var. elliottianum (O'Brien) Pfitzer, Pflanzenr. Heft 9: 58, 1903
Cordula rothschildiana (Rchb.f.) Rolfe, Orch. Rev. 20: 2, 1912
Paphiopedilum spicerianum (Rchb.f.) Pfitzer, Engl. Bot. Jahrb. 19 (1): 41, 1894
BM 6490
N.E. India, Assam - 1000-2000 m - T
o Cypripedium spicerianum Rchb.f., Gard. Chron.: 40, 1880
Cordula spiceriana (Rchb.f.) Rolfe, Orch. Rev. 20: 2, 1912
Paphiopedilum stonei (Hook.) Stein, Orchideenb.: 487, 1892
BM 5349
W. Borneo - up to 500 m - T
o Cypripedium stonei Hook., Bot. Mag.: t. 5349, 1862
Cordula stonei (Hook.) Rolfe, Orch. Rev. 20: 2, 1912
Paphiopedilum venustum (Wallich ex Sims) Pfitzer, Engl. Bot. Jahrb. 19 (1): 41, 1894
BM 2129
N.E. India, Bangladesh, Bhutan, Nepal - 1000-1500 m - T
o Cypripedium venustum Wallich ex Sims, Bot. Mag.: t. 2129, 1820
Cordula venusta (Wallich ex Sims) Rolfe, Orch. Rev. 20: 2, 1912
o **Paphilopedilum victoria-mariae** (Sander ex Masters) Rolfe, Orch. Rev. 4: 364, 1896
BM 7573
Sumatra - T
Cypripedium victoria-regina Sander, Gard. Chron.: 194, 1892
Cypripedium victoria-mariae Sander ex Masters, Gard. Chron.: 580, 1893 (nomen illeg.)
Cypripedium chamberlainianum forma victoria-mariae (Sander ex Masters) Rolfe, Orch. Rev. 1: 188, 1893
Cordula victoria-mariae Rolfe, Orch. Rev. 20: 2, 1912
Paphiopedilum victoria-regina (Sander) M.W. Wood subsp. victoriae-reginae (Sander) M.W. Wood, Orch. Rev. 84: 134, 1976
Paphiopedilum villosum (Lindl.) Stein, Orchideenb.: 490, 1892
BM 8126
Assam, Burma, Thailand, S. China, Vietnam - 1300-1700 m - T
Cypripedium boxallii Rchb.f., Gard. Chron.: 367, 1877
Paphiopedilum boxallii (Rchb.f.) Pfitzer, Nat. Pflanzenf. 2 (6): 84, 1889
o Paphiopedilum villosum var. annamense Rolfe, Bot. Mag.: t. 8126, 1907
Cordula boxallii (Lindl.) Rolfe, Orch. Rev. 20: 2, 1912
Cordula villosa (Lindl.) Rolfe, Orch. Rev. 20: 2, 1912
o **Paphiopedilum wardii** Summerh., Gard. Chron.: 446, 1932
BM 9481
Burma, S. W. China - T
Papilionanthe teres (Roxb.) Schltr., Orchis 9: 78, 1915
BM 4114
Nepal, Sikkim, N. India, Burma, Thailand, Laos - E
Dendrobium teres Roxb., Fl. Ind. 3: 485, 1832
o Vanda teres (Roxb.) Lindl., Gen. Sp. Orch. Pl.: 217, 1833
Papilionanthe vandarum (Rchb.f.) Garay, Bot. Mus. Leafl. Harv. Univ. 23 (10): 372, 1974
BM 4982
Nepal, Sikkim, Assam, Manipur - 1200-1700 m - E
o Aerides cylindrica auct. non Lindl.; Hook. Bot. Mag.: t. 4982, 1857
Aerides vandarum Rchb.f., Gard. Chron.: 997, 1867
Paraphalaenopsis denevei (J.J. Smith) A. Hawkes, Orquidea Rio de Janeiro 25: 212, 1963/64
BM 9445
W. Borneo - E
o Phalaenopsis denevei J.J. Smith, Rec. Trav. Bot. Néerl. 22: 264, 1925
Vanda denevei Zurow., Orch. Rev. 41: 76, 1933
Pecteilis susannae (L.) Raf., Fl. Tellur. 2: 38, 1836
BM 3374
Assam, Burma, S. China, Laos, Kampuchea, Vietnam, Malaya, Hong Kong, Java, Celebes, Buru, Ceram, Ambon, Timor - T
Orchis susannae L., Sp.Pl.: 939, 1753
Orchis gigantea Smith, Exot. Bot. 2: 79 t. 100, 1806
Habenaria susannae (L.) R.Br., Prodr.: 312, 1810
o Habenaria gigantea (Smith) D. Don, Prodr. Fl. Nepal.: 24, 1825
Platanthera gigantea (Smith) Lindl., Wall. Cat. 241: 7052, 1832
Platanthera susannae (L.) Lindl., Gen. Sp. Orch. Pl.: 295, 1835
Platanthera robusta Lindl., Gen. Sp. Orch. Pl.: 295, 1835
Pectilis gigantea (Smith) Raf., Fl. Tellur. 2: 38, 1837
Orchis altissima Buch-Ham. ex Hook.f., Fl. Tellur., 1890
Hemihabenaria susannae (L.) Finet, Rev. Gen. 13: 532, 1901
non Habenaria susannae & Platanthera susannae auct. quoad. Indian localities
Pelexia laxa (Poeppig & Endl.) Lindl., Gen. Sp. Orch. Pl.: 482, 1840
BM 9418
Costa Rica, Venezuela, Peru, Bolivia - T
Stenorrhynchos laxum Poeppig & Endl., Nov. Gen. Sp.Pl. 2: 7, 1836
Spiranthes longipetiolata Rchb.f., Beitr. Orch. Centr. Amer. 67, 1866
Gyrostachys longipetiolata (Rchb.f.) Kuntze, Rev. Gen. 2: 664, 1891
o Pelexia maculata Rolfe, Kew Bull.: 7, 1893
Pelexia longipetiolata (Rchb.f.) Schltr., Beih. Bot. Centralbl. 37 (2): 409, 1920
Spiranthes laxa (Poeppig & Endl.) C. Schweinf., Bot. Mus. Leafl. Harv. Univ. 10: 29, 1941
Spiranthes maculata (Rolfe) C. Schweinf., Bot. Mus. Leafl. Harv. Univ. 10: 30, 1941
o **Peristeria elata** Hook., Bot. Mag.: t. 3116, 1831
BM 3116
Trop. America, Costa Rica, Panama, Venezuela, Colombia - T
o **Peristeria pendula** Hook., Bot. Mag.: t. 3479, 1836
BM 3479
Panama, Venezuela, Guyana, Surinam, Peru - T, E
Peristeria maculata hort. ex Lindl., Bot. Reg. 29: Misc. p. 67, 1843
? Peristeria lentiginosa Lodd., Cat. ex Baxter Hort. Brit. Suppl. 3: 604, 1850
Peristylus plantagineus Lindl., Gen. Sp. Orch. Pl.: 300, 1835
BM 3397
Sri Lanka, India - T
o Habenaria goodyeroides Hook., Bot. Mag.: t. 3397, 1835 (non Lindl.)
Peristylus elatus Dalz., Hook., J. Bot. 3: 344, 1851
Habenaria wightii Trimen, Cat. Ceyl. Pl.: 91, 1885

Pescatoria cerina (Lindl. & Paxton) Rchb.f., Bot. Zeit. 10: 667, 1852
BM 5598
Costa Rica, Panama, Colombia - 600-2300 m - E
o Huntleya cerina Lindl. & Paxton, Paxt. Flow. Gard. 3: 62, 1852
Zygopetalum cerinum (Lindl. & Paxton) Rchb.f., Walp. Ann. 6: 651, 1863
o **Pescatoria dayana** Rchb.f. var. **rhodacra** Rchb.f., Gard. Chron.: 226, 1874
BM 6214
Colombia - 300-1500 m - E
Phaius flavus (Blume) Lindl., Gen. Sp. Orch. Pl.: 128, 1831
BM 2719, BM 3960
India, Nepal, Bhutan, Assam (Khasia), Thailand, China, Malaysia, Sumatra, Java, Philippines - up to 1500 m - E, T
Limodorum flavum Blume, Bijdr. 8: 375, 1825
o Bletia woodfordii Hook., Bot. Mag.: t. 2719, 1827
o Phaius maculatus Lindl., Gen. Sp. Orch. Pl.: 127, 1831
Bletia flava (Blume) Wallich ex Lindl., Gen. Sp. Orch. Pl.: 127, 1831
Hecabe lutea Raf., Fl. Tellur. 4: 44, 1838
Phaius flexuosus Blume, Mus. Bot. Lugd. Bat. 2: 179, 1856
Phaius crispus Blume, Mus. Bot. Lugd. Bat. 2: 180, 1856
Phaius platychilus Rchb.f., Xen. Orch. 1: 201, 1856
Phaius bracteosus Rchb.f., Bonpl. 5: 42, 1857
Phaius indigoferus Blume, Fl. Java Orch.: 9, 1858
Phaius woodfordii (Hook.) Merr., J. Arn. Arb. 29: 211, 1948
o **Phaius mishmensis** (Lindl.) Rchb.f., Bonpl. 5: 43, 1857
BM 7479
Sikkim, Assam, Burma, Thailand, Taiwan, Philippines - 1500-2000 m - T
Limatodes mishmensis Lindl., Paxt. Flow. Gard. 3: 36, 1852
Phaius roseus Rolfe, Kew Bull.: 6, 1893
Phaius gracilis Hayata, J. Coll. Sci. Imp. Univ. Tokyo 30: 322, 1911
o **Phaius pauciflorus** (Blume) Blume, Mus. Bot. 2: 181, 1852
BM 7086
Java, Sumatra, Malaya - 600-1000 m - T
Limatodes pauciflora Blume, Bijdr.: 375, 1825
Limatodes punctata Lindl., Fol. Orch. Limat.: 2, 1855
Phaius pallidus Ridley, J. Linn. Soc. 32: 313, 1896
Limatodes pallidus (Ridley) Ridley, Fl. Mal. Pen. 4: 124, 1924
Phaius pauciflorus var. pallidus (Ridley) Holttum, Gard. Bull. 11: 286, 1947
Phaius tankervilleae (Banks) Blume, Mus. Bot. Lugd. Bat. 2: 177, 1852
BM 1924, BM 4078, BM 6032, BM 7023
Sri Lanka, India, Himalaya, Burma, S. and S.E. Asia, Malaysia, China, Hong Kong, Taiwan, Japan, Philippines to Australia, New Caledonia - 600-1300 m - T
Limodorum tankervilleae Banks, Sert. Angl. 28: Jan., 1789
Phaius grandifolius Lour., Fl. Cochinch. 2: 529, 1790
Limodorum incarvillei Pers., Syn. Pl. 2: 520, 1807
Pachyne spectabilis Salisb., Trans. Hort. Soc. 1: 299, 1812
o Bletia tankervilleae (Banks) R.Br., Hort. Kew ed. 2, 5: 205, 1813
o Phaius wallichii Lindl., Wall., Pl. Asiat. Rarior 2: 46 t. 158, 1831
o Phaius bicolor Lindl., Gen. Sp. Orch. Pl.: 128, 1831
Phaius blumei Lindl., Gen. Sp. Orch. Pl.: 127, 1831
Limodorum tankervilleae Roxb., Fl. Ind. 3: 466, 1832 (non Banks)
Phaius grandifolius var. superbus Van Houtte, Fl. Serre 7: 259, 1852
Phaius carronii F. Muell., Ess. Pl. Esp. Burdekin: 19, 1860
Phaius grandiflorus Rchb.f., Walp. Ann. 6: 459, 1862
Phaius leucophoeus F. Muell., Fragm. Phyt. Austr. 4: 163, 1864
o Phaius blumei var. bernaysii Rchb.f., Gard. Chron.: 361, 1873
Phaius incarvillei (Pers.) Kuntze, Rev. Gen. 2: 675, 1891
Phaius tankervilleae var. superbus (Van Houtte) S.Y. Hu, Quart. J. Taiwan Mus. 27 (3.4): 464, 1974
Phaius tetragonus (Thouars) Rchb.f., Bonpl. 3: 221, 1855
BM 4442
Réunion, Mauritius, Seychelles - T
Epidendrum tetragonum Thouars, Fl. Iles Afr.: t. 34, 1804
o Pesomeria tetragona (Thouars) Lindl., Bot. Reg.: Misc. 6, 1838
Phaius villosus Blume, Mus. Bot. Lugd. Bat. 2: 182, 1856
o **Phaius tuberculosus** (Thouars) Blume, Mus. Bot. Lugd. Bat. 2: 181, 1856
BM 7307
Madagascar - T
Limodorum tuberculosum Thouars, Orch. Iles Afr.: t. 31, 1822
Bletia tuberculosa (Thouars) Sprengel, Syst. 3: 744, 1826
Phaius tuberculatus Blume, Orch. Arch. Ind.: t. 2, 1857
Phaius warpurii Weathers ex Gard. Chron.: 82, 1901
Gastrorchis tuberculosa (Thouars) Schltr., Fedde Rep. 33: 169, 1925
Phalaenopsis amabilis (L.) Blume, Bijdr. 7: 294, 1825
BM 5184
Sumatra, Java, Borneo, Palawan, New Guinea, Australia (Queensland) - E
Epidendrum amabile L., Sp. Pl.: 953, 1753
Cymbidium amabile (L.) Roxb., Hort. Beng. 63: 1814
Synadena amabilis (L.) Raf., Fl. Tellur. 4: 9, 1838
o Phalaenopsis grandiflora Lindl., Gard. Chron.: 39, 1848
Phalaenopsis amabilis var. grandiflora (Lindl.) Bateman, Second Cent. Orch. Pl.: t. 114, 1867
Phalaenopsis grandiflora var. gracillima Burb., The Garden 22: 118, 1882
Phalaeonopsis gloriosa Rchb.f., Gard. Chron.: 554, 1888
Phalaenopsis aphrodite var. gloriosa (Rchb.f.) Veitch, Man. Orch. Pl. pt. 7: 25, 1891
Phalaenopsis amabilis var. fournieri Cogn., Chron. Orch.: 166, 1898
Phalaenopsis amabilis var. rimestadiana Linden, Lindenia 16: 35 t. 736, 1901
Phalaenopsis rimestadiana (Linden) Rolfe, Orch. Rev. 13: 260, 1905
Phalaenopsis amabilis var. rimestadiana alba hort., Orchis 1: 27 t. 4, 1906
Phalaenopsis amabilis var. aphrodite subvar. gloriosa (Rchb.f.) Ames, Orchid. 2: 227, 1908
Phalaenopsis × elisabethae hort., Rev. Hort. n.s. 20: 534, 1927
Phalaenopsis amabilis var. ramosa van Deventer, Orchideeën 1: 94 figs. 1 & 2, 1935
Phalaenopsis amabilis var. gloriosa (Pleihari) van Brero, De Orchidee 6: 46, 1937
Phalaenopsis pleibury Burgeff, Cat. Bot. Gard. Wuerzburg, 1968 (nomen)
Phalaenopsis aphrodite Rchb.f., Hamb. Gartenz. 18: 35, 1862
BM 4297
Taiwan, Philippines (Babuyan Is., Sulu Archipelago), Java - E
o Phalaenopsis amabilis Lindl., Bot. Reg. 24: t. 34, 1838 (non Blume, 1825)
Phalaenopsis amabilis var. longifolia Don, Hort. Cantabr. ed. 13: 608, 1845
Phalaenopsis amabilis var. rotundifolia Don, Hort. Cantabr. ed. 13: 608, 1845
Phalaenopsis ambigua Rchb.f., Hamb. Gartenz. 18: 35, 1862
Phalaenopsis erubescens Burb., The Garden 9: 314, 1876
Phalaenopsis amabilis var. dayana hort. ex Warner & Williams, Orch. Alb. 1: t. 11, 1881
Phalaenopsis amabilis var. ambigua (Rchb.f.) Burb., The Garden 22: 119, 1882
Phalaenopsis amabilis var. erubescens (Burb.) Burb., The Garden 22: 119, 1882
Phalaenopsis aphrodite var. dayana (hort. ex Warner & Williams) Veitch, Man. Orch. Pl. 7: 24, 1891
Phalaenopsis amabilis var. aphrodite (Rchb.f.) Ames, Orchid. 2: 226, 1908
Phalaenopsis amabilis var. aphrodite subvar. erubescens (Burb.) Ames, Orchid. 2: 227, 1908
Phalaenopsis amabilis var. aphrodite subvar. dayana (hort. ex Warner & Williams) Ames, Orchid. 2: 227, 1908
Phalaenopsis amabilis var. formosa Shimadzu, Orch. Rev. 29: 68, 1921 (nomen)
Phalaenopsis formosana Miwa, Pract. Hort. 27: 115, fig., 1941 (nomen illeg.)
Phalaenopsis babuyana Miwa, Pract. hort. 27: 117, 1941 (nomen illeg.)
Phalaenopsis formosum hort. ex Sander's One-Table List of Orch. Hybr. 2: 862, 1961
Phalaenopsis cornu-cervi (Breda) Blume & Rchb.f., Hamb. Gartenz. 16: 116, 1860
BM 5570
Burma, Thailand, Java, Sumatra, Borneo - E
o Polychilos cornu-cervi Breda, Gen. Sp. Orch. Asclep.: t. 1, 1827
Polystylus cornu-cervi (Breda) Hassk., Nat. Tijdschr. Ned. Ind. 10: 3, 1856
Phalaenopsis devriesiana Rchb.f., Hamb. Gartenz. 16: 116, 1860
Phalaenopsis equestris (Schauer) Rchb.f., Linnaea 22: 864, 1850
BM 5212
Philippines, Taiwan - up to 400 m - E
Stauroglottis equestris Schauer, Nov. Acad. Cur. 19, Suppl. 1, 432, 1843
o Phalaenopsis rosea Lindl., Gard. Chron.: 671, 1848
Phalaenopsis stauroglottis hort. ex Rollinson, Gen. Cat.: 42, 1876 (nomen)
Phalaenopsis rosea var. deliciosa Burb., The Garden 22: 119, 1882
Phalaenopsis riteiwanensis Masam., Trans. Nat. Hist. Soc. Form. 24: 213, 1934
Stauroglottis riteiwanensis Masam., Trans. Nat. Hist. Soc. Form. 24: 213, 1934
o **Phalaenopsis kunstleri** Hook.f., Fl. Brit. Ind. 6: 30, 1890
BM 7885
Malaya (Perak) - E

o **Phalaenopsis lowii** Rchb.f., Bot. Zeit. 20: 214, 1862
BM 5351
Burma (Moulmein) – E, L
Phalaenopsis proboscidioides Parish ex Rchb.f., Xen. Orch. 2: 139, 1868 (nomen)
o **Phalaenopsis lueddemanniana** Rchb. f., Bot. Zeit. 23: 146, 1865
BM 5523
Philippines – E
Phalaenopsis lueddemannii Boxall ex Naves, Nov. App.: 243, 1882
o **Phalaenopsis mariae** Burb. ex Warner & Williams, Orch. Alb. 2: t. 80, 1883
BM 6964
Philippines (Sulu Archipelago), Borneo – up to 700 m – E
o **Phalaenopsis parishii** Rchb.f., Bot. Zeit. 23: 146, 1865
BM 5815
E. Himalaya, Burma – E
Grafia parishii (Rchb.f.) A. Hawkes, Phytol. 13: 306, 1966
o **Phalaenopsis schilleriana** Rchb.f., Hamb. Gartenz. 16: 115, 1860
BM 5530
Philippines (Luzon) – E
Phalaenopsis schilleriana var. viridi-maculata Duchartre, J. Soc. Imp. Hort. 8: 609 t. 17, 1862
Phalaenopsis schilleriana var. delicata Dean, Fl. Mag. n.s. 6: t. 257, 1877
Phalaenopsis schilleriana var. compacta nana hort., Gard. Chron.: 356, 1890 (nomen)
Phalaenopsis schilleriana var. odorata van Brero, De Orchidee 4: 23, 1935 (nomen illeg.)
Phalaenopsis speciosa Rchb. f. var. **tetraspis** (Rchb. f.) Sweet, Am. Orch. Soc. Bull. 37: 1092, 1968
BM 7321
Andaman Is., Nicobar Is. – E
o Phalaenopsis tetraspis Rchb. f., Xen. Orch. 2: 146, 1868
Phalaenopsis barrii King ex Hook., Ann. Roy. Bot. Gard. Calcutta 5: 38, 1895 (nomen nudum)
o **Phalaenopsis stuartiana** Rchb. f., Gard. Chron.: 748, 1881
BM 6622
Philippines (Mindanao) – E
Phalaenopsis stuartiana var. nobilis Rchb.f., Gard. Chron.: 748, 1881
Phalaenopsis schilleriana var. stuartiana (Rchb.f.) Burb., The Garden 22: 119, 1882
Phalaenopsis schilleriana var. vestalis Rchb.f., Gard. Chron.: 330, 1882
Phalaenopsis schilleriana var. alba Roebelen, Gard. Chron.: 459, 1890
Phalaenopsis schilleriana subvar. vestalis (Rchb.f.) Veitch, Man. Orch. Pl. pt. 7: 37, 1891
o **Phalaenopsis sumatrana** Korth. & Rchb.f., Hamb. Gartenz. 16: 115, 1860
BM 5527
Burma, Thailand, Malaya, Sumatra, Java, Borneo – E
Phalaenopsis zebrina Witte, Ann. Hort. Bot. Leiden 4: 145, 1860
Phalaenopsis acutifolia Linden, Lindenia 2: 11, 1886
o **Phalaenopsis violacea** Witte, Ann. Hort. Bot. Leiden 4: 129, 1860
BM 9198
Sumatra, Borneo, Malaya – E
Stauritis violacea (Witte) Rchb.f., Hamb. Gartenz. 18: 34, 1862
Stauropsis violacea (Witte) Rchb.f., Xen. Orch. 2: 7, 1862
Phragmipedium caricinum (Lindl. & Paxton) Rolfe, Orch. Rev. 4: 332, 1896
BM 5466
Peru, Bolivia, Brazil – T, E
o Cypripedium caricinum Lindl. & Paxton, Paxt., Flow. Gard. 1: 39, 1850
Selenipedium caricinum (Lindl. & Paxton) Rchb.f., Bonpl. 2: 116, 1854
Selenipedium pearcei Rchb.f., Fl. Serres 16: t. 1648, 1866
Cypripedium pearcei hort. ex Veitch, Man. Orch. Pl. pt. 4: 60, 1889
Paphiopedilum caricinum (Lindl. & Paxton) Pfitzer, Engl. Bot. Jahrb. 19: 41, 1894
Phragmopedilum caricinum (Lindl. & Paxton) Rolfe & Pfitzer, Pflanzenr. Heft 12: 46, 1903
Phragmipedium klotzscheanum (Rchb.f. ex Schomb.) Rolfe, Orch. Rev. 4: 332, 1896
BM 7178
Venezuela, Guyana, Brazil – up to 1000 m – T
o Cypripedium klotzscheanum Rchb.f. ex Schomb., Vers. Fl. Faun. Brit. Guyana: 1069, 1848
Selenipedium schomburgkianum Rchb.f., Xen. Orch. 1: 3, 1854
Cypripedium schomburgkianum (Rchb.f.) Klotzsch ex Schomb., Bot. Remin. Brit., Guyana: 59, 1876
Paphiopedilum klotzscheanum (ex Schomb.) Stein, Orchideenb.: 473, 1892
Selenipedium schomburgkianum (Rchb.f.) Desbois., Cypr.: 532, 1898

Phragmipedium longifolium (Rchb.f. & Warsc.) Rolfe, Orch. Rev. 4: 330 fig. 3, 1896
BM 5970
Costa Rica, Panama, Colombia, Ecuador – up to 2000 m – T
o Cypripedium longifolium Rchb.f. & Warsc., Bot. Zeit. 10: 690, 1852
Selenipedium longifolium (Rchb.f. & Warsc.) Rchb.f. & Warsc., Xen. Orch. 1: 3, 1854
Selenipedium reichenbachii Endres ex Rchb.f., Gard. Chron.: 1206, 1869 (nomen nudum)
Cypripedium reichenbachii Bull., Cat. 48: 4, 1869
Paphiopedilum longifolium (Rchb.f. & Warsc.) Pfitzer, Nat. Pflanzenf. 2, 4: 84, 1888
Phragmipedium roezlii (Rchb.f.) Garay, Orch. Digest. 43: 143, 1979
BM 6217
Costa Rica, Panama, Colombia – T
Selenipedium roezlii Rchb.f., Gartenfl. 63: t. 714, 1871
o Cypripedium roezlii (Rchb.f.) Regel, Gartenfl.: 97, 1873
Paphiopedilum roezlii (Rchb.f.) Pfitzer, Engl. Jahrb. Bot. Jahrb. 19: 42, 1894
Phragmipedium sargentianum (Rolfe) Rolfe, Orch. Rev. 4: 332, 1896
BM 7446
Brazil – T
o Selenipedium sargentianum Rolfe, Orch. Rev. 1: 239, 1893
Cypripedium sargentianum (Rolfe) Sander, Gard. Chron.: 781, 1894
Paphiopedilum sargentianum (Rolfe) Hallier, Ann. Jard. Bot. Buitenz. 14: 46, 1896
Phragmopedilum sargentianum (Rolfe) Pfitzer, Engl. Bot. Jahrb. 25: 527, 1898
Phragmipedium schlimii (Rchb.f.) Rolfe, Orch. Rev. 4: 330, 1896
BM 5614
Colombia – 1500–1800 m – T
Selenipedium schlimii Rchb.f., Bonpl. 2: 277, 1854
o Cypripedium schlimii (Rchb.f.) Bateman, Bot. Mag.: t. 5614, 1866
Paphiopedilum schlimii (Rchb.f.) Pfitzer, Engl. Bot. Jahrb. 19: 42, 1894
Physosiphon tubatus (Lodd.) Rchb.f., Walp. Ann. 6: 18, 1861
BM 4869, BM 9325
Mexico, Guatemala, El Salvador, Honduras, Nicaragua – up to 3500 m – E
Stelis tubatus Lodd., Bot. Cab.: t. 1601, 1830
o Physosiphon loddigesii Lindl., Bot. Reg. 21: sub. t. 1797, 1835
Physosiphon carinatus Lindl., Bot. Reg. 24: Misc. p. 72, 1838
Physosiphon ochraceus Rich. & Galeotti, Ann. Sci. Nat. s. 3, 3: 17, 1845
Physosiphon guatemalensis Rolfe, Kew Bull.: 197, 1891
o Physosiphon lindleyi Rolfe, Kew Bull.: 61, 1893
Physosiphon moorei hort., Kew Handl. Orch.: 189, 1896
Platanthera ciliaris (L.) Lindl., Gen. Sp. Orch. Pl.: 292, 1835
BM 1668
N. America, Canada – T
Orchis ciliaris L., Sp. Pl. 2: 939, 1753
o Habenaria ciliaris (L.) R.Br., Hort. Kew ed. 2, 5: 194, 1813
Blephariglottis flaviflora Raf., Fl. Tellur. 2: 38, 1836
Blephariglottis ciliaris (L.) Rydb., Britton Man.: 296, 1901
Platythelys maculata (Hook.) Garay, Bradea 2: 197, 1977
BM 5305
Guatemala, Honduras, Costa Rica, Venezuela, Colombia, Ecuador – T
o Physurus maculatus Hook., Bot. Mag.: t. 5305 fig. 83, 1862
Erythrodes maculata (Hook.) Ames, Orchid. 7: 72, 1922
Plectrelminthus caudatus (Lindl.) Summerh., Kew Bull. 3: 441, 1949
BM 4370
Guinea, Sierra Leone, Liberia, Ivory Coast, Ghana, Nigeria, W. Cameroun, C. African Rep., Zaire – E
o Angraecum caudatum Lindl., Cat.: t. 147, 1836
Listrostachys caudata (Lindl.) Rchb.f., F.T.A. 7: 153, 1864
Leptocentrum caudatum (Lindl.) Schltr., F.W.T.A. ed. 1, 2: 457, 1914
Pleione bulbocodioides (Franchet) Rolfe, Orch. Rev. 11: 291, 1903
BM 8106, BM 866 ns
China (Anhui, Gansu, Guizhou, Hubei, Sichuan, S.E. Tibet, Yunnan) – 1200–4600 m – E, L
Coelogyne bulbocodioides Franchet, Nouv. Arch. Mus. Paris s. 2, 10: 84, 1888
Coelogyne delavayi Rolfe, Bull. Misc. Inf. Kew: 195, 1896
Coelogyne henryi Rolfe, Bull. Misc. Inf. Kew, 1896
Coelogyne pogonioides Rolfe, Bull. Misc. Inf. Kew: 196, 1896
Pleione delavayi (Rolfe) Rolfe, Orch. Rev. 11: 291, 1903
Pleione pogonioides (Rolfe) Rolfe, Orch. Rev. 11: 291, 1903
Pleione mandarinorum (Kraenzlin ex Diels) Kraenzlin, Pflanzenr. Heft 32: 128, 1907
Pleione mairei Schltr., Fedde Rep. Sp. Nov. Beih. 4: 61, 1919
Pleione amoena Schltr., Fedde Rep. Sp. Nov. Beih. 4: 185, 1919
Pleione henry (Rolfe) Schltr., Fedde Rep. Sp. Nov. Beih. 4: 186, 1919

Pleione smithii Schltr., Act. Hort. Goth. 1: 149, 1924
Pleione communis Gagnepain, Bull. Soc. Bot. Fr. 78: 25, 1931
Pleione communis var. subobtusum Gagnepain, Bull. Soc. Bot. Fr., 1931
Pleione rhombilabia Hand.-Mazz., Symb. Sin. 7: 1348, 1936
○ (Pleione yunnanensis Rolfe, Orch. Rev.: 292, 1903; misidentified)
Pleione formosana Hayata, J. Coll. Sc. Tokyo 30, Art. 1: 326, 1911
BM 8729, BM 421 ns
E. China, Taiwan - T
○ Pleione pricei Rolfe, Bot. Mag.: t. 8729, 1917
Pleione hui Schltr., Fedde Rep. 19: 377, 1924
Pleione hookeriana (Lindl.) B.S. Williams, Orch. Grow. Man. ed. 6: 548, 1885
BM 6388, BM 862 ns
S. Tibet, C. & E. Nepal, Bhutan, N.E. India (Assam, Sikkim), Burma, N. Thailand, Laos - 2100-3900 m - T, L
○ Coelogyne hookeriana Lindl., Fol. Orch. Coelog.: 14, 1854
Coelogyne hookeriana var. brachyglossa Rchb.f., Gard. Chron.: 833, 1887
Pleione hookeriana var. brachyglossa (Rchb.f.) Rolfe, Orch. Rev. 11: 291, 1903
Pleione laotica Kerr, J. Siam. Soc. Nat. Hist. suppl. 9: 235, 1933
Pleione humilis (Smith) D. Don., Prod. Fl. Nepal. 37, 1825
BM 5674, BM 863 ns
Nepal, Sikkim, Assam, Manipur, Burma - 1850-3200 m - T, L
Epidendrum humile Smith, Exot. Bot. 2: 75 t. 98, 1806
○ Coelogyne humilis (Smith) Lindl., Coll. Bot.: 37, 1821
Cymbidium humile (Smith) Lindl., Coll. Bot.: sub. t. 37, 1825
Coelogyne humilis var. tricolor Rchb.f., Gard. Chron.: 394, 1880
Coelogyne humilis var. albata Rchb.f., Gard. Chron.: 392, 1888
Pleione diantha Schltr., Orchis 9: 44, 1915
Pleione × lagenaria Lindl., Paxt. Flow Gard. 2: 5 t. 39, 1851
BM 5370, BM 860 ns (in part)
Assam, S. China - 1500-2500 m - T
= Pleione maculata Lindl. × Pleione praecox D. Don
○ Coelogyne lagenaria Lindl., Paxt. Flow. Gard. 2: 5 t. 39 fig. 2, 1850
Pleione maculata (Lindl.) Lindl., Paxt. Flow. Gard. 2: 5 t. 39 fig. 1, 1851
BM 4691, BM 860 ns (in part)
Bhutan, Sikkim, Assam, Manipur, Burma, S. China, N. Thailand - 600-2600 m - T
Coelogyne candida Lindl., Wall. Cat. 54: 1964, 1829 (nomen nudum)
○ Coelogyne maculata Lindl., Gen. Sp. Orch. Pl.: 43, 1830
Pleione diphylla Lindl., Paxt. Flow. Gard. 2: 66, 1851
Coelogyne diphylla (Lindl.) Lindl., Fol. Orch. Coelog.: 15, 1854
Coelogyne arthuriana Rchb.f., Gard. Chron.: 40, 1881
Pleione maculata var. virginea Rchb.f., Gard. Chron.: 682, 1887
Pleione maculata var. arthuriana (Rchb.f.) Rolfe ex Pfitzer & Kraenzlin, Pflanzenr. Heft 32: 128, 1907
Gymnostylis candida (Lindl.) Wallich ex Pfitzer & Kraenzlin, Pflanzenr. Heft 32: 127, 1907
Pleione praecox (Smith) D. Don, Prod. Fl. Nepal: 37, 1825
BM 4496, BM 5753, BM 861 ns
Nepal, Sikkim, Bhutan, Burma, S. China, Thailand - 1500-2700 m - T
Epidendrum praecox Smith, Exot. Bot. 2: 73 t. 97, 1806
Coelogyne praecox (Smith) Lindl., Coll. Bot.: sub. t. 37, 1821
Cymbidium praecox (Smith) Lindl., Coll. Bot., 1825
Coelogyne wallichiana Lindl., Gen. Sp. Orch. Pl.: 43, 1830
○ Coelogyne wallichii Hook., Bot. Mag.: t. 4496, 1850
Pleione wallichiana (Lindl.) Lindl., Paxt. Flow. Gard. 1: 66, 185
Coelogyna praecox var. sanguinea Lindl., Fol. Orch. Coelog.: 16, 1854
Coelogyne praecox var. wallichiana (Lindl.) Lindl., Fol. Orch. Coelog.: 16, 1854
○ Coelogyne reichenbachiana T. Moore & Veitch, Gard. Chron.: 1210, 1868
Pleione reichenbachiana (T. Moore & Veitch) B.S. Williams, Orch. Grow. Man. ed. 4: 252, 1871
Coelogyne praecox var. tenera Rchb.f., Gard. Chron.: 294, 1883
Pleione concolor hort. ex B.S. Williams, Orch. Grow. Man. ed. 7: 681, 1894
Pleione birmanica (Rchb.f.) B.S. Williams, Orch. Grow. Man. ed. 7, 1894
Pleione praecox var. birmanica (Rchb.f.) Grant, Orch. Burm.: 167, 1895
Pleione praecox var. sanguinea (Lindl.) Pfitzer, Pflanzenr. Heft 32: 126, 1907
Pleione praecox var. candida Pfitzer, Pflanzenr. Heft 32: 126, 1907
Pleione praecox var. alba E.W. Cooper, Roy. Hort. Soc. Dict. Gard.: 1606, 1951
Pleione praecox var. wallichiana (Lindl.) E.W. Cooper, Roy. Hort. Soc. Dict., 1951
Pleione speciosa Ames & Schltr., Fedde Rep. Beih. 4: 61, 1919
BM 8588, BM 868 ns (in part)
C. China (Hubei, Sichuan, Yunnan?) - 1750-2250 m - T, L
Pleione fargesii Gagnepain, Bull. Soc. Bot. Fr. 78: 25, 1931
○ (Pleione pogonioides auct. non Rolfe, Orch. Rev.: 291, 1903; misidentified)
○ **Pleurothallis aristata** Hook., Ann. Mag. Nat. Hist. 1 (2): t. 15, 1839
BM 6886
W. Indies, Costa Rica, Panama, Venezuela, Guyana, Colombia, Ecuador - E
Pleurothallis urbaniana Rchb.f., Ber. Deutsch. Bot. Ges. 3: 279, 1855
Pleurothallis barberana Rchb.f., Gard. Chron.: 6, 1881
Humboldtia aristata (Hook.) Kuntze, Rev. Gen. 2: 667, 1891
Humboldtia barberana (Rchb.f.) Kuntze, Rev. Gen. 2: 667, 1891
Pleurothallis helenae Fawc. & Rendle, J. Bot. 47: 4, 1909
Pleurothallis dichotoma Ames, Sched. Orch. 6: 58, 1923 (non Schltr.)
Pleurothallis divexa Ames, Sched. Orch. 7: 20 t. 5, 1924
○ **Pleurothallis bicarinata** Lindl., Bot. Reg.: Misc. p. 14, 1839
BM 4142
Brazil - E
Humboldtia bicarinata (Lindl.) Kuntze, Rev. Gen.: 667, 1891
Pleurothallis biserrula Rchb.f., Bonpl. 3: 71, 1855
BM 7431
Venezuela, Colombia, Ecuador - 1500-1800 m - E
Pleurothallis sirene Rchb.f., Bonpl. 3: 71, 1855
○ Pleurothallis scapha Rchb.f., Gard. Chron.: 162, 1874
Humboldtia biserrula (Rchb.f.) Kuntze, Rev. Gen.: pt. 2: 667, 1891
Humboldtia sirene (Rchb.f.) Kuntze, Rev. Gen.: pt. 2: 668, 1891
Pleurothallis hoppii Schltr., Fedde Rep. Beih. 27: 46, 1924
Pleurothallis endotrachys Rchb.f., Linnaea 41: 95, 1876
BM 7129
Mexico, El Salvador, Nicaragua, Costa Rica, Venezuela, Colombia - up to 2200 m - E
Pleurothallis pfavii Rchb.f., Flora 69: 555, 1886
Masdevallia platyrachis Rolfe, Gard. Chron.: 178, 1888
○ Pleurothallis platyrachis (Rolfe) Rolfe, J. Bot. 28: 136, 1890
Humboldtia endotrachys (Rchb.f.) Kuntze, Rev. Gen. pt. 2: 667, 1891
Kraenzlinella platyrachis (Rolfe) Schltr., Orch. Rev. 23: 326, 1915
Pleurothallis spectabilis Ames & C. Schweinf., Sched. Orch. 8: 34, 1925
○ **Pleurothallis grandis** Rolfe, Kew Bull.: 234, 1918
BM 8853
Costa Rica - E
○ **Pleurothallis grobyi** Bateman ex Lindl., Bot. Reg. 21: t. 1797, 1835
BM 3682
Mexico to Bolivia, Brazil, W. Indies - up to 1500 m - E
Pleurothallis picta Lindl., Bot. Reg. 21: sub. t. 1797, 1835
Pleurothallis marginata Lindl., Bot. Reg. 24: Misc. p. 42, 1838
Pleurothallis surinamensis Focke, Tijdschr. nat. Wetensch. 2: 194, 1849
Pleurothallis marginalis Rchb.f., Bonpl. 3: 224, 1855
Pleurothallis perplexa Rchb.f., Hamb. Gartenz. 16: 15, 1860
Pleurothallis trilineata Barb. Rodr., Gen. & Sp. Orch. 1: 6, 1877
Pleurothallis crepidophylla Rchb.f., Otia Bot. Hamb. 1: 18, 1878
Lepanthes marmorata Barb. Rodr., Gen. & Sp. Orch. 2: 42, 1882
Lepanthes trilineata Barb. Rodr., Gen. & Sp. Orch. 2: 42, 1882
Pleurothallis choconiana Wats., Proc. Am. Acad. 23: 285, 1888
Humboldtia grobyi (Bateman ex Lindl.) Kuntze, Rev. Gen.: 668, 1891
Humboldtia marginalis (Rchb.f.) Kuntze, Rev. Gen.: 668, 1891
Humboldtia picta (Lindl.) Kuntze, Rev. Gen.: 668, 1891
Humboldtia marginata (Lindl.) Kuntze, Rev. Gen.: 668, 1891
Humboldtia crepidophylla Kuntze, Rev. Gen.: 667, 1891
Pleurothallis pergracilis Rolfe, Kew Bull.: 334, 1893
Pleurothallis marmorata (Barb. Rodr.) Cogn., Fl. Bras. 3, pt. 4: 490, 1896
Pleurothallis grobyi var. trilineata Cogn., Fl. Bras. 3, pt. 4: 496, 1896
Pleurothallis marmorata var. concolor Cogn., Fl. Bras. 3, pt. 6: 559, 1906
Pleurothallis panamensis Schltr., Fedde Rep. 17: 140, 1921
Pleurothallis biglandulosa Schltr., Notizbl. Bot. Gart. Berlin 8: 119, 1922
Pleurothallis subpicta Schltr., Anex. Inst. Butant. 1, pt. 4: 42, 1922
Pleurothallis dryadum Schltr., Fedde Rep. Beih. 19: 186, 1923
Pleurothallis arevaloi Schltr., Fedde Rep. Beih. 27: 43, 1924
Pleurothallis integrilabia Ames, Hubb. & C. Schweinf., Bot. Mus. Leafl. Harv. Univ. 3: 39, 1934
Pleurothallis ezechiasi Hoehne, Arqu. Bot. S. Paulo 11: pt. 2: 21, 1946
Pleurothallis grobyi var. marmorata Garay, Arq. Jard. Bot. Rio de Janeiro 11: 54, 1951
○ **Pleurothallis immersa** Linden & Rchb.f., Bonpl. 3: 224, 1855
BM 7189
Mexico to Panama, Venezuela, Colombia - E
Pleurothallis krameriana Rchb.f., Hamb. Gartenz. 21: 294, 1865

Humboldtia immersa (Linden & Rchb.f.) Kuntze, Rev. Gen.: 667, 1891
Humboldtia krameriana (Rchb.f.) Kuntze, Rev. Gen.: 667, 1891
Pleurothallis lasiosepala Schltr., Fedde Rep. 11: 43, 1912
Pleurothallis calerae Schltr., Fedde Rep. Beih. 19: 184, 1923
○ **Pleurothallis insignis** Rolfe, Gard. Chron.: 447, 1887
BM 6936
Venezuela, Colombia – up to 1600 m – E
Humboldtia insignis (Rolfe) Kuntze, Rev. Gen. 2: 667, 1891
○ **Pleurothallis prolifera** Herbert ex Lindl., Bot. Reg. 15: t. 1298, 1830
BM 3261
Venezuela, Brazil – up to 1500 m – E
Humboldtia prolifera (Herbert ex Lindl.) Kuntze, Rev. Gen. 2: 668, 1891
Pleurothallis litophila Barb. Rodr., Contrib. Jard. Bot. Rio de Janeiro 4: 100, 1907
Pleurothallis pubescens Lindl., Comp. Bot. Mag. 2: 355, 1836
BM 3897
Mexico to Nicaragua, Venezuela to Bolivia, Brazil – E
Pleurothallis vittata Lindl., Bot. Reg. 24: Misc. 73, 1838
○ Pleurothallis picta Hook., Bot. Mag.: t. 3897, 1842 (non Lindl.)
Pleurothallis smithiana Lindl., Bot. Reg. 29: Misc. 57, 1843
Pleurothallis polystachya A. Rich. & Galeotti, Ann. Sc. Nat. Bot. 3 (3): 16, 1845
Pleurothallis truxillensis Rchb.f., Bonpl. 2: 25, 1854
Pleurothallis bufonis Klotzsch, Allg. Gartenz. 22: 225, 1854
Pleurothallis riograndensis Barb. Rodr., Gen. & Sp. Orch. 2: 28, 1882
Pleurothallis janeirensis Barb. Rodr., Gen. & Sp. Orch. 2: 29, 1882
Humboldtia bufonis (Klotzsch) Kuntze, Rev. Gen. 2: 667, 1891
Humboldtia pubescens (Lindl.) Kuntze, Rev. Gen. 2: 668, 1891
Humboldtia polystachya (A. Rich. & Galeotti) Kuntze, Rev. Gen. 2: 668, 1891
Humboldtia smithiana (Lindl.) Kuntze, Rev. Gen. 2: 668, 1891
Humboldtia truxillensis (Rchb.f.) Kuntze, Rev. Gen. 2: 668, 1891
Humboldtia vittata (Lindl.) Kuntze, Rev. Gen. 2: 668, 1891
Pleurothallis bourgeaui Kraenzlin, Ark. Bot. 168: 15, 1920
Pleurothallis mandibularis Kraenzlin, Vidensk. Meddel. Dansk Nat. Foren Kjobenhaven 71: 169, 1920
○ **Pleurothallis punctulata** Rolfe, Gard. Chron.: 756, 1888
BM 8839
Venezuela, Colombia – 2400–2600 m – E
Humboldtia punctulata (Rolfe) Kuntze, Rev. Gen. 2: 668, 1891
Pleurothallis magnispatha Fold., Act. Bot. Venez. 3: 382, 1968
○ **Pleurothallis saurocephala** Lodd., Bot. Cab.: t. 1571, 1830
BM 3030
Brazil – E
Humboldtia saurocephala (Lodd.) Kuntze, Rev. Gen.: 668, 1891
Pleurothallis schiedei Rchb.f., Linnaea 22: 826, 1849
BM 7094
Mexico, Guatemala, El Salvador – up to 2200 m – E
○ Pleurothallis ornata Rchb.f., ex Wittm., Gartenz. 1: 106, 1882
Polycycnis barbata (Lindl.) Rchb.f., Bonpl. 3: 218, 1855
BM 4479
Costa Rica, S. America, Venezuela, Colombia, Brazil – 500–1100 m – E
○ Cycnoches barbatum Lindl., J. Hort. Soc. Lond. 4: 268, 1849
Polystachya affinis Lindl., Gen. Sp. Orch. Pl.: 73, 1830
BM 4161
Guinea, Sierra Leone, Liberia, Ivory Coast, Ghana, S. Nigeria, E. Cameroun, Gabon, C. African Rep., Zaire, Angola – 1000–1400 m – E
○ Polystachya bracteosa Lindl., Bot. Reg.: Misc. 48, 1840
Polystachya galeata (Sw.) Rchb.f., Walp. Ann. 6: 637, 1863
BM 3707
Guinea, Sierra Leone, Liberia, Ivory Coast, S. Nigeria, Gabon, Zaire – E
Limodorum cucullatum Afzel ex Sw., Kongl. Vet. Acad. Handl. Stockh.: 243, 1800
Dendrobium galeatum Sw., Schrad. Neues J. 1: 96, 1805
Bulbophyllum galeatum (Sw.) Lindl., Gen. Sp. Orch. Pl.: 57, 1830
○ Polystachya grandiflora Lindl., Bot. Mag.: t. 3707, 1839
○ **Polystachya lawrenceana** Kraenzlin, Gard. Chron.: 150, 1893
BM 8211
Malawi – E
○ **Polystachya paniculata** (Sw.) Rolfe, F.T.A. 7: 113, 1897
BM 8618
Guinea, Sierra Leone, Liberia, Ghana, S. Nigeria, Cameroun, Gabon, Zaire, Uganda – E
Dendrobium paniculatum Sw., Schrad. Neues J. 1: 97, 1805
○ **Polystachya pobeguinii** (Finet) Rolfe, Orch. Rev. 26: 107, 1918
BM 8772
Guinea, Sierra Leone, Liberia, Ivory Coast – E
Epiphora pobeguinii Finet, Notul. Syst. 2: 29, 1911
○ **Polystachya pubescens** (Lindl.) Rchb.f., Walp. Ann. 6: 643, 1863
BM 5586
S. Africa (Cape Province, Natal) – 500–1000 m – E
Epiphora pubescens Lindl., Comp. Bot. Mag. 2: 201, 1836
Lissochilus sylvaticus Ecklon ex Sonder, Linnaea 19: 71, 1847
Polystachya lindleyana Harvey, Thes. Cap. 2: 50 t. 178, 1859–63
○ **Ponthieva maculata** Lindl., Ann. Mag. Nat. Hist. 15: 385, 1845
BM 6637
Mexico to Panama, Venez., Colombia, Ecuador – up to 2500 m – E, T
Ponthieva wallisii Rchb.f., Linnaea 41: 101, 1876
Ponthieva formosa Schltr., Fedde Rep. Beih. 19: 12, 1923
Ponthieva brenesii Schltr., Fedde Rep. Beih. 19: 165, 1923
Ponthieva racemosa (Walter) C. Mohr., Contr. US. Nat. Herb. 6: 460, 1901
BM 842
USA (Florida), Mexico, C. America, W. Indies, Venezuela, Brazil, Peru – T
Arethusa racemosa Walter, Fl. Carol.: 222, 1788
○ Neottia glandulosa Sims, Bot. Mag. 21: t. 842, 1805
Ponthieva glandulosa (Sims) R.Br., Hort. Kew. ed. 2, 5: 200, 1813
Ponthieva rostrata Lindl., Ann. Mag. Nat. Hist. 15: 385, 1845
Ponthieva oblongifolia Rich. & Galeotti, Ann. Sci. Nat. s. 3, 3: 30, 1845
Ponthieva guatemalensis Rchb.f., Beitr. Orch. Centr.-Am.: 63, 1866
Ponthieva costaricensis Schltr., Rep. Sp. Nov. Beih. 19: 84, 1923
Porpax meirax (Parish & Rchb.f.) King & Pantl., Ann. Roy. Bot. Gard. Calcutta 8: 114 t. 158, 1898
BM 7329
Himalaya, Sikkim, Burma, Thailand, Malaya – E
Cryptochilus meirax Parish & Rchb.f., Trans. Linn. Soc. 30: 148, 1874
○ Eria meirax (Parish & Rchb.f.) N.E.Br., Gard. Chron.: 603, 1880
Eria elwesii Rchb.f., Gard. Chron. 1: 402, 1883
Porroglossum echidnum (Rchb.f.) Garay, Svensk. Bot. Tidskr. 47: 201, 1953
BM 7664
Venezuela, Colombia, Ecuador – up to 2500 m – E, L, T
Masdevallia echidna Rchb.f., Bonpl. 3: 69, 1855
○ Masdevallia muscosa Rchb.f., Gard. Chron.: 460, 1875
Porroglossum muscosum (Rchb.f.) Schltr., Fedde Rep. Beih. 7: 83, 1920
○ **Promenaea microptera** Rchb.f., Gard. Chron.: 134, 1881
BM 8631
Trop. S. America, Brazil – E
Zygopetalum micropterum Rchb.f., Gard. Chron.: 134 in adnot., 1881
Promenaea stapelioides (Link & Otto) Lindl., Bot. Reg.: Misc. 13, 1843
BM 3877
Brazil – E
Cymbidium stapelioides Link & Otto, Ic. Pl. Sel. Hort. Berol. 111: t. 52, 1828
○ Maxillaria stapelioides (Link & Otto) Lindl., Gen. Sp. Orch. Pl.: 146, 1832
Zygopetalum stapelioides (Link & Otto) Rchb.f., Walp. Ann. 6: 658, 1863
Psychopsis papilio (Lindl.) H.G. Jones, J. Barbados Mus. Hist. Soc. 35 (1): 32, 1975
BM 2795, BM 3733
Trinidad, Venezuela, Colombia, Ecuador, Peru – 500–1000 m – E
○ Oncidium papilio Lindl., Bot. Reg. 2: t. 910, 1825
Psychopsis picta Raf., Fl. Tellur. 4: 40, 1838
○ Oncidium papilio var. limbatum Hook., Bot. Mag.: t. 3733, 1839
Oncidium papilio var. majus Rchb.f., Cat. Hort. Pescatore: 30, 1849
Oncidium papilio var. pictum hort. ex Jennings, Orch.: t. 11, 1875
Oncidium papilio var. eckhardti Linden, Ill. Hort. 30: t. 500, 1883
Psychopsis sanderae (Rolfe) Lueckel & Braem, Die Orchidee 33: 1, 1982
BM 8374
Peru, Bolivia – up to 1500 m – E
Oncidium versteegianum Pulle, Rec. Trav. Bot. Neerl. 6: 255, 1909
○ Oncidium sanderae Rolfe, Gard. Chron.: 67, 1910
Psychopsis versteegianum (Pulle) Lueckel & Braem, Die Orchidee 33 (1), 1982
Pteroglossa euphlebia (Oliver ex Rchb.f.) Garay, Bot. Mus. Leafl. Harv. Univ. 28 (4): 350, 1980
BM 6690
Brazil – T
○ Spiranthes euphlebia Oliver ex Rchb.f., Gartenfl. 32: 3, 1883
Stenorrhynchus euphlebius Oliver ex Rchb.f., Gartenfl. 32: 3, 1883
Cogniauxiocharis euphlebius (Oliver ex Rchb.f.) Hoehne, Arq. Bot. Estad. S. Paulo s. 2, 1: 132 t. 148, 1944

○ **Pterostylis acuminata** R. Br., Prodr. Fl. Nov. Holl.: 326, 1810
BM 3401
Australia (Queensland, New South Wales) – T
○ **Pterostylis banksii** R. Br. ex Cunn., Bot. Mag.: t. 3172, 1832
BM 3172
New Zealand – T
○ **Pterostylis baptistii** Fitzg., Austr. Orch. 1: pt. 1, 1875
BM 6351
E. Australia – T
○ **Pterostylis concinna** R. Br., Prodr. Fl. Nov. Holl.: 326, 1810
BM 3400
E. Australia, Tasmania – T
○ **Pterostylis curta** R. Br., Prodr. Fl. Nov. Holl.: 326, 1810
BM 3086
New Caledonia, E. Australia, Tasmania – T
○ **Pterostylis nutans** R. Br., Prodr. Fl. Nov. Holl.: 327, 1810
BM 3085
E. Australia – T
○ **Renanthera annamensis** Rolfe, Bot. Mag.: t. 8116, 1907
BM 8116
Vietnam – E
○ **Renanthera coccinea** Lour., Fl. Cochinch. 2: 521, 1790
BM 2997, BM 2998
Burma, Thailand, S. China, Kampuchea, Laos, Vietnam, Philippines, Java – E
Epidendrum renanthera Räusch., Nom. ed. 3: 265, 1797
Gongora phillippica Llanos, Mem. Acad. Cien. Madr. 2: 498, 1859
○ **Renanthera imschootiana** Rolfe, Kew Bull.: 200, 1891
BM 7711
Assam, Burma, Kampuchea, Laos, Vietnam – E
Renanthera papilio King & Pantl., J. As. Soc. Beng. 64 (2): 388, 1895
○ **Renanthera storiei** Rchb. f., Gard. Chron.: 296, 1880
BM 7537
Philippines – E
Vanda storiei Storie ex Rchb. f., Gard. Chron.: 296, 1880
○ **Restrepia elegans** Karsten, Allg. Gartenz. 15: 202, 1847
BM 5966
Venezuela – E
Restrepia punctulata Lindl., Fol. Orch. Restrepia 2: 2, 1859
Restrepia guttulata Lindl., Comp. Mag. 2: 357, 1836
BM 6288
Venezuela, Colombia, Ecuador – E
Restrepia maculata Lindl., Orch. Lond.: 4, 1846
Restrepia pardina Lemaire, Ill. Hort. 16: 8 t. 601, 1869
Restrepia leopardina hort. ex Orch. Rev. 7: 94, 1899
Restrepia leopardina var. rosea hort., Orch. Rev. 12: 211, 1904
○ (Restrepia antennifera auct. non Kunth, Nov. Gen. Sp. 1: 294, 1816; misidentified)
Restrepia hemsleyana Schltr., Fedde Rep. 15: 266, 1918
BM 7930
Colombia – E
Restrepia antennifera Hemsley, Bot. Mag.: t. 7930, 1903 (non Kunth)
○ (Restrepia antennifera Kunth, Nov. Gen. Sp. 1: 294, 1816; misidentified)
○ **Restrepia striata** Rolfe, Gard. Chron.: 137, 1891
BM 7233
Colombia, Ecuador – E
Restrepia xanthophthalma Rchb. f., Hamb. Gartenz. 21: 300, 1865
BM 5257
Mexico, Guatemala, El Salvador, Honduras, Costa Rica, Panama – up to 1300 m – E
○ Restrepia langbergii Rchb. f. sensu Hook., Bot. Mag.: t. 5257, 1861
Restrepia powellii Schltr., Fedde Rep. Beih. 17: 25, 1922
Restrepia tonduzii Schltr., Fedde Rep. Beih. 19: 291, 1923
Pleurothallis xanthophthalma (Rchb. f.) L. O. Williams, Bot. Mus. Leafl. Harv. Univ. 8: 144, 1940
Restrepiella ophiocephala (Lindl.) Garay & Dunsterv., Venez. Orch. Ill. 4: 266, 1966
BM 9128
Mexico to Costa Rica – E
Pleurothallis peduncularis Hook., J. Bot. 3: 308, t. 9, 34, 1838
○ Pleurothallis ophiocephala Lindl., Bot. Reg. 24: Misc. p. 34, 1838
Pleurothallis puberula Klotzsch, Allg. Gartenz. 22: 393, 1854
Restrepia ophiocephala (Lindl.) Rchb. f., Bonpl. 2: 88, 1854
Pleurothallis stigmatoglossa Rchb. f. ex Lindl., Fol. Orch. Pleuroth. 2: 18, 1859
Rhyncholaelia digbyana (Lindl.) Schltr., Beih. Bot. Centralbl. 36: Abt. 2: 477, 1918
BM 4474
Mexico, Guatemala, Belize, Honduras – E
○ Brassavola digbyana Lindl., Bot. Reg. 32: t. 53, 1846
Bletia digbyana (Lindl.) Rchb. f., Walp. Ann. 6: 422, 1861
Laelia digbyana (Lindl.) Benth. ex Jackson, Ind. Kew. 2: 21, 1895
Laelia digbyana var. fimbripetala Ames, Am. Orch. Soc. Bull. 1: 59, 1932
Rhyncholaelia glauca (Lindl.) Schltr., Beih. Bot. Centralbl. 36: Abt. 2: 477, 1918
BM 4033
Mexico, Guatemala, Honduras, Nicaragua, Panama – E
○ Brassavola glauca Lindl., Bot. Reg. 25: Misc. p. 47, 1839
Bletia glauca (Lindl.) Rchb. f., Walp. Ann. 6: 422, 1862
Laelia glauca (Lindl.) Benth. ex Jackson, Index Kew 2: 21, 1895
Rhynchostylis gigantea (Lindl.) Ridley, J. Linn. Soc. 32: 356, 1896
BM 5635
Burma, Thailand, Kampuchea, Laos, Vietnam – E
○ Saccolabium giganteum Lindl., Wall. Cat.: 7306, 1832
Saccolabium densiflorum Lindl., Gen. Sp. Orch. Pl.: 220, 1833
Vanda densiflora (Lindl.) Lindl., Paxt. Flow. Gard. 2: 21 t. 42, 1851/52
Anota densiflora (Lindl.) Schltr., Orchideen: 588, 1915
Rhynchostylis densiflora (Lindl.) L. O. Williams, Bot. Mus. Leafl. Harv. Univ.: 5 (4): 58, 1937
Anota gigantea (Lindl.) Fukuyama, Trans. Nat. Hist. Soc. Taiwan 34: 3, 1944
Rhynchostylis gigantea (Lindl.) Ridley var. harrisoniana (Hook.) Holttum, Gard. Bull. 11: 287, 1947
BM 5433
China, Malaya – E
○ Saccolabium harrisonianum Hook., Bot. Mag.: t. 5433, 1864
Rhynchostylis retusa (L.) Blume, Bijdr.: 286 t. 49, 1825
BM 4108
Sri Lanka, S. India, Himalaya, Sikkim, Assam, Burma, Kampuchea, Laos, Vietnam, Malaya, Java, Philippines – E
Epidendrum retusum L., Sp. Pl.: 953, 1753
Limodorum retusum (L.) Sw., Nov. Act. Upsal. 6: 80, 1799
Aerides retusa (L.) Sw., J. Bot. 2: 233, 1799
Aerides praemorsa Willd., Sp. Pl. 4: 130, 1805
Rhynchostylis praemorsa (Willd.) Blume, Sp. Pl. 4: 130, 1805
Aerides guttata Roxb., Hort. Beng.: 63, 1814
Aerides spicata D. Don, Prodr. Fl. Nep.: 31, 1825
Epidendrum hippium Buch.-Ham. ex D. Don, Prod. Fl. Nepal: 32, 1825
Sarcanthus guttatus (Roxb.) Lindl., Bot. Reg.: t. 1443, 1831
○ Saccolabium guttatum (Roxb.) Lindl., Wall. Cat.: 7308, 1832 (nomen nudum)
Saccolabium praemorsum (Willd.) Lindl., Gen. Sp. Orch. Pl.: 221, 1833
Saccolabium spicatum (D. Don) Lindl., Gen. Sp. Orch. Pl.: 221, 1833
Orchis lanigera Blanco, Fl. Filip.: 641, 1837
Saccolabium blumei Lindl., Sert. Orch.: 47, 1841
Saccolabium macrostachyum Lindl., Sert. Orch.: 47, 1841
Saccolabium retusum (L.) Voight, Hort. Suburb. Calcutta: 630, 1845
Saccolabium rheedii Wight, Ic. Pl. Ind. Or. 5 (1): 19 pl. 1745/46, 1851
Rhynchostylis guttata (Roxb.) Rchb. f., Bonpl. 2: 93, 1854
Saccolabium violaceum Rchb. f., Bonpl. 2: 93, 1854
Saccolabium garwalicum Lindl., J. Linn. Soc. 3: 32, 1859
Rhynchostylis garwalica (Lindl.) Rchb. f., Walp. Ann. 6: 888, 1864
Saccolabium littorale Rchb. f., Gard. Chron.: 198, 1881
Saccolabium berkeleyi Rchb. f., Gard. Chron.: 814, 1883
Saccolabium heathii hort., Gard. Chron.: 369, 1885
Gastrochilus blumei Kuntze, Rev. Gen.: 661, 1891
Gastrochilus gorwalicus Kuntze, Rev. Gen.: 661, 1891
Gastrochilus retusus Kuntze, Rev. Gen.: 661, 1891
Gastrochilus rheedii Kuntze, Rev. Gen.: 661, 1891
Gastrochilus spicatus Kuntze, Rev. Gen.: 661, 1891
Gastrochilus praemorsus Kuntze, Rev. Gen.: 661, 1891
Saccolabium furcatum hort. ex Williams, Orch. Grow. Man. ed. 7: 700, 1894
○ **Robiquetia mooreana** (Rolfe) J. J. Smith, Nat. Tijds. Nederl. Ind.: 44, 1912
BM 7428
New Guinea, Solomon Is. – E
○ Saccolabium mooreanum Rolfe, Kew Bull.: 64, 1893
Saccolabium sayerianum F. Muell. & Kraenzlin, Oesterr. Bot. Zeit. 44: 253, 1894
Saccolabium sanderianum Kraenzlin, Xen. Orch. 3: 134 t. 276 II, 1894
Saccolabium kerstingianum Kraenzlin, Fl. Dtsch. Schutzgeb. Südsee: 251, 1901
Rodriguezia decora (Lemaire) Rchb. f., Bot. Zeit. 10: 771, 1852
BM 4834, BM 5419
Brazil – E
○ Burlingtonia decora Lemaire, Jard. Fleur. 2: t. 188, 1852
Burlingtonia amoena Planchon, Fl. Serres 7: 195, 1852
○ Burlingtonia decora var. picta Hook., Bot. Mag.: t. 5419, 1863
Rodriguezia lanceolata Ruiz Lopez & Pavón, Syst. Veg. Fl. Peru. Chil. 1: 219, 1798
BM 3524

Panama, Venezuela, Trinidad, Guyana, Colombia, Ecuador, Brazil – E
o Rodriguezia secunda Kunth, Nov. Gen. Sp. 1: 367, 1815
Pleurothallis coccinea Hook., Exot. Fl. 2: t. 129, 1815
Rodriguezia lanceolata Lodd., Bot. Cab. 7: t. 696, 1822 (non Ruiz Lopez & Pavón)
Burlingtonia rosea hort. ex Rand, J. Orch. 5: 14, 1894
Rodriguezia secunda var. panamensis Schltr., Fedde Rep. Beih. 17: 75, 1922
Rossioglossum grande (Lindl.) Garay & G.C. Kennedy, Orch. Digest 40 (4): 142, 1976
BM 3955
Mexico, Guatemala – up to 2700 m – E
o Odontoglossum grande Lindl., Bot. Reg. 26: 47, 1840
Rudolfiella aurantiaca (Lindl.) Hoehne, Ic. Orch. Bras.: 220 t. 197, 1949
BM 3597
Brazil, Guyana, Surinam, Trinidad, Venezuela, Colombia, Peru – E
o Bifrenaria aurantiaca Lindl., Bot. Reg. 22: t. 1875, 1836
Lindleyella aurantiaca (Lindl.) Schltr., Orchideen: 414, 1914
Sacoila lanceolata (Aublet) Garay, Bot. Mus. Leafl. 28 (4): 352 t. 45, 1980
BM 1036, BM 2797
Florida to Panama, W. Indies, S. America – T
Limodorum lanceolatum Aublet, Pl. Guian. 2: 821, 1775
Satyrium orchioides Sw., Prodr. Veg. Ind. Occ.: 118, 1788
Neottia lanceolata (Aublet) Willd., Sp. Pl. 4: 73, 1805
o Neottia orchioides (Sw.) Willd., Sp. Pl. 4: 75, 1805
Ibidium cristalligerum Salisb., Trans. Hort. Soc. 1: 292, 1812 (nomen illeg.)
Neottia squamulosa Kunth, Nov. Gen. Sp. 1: 332, 1816
Stenorrhynchos orchioides (Sw.) L.C. Rich., Mém. Mus. Par. 4: 59, 1817
Stenorrhynchos lanceolatum (Aublet) L.C. Rich., Mém. Mus. Par. 4: 59, 1817
Stenorrhynchos squamulosus (Kunth) Spreng., Syst. Veg. 3: 710, 1826
Serapias coccinea Vell., Fl. Flum. Ic. 9: t. 48, 1827
Serapias tomentosa Vell., Fl. Flum. Ic. 9: t. 51, 1827
o Neottia plantaginea Hook., Exot. Fl. 3: t. 226, 1827
Neottia aphylla Hook., Bot. Mag.: t. 2797, 1828
Sacoila lurida Raf., Fl. Tellur. 2: 86, 1836 (nomen illeg.)
Stenorrhynchos australis Lindl., Gen. Sp. Orch. Pl.: 477, 1840
Stenorrhynchos orchioides var. plantaginea Lindl., Gen. Sp. Orch. Pl.: 478, 1840
Stenorrhynchos aphyllus (Hook.) Lindl., Gen. Sp. Orch. Pl.: 478, 1840
Spiranthes orchioides (Sw.) A. Rich., Sagra Hist. Cuba 11: 252, 1850
Stenorrhynchos australis var. luteoalbus Rchb.f. & Warm., Otia Bot. Hamb. 2: 82, 1881
Spiranthes jaliscana S. Watson, Proc. Am. Acad. 26: 153, 1891
Gyrostachys stenorrhynchus Kuntze, Rev. Gen. pt. 2: 664, 1891
Gyrostachys lanceolata (Aublet) Kuntze, Rev. Gen. pt. 2: 664, 1891
Gyrostachys aphylla (Hook.) Kuntze, Rev. Gen. pt. 2: 664, 1891
Gyrostachys orchioides (Sw.) Kuntze, Rev. Gen. pt. 2: 664, 1891
Stenorrhynchos jaliscana (S. Watson) Nash, Bull. Torrey Club 22: 158, 1895
Stenorrhynchos orchioides var. australis Cogn., Fl. Bras. 3, pt. 4: 178, 1895
Stenorrhynchos pedicellatus Cogn., Bull. Herb. Bois, s. 2, 3: 932, 1903
Stenorrhynchos pedicellatus var. major Cogn., Bull. Herb. Bois s. 2, 3: 932, 1903
Stenorrhynchos sancti-antoni Kraenzlin, Engl. Bot. Jahrb. 36 Beibl. 80: 8, 1905
Stenorrhynchos apetalus Kraenzlin, Fedde Rep. 6: 23, 1908
Stenorrhynchos riograndensis Kraenzlin, Svensk. Vet. Akad. Handl. 46: No. 10: 28, 1911
Stenorrhynchos guatemalensis Schltr., Beih. Bot. Centralbl. 37, pt. 2: 376, 1918
Pelexia tomentosa (Vell.) Schltr., Beih. Bot. Centralbl. 37, pt. 2: 376, 1918
Stenorrhynchos secundiflorus Lillo & Hauman, Anal. Soc. Cienc. Argent. 90: 134, 1921
Spiranthes lanceolata (Aublet) León, Cont. Ocas. Mus. Hist. Nat. Coll. De la Salle, Cuba 8: 358, 1946
Stenorrhynchos coccineus (Vell.) Hoehne, Arq. Bot. Estad. S. Paulo n.s. 2: 146, 1952
o **Sarcochilus hartmannii** F. Muell., Fragm. Phyt. Aust. 8: 248, 1874
BM 7010
Australia (Queensland, New South Wales) – E, L
Thrixspermum hartmanni (F. Muell.) Rchb.f., Gard. Chron.: 716, 1877
Sarcochilus rubicentrum Fitzg., Aust. Orch. 2: pt. 1, 1884
Sarcochilus moorei (Rchb.f.) Schltr., Orch. Deutsch. Neu Guin. 967, 1914
BM 8737
Solomon Is., New Guinea, Australia (Cape York Peninsula) – E, L
Thrixspermum moorei Rchb.f., Gard. Chron.: 104, 1880
Thrixspermum beccarii Rchb.f., Bot. Centralbl. 28: 343, 1886
Sarcochilus papuanum Kraenzlin, K. Schum. & Hollr. Fl. Kais. Willheld.: 34, 1889
Sarcochilus beccarii (Rchb.f.) F. Muell., Descr. Notes Pl.: 9, 1890
Renanthera ramuana Kraenzlin, K. Schum. & Laut. Fl. Deutsch. Schutzg. Südsee: 252, 1901
Sarcochilus englerianum Kraenzlin, K. Schum. & Laut. Fl. Deutsch. Schutzg. Südsee: 252, 1901
Sarcochilus ramuanus (Kraenzlin) Schltr., K. Schum. & Laut. Nachtr.: 232, 1905
o Sarcochilus solomonensis Rolfe, Kew Bull.: 72, 1908
Sarcoglottis acaulis (Smith) Schltr., Fedde Rep. Beih. 6: 53, 1919
BM 1562
Trop. America, Mexico to Argentina – T
Neottia acaulis Smith, Exot. Bot. 2: 91 t. 105, 1806
Arethusa picta Anders., Trans. Soc. Arts 25: 199, 1807 (nomen)
o Neottia picta Sims, Bot. Mag.: t. 1562, 1813
Neottia picta R.Br., Hort. Kew ed. 2, 5: 199, 1813
Spiranthes picta (Sims) Lindl., Bot. Reg. 10: sub.t. 823, 1824
Sarcoglottis speciosa Presl, Rel. Haenk. 1: 96 t. 15, 1827
Narica moschata Raf., Fl. Tellur. 2: 87, 1837
Synoplectris picta (Sims) Raf., Fl. Tellur. 2: 90, 1837
Spiranthes speciosa (Presl) Lindl., Gen. Sp. Orch. Pl.: 475, 1840
Sarcoglottis picta (Sims) Klotzsch, Allg. Gartenz. 10: 107, 1842
Sarcoglottis picta var. variegata Klotzsch, Allg. Gartenz. 10: 107, 1842
Gyrostachys picta (Sims) Kuntze, Rev. Gen. 2: 664, 1891
Spiranthes acaulis (Smith) Cogn., Fl. Bras. 3 (4): 221, 1895
Sarcoglottis hunteriana Schltr., Fedde Rep. Beih. 17: 13, 1922
Sarcoglottis powellii Schltr., Fedde Rep. Beih. 17: 14, 1922
Sarcoglottis purpusiorum Schltr., Fedde Rep. Beih. 21: 333, 1925
Sarcoglottis grandiflora (Lindl.) Klotzsch, Allg. Gartenz. 10: 107, 1842
BM 2730
Venezuela, Surinam, Brazil, Argentina, Paraguay, Ecuador – T
Spiranthes grandiflora Lindl., Bot. Reg.: t. 1043, 1826
o Neottia grandiflora (Lindl.) Hook., Bot. Mag.: t. 2730, 1827
o **Satyrium carneum** (Dryander) R.Br., Hort. Kew ed. 2, 5: 193, 1813
BM 1512
S. Africa – T
Orchis carnea Dryander, Hort. Kew 3: 294, 1789
Satyrium cucullatum Thunb., Fl. Cap.: 88, 1807
o **Satyrium coriifolium** Sw., Kongl. Vet. Acad. Handl. 21: 216, 1800
BM 2172
S. Africa – T
Orchis lutea F. Buxb., Cent. 3: 7 t. 10, 1729
Orchis cornuta Houtt., Handl. 12: 456 t. 80 fig. 2, 1773–83
Diplecthrum coriifolium (Sw.) Pers. syn. 2: 509, 1807
Diplecthrum erectum (Lindl.) Pers., Syn. 2: 509, 1807
Satyrium cucullatum Lodd., Bot. Cab.: t. 104, 1818 (non Jacq.)
Satyrium erectum Lindl., Gen. Sp. Orch. Pl.: 340, 1838 (non Sw.)
Satyrium chrysostachyum Herschel, Bot. Reg.: sub.t. 154, 1838
Satyrium aureum Paxton, Mag. Bot. 15: 31, 1848
o **Satyrium coriifolium** Sw. var. **maculatum** Hook.f., Bot. Mag.: t. 7289, 1893
BM 7289
S. Africa – T
o **Satyrium nepalense** D. Don, Prodr. Fl. Nepal: 26, 1825
BM 6625
Sri Lanka, India, E. Tibet, Sikkim, N. Burma, W. China – 1200–3000 m – T
Satyrium wightianum Lindl., Gen. Sp. Orch. Pl.: 340, 1838
Satyrium ciliatum Lindl., Gen. Sp. Orch. Pl.: 341, 1838
Satyrium perrottetianum A. Rich., Ann. Sc. Nat. s. 2, 15: 76 t. 53, 1841
Satyrium albiflorum A. Rich., Ann. Sc. Nat. s. 2, 15: 76 t. 53, 1841
Satyrium pallidum A. Rich., Ann. Sc. Nat. s. 2, 15: 77, 1841
Satyrium princeps Bolus, Hook. Ic. Pl.: t. 1729, 1888
BM 7104
S. Africa – T
o Satyrium membranaceum N.E.Br., Gard. Chron.: 136, 1889 (non of Sw.)
o **Satyrium sphaerocarpum** Lindl., Gen. Sp. Orch. Pl.: 337, 1838
BM 7295
S. Africa, Mozambique – up to 1500 m – T
Satyrium militare Lindl., Gen. Sp. Orch. Pl.: 342, 1838
Satyrium beyrichianum Kraenzlin, Engl. Bot. Jahrb. 24: 508, 1898

Scaphosepalum gibberosum (Rchb.f.) Rolfe, J. Bot. 23: 136, 1890
BM 6990
Colombia – E
○ Masdevallia gibberosa Rchb.f., Gard. Chron.: 8, 1876
○ **Scaphosepalum pulvinare** (Rchb.f.) Rolfe, J. Bot.: 137, 1890
BM 7151
Colombia – E
Masdevallia pulvinaris Rchb.f., Gard. Chron.: 200, 1880
Scaphosepalum punctatum (Rolfe) Rolfe, J. Bot.: 137, 1890
BM 7165
Colombia – E
○ Masdevallia punctata Rolfe, Gard. Chron.: 233, 1888
○ **Scaphyglottis violacea** Lindl., Bot. Reg. 22: t. 1901, 1836
BM 4071
Venezuela, Guyana, Brazil, Amazonas – E
Cladobium violaceum Lindl., Introd. Neat. Syst. Bot. ed. 2: 446, 1836
Scaphyglottis rosea Hook., Ic. Pl. 4: t. 313, 1841
Ponera violacea (Lindl.) Rchb.f., Bonpl. 2: 22, 1854
Ponera rosea (Hook.) Rchb.f., Bonpl. 2: 22, 1854
Schomburgkia gloriosa Rchb.f., Hamb. Gartenz. 16: 178, 1860
BM 3729
Venezuela, Guyana, Surinam, Brazil – E
Epidendrum fimbriatum Vell., Fl. Flum. 9: t. 14, 1827
○ Schomburgkia marginata Hook., Bot. Mag.: t. 3729, 1840
Schomburgkia crispa Lindl., Bot. Reg. 30: t. 23, 1844 (non Lindl. 1838)
Schomburgkia fimbriata (Vell.) Hoehne, Arq. Bot. Estad. S. Paulo 2 (6): 142, 1952
Cattleya crispa Beer, Prakt. Stud. Orch.: 209, 1854 (non Lindl.)
Bletia crispina Rchb.f., Walp. Ann. 6: 419, 1862
Bletia gloriosa (Rchb.f.) Rchb.f., Walp. Ann. 6: 419, 1862
Laelia gloriosa (Rchb.f.) L.O. Williams, Darwiniana 5: 76, 1941
○ **Schomburgkia lyonsii** Lindl., Gard. Chron.: 615, 1853
BM 5172
Jamaica – 100–1000 m – L, E
Schomburgkia carinata Griseb., Fl. Brit. W. Ind.: 621, 1864
Schomburgkia superbiens (Lindl.) Rolfe, Orch. Rev. 25: 49, 1917
BM 4090
Mexico, Guatemala, Honduras, Nicaragua – E
○ Laelia superbiens Lindl., Bot. Reg. 26: Misc. p. 46, 1840
Cattleya superbiens (Lindl.) Beer, Prakt. Stud. Orch.: 214, 1854
Bletia superbiens (Lindl.) Rchb.f., Walp. Ann. 6: 418, 1862
○ **Schomburgkia thomsoniana** Rchb.f. var. **minor** Hook.f., Bot. Mag.: t. 7815, 1902
BM 7815
W. Indies – E
Schomburgkia thomsoniana Rchb.f., Gard. Chron.: 38, 1857
Myrmecophila thomsoniana (Rchb.f.) Rolfe, Orch. Rev. 25: 50, 1917
Schomburgkia undulata Lindl., Bot. Reg.: sub. t. 28, 1844
BM 8427
Costa Rica, Panama, Venezuela – up to 1000 m – E
Schomburgkia violacea Paxton, Mag. Bot. 16: 123, 1849
Cattleya undulata (Lindl.) Beer, Prakt. Stud. Orch.: 215, 1854
Bletia undulata (Lindl.) Rchb.f., Walp. Ann. 6: 420, 1861
○ Schomburgkia lueddemanii Prill, J. Soc. Imp. Hort. Pow. 8: 123, 1862
Laelia lueddemanii (Prill) L.O. Williams, Ann. Missouri Bot. Gard. 27: 282, 1940
○ **Scuticaria hadwenii** (Lindl.) hort. ex. Hook., Bot. Mag.: sub. t. 4629, 1852
BM 4629
Brazil, Guyana – E
Bifrenaria hadwenii Lindl., Paxt. Flow. Gard. 1: 67, 1851
Scuticaria strictifolia Hoehne, Arq. Bot. Estad. S. Paulo n. s. 2 (4): 88, 1947
Scuticaria steelei (Hook.) Lindl., Bot. Reg. 29: Misc. p. 14, 1843
BM 3573
Venezuela, Guyana, Brazil, Amazonas – E
○ Maxillaria steelei Hook., Bot. Mag.: t. 3573, 1837
Maxillaria flabellifera Lindl., Bot. Reg. 23: sub. t. 1986, 1837
Scuticaria keyseriana hort., J. Hort. 16: 421, 1888
Sedirea japonica (Linden & Rchb.f.) Garay & Sweet, Orch. S. Ryukyu Is.: 149, 1974
BM 5798
Japan, Ryukyu Is., Korea – E
○ Aerides japonica Linden & Rchb.f., Hamb. Gartenz. 19: 210, 1863
Seidenfadenia mitrata (Rchb.f.) Garay, Bot. Mus. Leafl. Harv. Univ. 23 (4): 204, 1972
BM 5728
Burma, Thailand – E
○ Aerides mitrata Rchb.f., Bot. Zeit.: 415, 1864
○ **Serapias cordigera** L., Sp. Pl. ed. 2: 1345, 1763
BM 5868 A
Azores, Mediterranean Europe, Asia Minor – T
Serapias lingua var. β Savi, Fl. Pis. 2: 304, 1798
Helleborine cordigera (L.) Pers., Syn. 2: 512, 1807
Serapias ovalis L.C. Rich. Mém. Mus. Paris 4: 54, 1817
Serapias oxyglottis Cocc., Fl. Prov. Bologne: 480, 1883 (non Bertol. nec Willd. nec Rchb.f.)
Lonchitis cordigera (L.) Bubani, Fl. Pyr. 4: 50, 1901
Serapiastrum cordigerum (L.) A.A. Eaton, Proc. Biol. Soc. Wash. 21: 67, 1908
Serapias cordigera var. genuina Briq., Prodr. Fl. Corse 1: 379, 1910
○ **Serapias lingua** L., Sp. Pl.: 950, 1753
BM 5868 B
S.W. Europe, Mediterranean region – T
Orchis lingua (L.) Scop., Fl. Carn. ed. 2, 11: 187, 1772
Helleborine oxyglottis Pers., Syn. 2: 512, 1807
Serapias glabra Lapeyr, Hist. Albr. Pl. Pyr.: 552, 1813
Helleborine lingua (L.) Sebast. & Mauri, Fl. Rom. Prodr.: 313, 1818
Serapias oxyglottis (Pers.) Bertol., Am. It.: 202, 1819 (non Willd.)
Helleborine leucoglottis Steudel, Nom.: 398, 1840
Serapias brevibracteata St. Lager, Ann. Soc. Bot. Lyon 7: 134, 1880
Serapias algarbiensis Gand., Fl. Europ. 23: 136, 1890
Lonchitis oxyglottis (Pers.) Bubani, Fl. Pyr. 4: 50, 1901
Serapiastrum lingua (L.) A.A. Eaton, Proc. Biol. Soc. Wash. 21: 67, 1908
○ **Sievekingia reichenbachiana** (F. Lehm.) Rolfe, Bot. Mag.: t. 7576, 1898
BM 7576
Ecuador – E
Gorgoglossum reichenbachianum F. Lehm., Gard. Chron.: 346, 1897
○ **Sievekingia shepheardii** Rolfe, Bot. Mag.: t. 8635, 1915
BM 8635
Colombia – E
Sigmatostalix guatemalensis Schltr., Fedde Rep. 10: 253, 1911
BM 8825
Mexico, Guatemala, Costa Rica, Panama – up to 1000 m – E
○ Sigmatostalix costaricensis Rolfe, Kew Bull.: 78, 1916
Sigmatostalix poikilostalix Kraenzlin, Pflanzenr. Heft 80: 310 fig. 26 D, 1922
Sobralia decora Bateman, Orch. Mex. & Guat.: t. 26, 1841
BM 4570
Mexico, Guatemala, El Salvador, Nicaragua, Honduras, Venezuela – T
Sobralia galeottiana A. Rich., Ann. Soc. Nat. s. 3, 3: 30, 1845
○ (Sobralia sessilis Lindl., Bot. Reg.: Misc. 11, 1841; misidentified)
○ **Sobralia fragrans** Lindl., Gard. Chron.: 598, 1853
BM 4882
Belize, Honduras, Nicaragua, Costa Rica, Panama, S. America to Ecuador – T, E
Sobralia eublepharis Rchb.f. ex Kraenzlin, Fedde Rep. 26: 255 t. 78, 1929
○ **Sobralia leucoxantha** Rchb.f., Beitr. Orch. Cent. Am.: 68, 1866
BM 7058
Costa Rica, Panama – T
Sobralia powellii Schltr., Fedde Rep. Beih. 17: 11, 1928
○ **Sobralia macrantha** Lindl., Sert. Orch.: sub. t. 29, 1836
BM 4446
Mexico, Guatemala, El Salvador, Honduras, Nicaragua, Costa Rica – T, L
Sobralia macrantha var. purpurea Lindl., Fol. Orch. Sobralia: 8, 1854
Sobralia macrantha var. alba Lindl., Fol. Orch. Sobralia: 8, 1854
Sobralia macrophylla Rchb.f., Bot. Zeit. 10: 713, 1852
BM 4682
Costa Rica, Panama, Venezuela, Colombia, Brazil, Ecuador – T
○ Sobralia chlorantha Hook., Bot. Mag.: t. 4682, 1852
Cattleya chlorantha (Hook.) Beer, Prakt. Stud. Orch.: 209, 1854
Cyathoglottis macrantha Lemaire, Jard. Fleur. 4: t. 355, 1854
Sobralia aurantiaca Linden & Rchb.f., Bonpl. 2: 278, 1854
Sobralia rolfeana Schltr., Fedde Rep. Beih. 17: 12, 1922
○ **Sobralia sessilis** Lindl., Bot. Reg. 27: Misc. p. 3 t. 17, 1841
BM 7376
Brazil, Guyana, Venezuela, Colombia, Peru – T, E
Sobralia galeottiana Lindl., Fol. Orch. Sobralia: 6, 1854 (non A. Rich.)
Cattleya sessilis (Lindl.) Beer, Prakt. Stud. Orch.: 214, 1854
○ **Sobralia xantholeuca** hort. ex Williams, Orch. Grow. Man. ed. 6: 576, 1885
BM 7332
Guatemala, El Salvador – up to 1700 m – T
○ × **Sophrolaelia psyche** Rolfe, Orch. Rev. 10: 55, 1902
BM 8654
= Laelia cinnabarina Lindl. × Sophronotis grandiflorum Lindl.
Sophronitella violacea (Lindl.) Schltr., Fedde Rep. Beih. 35: 76, 1925
BM 6880
Brazil – E
○ Sophronitis violacea Lindl., Bot. Reg. 26: Misc. 18, 1840

Cattleya violacea (Lindl.) Beer, Prakt. Stud. Orch.: 209, 1854 (non Rolfe)
○ **Sophronitis cernua** Lindl., Bot. Reg. 13: sub.t. 1129, 1827
BM 3677
Brazil – E
Epidendrum humile Vell., Fl. Flum. Ic. 9: t. 24, 1827
Sophronia cernua Lindl., Bot. Reg.: t. 1129, 1827
Sophronitis modesta Lindl., Bot. Reg. 14: sub.t. 1147, 1828
Sophronitis hoffmannseggii Rchb.f., Linnaea 16: 286, 1842
Sophronitis isopetala Hoffsgg., Verz. Orch.: 60, 1842
Sophronitis nutans Hoffsgg., Verz. Orch.: 61, 1842
Sophronitis pterocarpa Lindl. & Paxton, Flow. Gard. 3: 11 fig. 239, 1852
Cattleya cernua (Lindl.) Beer, Prakt. Stud. Orch.: 209, 1854
Sophronitis coccinea (Lindl.) Rchb.f., Walp. Ann. 6: 465, 1862
BM 3709
Brazil – E
Cattleya coccinea Lindl., Bot. Reg. 22: sub.t. 1919, 1836
Sophronitis grandiflora Lindl., Sert. Orch.: t. 5 fig. 2, 1838
○ Cattleya grandiflora (Lindl.) Beer, Prakt. Stud. Orch.: 209, 1854
Sophronitis militaris Rchb.f., Walp. Ann. 6: 465, 1862
Spathoglottis aurea Lindl., J. Hort. Soc. Lond.: 34, 1850
BM 7443
Malaya, Borneo – T
Spathoglottis kimballiana hort. Sander ex Gartenfl. 41: 184, 1892
○ Spathoglottis kimballiana Hook.f., Bot. Mag.: t. 7443, 1895
○ **Spathoglottis gracilis** Rolfe ex Hook.f., Bot. Mag.: t. 7366, 1894
BM 7366
Borneo – up to 1000 m – T
○ **Spathoglottis hardingiana** Parish & Rchb.f., Otia Bot. Hamb. Fasc. 1: 45, 1878
BM 7964
Burma, Thailand, Malaya – T, L
○ **Spathoglottis ixioides** (Don) Lindl., Wall. Cat.: 3745, 1831
BM 7060
Sikkim, Himalaya – up to 3000 m – T
Cymbidium ixioides Don, Prodr. Fl. Nep.: 36, 1825
Pachystoma josephii Rchb.f., Walp. Ann. 6: 464, 1862
○ **Spathoglottis petri** Rchb.f., Gard. Chron.: 392, 1877
BM 6354
Pacific Is. – T
Spathoglottis plicata Blume, Bijdr. 8: 401, 1825
BM 7013
Australia, New Caledonia, Solomon Is., Bougainville, Tonga, Samoa, New Guinea, Philippines, Java, Malaya, Thailand, Burma, India – T
Bletia angustata Gaudin, Frey, Voy. Bot.: 421, 1829
Bletia angustifolia Gaudin, Frey, Voy. Bot.: t. 32, 1829
Paxtonia rosea Lindl., Bot. Reg. 24: Misc.p. 61, 1838
Spathoglottis lilacina Griffith, Notul 3: 323, 1851
Phaius rumphii Blume, Mus. Bot. Lugd. Bat. 2: 179, 1856
Spathoglottis spicata Lindl., J. Linn. Soc. 3: 9, 1859
○ Spathoglottis vieillardii Rchb.f., Linnaea 41: 85, 1877
Spathoglottis angustorum Rchb.f., Gard. Chron.: 9, 1886
Spathoglottis plicata var. alba Ridley, Mat. Fl. Mal. Pen. 1: 117, 1907
Spathoglottis daenikeri Kraenzlin, Vierteljahrschr. Nat. Ges. Zürich 74: 80, 1929
○ **Spiranthes cernua** (L.) L.C. Rich., Mém. Mus. Hist. Nat. Paris 4: 59, 1818
BM 1568, BM 5277
USA (Virginia), Canada – T
Ophrys cernua L., Sp. Pl. 2: 946, 1753
○ Neottia cernua (L.) Sw., Schrad. Neues J. 1: 52, 1805
Gyrostachys cernua (L.) Kuntze, Rev. Gen. Pl. 2: 664, 1891
Gyrostachys constricta Smith, Bull. Torrey Club 25: 609, 1898
Spiranthes constricta (Smith) K. Schumann, Bot. Jahrb. 26 (1): 339, 1900
Ibidium cernuum (L.) House, Bull. Torrey Club 32: 381, 1905
Triorchis cernua (L.) Nieuwl., Am. Midl. Nat. 3: 122, 1913
○ **Stanhopea costaricensis** Rchb.f., Hamb. Gartenz. 16: 424, 1860
BM 8830
Guatemala, El Salvador, Nicaragua, Costa Rica, Panama – E
○ **Stanhopea ecornuta** Lemaire, Fl. Serres 2: t. 181, 1846
BM 4885
Guatemala, Honduras, Nicaragua, Costa Rica, Panama – up to 1200 m – E
Stanhopeastrum ecornutum (Lemaire) Rchb.f., Bot. Zeit. 10: 927, 1852
Stanhopea florida Rchb.f., Gard. Chron.: 615, 1879
BM 8417
Peru – 1000–1500 m – E
○ Stanhopea peruviana Rolfe, Bot. Mag.: t. 8417, 1912
Stanhopea grandiflora (Lodd.) Lindl., Gen. Sp. Orch. Pl.: 158, 1832 (non (Humb. & Bonpl.) Rchb.f.)
BM 3359
Brazil, Guyana, Venezuela, Trinidad, Colombia – E
Ceratochilus grandiflorus Lodd., Bot. Cab. 15: t. 1414, 1828
○ Stanhopea eburnea Lindl., Bot. Reg. 18: t. 1529, 1832
Stanhopea calceolata Drap., Hort. Univ. 2: 264, 1841
○ **Stanhopea haseloviana** Rchb.f., Allg. Gartenz. 23: 322, 1855
BM 7452
Peru, Ecuador – 1000–1200 m – E
Stanhopea hernandezii (Kunth) Schltr., Beih. Bot. Centralbl. 2: 490, 1918
BM 4197
Mexico, Guatemala, Venezuela, Guyana, Brazil – 1000–1200 m – E
Anguloa hernandezii Kunth, Syn. 1: 332, 1822
Stanhopea devoniensis Lindl., Sert. Orch.: t. 1, 1838
non Stanhopea martiana Bateman ex Lindl., Bot. Reg. 26: Misc. 109, 1840
○ (Stanhopea tigrina Bateman, Orch. Mex. & Guat.: 7, 1839; misidentified)
○ **Stanhopea insignis** Frost ex Hook., Bot. Mag.: t. 2948/49, 1829
BM 2948, BM 2949
Brazil – E
Stanhopea jenishiana Kramer ex Rchb.f., Bot. Zeit. 10: 934, 1852
BM 8517
Panama, Venezuela, Colombia, Ecuador – up to 1700 m – E
Epidendrum grandiflorum Kunth, Pl. Aequin. 1: 94 t. 27, 1806
Anguola grandiflora (Kunth) Kunth, Nov. Gen. Sp. 1: 345, 1816
○ Stanhopea grandiflora (Kunth) Rchb.f., Walp. Ann. 6: 587, 1863
Stanhopea grandiflora var. jenishiana (Kramer ex Rchb.f.) Rchb. f., Walp. Ann. 6: 588, 1863
Stanhopea hoppii Schltr., Fedde Rep. Beih. 27: 82, 1924
non Stanhopea grandiflora (Lodd.) Lindl., Gen. Sp. Orch. Pl.: 158, 1832
non Stanhopea bucephalus Lindl., Gen. Sp. Orch. Pl.: 157, 1832
○ **Stanhopea oculata** (Lodd.) Lindl., Gen. Sp. Orch. Pl.: 158, 1832
BM 5278, BM 5300
Mexico, Guatemala, Belize, Honduras, El Salvador, Nicaragua, Costa Rica, Panama, Venezuela, Colombia – E
Stanhopea lindleyi Zucc., Abh. Akad. Muench. 2: 320, 1831–36
Ceratochilus oculatus Lodd., Bot. Cab.: t. 1764, 1832
○ Stanhopea bucephalus Lindl., Gen. Sp. Orch. Pl.: 157, 1832
Stanhopea oculata var. barkeriana Lindl., Bot. Reg. 25: Misc. p. 69, 1839
Stanhopea oculata var. lindleyi Zucc. ex Lindl., Fol. Orch. Stanh.: 3, 1852
Stanhopea guttata K. Koch, Allg. Gartenz.: 364, 1858
Stanhopea ornatissima Lemaire, Ill. Hort. 9: t. 325, 1862
Stanhopea cymbiformis Rchb.f., Xen. Orch. 2: 84 t. 124, 1865
Epidendrum cornutum Sessé & Mociño, Fl. Mex. ed. 2: 225, 1887
Stanhopea oculata var. crocea Regel, Ind. Sem. Hort. Petrop. 17: 15, 1898
Stanhopea oculata var. geniculata Klotzsch, Act. Hort. Petrop. 17: 143, 1898
Stanhopea purpusii Schltr., Orchis 10: 186, 1916
Stanhopea minor Schltr., Notizbl. Bot. Gart. Berl. 6: 483, 1917
Stanhopea tricornis Lindl., J. Hort. Soc. 4: 263, 1849
BM 8507
Colombia, Ecuador, Peru – E
Stanhopea wallisii Rchb.f., Linn. 41: 109, 1877
Stanhopea stenochila Lehm. & Kraenzlin, Gard. Chron.: 369, 1900
Stanhopea langlasseana Cogn., Gard. Chron.: 426, 1901
○ Stanhopea convoluta Rolfe, Kew Bull.: 366, 1909
○ **Stanhopea wardii** Lodd. ex Lindl., Sert. Orch.: t. 20, 1838
BM 5289
Mexico to Panama, Venezuela to Peru – E
Stanhopea aurea Lodd. ex Lindl., Bot. Reg. 27: Misc.p. 11, 1841
Stanhopea venusta Lindl., Bot. Reg. 27: Misc.p. 11, 1841
Stanhopea amoena Klotzsch, Allg. Gartenz. 20: 273, 1852
Stanhopea wardii var. venusta Rolfe, Lindenia 7: t. 315, 1892
Stelis eublepharis Rchb.f., Bonpl. 3: 240, 1855
BM 6521
Costa Rica, Venez., Colombia, Ecuador, Peru – up to 2000 m – E
○ Stelis bruchmuelleri Rchb.f. ex Hook., Bot. Mag.: t. 6521, 1880
○ **Stenoglottis fimbriata** Lindl., Comp. Bot. Mag. 2: 210, 1836
BM 5872
S. Africa (Cape Colony, Natal, Transvaal), Swaziland, Zimbabwe, Malawi, Tanzania – 1000–2000 m – T, L
○ **Stenoglottis longifolia** Hook.f., Bot. Mag.: t. 7186, 1891
BM 7186
S. Africa (Natal, Zululand) – 300–700 m – T, L
Stenoglottis fimbriata N.E.Br., Gard. Chron.: 438, 1889 (non Lindl.)

Stenorrhynchos speciosum (Jacq.) Rich. ex Sprengel, Syst. Veg. 3: 709, 1826
BM 1374
Mexico, Guatemala, Honduras, Costa Rica, Panama, Ecuador, W. Indies - up to 3000 m - E, T
o Neottia speciosa Jacq., Coll. 3: 174, 1790
Serapias speciosa (Jacq.) J. Gmelin, Syst. Nat. 2: 59, 1791
Spiranthes speciosa (Jacq.) A. Rich., Sagra Hist. Cuba 11: 252, 1850 (non Lindl., 1840)
Spiranthes colorata N. E. Br., Gard. Chron.: 210, 1883
Spiranthes colorata var. maculata N. E. Br., Gard. Chron.: 210, 1883
Spiranthes richardi Autran & Durand, Hort. Bois.: 351, 1896
Stenorrhynchos millei Schltr., Fedde Rep. 15: 51, 1917
Stereochilus erinaceus (Rchb. f.) Garay, Bot. Mus. Leafl. Harv. Univ. 23: 4, 1972
BM 5630
Burma - E
o Sarcanthus erinaceus Rchb. f., Bot. Zeit. 22: 298, 1864
Sarcanthus stowellianus Bateman, Bot. Mag.: sub. t. 5630, 1867
Aerides dasypogon hort. ex Bateman, Bot. Mag.: sub. t. 5630, 1867 (non Lindl.)
Sunipia paleacea (Lindl.) P. Hunt, Kew Bull. 26: 184, 1971
BM 6344
Nepal to Bhutan - up to 2000 m - E
o Ione paleacea Lindl., Fol. Orch. Ione: 2, 1853
Bulbophyllum paleaceum (Lindl.) Hook. f., Fl. Brit. Ind. 5: 769, 1890
Symphyglossum sanguineum (Rchb. f.) Schltr., Orchis 13: 9, 1919
BM 5627
Peru, Ecuador - E
o Mesospinidium sanguineum Rchb. f., Walp. Ann. 6: 858, 1864
Cochlioda sanguinea (Rchb. f.) Benth. & Hook. f., Gen. Pl. 3: 560, 1883
Tetramicra canaliculata (Aublet) Urban, Rep. Sp. Nov. 15: 306, 1919
BM 3098
USA (Florida), W. Indies - E, L
Limodorum foliis subulatis Burman, Cat. Pl. Am.: 176 pl. 181 fig. 1, 1758
Limodorum canaliculatum Aublet, Pl. Guian. 2: 821, 1775
Cymbidium rigidum Willd., Sp. Pl. 4: 105, 1805
Epidendrum canaliculatum (Aublet) Poir., Encyc. Suppl. 1: 375, 1810
Cyrtopodium elegans Ham., Prodr. Pl. Ind. Occ.: 53, 1825
Tetramicra rigida (Willd.) Lindl., Gen. Sp. Orch. Pl. 8: 119, 1831
o Brassavola elegans (Ham.) Hook., Bot. Mag.: t. 3098, 1831
Bletia rigida (Willd.) Rchb. f., Walp. Ann. 6: 438, 1862
Bletia subaequalis Rchb. f., Flora 69: 503, 1886
Brassavola rigida (Willd.) Bold., Fl. Dutch W. Ind. Is. 1: 43, 1909
Tetramicra elegans (Ham.) Cogn., Urban, Symb. Antill. 6: 548, 1910
Thrixspermum amplexicaulis (Blume) Rchb. f., Xen. Orch. 2: 121, 1867
BM 7754
Malaya, Sumatra, Java, Philippines - E, T
Dendrocolla amplexicaulis Blume, Bijdr.: 288, 1825
Aerides amplexicaulis (Blume) Lindl., Gen. Sp. Orch. Pl.: 239, 1838
o Sarcochilus lilacinus Griffith, Notul 3: 334, 1851
Orsidice amplexicaulis (Blume) Rchb. f., Bonpl. 2: 93, 1854
Orsidice lilacina (Griffith) Rchb. f., Bonpl. 2: 93, 1854
Sarcochilus amplexicaulis (Blume) Rchb. f., Walp. Ann. 6: 498, 1863
Thrixspermum lilacinum (Griffith) Rchb. f., Xen. Orch. 2: 121, 1867
Thrixspermum hainanense (Rolfe) Schltr., Orchis: 55, 1911
BM 7489
Hainan, China - E
o Sarcochilus hainanensis Rolfe, Kew Handl. Orch.: 201, (not publ.)
Thunia alba (Lindl.) Rchb. f., Bot. Zeit. 10: 764, 1852
BM 3991
Himalaya, Assam, Burma - 1200-2000 m - T
Limodorum bracteatum Roxb., Hort. Beng.: 63, 1814 (nomen nudum)
o Phaius albus Lindl., Wall. Cat.: 3749, 1831 (nomen nudum)
Thunia pulchra Rchb. f., Gard. Chron.: 166, 1881
Thunia bracteata (Roxb.) Schltr., Fedde Rep. Beih. 4: 205, 1919
o **Thunia bensoniae** Hook. f., Bot. Mag.: t. 5694, 1868
BM 5694
Himalaya, Assam, Burma - T
Phaius bensoniae (Hook. f.) Hemsley, Gard. Chron.: 565, 1882
Ticoglossum oerstedii (Rchb. f.) R. Rodriguez ex Halbinger, Orquidea (Méx.) 9 (1): 5, 1983
BM 6820
Costa Rica, Panama - up to 4000 m - E
o Odontoglossum oerstedii Rchb. f., Bonpl. 3: 124, 1855
o **Trevoria chloris** F. Lehm., Gard. Chron.: 346, 1897
BM 7805
Colombia - E
Trevoria lehmannii Rolfe, Orch. Rev. 18: 298, 1897
o **Trias picta** (Parish & Rchb. f.) Parish ms. ex Hemsley, Gard. Chron.: 427, 1882
BM 9150
Thailand, Burma - E
Bulbophyllum pictum Parish & Rchb. f., Trans. Linn. Soc. 30: 150, 1874
o **Trichocentrum albopurpureum** Linden & Rchb. f. ex Rchb. f., Gard. Chron.: 219, 1866
BM 5688
Peru, Brazil. Amazonas - up to 1200 m - E
Trichocentrum albo-coccineum Linden, Belg. Hort. 15: 103, 1865
Trichocentrum atropurpureum Linden ex Regel, Ind. Sem. Hort. Petrop.: 79, 1868
Trichocentrum amazonicum Barb. Rodr., Orch. Nov. 2: 140, 1877
o **Trichocentrum fuscum** Lindl., Bot. Reg. 23: t. 1951, 1837
BM 3969
Mexico, Brazil - E
Acoidium fuscum Lindl., Bot. Reg. 23: t. 1951, 1837
o **Trichocentrum tigrinum** Linden & Rchb. f., Gard. Chron.: 892, 1869
BM 7380
C. America, Ecuador - E
Trichopilia fragrans (Lindl.) Rchb. f., Hamb. Gartenz. 14: 229, 1858
BM 5035
W. Indies, Venezuela, Colombia, Ecuador, Peru, Bolivia - up to 1000 m - E
o Pilumna fragrans Lindl., Bot. Reg. 30: Misc. p. 74, 1844
Trichopilia candida Linden ex Lindl., Orch. Linden.: 13, 1846
Trichopilia albida Wendl. f., Allg. Gartenz. 19: 362, 1851
Pilumna wageneri Rchb. f., Bonpl. 2: 13, 1854
Trichopilia wageneri (Rchb. f.) Rchb. f., Hamb. Gartenz. 14: 229, 1858
Trichopilia lehmannii Regel, Gartenfl. 37: 355 t. 1276, 1888
Trichopilia galeottiana A. Rich., Ann. Sci. Nat. s. 3, 3: 26, 1845
BM 5550
Mexico - E
Trichopilia picta Lemaire, Ill. Hort.: Misc. p. 68 t. 225, 1859
o Trichopilia turialvae Rchb. f. sensu Bateman, Bot. Mag.: t. 5550, 1865 (non Rchb. f.)
Trichopilia marginata Henfrey, Gard. Mag. Bot. 3: 185, 1851
BM 4857
Guatemala, Honduras, Costa Rica, Panama - 1000-1700 m - E
o Trichopilia coccinea Warsc. ex Lindl. & Paxton, Flow. Gard. 2: 79 t. 54, 1851
Trichopilia crispa Lindl., Gard. Chron.: 342, 1857
Trichopilia lepida hort. ex Fl. Mag. n. s.: t. 98, 1874
o **Trichopilia suavis** Lindl. & Paxton, Paxt. Flow. Gard. 1: 44, 1850-51
BM 4654
Costa Rica, Panama, Colombia - 1300-1800 m - E
Trichopilia kienastiana Rchb. f., Gard. Chron.: 166, 1883
o **Trichopilia tortilis** Lindl., Nat. Syst. Bot. ed. 2: 446, 1836
BM 3739
Mexico, Guatemala, Honduras, El Salvador - up to 1500 m - E
Trisetella huebneri (Schltr.) Luer, Phytol. 47 (2): 57, 1980
BM 6268
Costa Rica, Panama, Venezuela, Brazil, Amazonas, Colombia, Ecuador, Peru, Bolivia - E
Masdevallia huebneri Schltr., Beih. Bot. Centralbl. 62: pt. 2, 88, 1925
Triaristella huebneri (Schltr.) Luer, Selbyana 2: 205, 1978
Triaristellina huebneri (Schltr.) Rauschert, Fedde Rep. 94: 469, 1983
o (Masdevallia triaristella Rchb. f., Gard. Chron.: 266 & 559, 1876; misidentified)
o **Vanda amesiana** Rchb. f., Gard. Chron.: 764, 1887
BM 7139
Burma, Thailand, China, Kampuchea, Laos, Vietnam - 1200-1600 m - E
o **Vanda bensonii** Bateman, Bot. Mag.: t. 5611, 1866
BM 5611
Thailand, Burma - E
o **Vanda coerulescens** Griffith, Notul. 3: 352, 1851
BM 5834
Thailand, Burma - 300-500 m - E
Vanda concolor Blume, Rumphia 4: 49, 1848
BM 3416
India, Thailand, China - E
o Vanda roxburghii var. unicolor Hook., Bot. Mag.: t. 3416, 1835
Vanda furva Lindl., Bot. Reg.: Misc. 42, 1844 (non Blume)
Vanda confusa Rolfe, Orch. Rev. 10: 196, 1902
BM 6328
India, Burma - E
o Vanda coerulescens subvar. boxallii Griffith, Gard. Chron.: 749, 1877
o **Vanda cristata** Lindl., Gen. Sp. Orch. Pl.: 216, 1833
BM 4304
Tibet, Nepal, Sikkim, Bhutan - 800-2000 m - E
Aerides cristata Wallich ex Lindl., Gen. Sp. Orch. Pl.: 216, 1832

Vanda alpina auct. non Lindl.; Tuyama, Hara Fl. E. Himalaya: 452, 1966
o **Vanda denisoniana** Benson & Rchb.f., Gard. Chron.: 528, 1869
BM 5811
Burma, Thailand - 800–1000 m - E
o **Vanda insignis** Blume, Rumphia 4: 49 t. 192 fig. 2, 1848
BM 5759
Moluccas, Java - E
o **Vanda limbata** Blume, Rumphia 4: 49, 1848
BM 6173
Java Philippines - E
o **Vanda luzonica** Loher ex Rolfe, Orch. Rev. 23: 137, 1915
BM 8709
Philippines - E
Vanda parviflora Lindl., Bot. Reg. 30: Misc. 45, 1844
BM 5138
Sri Lanka, India, Himalaya (Kumaun to Sikkim), Assam, Burma, Thailand - E
o Aerides wightiana Lindl., Wall. Cat.: 7320, 1832 (nomen nudum)
Aerides testacea Lindl., Gen. Sp. Orch. Pl.: 238, 1833
Vanda testacea (Lindl.) Rchb.f., Gard. Chron.: 166, 1877
Vanda vitellina Kraenzlin, Gard. Chron.: 206, 1892
non Vanda wightianum Lindl. ex Wight 5: 9 t. 1670, 1851
o **Vanda pumila** Hook.f., Fl. Brit. Ind. 6: 53, 1890
BM 7968
Sikkim, Bhutan, Thailand, N. Sumatra - E
Vanda cristata var. β Lindl., Fol. Orch.: 10, 1853
Vanda tessellata (Roxb.) Lodd. ex G. Don, Hort. Brit.: 372, 1832
BM 2245
Sri Lanka, India, Nepal, Burma, China - E
Epidendrum tesellatum Roxb., Pl. Corom. 1: 34, 1795
Cymbidium tessellatum (Roxb.) Sw., Nov. Act. Upsal. 6: 75, 1799
o Vanda roxburghii R.Br., Bot Reg. 6: pl. 506, 1820
Cymbidium tesselloides Roxb., Fl. Ind. 3: 463, 1832
Cymbidium alagnata Ham. ex Wallich, Cat.: 7327, 1832
Aerides tessellata (Roxb.) Wight, Wall. Cat.: 7318, 1832
Vanda unicolor Steudel, Nom. Bot. ed. 2, 2: 744, 1841
Epidendrum tesselloides (Roxb.) Steudel, Nom. Bot. ed. 2, 1: 558, 1841
Vanda tesselloides (Roxb.) Rchb.f., Walp. Ann. 6: 864, 1861
o **Vanda tricolor** Lindl., Bot. Reg.: sub.t. 59, 1847
BM 4432
Laos, Java, N. Australia - E
Vanda suaveolens Blume, Rumphia 4: 49, 1848
Vanda hindsii Benth., Fl. Austr. 6: 297, 1873 (non Lindl.)
Vanda tricolor Lindl. var. **suavis** (Lindl.) Rchb.f., Walp. Ann. 6: 866, 1862
BM 5174
Laos, Java - E
o Vanda suavis Lindl., Gard. Chron.: 351, 1848
o **Vanda watsonii** Rolfe, Gard. Chron.: 83 & 123 fig. 52, 1905
BM 8109
Thailand, Vietnam - up to 1600 m - E
Vandopsis gigantea (Lindl.) Pfitzer, Nat. Pflanzenf. 2 (6): 210, 1889
BM 5189
China, Burma, Thailand, N. Malaya - E
Vanda lindleyana Griffith ex Lindl., Paxt. Flow. Gard. 2: 22, 1851/52
o Vanda gigantea Lindl., Gen. Sp. Orch. Pl., 1853
Fieldia gigantea (Lindl.) Rchb.f., Xen. Orch. 2: 39 t. 112, 1862
Stauropsis giganteus (Lindl.) Benth. ex Pfitzer, Vergl. Morph. Orch.: 14, 1881
Vandopsis imthurnii (Rolfe) P. Hunt. Kew Bull.: 98, 1970
BM 8714
Solomon Is. - E
o Stauropsis imthurnii Rolfe, Bot. Mag.: t. 8714, 1917
Arachnis imthurnii (Rolfe) L.O. Williams, Bot. Mus. Leafl. Harv. Univ. 5 (4): 58, 1937
o **Vanilla humblotii** Rchb. f., Flora: 378, 1885
BM 7996
Madagascar, Comoro Is. - E
o **Vanilla planifolia** Jackson, Andrews Bot. Rep. 8: t. 538, 1808
BM 7167
W. Indies, Mexico, Brazil, Ecuador - E
Lobus oblongus aromaticus Clusius Exot. Libr.: 72, 1605
Araco aromatica Hernandez, Thes. Rev. Med. Nov. Hisp.: 38 cum icon., 1651
Lobus aromaticus C. Bauhin, Pinax: 404, 1671
Volubilis siliquosa mexicana Catesby, Carol. 3, 7: t. 7, 1748
Vanilla mexicana Miller, Dict. ed. 8 No. 1 trad. franç. 7: 505, 1785
Vanilla aromatica Willd., Sp. Pl. 4: 121, 1805
Myrobroma fragrans Salisb., Parad. Lond. 2: t. 82, 1807 (nomen illeg.)
Vanilla viridiflora Blume, Bijdr.: 422, 1825
Vanilla sativa Schiede, Linnaea 4: 573, 1829
Vanilla sylvestris Schiede, Linnaea 4: 573, 1829
Vanilla fragrans (Salisb.) Ames, Sched. Orch. 7: 36, 1924
Warrea warreana (Lodd. ex Lindl.) C. Schweinf., Bot. Mus. Leafl. Harv. Univ. 17: 55, 1955
BM 4235
Venezuela, Colombia, Peru, Ecuador, Brazil - T
o Maxillaria warreana Lodd. ex Lindl., Gen. Sp. Orch. Pl.: 148, 1832
Warrea tricolor Lindl., Bot. Reg. 29: Misc. p. 14, 1843
Warrea bidentata Lindl., Bot. Reg.: Misc. 16, 1844
Warrea unijugata Regel, Ind. Sem. Hort. Petrop.: 22, 1855
Aganisia tricolor (Lindl.) Bois, Orch.: 128, 1893 (non Benth. & Hook., non N.E.Br.)
Warrea speciosa Schltr., Fedde Rep. Beih. 9: 98, 1921
o **Xylobium leontoglossum** (Rchb.f.) Rolfe, Gard. Chron.: 485, 1889
BM 7085
Venezuela, Colombia, Peru - up to 2000 m - E
Maxillaria leontoglossa Rchb.f., Bonpl. 3: 67, 1855
Xylobium gracile Schltr., Fedde Rep. Beih. 8: 92, 1921
Xylobium squalens var. gracile (Schltr.) C. Schweinf., Bot. Mus. Leafl. Harv. Univ. 11: 198, 1944
Xylobium pallidiflorum (Hook.) Nicholson, Dict. Gard. 4: 225, 1887
BM 2806
W. Indies, Nicaragua, Venezuela, Trinidad, Brazil, Colombia, Ecuador, Peru, Bolivia - E
o Maxillaria pallidiflora Hook., Bot. Mag.: t. 2806, 1828
Maxillaria stenobulbon Klotzsch, Ind. Sem. Hort. Berol.: 11, 1853
Xylobium palmifolium (Sw.) Benth. ex Fawcett, Fl. Pl. Jam. 39, 1893
BM 3981
Trinidad, Jamaica - E, L
Epidendrum palmifolium Sw., Prodr. Veg. Ind. Occ.: 123, 1788
Dendrobium palmifolium (Sw.) Sw., Nov. Act. Upsal. 6: 82, 1799
Colax palmifolius (Sw.) Lindl., Bot. Reg. 11: sub.t. 897, 1825
Maxillaria palmifolia (Sw.) Lindl., Gen. Sp. Orch. Pl.: 148, 1832
o Maxillaria decolor Lindl., Bot. Reg.: t. 1549, 1833
Xylobium decolor (Lindl.) Nicholson, Dict. Gard. 4: 223, 1887
Xylobium variegatum (Ruiz Lopez & Pavón) Garay & Dunsterv., Venez. Orch. Ill. 2: 342, 1961
BM 2955
Costa Rica, Venezuela, Colombia, Ecuador, Peru, Bolivia, Brazil - E
Maxillaria variegata Ruiz Lopez & Pavón, Syst. Veg. 1: 222, 1798
Dendrobium variegatum Pers., Syn. Pl. 2: 524, 1807
Dendrobium squalens Lindl., Bot. Reg. 9: t. 732, 1823
Xylobium squalens (Lindl.) Hook., Bot. Reg. 11: sub.t. 897, 1825
o Maxillaria squalens (Lindl.) Hook., Bot. Mag.: t. 2955, 1829
Dendrobium carnosum C. Presl., Symb. Bot. 35: t. 24, 1832
Cyrtopera scabrilinguis Lindl., Gen. Sp. Orch. Pl.: 189, 1833
Maxillaria supina Poeppig & Endl., Nov. Gen. Sp. Pl. 1: 39, 1836
Xylobium houtei Makoi ex Mutel, Mém. sur Plus. Orch. 1: 16, 1840
Maxillaria scabrilinguis (Lindl.) Schltr., Bot. Reg. 30: Misc. p. 71, 1844
Xylobium dusenii Kraenzlin, Svensk Vet. Akad. Handl. 46: No. 10, 65, 1911
Xylobium scabrilingue (Lindl.) Schltr., Orchis 7: 23, 1913
Xylobium supinum (Poeppig & Endl.) Schltr., Orchis 7: 24, 1913
Xylobium carnosum (C. Presl.) Schltr., Fedde Rep. Beih. 9: 160, 1921
Zootrophion atropurpureum (Lindl.) Luer, Selbyana 7: 80, 1982
BM 4164
Cuba, Jamaica, Panama, Colombia, Ecuador, Peru, Bolivia - E
Specklinia atropurpurea Lindl., Bot. Reg.: t. 1797, 1836
Pleurothallis atropurpurea (Lindl.) Lindl., Bot. Reg. 28: Misc. 81, 1842
o Masdevallia fenestrata Lindl. ex Hook., Bot. Mag.: t. 4164, 1845
Cryptophoranthus atropurpureus (Lindl.) Rolfe, Gard. Chron. 2: 693, 1887
Cryptophoranthus alvaroi Garay, Orquideologia 5: 15, 1970
Zootrophion dayanum (Rchb.f.) Luer, Selbyana 7: 82, 1982
BM 8740
Colombia, Venezuela, Ecuador, Peru, Bolivia - E
Masdevallia dayana Rchb.f., Gard. Chron.: 295, 1880
o Cryptophoranthus dayanus (Rchb.f.) Rolfe, Gard. Chron.: 693, 1887
Cryptophoranthus lehmannii Rolfe, Orch. Rev. 11: 303, 1903
Cryptophoranthus argus Rchb.f. ex Kraenzlin, Fedde Rep. 17: 437, 1921
Cryptophoranthus beloglottis Schltr., Fedde Rep. Beih. 8: 50, 1921
Cryptophoranthus hologlottis Schltr., ex Kraenzlin, Fedde Rep. Beih. 34: 225, 1925
× **Zygopabstia veitchii** (Rolfe) Dressler, Baileya 20 (1): 30, 1976
BM 7980
Brazil - E
= Pabstia jugosa (Lindl.) Garay × Zypogetalum crinitum Lodd.
Zygopetalum × veitchii J.H. Veitch, Gard. Chron.: 425, 1887

○ × Zygocolax veitchii Rolfe, Gard. Chron.: 765, 1887
Zygopetalum crinitum Lodd., Bot. Cab. 17: t. 1637, 1830
BM 3402
Brazil - E, T
○ Zygopetalum mackayi var. crinitum (Lodd.) Lindl., Gen. Sp. Orch. Pl.: 187, 1833
Zygopetalum stenochilum Lodd., Bot. Cab. 20: t, 1923, 1833
Zygopetalum pubescens Hoffsgg., Verz. Orch.: 63, 1843
Zygopetalum microtos Hoffsgg. ex Rchb. f., Walp. Ann. 6: 661, 1863
Zygopetalum crepeauxii Carrière, Rev. Hort.: 420, 1887
Zygopetalum claesianum hort., Orch. Rev. 2: 62, 1894
Zygopetalum lamellosum (Rchb. f.) Rchb. f., Gen. Pl. 3: 543, 1883
BM 6240
Colombia - E
○ Pescatorea lamellosa Rchb. f., Gard. Chron.: 225, 1875
○ **Zygopetalum mackaii** Hook., Bot. Mag.: t. 2748, 1827
BM 2748
Brazil - 1300–1700 m - E

○ **Zygopetalum maxillare** Lodd., Bot. Cab.: t. 1776, 1831
BM 3686
Brazil, Argentina, Paraguay - E
Zygopetalum mandibulare Rchb. f., Gard. Chron.: 684, 1877
Zygopetalum hasslerianum Kraenzlin, Engl. Bot. Jahrb. 37: 389, 1906
Zygosepalum labiosum (L. C. Rich.) C. Schweinf., Mem. N. Y. Bot. Gard. 14 (3): 184, 1967
BM 2819
Venezuela, Guyana, Brazil, Amazonas - E
Epidendrum labiosum L. C. Rich. Cat. Pl. Le Blond, Act. Soc. Hist. Nat. Paris 1: 112, 1792
○ Zygopetalum rostratum Hook., Bot. Mag.: t. 2819, 1828
Menadenium rostratum (Hook.) Raf., Fl. Tellur. 4: 45, 1836
Zygosepalum rostratum (Hook.) Rchb. f., Ned. Kruidk. Arch. 4: 330, 1859
Menadenium labiosum (L. C. Rich.) Cogn., Fl. Bras. 3 pt. 5: 582, 1902
Zygopetalum labiosum (L. C. Rich.) L. O. Williams, Caldasia 1 (5): 16, 1942

KATALOG

Orchideentafeln aus Curtis's Botanical Magazine (1948–1983)

○ **Aerangis coriacea** Summerh., Gard. Chron.: 96 fig. 44, 1952
BM 297 ns
Kenya, N. Tanganyika – E
Aerangis sp. nov. Orch. Rev. 60: 45, 46, 48, 1952

○ **Aerangis jacksonii** J. Stewart, Bot. Mag.: sub. t. 754 ns., 1978
BM 754 ns
Uganda (Toro and Mengo districts) – E

Aerangis luteo-alba (Kraenzlin) Schltr. var. **rhodosticta** (Kraenzlin) J. Stewart, Kew Bull. 34: (2), 1979
BM 276 ns
Trop. Africa (Cameroun, Central Afr. Rep., Ethiopia, Kenya, Tanganyika) – E
Angraecum rhodostictum Kraenzlin, Notizbl. Bot. Gart. Berlin 1: 154, 1896
Angorchis rhodosticta (Kraenzlin) Kuntze, Deutsch. Bot. Monatschr. 21: 173, 1903
Angraecum albido-rubrum De Wild, Bull. Jard. Bot. Brux. 5: 180, 1916
Aerangis albido-rubra (De Wild) Schltr., Beih. Bot. Centralbl. 36 (2): 113, 1918

○ Aerangis rhodosticta (Kraenzlin) Schltr., Beih. Bot. Centralbl. 36 (2): 119, 1918
Angraecum mirabile hort., Gard. Chron.: 17 fig. 7, 1923

○ **Aeranthes caudata** Rolfe, Kew Bull.: 149, 1901
BM 685 ns
Madagascar, Comoro Is. – E
Aeranthes imerinensis H. Perrier, Not. Syst. Paris 7: 44, 1938

○ **Aerides houlletiana** Rchb. f., Gard. Chron.: 1194, 1872
BM 260 ns
Thailand, S. China, Kampuchea, Laos, Vietnam – E
Aerides ellisii J. Anderson, Gard. Chron.: 520, 1880
Aerides picotiana hort. ex Rchb. f. Gard. Chron: 378, 1888
Aerides falcata var. houlletiana (Rchb. f.) Veitch., Man. Orch. 7: 68, 1891

○ **Ancistrochilus rothschildianus** O'Brien, Gard. Chron.: 51, 1907
BM 786 ns
Sierra Leone, Guinea to Cameroun, W. Uganda – up to 1200 m – E
Ancistrochilus hirsutissimus Kraenzlin, Engl. Bot. Jahrb. 51: 386, 1914
Pachystoma rothschildianum (O'Brien) Sander, Orch. Guide: 363, 1927

○ **Angraecum magdalenae** Schltr. & Perrier, Fedde Rep. Beih. 33: 354, 1925
BM 591 ns
Madagascar – L
Angraecum magdalenae var. latilabellum Bosser, Adans. 5: 408 t. 11 (1–5), 1965

○ **Bulbophyllum frostii** Summerh., Kew Bull.: 76, 1928
BM 121 ns
Vietnam (Annan) – E

○ **Camarotis rostrata** (Roxb.) Rchb. f., Walp. Ann. 6: 881, 1864
BM 537 ns
India, E. Pakistan, Thailand – E
Aerides rostrata Roxb., Fl. Ind. 3: 474, 1832
Camarotis purpurea Lindl., Wall. Cat.: 7329, 1832 (nomen)
Sarcochilus purpureus (Lindl.) Hook. f., Fl. Brit. Ind. 6: 36, 1891

○ **Cattleya bowringiana** O'Brien, Gard. Chron.: 683, 1885
BM 451 ns
Guatemala, Honduras – E, T

○ **Ceratostylis retisquama** Rchb. f., Bonpl. 5: 53, 1857
BM 640 ns
Philippines (Luzon and Mindanao) – E
Ceratostylis rubra Ames, Philipp. J. Sc. 4: 670, 1909
Ceratostylis latipetala Ames, Philipp. J. Sc. 4: 671, 1909

○ **Coelogyne dayana** Rchb. f., Gard. Chron.: 826, 1884
BM 309 ns
Malaya, Java, Borneo – E

○ **Coelogyne pulchella** Rolfe. Kew Bull.: 194, 1898
BM 28 ns
S. Burma (Tenasserim) – E

Corybas diemenicus (Lindl.) Rupp, Proc. Linn. Soc. N. S. W. 53: 55, 1928
BM 836 ns
S. Australia, Tasmania – T
Corysanthes diemenica Lindl., Gen. Sp. Orch. Pl.: 393, 1840
Corysanthes fimbriata var. diemenica (Lindl.) Benth., Fl. Austr. 6: 351, 1873

○ Corybas dilatus sensu Dransfield, Bot. Mag.: t. 836 ns., 1980 non (Rupp & Nicholls) Rupp

○ **Cryptostylis subulata** (Labill.) Rchb. f., Beitr. Syst. Pfl.: 15, 1871
BM 573 ns
Australia – T
Malaxis subulata Labill., Nov. Holl. Pl. Sp. 2: 62 t. 212, 1806
Cryptostylis longifolia R. Br., Prodr. Fl. Nov. Holl.: 317, 1810 (nomen illeg.)

○ **Cymbidium goeringii** (Rchb. f.) Rchb. f., Walp. An.. 3: 547, 1852
BM 413 ns
China, Korea, Ryukyu Is., Japan, Taiwan – T
Cymbidium virescens Lindl., Bot. Reg.: Misc. 37, 1838
Maxillaria goeringii Rchb. f., Bot. Zeit. 3: 334, 1845
Cymbidium virens Lindl., Walp. Ann. 6: 626, 1861
Cymbidium formosum Hayata, J. Coll. Sc. Tokyo 30: 335, 1911
Cymbidium forrestii Rolfe ex Downie, Notes Roy. Bot. Gard. Edinb. 8: 23, 1913
Cymbidium serratum Schltr., Fedde Rep. Beih. 4: 73, 1919
Cymbidium yunnanense Schltr., Fedde Rep. Beih. 4: 273, 1919
Cymbidium pseudovirens Schltr., Fedde Rep. Beih. 12: 351, 1922
Cymbidium tortisepalum Fuk., Bot. Mag. Tokyo 48: 304 t. 1, 1931
Cymbidium gracillimum Fuk., Trans. Nat. Hist. Soc. Form. 22: 413, 1932
Cymbidium uniflorum Yen., Ic. Cymb. Amoy. A–Z, 1964
Cymbidium longibracteatum Wu & Chen, Acta Phytotax. Sin. 11: 31, 1966
Cymbidium goeringii var. angustatum F. Maekawa, The Wild Orch. Jap. in colour.: 416 t. 171, 1971 (nomen nudum)
Cymbidium tortisepalum var. viridiflorum Ying, Coll. Ill. Ind. Orch. Taiwan: 415, 1977
Cymbidium formosanum var. gracillimum (Fuk.) Liu & Su, Fl. Taiwan 5: 943, 1978
Cymbidium goeringii var. serratum (Schltr.) Wu & Chen, Acta Phytotax. Sin. 18: 300, 1980
Cymbidium goeringii var. longibracteatum (Wu & Chen) Wu & Chen, Acta Phytotax. Sin. 18: 300, 1980
Cymbidium goeringii var. tortisepalum (Fuk.) Wu & Chen, Acta Phytotax. Sin. 18: 300, 1980

○ **Cymbidium suavissimum** Sander ex C. H. Curtis, Gard. Chron.: 137 & 157 fig. 67, 1928
BM 671 ns
N. Burma – E

○ **Cymbidium tracyanum** hort. ex O'Brien, Gard. Chron.: 718, 1890
BM 56 ns
Burma, Thailand – E
Cyperorchis tracyana (hort. ex O'Brien) Schltr., Fedde Rep. 20: 108, 1924

Cymbidium wilsonii (Rolfe ex T. Cooke) Rolfe, Orch. Rev. 12: 79, 1904
BM 704 ns
China (Yunnan) – E
Cymbidium giganteum var. wilsonii Rolfe ex T. Cooke, The Garden 65: 158, 1904

Cyperorchis wilsonii (Rolfe ex T. Cooke) Schltr., Fedde Rep. 20: 108, 1924
o Cymbidium giganteum Wallich ex Lindl. cv. Wilsonii (Rolfe ex T. Cooke) P. Taylor & P. Woods, Bot. Mag.: t. 704 n.s., 1976
o **Dendrobium bracteosum** Rchb.f., Gard. Chron.: 809, 1886
BM 389 ns
New Guinea, New Ireland - E
Dendrobium chrysolabium Rolfe, Gard. Chron.: 770, 1889
Dendrobium novae-hiberniae Kraenzlin, Oesterr. Bot. Zeit. 44: 301, 1894
Dendrobium dixsonii F.M. Bailey, Queensl. Dept. Agr. Bot. Bull. 13: 33, 1896
Dendrobium trisaccatum Kraenzlin, Pflanzenr. Heft 45: 107, 1910
Dendrobium sp. Foote, Orch. Rev. 43: 31, 1935
o **Dendrobium engae** Reeve, Orchadian 6 (6): 123, 1979
BM 872 ns
New Guinea, - 2000–2700 m - E
o **Dendrobium harveyanum** Rchb.f., Gard. Chron.: 624, 1883
BM 790 ns
Burma, N. Thailand - E
o **Dendrobium johnsoniae** sensu P.F. Hunt, Bot. Mag.: t. 560 n.s., 1969/70 (non F. Muell.)
BM 560 ns - E
Hybrid of Dendrobium johnsoniae × Dendrobium macrophyllum or a secundary hybrid
o **Dendrobium lawesii** F. Muell., Austr. Chem. Drug. 7: 14, 1884
BM 524 ns
New Guinea - E
Dendrobium warburgianum Kraenzlin, Engl. Bot. Jahrb. 13: 281, 1891
Dendrobium pseudomohlianum Kraenzlin, K. Schum. & Laut., Nachtr. Fl. Deutsch. Schutzgeb. Südsee 178, 1905
Dendrobium lawesii var. salmonicolor Schltr., Fedde Rep. Beih. 1: 513, 1912
Pedilonum lawesii (F. Muell.) Rauschert, Fedde Rep.: 461, 1983
o **Dendrobium polysema** Schltr., K. Schum. & Laut. Nachtr. Fl. Deutsch. Schutzgeb. Südsee: 163, 1905
BM 798 ns
New Guinea - E
Dendrobium macrophyllum var. stenopterum Rchb.f., Gard. Chron.: 393, 1888
Dendrobium polysema var. pallidum Chadium, Orch. Rev. 29: 30–32, 1964
Sayeria polysema (Schltr.) Rauschert, Fedde Rep.: 468, 1983
o **Dendrobium ruppianum** A. Hawkes, Austr. Orch. Rev. 29: 40, 1964
BM 749 ns
Australia (N.E. Queensland) - E
Dendrobium speciosum var. fusiforme Bailey, Syn. Queensland Fl.: 509, 1883
Dendrobium fusiforme (Bailey) Bailey, Queensland Fl. 5: 1527, 1902 (non Thouars 1822)
o **Dendrobium stratiotes** Rchb. f., Gard. Chron.: 266, 1886
BM 436 ns
New Guinea - E
o **Dendrobium unicum** Seidenf., Bot. Tidsskr. 65: 332, 1970
BM 616 ns
Laos, Thailand - E
Dendrobium woodsii Cribb, Orchadian 6 (12): 282 fig. 3, 1981
BM 727 ns
New Guinea - E
o Dendrobium fantasticum sensu P. Taylor & J.J. Wood, Bot. Mag.: t. 727 n.s. 1976/77 (non L.O. Williams, Bot. Mus. Leafl. Harv. Univ. 12: n. 5: 158, 1940)
Sayeria woodsii (Cribb) Rauschert, Fedde Rep.: 468, 1983
Encyclia baculus (Rchb.f.) Dressler & Pollard, Phytol. 21: 436, 1971
BM 702 ns
Mexico, Guatemala, El Salvador, Honduras, Nicaragua, Colombia, possibly Brazil - E
Epidendrum fragrans var. megalanthum Lindl., J. Hort. Soc. Lond. 4: 223, 1849
o Epidendrum baculus Rchb.f., Bonpl. 4: 214, 1856
Epidendrum pentotis Rchb.f., Linnaea 41: 81, 1876
Epidendrum acuminatum Sessé & Mocino, Fl. Mex. ed. 2: 202, 1894 (non Ruiz Lopez & Pavón, 1798)
Epidendrum confusum Rolfe, Orch. Rev. 7: 197, 1899
Epidendrum beyrodtianum Schltr., Orchis 9: 49, 1915
Encyclia pentotis (Rchb.f.) Dressler, Brittonia: 13–265, 1961
Encyclia calamaria (Lindl.) Pabst., Orquidea 29 (6): 276, 1967
BM 775 ns
Brazil - E
o Epidendrum calamarium Lindl., Bot. Reg.: 24 Misc. 88, 1838

Encyclia chondylobulbon (A. Rich. & Galeotti) Dressler & Pollard, Phytol. 21: 436, 1971
BM 160 ns
Mexico - E
o Epidendrum chondylobulbon A. Rich. & Galeotti, Ann. Sc. Nat. 3, 3: 20, 1845
o **Encyclia cordigera** (Kunth) Dressler, Taxon 13: 247, 1964
BM 290 ns, BM 3534
Mexico to Panama, W. Indies, Venezuela, Trinidad, Peru - E
o **Encyclia ghillanyi** Pabst, Bradea 2 (14): 80, 1976
BM 812 ns
Brazil - E
Encyclia radiata (Lindl.) Dressler, Brittonia 13: 265, 1961
BM 662 ns
Mexico, Guatemala, Honduras, Costa Rica, Venezuela - E
o Epidendrum radiatum Lindl., Bot. Reg. 27: Misc. 58, 1841
Epidendrum marginatum Link, Klotzsch & Otto Ic. Pl. Rar. 2: 90 t. 36, 1842
Encyclia sima Dressler, Orquideologia 4 (2): 91, 1969
BM 757 ns
Panama - E
o Epidendrum simum (Dressler) P. Taylor, Bot. Mag.: t. 757 n.s., 1978
o **Epidendrum oerstedii** Rchb.f., Bot. Zeit. 10: 937, 1852
BM 375 ns
Nicaragua, Costa Rica, Panama - E
Epidendrum costaricense Rchb.f., Bot. Zeit. 10: 937, 1852
Epidendrum umlauftii Zahlbr., Wiener Ill. Gartenz. 18: 209 t. 2, 1893
Epidendrum ciliare var. oerstedii (Rchb.f.) L.O. Williams, Ann. Missouri Bot. Gard. 33: 327, 1946
o **Eria globifera** Rolfe, Gard. Chron.: 449, 1905
BM 83 ns
Vietnam (Annam) - E
Eria langbianensis Gagnepain, Bull. Mus. Paris s. 2, 2: 308, 1930
o **Eria pannea** Lindl., Bot. Reg. 28: 64 Misc. 79, 1842
BM 570 ns
Bhutan, Sikkim, Burma, Laos, Kampuchea, Vietnam, China, Malaya, Sumatra, Riau Arch., Bangka, Borneo - E
Eria teretifolia Griffith, Itin. Not.: 202, 1848 (non Griffith, 1851)
Eria calamifolia Hook.f., Fl. Brit. Ind. 6: 191, 1890
Pinalia calamifolia (Hook.f.) Kuntze, Rev. Gen. 2: 679, 1891
Pinalia pannea (Lindl.) Kuntze, Rev. Gen. 2: 679, 1891
Eria nivosa Ridley, J. Nat. Hist. Siam Soc. 4: 116, 1921
o **Eriopsis biloba** Lindl., Bot. Reg. 33: sub.t. 9, 1847
BM 611 ns, BM 4437
Costa Rica, Panama, Venezuela, Guyana, Brazil, Colombia, Ecuador, Peru - E, T
o **Eulophia guineensis** Lindl., Bot. Reg. 8: t. 686, 1823
BM 267 ns, BM 2467
Gambia, Mali, Guinea, Sierra Leone, Ivory Coast, Ghana, Nigeria, Zaire, Uganda, Tanzania, Angola - T
o **Eulophiella elisabethae** Linden & Rolfe, Lindenia 7: 29 t. 325, 1892
BM 656 ns, BM 7387
Madagascar - E
o **Grobya amherstiae** Lindl., Bot. Reg.: t. 1740, 1835
BM 720 ns
Brazil - E
o **Habenaria engleriana** Kraenzlin, Engl. Bot. Jahrb. 17: 68 t. 5 A, 1893
BM 631 ns
Trop. W. Africa (Guinea, Sierra Leone, Ghana, Togo, N.S. Nigeria) - T
Habenaria hunteri Rolfe, Kew Bull.: 238, 1918
o **Lacaena bicolor** Lindl., Bot. Reg.: Misc.p. 68, 1843
BM 330 ns
Mexico, Honduras, Costa Rica - E
Peristeria longiscapa A. Rich. & Galeotti, Ann. Sc. Nat. s. 3, 3: 25, 1845
Lacaena bicolor var. glabrata Lemaire, Ill. Hort. 1: t. 33 & Misc.p. 56, 1854
Acineta wrightii J. Fraser, Gard. World.: 673, 1889
Lueddemannia sanderiana Kraenzlin, Gard. Chron.: 138, 1897
Acineta hrubyana hort., Gard. Chron.: 427, 1907 (non Rchb.f.)
Lacaena bicolor var. alba Rolfe, Orch. Rev. 18: 208, 1910
o **Liparis makinoana** Schltr., Fedde Rep. Beih. 4: 63 & 200, 1919
BM 458 ns
Japan, Korea, U.S.S.R., China - T
Liparis liliifolia auct. non L.C. Rich.; Ridley, J. Linn. Soc. Lond. 22: 269, 1887
o **Lycaste ciliata** (Ruiz Lopez & Pavón) Lindl. ex Rchb.f., Bonpl. 4: 324, 1856
BM 767 ns, BM 5706
Colombia, Ecuador, Peru, Bolivia - T

○ **Maxillaria camaridii** Rchb. f., Hamb. Gartenz. 19: 547, 1863
BM 472 ns, BM 3306, BM 4141
Guatemala, Honduras, Costa Rica, Panama, W. Indies, Venezuela, Trinidad, Guyana, Surinam, Brazil, Colombia, Peru, Bolivia – E
○ **Miltonia flavescens** (Lindl.) Lindl., Sert. Orch. Miltonia: 3, 1853
BM 849 ns
Brazil, Paraguay, Argentina – 200–700 m – E
Cyrtochilum flavescens Lindl., Bot. Reg.: t. 1627, 1833
Cyrtochilum stellatum Lindl., Sert. Orch.: t. 7, 1838
Oncidium flavescens (Lindl.) Rchb. f., Walp. Ann. 6: 757, 1863
○ **Odontoglossum armatum** Rchb. f., Linnaea 41: 32, 1877
BM 825 ns
Colombia, Ecuador – 2000–2500 m – E
Odontoglossum denticulatum Lehm., ined.
Odontoglossum cristatum var. lehmannii Regel, Gartenfl. 39: 58 t. 1313, 1890
○ **Oeceoclades saundersiana** (Rchb. f.) Garay & Taylor, Bot. Mus. Leafl. Harv. Univ. 24 (9): 270, 1976
BM 731 ns
Trop. Africa – T
Eulophia saundersiana Rchb. f., Bot. Zeit. 24: 378, 1866
Graphorchis saundersiana (Rchb. f.) Kuntze, Rev. Gen. 2: 662, 1891
Eulophidium saundersianum (Rchb. f.) Summerh., Bull. Jard. Bot. Brux. 27: 401, 1957
○ **Oncidium oblongatum** Lindl. Bot. Reg.: Misc. p. 4, 1844
BM 5 ns
Mexico – E
Oncidium xanthochlorum Klotzsch, Ind. Sem. Hort. Berol. App.: 2, 1852
○ **Paphiopedilum acmodontum** Schoser ex M. W. Wood, Orch. Rev. 84: 350, 1976
BM 820 ns
Philippines – T
○ **Paphiopedilum appletonianum** (Gower) Rolfe, Orch. Rev. 4: 364, 1896
BM 833 ns
Thailand, Laos, Kampuchea – T
Cypripedium appletonianum Gower, The Garden 1: 93, 1893
Cypripedium bullenianum var. appletonianum (Gower) Rolfe, Orch. Rev. 1: 135, 1893
Cypripedium poyntzianum O'Brien, Gard. Chron.: 36, 1894
Cypripedium wolterianum Kraenzlin, Gard. Chron.: 166, 1895
Paphiopedilum wolterianum (Kraenzlin) Pfitzer, Xen. Orch. 3: 142 t. 282, 1896
Paphiopedilum appletonianum var. poyntzianum (O'Brien) Pfitzer, Pflanzenr. Orch. Pleonandr.: 79, 1903
Cordula appletoniana (Gower) Rolfe, Orch. Rev. 20: 2, 1912
Paphiopedilum johorense Fowlie & Yap, Orch. Digest 36: 73, 1972
○ **Paphiopedilum bellatulum** (Rchb. f.) Stein. Orchideenb.: 456, 1892
BM 880 ns
Burma, Thailand, S. China, Laos – 1000–1500 m – T, L
Cypripedium bellatulum Rchb. f., Gard. Chron.: 648 & 747, 1888
Cordula bellatula (Rchb. f.) Rolfe, Orch. Rev. 20: 2, 1912
Paphiopedilum ciliolare (Rchb. f.) Stein, Orchideenb.: 462, 1892
BM 803 ns
Philippines (Luzon & Mindanao) – 300–1800 m – T
Cypripedium ciliolare Rchb. f., Gard. Chron.: 488, 1852
Cypripedium miteauanum Masters, Gard. Chron.: 326, 1888
Paphiopedilum ciliolare var. miteauanum (Masters) Pfitzer, Pflanzenr. Heft 12: 89, 1903
Cordula ciliolaris (Rchb. f.) Rolfe, Orch. Rev. 20: 2, 1912
○ Paphiopedilum superbiens subsp. ciliolare (Rchb. f.) M. W. Wood, Bot. Mag.: t. 803 ns., 1981
○ **Paphiopedilum dayanum** (Lindl.) Pfitzer, Engl. Bot. Jahrb. 19: 40, 1894
BM 594 ns
Borneo – T
Cypripedium dayi Stone mss., vide Gard. Chron.: 693, 1860
Cypripedium superbiens var. dayanum Lindl., Gard. Chron.: 693, 1860
Cypripedium dayanum Lindl., Proc. Roy. Hort. Soc. 1: 245, 1860
Cypripedium petri Rchb. f., Gard. Chron.: 680, 1880
Cypripedium ernestianum Castle, J. Hort. s. 3, 14: 375 t. 67, 1887
Cypripedium dayanum vars. smithianum, splendens & superbum Pucci, Cyprip.: 77, 1891
Cypripedium dayanum var. ernestianum (Castle) Desbois, Cypr. ed. 2: 155, 1898
Paphiopedilum dayanum var. petri (Rchb. f.) Pfitzer, Pflanzenr. Heft 12: 86, 1903
Cordula dayana (Lindl.) Rolfe, Orch. Rev. 20: 2, 1912
Cordula petri (Rchb. f.) Rolfe, Orch. Rev. 20: 2, 1912
○ **Paphiopedilum delenatii** Guillaumin, Bull. Soc. Bot. Fr. 71: 554 & 558, 1924
BM 89 ns
Vietnam – T
Cypripedium delenatii hort., Orch. Rev. 39: 120, 1931
○ **Paphiopedilum druryi** (Beddome) Stein, Orchideenb.: 466, 1892
BM 764 ns
S. India – T
Cypripedium druryi Beddome, Ic. Pl. Ind. Occ. 1: 23 t. 112, 1874
Cordula druryi (Beddome) Rolfe, Orch. Rev. 20: 2, 1912
○ **Paphiopedilum liemianum** (Fowlie) Karasawa & Saito, Bull. Hirosh. Bot. Gard. 5: 57, 1982
BM 729 ns
Sumatra – T
Paphiopedilum chamberlainianum (O'Brien) Stein subsp. liemianum Fowlie, Orch. Digest 35: 53–55, 1971
○ Paphiopedilum victoria-regina (Sander) M. W. Wood subsp. liemianum (Fowlie) M. W. Wood, Orch. rev. 84: 138, 1976
○ **Paphiopedilum praestans** (Rchb. f.) Pfitzer, Engl. Bot. Jahrb. 19: 41, 1894
BM 743 ns
New Guinea – T
Cypripedium praestans Rchb. f., Gard. Chron.: 776, 1886
Cypripedium gardineri Guillemard, The Cruise of the Marchesa to Kamschatka and New Guinea 2: 309, 1886
Cypripedium praestans var. kimballianum Linden & Rodigas, Lindenia 6: t. 249, 1890
Paphiopedilum gardineri (Guillemard) Pfitzer, Bot. Jahrb. 19: 41, 1894
Paphiopedilum praestans var. kimballianum (Linden & Rodigas) Pfitzer, Pflanzenr. Heft 9: 50 & 61, 1903
Cordula praestans (Rchb. f.) Rolfe, Orch. Rev. 20: 2, 1912
○ **Paphiopedilum sukhakulii** Schoser & Senghas, Die Orchidee 16: 110 & 224, 1965
BM 855 ns
N. E. Thailand – T
○ **Paphiopedilum superbiens** (Rchb. f.) Stein, Orchideenb.: 487, 1892
BM 803 ns
Sumatra (Barisan Mts. and near Lake Toba) – T
Cypripedium superbiens Rchb. f., Bonpl. 3: 227, 1855
Cypripedium barbatum var. veitchii hort. ex Van Houtte, Fl. Serres s. 2, 4: 161 t. 1453, 1861
Cypripedium veitchianum hort. ex Lemaire, l'Ill. Hort. 12: t. 429, 1865
Cypripedium barbatum var. superbum hort. ex Morren, Belg. Hort.: 97, 1883
Cypripedium curtisii Rchb. f., Gard. Chron.: 8, 1883
Paphiopedilum curtisii (Rchb. f.) Stein, Orchideenb.: 464, 1892
Cordula superbiens (Rchb. f.) Rolfe, Orch. Rev. 20: 2, 1912
Cordula curtisii (Rchb. f.) Kuntze, Orch. Rev. 20: 2, 1912
○ **Paphiopedilum tonsum** (Rchb. f.) Stein, Orchideenb.: 488, 1892
BM 838 ns
N. C. Sumatra – T
Cypripedium tonsum Rchb. f., Gard. Chron.: 262, 1883
Cordula tonsa (Rchb. f.) Rolfe, Orch. Rev. 20: 2, 1912
○ **Pecteilis sagarikii** Seidenf., Bot. Tidsskr. 68: 46, 1973
BM 877 ns
Thailand – T
○ **Phaius francoisii** (Schltr.) Summerh., Kew Bull. 17: 558, 1964
BM 738 ns
Madagascar – T
Gastrorchis francoisii Schltr., Fedde Rep. Beih. 33: 168, 1924
○ **Pleione Alishan** (P. formosa × P. Versailles)
BM 869 ns (in part)
○ **Pleione Brigadoon** (P. speciosa × P. confusa)
BM 869 ns (in part)
○ **Pleione bulbocodioides** (Franchet) Rolfe, Orch. Rev. 11: 291, 1903
BM 866 ns, BM 8106
China (Anhui, Gansu, Guizhou, Hubei, Sichuan, S. E. Tibet, Yunnan) – T, E
Pleione × confusa Cribb & C. Z. Tang, Bot. Mag.: 126 n. s., 1983
BM 501 ns
= Pleione forrestii Schltr. × Pleione albiflora Cribb & C. Z. Tang
○ Pleione forrestii sensu P. F. Hunt, Bot. Mag.: t. 501 n. s., 1967 (non Schltr.)
○ **Pleione Eiger** (P. formosana × P. humilis)
BM 871 ns (in part)
○ **Pleione formosana** Hayata, J. Coll. Sc. Tokyo 30, art. 1: 326, 1911
«Polar Sun», «Blush of Dawn», «Oriental Grace»
BM 867 ns
○ **Pleione formosana** Hayata, J Coll. Sc. Tokyo 30: 326, 1911
BM 421 ns, BM 8729
E. China, Taiwan – T

○ **Pleione forrestii** Schltr., Notes Roy. Bot. Gard. Edin. 5: 106, 1912
BM 864 ns
N. Burma, S.W. China (W. Yunnan) - 2400–3100 m - L

○ **Pleione Hekla** (P. formosana × P. humilis)
BM 871 ns (in part)

○ **Pleione hookeriana** (Lindl.) Williams, Orch. Grow. Man. ed. 6, 548, 1855
BM 862 ns, BM 6388
S. Tibet, C. & E. Nepal, Sikkim, Bhutan, Assam, Burma, N. Thailand, Laos - E, L

○ **Pleione humilis** (Smith) D. Don, Prod. Fl. Nepal.: 37, 1825
BM 863 ns, BM 5674
Nepal, Sikkim, Assam, Manipur, Burma - 1850–3200 m - E, L

○ **Pleione × lagenaria** (Lindl.) Lindl., Paxt. Flow. Gard. 2: 5 t. 39, 1851
BM 860 ns, BM 5370
Assam, S. China - 1500–2500 m - E, L

○ **Pleione limprichtii** Schltr., Fedde Rep. Beih. 12: 346, 1922
BM 397 ns, BM 868 ns (in part)
China (Sichuan), Burma? - 2000–2500 m - T, L

○ **Pleione maculata** (Lindl.) Lindl., Paxt. Flow. Gard. 2: 5 t. 39 fig. 1, 1851
BM 860 ns (in part), BM 4691
Sikkim, Bhutan, Assam, Manipur, Burma, S. China, N. Thailand - 600–2600 m - T

○ **Pleione praecox** (Smith) D. Don, Prod. Fl. Nepal: 37, 1825
BM 861 ns, BM 4496, BM 5753
Nepal, Sikkim, Bhutan, Burma, S. China, Thailand - 1500–2700 m - T

○ **Pleione Shantung** (P. formosana × P. confusa)
BM 870 ns (in part)

○ **Pleione Soufrière** (P. Versailles × P. confusa)
BM 870 ns (in part)

○ **Pleione speciosa** Ames & Schltr., Fedde Rep. Beih. 4: 61, 1919
BM 868 ns (in part), BM 8588
C. China (Hubei, Sichuan, Yunnan?) - 1750–2250 m - T, L

○ **Pleione Stromboli** (P. speciosa × P. bulbocodioides)
BM 869 ns (in part)

○ **Pleione Versailles** (P. formosana × P. limprichtii)
BM 871 ns (in part)

○ **Pleione Vesuvius** (P. bulbocodioides × P. confusa)
BM 870 ns (in part)

○ **Pleione yunnanensis** (Rolfe) Rolfe, Orch. Rev. 11: 291, 1903
BM 865 ns
China (Yunnan, Sichuan, Guizhou Provinces), N. Burma - 1350–3200 m - T, L
Coelogyne yunnanensis Rolfe, J. Linn. Soc. 36: 23, 1903
Pleione ganchuanensis Gagnepain, Bull. Soc. Bot. Fr. 78: 25, 1931
Pleione chiwuana Tang & Wang, Act. Phytotax. Sin. 1: 78, 1951

○ **Pleurothallis tuerckheimii** Schltr., Fedde Rep. 10: 292, 1912
BM 170 ns
Mexico, Guatemala, Costa Rica, Panama - E
Pleurothallis megachlamys Schltr., Fedde Rep. Beih. 19: 108, 1923
Masdevallia jalapensis Kraenzlin, Fedde Rep. Beih. 34: 117, 1925

○ **Podangis dactyloceras** (Rchb. f.) Schltr., Beih. Bot. Centralbl. 36 pt. 2: 82, 1918
BM 540 ns
Guinea, Sierra Leone, Ghana, Nigeria, Cameroun, Zaire (Kinshasa), Uganda, Tanzania, Angola - E
Listrostachys dactyloceras Rchb. f., Flora 48: 190, 1865
Angorchis dactyloceras (Rchb. f.) Kuntze, Rev. Gen.: 651, 1891
Listrostachys forcipata Kraenzlin, Engl. Bot. Jahrb. 19: 254, 1894
Angraecum forcipatum (Kraenzlin) Engl., Pflanzenw. Afr. 2: 420, 1908
Listrostachys saxicola Kraenzlin, Engl. Bot. Jahrb. 48: 399, 1912

○ **Polystachya bella** Summerh., Kew Bull. 14: 137, 1960
BM 476 ns
Kenya, Uganda - E
Polystachya obanensis W. M. Moreau, J. E. Afr. Nat. Hist. Soc. 17: 30, 1943 (non Rendle)

○ **Promenaea xanthina** (Lindl.) Lindl., Bot. Reg. 29: Misc. 13, 1843
BM 697 ns
Brazil - E
Maxillaria xanthina Lindl., Bot. Reg. 25: sub. t. 17, 1839
Maxillaria citrina Don, Hort. Cantabr. ed. 13: 602, 1845
Promenaea citrina Don, Hort. Cantabr. ed. 13: 720, 1845
Maxillaria guttata hort. ex Rchb. f., Bot. Zeit. 10: 672, 1852
Zygopetalum xanthinum (Lindl.) Rchb. f., Walp. Ann. 6: 659, 1863
Zygopetalum citrinum (Don) Nicholson, Dict. Gard. 4: 245, 1887

Psychopsis krameriana (Rchb. f.) H. G. Jones, Novosti Sist. Vyssh. Rast. 12: 141, 1975
BM 134 ns
Costa Rica, Panama, Colombia, Ecuador - E
○ Oncidium kramerianum Rchb. f., Allg. Gartenz. 23: 9, 1855
Oncidium papilio var. kramerianum Lindl., Fol. Orch. Oncid.: 56, 1855
Oncidium nodosum Morren, Belg. Hort. 24: 258, in Obs., 1874
Papiliopsis nodosus Morren, Belg. Hort. 24: 258, 1874
Papiliopsis krameriana (Rchb. f.) Morren ex Cogn. & Marsch, Pl. Feuill. Ornam. 2: 55, 1874
Oncidium papilioniforme Regel, Act. Hort. Petrop. 6: 292, 1880
Oncidium krameri hort., Orchidoph.: 552, 1883
Oncidium kramerianum var. resplendens Rchb. f., Gard. Chron.: 360, 1888

○ **Sarcochilus fitzgeraldii** F. Muell., Fragm. Phyt. Austr. 7, 115, 1870
BM 201 ns
Australia (N. New South Wales, S. Queensland) - E, L
Sarcochilus fitzergeraldii var. alba hort. ex Schmidt, Orch. Rev. 35: 225, 1927
Sarcochilus fitzgeraldii var. aemula Rupp, Proc. Linn. Soc. N. S. W. 69: 73, 1944

○ **Sobralia lucasiana** hort. ex Gard. Chron.: 816, 1892
BM 144 ns
Cultivated plant - T

○ **Solenidium racemosum** Lindl., Orch. Linden.: 15, 1846
BM 709 ns
Colombia, Venezuela - E
Oncidium racemosum (Lindl.) Rchb. f., Walp. Ann. 6: 771, 1863

○ **Stanhopea connata** Klotzsch, Allg. Gartenz. 22: 226, 1854
BM 779 ns
Colombia, Ecuador, N. Peru - E
Stanhopea graveolens Klotzsch ex Rchb. f., Xen. Orch. 1: 118, 1855 (non Lindl.)

○ **Stanhopea graveolens** Lindl., Bot. Reg. 26: Misc. 59, 1840
BM 796 ns
Mexico, Belize, Guatemala, Honduras, El Salvador - E, L

○ **Warmingia eugenii** Rchb. f., Otia Bot. Hamb.: 87, 1881
BM 725 ns
Brazil - E
Warmingia loefgrenii Cogn., Fl. Bras. 3 (4): 119, 1904

REGISTER

Angraecopsis
– falcata = Neofinetia falcata
Angraecum
ns – albido-rubrum = Aerangis luteo-alba var. rhodosticta
– apiculatum = Aerangis biloba
– aschersonii = Cyrtorchis monteiroae
– bidens = Diaphananthe bidens
– bilobum = Aerangis biloba
– bistortum = Cyrtorchis ringens
– brongniartianum = Angraecum eburneum
– campyloplectron = Aerangis biloba
– caudatum = Plectrelminthus caudatus
– chailluanum = Cyrtorchis chailluana
– citratum = Aerangis citrata
– comorense = Angraecum eburneum
– crumenatum = Dendrobium crumenatum
4145 – **distichum**
4761 – **eburneum**
5170 – **eburneum**
– eburneum var. virens = Angraecum eburneum
7813 – **eichlerianum**
– falcatum = Neofinetia falcata
– fastuosum = Aerangis fastuosa
ns – forcipatum = Podangis dactyloceras
– fragrans = Jumellea fragrans
– funale = Dendrophylax funalis
– germinyanum = Angraecum ramosum
– gracilipes = Jumellea sagittata
– grantii = Aerangis kotschyana
– gyriamae = Angraecum eburneum
8153 – **infundibulare**
– kotschyanum = Aerangis kotschyana
– kotschyi = Aerangis kotschyana
ns 591 – magdalenae
ns – magdalenae var. latilabellum = Angraecum magdalenae
ns – mirabile = Aerangis luteo-alba var. rhodosticta
– modestum = Aerangis modesta
– pertusum = Listrostachys pertusa
7061 – **ramosum**
– reichenbachianum = Angraecum scottianum
ns – rhodostictum = Aerangis luteo-alba var. rhodosticta
– sanderianum = Aerangis modesta
6723 – **scottianum**
– semipedale = Aerangis kotschyana
5113 – **sesquipedale**
– superbum = Angraecum eburneum
– virens = Angraecum eburneum
– voeltzkowianum = Angraecum eburneum
Anguloa
9381 – **brevilabris**
5384 – **brevilabris** var. **sanguinea**
8700 – **cliftonii**
– clowesiana = Anguloa clowesii
4313 – **clowesii**
– clowesii var. eburnea = Anguloa clowesii
– clowesii var. flava = Anguloa clowesii
– clowesii var. macrantha = Anguloa clowesii
– eburnea = Anguloa uniflora
– grandiflora = Stanhopea jenishiana
– hernandezii = Stanhopea hernandezii
– lurida = Catasetum luridum
– purpurea = Anguloa brevilabris var. sanguinea
– ruckeri = Anguloa brevilabris
– ruckeri var. sanguinea = Anguloa brevilabris var. sanguinea
– sagittata = Anguloa brevilabris
– turneri = Anguloa uniflora
4807 – **uniflora**
– virginalis = Anguloa uniflora
Ania
9553 – **hookeriana**
7563 – **penangiana**
4669 – **viridifusca**
Anisopetalon
– careyanum = Bulbophyllum careyanum
Anneliesia
3793 – **candida**
Anoectochilus
– clarkei = Anoectochilus lanceolatus
– dawsonianus = Ludisia discolor
– flavus = Anoectochilus lanceolatus
– grandiflorus = Anoectochilus lanceolatus
8753 – **lanceolatus**
– lobbianus = Anoectochilus roxburghii
– luteus = Anoectochilus lanceolatus
– petelotii = Ludisia discolor
– regalis = Anoectochilus setaceus
4123 – **reinwardtii**
9529 – **roxburghii**
– sanderianus = Macodes sanderiana
* – setaceus = Anoectochilus reinwardtii
5208 – **setaceus**
– setaceus Schltr. = Anoectochilus roxburghii
– setaceus var. inornatus = Anoectochilus setaceus
– siamensis auct. non Schltr. = Anoectochilus roxburghii
Anota
– densiflora = Rhynchostylis gigantea
– gigantea = Rhynchostylis gigantea
Ansellia
4965A,B– **africana**
– africana var. nilotica = Ansellia africana
– confusa = Ansellia africana
– congoensis = Ansellia africana
– gigantea = Ansellia africana
– gigantea var. nilotica = Ansellia africana
– humilis = Ansellia africana
– nilotica = Ansellia africana
Apatostelis
3975 – **ciliaris**
Aplostellis
– velutina = Nervilia plicata
Aporum
– anceps = Dendrobium anceps
– crumenatum = Dendrobium crumenatum
– leonis = Dendrobium leonis
Arachnanthe
– annamensis = Arachnis annamensis
– cathcartii = Esmeralda cathcartii
– clarkei = Esmeralda clarkei
– lowii = Dimorphorchis lowii
Arachnis
8062 – **annamensis**
– bella = Esmeralda clarkei
– cathcartii = Esmeralda cathcartii
– clarkei = Esmeralda clarkei
– imthurnii = Vandopsis imthurnii
– lowii = Dimorphorchis lowii
Arachnites
– fuciflora = Ophrys holoserica
Araco
– aromatica = Vanilla planifolia
Arethusa
2204 – **bulbosa**
– bulbosa L. forma albiflora = Arethusa bulbosa
– bulbosa L. forma subcaerulea = Arethusa bulbosa
– catenata = Caladenia catenata
– ciliaris = Bartholina burmanniana
– picta = Sarcoglottis acaulis
– plicata = Nervilia plicata
– racemosa = Ponthieva racemosa
– sinensis = Bletilla sinensis
Arethusantha
– bletioides = Cymbidium elegans
Argyrorchis
– javanica = Macodes javanica
Arietinum
– americanum = Cypripedium arietinum
Arpophyllum
– cardinale = Arpophyllum giganteum
6022 – **giganteum**
– jamaicense = Arpohyllum giganteum
– spicatum = Arpophyllum giganteum
– squarrosum = Arpophyllum giganteum
– stenostachyum = Arpophyllum giganteum
Arundina
– affinis = Arundina graminifolia
– bambusifolia = Arundina graminifolia
– chinensis = Arundina graminifolia
– densa = Arundina graminifolia
– densiflora = Arundina graminifolia
7284 – **graminifolia**
– meyenii = Arundina graminifolia
– minor = Arundina graminifolia
– philippii = Arundina graminifolia
– pulchella = Arundina graminifolia
– pulchra = Arundina graminifolia
– speciosa = Arundina graminifolia
Asarca
– berteri = Asarca sinuata
– chlorosticta = Chloraea virescens
– crispa = Chloraea crispa
– cygnaea = Chloraea crispa
– fimbriata = Chloraea virescens
– incisa = Chloraea virescens
– odontoglossa = Chloraea virescens
– patagonica = Chloraea virescens
7909 – **sinuata**
– unguis-cati = Chloraea virescens
Ascocentrum
5595 – **ampullaceum**
5326 – **curvifolium**
6222 – **hendersonianum**
8121 – **rubescens**
Ascotaina
– hookeriana = Ania hookeriana
Aspasia
3962 – **epidendroides**
– fragrans = Aspasia epidendroides
– interrupta = Aspasia variegata
– liturata = Aspasia variegata
– lunata = Aspasia variegata
3679 – **variegata**
Auliza
– ciliaris = Epidendrum ciliare
– difformis = Epidendrum difforme
– nocturna = Epidendrum nocturnum
– parkinsonianum = Epidendrum parkinsonianum
– stamfordiana = Epidendrum stamfordianum
Aulizeum
– ciliare = Epidendrum ciliare
– cochleatum = Encyclia cochleata
– pygmaeum = Encyclia pygmaea
– variegatum = Ecyclia vespa
Barkeria
– elegans = Epidendrum elegans Rchb. f.
6098 – **lindleyana**
3951 – **skinneri**
– skinneri Paxton = Barkeria skinneri
– skinneri var. major = Barkeria skinneri
– skinneri var. superba = Barkeria skinneri
4094 – **spectabilis**
Bartholina
7450 – **burmanniana**

Calanthe
4671 **– vestita**
– violacea = Calanthe triplicata
– viridifusca = Ania viridifusca
– volkensii = Calanthe sylvatica
– warpurii = Calanthe sylvatica
– wightii = Calanthe masuca
Calceolus
– candidus = Cypripedium candidum
– hirsutus = Cypripedium calceolus var. pubescens
– parviflorus = Cypripedium calceolus var. parviflorum
– reginae = Cypripedium reginae
Callista
– adunca = Dendrobium aduncum
– aemulum = Dendrobium aemulum
– aggregata = Dendrobium lindleyi
– albosanguinea = Dendrobium albo-sanguineum
– amabilis = Dendrobium amabile
– amboinensis = Dendrobium amboinense
– amethystoglossa = Dendrobium amethystoglossum
– amoena = Dendrobium amoenum
– anceps = Dendrobium anceps
– anosma = Dendrobium anosmum
– aphrodite = Dendrobium aphrodite
– aphylla = Dendrobium aphyllum
– aquea = Dendrobium aqueum
– aurea = Dendrobium heterocarpum
– barbatula = Dendrobium barbatulum
– bensoniae = Dendrobium bensoniae
– bigibba = Dendrobium bigibbum
– boxallii = Dendrobium gratiosissimum
– brymeriana = Dendrobium brymerianum
– bursigera = Dendrobium secundum
– calceola = Dendrobium moschatum
– canaliculata = Dendrobium canaliculatum
– capillipes = Dendrobium capillipes
– carinifera = Dendrobium cariniferum
– chrysocrepis = Dendrobium chrysocrepis
– chrysotoxa = Dendrobium chrysotoxum
– ciliata = Dendrobium delacourii
– clavata = Dendrobium denneanum
– crassinodis = Dendrobium pendulum
– crepidata = Dendrobium crepidatum
– cretacea = Dendrobium cretaceum
– crumenata = Dendrobium crumenatum
– crystallina = Dendrobium crystallinum
– cucumerina = Dendrobium cucumerinum
– cumulata = Dendrobium cumulatum
– denudans = Dendrobium denudans
– densiflora = Dendrobium densiflorum
– devoniana = Dendrobium devonianum
– dixantha = Dendrobium dixanthum
– draconis = Dendrobium draconis
– fairfaxii = Dendrobium teretifolium
– falconeri = Dendrobium falconeri
– farmeri = Dendrobium farmeri
– fimbriata = Dendrobium fimbriatum
– findlayana = Dendrobium findlayanum
– fytchiana = Dendrobium fytchianum
– gibsonii = Dendrobium gibsonii
– gouldii = Dendrobium gouldii
– gracilicaulis = Dendrobium gracilicaule
– griffithiana = Dendrobium griffithianum
– hercoglossa = Dendrobium hercoglossum
– heterocarpa = Dendrobium heterocarpum
– hookeriana = Dendrobium hookerianum
– infundibula = Dendrobium infundibulum
– japonica = Dendrobium monoliforme
– jenkinsii = Dendrobium lindleyi
– jerdoniana = Dendrobium nutans
– johannis = Dendrobium johannis
– kingiana = Dendrobium kingianum
– lasioglossa = Dendrobium lasioglossum
– leonis = Dendrobium leonis
– linawiana = Dendrobium linawianum
– linguiformis = Dendrobium linguiforme
– lituiflora = Dendrobium lituiflorum
– loddigesii = Dendrobium loddigesii
– lowii = Dendrobium lowii
– luteola = Dendrobium luteolum
– maccarthiae = Dendrobium maccarthiae
– macrophylla = Dendrobium macrophyllum
– marginata = Dendrobium xanthophlebium
– moniliformis = Dendrobium moniliforme
– moschata = Dendrobium moschatum
– moulmeinensis = Dendrobium dixanthum
– mutabilis = Dendrobium mutabile
– nutans = Dendrobium nutans
– ochreata = Dendrobium ochreatum
– palpebrae = Dendrobium palpebrae
– parishii = Dendrobium parishii
– pendula = Dendrobium pendulum
– phalaenopsis = Dendrobium bigibbum
– primulina = Dendrobium primulinum
– revoluta = Dendrobium revolutum
– rigescens = Dendrobium mutabile
– rigida = Dendrobium mutabile
– scabrilinguis = Dendrobium scabrilingue
– scortechinii = Dendrobium anosmum
– secunda = Dendrobium secundum
– senilis = Dendrobium senile
– speciosa = Dendrobium speciosum
– spectabilis = Dendrobium spectabile
– suavissima = Dendrobium chrysotoxum
– sulcata = Dendrobium sulcatum
– sumneri = Dendrobium bigibbum
– tattoniana = Dendrobium canaliculatum
– teretifolia = Dendrobium teretifolium
– tetragona = Dendrobium tetragonum
– tortilis = Dendrobium tortile
– transparens = Dendrobium transparens
– veitchiana = Dendrobium macrophyllum
– vexans = Dendrobium hercoglossum
– villosula = Dendrobium nutans
– wardiana = Dendrobium wardianum
– williamsonii = Dendrobium williamsonii
– xanthophlebia = Dendrobium xanthophlebium
Calochilus
3187 **– campestris**
– cupreus = Calochilus campestris
Caloglossum
– humblotii = Cymbidiella falcigera
Calopogon
– pulchellus = Calopogon tuberosus
– pulchellus var. latifolius = Calopogon tuberosus
– pulchellus var. simpsonii = Calopogon tuberosus
116 **– tuberosus**
Calypso
– americana = Calypso bulbosa var. americana
– borealis = Calypso bulbosa var. americana
– bulbosa = Calypso bulbosa var. americana
2763 **– bulbosa** var. **americana**
Camaridium
– affine = Maxillaria camaridii
– amazonicum = Maxillaria camaridii
– cryptopodanthum = Maxillaria camaridii
– ochroleucum = Maxiallaria camaridii
– xylobiichilum = Maxillaria curtipes
Camarotis
ns – purpurea = Camarotis rostrata
ns 537 – rostrata
Catachaetum
– claveringii = Catasetum macrocarpum
– floribundum = Catasetum macrocarpum
– lituratum = Catasetum luridum
– purum = Catasetum purum
– semiapertum = Catasetum purum
– squalidum = Catasetum luridum
Catasetum
– abruptum = Catasetum luridum
– adnatum = Catasetum atratum
– appendiculatum = Catasetum barbatum
– arachnoidium = Catasetum callosum
5202 **– atratum**
– baraquinianum = Catasetum saccatum var. christyanum
3514 **– barbatum**
3802 **– barbatum**
7069 **– barbatum**
7470 **– barbatum**
– barbatum var. barbatum = Catasetum barbatum
– barbatum var. proboscideum = Catasetum barbatum
– barbatum var. spinosum = Catasetum barbatum
– brachybulbon = Catasetum barbatum
– brenesii = Catasetum integerrimum
– buchtienii = Catasetum barbatum
– bungerothii = Catasetum pileatum
– calceolatum = Clowesia russelliana
4219 **– callosum**
6648 **– callosum**
– callosum var. carunculatum = Catasetum callosum
– callosum var. crenatum = Catasetum callosum
– callosum var. eucallosum = Catasetum callosum

Catasetum
- callosum var. grandiflorum = Catasetum callosum
- carunculatum = Catasetum callosum

3262 – **cernuum**
5399 – **cernuum**
- christyanum = Catasetum saccatum var. christyanum
- christyanum var. obscurum = Catasetum saccatum var. christyanum
- ciliatum = Catasetum discolor var. roseo-album
- claveringii = Catasetum macrocarpum
- cogniauxii = Catasetum fimbriatum
- collossus = Catasetum saccatum var. christyanum
- comosum = Catasetum barbatum
- craniomorphum = Catasetum luridum
- crinitum = Catasetum barbatum
- cristatum var. spinigerum = Catasetum barbatum
- cristatum var. spinosum = Catasetum barbatum
- cruciatum = Catasetum saccatum var. christyanum
- darwinianum = Catasetum callosum

3923 – **deltoideum**
3708 – **discolor** var. **fimbriatum**
3796 – **discolor roseo-album**
3832 – **discolor roseo-album**
3601 – **discolor** var. **viridiflorum**
7158 – **fimbriatum**
- fimbriatum var. aurantiacum = Catasetum fimbriatum
- fimbriatum var. brevipetalum = Catasetum fimbriatum
- fimbriatum var. callosum = Catasetum fimbriatum
- fimbriatum var. cogniauxii = Catasetum fimbriatum
- fimbriatum var. fissum = Catasetum fimbriatum
- fimbriatum var. micranthum = Catasetum fimbriatum
- fimbriatum var. morrenianus = Catasetum fimbriatum
- fimbriatum var. ornithorrhynchum = Catasetum fimbriatum
- fimbriatum var. subtropicale = Catasetum fimbriatum
- fimbriatum var. viridulum = Catasetum fimbriatum
- floribundum = Catasetum macrocarpum
- fuliginosum = Catasetum callosum

8093 – **galeritum**
- galeritum var. galeritum = Catasetum galeritum
- galeritum var. pachyglossum = Catasetum galeritum
- gardneri = Catasetum discolor var. fimbriatum
- garnettianum = Catasetum barbatum
- globiferum = Catasetum globiflorum

3942 – **globiflorum**
- inapertum = Catasetum purum
- inconstans = Catasetum fimbriatum
- incurvum = Catasetum saccatum var. christyanum

3823 – **integerrimum**
3937 – **integerrimum**
- integerrimum var. purpurascens = Catasetum integerrimum
- integerrimum var. viridiflorum = Catasetum integerrimum
- lanciferum = Catasetum barbatum
- lansbergii = Catasetum callosum

7444 – **lemosii**
- linguiferum = Catasetum macrocarpum

3819 – **longifolium**
3590 – **luridum**
3929 – **luridum**
2559 – **macrocarpum**
3329 – **macrocarpum**
- macrocarpum Stein = Catasetum barbatum

9347 – **maculatum**
- maculatum Bateman = Catasetum integerrimum
- mentosum = Catasetum atratum

8514 – **microglossum**
- naso = Catasetum sanguineum
- oerstedii = Catasetum maculatum
- ornithorrhynchus = Catasetum fimbriatum
- pallidum = Catasetum atratum
- pflanzii = Catasetum fimbriatum

6998 – **pileatum**
- polydactylon = Catasetum barbatum
- proboscideum = Catasetum barbatum

3388 – **purum**
7864 – **quadridens**
- randii = Catasetum barbatum
- rivularium = Catasetum barbatum
- roseo-album = Catasetum discolor var. roseo-album
- roseum = Catasetum lemosii
- rostratum = Catasetum integerrimum
- russellianum = Clowesia russelliana

8007 – **saccatum** var. **christyanum**
4792 – **sanguineum**
- sanguineum var. integrale = Catasetum sanguineum
- scurra = Clowesia warczewitzii
- secundum = Catasetum saccatum var. christyanum
- semiapertum = Catasetum purum
- serratum = Catasetum viridiflavum
- spinosum = Catasetum barbatum
- stupendum = Catasetum saccatum var. christyanum

9086 – **tenebrosum**
- tricolor = Catasetum macrocarpum
- tridentatum Hook. = Catasetum macrocarpum
- tridentatum Pfitzer = Catasetum barbatum
- trifidum = Catasetum cernuum
- viride = Catasetum cernuum

4017 – **viridiflavum**
- wailesii = Catasetum integerrimum
- warczewiczii = Clowesia warczewitzii
- wredeanum = Catasetum fimbriatum

Cathea
- tuberosa = Calopogon tuberosus

Cattleya

5039 – **acklandiae**
- aclandiae var. schilleriana = Cattleya schilleriana
- acuminata = Laelia rubescens
- albida = Laelia albida
- alexandrae = Cattleya elongata
- alexandrae var. elegans = Cattleya elongata
- aliciae = Cattleya mossiae
- amabilis = Cattleya intermedia
- amethystina = Cattleya intermedia

5683 – **amethystoglossa**
- amethystoglossa var. sulphurea = Cattleya amethystoglossa
- anceps = Laelia anceps
- aquinii = Cattleya intermedia
- autumnalis Beer = Laelia autumnalis
- autumnalis hort. = Cattleya labiata

4909 – **bicolor**
- bogotensis = Cattleya trianae

ns 451 – bowringiana
- carrieri = Cattleya mossiae
- cernua = Sophronitis cernua
- chlorantha = Sobralia macrophylla
- cinnabarina = Laelia cinnabarina
- citrina = Encyclia citrina
- coccinea = Sophronitis coccinea
- ? concolor = Cattleya harrisoniana
- crispa Lindl. = Laelia crispa
- crispa Beer = Schomburgkia gloriosa

4916 – **deckeri**
5618 – **dowiana**
- edithiana = Cattleya mossiae
- elegans = Laelia elegans

7543 – **elongata**
- epidendroides = Cattleya luteola
- florida = Cattleya luteola

3265 – **forbesii**
- fulva = Cattleya forbesii
- furfuracea = Laelia furfuracea
- grahami = Laelia speciosa
- grandiflora = Sophronitis coccinea

5048 – **granulosa**
- grossi = Cattleya bicolor
- guatemalensis = Cattleya deckeri
- guttata = Cattleya leopoldii
- guttata var. keteleerii = Cattleya amethystoglossa
- guttata var. leopoldii = Cattleya leopoldii
- guttata var. prinzii = Cattleya amethystoglossa
- guttata var. russelliana = Cattleya leopoldii
- harrisoniae = Cattleya harrisoniana

4085 – **harrisoniana**
- harrisonie = Cattleya harrisoniana
- harrisonii = Cattleya harrisoniana
- ? ianthina = Cattleya intermedia
- integerrima var. angustifolia = Laelia perrinii

2851 – **intermedia**
- intermedia var. angustifolia = Laelia perrinii
- intermedia var. variegata = Cattleya harrisoniana

7287 – **iricolor**
- isopetala = Cattleya forbesii
- karwinskii = Encyclia citrina
- kimballiana = Cattleya trianae

3998 – **labiata**
- labiata var. atropurpurea = Cattleya mossiae
- labiata var. autumnalis = Cattleya labiata
- labiata var. candida = Cattleya mossiae
- labiata var. dowiana = Cattleya dowiana
- labiata var. genuina = Cattleya labiata
- labiata var. lindigii = Cattleya trianae
- labiata var. mossiae = Cattleya mossiae
- labiata var. picta = Cattleya mossiae
- labiata var. warocqueana = Cattleya labiata
- labiata var. whitei = Cattleya whitei

7133 – **lawrenceana**
- lemoniana = Cattleya labiata

3693 – **leopoldii**
- lindleyana = Brassocattleya lindleyana
- loddigesii var. amethystina = Cattleya intermedia
- loddigesii var. harrisoniae = Cattleya harrisoniana
- loddigesii var. harrisoniana = Cattleya harrisoniana
- loddigesii var. intermedia = Cattleya intermedia

5032 – **luteola**
- luteola var. roezlii = Cattleya luteola

Cattleya
– majalis = Laelia speciosa
– malouana = Cattleya maxima
– marginata = Laelia pumila
– maritima = Cattleya intermedia
4902 – **maxima**
– measuresiana = Cattleya bicolor
– meyeri = Cattleya luteola
3669 – **mossiae**
– nalderiana = Cattleya labiata
– ? nilsonii = Cattleya elongata
– ovata = Cattleya intermedia
– pallida = Cattleya labiata
– papeiansiana = Cattleya harrisoniana
– pauper = Cattleya forbesii
– peduncularis = Laelia rubescens
– perrinii Endl. = Cattleya labiata
– perrinii Lindl. = Laelia perrinii
– pinellii = Laelia pumila
– pinellii var. marginata = Laelia pumila
– pumila Hook. = Laelia pumila
– pumila Schomb. = Cattleya lawrenceana
– purpurina = Cattleya amethystoglossa
– quadricolor = Cattleya trianae
– regalis = Cattleya labiata
8377 – **rex**
– rubescens = Laelia rubescens
– ? russeliana = Cattleya whitei
5150 – **schilleriana**
– schilleriana var. concolor = Cattleya schilleriana
– schomburgkii = Cattleya violacea
– sessilis = Sobralia sessilis
4270 – **skinneri**
– skinneri var. parviflora = Cattleya deckeri
– spectabilis = Laelia pumila
– sulphurea = Cattleya luteola
– superba = Cattleya violacea
– superbiens = Schomburgkia superbiens
– tibicinis = Myrmecophila tibicinis
– tigrina = Cattleya leopoldii
5504 – **trianae**
– undulata = Schomburgkia undulata
– vestalis = Cattleya forbesii
– violacea Beer = Sophronitella violacea
4083 – **violacea**
– warocquena = Cattleya labiata
7727 – **× whitei**
Caularthron
3332 – **bicornutum**
– umbellatum = Epidendrum difforme
Centrogenium
– setaceum = Eltroplectris calcarata
Centropetalum
5718 – **hartwegii**
– punctatum = Centropetalum hartwegii
Centrosis
– sylvatica = Calanthe sylvatica
Cephalanthera
– royleana = Epipactis gigantea
Cephalantheropsis
4714 – **gracilis**
Ceratochilus
– grandiflorus = Stanhopea grandiflora
– oculatus = Stanhopea oculata
Ceratostylis
ns – latipetala = Ceratostylis retisquama
ns 640 – retisquama
– rubra = Ceratostylis retisquama
Cheiropterocephalus
– sertuliferus = Malaxis excavata
Chelonanthera
– speciosa = Coelogyne speciosa
Chelonistele
8203 – **perakensis**
9046 – **pusilla**
Chiloschista
7044 – **lunifera**
Chloraea
2956 – **bletioides**
– chlorosticta = Chloraea virescens
– chrysantha = Chloraea virescens
7955 – **crispa**
– cygnaea = Chloraea crispa
– fimbriata = Chloraea virescens
– grandis = Chloraea bletioides
– incisa = Chloraea virescens
– longibracteata = Asarca sinuata
– odontoglossa = Chloraea virescens
– patagonica = Chloraea virescens
– pigichen = Chloraea virescens
– piquichen = Chloraea virescens
– pleistodactyla = Chloraea virescens
– spectabilis = Chloraea crispa
– ulantha = Chloraea bletioides
– ulanthoides = Chloraea bletioides
– unguis-cati = Chloraea virescens
8100 – **virescens**
Chondrorhyncha
– discolor = Cochleanthes discolor
– lipsicombiae = Mendoncella marginata
– marginata = Mendoncella marginata
Chrysobaphus
– roxburghii = Anoectochilus roxburghii
Chusua
7601 – **monophylla**
Chysis
3617 – **aurea**
– aurea var. bractescens = Chysis bractescens
– aurea var. limminghei = Chysis limminghei
– aurea var. maculata = Chysis maculata
5186 – **bractescens**
– costaricensis = Chysis maculata
5265 – **limminghei**
4576 – **maculata**
Cirrhaea
2978 – **dependens**
– fusco-lutea Hook. = Cirrhaea saccata
– fusco-lutea Lindl. = Cirrhaea dependens
– hoffmannseggii = Cirrhaea dependens
– livida = Cirrhaea dependens
– loddigesii = Gongora galeata
– purpurascens = Cirrhaea dependens
– russelliana = Cirrhaea dependens
3726 – **saccata**
– tristis = Cirrhaea dependens
– violaceo-virens = Cirrhaea dependens
– violascens = Cirrhaea dependens
– viridipurpurea = Cirrhaea dependens
– warreana = Cirrhaea dependens
Cirrhopetalum
– africanum = Bulbophyllum longiflorum
– amesianum = Bulbophyllum cumingii
– appendiculatum = Bulbophyllum putidum
– auratum = Bulbophyllum auratum
– autumnale = Bulbophyllum macraei
– biflorum = Bulbophyllum biflorum
– boninense = Bulbophyllum macraei
– borneense = Bulbophyllum auratum
– breviscapum = Bulbophyllum lasiochilum
– campanulatum = Bulbophyllum auratum
– clavigerum = Bulbophyllum longiflorum
– collettii = Bulbophyllum wendlandianum
– compressum = Bulbophyllum uniflorum
– concinnum var. purpureum = Bulbophyllum corolliferum
– cornutum = Bulbophyllum helenae
– cumingii = Bulbophyllum cumingii
– curtisii = Bulbophyllum corolliferum
– eberhardtii = Bulbophyllum picturatum
– farreri = Bulbophyllum farreri
– fascinator = Bulbophyllum putidum
– fimbriatum = Bulbophyllum fimbriatum
– flaviflorum = Bulbophyllum flaviflorum
– fletcherianum = Bulbophyllum fletcherianum
– graveolens = Bulbophyllum graveolens
– guttulatum = Bulbophyllum guttulatum
– hookeri = Bulbophyllum hookeri
– kenejianum = Bulbophyllum longiflorum
– lasiochilum = Bulbophyllum lasiochilum
– ? layardii = Bulbophyllum longiflorum
– leopardinum = Bulbophyllum binnendijkii
– longiflorum = Bulbophyllum longiflorum
– longissimum = Bulbophyllum longissimum
– macraei = Bulbophyllum macraei
– makinoanum = Bulbophyllum macraei
– makoyanum = Bulbophyllum makoyanum
– mastersianum = Bulbophyllum mastersianum
– medusae = Bulbophyllum medusae
– miniatum = Bulbophyllum flaviflorum
– nutans = Bulbophyllum othonis
– ornatissimum Rchb. f. = Bulbophyllum ornatissimum
– ornatissimum auct. non Rchb. f. = Bulbophyllum putidum
– picturatum = Bulbophyllum picturatum
– proliferum = Bulbophyllum wendlandianum
– putidum = Bulbophyllum putidum
– refractum Bulbophyllum tripudians
– robustum = Bulbophyllum graveolens
– stramineum = Bulbophyllum cumingii
– tanegasimense = Bulbophyllum macraei
– thouarsii Lindl. 1830 = Bulbophyllum longiflorum
– thouarsii Lindl. 1839 = Bulbophyllum weberi
– thouarsii var. concolor = Bulbophyllum longiflorum
– tripudians = Bulbophyllum tripudians
– umbellatum = Bulbophyllum longiflorum
– uraiense = Bulbophyllum macraei
– walkerianum = Bulbophyllum macraei
– wallichii = Bulbophyllum fimbriatum
– weberi = Bulbophyllum weberi
– wendlandianum = Bulbophyllum wendlandianum
Cladobium
– violaceum = Scaphyglottis violacea

Cleisostoma
4639 – **filiforme**
5217 – **parishii**
– Seidenfadenii = Cleisostoma simondii
3571 – **simondii**
– teres = Cleisostoma simondii
– vacherotiana = Aerides multiflora
Clowesia
3777 – **russelliana**
9619 – **warczewiczii**
Cochleanthes
4830 – **discolor**
3585 – **flabelliformis**
– fragrans = Cochleanthes flabelliformis
– marginata = Mendoncella marginata
Cochlioda
7474 – **noezliana**
6084 – **rosea**
– sanguinea = Symphyglossum sanguineum
6001 – **vulcanica**
Coelia
– bella = Bothriochilus bellus
4712 – **macrostachya**
– macrostachya var. genuina = Coelia macrostachya
– macrostachya var. integrilabia = Coelia macrostachya
– picta = Bothriochilus bellus
Coeloglossum
– cordatum = Gennaria diphylla
– diphyllum = Gennaria diphylla
Coelogyne
– angustifolia = Coelogyne trinervis
– arthuriana = Pleione maculata
– bimaculata = Coelogyne flexuosa
8582 – **brachyptera**
– brunnea = Coelogyne fuscescens var. brunnea
– bulbocodioides = Pleione bulbocodioides
– candida = Pleione maculata
– cinnamomea = Coelogyne trinervis
– cinnamomea var. angustifolia = Coelogyne trinervis
– conferta = Coelogyne nitida
– corrugata = Coelogyne nervosa
6955 – **corymbosa**
8477 – **cristata**
4645 – **cumingii**
– cymbidioides = Coelogyne massangeana
ns 309 – dayana
– dayana var. massangeana = Coelogyne massangeana
– delavayi = Pleione bulbocodioides
– densiflora = Coelogyne massangeana
– decipiens = Chelonistele pusilla
– diphylla = Pleione maculata
– elata = Coelogyne holochila
– fimbriata = Coelogyne fuliginosa
3318 – **flaccida**
– fleuryi = Coelogyne lawrenceana
9563 – **flexuosa**
4440 – **fuliginosa**
– fusca = Otochilus fusca
– fuscescens = Coelogyne fuscescens var. brunnea
5494 – **fuscescens** var. **brunnea**
– glandulosa = Coelogyne nervosa
– goweri = Coelogyne nitida
– graminifolia = Coelogyne viscosa
– henryi = Pleione bulbocodioides
5001 – **holochila**
– hookeriana var. brachyglossa = Pleione hookeriana
– hookeriana = Pleione hookeriana
– hookeriana var. brachyglossa = Pleione hookeriana
– humilis = Pleione humilis
– humilis var. albata = Pleione humilis
– humilis var. tricolor = Pleione humilis
8856 – **integerrima**
– lagenaria = Pleione lagenaria
8164 – **lawrenceana**
5958 – **lentiginosa**
– ? longeciliata = Coelogyne fuliginosa
– maculata = Pleione maculata
6979 – **massangeana**
8297 – **mooreana**
5601 – **nervosa**
4661 – **nitida**
– nitida (Roxb.) Hook. f. = Coelogyne punctulata
– ocellata = Coelogyne punctulata
– ochracea = Coelogyne nitida
– ochracea subsp. conferta = Coelogyne nitida
– ochracea var. foliata = Coelogyne nitida
– odoratissima = Coelogyne trifida
9255 – **ovalis**
– ovalis Rchb. f. = Coelogyne fuliginosa
– pachybulbon = Coelogyne trinervis
5084 – **pandurata**
5323 – **parishii**
– parishii Gagnepain = Coelogyne brachyptera
– parishii var. brachyptera = Coelogyne brachyptera
– perakensis = Chelonistele perakensis
– pilosissima = Coelogyne ovalis
– pogonioides = Pleione bulbocodioides
ns – pogonioides = Pleione bulbocodioides
– praecox = Pleione praecox
– praecox var. sanguinea = Pleione praecox
– praecox var. tenera = Pleione praecox
– praecox var. wallichiana = Pleione praecox
ns 28 – pulchella
3767 – **punctulata**
– punctulata (»punctata«) var. conferta = Coelogyne nitida
– pusilla = Chelonistele pusilla
– quadrangularis = Coelogyne swaniana
– reichenbachiana = Pleione praecox
– rhodeana = Coelogyne trinervis
– rossiana = Coelogyne trinervis
5072 – **schilleriana**
4889 – **speciosa**
9539 – **speciosa** var. **alba**
7602 – **swaniana**
4785 – **testacea**
– tomentosa var. cymbidoides = Coelogyne massangeana
– tomentosa var. massangeana = Coelogyne massangeana
5462 – **trifida**
7176 – **trinervis**
– triplicatula = Coelogyne ovalis
– triptera = Encyclia pygmaea
7764 – **veitchii**
8262 – **venusta**
– virescens = Coelogyne brachyptera
7006 – **viscosa**
– wallichiana = Pleione praecox
– wallichii = Pleione praecox
– ? wettsteinianua = Coelogyne trinervis
ns – yunnanensis = Pleione yunnanensis
Cogniauxiocharis
– euphlebius = Pteroglossa euphlebia
Coilostylis
– emarginata = Epidendrum ciliare
Colax
– aromaticus = Lycaste aromatica
– barringtoniae = Lycaste barringtoniae
– grandiflorus = Bifrenaria harrisoniae
– harrisoniae = Bifrenaria harrisoniae
– jugosus = Pabstia jugosa
– palmifolius = Xylobium palmifolium
– parkeri = Maxillaria parkeri
– placanthera = Pabstia placanthera
– racemosus = Bifrenaria racemosa
– viridis var. placanthera = Pabstia placanthera
– viridis var. pluriflora = Pabstia jugosa
Comparettia
4980 – **falcata**
6679 – **macroplectron**
– rosea = Comparettia falcata
Coppensia
– bifolia = Oncidium bifolium
Cordula
ns – appletoniana = Paphiopedilum appletonianum
– argus = Paphiopedilum argus
– barbata = Paphiopedilum barbatum
ns – bellatula = Paphiopedilum bellatulum
– boxallii = Paphiopedilum villosum
– callosa = Paphiopedilum callosum
– chamberlainiana = Paphiopedilum chamberlainianum
– charlesworthii = Paphiopedilum charlesworthii
ns – ciliolaris = Paphiopedilum ciliolare
– concolor = Paphiopedilum concolor
ns – curtisii = Paphiopedilum superbiens
ns – dayana = Paphiopedilum dayanum
ns – druryi = Paphiopedilum druryi
– exul = Paphiopedilum exul
– fairrieana = Paphiopedilum fairrieanum
– glaucophylla = Paphiopedilum glaucophyllum
– godefroyae = Paphiopedilum godefroyae
– haynaldiana = Paphiopedilum haynaldianum
– hirsutissima = Paphiopedilum hirsutissimum
– hookerae = Paphiopedilum hookerae
– lawrenceana = Paphiopedilum lawrenceanum
– mastersiana = Paphiopedilum mastersianum
– nivea = Paphiopedilum niveum
– parishii = Paphiopedilum parishii
ns – petri = Paphiopedilum dayanum
– philippinensis = Paphiopedilum philippinense
ns – praestans = Paphiopedilum praestans
– purpurata = Paphiopedilum purpuratum
– rothschildiana = Paphiopedilum rothschildianum
– spiceriana = Paphiopedilum spicerianum
– stonei = Paphiopedilum stonei
ns – superbiens = Paphiopedilum superbiens
ns – tonsa = Paphiopedilum tonsum
– venusta = Paphiopedilum venustum
– victoria-mariae = Paphiopedilum victoria-mariae
– villosa = Paphiopedilum villosum
Cordyla
– discolor = Nervilia plicata
Coryanthes
– albertinae = Coryanthes speciosa
– barkeri = Coryanthes speciosa
– eximia = Coryanthes speciosa
– hunteriana = Coryanthes speciosa

Cymbidium
– grandiflorum var. punctulatum = Cymbidium hookerianum
– gyokuchin var. arrogans = Cymbidium ensifolium
– haematodes = Cymbidium ensifolium
– hillii = Cymbidium canaliculatum
– hirsutum = Elleanthus caravata
5574 **– hookerianum**
– hookerianum var. hookerianum = Cymbidium hookerianum
– hoosai = Cymbidium sinense
– humblotii = Cymbidiella falcigera
– humile = Pleione humilis
– huttonii = Grammatophyllum stapeliiflorum
– hyacinthinum = Bletilla striata
8312 **– insigne**
– insigne var. album = Cymbidium insigne
– intermedium = Cymbidium aloifolium
– iridifolium = Oberonia iridifolia
4844 **– iridioides**
– ixioides = Spathoglottis ixioides
– juncifolium = Oncidium cebolleta
– kanran var. misericors = Cymbidium ensifolium
– koran = Cymbidium ensifolium
– leachianum = Cymbidium dayanum
ns – longibracteatum = Cymbidium goeringii
– luteum = Chloraea crispa
– mannii = Cymbidium aloifolium
– marginatum = Cymbidium dayanum
– meyenii = Arundina graminifolia
– micans = Cymbidium ensifolium
– misericors = Cymbidium ensifolium
– montanum = Octadesmia montana
– moschatum = Dendrobium moschatum
– munronianum King & Pantl. = Cymbidium ensifolium
– munronianum Holtum = Cymbidium ensifolium
– munronianum Ridley = Cymbidium ensifolium
– nitidum Roxb. = Coelogyne punctulata
– nitidum Wallich = Coelogyne nitida
– niveo-marginatum = Cymbidium ensifolium
– nodosum = Brassavola nodosa
– ochroleucum = Maxillaria camaridii
– pendulum Sw. = Cymbidium aloifolium
– pendulum sensu Vidal = Cymbidium atropurpureum
– pendulum var. atropurpureum = Cymbidium atropurpureum
– poilanei = Cymbidium dayanum
ns – pseudovirens = Cymbidium goeringii
– pulchellum = Cymbidium chloranthum
– praecox = Pleione praecox
– pulcherrimum = Cymbidium dayanum
– reflexum = Liparis reflexa
– rhodochilum = Cymbidiella pardalina
– rigidum = Tetramicra canaliculata
– rubigemmum = Cymbidium ensifolium
– rubrum = Ascocentrum ampullaceum
– sanderi = Cymbidium insigne
– sanderi var. sanderi = Cymbidium insigne
– sanguineanum = Cymbidium chloranthum
– sanguinolentum = Cymbidium chloranthum
– scarabaeiforme = Luisia psyche
9637 **– schroederi**
– scriptum = Grammatophyllum scriptum
ns – serratum = Cymbidium goeringii
– shimaran = Cymbidium ensifolium
– siamense = Cymbidium ensifolium
– sikkimense = Cymbidium devonianum
– simonsianum = Cymbidium dayanum
– simonsianum forma vernale = Cymbidium dayanum
– simulans = Cymbidium aloifolium
888 **– sinense**
– sinense var. albojucundissimum = Cymbidium sinense
– sinense var. album = Cymbidium sinense
– sinense var. bellum = Cymbidium sinense
– sinense var. margicoloratum = Cymbidium sinense
– sinense forma albojucundissimum = Cymbidium sinense
– sinense forma margicoloratum = Cymbidium sinense
– sparkesii = Cymbidium canaliculatum
– speciosissimum = Coelogyne cristata
– stapeliiflorum = Grammatophyllum stapeliiflorum
– stapelioides = Promenaea stapelioides
– striatum = Bletilla striata
ns 671 – suavissimum
– subulatum = Leucohyle subulata
– sundaicum = Cymbidium ensifolium
– sundaicum var. estriata = Cymbidium ensifolium
– sutepense = Cymbidium dayanum
– syringodorum = Cymbidium eburneum
– tessellatum = Vanda tessellata
– tesselloides = Vanda tessellata
– tetrapetalum = Oncidium tetrapetalum
5457 **– tigrinum**
ns – tortisepalum = Cymbidium goeringii
ns – tortisepalum var. viridiflorum = Cymbidium goeringii
ns 56 – tracyanum
– trinerve = Cyrtopodium punctatum
– triquetrum = Oncidium triquetrum
– triste = Luisia platyglossa
– umbellatum = Bulbophyllum longiflorum
ns – uniflorum = Cymbidium goeringii
– utriculatum = Govenia utriculata
– variciferum = Cymbidium chloranthum
– verecundum = Bletia purpurea
– violaceum = Cattleya violacea
ns – virens = Cymbidium goeringii
ns – virescens Lindl. = Cymbidium goeringii
– virescens Willd. = Chloraea virescens
– wallichii = Cymbidium aloifolium
ns 704 – wilsonii
– xiphiifolium = Cymbidium ensifolium
– yakibaran = Cymbidium ensifolium
– yakibaran var. albo-marginatum = Cymbidium ensifolium
– yakibaran var. niveo-marginatum = Cymbidium ensifolium
ns – yunnanense = Cymbidium goeringii

Cymbiglossum
– bictoniense = Lemboglossum bictoniense
– cervantesii = Lemboglossum cervantesii
– cordatum = Lemboglossum cordatum
– maculatum = Lemboglossum maculatum
– majale = Lemboglossum majale

Cynorkis
8053 **– compacta**
7554 **– grandiflora**
7551 **– lowiana**
7852 **– purpurascens**
7845 **– villosa**

Cynosorchis
– calanthoides = Cynorchis purpurascens
– compacta = Cynorkis compacta
– purpurascens = Cynorkis lowiana
– purpurascens var. praecox = Cynorchis purpurascens
– praecox = Cynorchis purpurascens
– uniflora = Cynorkis grandiflora

Cyperorchis
– eburnea = Cymbidium eburneum
– elegans = Cymbidium elegans
– elegans var. blumei = Cymbidium elegans
– erythrostyla = Cymbidium erythrostylum
– gigantea = Cymbidium iridioides
– grandiflora = Cymbidium hookerianum
– insignis = Cymbidium insigne
– schroederi = Cymbidium schroederi
– tigrina = Cymbidium tigrinum
ns – tracyana = Cymbidium tracyanum
ns – wilsonii = Cymbidium wilsonii

Cypripedium
192 **– acaule**
– acaule forma albiflorum = Cypripedium acaule
– acaule var. album = Cypripedium acaule
– album = Cypripedium reginae
ns – appletonianum = Paphiopedilum appletonianum
– argus = Paphiopedilum argus
1569 **– arietinum**
– assurgens = Cypripedium calceolus var. pubescens
– atsmori = Cypripedium macranthum var. speciosum
– aureum = Cypripedium calceolus var. pubescens
– barbatum Lindl. = Paphiopedilum barbatum
– barbatum Ridley = Paphiopedilum robinsonii
– barbatum var. argus = Paphiopedilum argus
ns – barbatum var. superbum = Paphiopedilum superbiens
ns – barbatum var. veitchii = Paphiopedilum superbiens
ns – bellatulum = Paphiopedilum bellatulum
– bifidum = Cypripedium calceolus var. parviflorum
– boxallii = Paphiopedilum boxallii
– bulbosum L. = Calypso bulbosa var. americana
– bulbosum Miller = Cypripedium calceolus var. pubescens
– bulbosum var. flavescens = Cypripedium calceolus var. pubescens
– bulbosum var. parviflorum = Cypripedium calceolus var. parviflorum
ns – bullenianum var. appletonianum = Paphiopedilum appletonianum
– calceolus = Cypripedium calceolus var. pubescens
– calceolus var. γ = Cypripedium reginae

Cypripedium

- calceolus var. atsmori = Cypripedium macranthum var. speciosum

3024 **– calceolus** var. **parviflorum**

911 **– calceolus** var. **pubescens**

7188 **– californicum**

- callosum = Paphiopedilum callosum
- canadensis = Cypripedium reginae

5855 **– candidum**

- cardiophyllum = Cypripedium debile
- caricinum = Phragmipedium caricinum
- chamberlainianum = Paphiopedilum chamberlainianum
- chamberlainianum forma victoria-mariae = Paphiopedilum victoria-regina
- charlesworthii = Paphiopedilum charlesworthii

ns – ciliolare = Paphiopedilum ciliolare

- concolor = Paphiopedilum concolor
- concolor var. godefroyae = Paphiopedilum godefroyae

9364 **– cordigerum**

ns – curtisii = Paphiopedilum superbiens

ns – dayanum = Paphiopedilum dayanum

- dayanum var. ernestianum = Paphiopedilum dayanum

ns – dayanum var. smithianum = Paphiopedilum dayanum

ns – dayanum var. splendens = Paphiopedilum dayanum

- dayanum var. superbum = Paphiopedilum dayanum

ns – dayi = Paphiopedilum dayanum

8183 **– debile**

ns – delenatii = Paphiopedilum delenatii

ns – druryi = Paphiopedilum druryi

- elliottianum = Paphiopedilum rothschildianum

ns – ernestianum = Paphiopedilum dayanum

- exul = Paphiopedilum exul
- fairrieanum = Paphiopedilum fairrieanum

7275 **– fasciculatum**

- fasciculatum var. pusillum = Cypripedium fasciculatum
- flavescens = Cypripedium calceolus var. pubescens
- furcatum = Cypripedium calceolus var. pubescens

ns – gardineri = Paphiopedilum praestans

- glaucophyllum = Paphiopedilum glaucophyllum
- godefroyae = Paphiopedilum godefroyae
- godefroyae var. leucochilum = Paphiopedilum godefroyae

7746 **– guttatum**

- haynaldianum = Paphiopedilum haynaldianum

8965 **– himalaicum**

- hirsutissimum = Paphiopedilum hirsutissimum
- hirsutum forma album = Cypripedium reginae
- hirsutum Miller 1894 = Cypripedium calceolus var. pubescens
- hirsutum Miller 1905 = Cypripedium reginae
- hirsutum Miller 1917 = Cypripedium acaule
- hirsutum var. parviflorum = Cypripedium calceolus var. parviflorum
- hookerae = Paphiopedilum hookerae
- humile = Cypripedium acaule
- insigne = Paphiopedilum insigne
- insigne var. exul = Paphiopedilum exul

9520 **– japonicum**

- javanicum = Paphiopedilum barbatum
- klotzscheanum = Phragmipedium klotzscheanum
- knightae = Cypripedium fasciculatum
- laevigatum = Paphiopedilum philippinense
- lawrenceanum = Paphiopedilum lawrenceanum
- longifolium = Phragmipedium longifolium
- luteum = Cypripedium calceolus var. parviflorum
- luteum var. angustifolium = Cypripedium calceolus var. pubescens
- luteum var. biflorum = Cypripedium calceolus var. pubescens
- luteum var. concolor = Cypripedium calceolus var. pubescens
- luteum var. glabrum = Cypripedium calceolus var. pubescens
- luteum var. maculatum = Cypripedium calceolus var. pubescens
- luteum var. parviflorum = Cypripedium calceolus var. parviflorum
- luteum var. pubescens = Cypripedium calceolus var. pubescens
- macranthon var. album = Cypripedium ventricosum var. album
- macranthon auct. non Sw. = Cypripedium himalaicum
- macranthon Rchb. f. = Cypripedium ventricosum var. album

2938 **– macranthum**

- macranthon var. himalaicum = Cypripedium himalaicum
- macranthon var. ventricosum = Cypripedium ventricosum var. album
- macranthon var. ventricosa = Cypripedium tibeticum
- macranthon var. ventricosum = Cypripedium ventricosum var. album
- macranthos var. tibeticum = Cypripedium tibeticum
- macranthos var. ventricosa = Cypripedium ventricosum var. album
- macranthos var. vulgare = Cypripedium macranthum

8386 **– macranthum** var. **speciosum**

- makasin = Cypripedium calceolus var. pubescens
- manchuricum var. virescens = Cypripedium ventricosum var. album
- mastersianum = Paphiopedilum mastersianum

ns – miteauanum = Paphiopedilum ciliolare

7319 **– montanum**

- neo-guineense = Paphiopedilum rothschildianum
- niveum = Paphiopedilum niveum
- occidentale = Cypripedium montanum
- orientale = Cypripedium guttatum
- parishii = Paphiopedilum parishii
- parviflorum Salisb. = Cypripedium calceolus var. parviflorum
- parviflorum Sims = Cypripedium calceolus var. pubescens
- parviflorum var. pubescens = Cypripedium calceolus var. pubescens
- pearcei = Phragmipedium caricinum

ns – petri = Paphiopedilum dayanum

- philippinense = Paphiopedilum philippinense
- pitcherianum = Paphiopedilum argus

ns – poyntzianum = Paphiopedilum appletonianum

ns – praestans = Paphiopedilum praestans

ns – praestans var. kimballianum = Paphiopedilum praestans

- pubescens = Cypripedium calceolus var. pubescens
- pubescens var. makasin = Cypripedium calceolus
- purpuratum = Paphiopedilum purpuratum
- pusillum = Cypripedium fasciculatum

216 **– reginae**

- reginae var. album = Cypripedium reginae
- reichenbachii = Phragmipedium longifolium
- robinsoni = Paphiopedilum robinsonii
- roebellini = Paphiopedilum philippinense
- roezlii = Phragmipedium roezlii
- rothschildianum = Paphiopedilum rothschildianum
- sargentianum = Phragmipedium sargentianum
- schlimii = Phragmipedium schlimii
- schmidtianum = Paphiopedilum callosum
- schomburgkianum = Phragmipedium klotzscheanum
- sinicum = Paphiopedilum purpuratum
- speciosum = Cypripedium macranthum var. speciosum
- spectabile = Cypripedium reginae
- spicerianum = Paphiopedilum spicerianum
- stonei = Paphiopedilum stonei

ns – superbiens = Paphiopedilum superbiens

ns – superbiens var. dayanum = Paphiopedilum dayanum

- thunbergii Blume = Cypripedium macranthum
- thunbergii Matsum. = Cypripedium macranthum var. speciosum

8070 **– tibeticum**

ns – tonsum = Paphiopedilum tonsum

- undatum = Cypripedium calceolus var. pubescens
- veganum = Cypripedium calceolus var. pubescens

ns – veitchianum = Paphiopedilum superbiens

- ventricosum = Cypripedium ventricosum album

9117 **– ventricosum album**

- venustum = Paphiopedilum venustum
- victoria-mariae = Paphiopedilum victoria-mariae
- victoria-regina = Paphiopedilum victoria-mariae
- villosum = Paphiopedilum villosum

ns – wolterianum = Paphiopedilum appletonianum

- yauaperyense = Eriopsis sceptrum

Cyrtochilum

- aemulum = Oncidium superbiens
- bictoniense = Lemboglossum bictoniense
- citrinum = Oncidium concolor

Epidendrum
– tessellatum Bateman ex Lindl. = Encyclia livida
– tessellatum Roxb. = Vanda tessellata
– tesselloides = Vanda tessellata
– tetragonum = Phaius tetragonus
– tetrapetalum = Oncidium tetrapetalum
– tibicinis = Myrmecophila tibicinis
– tigrinum = Encyclia vespa
– tomentosum = Eria tomentosa
– tonduzii = Oerstedella endresii
– triandrum = Encyclia cochleata
– tridens = Epidendrum nocturnum
– tripartitum = Encyclia bractescens
– triquetrum = Oncidium triquetrum
– tuberosum = Bletilla striata
– tunguraguae = Epidendrum nocturnum
– turialvae = Epidendrum paniculatum
– umbellatum Forster = Bulbophyllum longiflorum
– umbellatum Sw. = Epidendrum difforme
– umbellatum Vell. = Malaxis excavata
– umbellatum var. latilabre = Epidendrum difforme
– umbelliferum = Epidendrum difforme
ns – umlauftii = Epidendrum oerstedii
– undulatum = Oncidium carthagenense
– uniflorum Lindl. = Encyclia pygmaea
– ? uniflorum Vell. = Maxillaria picta
– utricularioides = Ionopsis utricularioides
– vaginatum = Encyclia fragrans
– variegatum = Encyclia vespa
– verrucosum = Encyclia adenocaula var. adenocaula
– verrucosum var. myrianthum = Oerstedella myriantha
– versicolor = Epidendrum elongatum
– vespa = Encylia vespa
– violaceum = Cattleya violacea
– virens = Epidendrum difforme
– virescens = Epidendrum secundum
– viridiflorum = Encyclia viridiflora
– viridipurpureum = Epidendrum secundum
– viscidum = Epidendrum ciliare
– vitellinum = Encyclia vitellina
– vitellinum var. autumnale = Encyclia vitellina
– vitellinum var. giganteum = Encyclia vitellina
– vitellinum var. majus = Encyclia vitellina
7586 **– xanthinum**
– xytriophorum = Epidendrum elongatum
Epigeneium
9191 **– acuminatum**
4755 **– cymbidioides**
6591 **– treacherianum**
Epipactis
– americana = Epipactis gigantea
– arachnites = Ophrys holoserica
– epipogium = Epipogium aphyllum
7690 **– gigantea**
– plicata = Nervilia plicata
– pubescens = Goodyera pubescens
– royleana = Epipactis gigantea
– thunbergii = Epipactis gigantea
– willdenovii = Goodyera pubescens
Epiphora
– pobeguinii = Polystachya pobeguinii
– pubescens = Polystachya pubescens
Epipogium
4821 **– aphyllum**
Epipogon
– epipogium = Epipogium aphyllum
– epipogon = Epipogium aphyllum
– gmelinii = Epipogium aphyllum
Epistephium
5485 **– williamsii**
Eria
– affinis = Eria bractescens
9453 **– amica**
– andersonii = Eria amica
– armeniaca = Eria ornata
– bidens = Eria iridifolia
4163 **– bractescens**
– bractescens var. latipetala = Eria rhodoptera
ns – calamifolia = Eria pannea
– cochleata = Eria javanica
– confusa = Eria amica
– decipiens = Eria summerhayesiana
– dillwynii = Eria bractescens
– elwesii = Porpax meirax
– endymion = Eria hyacinthoides
– excavata = Eria amica
– extinctoria = Eria summerhayesiana
– fragrans = Eria javanica
– fuerstenbergiana = Eria tomentosa
ns 83 – globifera
– griffithii = Eria bractescens
8229 **– hyacinthoides**
– hypomelana = Eria amica
8171 **– iridifolia**
3605 **– javanica**
ns – langbianensis = Eria globifera
7605 **– latibracteata**
– latifolia = Eria iridifolia
– laucheana = Eria rhodoptera
– lindleyana = Eria obesa
– littoralis = Eria bractescens
– longispica = Eria iridifolia
7238 **– marginata**
– meirax = Porpax meirax
5415 **– myristiciformis**
ns – nivosa = Eria pannea
5391 **– obesa**
8642 **– ornata**
– ornata auct. non (Blume) Lindl. = Eria tomentosa
ns 570 – pannea
– prainii = Eria obesa
– pubescens = Eria amica
– pulchella = Eria bractescens
8296 **– rhodoptera**
8234 **– rhynchostyloides**
– rolfei = Eria latibracteata
– rugosa = Eria javanica
– stellata = Eria javanica
– striolata = Eria javanica
5910 **– summerhayesiana**
ns – teretifolia = Eria pannea
8662 **– tomentosa**
– vaginata = Eria javanica
– validissima = Eria iridifolia
5807 **– vestita**
Eriopsis
ns 611 – biloba
4437 **– biloba**
– colombiana = Eriopsis biloba
– fuerstenbergii = Eriopsis biloba
– grandibulbosa = Eriopsis biloba
– helenae = Eriopsis sceptrum
– mesae = Eriopsis biloba
– rhytidobulbon = Eriopsis biloba
– rutidobulbon = Eriopsis biloba
8462 **– sceptrum**
– schomburgkii = Eriopsis biloba
– sprucei = Eriopsis sceptrum
– werckleyi = Eriopsis biloba
Erycina
7389 **– echinata**
– major = Erycina echinata
Erythrodes
– maculata = Platythelys maculata
Esmeralda
– bella = Esmeralda clarkei
5845 **– cathcartii**
7077 **– clarkei**
– sanderiana = Euanthe sanderiana
Euanthe
6983 **– sanderiana**
Eulophia
1814 **– alta**
8044 **– angolensis**
– bicolor Dalz. = Eulophia nuda
– bicolor Rchb. f. & Sonder = Eulophia welwitschii
– cochleare = Cochleanthes flabelliformis
– cochlearis = Cochleanthes flabelliformis
– congoensis = Eulophia guineensis
7921 **– cristata**
8397 **– cucullata**
– dilecta = Eulophia cucullata
– dusenii = Eulophia euglossa
5579 **– epidendraea**
– epidendroides = Eulophia epidendraea
5561 **– euglossa**
8470 **– flavopurpurea**
– fusca = Eulophia nuda
– graminea = Eulophia epidendraea
– guamensis = Eulophia pulchra
2467 **– guineensis**
ns 267 – guineensis
– helleborina = Brachycorthis macrantha
– hians = Herschelianthe hians
5486 **– horsfallii**
6858 **– horsfallii**
8047 **– horsfallii**
– involuta = Eulophia orthoplectra
– krebsii = Eulophia streptopetala
– krebsii var. purpurata = Eulophia streptopetala
– latifolia = Eulophia angolensis
– longifolia = Eulophia alta
– macrorhizon = Eulophia sanguinea
– macrostachya = Eulophia pulchra
– mahonii = Eulophia horsfallii
– milanjiana = Eulophia welwitschii
– millsonii = Eulophia flavopurpurea
– murrayana = Neogardneria murrayana
8057 **– nuda**
7546 **– orthoplectra**
– paivaeana = Eulophia streptopetala
– porphyroglossa = Eulophia horsfallii
6246 **– pulchra**
– quartiniana = Eulophia guineensis
– rouxii = Eulophia pulchra
– sandersonii = Eulophia horsfallii
6161 **– sanguinea**
ns – saundersiana = Oeceoclades saundersiana
– squalida = Eulophia nuda
2931 **– streptopetala**
5861 **– streptopetala**
– ugandae = Eulophia angolensis
– virens = Eulophia epidendraea
7330 **– welwitschii**
– woodfordii = Eulophia alta
– woodii = Eulophia welwitschii
– zeyheri = Eulophia welwitschii
Eulophidium
– pulchrum = Eulophia pulchra
ns – saundersianum = Oeceoclades saundersiana
Eulophiella
7387 **– elisabethae**
ns 656 – elisabethae
– hamelinii = Eulophiella roempleriana
– perrieri = Eulophiella elizabethae
– petersiana = Eulophiella roempleriana
7612 **– roempleriana**
7613 **– roempleriana**
Euphlebium
– amboinense = Dendrobium amboinense
– inaequale = Dendrobium inaequale
Euthonaea
– imbricata = Hexisea bidentata

Euthonaea
– oppositifolia = Hexisea bidentata
Evelyna
– caravata = Elleanthus caravata
– lepida = Elleanthus caravata
Exophya
– fuscata = Epidendrum patens
Fernandezia
– elegans = Lockhartia elegans
– robusta = Lockhartia oerstedii
Fieldia
– gigantea = Vandopsis gigantea
Finetia
– falcata = Neofinetia falcata
Fissipes
– acaulis = Cypripedium acaule
– hirssuta = Cypripedium acaule
Gabertia
– scripta = Grammatohpyllum scriptum
Galeandra
4701 **– baueri**
4610 **– devoniana**
– quartiniana = Eulophia guineensis
Galeottia
– grandiflora = Mendoncella grandiflora
Gastrochilus
4772 **– acutifolius**
7142 **– bellinus**
5767 **– bigibbus**
– curvifolius = Ascocentrum curvifolium
Gastrorchis
ns – francoisii = Phaius francoisii
– tuberculosa = Phaius tuberculosus
Gavilea
– sinuata var. A = Asarca sinuata
Gennaria
3164 **– diphylla**
Geodorum
2195 **– citrinum**
Gomesa
3497 **– barkeri**
2746 **– foliosa**
3504 **– planifolia**
– planifolia var. laxa = Gomesa planifolia
– reclinata = Gomesa planifolia
1748 **– recurva**
– recurva Lodd. = Gomesa planifolia
Gomezia
– densiflora = Gomesa recurva
Gongora
5501 **– armeniaca**
– atropurpurea = Gongora quinquenervis
– boothiana = Gongora quinquenervis
– bufonia = Gongora quinquenervis
– bufonia var. leucochila = Gongora quinquenervis
– fulva = Gongora quinquenervis
– fulva var. vitellina = Gongora quinquenervis
3563 **– galeata**
7224 **– gratulabunda**
8562 **– grossa**
– histrionica = Gongora quinquenervis
– jenischii = Gongora quinquenervis
8766 **– latisepala**
– leucochila = Gongora quinquenervis
– macrantha = Coryanthes macrantha
– maculata = Gongora quinquenervis
– maculata var. alba = Gongora quinquenervis
– maculata var. tricolor = Gongora tricolor
– maculata forma odoratissima = Gongora quinquenervis
– nigrita = Gongora quinquenervis
– odoratissima = Gongora quinquenervis
– odoratissima var. jenischii = Gongora quinquenervis
– phillipica = Renanthera coccinea
6284 **– portentosa**
– powellii = Gongora quinquenervis
– quadricornis = Gongora quinquenervis
3220 **– quinquenervis**
3687 **– quinquenervis**
– quinquevulneris = Gongora quinquenervis
– retrorsa = Gongora quinquenervis
– shepherdii = Gongora quinquenervis
– speciosa = Coryanthes speciosa
– superflua = Gongora quinquenervis
7530 **– tricolor**
– truncata var. alba = Gongora quinquenervis
– unicolor = Gongora quinquenervis
– viridipurpurea = Cirrhaea dependens
– vitellina = Gongora quinquenervis
Gonogona
– discolor = Ludisia discolor
Goodyera
– discolor = Ludisia discolor
2540 **– pubescens**
– pubescens var. minor = Goodyera pubescens
Gorgoglossum
– reichenbachianum = Sievekingia reichenbachiana
Govenia
– boliviense = Govenia utriculata
– ernstii = Govenia utriculata
– fasciata = Govenia superba
– gardneri = Govenia utriculata
– lagenophora = Govenia superba
– liliacea = Govenia utriculata
– platyglossa = Govenia superba
– sodiroi = Govenia utriculata
– stictoglossa = Govenia superba
– sulphurea = Govenia superba
8794 **– superba**
8768 **– tingens**
3660 **– utriculata**
4151 **– utriculata**
Grafia
– parishii = Phalaenopsis parishii
Grammangis
5179 **– ellisii**
– falcigera = Cymbidiella falcigera
– pardalina = Cymbidiella pardalina
– stapeliiflora = Grammatophyllum stapeliiflorum
Grammatophyllum
– elegans = Cymbidium elegans
– ellisii = Grammangis ellisii
– fastuosum = Grammatophyllum speciosum
– fenzlianum = Grammatophyllum scriptum
– finlaysonianum = Bromheadia finlaysoniana
– giganteum = Grammatophyllum speciosum
– guilelmii = Grammatophyllum scriptum
– macranthum = Grammato-phyllum speciosum
– measuresianum = Grammato-phyllum scriptum
– multiflorum = Grammatophyllum scriptum
– paludosum = Dipodium paludosum
– roemplerianum = Eulophiella roempleriana
– rumphianum = Grammatophyllum scriptum
– sanderianum = Grammatophyllum speciosum
– scandens = Dipodium pictum
7507 **– scriptum**
– seegerianum = Grammatophyllum scriptum
5157 **– speciosum**
5676 **– stapeliiflorum**
– wallisii = Grammatophyllum speciosum
Graphorchis
– cristata = Eulophia cristata
– guineensis = Eulophia guineensis
– nuda = Eulophia nuda
– pulchra = Eulophia pulchra
– sanguinea = Eulophia sanguinea
ns – saundersiana = Oeceoclades saundersiana
Grobya
ns 720 – amherstiae
Gyas
– humilis = Bletilla striata
Gymnadenia
– diphylla = Gennaria diphylla
– macrantha = Brachycorthis macrantha
– purpurascens = Cynorchis purpurascens
– uniflora = Cynorkis grandiflora
Gymnostylis
– candida = Pleione maculata
Gyrostachys
– aphylla = Sacoila lanceolata
– cernua = Spiranthes cernua
– constricta = Spiranthes cernua
– lanceolata = Sacoila lanceolata
– longipetiolata = Pelexia laxa
– orchioides = Sacoila lanceolata
– ovalifolia = Beadlea elata
– picta = Sarcoglottis acaulis
– stenorrhynchus = Sacoila lanceolata
Habenaria
7798 **– armatissima**
– armondiana = Habenaria leptoceras
– bonatea = Bonatea speciosa
– ciliaris = Platanthera ciliaris
– cordata = Gennaria diphylla
– decipiens = Habenaria longecalcarata
9663 **– dentata**
– dinteriana = Habenaria artissima
– diphylla = Gennaria diphylla
7478 **– elwesii**
ns 631 **– engleriana**
– finetiana = Habenaria dentata
– geniculata = Habenaria dentata
– geniculata var. yunnanensis = Habenaria dentata
– gigantea = Pecteilis susannae
– goodyeroides = Peristylus plantagineus
– gracilis = Habenaria longecalcarata
– helleborina = Brachycorthis macrantha
ns – hunteri = Habenaria engleriana
– incarnata = Disa incarnata
2726 **– leptoceras**
7278 **– longicalcarata**
2957 **– longicauda**
– longicorniculata = Habenaria longecalcarata
– lugardii = Habenaria armatissima
– macrantha = Habenaria splendens
– macroceras = Habenaria quinqueseta
– macroceratitis = Habenaria quinqueseta
– macroceratitis var. brevicalcarata = Habenaria quinqueseta
– miersiana = Habenaria dentata
– miersiana var. yunnanensis = Habenaria dentata
– militaris = Habenaria rhodocheila
– militaris var. philippinensis = Habenaria rhodocheila
– monophylla = Chusua monophylla
– montana = Habenaria longecalcarata
– pusilla = Habenaria rhodocheila
2947 **– quinqueseta**
– radiata = Habenaria dentata
7570 **– rhodocheila**
– robusta = Bonatea speciosa

Maxillaria
2729 – **parkeri**
– pertusa = Maxillaria lepidota
3154 – **picta**
– picta Rchb. f. = Maxillaria chrysantha
– placanthera = Pabstia placanthera
6477 – **porphyrostele**
– praestans = Maxillaria cucullata
– pubigera = Bifrenaria harrisoniae
3613 – **pumila**
– puncto-striata = Maxillaria cucullata
– racemosa = Bifrenaria racemosa
– regaliana = Maxiallaria chrysantha
– revoluta = Maxillaria variabilis
– rhombea = Maxillaria cucullata
– rupestris = Maxillaria picta
7518 – **sanderiana**
– saxicola = Maxillaria lepidota
– scabrilinguis = Xylobium variegatum
– serotina = Maxillaria chrysantha
4434 – **setigera**
– setigera var. angustifolia = Maxillaria setigera
– skinneri = Lycaste skinneri
– spathacea = Bifrenaria harrisoniae
– squalens = Xylobium variegatum
– stapelioides = Promenaea stapelioides
– steelei = Scuticaria steelei
– stenobulbon = Xylobium pallidiflorum
– stenopetala = Bifrenaria aureo-fulva
– superba = Govenia superba
– supina = Xylobium variegatum
– tetragona = Lycaste tetragona
– triangularis = Maxillaria elatior
– tyrianthina = Bifrenaria tyrianthina
3614 – **variabilis**
– variegata = Xylobium variegatum
5296 – **venusta**
– virginalis = Lycaste skinneri
– viridis var. pluriflora = Pabstia jugosa
– viridis var. stenosepala = Pabstia placanthera
– warreana = Warrea warreana
ns – xanthina = Promenaea xanthina
Megaclinium
– angustum = Bulbophyllum melanorrhachis
– bufo = Bulbophyllum purpureorhachis
– endotrachys = Bulbophyllum falcatum
– falcatum = Bulbophyllum falcatum
– leucorrhachis = Bulbophyllum leucorrhachis
– maximum = Bulbophyllum maximum
* – maximum = Bulbophyllum falcatum
– millenii = Bulbophyllum melanorrhachis
– minutum = Bulbophyllum melanorrhachis
– platyrhachis = Bulbophyllum platyrhachis
– purpuratum = Bulbophyllum maximum
– purpureorhachis = Bulbophyllum purpureorhachis
– oxypterum = Bulbophyllum maximum
Menadena
– parkeri = Maxillaria parkeri
Menadenium
– labiosum = Zygosepalum labiosum
– rostratum = Zygosepalum labiosum
Mendoncella
5567 – **grandiflora**
4766 – **marginata**
5582 – **marginata**
8610 – **prainiana**
Mesospinidium
– aurantiacum = Ada aurantiaca
– cinnabarinum = Ada aurantiaca
– roseum = Cochlioda rosea
– sanguineum = Symphyglossum sanguineum
– vulcanicum = Cochlioda vulcanica
Microstylis
– calophylla = Malaxis socttii
– carpinterae = Malaxis excavata
– discolor = Malaxis discolor
– excavata = Malaxis excavata
– hastilabia = Malaxis excavata
– humilis = Encyclia pygmaea
– josephiana = Malaxis josephiana
– metallica = Malaxis metallica
– muelleri = Malaxis excavata
– ottonis = Malaxis excavata
– paranaensis = Malaxis excavata
– quadrangularis = Malaxis excavata
– scottii = Malaxis scottii
– sertulifera = Malaxis excavata
– simillima = Malaxis excavata
– spiralipetala = Malaxis excavata
Microtis
3378 – **media**
3377 – **parviflora**
Miltonia
3572 – **anceps**
– candida = Anneliesia candida
– candida var. flavescens = Anneliesia candida
– cereola = Miltonia regnellii
4109 – **clowesii**
– endresii = Miltoniopsis warscewiczii
ns 849 – flavescens
– illustris = Miltonia spectabilis var. moreliana
– laevis = Miltonioides laevis
– leucomelas = Miltonioides laevis
– moreliana = Miltonia spectabilis var. moreliana
– pinelii = Miltonia anceps
5436 – **regnellii**
– roezlii = Miltoniopsis roezlii
4204 – **spectabilis**
4425 – **spectabilis var. moreliana**
– spectabilis var. purpureo-violacea = Miltonia spectabilis var. moreliana
– superba = Miltoniopsis warscewiczii
– vexillaria = Miltoniopsis vexillaria
– warneri = Miltonia spectabilis var. moreliana
– warscewiczii = Miltonioides warscewiczii
Miltonioides
6265 – **laevis**
5843 – **warscewiczii**
Miltoniopsis
6085 – **roezlii**
6037 – **vexillaria**
6163 – **warscewiczii**
Mischobulbon
– scapigerum = Nephelaphyllum scapigerum
Monachanthus
– bushnanii = Catasetum discolor var. roseo-album
– bushnanii var. fimbriatum = Catasetum discolor var. fimbriatum
– bushnanii var. vinosum = Catasetum discolor var. roseo-album
– discolor var. bushnanii = Catasetum discolor var. viridiflorum
– discolor var. viridiflorus = Catasetum discolor var. viridiflorum
– fimbriatus = Catasetum discolor var. fimbriatum
– longifolius = Catasetum longifolium
– roseo-albus = Catasetum discolor var. roseo-album
– viridis Lindl. 1832 = Catasetum cernuum
– viridis Lindl. 1836 = Catasetum macrocarpum Rich. ex Kunth
– viridis Schomb. = Catasetum barbatum
Monomeria
8160 – **dichroma**
Moorea
– irrorata = Neomoorea wallisii
Mormodes
– amazonicum = Mormodes buccinator
– atropurpureum = Mormodes hookeri
– barbatum = Mormodes hookeri
– brachystachya = Mormodes buccinator
4455 – **buccinator**
8041 – **buccinator** var. **aurantiacum**
4214 – **cartoni**
5840 – **colossus**
– flavida = Mormodes buccinator
– greenei = Mormodes uncium
4577 – **hookeri**
– incisa = Mormodes uncium
– lentiginosa = Mormodes buccinator
– leucochila = Mormodes buccinator
– macranthum = Mormodes colossus
3900 – **maculata**
3879 – **maculatum** var. **unicolor**
– marmorea = Mormodes buccinator
6496 – **ocanae**
– pardina = Mormodes maculata
– pardina var. unicolor = Mormodes maculatum var. unicolor
– powellii = Mormodes colossus
8390 – **revolutum**
7438 – **rolfeanum**
8597 – **tigrinum**
5802 – **uncium**
– vitellina = Mormodes buccinator
– wagneriana = Mormodes buccinator
– wendlandii = Mormodes colossus
Myanthus
– barbatus = Catasetum barbatum
– cernuus = Catasetum cernuum
– deltoideus = Catasetum deltoideum
– fimbriatus = Catasetum fimbriatum
– grandiflorus = Catasetum callosum
– spinosus = Catasetum barbatum
– warczewiczii = Clowesia warczewitzii
Mycaranthes
– latifolia = Eria iridifolia
Myoda
– rufescens = Ludisia discolor
Myoxanthus
5885 – **reymondii**
Myrmecophila
4476 – **tibicinis**
– thomsoniana = Schomburgkia thomsoniana var. minor
Myrobroma
– fragrans = Vanilla planifolia
Mystacidium
– distichum = Angraecum distichum
– germinyanum = Angraecum ramosum
– infundibulare = Angraecum infundibulare
– productum = Diaphananthe bidens
– sesquipedale = Angraecum sesquipedale
Nanodes
5723 – **medusae**
Narica
– moschata = Sarcoglottis acaulis
Nasonia
– hartwegii = Centropetalum hartwegii
– punctata = Centropetalum hartwegii

Nauenia
– spectabilis = Lacaena spectabilis
Neippergia
– chrysantha = Acineta chrysantha
Neobenthamia
7221 **– gracilis**
Neocogniauxia
6683 **– monophylla**
Neofinetia
2097 **– falcata**
Neogardneria
– binotii = Neogardneria murrayana
3674 **– murrayana**
Neolehmannia
– difformis = Epidendrum difforme
– medusae = Nanodes medusae
Neomoorea
– irrorata = Neomoorea wallisii
7262 **– wallisii**
Neottia
– acaulis = Sarcoglottis acaulis
– aphylla = Sacoila lanceolata
– calcarata = Eltroplectris calcarata
– cernua = Spiranthes cernua
– discolor = Ludisia discolor
– elata = Beadlea elata
– glandulosa = Ponthieva racemosa
* – grandiflora = Chloraea bletioides
– grandiflora = Sarcoglottis grandiflora
– lanceolata = Sacoila lanceolata
– minor = Beadlea elata
– orchioides = Sacoila lanceolata
– picta = Sarcoglottis acaulis
– plantaginea = Sacoila lanceolata
– pubescens = Goodyera pubescens
– speciosa = Stenorrhynchus speciosum
– squamulosa = Sacoila lanceolata
Nephelaphyllum
5332 **– pulchrum**
5390 **– scapigerum**
Nervilia
– ? biflora = Nervilia plicata
– dallachyana = Nervilia plicata
– discolor = Nervilia plicata
6851 **– fordii**
– fordii auct. non Hance = Nervilia plicata
6671 **– gammieana**
6125 **– plicata**
– velutina = Nervilia plicata
Neuwiedia
7425 **– griffithii**
– lindleyi = Neuwiedia veratrifolia
7368 **– veratrifolia**
Nipponorchis
– falcata = Neofinetia falcata
Notylia
6311 **– albida**
– angustilancea = Notylia barkeri
8306 **– barkeri**
– bernoullii = Notylia barkeri
5609 **– bicolor = Macroclinium bicolor**
– bipartita = Notylia barkeri
– brenesii = Notylia barkeri
– guatemalensis = Notylia barkeri
– huegelii = Notylia barkeri
– multiflora = Notylia barkeri
– panamensis = Notylia albida
– pittieri = Notylia barkeri
– tamaulipensis = Notylia barkeri
– tridachne = Notylia barkeri
– trisepala = Notylia barkeri
– turialbae = Notylia barkeri
Nyctosma
– nocturna = Epidendrum nocturnum
Oberonia
5056 **– acaulis**
– denticulata = Oberonia iridifolia
4517 **– iridifolia**
– myriantha = Oberonia acaulis
– sikkimensis = Oberonia acaulis
Octadesmia
– monophylla = Neocogniauxia monophylla
2823 **– montana**
Octomeria
2764 **– graminifolia**
– serratifolia = Octadesmia montana
– stellata = Eria javanica
– vaginata = Eria javanica
× Odontioda
8133 **– heatonensis**
7990 **– vuylstekeae**
Odontochilus
– flavus = Anoectochilus lanceolatus
– lanceolatus = Anoectochilus lanceolatus
– petelotii = Ludisia discolor
Odontoglossum
– alexandrae = Odontoglossum crispum
– alexandrae var. guttatum = Odontoglossum crispum
– anceps Klotzsch = Miltonia anceps
– anceps Lemaire = Lemboglossum maculatum
ns 825 – armatum
– aspasia = Aspasia epidendroides
– × aspersum = Odontoglossum hallii
– × baphicanthum = Odontoglossum odoratum
– barkeri = Gomesa barkeri
– bictoniense = Lemboglossum bictoniense
– brevifolium = Otoglossum brevifolium
4919 **– cariniferum**
– cervantesii = Lemboglossum cervantesii
– cervantesii var. membranaceum = Lemboglossum cervantesii
– × chaetostroma = Odontoglossum hallii
– chiriquense = Otoglossum chiriquense
6317 **– cirrhosum**
– clowesii = Miltonia clowesii
– constrictum = Odontoglossum sanderianum
– constrictum var. majus = Odontoglossum sanderianum
– cordatum = Lemboglossum cordatum
– coronarium var. chiriquense = Otoglossum chiriquense
– coronarium var. miniatum = Otoglossum brevifolium
5691 **– crispum**
5697 **– crispum**
8809 **– cristatum**
ns – cristatum var. lehmannii = Odontoglossum armatum
ns – denticulatum = Odontoglossum armatum
– edithiae = Odontoglossum crispum
6771 **– edwardii**
– foliosum = Gomesa foliosa
– ghiesbreghtianum = Oncidium tigrinum
– glonerianum = Odontoglossum odoratum
– gloriosum = Ondotoglossum odoratum
– grande = Rossioglossum grande
6237 **– hallii**
– hastilabium = Oncidium hastilabium
– hastilabium var. fuscatum = Odontoglossum cariniferum
– hookeri = Lemboglossum cordatum
8873 **– × humeanum**
– johnsonorum = Oncidium maculatum
5778 **– krameri**
– laeve = Miltonioides laevis
– latimaculatum = Odontoglossum crispum
8142 **– leeanum**
– leucomelas = Miltonioides laevis
– lueddemannii = Lemboglossum cordatum
– maculatum Hook. = Lemboglossum cordatum
– maculatum Llave & Lex. = Lemboglossum maculatum
– majale = Lemboglossum majale
6144 **– maxillare**
– membranaceum = Lemboglossum cervantesii
– miniatum = Otoglossum brevifolium
8097 **– naevium**
– noetzlianum = Cochlioda noetzliana
6502 **– odoratum**
– odoratum var. leeanum = Odontoglossum leeanum
– oerstedii = Ticoglossum oerstedii
5993 **– pardinum**
– planifolium = Gomesa planifolia
– platycheilum = Lemboglossum majale
6229 **– praenitens**
8780 **– × praevisum**
– pulchellum = Osmoglossum pulchellum
8031 **– ramulosum**
– recurvum = Gomesa revurva
7569 **– retusum**
– roezlii = Miltoniopsis roezlii
– roseum = Cochlioda rosea
5736 **– sanderianum**
– spathaceum = Odontoglossum pardinum
– spilotanthum = Odontoglossum pardinum
– subcruciforme = Oncidium maculatum
– tigrinum = Oncidium tigrinum
6029 **– tripudians**
– variegatum = Aspasia variegata
– vexillarium = Miltoniopsis vexillaria
– warocqueanum = Odontoglossum crispum
– warscewiczianum = Miltoniopsis warscewiczii
– warscewiczii = Miltoniopsis warscewiczii
– weltonii = Miltonioides warscewiczii
– zebrinum = Oncidium zebrinum
Oeceoclades
– falcata = Neofinetia falcata
– funalis = Dendrophylax funalis
– lindleyana = Neofinetia falcata
– lindleyi = Neofinetia falcata
ns 731 – saundersiana
Oerstedella
7855 **– endresii**
5556 **– myriantha**
9170 **– pumila**
Olgasis
– triquetra = Oncidium triquetrum
Oncidium
– aemulum = Oncidium superbiens
– alboviolaceum = Oncidium incurvum
3603 **– altissimum**
* – altissimum = Oncidium jacquinianum
– anceps = Miltonia anceps
– aurosum = Oncidium excavatum
– barkeri = Oncidium tigrinum
– batemanianum = Oncidium bifolium
4148 **– bicallosum**
– bicornutum = Oncidium pubes
– bidens = Brassia bidens
1491 **– bifolium**
– boydii = Oncidium altissimum
– brachyphyllum = Oncidium cebolleta
– brassia = Brassia maculata
– candidum Beer = Anneliesia candida
– candidum Lindl. = Palumbina candida

Sobralia
– caravata = Elleanthus caravata
– chlorantha = Sobralia macrophylla
– citrina = Encyclia citrina
4570 **– decora**
– eublepharis = Sobralia fragrans
4882 **– fragrans**
– galeottiana A. Rich. = Sobralia decora
– galeottiana Lindl. = Sobralia sessilis
7058 **– leucoxantha**
ns 144 – lucasiana
4446 **– macrantha**
– macrantha var. purpurea = Sobralia macrantha
– macrantha var. alba = Sobralia macrantha
4682 **– macrophylla**
– powellii = Sobralia leucoxantha
– rolfeana = Sobralia macrophylla
7376 **– sessilis**
* – sessilis = Sobralia decora
7332 **– xantholeuca**
Solenidium
ns 709 – racemosum
× Sophrolaelia
8654 **– psyche**
Sophronia
– cernua = Sophronitis cernua
Sophronitella
6880 **– violacea**
Sophronitis
3677 **– cernua**
3709 **– coccinea**
– grandiflora = Sophronitis coccinea
– hoffmannseggii = Sophronitis cernua
– isopetala = Sophronitis cernua
– militaris = Sophronitis coccinea
– modesta = Sophronitis cernua
– nutans = Sophronitis cernua
– pterocarpa = Sophronitis cernua
– violacea = Sophronitella violacea
Spathoglottis
– angustorum = Spathoglottis plicata
7443 **– aurea**
– daenikeri = Spathoglottis plicata
7366 **– gracilis**
7964 **– hardingiana**
7060 **– ixioides**
– kimballiana = Spathoglottis aurea
– lilacina = Spathoglottis plicata
6354 **– petri**
7013 **– plicata**
– plicata var. alba = Spathoglottis plicata
– speciosa = Ipsea speciosa
– spicata = Spathoglottis plicata
– vieillardii = Spathoglottis plicata
Specklinia
– atropurpurea = Zootrophion atropurpureum
Spiranthes
– aucaulis = Sarcoglottis acaulis
1568 **– cernua**
5277 **– cernua**
– colorata = Stenorrhynchus speciosum
– colorata var. maculata = Stenorrhynchus speciosum
– comosa = Beadlea elata
– constricta = Spiranthes cernua
– elata = Beadlea elata
– elata var. ovata = Beadlea elata
– euphlebia = Pteroglossa euphlebia
– grandiflora = Sarcoglottis grandiflora
– jaliscana = Sacoila lanceolata
– lanceolata = Sacoila lanceolata
– laxa = Pelexia laxa
– lineata Lindl. = Beadlea elata
– lineata Stuckert = Beadlea elata
– longipetiolata = Pelexia laxa
– maculata = Pelexia laxa
– orchioides = Sacoila lanceolata
– pamii = Beadlea elata
– picta = Sarcoglottis acaulis
– preslii = Beadlea elata
– richardii = Stenorrhynchus speciosum
– speciosa A. Rich. = Stenorrhynchus speciosum
– speciosa Lindl. = Sarcoglottis acaulis
– variegata = Beadlea elata
Stanhopea
– amoena = Stanhopea wardii
– aurea = Stanhopea wardii
– bucephalus = Stanhopea oculata
– calceolata = Stanhopea grandiflora
ns 779 – connata
– convoluta = Stanhopea tricornis
8830 **– costaricensis**
– cymbiformis = Stanhopea oculata
– devoniensis = Stanhopea hernandezii
– eburnea = Stanhopea grandiflora
4885 **– ecornuta**
8417 **– florida**
3359 **– grandiflora**
– grandiflora Rchb. f. = Stanhopea jenishiana
– grandiflora var. jenishiana = Stanhopea jenishiana
ns – graveolens Klotzsch = Stanhopea connata
ns 796 – graveolens Lindl.
– guttata = Stanhopea oculata
– harrisoniae = Bifrenaria harrisoniae
7452 **– haseloviana**
4197 **– hernandezii**
– hoppii = Stanhopea jenishiana
2948 **– insignis**
2949 **– insignis**
8517 **– jenishiana**
– langlasseana = Stanhopea tricornis
– lindleyi = Stanhopea oculata
– minor = Stanhopea oculata
5278 **– oculata**
5300 **– oculata**
– oculata var. barkeriana = Stanhopea oculata
– oculata var. crocea = Stanhopea oculata
– oculata var. geniculata = Stanhopea oculata
– oculata var. lindleyi = Stanhopea oculata
– ornatissima = Stanhopea oculata
– peruviana = Stanhopea florida
– purpusii = Stanhopea oculata
– rodigasiana = Embreea rodigasiana
– stenochila = Stanhopea tricornis
* – tigrina = Stanhopea hernandezii
8507 **– tricornis**
– venusta = Stanhopea wardii
– wallisii = Stanhopea tricornis
5289 **– wardii**
– wardii var. venusta = Stanhopea wardii
Stanhopeastrum
– ecornutum = Stanhopea ecornuta
Stauritis
– violacea = Phalaenopsis violacea
Stauroglottis
– equestris = Phalaenopsis equestris
– riteiwanensis = Phalaenopsis equestris
Stauropsis
– giganteus = Vandopsis gigantea
– imthurnii = Vandopsis imthurnii
– violacea = Phalaenopsis violacea
Stelis
– atropurpurea = Apatostelis ciliaris
– bruchmuelleri = Stelis eublepharis
– ciliaris = Apatostelis ciliaris
– confusa = Apatostelis ciliaris
6521 **– eublepharis**
– jimenezii = Apatostelis ciliaris
– micrantha var. atropurpurea = Apatostelis ciliaris
– tubatus = Physosiphon tubatus
Stenocoryne
– aureo-fulva = Bifrenaria aureo-fulva
– harrisoniae = Bifrenaria harrisoniae
– racemosa = Bifrenaria racemosa
– secunda = Bifrenaria aureo-fulva
Stenoglottis
5872 **– fimbriata**
– fimbriata N. E. Br. = Stenoglottis longifolia
7186 **– longifolia**
Stenorrhynchos
– apetalus = Sacoila lanceolata
– aphyllus = Sacoila lanceolata
– australis = Sacoila lanceolata
– australis var. luteoalbus = Sacoila lanceolata
– coccineus = Sacoila lanceolata
– euphlebius = Pteroglossa euphlebia
– guatemalensis = Sacoila lanceolata
– jaliscana = Sacoila lanceolata
– lanceolatum = Sacoila lanceolata
– laxum = Pelexia laxa
– millei = Stenorrhynchos speciosum
– orchioides = Sacoila lanceolata
– orchioides var. australis = Sacoila lanceolata
– orchioides var. plantaginea = Sacoila lanceolata
– pedicellatus = Sacoila lanceolata
– pedicellatus var. major = Sacoila lanceolata
– riograndensis = Sacoila lanceolata
– sancti-antoni = Sacoila lanceolata
– secundiflorus = Sacoila lanceolata
1374 **– speciosum**
– squamulosus = Sacoila lanceolata
Stereochilus
5630 **– erinaceus**
Sturmia
– reflexa = Liparis reflexa
Styloglossum
– nervosum = Calanthe pulchra
Sunipia
6344 **– paleacea**
Symphyglossum
5627 **– sanguineum**
Synadena
– amabilis = Phalaenopsis amabilis
Synoplectris
– picta = Sarcoglottis acaulis
Tainia
– hookeriana = Ania hookeriana
– penangiana = Ania penangiana
– stellata = Eria javanica
– viridifusca = Ania viridifusca
Telipogon
– buenaventurae = Dimerandra emarginata
Tetramicra
– bicolor = Leptotes bicolor
3098 **– canaliculata**
– elegans = Tetramicra canaliculata
– montana = Octadesmia montana
– serrulata = Leptotes bicolor
– rigida = Tetramicra canaliculata
Thiebautia
– nervosa = Bletia purpurea
Thorvaldsenia
– speciosa = Chysis bractescens
Thrixspermum
7754 **– amplexicaulis**
– beccarii = Sarcochilus moorei
7489 **– hainanense**
– hartmannii = Sarcochilus hartmannii
– lilacinum = Thrixspermum amplexicaulis
– luniferum = Chiloschista lunifera
– moorei = Sarcochilus moorei
Thunia
3991 **– alba**
5694 **– bensoniae**
– bracteata = Thunia alba
– pulchra = Thunia alba

Ticoglossum
6820 – **oerstedii**
Tolumnia
– pulchella = Oncidium pulchellum
Trevoria
7805 – **chloris**
– lehmannii = Trevoria chloris
Triaristella
– huebneri = Trisetella huebneri
Trias
– dayanum = Bulbophyllum dayanum
9150 – **picta**
Tribrachia
– purpurea = Bulbophyllum careyanum
Trichocentrum
– albo-coccineum = Trichocentrum albopurpureum
5688 – **albopurpureum**
– amazonicum = Trichocentrum albopurpureum
– atropurpureum = Trichocentrum albopurpureum
3969 – **fuscum**
7380 – **tigrinum**
Trichopilia
– albida = Trichopilia fragrans
– candida = Trichopilia fragrans
– coccinea = Trichopilia marginata
– crispa = Trichopilia marginata
5035 – **fragrans**
5550 – **galeottiana**
– hymenantha = Leucohyle subulata
– jamaicensis = Leucohyle subulata
– kienastiana = Trichopilia suavis
– lehmannii = Trichopilia fragrans
– lepida = Trichopilia marginata
4857 – **marginata**
– picta = Trichopilia galeottiana
– sanguinolenta = Helcia sanguinolenta
4654 – **suavis**
– subulata = Leucohyle subulata
3739 – **tortilis**
– turialvae = Trichopilia galeottiana
– wageneri = Trichopilia fragrans
Trichotosia
– vestita = Eria vestita
Tridachne
– virens = Notylia barkeri
Trigonidium
– monophyllum = Neocogniauxia monophylla
Triorchis
– cernua = Spiranthes cernua
Trisetella
6268 – **huebneri**
Tropilis
– aemula = Dendrobium aemulum
– gracilicaulis = Dendrobium gracilicaule
– kingiana = Dendrobium kingianum
– speciosa = Dendrobium speciosum
– tetragona = Dendrobium tetragonum
Tryphia
– orthoceras = Holothrix orthoceras
Ulantha
* – grandiflora = Chloraea bletioides
Vanda
– alpina = Vanda cristata
7139 – **amesiana**
5611 – **bensonii**
– cathcartii = Esmeralda cathcartii
– clarkei = Esmeralda clarkei
5834 – **coerulescens**
– coerulescens subvar. boxallii = Vanda confusa
3416 – **concolor**
6328 – **confusa**
4304 – **cristata**
– cristata var. β = Vanda pumila
– denevei = Paraphalaenopsis denevei
5811 – **denisoniana**
– densiflora = Rhynchostylis gigantea
– furva = Vanda concolor
– gigantea = Vandopsis gigantea
– hindsii = Vanda tricolor
5759 – **insignis**
– kimballiana = Holcoglossum kimballianum
6173 – **limbata**
– lindleyana = Vandopsis gigantea
– lowii = Dimorphorchis lowii
8709 – **luzonica**
5138 – **parviflora**
– peduncularis = Cottonia peduncularis
7968 – **pumila**
– roxburghii = Vanda tessellata
– roxburghii var. unicolor = Vanda concolor
– sanderiana = Euanthe sanderiana
– saprophytica = Holcoglossum kimballianum
– scripta = Grammatophyllum scriptum
– simondii = Cleisostoma simondii
– storiei = Renanthera storiei
– suaveolens = Vanda tricolor
– suavis = Vanda tricolor var. suavis
– teres = Papilionanthe teres
– teretifolia = Cleisostoma simondii
2245 – **tessellata**
– tesselloides = Vanda tessellata
– testacea = Vanda parviflora
4432 – **tricolor**
5174 – **tricolor** var. **suavis**
– unicolor = Vanda tessellata
– vitellina = Vanda parviflora
8109 – **watsonii**
Vandopsis
5189 – **gigantea**
8714 – **imthurnii**
– lowii = Dimorphorchis lowii
Vanilla
– aromatica = Vanilla planifolia
– fragrans = Vanilla planifolia
7996 – **humblotii**
– mexicana = Vanilla planifolia
7167 – **planifolia**
– sativa = Vanilla planifolia
– sylvestris = Vanilla planifolia
– viridiflora = Vanilla planifolia
Volubilis
– siliquosa = Vanilla planifolia
Wailesia
– paludosa = Dipodium paludosum
– picta = Dipodium pictum
Warmingia
ns 725 – eugenii
ns – loefgrenii = Warmingia eugenii
Warrea
– bidentata = Warrea warreana
– discolor = Cochleanthes discolor
– marginata = Mendoncella marginata
– quadrata = Mendoncella marginata
– speciosa = Warrea warreana
– tricolor = Warrea warreana
– unijugata = Warrea warreana
4235 – **warreana**
Warscewiczella
– cochlearis = Cochleanthes flabelliformis
– cochleata = Cochleanthes flabelliformis
– discolor = Cochleanthes discolor
– flabelliformis = Cochleanthes flabelliformis
– gibeziae = Cochleanthes flabelliformis
– marginata = Mendoncella marginata
– velata = Mendoncella marginata
Xiphizusa
– weddelii = Bulbophyllum weddellii
Xylobium
– carnosum = Xylobium variegatum
– decolor = Xylobium palmifolium
– dusenii = Xylobium variegatum
– gracile = Xylobium leontoglossum
– houtei = Xylobium variegatum
7085 – **leontoglossum**
2806 – **pallidiflorum**
3981 – **palmifolium**
– scabrilingue = Xylobium variegatum
– squalens = Xylobium variegatum
– squalens var. gracile = Xylobium leontoglossum
– supinum = Xylobium variegatum
2955 – **variegatum**
Zoduba
– masuca = Calanthe masuca
Zootrophion
4164 – **atropurpureum**
8740 – **dayanum**
Zosterostylis
– arachnites = Cryptostylis arachnites
– walkerae = Cryptostylis arachnites
– zeylanica = Cryptostylis arachnites
× Zygocolax
– veitchii = × Zygopabstia veitchii
× Zygopabstia
7980 – **veitchii**
Zygopetalum
– africanum = Lemboglossum bictoniense
– binotii = Neogardneria murrayana
– cerinum = Pescatoria cerina
ns – citrinum = Promenaea xanthina
– claesianum = Zygopetalum crinitum
– cochleare = Cochleanthes flabelliformis
– cochleatum = Cochleanthes flabelliformis
– coeleste = Bollea coelestis
– conchaceum = Cochleanthes flabelliformis
– crepeauxii = Zygopetalum crinitum
3402 – **crinitum**
– discolor = Cochleanthes discolor
– flabelliforme = Cochleanthes flabelliformis
– gibeziae = Cochleanthes flabelliformis
– gramineum = Kefersteinia graminea
– grandiflorum = Mendoncella grandiflora
– hasslerianum = Zygopetalum maxillare
– jugosum = Pabstia jugosa
– labiosum = Zygosepalum labiosum
– lalindei = Bollea lalindei
6240 – **lamellosum**
2748 – **mackaii**
– mackayi var. crinitum = Zygopetalum crinitum
– mandibulare = Zygopetalum maxillare
– marginatum = Mendoncella marginata
3686 – **maxillare**
– micropterum = Promenaea microptera
– microtos = Zygopetalum crinitum
– murrayanum = Neogardneria murrayana
– patini = Bollea lalindei
– placantherum = Pabstia placanthera
– prainianum = Mendoncella prainiana
– pubescens = Zygopetalum crinitum
– pulvinare = Bollea coelestis
– quadratum = Mendoncella marginata
– rostratum = Zygosepalum labiosum
– stapelioides = Promenaea stapelioides
– stenochilum = Zygopetalum crinitum
– × veitchii = × Zygopabstia veitchii
– velatum = Mendoncella marginata
ns – xanthinum = Promenaea xanthina
Zygosepalum
2819 – **labiosum**
– rostratum = Zygosepalum labiosum